# MASTERPLOTS II

## AMERICAN FICTION
## SERIES

# MASTERPLOTS II

---

## AMERICAN FICTION
## SERIES

## 5

Supplement

*Edited by*

# FRANK N. MAGILL

SALEM PRESS

Pasadena, California   Englewood Cliffs, New Jersey

∞ The paper used in these volumes conforms to the
American National Standard for Permanence of Paper
for Printed Library Materials, Z39.48-1984.

**Library of Congress Cataloging-in-Publication Data**
Masterplots II: American fiction series. Supplement /
edited by Frank N. Magill.
    p.  cm.
  Includes bibliographical references and indexes.
  1. America—Literatures—Stories, plots, etc.  2.
America—Literatures—History and criticism. 3. Fic-
tion—20th century—Stories, plots, etc. 4. Fiction—
20th century—History and criticism. I. Magill, Frank
Northen, 1907-   . II. Title: Masterplots 2. American
fiction series. Supplement. III. Title: Masterplots two.
American fiction series. Supplement.
PN846.M37   1994                 94-21511
809.3'0097—dc20                        CIP
ISBN 0-89356-719-1 (set)
ISBN 0-89356-720-5 (volume 1)

# PUBLISHER'S NOTE

The four volumes of *Masterplots II, American Fiction Series* (1986) explored 383 works by some of the most important writers of the Americas—North, Central, and South. This two-volume supplement updates and extends the original series' coverage by examining 180 additional works of fiction by contemporary or hitherto neglected writers who have had, and in many cases continue to have, a substantial effect on the evolution of American literature.

The increasing prominence of ethnic voices in American fiction is reflected by articles on works by such writers as Louise Erdrich, Ernest J. Gaines, and Rolando Hinojosa. Important developments in women's literature are treated in discussions of works by such authors as Barbara Kingsolver, Terry McMillan, and Amy Tan. Discussion of works by such best-selling writers as Stephen King and Scott Turow reflects the state of American popular fiction. Essays on books by such past writers as D'Arcy McNickle and John Okada help to give a more complete picture of America's literary history.

Each article begins with ready-reference information that presents the date of the author's birth (and death, if applicable); the type, time, and locale of the work's plot; and the date of the work's first publication. A brief description of the work's principal characters precedes a more extensive analysis.

This analysis begins with a summary of the work's major plot elements and continues with separate sections that explore the work in depth. "The Characters" delves into the motivations and development of the individuals portrayed; "Themes and Meanings" examines the work's larger concerns; and "Critical Context" assesses the work's place in the American literary tradition and summarizes its reception. Each entry concludes with a feature new to the *Masterplots II* series: an annotated bibliography that directs readers to sources for further study.

The two volumes of *Masterplots II, American Fiction Series Supplement* continue the volume numbering and pagination of the original series. The articles are arranged alphabetically by title; indexes at the end of volume 6 are designed to assist the reader in selecting articles of interest. The Cumulative Author Index lists all entries for each writer surveyed, while the Cumulative Title Index locates specific works. Both indexes reference the contents of the entire *Masterplots II, American Fiction Series Supplement*.

We would like to thank the many academicians and other writers who contributed to this set. A list of their names and affiliations appears at the beginning of volume 5.

# CONTRIBUTING REVIEWERS

Michael Adams
*Fairleigh Dickinson University*

Patrick Adcock
*Henderson State University*

Diane M. Almeida
*University of Massachussets at Boston*

Terry L. Andrews
*Independent Scholar*

Edwin T. Arnold
*Appalachian State University*

Jane H. Babson
*Willamette University*

Margot Gayle Backus
*St. John Fisher College*

Jim Baird
*University of North Texas*

JoAnn Balingit
*Independent Scholar*

Melissa E. Barth
*Appalachian State University*

Barbara G. Bartholomew
*University of Houston, Downtown*

Margaret Kent Bass
*St. Lawrence University*

Emilio Bejel
*University of Colorado at Boulder*

Robert Bensen
*Hartwick College*

Stephen Benz
*Barry University*

Margaret Boe Birns
*New York University*

Nicholas Birns
*Western Connecticut State University*

J. H. Bowden
*Indiana University, Southeast*

Harold Branam
*Savannah State College*

Gerhard Brand
*California State University, Los Angeles*

Ludger Brinker
*Macomb College*

Silvester J. Brito
*University of Wyoming*

C. L. Brooke
*Cleveland State University*

David Buehrer
*Valdosta State University*

Jeffrey L. Buller
*Georgia Southern University*

Charles Cameron
*Independent Scholar*

Mary LeDonne Cassidy
*South Carolina State University*

Thomas J. Cassidy
*South Carolina State College*

Balance Chow
*San Jose State University*

C. L. Chua
*California State University, Fresno*

Virginia Crane
*California State University, Los Angeles*

Mary Virginia Davis
*California State University, Sacramento*

Frank Day
*Clemson University*

Bill Delaney
*Independent Scholar*

James E. Devlin
*State University of New York College at Oneonta*

Clifford Edwards
*Fort Hays State University*

Robert P. Ellis
*Worcester State College*

James Feast
*Baruch College of the City University of New York*

John W. Fiero
*University of Southwestern Louisiana*

Edward A. Fiorelli
*St. John's University, New York*

Gustavo Pérez Firmat
*Duke University*

Sandra K. Fischer
*State University of New York at Albany*

Jean C. Fulton
*Maharishi International University*

Ann D. Garbett
*Averett College*

Jill B. Gidmark
*University of Minnesota*

Marc Goldstein
*University of Rochester*
*New York University*

Linda Silverstein Gordon
*Worcester State College*

Joyce Ann Hancock
*Jefferson Community College, Kentucky*

Joseph W. Hinton
*Portland State University*

Rebecca Stingley Hinton
*Indiana University, East*

Dennis Hoilman
*Ball State University*

W. Kenneth Holditch
*University of New Orleans*

John R. Holmes
*Franciscan University of Steubenville*

Janice A. Jaffe
*Bowdoin College*

Philip K. Jason
*United States Naval Academy*

Sheila Golburgh Johnson
*Independent Scholar*

Eunice Pedersen Johnston
*North Dakota State University*

Jane Anderson Jones
*Manatee Community College*

Steven G. Kellman
*University of Texas*

W. P. Kenney
*Manhattan College*

Grove Koger
*Boise Public Library*

Paula D. Kopacz
*Eastern Kentucky University*

Geeta Kothari
*University of Pittsburgh*

Eugene Larson
*Los Angeles Pierce College*

Leon Lewis
*Appalachian State University*

James Livingston
*Northern Michigan University*

Marcus "C" López
*Solano Community College*

Janet Lorenz
*Independent Scholar*

Michael Loudon
*Eastern Illinois University*

Janet McCann
*Texas A&M University*

Barbara McCaskill
*University of Georgia*

Andrew Macdonald
*Loyola University of*
*New Orleans*

Gina Macdonald
*Loyola University of*
*New Orleans*

Victoria E. McLure
*South Plains College*

Jim McWilliams
*Southern Illinois University at Carbondale*

Edward A. Malone
*University of Missouri, Rolla*

Barry Mann
*Independent Scholar*

Lois A. Marchino
*University of Texas at El Paso*

George Mariscal
*University of California,*
*San Diego*

Peter Markus
*Western Michigan University*

William Matta
*University of Guam*

Charles E. May
*California State University, Long Beach*

Laurence W. Mazzeno
*Ursuline College*

D. Jan Mennell
*North Carolina State University*

Christian H. Moe
*Southern Illinois University at Carbondale*

Robert A. Morace
*Daemen College*

Robert E. Morsberger
*California State Polytechnic University, Pomona*

John M. Muste
*Ohio State University*

George Thomas Novotny
*University of South Florida*

George O'Brien
*Georgetown University*

Lisa Paddock
*Independent Scholar*

Janet Taylor Palmer
*Caldwell Community College*

Phillip Parotti
*Sam Houston State University*

David Peck
*California State University, Long Beach*

Robert W. Peckham
*Sacred Heart Major Seminary*

Victoria Price
*Lamar University*

Rosemary M. Canfield Reisman
*Independent Scholar*

Mary Rohrberger
*University of Northern Iowa*

Carl Rollyson
*Baruch College of the City University of New York*

Paul Rosefeldt
*Delgado Community College*

Chaman L. Sahni
*Boise State University*

Wilma Shires
*Cisco Junior College*

R. Baird Shuman
*University of Illinois at Urbana-Champaign*

Carl Singleton
*Fort Hays State University*

Genevieve Slomski
*Independent Scholar*

Nick David Smart
*New York University*

Ira Smolensky
*Monmouth College, Illinois*

A. J. Sobczak
*Independent Scholar*

Francisco Soto
*City University of New York College of
Staten Island*

Gerald H. Strauss
*Bloomsburg University*

James Sullivan
*California State University, Los Angeles*

Catherine Swanson
*Independent Scholar*

Roy Arthur Swanson
*University of Wisconsin— Milwaukee*

Teresia Langford Taylor
*Hardin-Simmons University*

Betty Taylor-Thompson
*Texas Southern University*

Terry Theodore
*University of North Carolina at Wilmington*

Tiffany Elizabeth Thraves
*Randolph-Macon Woman's College*

Daniel Torres
*Ohio University*

Dennis Vannatta
*University of Arkansas at Little Rock*

Mary E. Virginia
*Independent Scholar*

Catherine Carnell Watt
*University of California, Riverside*

James M. Welsh
*Salisbury State University*

Michael Witkoski
*Independent Scholar*

Pat M Wong
*Binghamton University*

Clifton K. Yearly
*State University of New York at Buffalo*

Weihua Zhang
*State University of New York at Albany*

# LIST OF TITLES IN VOLUME 5

# LIST OF TITLES IN VOLUME 5

# MASTERPLOTS II

## AMERICAN FICTION
## SERIES

# THE ACCIDENTAL TOURIST

*Author:* Anne Tyler (1941-    )
*Type of plot:* Domestic realism
*Time of plot:* The 1980's
*Locale:* Baltimore, Maryland
*First published:* 1985

> *Principal characters:*
> MACON LEARY, the middle-aged author of a series of guidebooks for
>     travelers who would prefer to remain at home
> SARAH LEARY, Macon's estranged wife
> EDWARD, Macon's dog, an undisciplined Welsh corgi
> MURIEL PRITCHETT, Edward's trainer, who transforms Macon's life
> ALEXANDER PRITCHETT, Muriel's son
> ROSE LEARY, Macon's sister
> JULIAN EDGE, Macon's publisher, who marries Rose
> PORTER LEARY, Macon's brother
> CHARLES LEARY, Macon's brother

## The Novel

Macon Leary learns to cope with the murder of his twelve-year-old son and separation from his wife in Anne Tyler's *The Accidental Tourist*. With the assistance of Muriel, a flamboyant young dog trainer with whom he becomes romantically involved, Macon assuages his grief, learns to assume control over his life, and becomes more contented than ever before.

As the novel begins, Macon and Sarah are returning early from a vacation on the beach. Neither, it seems, "had the heart for it." Nor have they had the heart for much else since the murder of their son during a robbery the previous year. During the short car trip, the flaws of their marriage are revealed. Macon refuses to stop driving during a rainstorm, informing Sarah that he has a system for safe driving. Meantime, Sarah longs for a more spontaneous, less systematic man. When she announces that she is leaving him and abandoning their twenty-year marriage, Macon is stunned.

With Sarah gone, Macon is alone and lonely in his home in an upper-class Baltimore neighborhood. His sole companions are his son's intractable dog, Edward, and Helen, a cat. Macon seldom ventures from his house, where he writes guidebooks for Americans who must travel but long for domestic routines. While others sit in armchairs and dream of travel, "accidental tourists" travel dreaming of home.

Always a methodical man, Macon becomes obsessive when Sarah departs. Preoccupied with conserving energy, he stops using the clothes dryer, although he often has to wear damp clothes. He attaches the popcorn maker—he eschews eggs, fearing food poisoning—to his bedside clock to avoid any unessential steps while preparing breakfast. To eliminate the inconvenience of making the bed, he sleeps in "body bags," sheets that are sewn together to form a giant envelopes.

As his compulsions intensify, he is overwhelmed by his systems; even his pets cannot adapt. Edward refuses to enter the basement, where his dog food awaits him after Macon dumps it in a coal chute, and Helen must use the dryer vent as a cat door to conserve litter. When Helen is inadvertently caught in the vent as the dryer is running, her howling causes Edward—who is too frightened to travel down the stairs on his own and therefore is being carried by Macon—to panic. Macon collides with his new energy-saving, wheeled laundry basket and breaks his leg. The three move into Macon's grandparents' home, where his two divorced brothers are already being cared for by Rose, their unmarried sister.

The Leary siblings are mired in routine, spending each evening playing Vaccination, a card game that they designed as children that has grown so convoluted that it proves impossible for outsiders, even spouses, to learn. They eat meticulously prepared and ritually consumed "conservative" baked potatoes nightly. They are aggressively orderly, with allspice stored next to ant poison in Rose's alphabetized kitchen pantry. Initially comforted by his siblings, Macon is before long appalled by their stasis. He descends into a mind-numbing depression.

Macon's emotional state as he returns home is mirrored by Edward, whose behavior grows alarmingly erratic and aggressive. He attacks bikers, trees visitors, and panics when family members attempt to leave the house, even biting Macon. Forced to call a trainer when his brother Charles threatens to have the dog destroyed, Macon turns to Muriel, whom he met at the Meow-Bow animal hospital.

Muriel, a thin young woman with a halo of frizzy black hair and an "unluxurious" body, aggressively pursues Macon as she simultaneously tames Edward. Macon, an accidental tourist trapped in his own life, seems unable to resist her. He gradually moves into Muriel's old row house, where he happily repairs some of the many leaks, holes, and deficiencies. Meanwhile, Muriel's strength and resiliency act as a palliative to Macon's grief. In turn, Muriel's son Alexander benefits from Macon's attentions. Disabled psychologically as well as physically by allergies and asthma, Alexander gains self-esteem as Macon and Edward draw him into their competent, male world. Macon is a passenger in Muriel's world for several months before he is forced to decide whether to remain with her or to reconcile with Sarah.

As Macon's life is being refashioned, so too are the lives of Julian, Macon's publisher, and his sister Rose as the unlikely pair move toward marriage. One of the novel's most convincing moments occurs when Julian moves into the Leary household, where he joins in the nightly ritual of Vaccination.

## The Characters

To please Sarah when he was courting her, teenaged Macon adopted a cool and mysterious façade. Somehow, although he was never comfortable in the role, he became trapped by the persona he had created, unable even at his son's death to provide comfort or receive it from Sarah. Even before Ethan's death, however, Macon had difficulty finding meaning in his life, relying, therefore, on "systems" and routine to provide order and stability, if not happiness. Although he writes travel books, Macon despises travel, invariably longing for the routines of home. With Sarah and Ethan gone, however, even his routines fail to soothe him, and Macon slides into depression.

Muriel, one of Tyler's most memorable characters, is a flamboyantly dressed, unpredictable, and resourceful young woman. After a brief early marriage, she works at an assortment of unconventional jobs to support her seven-year-old son Alexander, whom she alternately coddles and ignores. When she pursues Macon, he is swept along by her strength into a world that seems both exotic and appealing. Through Muriel, Macon is drawn into a world of women: Muriel's sister, her friends, and her neighbors. As Muriel successfully trains Edward, Macon is also nurtured and strengthened. She is the catalyst through which a happier, more emotionally satisfied man emerges.

Edward is given rare depth and provides the novel with some of its best comic moments. As Macon's emotional state deteriorates, Edward, who was also traumatized by Ethan's death, is increasingly aggressive. He becomes a nuisance at best and a menace at worst. He is, however, unfailingly amusing.

The Leary siblings, Charles, Porter, Macon, and Rose, were somber and orderly as children and frequently dismayed by their widowed mother, who virtually worshipped change for its own sake. Stodgy even as children, the Learys were unnerved by their mother's enthusiasm for life. After marrying a traveling engineer, she sent her children to Baltimore to live with her parents, two "thin, severe," and "distinguished" people of whom the children immediately approved. The Leary siblings are firmly rooted in Tyler's tradition of idiosyncratic and eccentric characters. Afflicted with "geographic dyslexia," unable to avoid getting lost on the most routine trips, they dread any foray into the outside world. They are wrapped in a safe cocoon where even the ringing telephone is ignored.

Rose, unlike her divorced brothers Charles and Porter, never married. She has chosen instead to remain in the house, caring for her brothers and the many elderly neighbors who call upon her for everything from chauffeuring to plumbing. Yet Rose's fundamental dissatisfaction is evident in her nearly obsessive attention to an afternoon soap opera. While Charles and Porter remain static throughout *The Accidental Tourist*, providing a backdrop against which the others' transformations can be gauged, Rose's life changes when she meets Julian.

Although initially amused by the eccentric Macon, Julian becomes infatuated with Rose and with the hominess of the life she has created. In his mid-thirties, he is two years younger than Rose; like her, he has never married. Instead, he lives in a singles apartment, dresses nattily, frequents singles bars, and spends his leisure sailing on the Chesapeake Bay. He is the sort, according to Macon, who makes purchases without the use of *Consumer Reports*. Rose and Julian's romance provides some of the novel's most comic moments.

*Themes and Meanings*

The centrality of sibling relationships, a common theme in many of Tyler's novels, is the backdrop against which the events of *The Accidental Tourist* occur. It is also the litmus against which Tyler measures the degree of change occurring in her characters. In *The Accidental Tourist*, Tyler explores the effects people have on one another and the changes wrought by their interactions.

Julian, the quintessential preppy playboy, is enthralled by the homey atmosphere in the Leary house. He abandons his single life for a pedantic upper-middle-class world. Driven by his desire, Julian even manages to learn Vaccination, the only spouse to do so. For her part, Rose steps out of the groove into which she appears firmly entrenched and goes sailing on the Chesapeake.

When Sarah first leaves Macon, his grief over Ethan's death and his own sudden bachelorhood nearly overwhelm him. When he moves into the working-class neighborhood in which Muriel rents a broken-down row house, he leaves behind a persona that is at least partially an artificial construct formed during his courtship of Sarah. Muriel's flamboyance, her inner strength, and her *joie de vivre* in the face of nearly overwhelming hardship allow Macon at once to heal and to become, as Muriel calls him, soft-hearted. The original accidental tourist, Macon even finds himself extolling the virtues of San Francisco to a weary native Baltimorean who is a devotee of Macon's books.

*The Accidental Tourist* is, of course, a metaphor for Macon's life. He is passively swept along by events. While he is a competent and basically goodhearted man, Macon lacks Muriel's inner strength. Through her influence, he is forced finally to make decisions in his life.

With its diverse historical traditions and distinctive neighborhoods, Baltimore provides a rich background for Tyler's eccentric characters. Two sections of this multifaceted city are given clarity in *The Accidental Tourist*, Macon's upper-class Logan Park and Muriel's inner-city neighborhood of row houses. Before he meets Muriel, Macon's entire life is spent in an old neighborhood of detached houses and tree-lined streets. The houses are spacious and private compared to Muriel's domain, which consists of decrepit row houses with fake stone fronts, families sitting on front steps leading directly to the pavement, and unemployed men standing on streetcorners making small talk. Macon is a visitor in a strange world, a world in which he initially wonders how anyone can feel safe, but a world that ultimately he finds vibrant and thriving.

Social class consciousness permeates *The Accidental Tourist* as it does Baltimore. Because of their different classes, Macon's family disapproves of his relationship with Muriel. His brothers refer to her as "this Muriel person," and Sarah tells Macon that with Muriel he will be permanently on the fringe, a member of one of those couples who fit nowhere. It is a measure of Macon's growth that he rejects these class biases and makes an active decision to return to Muriel.

*Critical Context*

With the publication of *The Accidental Tourist*, Tyler's professional and popular reputation expanded. The third of her books to be nominated for the National Book Critics Circle Award—after *Morgan's Passing* (1980) and *Dinner at the Homesick Restaurant* (1982)—*The Accidental Tourist* was the first to be awarded the prize. Aided by the release of a Hollywood film version of the book, Tyler's readership expanded measurably. As a result of her growing reputation, several of her earlier works that had enjoyed limited success were reprinted. In addition, her eleventh novel, *Breathing Lessons* (1988), won the Pulitzer Prize in fiction. Tyler later published a twelfth novel, *Saint Maybe* (1991). She has also written numerous book reviews and short stories.

While Tyler credits the Southern writer and master of eccentric characterizations Eudora Weltey as an early and principal influence, her own writing defies classification. While there are Southern qualities in her writing, including depictions of eccentric individuals and regional speech patterns, her style is unique and immediately identifiable as her own. The setting of her latter novels is Baltimore, but her writing captures a universality of human experience. She admirably describes nuances of behavior in her characters, and she explores the depths of their natures through minutiae. Situations that would be merely banal in the hands of most other writers become profound tools for Tyler. Although her characters are often eccentric, they are nevertheless recognizably human.

Her books share common themes: relationships between siblings, between parents and children, or between husbands and wives. Families, especially brothers and sisters, are drawn together by an inexorable pull. Characters are seen reacting in unpredictable but understandable ways to the often confusing and difficult world in which they live. Because Tyler explores similar human relationships, the characters in *The Accidental Tourist* are similar to those in her other works. Yet her characterizations are sufficiently unique to hold reader interest through several books. Many characters, Muriel in this instance, are truly memorable. Edward, moreover, has become a standard by which other fictional dogs are compared.

*Bibliography*

Almond, Barbara R. "The Accidental Therapist: Intrapsychic Change in a Novel." *Literature and Psychology* 38 (Spring/Summer, 1992):84-105. Discusses Macon's character development in psychological terms. Sees Muriel as functioning as Macon's therapist.

Eder, Richard. "*The Accidental Tourist*." *Los Angeles Times Book Review*, September 15, 1985, 3, 10. In a highly laudatory review, Eder discusses Tyler's techniques of characterization, including the "made-up quality" of her characters who are designed to instruct and entertain. "They are odd but utterly recognizable: mirrors set at an extravagant angle to catch what is going by," writes Eder.

Evans, Elizabeth. *Anne Tyler*. New York: Twayne, 1993. Discusses Tyler's books, including *The Accidental Tourist*, in the context of broader issues in her work.

Evans sees humor as a central feature in Tyler's work and notes that the author examines women's roles in society and familial relationships in detail.

McMurtry, Larry. "Life Is a Foreign Country." *The New York Times Book Review* 90 (September 8, 1985): McMurtry places Macon firmly in the tradition of many of Tyler's male characters who are unusually influenced by strong women. McMurtry views Tyler's metaphor of the accidental tourist as strong, capturing the essence of most of her male characters, who live as accidental tourists in their own lives. He also discusses another common theme in her work, the magnetism of sibling relationships.

Petry, Alice Hall. *Understanding Ann Tyler*. Columbia: University of South Carolina Press, 1990. After providing context for Tyler's fiction in an overview that discusses her work in relation to other authors, Petry then devotes individual chapters to each of Tyler's books. She discusses in detail the plot of *The Accidental Tourist* and provides basic interpretations of characters and events.

*Mary E. Virginia*

# ALBURQUERQUE

*Author:* Rudolfo A. Anaya (1937-        )
*Type of plot:* Magical realism
*Time of plot:* 1992
*Locale:* Albuquerque, New Mexico
*First published:* 1992

> *Principal characters:*
> ABRÁN GONZÁLEZ, a twenty-one-year-old former Golden Gloves boxing champion who is now a first-year student at the University of New Mexico
> BEN CHÁVEZ, a writer and teacher of writing at the University of New Mexico
> FRANK DOMINIC, a wealthy attorney who is running for mayor and who has plans to turn Albuquerque into a city of canals and casinos
> MARISA MARTÍNEZ, the beautiful and honest mayor of Albuquerque, who opposes Dominic's plan
> LUCINDA CÓRDOVA, a nurse at the hospital where Abrán's mother dies
> JOSE CALABASA, a Santo Domingo Indian and Vietnam veteran who is Abrán's friend
> WALTER JOHNSON, a wealthy developer and candidate for mayor

*The Novel*

*Alburquerque* is Anaya's exploration of the ethnically and culturally diverse world of New Mexico in the 1990's. The book focuses on the conflict between the heritage of the past and the challenges to it posed by economic growth unscrupulously promoted by developers and politicians. In its structure, the novel parallels a young man's search for the identity of his father to the city's search for a sense of community amid divisive political and ethnic tensions. Anaya's spelling of the city's name in the title reflects the city's history; according to legend, a gringo stationmaster dropped the first "r" from the town's name "in a move," Anaya says, "that symbolized the emasculation of the Mexican way of life."

Near death from cancer, Cynthia Johnson, a highly respected New Mexico painter, sends for Abrán González, a former Golden Gloves boxing champion who is now a college student, telling him that he is the son she gave up for adoption twenty-one years ago. Intensely proud of his Mexicanness and of the culture of the Barelas barrio where he was reared by his adoptive parents, Abrán is shocked to learn that he has an Anglo mother and naturally wants to know who his father is. By the time he arrives at the hospital, however, Cynthia is too weak to speak, and she dies without revealing the identity of her lover, a secret she confided to no one, not even her parents. Abrán turns for help and companionship to Lucinda Córdova, a nurse who had been close to Cynthia during her final days and to whom he is deeply attracted. Together, they begin a search for the identity of Abrán's father.

This quest takes Abrán first to one of Cynthia's high school classmates, Frank Dominic, who is now a wealthy lawyer running for mayor on a platform of legalized gambling and commercial development. Dominic promises to use his resources to find Abrán's father, but only if Abrán agrees to return to the ring for a fight to be held as a part of an elaborate celebration Dominic has scheduled to kick off his campaign.

Drawn into the orbit of power, Abrán succumbs—but only once—to the charms of the present mayor, Marisa Martínez, a beautiful and highly capable woman whose election was in large part the result of Cynthia's support. Unaware of Abrán's intimacy with Marisa, Lucinda takes him to northern New Mexico to meet her parents in the small village where they live. Dominic, furious when he learns that Abrán has broken training, arranges for Lucinda to be told about Abrán's infidelity, causing Lucinda to break off their relationship.

Additional complication results from Dominic's attempts to convince the Indian pueblos to sell their water rights to supply enough water for the canals envisioned in his urban development plan. Abrán's friend Jose Calabasa has returned to his pueblo to try to dissuade the council from selling out, but he is unsuccessful. Discouraged and depressed, he awakens after a two-day binge to learn that it is the day of Abrán's fight. Having promised to be there, Jose rushes back to Albuquerque. After a series of wildly comic adventures, he learns that a lawyer from Santa Fe has been trying to get in touch with Abrán about one of Cynthia's paintings, which may depict Abrán's father. Jose remembers having seen the painting at the house of Ben Chávez, a writer and teacher at the university who was another of Cynthia's high school classmates. Rushing there, Jose confronts Ben, who admits to being Abrán's father. Hoping to reveal Ben's secret to Abrán and make it unnecessary for him to go through with the fight, Jose rushes to the convention center where the fight is being held. Lucinda, having talked with Marisa and forgiven Abrán, is also rushing to the convention center. She arrives to find that Jose has been badly beaten trying to get to Abrán. As he is being taken to a waiting ambulance, Jose manages to tell Lucinda that Ben Chávez is Abrán's father.

Yet the match has already started, and Abrán is taking a bad beating. It is not until the end of the ninth round that Lucinda is able to make her way to ringside, where she is joined by Ben, and together they tell Abrán the truth. Still, he decides to continue the fight although he no longer needs Dominic's help. Inspired by the discovery of his father's identity and the return of Lucinda, Abrán makes an incredible comeback, knocking out his opponent in the tenth round and giving the people of Albuquerque the hero they need. Dominic's plans to change the city collapse, and both Abrán and the city have found who they really are.

*The Characters*

Abrán has always been an outsider in the Mexican community in which he was reared. Because his skin was lighter, he was teased and harassed by his classmates. He began fighting, first on the playground and later in the ring, to prove that he was as good a Mexican as any of the other boys in the barrio. When he discovers that his mother is an Anglo, his sense of identity is shaken, and he is driven to find his father. Uncomfortable in the world of power, wealth, and glamour, Abrán instinctively recognizes his proper place in the mountains of northern New Mexico. He is drawn to their "pure light" and their traditional Mexican culture, and it is here that he and Lucinda plan to settle down, rear a family, and open a much-needed health clinic.

Ben Chávez, the writer and teacher, is a partly autobiographical version of the author and is the most fully realized of the novel's characters. While still in high school, Chávez was injured in a street fight and thus was hospitalized when Cynthia Johnson gave birth to his son. More comfortable with his fictional characters than with Abrán, the son he has fathered, Ben is working on a novel, which he feels compelled to write, about his love for Cynthia. He is an observer rather than a man of action, and it is largely through his consciousness that the reader understands and evaluates the other characters.

Frank Dominic, the son of a hardworking shoemaker of indefinite ethnic background, is one of the two thoroughly unsympathetic characters and the focus of the novel's pointed and often personal political satire. He is interested only in gaining power and in self-aggrandizement. An expert on image-building, Dominic has tried to link himself with the old Spanish blood in New Mexico; he married a woman who is supposed to be distantly related to the original duke of Albuquerque, and he affects a phony good-old-boy style that Ben finds offensive despite the fact that they have known each other since childhood. A person whose only loyalty is to himself, Dominic uses people ruthlessly and even bets against his own fighter, Abrán, in the big fight he has arranged. At the end of the novel, however, his empire crumbles; despite his extensive knowledge of the history of Albuquerque, he has no feel for its people or their heritage. His attempt to change the city into something it is not grows out of his own need for power and recognition, not out of the spirit and character of the people.

Walter Johnson is the other unsympathetic character. He first came to Albuquerque nearly dead from tuberculosis but was nursed back to health by Vera, whom he eventually marries. As he gains wealth and power, though, her Jewish background turns out to be a detriment to his acceptance by Albuquerque society. He buys a Spanish genealogy for Vera and gains entrance to the country-club circle to which he aspires, but he lacks an heir. Vera, in desperation, has an affair with her gynecologist, never revealing to Walter that Cynthia is not his daughter. When Cynthia becomes pregnant and Walter learns that her lover is a Mexican, he insists that she put the child up for adoption and that neither she nor Vera ever have any contact with it.

Lucinda Córdova is selfless and committed to the plain, simple, honest values of her upbringing in the remote and isolated villages of northern New Mexico. She nursed Cynthia in her last illness and feels an immediate bond with Abrán. After an idyllic week with Abrán at her parents' home in the north, she feels totally committed to him, and when she learns of Abrán's infidelity, she is shocked and profoundly hurt. Nevertheless, she overcomes her hurt and takes her place at his side when he needs her at the fight.

Marisa Martínez, the mayor of Albuquerque, is talented, beautiful, tough, and an excellent mayor. She is divorced and content to live alone; however, her powerful sexuality is roused by Abrán's physicality and youth. She refuses to pull out of the campaign when Dominic arranges for the publication of nude photographs, taken by a detective that Dominic hired, of Marisa and Abrán together.

## Themes and Meanings

The novel is a complex weaving together of themes and meanings and even of literary styles. On one level, it is the love story of Abrán and Lucinda. Related closely to this theme is the conflict between urbanization, with its ethnic diversity and impetus toward continual expansion and flux, and pastoralism, which leads Abrán and Lucinda to see their future in terms of a return to the mountains, to the simplicity and cultural purity of village life, and to the spirituality that is engendered through a closer contact with nature than the city allows.

The novel also presents a critique of New Mexico politics and politicians, and many of its characters are drawn from real life. It presents an especially harsh indictment of Anglo bigotry and of unscrupulous and materialistic politicians. Contrasted to the politicians are the artists, primarily Ben and Cynthia, whose function it is to interpret the people to themselves, to show them who they are and thus to give them the sense of identity and cultural heritage of which the politicians constantly threaten to rob them. It is in this light that Anaya's use of Magical Realism can best be understood. He introduces la Llorona, the wailing woman of Mexican folklore, the trickster figure of Coyote from Indian mythology, two "fictional" characters—Juan and Al—from Ben's poem, and a figment of Ben's imagination, doña Loneliness, who suddenly becomes a flesh-and-blood whore dressed in red. These fantastic characters function side-by-side with the "real" characters to emphasize Anaya's view that the artist's creation is as much a reality as is the so-called reality it imitates. In the struggle to create the future, the artist is more important and much more to be trusted than the politician.

The man of the future that the artist has created—Cynthia as mother, Ben as father, and Anaya as author—is Abrán. He is to be the father of the people; as Anaya says, "Abrán, born of the Mexican father and the gringa mother, was the new Chicano, and he could create his own image, drawing the two worlds together, not letting them tear him apart." The future belongs not to the urban developers but to the people of mixed blood who can find a common ground for community within the diversity of ethnic heritages that threatens to tear it apart. Albuquerque, Anaya implies, is not merely a city in New Mexico; it is a microcosm of the United States—more, it is a microcosm of the planet.

## Critical Context

*Alburquerque* brings Anaya's history of his people and of New Mexico up to the present. The history begins with the first and most famous novel, *Bless Me, Ultima* (1972), and continues in *Heart of Aztlán* (1976) and *Tortuga* (1979), between which and *Alburquerque* there is a lapse of some twenty years. It contains the elements for which Anaya has become best known—the celebration of the Mexican heritage of the Southwest, including its folklore and its deep commitment to family, to the land, and to the sense of mystery beyond the reach of science to explain. As does *Heart of Aztlán*, *Alburquerque* makes use of Old Testament typology; Clemente Chávez, the protagonist of *Heart of Aztlán*, leads the workers in a strike against the railroad, much as Moses led his people out of bondage, and Abrán, his grandson, is the Abraham who will be the founder of a new nation of chosen people, people of mixed blood.

The literary influence most apparent in this novel is that of the school of Magical Realism, an influence that places Anaya in the company of many distinguished Latin American writers. Perhaps equally important is the influence of a number of New Mexico writers who have anticipated various themes developed in *Alburquerque*. Leslie Silko, in her well-known novel *Ceremony* (1977), developed the theme of the person of mixed blood as the progenitor of a race better suited to the needs of the future than people of "pure" blood. Silko's sense that it is the storytellers who will find the answers to the problems of humankind, who will create out of the materials of the past stories to defeat the powers of the destroyers who threaten the future, represents a somewhat mystical faith in the power of art similar to that developed by Anaya in *Alburquerque*. The influence of Frank Waters can be seen in Anaya's depiction of life in the Mexican villages of the north and in his sensitivity to the spiritual as well as the physical beauties of the land. The influence of N. Scott Momaday is apparent in Anaya's treatment of the rituals and ceremonies of Indian and Mexican life as well as in the theme of the creative power of the word, a theme that is thematically as well as structurally central to *Alburquerque*.

In this novel, Anaya takes his place in the forefront not only of Latino writers but also of all those writers who celebrate the beauty of the people and the land of the American Southwest.

*Bibliography*

Augenbraum, Harold. Review of *Alburquerque*, by Rudolfo A. Anaya. *Library Journal* 117 (July, 1992) 119. Calls the novel "an archetypal quest for the father" and says that though "at times melodramatic, the work has an intense spirituality that ultimately makes it mesmerizing."

Candelaria, Cordelia. "Anaya, Rudolfo Alfonso." In *Chicano Literature: A Reference Guide*, edited by Julio A. Martínez and Francisco A. Lomelí. Westport, Conn.: Greenwood Press, 1985. Candelaria provides a convenient summary of Anaya's career prior to 1983 as well as plot summaries of *Bless Me, Ultima, Heart of Aztlán*, and *Tortuga*. She argues that the first two novels are linked in a way suggestive of William Faulkner's Yoknapatawpha stories.

Cazemajou, Jean. "Mediators and Mediation in Rudolfo Anaya's Trilogy: *Bless Me, Ultima, Heart of Aztlán*, and *Tortuga*." In *European Perspectives on Hispanic Literature of the United States*, edited by Genvieve Fabre. Houston: Arte Público Press, 1988. This important article provides background for an understanding of the place of *Alburquerque* in the context of Anaya's earlier novels. Cazemajou sees "myth, not militancy," as Anaya's major literary tool and argues that Anaya's romanticism enables him to avoid the "pitfalls of naturalism that await most minority writers."

Márquez, Antonio. "The Achievement of Rudolfo A. Anaya." In *The Magic of Words: Rudolfo A. Anaya and His Writings*, edited by Paul Vassallo. Albuquerque: University of New Mexico Press, 1982. Márquez sees Anaya's work as leading Chicano literature into the "canons of world literature" and argues that the discussion of myth is crucial to an understanding of his work. Márquez also anticipates a major theme in *Alburquerque* when he discusses Anaya's work as an "eloquent testament that art can teach us to recognize our humanity."

*Publishers Weekly.* Review of *Alburquerque*, by Rudolfo A. Anaya. 239 (May 25, 1992): 36-37. Sees the novel as an "explosive study of political patronage and the search for ethnic roots," a "touching love story woven into a tale of treachery," and a penetrating analysis of "the social and economic dislocations squeezing the American Southwest."

*Dennis Hoilman*

# ALL THE PRETTY HORSES

*Author:* Cormac McCarthy (1933-      )
*Type of plot:* Bildungsroman
*Time of plot:* 1949
*Locale:* Southern Texas and northern Mexico
*First published:* 1992

>        *Principal characters:*
>            JOHN GRADY COLE, a sixteen-year-old boy who rides out of Texas on
>                horseback to escape the collapse of his family and the pressures of
>                modern life
>            LACEY RAWLINS, John Grady's friend, who rides with him
>            JIMMY BLEVINS, a waif even younger than John Grady and Lacey and
>                eccentric beyond his years
>            ALEJANDRA ROCHA Y VILLARÉAL, a beautiful young Mexican woman
>                who becomes John Grady's lover

*The Novel*

*All the Pretty Horses* (the title comes from a popular lullaby) is a rousing adventure story. Set in southern Texas and northern Mexico in 1949, the book has all the features of the standard apprenticeship novel: A young man leaves home with a companion, is introduced to evil in the world, loses his virginity to a beautiful young woman, and finally comes home a much wiser man.

McCarthy divides *All the Pretty Horses* into four sections of roughly equal length and tells the story from the third-person omniscient point of view. The colloquial speech of the three young men casts a spell. It is charming, vivid, and pungent without being obscene, and it provides one of the many great pleasures of the novel. The narrator's commentary sometimes strains after poetic moods in the spirit of William Faulkner, but these rare embarrassments fade in comparison with the real beauty of McCarthy's best descriptions.

For example, the three young men, riding tired in their saddles one night, are confronted with an ominous storm front: "Shrouded in the black thunderheads the distant lightning glowed mutely like welding seen through foundry smoke. As if repairs were under way at some flawed place in the iron dark of the world." Such a passage is hardly mere ornament; the menace of the image foreshadows the nightmare events that await the travelers.

Part 1 opens with the death of John Grady's grandfather and depicts John Grady at loose ends, with his parents separated as his mother pursues a career on the stage. Too young to take over the family spread, John Grady one night saddles up Redbo, the first of the pretty horses featured so lovingly in the novel, and rouses his friend Rawlins; the two ride off to seek their fortunes. Their beginning is a boys' idyll of zestfully eating bad food, lying around rolling cigarettes, and reveling in the natural world.

Soon they find themselves being followed by a bedraggled boy, even younger than they, who calls himself Jimmy Blevins. Despite Rawlins' scornful protestations, they become a threesome.

Blevins is an astonishing personage. John Grady carries a "thumb-buster" of a pistol and Rawlins a small carbine, but Blevins cherishes a powerful Colt pistol with which he is extraordinarily accurate and which establishes his bona fides with his new companions. Blevins also suffers from a pathological fear of electrical storms induced by the deaths by lightning of several of his family members, and this terror eventually contributes to his death.

During a bad storm, the frightened Blevins loses his clothes and his horse. This misfortune sets off a chain of events that will eventually lead to Blevins' death and much misery for the other two, for when they find Blevins' horse later in a little village corral, the impetuous Blevins liberates it and rides off. As a result, they are all identified as horse thieves.

With no knowledge of Blevins' fate, John Grady and Rawlins sign on as ranch hands at a hacienda in northern Mexico. John Grady's affinities with horses earn him a special job and much favored treatment. The owner's daughter, the beautiful Alejandra Rocha y Villaréal, falls in love with John Grady and seduces him. When her father discovers the love affair, he sets the Mexican authorities after the two young men. They are hauled off, charged with horse theft, and reunited with the long-suffering Blevins in a vile jail. As they are being transported to more permanent quarters of incarceration, Blevins is taken into the woods and unceremoniously shot. John Grady nearly dies in a vicious prison knife fight, but the two youths are saved by the intervention of Alejandra's haughty, aristocratic grandaunt, the duenna Alfonsa.

Rawlins goes home, but John Grady returns to the hacienda to plead his romantic case with the duenna. He fails, being instructed on the gap between Alejandra's high birth and his own low prospects. After a last passionate assignation with the girl, John Grady leaves for Texas. First, though, he kidnaps the cruel jailer and then escapes with the three horses he and his companions had ridden into Mexico, visiting severe retribution on his jailer hostage in the process. Back home, he visits Rawlins, now apparently converted to a settled life, and in the last paragraph is seen riding through the dust of a Texas sunset: "He rode with the sun coppering his face and the red wind blowing out of the west across the evening land and the small desert birds flew chittering among the dry bracken and horse and rider and horse passed on and their long shadows passed in tandem like the shadow of a single being. Passed and paled into the darkening land, the world to come."

### The Characters

John Grady Cole enjoys deep ties to his Texas homeland. When his maternal grandfather dies, the Grady name dies, and his mother—who has abandoned John Grady's sickly father for a stage career—is letting go of the ranch. With these ties cut, John Grady saddles up Redbo and summons Lacey Rawlins to help him learn what the world has to offer a boy at loose ends. John Grady has depth. He is intelligent, honorable, and courageous; he is, in short, an old-fashioned hero in the making. His uncanny feeling for horses verges on the occult, and this feeling is matched by the intensity of his responses to the natural world of weather and landscapes.

When Rawlins, in a display of coldheartedness that is more affected than real, wants to leave the hapless Blevins behind, it is John Grady who stands up for the boy. When John Grady gets back to Texas with Blevins' horse, he tries his best to find a relative to whom to give the horse. He is one who knows what is right and seeks to do it straightforwardly. Nothing suggests that he is to become a cynic, despite his grueling initiation into the world's evils.

Rawlins is a less substantial, less complex young man, a follower who would saddle up for Mexico only under the sway of the stronger personality of John Grady. He has the qualities demanded of a hero's sidekick—courage, loyalty, and innate decency— but he will never have a hero's touch with strong-willed horses and women. Rawlins will settle down to the good homeowner's life in south Texas, and his adventure south of the border will warm his memories far into old age. He will not grow as a human being in the way that John Grady can be expected to.

Jimmy Blevins is an original creation. His origins are totally obscure, his name problematic, his habits eccentric, and his inner loneliness immediately ingratiating. He is a young teenager who is already competent with guns and horses, revealing experience that bespeaks a difficult childhood. Despite this unsought worldliness, however, when he catches up to John Grady and Rawlins, he is that most helpless of children—the kid who just wants to go along with and be accepted by the older boys. He is comic in his first appearances, but when he gives John Grady his last scraps of Mexican money before being led off to be shot in the woods, he is tragic. His determination to get his horse back, whatever the odds, is admirable. His death hurts.

Neither Alejandra nor the haughty duenna is completely convincing. The girl is what every young man wants when he rides off on a quest, but if she were truly the spirited young woman that her horsy, aristocratic culture means for her to be, she would say "duennas be damned" and ride off into the sunset. John Grady Cole will find a better mate. The duenna's enameled hardness, despite her intervention to rescue John Grady, is not appealing. It is hard to find in her lecture to John Grady any trace of human understanding, even though it is her confidence in precisely this capacity on which she bases her authority. She is an anachronism.

### Themes and Meanings

*All the Pretty Horses* is first an apprenticeship novel, or *Bildungsroman*, the story of a young man and his companion assuaging the hungers of youth by literally riding off into the unknown. The novel's brilliant success ensues mainly from the skill with which the protagonists are made not merely believable but extremely likable as well. Although their stories resemble the string of adventures of the picaresque novel, these boys are not picaros, or rogues; and though they are hardly genteel youth, even when they are breaking the letter of the law they inspire confidence in their devotion to its spirit. When John Grady kidnaps the brutal jailer and retrieves the boys' horses, good has clearly triumphed, whatever is written in the code of criminal justice.

As a backdrop to the moving figures, there is always the harsh but beautiful landscape, as in this cruel tableau: "Bye and bye they passed a stand of roadside cholla against which small birds had been driven by the storm and there impaled. Gray nameless birds espaliered in attitudes of stillborn flight or hanging loosely in their feathers. Some of them were still alive and they twisted on their spines as the horses passed and raised their heads and cried out but the horsemen rode on."

This living land of John Grady's grandfather is rapidly giving way to highways and pickup trucks, a new world that is struggling to be born, and John Grady is caught in the transition. The brave new world that is to come will not have much time for pretty horses. His grandfather Grady is dead, his dying father cannot advise him, and his mother has been drawn to the Vanity Fair of a life on stage. What John Grady finds in Mexico is hardly reassuring: Besides a few Wordsworthian peasants masquerading as mozos, or ranch hands, humanity there seems to be a small, decaying aristocracy presiding over a degrading civil system.

The language of this novel must be given its due. With the exception of several passages that careen into Faulknerian silliness, it is almost always gorgeous. The speech of the three boys is rich and satisfying, and the still lifes are often beautiful. Language is a major theme of the novel.

*Critical Context*

*All the Pretty Horses* was preceded in McCarthy's career by five earlier novels. *The Orchard Keeper* (1965) tells the story of John Wesley Rattner's coming into manhood in East Tennessee. *Outer Dark* (1968) is a grim story of incest, guilt, and retribution. *Child of God* (1974) and *Suttree* (1979), both also set in East Tennessee, are tales of social outcasts. *Blood Meridian: Or, The Evening Redness in the West* (1985) is a harrowing tale of scalp hunters on the Texas-Mexico border in the mid-nineteenth century. The Tennessee settings are natural for McCarthy. Although he was born in Rhode Island, he came to Knoxville as a child. (Originally named Charles, he was renamed Cormac after the fifteenth century Irish king who built Blarney Castle, site of the famed Blarney Stone, which has the name "Cormac McCarthy" inscribed on it.)

McCarthy is usually identified as a Southern writer. He has the Southern writer's feeling for place, and he evinces a true pastoral nostalgia, dishes up violence and the grotesque, and is frequently linked to Faulkner. His six novels show a progression in accomplishment, readership, and critical acclaim, with *All the Pretty Horses*, winning the National Book Award for fiction in 1992. The title page describes *All the Pretty Horses* as volume one of "The Border Trilogy," and the novel ends with a sense that life is not yet through with John Grady Cole—or he with it. McCarthy's career suggests that the full story of John Grady Cole, if continued in two more books, will be a significant achievement in American fiction.

*Bibliography*

Bell, Vereen. "'Between the Wish and the Thing the World Lies Waiting." *The Southern Review* 28 (Autumn, 1992): 920-927. Bell agrees with other critics who find *All the Pretty Horses* more accessible than McCarthy's previous novels. The novel proves that McCarthy is "a genuine—if somehow secular—mystic" and "a serious student of history." His narratives "always seem to verge upon" allegory.

Cheuse, Alan. "A Note on Landscape in *All the Pretty Horses*." *The Southern Quarterly* 30 (Summer, 1992): 140-142. One of several essays in a special issue devoted to McCarthy. This is a short piece, but it appreciates one of the most admired features of *All the Pretty Horses*.

Jones, Malcolm. "Literary Lion in the Desert." *Newsweek* 113 (May 18, 1992): 68. Jones judges *All the Pretty Horses* not only admirable but also likable. He praises the book as a sweet-tempered "hymn to youth" that, although a Western, "transcends the bounds of its genre."

Luce, Dianne. "Cormac McCarthy." *The Southern Quarterly* 30 (Summer, 1992): 143-151. Although this bibliography was published too early to provide many items devoted specifically to *All the Pretty Horses*, it is still of interest to McCarthy's readers.

Wallace, Garry. "Meeting McCarthy." *The Southern Quarterly* 30 (Summer, 1992): 134-139. A brief but revealing glimpse of McCarthy, who has good words for Ken Follett and Stephen King and identifies Bruce Chatwin and John McPhee as two other authors whom he has read.

*Frank Day*

# ALMANAC OF THE DEAD

*Author:* Leslie Marmon Silko (1948-          )
*Type of plot:* Psychological realism
*Time of plot:* The 1990's
*Locale:* Tucson, Arizona
*First published:* 1991

>    *Principal characters:*
>        SEESE, a young white woman whose child is lost, "nurse" to Lecha
>        STERLING, a Laguna Pueblo Indian banished from his reservation
>        LECHA, a Yaqui Indian psychic who transcribes ancient notebooks
>        CALABAZAS, an Indian cocaine smuggler
>        BEAUFREY, a white cocaine smuggler
>        MAX BLUE, the head of an Italian American crime family
>        MENARDO, a Mexican mestizo who becomes wealthy dealing drugs and
>            weapons
>        CLINTON, a homeless African American Vietnam veteran
>        ROY, a homeless Vietnam veteran, chief organizer of the Army of the
>            Homeless
>        THE TWIN BROTHERS, TACHO and EL FEO, Indian brothers of prophecy

*The Novel*

The narrative of Leslie Marmon Silko's *Almanac of the Dead* centers on Tucson, Arizona, and the intertwining lives and events of its numerous people, among whom are "speculators, confidence men, embezzlers, lawyers, judges, police and other criminals, as well as addicts and pushers." Hauntingly, Silko's novel depicts a society of almost utter depravity, identifies as the source of this state the atrocities committed against Native Americans, and finally predicts the coming end of this cruel reign with the rise of indigenous peoples and the endurance of the sacred Earth.

*Almanac of the Dead* begins with a prophecy contained in the ancient tribal texts of the Americas: "Ancient prophecies foretold the arrival of Europeans in the Americas. The ancient prophecies also foretell the disappearance of all things European." Silko's story echoes that of the prophecy, depicting the downfall of the "criminals" in her novel and the commencement of indigenous people's struggle to regain stolen land. The novel consists of six sections, each divided into books and further divided into short vignettes that adopt more than thirty characters' points of view. Silko uses this structure to approximate oral tradition, thus making *Almanac of the Dead* a calendar of movement through the motion of people, events, and spirits that make up the book's present, past, and future society.

Tucson, the location to which all the characters have some tie as well as the place where the majority of the action takes place, is established as a city of witchery, presently and historically. It is peopled with whites and "breeds" whose ancestors profited from the U.S.-Apache wars and with Indians who deny their heritage. The majority of the characters, of European, Mexican, and Native American descent, participate in illegal activities: smuggling of guns, alcohol, and drugs; murdering for hire or for individual profit; and manufacturing and distributing "pornographic" films of fetus dissections, torture, and fake autopsies. The cocaine-dealing profession is not limited to the white Beaufrey and the Italian American Blue crime family but also extends to Indian descendants such as Zeta, Ferro, and Calabazas. Additionally, varying degrees of scandalous enterprises are perpetrated by the corrupt government officials, including Judge Arne, the Police Chief, and the Senator.

Mexico, as well, is mired in witchery; it is, according to history, the place of the old-world Indians who became obsessed with the power of sacrifice and bloodshed. In the beginning of the novel, cocaine smuggled across the border to the United States finances the criminals in both countries and weakens subjugated people. Indians are "disappeared," as are suspected communists. The rich white supremacist Beaufrey and his lover plan the creation of underground survival stations for when the "savages" overpopulate and dirty the aristocratic bloodlines of the world.

Silko suggests that the origins of this depravity are the horrors committed against indigenous peoples and the subsequent loss of tribal thinking; she reveals these horrors through the telling of suppressed history. The relatively recent history of Tucson during the Apache wars, when citizens profited from the deaths of their own relatives, and the long-past history of the coming of the Europeans to the Americas, when Montezuma and Hernán Cortés (kindred sorcerers who "worshiped destruction and blood" and "secretly knew one another") began the undoing of all people, are told to characters by their grandmothers and through an ancient manuscript. Suppressed history is also presented in a speech by La Escapía, the Indian wife of El Feo the Mountain Twin. Additionally, Clinton plans radio shows that will aid the rise of the people by educating them about their history and their spirits; the text of his shows describes the kinship of African spirits and Native American spirits, thus also uniting African Americans and Native Americans. The manuscript and the oral stories continually help the reader to decipher the novel as a whole.

The heyday of the current injustices is already passing, however, and the criminals begin to be destroyed. Prophetically, the wicked bring about their own destruction by the hands of their servants. The sacred Twins begin their pilgrimage north from Mexico to the U.S. border, leading hundreds of thousands of people to reclaim the land. The Giant Stone Snake proves to be a message from the spirits pointing south toward Mexico, both the original source of witchery and the source for prophecy fulfillment. The Army of the Homeless is established; a barefoot Hopi begins to organize the incarcerated across the United States; Wilson Weasel Tail preaches the need to retake the land; and Awa Gee plans to plant a virus in the computers of power stations all over the country just as the people revolt. The novel ends with Tucson in chaos but with nearby cities unaware of the turmoil.

*The Characters*

The sheer multitude of characters serves to emphasize the novel's focus on the interplay between characters and events. The short sections of the novel move from character to character. Sometimes the point of view changes even within the short sections. Nearly all these characters are developed fully, and they make up a wide array of bizarre, sometimes perverse individuals. The characters are clustered, and each cluster is eventually tied to other clusters of characters; this movement unravels the narrative in the novel, emphasizing each event's and person's interplay in the novel's nonstop motion.

Though no character dominates the novel, Sterling emerges as its conscience. Sterling, appearing near the beginning and at the end of the book, is unique among the characters in that he enters Tucson by accident, wandering into town with no real purpose, and then leaves it behind, taking only the awareness he has gained. His eventual gain of understanding for the endurance of the Earth and the importance of tribal spirits is the very heart of the novel. At the beginning, Sterling is immersed in the white system, and his self-delusion is rooted in his European thinking, symbolized by his obsession with crime magazines. Sterling's fascination with the white image of "Geronimo" (his favorite "criminal") illustrates his inability to understand reality in a tribal sense. Silko educates the reader about Geronimo's "true" existence, as Sterling should have been educated, through the oral stories of an Indian matriarch. The crime magazines and other trappings of white culture are abandoned once Sterling returns to his culture and begins to think in a more tribal-centered manner. Sterling leaves the corrupt world of the novel behind and returns to the Stone Snake and to his reservation. Once home, he recalls the old-time ways he was taught as a child, realizes the sacredness of the Earth, and knows that the Twin Brothers and the people will come from the south.

Seese's fate is precarious but hopeful. Her addiction to cocaine and her connection to that world of depravity, is directly responsible for the loss of her child, Monte. While she searches for Monte, she begins to wean herself from her addiction; she lapses back into drug use, but her experiences while using again prove so horrifying that she apparently commits to permanent cessation. Through her dreams, she eventually realizes that Monte is dead and lost to her forever. Seese continues to survive and, at the close of the novel, remains with Lecha, who has completed the transcription of the ancient manuscript and who predicts that the unrest of the people will be followed by natural disasters and civil war. Seese's future and her beliefs regarding the prophecy are unknown, as she does nothing but cry during the final pages. Yet Silko has Lecha and Sterling rescue Seese from the crumbling Tucson, promising at least a potential future.

Silko creates the character of Lecha with many characteristics of Coyote, a Native American mythic character who is half creator, half fool and renowned for greediness and trickery. Her desertion of Ferro, her son, and her playfulness with the corrupt world—even while she translates the manuscript and believes in her grandmother Yeome's teachings—display luck, creativity, and craftiness, those attributes of Coyote that maintain vitality even in the midst of desolation. Yeome has given Lecha a gift of psychic power, which she has used to gain wealth; like many old families of Tucson, she profits from others' misfortunes, for she soon realizes that she has psychic powers only to discover the dead. Nevertheless, Lecha is the keeper of the ancient manuscript, the calendar that will predict the coming catastrophes. She holds the key to the prophecy, to the future.

## Themes and Meanings

Vital to *Almanac of the Dead* is the acceptance of what Native American writer Paula Gunn Allen terms "ceremonial time," a sense of reality that transcends linear time and embraces the fluidity of past, present, and future. Silko's structural technique, which gracefully connects people and events while shifting from perspective to perspective, establishes the imperative of reading in this mindframe. The lack of an easily definable plot and protagonist is disconcerting until the accretion is recognized; then characters and occurrences become more fully understood as the multiple stories begin to unite, forming a whole instead of related parts. The reader, like Sterling, is guided toward understanding through accretion and a vision of synthesis. Only when viewed as interlocking and interrelated do the fragmented, jumbled accounts reveal a comprehensible message.

Silko insists that her narratives of the characters' lives become united, and she similarly merges specific times and places into a boundless reality. Time becomes fluid as events of the past illuminate the future, present illuminates past, and so on. Her literal movement from place to place, character to character, and time to time elucidates the novel's theme of reality as movement; she demands that characters not be conceptualized as isolated individuals and demands that time not be deciphered linearly. Only witchery enforces the notion of distinct beings in a particular place and time. Rather, the unifying elements of the novel—and, Silko suggests, of reality itself—are the connection to ritual and ceremony and the endurance of the Earth.

*Almanac of the Dead* shows the Feminine Power, a principal central to Silko's own Keres Pueblo, rising from forgotten history to reassert its rightful role in Native American cosmology. The passing down of the almanac itself has been matrilineal; the ancient manuscript is passed to Yeome and from her to her granddaughters. Yeome and Old Mahawala, another matriarch in the novel, both ensure the education of their children to the old ways through their written and oral tales. Once Sterling returns to his reservation and begins to compile the knowledge he has gleaned from multiple sources, he finally begins to remember these old tales from his grandmother, tales he had long ago forgotten. He knows that, regardless, the Earth will continue, for "she" will always be sacred; people only "desecrated themselves," for humanity is "too insignificant to desecrate her." The taking back of the Native Lands is itself a reclaiming of the feminine; when indigenous peoples identify themselves with the Mother Earth, they become the land, endure, and continue.

*Critical Context*

Like N. Scott Momaday and James Welch, two highly successful contemporary Native American writers, Silko writes within the Native American oral tradition— appropriately so, since her main agenda is the reaffirmation of tribal ways and tribal reality. She has been hailed as one of the most important writers of her time, and *Almanac of the Dead* is, to say the least, a massive undertaking. The novel, nearly eight hundred pages in length, is nothing short of Silko's personally constructed view of the apocalypse. As in her previous work, especially her novel *Ceremony* (1977), she maintains the imperative need for a return to spirituality and to traditional beliefs. *Almanac of the Dead*, however, is rampant with graphic violence and can be a disturbing, even agonizing, reading experience; Silko, no doubt, purposefully intensifies the witchery in her novel with this vivid manner of depiction in order to indelibly print the harsh realities into the minds of her readers. The novel, despite its weaknesses, is amazingly successful, inescapably haunting.

*Bibliography*

Allen, Paula Gunn. "Leslie Marmon Silko and Gerald Vizenor: Healing and Ritual." In *The Sacred Hoop: Recovering the Feminine in American Indian Traditions.* Boston: Beacon Press, 1986. Allen discusses the central themes of environmental integrity and pacifism in Silko's novel *Ceremony*. Comparison of *Ceremony* and *Almanac of the Dead* is interesting, especially in light of Allen's points. The book contains invaluable information on Native American culture and literature.

Benediktsson, Thomas E. "The Reawakening of the Gods: Realism and the Supernatural in Silko and Hulme." *Critique: Studies in Contemporary Fiction* 33 (Winter, 1992): 121-131. Benediktsson does not deal specifically with *Almanac of the Dead* but his analysis of Silko's work is illuminating. For the scholarly reader.

Birkerts, Sven. "Apocalypse Now: *Almanac of the Dead* by Leslie Silko." *The New Republic* 205 (November 4, 1991): 39-41. Birkerts describes Silko's process of stage development in the first two-thirds of the novel and sketches outlines of the events and characters. Birkerts finds fault with the last third of the novel, reasoning that Silko unwinds too quickly what she has spent such effort in originally spinning. His review is quite useful and interesting.

Jones, Malcolm, Jr. "*Almanac of the Dead.*" *Newsweek* 118 (November 18, 1991): 84. Jones finds *Almanac of the Dead* powerful but also maddening. He claims that the novel is Silko's unfair vision of payback, peopled with "good characters and white characters." Brief and entertaining, though not very informative.

Seyersted, Per. *Leslie Marmon Silko.* Boise, Idaho: Boise State University, 1980. This short book contains a biography of Silko with discussion of some of her stories, poems, and *Ceremony*. The main interest of the study is Seyersted's discussion of Silko as a storyteller. The book is written for the general reader and provides a good base knowledge of the author of *Almanac of the Dead*.

*Tiffany Elizabeth Thraves*

# ALNILAM

*Author:* James Dickey (1923-      )
*Type of plot:* Philosophical realism
*Time of plot:* January, 1943
*Locale:* Peckover and adjoining Latham Field, North Carolina
*First published:* 1987

> *Principal characters:*
> FRANK CAHILL, a crusty, emotionally shallow Atlanta amusement park
>   owner
> JOEL CAHILL, Frank's recently disappeared and presumed-dead son
> BOYD MCCLENDON, a Peckover hotel owner who befriends Cahill while
>   he is staying there
> COLONEL VERNON HOCCLEVE, the military commander of Latham Air
>   Field, where Joel trained
> MCCLINTOCK MCCAIG, a Latham flight instructor, Joel's friend
> STATHIS HARBELIS, a Latham aviator cadet, Joel's friend
> MAJOR BRUNO IANNONE, a medical doctor at Latham
> HANNAH PELHAM, a Peckover girl who loved Joel

*The Novel*

Inspired, perhaps, by his own World War II flying experiences for the Army Air Corps, James Dickey's novel *Alnilam* is set in the fictional town of Peckover adjoining a military airfield near Fayetteville, North Carolina. The central character, Frank Cahill, officially notified of the accidental flying death of his son, Joel, whom he has never seen, journeys to the airbase to meet the officers and aviation cadets.

*Alnilam* is not divided into chapters or major parts. All the events center around Frank Cahill, recently blind from diabetes, and his quest to find out about his son and the manner of his death. Lengthy passages of the novel are set in parallel columns reflecting darkness and light, the bold left type reflecting Cahill's internal sensations and thoughts, and the right side the objective narrative of speech and events.

*Alnilam* opens with an interesting account of Cahill's attempt to find his way out of a boardinghouse in the middle of a winter night to relieve himself. He is accompanied by Zack, his faithful, untrained dog. This hallucinatory opening is followed by flashbacks of Cahill's life, fleshing out some biographical details and clarifying his present situation. He is the owner of Willow Plunge Amusement Park in Atlanta. Nineteen years ago, his pregnant wife, Florence, left him forever. He has never once seen or contacted his son, Joel. Cahill's blindness, the result of the sudden onset of adult diabetes, occurred less than four months ago.

The novel's events occur within a week in January, 1943. Cahill has just received a military telegram inviting him to the airbase where his son was training. The military cadets are graduating, and they want Cahill to attend the ceremonies. On a selfish whim, he decides to go and arrives with Zack in Peckover, which adjoins the base. He is enthusiastically welcomed by Colonel Vernon Hoccleve, the military commanding officer, who allows him to meet with officers, friends, and fellow cadets—anyone, in short, who knew Joel. Cahill questions all of them about his son. Cahill also meets Hannah Pelham, Joel's wild girlfriend. She reveals Joel to be somewhat sadistic. Hannah seduces a somewhat surprised Cahill.

Soon a contradictory picture of Joel emerges from the various exchanges. Joel, it turns out, was a charismatic, although secretive and mystical individual. He founded a strange cult among his fellow students named "Alnilam," which is Arabic for "string of pearls." The name comes from the middle star in the belt of the constellation Orion. Joel believed that man and flying machine were extensions of one another, and he inculcated this belief through cryptic statements that his followers have elevated to the status of gospel.

Cahill's investigative mystery deepens when he discovers that cadet-pilot Joel's plane came down because of a downdraft while he was swooping over a brush fire. He was pulled out of his plane by a farmer and taken to a farmhouse. While the farmer fought the blaze, Joel escaped back into the fire. He then made his way to a river and disappeared forever. The investigating officials were sure his body would show up soon.

Cahill does not share their confidence; neither do the Alnilam cadets, nor McClintock McCaig, Joel's flight trainer and friend. McCaig manages to get Cahill into an airplane and takes him for a flight so he can better understand Joel's love of flying. Through it all, Cahill expresses curiosity but no grief. He is neither excited nor repelled by his observations and discoveries.

Cahill's presence begins to have a negative effect at the base. Zack bites one of the cadets and attacks and kills a pack of dogs. Colonel Hoccleve orders Cahill to leave the base and not attend the ceremonies. The Alnilam group persuades Cahill to remain. They reveal to him Joel's secret philosophy and the son's prediction of his own disappearance and the appearance of his father. The cadets, allied with others at various bases, are planning a special surprise at graduation. Cahill enters the base secretly and wanders onto the airfield when chaos breaks loose. The cadets have initiated an insurrection by destroying airplanes, leading to the death of an older pilot and Zack's decapitation. The novel ends with Cahill returning home and asking Hannah to come live with him. She refuses. Cahill boards his bus, realizing he has come to terms with himself.

*The Characters*

Frank Cahill is a newly blind, self-sufficient, irascible individual who has been a loner all of his life. Even his marriage, recounted in flashbacks, never brought him close to his wife. She left him while pregnant, and he never tried to contact her or his child until he received the military telegram. Dickey portrays a very unsympathetic character, a cursed, blind Oedipal figure searching not for a father but for a son. He finds some measure of salvation and meaning to life in his quest to understand Joel's life and death.

Zack, Cahill's constant companion, is a large, black, wolflike dog that everybody fears, and with good reason. Untrained and newly acquired because of Cahill's sudden blindness, Zack attains mythical proportions. Afraid of nothing, the canine attacks an air cadet, kills a marauding pack of wild dogs, and is finally stopped only by whirling propellers at the novel's end. Cahill carries the dog's head in his hands in a rousing conclusion to the bloody carnage at the Latham Field graduation ceremonies.

Joel Cahill, Frank's son, is never seen but is described by most all the other characters. Dickey portrays him as a Shelley-like figure, enigmatic, brilliant, and defiant. He is also cruel, and he creates and leads a dictatorial military unit. He dies (or mysteriously disappears) and remains to the reader a creepy, sadistic character.

Boyd McClendon is the garrulous, whiskey-drinking owner of a hotel/diner in Peckover who takes a liking to Cahill. He attempts to comfort and aid him during his week-long ordeal. His presence is crucial to the newly arrived blind hero unfamiliar with Peckover.

Hannah Pelham, who loved Joel, is the wild mountain maid working in the local mill. She sees the messianic cadet clearly, particularly his sadistic impulses. Through her, Cahill attempts to express his welling emotional breakthrough by novel's end.

At Latham Air Field, Cahill meets a number of individuals. Colonel Vernon Hoccleve, a military commander, is depicted as a straightforward, no-nonsense officer who runs a tight organization. Disliked by Joel and most of the cadets, he is sympathetic to Cahill and Zack, at first, but realizes later the twosome are a disturbing presence. Sensing trouble, he attempts to bar Cahill from the ceremonies, but he is too late to stop the tragic events.

Joel's flight instructor and friend McClintock McCaig is skeptical about the pilot's reported death and disappearance. Through his investigative efforts, he discovers physical evidence that Joel may still be alive. Stathis Harbelis is also Joel's friend and a member of the secretive Alnilam conspiracy. He comes across as naïve at first, but he is a committed true believer, dedicated to carrying out Joel's cryptic commands to the very end. Finally, there is Major Bruno Iannone, the skeptical medical officer who sees Joel clearly as a dangerous demagogue and a menace to his unit and the U.S. military.

*Themes and Meanings*

One of Dickey's major themes in *Alnilam* is sight versus blindness. The blind father often sees more clearly than the sighted characters. Dickey repeatedly emphasizes the unreliability of the senses. He contrasts the physical power of seeing and the luminous inner sight of understanding. His use of parallel texts between the dark and the light, although clumsy, underscores his point.

Dickey is also interested in father-son relationships. He is influenced by classical mythology, particularly Sophocles' blind hero Oedipus. Cahill, like his mythical counterpart, is intrigued by his family roots. It is Cahill who comes to an understanding of himself and discovers the truth about his son and, perhaps unknowingly, a part of himself. Both Oedipus and Cahill have to contend with hubris, the classical sin of pride. Cahill listens to no one, a trait the classical hero also shares. Yet unlike Oedipus, who searches for his father, the sightless Cahill searches for his Icarus-like son, who flew too close to the flames.

Dickey, poet that he is, is interested in the meaning and mystery of flight. He writes highly mystical passages about the air, perhaps drawing on his own experiences as a World War II fighter pilot. The best sequences in the book occur when he is describing the mystique of flying, as, for example, when the novelist has two airmen describe their flying experiences during the war and later when Cahill takes his first flight.

Dickey is also concerned thematically about power and its abuse. Joel, the poetry-spouting cadet, pulls people toward him in a conspiratorial circle. He is a mysterious, almost mystical figure, inspiring everyone around him. Joel says he is one with the airplane while in flight. Everyone agrees, including the flight instructors; he was born to fly. Joel is someone people not only remember but also trust. He becomes a messiah figure with believers who would follow him to the grave. Dickey points out that people such as Joel are potentially destructive.

The conflict of leadership and the revolt against rational authority is another theme explored by Dickey. All the Alnilam cadets, under Joel's leadership, conspire mutiny within the military system. They plan to take it over one day and, in time, to take over America and eventually the world. Cahill's arrival galvanizes them into overt action, hence the need for him to witness the destruction planned for the graduation ceremonies. Their plotting and subsequent infamy, Dickey says, serve as a reminder of the cabals that launched Adolf Hitler, Vladimir Ilich Lenin, and Benito Mussolini.

Perhaps the book's weakest thematic development revolves around the whole concept of Alnilam and its ultimate meaning. Dickey is too vague and cryptic on the subject to engage the reader's attention. Often long-winded in other areas, he never comes to grips with the topic. Also, the demonstration of Alnilam's power is awkwardly contrived and melodramatically conceived, robbing the novel's denouement of its intended impact.

*Critical Context*

*Alnilam* was Dickey's first novel since the highly acclaimed *Deliverance* (1987). Unlike his first novel, which was a straightforward, macho tale of four innocent people forced to confront their killer instincts in the wild, *Alnilam* was poetic, intricate, laced heavily with symbolism and given to visionary idealism. It was also less dramatic and less accessible to the reader. Yet *Alnilam* and *Deliverance*, while different in stylistic approach, plots, and characters, are remarkably similar in philosophy. The heroes in both novels come to an enlightened understanding of themselves through their remarkable experiences and move away from their meaningless lives.

Dickey exhibits a consistency in his writings. Years earlier, he wrote a poem stating that a man would never see until he either went blind or, like the mythical hunter Orion, became a part of the stars and light. Dickey's major character in *Alnilam*, Cahill, fulfills that earlier poetic prophecy. Cahill, recently blind, achieves his own glorious transformation by searching for the truth about his son. In his struggle with himself and the strange world he is visiting, Cahill becomes like the warrior-hunter Orion, with his faithful companion Zack symbolizing the dog Sirius.

In his work, Dickey has always been intoxicated with the power of language. In *Alnilam*, he uses that power to do for air what Melville achieved with water in *Moby Dick: Or, The Whale* (1851). For Dickey, air is more fundamental to human existence than water. He examines the kind of emotional state humans achieve when flying. His aim is to show how the human body reacts to leaving the ground. His passages on flying, the importance of flight, and aerial combat are easily the best parts of the book.

Dickey attempted to break new ground in fiction with *Alnilam* but was only partially successful. Critics complained that the novel was far too long, overblown, and pretentious and was marred by slow pacing. Although the book is ostensibly a mystery, it is shaped less by plot than by poetic impulses. At his best, however, Dickey creates vivid characters, especially Southerners, and is able to create a richly detailed picture of a region.

*Bibliography*

Baughman, Ronald. "James Dickey." In *Dictionary of Literary Biography Documentary Series*. Vol. 7, edited by Margaret A. Van Antwerp. Detroit: Gale Research, 1989. Study devoted to three American poets, James Dickey, Robert Frost, and Marianne Moore. Baughman gives a comprehensive look at Dickey's life and work. He intersperses critical commentary, Dickey's letters and interviews, book reviews, and numerous photographs.

Calhoun, Richard J., and Robert W. Hill. *James Dickey*. Boston: Twayne, 1983. Good overall introduction to Dickey's pre-*Alnilam* work. Opens with a biographical sketch and then examines his work chronologically. Emphasis is placed on the poetry, but his prose work, including *Deliverance*, is also examined in a separate chapter. Dickey's critical contributions are placed in context with his literary output. Afterword, chronology, select bibliography, and index.

Kirschten, Robert. *James Dickey and the Gentle Ecstasy of Earth*. Baton Rouge: Louisiana State University Press, 1988. The book's title is taken from the minor nineteenth century poet Joseph Trumbull Stickney, whom Dickey engages in a poetic dialogue in "Exchanges." Examines the entire range of Dickey's poetry and labels him as a mystic, neoplatonist, romantic, and primitive. Sees Dickey as a poetic gambler willing to take creative risks. Helpful in understanding Dickey's poetic flights of fancy in *Alnilam*.

Van Ness, Gordon. *Outbelieving Existence: The Measured Motion of James Dickey*. Columbia, S.C.: Camden House, 1992. Solid study of Dickey's whole corpus, with five chapters on poetry and separate chapters on his children's poetry, novels, other prose writings, and criticism. Excellent examination of *Deliverance* and *Alnilam*, with a fine summary of critical opinion on the latter. Offers a good overview of Dickey's career and a valuable bibliography.

Weigl, Bruce, and T. R. Hummer, eds. *The Imagination as Glory: The Poetry of James Dickey*. Urbana: University of Illinois Press, 1984. Collection of a dozen essays on

Dickey by well-known writers, including novelist Joyce Carol Oates, critic Ralph J. Mills, and poet Laurence Lieberman. Also includes two essays by Dickey about his own work. Critical commentary varies from adulation to skepticism. Closes with a valuable bibliography.

*Terry Theodore*

# THE ANCIENT CHILD

*Author:* N. Scott Momaday (1934-      )
*Type of plot:* Psychological
*Time of plot:* The 1980's
*Locale:* San Francisco, the Oklahoma Plains, and the Navajo lands
*First published:* 1989

> *Principal characters:*
> LOCKE SETMAN, also called SET and LOKI, a middle-aged Native American and a successful painter
> GREY, a young medicine woman of mixed Kiowa and Navajo descent
> BILLY THE KID, a legendary outlaw who figures prominently in Grey's fantasies
> KOPE'MAH, Grey's grandmother, an ancient medicine woman
> LOLA BOURNE, Set's girlfriend, a beautiful and sophisticated music teacher
> BENT SANDRIDGE, Set's philosophical adoptive father
> THE BEAR BOY, a figure from Kiowa myth

*The Novel*

This story of a Native American's search for identity alternates scenes from the lives of the two main characters, Set and Grey. Interspersed among these scenes are tales from Kiowa myths and Western legends, each with relevance to the main characters' quest for identity.

Early in the novel, Grey watches over the deathbed of her ancient grandmother, Kope'mah. She dreams of the legendary outlaw Billy the Kid, and imagines herself as his lover and companion. She is at this time also growing gradually aware of her powers as a medicine woman.

Set, in San Francisco, is at the peak of his career as a painter. Orphaned at the age of seven, Set has been reared by his adoptive father Bent with love but with little or no sense of his heritage as a Native American. Now in middle age, he enjoys a strong and mutually supportive relationship with Lola, although he and Lola remain fairly independent of one another. When a cryptic telegram summons him to Oklahoma by telling him that Grandmother Kope'mah is near death, he is intrigued. He has never heard of Grandmother Kope'mah and almost believes the telegram has been sent to him in error except for its tantalizing mention of his biological father, Cate. He goes to Oklahoma but arrives too late; the grandmother is dead. There, however, he meets Grey and is unsettled and captivated by her beauty and dignity. His other relatives convince him to attend an Indian gathering before returning to San Francisco. At the gathering, Grey asks Set to paint her face for a dance, and she presents him with a medicine bundle that contains "bear medicine" that she says belongs to him. This brief exchange creates a bond between them that Set cannot yet fathom.

Back in his own world, Set's stature as a painter continues to grow. His agent, Jason, arranges an opening for Set in Paris, and he travels there with Lola. When they learn that Bent has had a small stroke, Lola returns to San Francisco to attend him. Set has a one-night affair with the Parisienne owner of the gallery where his paintings are being shown; on returning to his hotel, he finds a frantic massage from Lola telling him that Bent's condition has worsened. He returns immediately but finds that his father has already died.

Orphaned a second time, Set is plunged into grief and depression. Lola suspects Set's infidelity, and their relationship suffers. Cut off from his only loving relationships, the lost and alienated Set experiences a kind of mental breakdown. He wanders the streets aimlessly and spends days on end in his studio, painting and drinking, often forgetting to eat or sleep. Lola and Jason eventually have Set hospitalized.

Meanwhile, on the Oklahoma plains, Grey is slowly, intuitively becoming aware both of Set's crisis and of her own role as his savior. Touched by the spirit of her grandmother, she feels her powers as a medicine woman growing. She begins writing an account of her dream life with Billy the Kid and also begins creating masks. She waits, knowing that Set will be drawn to her. One stormy day, he arrives.

With Grey's aid, Set begins to recover from his breakdown. As she leads him on a journey, both physical and spiritual, to the Navajo lands of her mother's tribe, Set and Grey begin to fall in love. Along the journey, she guides him through a spiritual metamorphosis into a bear, a necessary part of his spiritual recovery and of his discovering his identity as a Native American. At home with Grey's mother, sister, and niece in Navajo country, Set is completely healed. He and Grey are married and conceive a child. At the novel's close, Set goes alone on a "vision quest" to capture the full power of his bear medicine and to complete and solidify his identity as an American Indian.

The Kiowa myths and legends interspersed throughout the story are an important part of the novel. One myth tells of a boy who is suddenly transformed into a bear while he is playing with his sisters. Another is the story of the "lost boy," a lone child who one day appears at a Kiowa camp. The Kiowa are astonished, because the boy has appeared as if from nowhere; he speaks a strange language and amazes them by his total lack of fear. They give him food and shelter and are ready to adopt him as one of their own, but when they awake the next day he is gone. The mystery of the lost boy is so troubling to them that they find they must invent a story to explain his sudden appearance and equally sudden disappearance. Another legend that recurs throughout the novel is of the historical figure Set-Angya ("Sitting Bear"), a Kiowa chief whose courage was so great it seemed a kind of madness. The figures in these stories all provide parallels to Set's experiences.

*The Characters*

At the novel's opening, Grey is a self-assured, uninhibited adolescent. She develops mainly in terms of the natural maturation that comes with age. She already has a powerful sense of self, is equally at home in her two worlds (Kiowa and Navajo), and understands the sources of her strength. "Never had Grey to quest after visions,"

Momaday repeats throughout the novel; she easily creates her own. Early on, she manifests these qualities of strength and self-assurance in a fairly adolescent way— declaring herself mayor of the collection of abandoned sod-houses where she lives and daydreaming about life with Billy the Kid. Her power and freedom reach their apotheosis in her fantasies about life with Billy the Kid; in these fantasies, she is totally free, brave, supremely capable, and loved. As she matures, and especially after she meets Set, the same qualities she has in abundance in her dreams begin to exhibit themselves more strongly in her real life. At the age of twenty, she understands her responsibility to guide and heal Set, a worldy, successful man approximately twice her age. Grey engineers Set's rites of passage and brings him into a stable and supportive Indian family. Grey's development mirrors Set's, without the turmoil and emotional and spiritual confusion. Because Grey has always been deeply connected with her native culture, she knows and understands her own identity.

Set is the product of a very different environment. An orphan, he is cut off completely from the Indian world. In adulthood, Set seems happy and successful but has no real connection to the community around him. His only true sense of himself is found through his art. When Bent dies and his relationship with Lola sours, Set is cast adrift. He experiences a nervous breakdown of sorts that leaves him physically and mentally weakened and vulnerable. With Grey's help, he is able to rediscover and connect with the culture of his ancestors, and thus become whole again.

Lola is a foil for Grey. She is beautiful, convivial, and talented, but she is thoroughly Anglo-American in orientation: ambitious, cultured, and materialistic. Although she and Set share an emotional bond through their art, her values are contrasted to the traditional spirituality of Grey. While she is not to play as important a role in Set's life as Grey, her love and assistance form a critical part of Set's progress toward under- standing his identity.

Billy the Kid lives entirely in Grey's imagination in *The Ancient Child*. Her fantasy relationship with him serves as an important bridge, connecting Grey not only to the past of her grandmother's era and to the non-Indian world, but also to a vision of herself as powerful, courageous, and sensuous. Billy, like many of the characters, is kind of an "ancient child"—young in years, but hardened and cynical in outlook. Despite his notoriously cold-blooded nature, Billy exhibits the charm, playfulness, and respectful courtesy of a child.

Kope'mah, the ancient medicine woman, is Grey's guide on her journey toward becoming a medicine woman. In Kope'mah's memory live vivid images of her tribe's glorious past and also their deepest suffering; like Billy, she provides Grey with a powerful connection to the past. Even in death, Kope'mah remains a vital force in Grey's and Set's lives. Her funeral is the occasion of their first meeting, and her spirit continues to inform and inspire Grey as she develops as a medicine woman.

The "bear boy" connects Set to Kiowa legend and hence to his Native American heritage. Set's development parallels the ancient tale of the bear boy: He has the bear's "medicine," and one of Grey's roles is to help Set make the transformation to the potent bear and back to manhood again. The bear boy's connection to Set is never defined explicitly; rather, he serves as one of the novel's many "ancient children" through whom the protagonists discover themselves, as they identify with these mythic figures and interpret their lives within the framework of these powerful ancient stories.

## Themes and Meanings

A major theme of *The Ancient Child* is the importance of finding one's true self and finding a home. The novel revolves around a Native American man, comfortable and successful but not quite at home in the Anglo-American world, who must discover his native culture and his own identity and role therein. Momaday's own experiences of living equally in the Anglo and Indian worlds offer him a unique and powerful insight into this question of discovering one's sense of self and one's place in the world. This, however, is not a uniquely "Indian" theme; the question of assimilating into a dominant culture while retaining one's unique cultural identity is an important part of the American experience, and the need to understand oneself and one's place in the world is universal.

Momaday believes that one of the ways for an individual to find this identity is to use stories, such as the Kiowa myths and Western legends that figure so prominently in the novel, to interpret and understand experiences. This is clearly seen in the case of Grey, who builds up a personal fantasy around the legendary character of Billy the Kid and uses the fantasy to explore and strengthen the qualities she wishes to have. Set is not an active dreamer like Grey, but Momaday shows the importance of stories to Set's life by setting up clear parallels between Set's experiences and ancient myths through the stories of the bear boy and the lost boy.

Tied to Momaday's belief in the power of stories is his theory that there is really only one essential story, told and retold in many variations. In *The Ancient Child*, he enunciates this theory through the character of Set. "Yes, he believed, there is only one story, after all, and it is about the pursuit of man by God, and it is about a man who ventures out to the edge of the world, and it is about his holy quest, and it is about his faithful or unfaithful wife, and it is about the hunting of a great beast." Part of the individual's development rests on one's ability to understand and place oneself within this story and to create one's own unique version of it.

Momaday's work exemplifies this belief; he incorporates pieces of past works and elements of his own experiences to create *The Ancient Child*. For example, Grey's writings about Billy the Kid are taken from a previously unpublished sequence of poems by Momaday entitled "The Strange and True Story of My Life with Billy the Kid." Even the book that inspires Grey to write bears a striking resemblance to Momaday's 1976 work *The Names*. In subtler ways, Momaday incorporates motifs that have occurred elsewhere in his writings: the landscape that shapes the protagonists' lifestyles, the portentous thunderstorm, the visit to the burial site of one's ancestors, and the vision quest. This is not mere recycling of previous work; rather, it is Momaday's own demonstration of how a single story (or elements of a story) can be reinterpreted to mean different things and to create different identities. By synthesizing the diverse elements of ancient myth, past writings, his own experiences, and pure fictive imagination, Momaday creates a novel that is at once a unique piece of fiction, his own story, and a universal story.

An understanding of Momaday's beliefs about telling and retelling a single story help to explain the significance of the novel's title. Ancient characters, young or old (such as the boys in the Kiowa myths), can be revived and rejuvenated by a retelling of their story. New stories (or characters) have an ancient quality because they are part of one timeless story. Grey is a kind of ancient child, a young woman undergoing a maturation process (the "story" of growing up) that is itself as old as humanity; even in youth, she has a wisdom beyond her years. ("An ancient woman inhabits the body of a girl," writes Momaday.) Set must become like a child in order to realize his full, adult identity. As the children have an ancient quality, so do the ancients have a childlike quality. Kope'mah and Worcester Meat, Grey's ancient relatives, easily conjure up and reexperience scenes from their lives through their imaginative powers. They remain simple and playful even in advanced age.

*Critical Context*

*The Ancient Child* is in many ways a natural continuation and synthesis of Momaday's earlier works. In light of Momaday's view that there is "only one story," the reader is not surprised to see themes and images repeated from such works as *The Way to Rainy Mountain* (1969) and *House Made of Dawn* (1969), chiefly the belief in the individual's power to re-create the self through the imaginative use of powerful stories.

*The Ancient Child* also shares with Momaday's earlier works a fascination with the power of language; Momaday has even coined the term "wordwalker" to describe his view of himself as an artist. Momaday's work displays an acute awareness of words, language, and tone—seen, for example, in Set's obsessive meditation on his own name during his mental breakdown, and in the difference between the rough frankness of Grey's (imagined) spoken dialogues with Billy the Kid and the even elegance of her writings about him. Momaday has expressed an admiration for the linguistic purity and force of the poems of Emily Dickinson and of formal Indian orations; his work shows a similar striving toward a powerful simplicity and clarity of language.

Closely linked to Momaday's feel for words is his interest in different narrative forms, a feature also found in his earlier works. In *The Ancient Child*, Momaday combines modern narrative fiction with poetry, the Western lore of the dime novel, and the oral storytelling tradition of the Kiowa people, constantly shifting time, place, and perspective. The resulting narrative is disjointed, but this is critical to the theme of the novel. The "story" of this novel synthesizes these diverse elements, just as the vision of Set's own personal "story" synthesizes the fragmented elements of his life.

Momaday, like his protagonist Grey, is of mixed Kiowa descent and spent much of his youth on Navajo reservations in the Southwest. In addition to being a writer and poet, he is, like Set, a painter. *The Ancient Child* is in many ways Momaday's own story; in it, Momaday draws heavily on his own experiences as a Native American artist balancing his life between the Indian and Anglo-American worlds.

To categorize Momaday as an "Indian" writer, however, would be to limit the scope of his work. Momaday resists being pigeonholed as a spokesman for the American Indian. *The Ancient Child*, with its thematic concerns about cultural assimilation, its emphasis on discovering individual identity, and its reliance on landscape for defining moods and developing themes, is a thoroughly American novel.

*Bibliography*
Meredith, Howard. "The Ancient Child." *World Literature Today* 64 (Summer, 1990): 510-511. Discusses the structure of *The Ancient Child* and its relation to the novel's themes. Notes the importance of art as "affirmation" and "resistance" for both the protagonists (Set and Grey). Focuses on the importance of the geometrical symbolism of the titles of the novel's four sections and of cultural images as the framework of the story.
Roemer, Kenneth M. "The Ancient Child, A Novel." *The American Indian Quarterly* 15 (Winter, 1991): 269-271. Places *The Ancient Child* in the context of Momaday's other works. Identifies recurring themes and images and discusses how Momaday's incorporation of existing material into this work typifies his aesthetic theory. Discusses the importance of structure and image in developing the novel's themes and examines Momaday's belief in the "transformative powers" of storytelling.
Schubnell, Matthais. *N. Scott Momaday: The Cultural and Literary Background*. Norman: Oklahoma University Press, 1985. The biographical section offers insight into Momaday's bicultural orientation and discusses his literary influences. Also includes critical discussion of Momaday's works (novels and poetry) through *The Names*. Of particular interest for readers of *The Ancient Child* is an extended examination of Momaday's then-unpublished group of poems, "The Strange and True Story of My Life with Billy the Kid," sections of which are incorporated into *The Ancient Child*.
Woodard, Charles L. *Ancestral Voice: Conversations with N. Scott Momaday*. Lincoln: University of Nebraska Press, 1989. A lengthy interview in which Momaday discusses the relation between his life and works, his aesthetic theories, the legend of Billy the Kid, and Indian myths. He talks about the transformative power of stories and storytelling and discusses his personal connection to the Kiowa myth of the bear boy. *The Ancient Child* is discussed as a work in progress.
Zachrau, Thekla. "N. Scott Momaday: Towards an Indian Identity." *American Indian Culture and Research Journal* 3, no. 1 (1979): 39-56. An excellent source for the themes and motifs that recur throughout Momaday's work. Gives a detailed analysis of such elements as cultural alienation, Indian mythology, Kiowa oral tradition, the legend of the bear boy, autobiographical details, and the role of language and narrative technique in Momaday's writings. Although Zachrau does not discuss *The Ancient Child* itself, the reader will find a wealth of information about themes and episodes that are carried over from previous works.

*Catherine Swanson*

# ANNIE JOHN

*Author:* Jamaica Kincaid (Elaine Potter Richardson, 1949-     )
*Type of plot:* Autobiographical
*Time of plot:* The 1950's and the early 1960's
*Locale:* Antigua, the West Indies
*First published:* 1985

> *Principal characters:*
> ANNIE VICTORIA JOHN, the protagonist, a young West Indian girl
> ANNIE JOHN, her mother, whose identity her daughter adores and against
> whom she rebels
> ALEXANDER JOHN, the protagonist's aging father, a kind but aloof car-
> penter
> GWEN, Annie's first childhood friend, the model of innocence
> THE RED GIRL, a "wild" girl who introduces Annie to erotic love
> MA CHESS, Annie's grandmother, who embraces an African worldview

## The Novel

Narrated exclusively by the fifteen-year-old, first-person protagonist, *Annie John* explores the inseparable bond between mother and daughter as it provides both the illusion of security and the movement toward psychological separation. Influenced greatly by autobiographical elements, the novel traces Annie's coming of age, from her innocent adoration of her mother, who has the same name, through her rejection of her mother in the effort to establish her own individual identity, to her departure from home, the island of Antigua in the West Indies. Annie's quest is not only to emerge in adolescence with her own self-identity but also to integrate the complexity of her Caribbean heritage with its legacies of colonization, cultural differences, and pluralist ideologies. She seeks an individuality based on her separateness from all those around her.

In the opening chapters, the book's languid rhythms, sensuous imagery, and sharply honed sentences revolved around the dominant image of Annie's mother's hand. At ten, Annie learns of the death of a girl younger than herself who has died in her mother's arms. She spends her childhood completely within her mother's world. She studies her shopping in the market, talking to her friends, eating her meals, and laughing with her father. She bathes in her mother's intimacy, reveling in the scents of oils and flowers in their common bath. When Annie learns that her mother has helped to prepare a dead girl's body for burial, she recoils in horror. Her innocence broken by the reality of death foreshadows the end of her childhood and initiates the inevitable separation from her mother as Annie moves toward adulthood.

Arriving home early one day, Annie finds her mother and father in bed together, and she sees her mother's hand circling on her father's back. Having established her innocence in a world of female activities, she recognizes intuitively that her father is her chief rival for her mother's attention; she feels in danger of being shut out of her mother's world. Her ambivalence toward her mother becomes a unifying thread throughout the novel; she longs for her mother's love, yet she fears that it could suffocate her.

As Annie experiences the onset of puberty, her imminent separation from her mother is painfully felt as her mother moves further into the distance, even forbidding her to wear dresses made from the same fabric, as had been common practice when she was younger. Annie begins to move away from her mother as well. Her first close friendship is with Gwen, who is neatly dressed, always clean, and a serious student. Gwen smells like lavender, her mother's favorite scent. As Annie moves into the circle of girlfriends at school, her association with school itself becomes one of rejection. Identifying school with her mother's desires and her earlier innocence, Annie becomes a "rebel" leader, leading the girls in bawdy songs, swearing, and displaying parts of her body to the other girls.

After shifting her love for her mother to Gwen and the other schoolgirls, Annie engages in her most rebellious act yet. She explores her sexuality with the Red Girl, the opposite of all that her mother has taught her to admire in a woman. The Red Girl never bathes, never goes to church, never obeys her elders. She represents the onset of Annie's separation from her mother when she begins menstruation. With the Red Girl, Annie plays marbles, hiding them from her disapproving mother; her friendship takes on a secret, underground existence, and Annie explores her new erotic impulses. She lies with ease and pride, and she steals from her mother to buy gifts for the Red Girl.

Forced to end the friendship with the Red Girl by her mother, Annie moves further into her own world, alternately dreaming of rescuing the Red Girl and fearful of other women who have been her father's previous lovers. She fears they will use obeah, an African-based belief in power over spirits, to harm her in order to punish her father for leaving them. When a boy humiliates her, Annie's mother blames her for acting like a slut.

Annie retreats into illness, falling silent and possessed by dark, fragmented images of her early childhood. As an unusually long period of rain soaks the island, Annie becomes obsessed with cleansing her past, even washing the family's faces away from photographs. Recalling a moment of sexual arousal and fear while sitting on her father's lap, Annie retreats from her sexuality altogether and begins recasting her past and emergent maturation with the nurturing care of her maternal grandmother, Ma Chess.

As Annie recovers from her breakdown, she feels gripped by loss. Embedded in the association of images with her parents, she longs intensely to flee everything. Caught between childhood and adulthood, she wants only to escape from all that she has known. When she wins a scholarship to study in England, she has her chance. As Annie departs, however, her mother reminds her that she will always be her daughter and that Antigua will always be her home.

## The Characters

Annie Victoria John, as she imagines her mother might address letters to her, is the figure of fear both of changing and not changing that is present in every adolescent. She dominates the poetic narrative through her internal monologues, her dreams, her fantasies, her distant associations, and her precise observations of all that goes on around her. Her steady pace through anxieties over origins, identity, sexuality, and maturation arrives at an uneasy anticipation of independence in England—ironically so, given that Antigua, in Kincaid's childhood, was still a British colony. Similarly, it is just as Annie leaves that she realizes the potential for a reunion with her mother's love, yet she knows too that she must leave her mother for that reunion to become real in the future.

The protagonist's mother emerges from the ambivalent images bestowed on her by her daughter's passage from childhood to adolescence. Annie's mother appears at times as tender and at others as nearly monstrous. Her compassion, however, is never far from the reader's grasp; she cares for Annie's father, modeling loving adult relationships. Yet she also knows that Annie must become herself, and her seemingly harsh responses to her daughter are only typical, caring parental warnings and discipline.

Alexander John, Annie's father, is perceived by her as distant and aloof until she moves into puberty. Actually, her father is a kind and nurturing man but is representative of West Indian male attitudes. He regards himself as free to assert his manhood in the society, yet he is particularly attentive to Annie's mother. Both Annie's initial bonds with her mother and her refuge in her father's attention as she separates from her mother are the result of his distant but dominating presence.

Gwen, Annie's first girlfriend, is the type of character that Annie must both accept and later reject if she is to reach adulthood with her own identity. She is a comfortable bridge from Annie's early security in her mother's intimacy to her first taste of independence.

The Red Girl, embraced as Annie rejects the motherlike qualities of Gwen, evokes Annie's sexual awakening. When Annie fears her father's appeal, she moves outside the home but remains in the safety of woman's bonding. The Red Girl is wild and free, signaling Annie's own yearning for defiance and personal freedom.

Ma Chess, Annie's maternal grandmother, plays a vital role in Annie's recovery from her self-induced illness. Offering both sustenance and security, she feeds her and bathes her, just as her mother had once done. Consequently, Ma Chess preserves the potential for a loving mother-daughter relationship.

## Themes and Meanings

The stages of Annie's maturation and her quest for a sense of self are rooted not only in Kincaid's admitted autobiographical fashioning of her fiction but also in the context of Caribbean beliefs and customs. Annie's fear of losing her mother, which in turn spurs her independent development, begins when Annie realizes that her mother's social life and responsibilities are anchored in a community outside her own perceptions and understanding. Her mother must be available to her neighbors when sickness or death occurs, and her bathing of the dead girl's body as a gesture of social obligation raises the fear in Annie that her mother could die, leaving her alone in the world. Her father's handmade coffin for the girl further raises the possibility that she could be left with no parents at all, but Annie does not yet grasp the community's compassion for all of its children.

Up to the point where Annie reaches puberty, her mother has modeled every detail in order for her daughter to become an ideal woman. When Annie becomes a sexually potent female, however, she does not think her mother has noticed. Of course she has, but she says nothing; Kincaid suggests that modeling for this Caribbean mother stops at puberty. Annie's mother retreats into silence, paralleling her daughter's eventual illness. This failure to confront and to address sexuality directly and openly becomes a source of further fear for Annie.

Although Annie attempts to seek her father's attention when she rejects her mother, she also knows that, sexually, he belongs to her mother's world. Alexander's previous "outside children," in the Caribbean phrase, whom he does not acknowledge as his own, reflects a historical reality of Caribbean society. Hence Annie not only fears their wrath through obeah but also learns that there is silent shame inherent in sexuality. Kincaid implies that male sexuality has few consequences but that, for females, the consequence can be abandonment and a subsequent life of poverty.

Ma Chess dwells in an African world; she is an obeah woman who embraces an African sense of herself. Her beliefs are not for sale. Ma Chess helps Annie to recognize that she must choose her own values, which need not suppress or diminish any part of her complex cultural history. The security in the relationship between grandmother and granddaughter becomes the tension-free security of Annie's past. When she leaves to set her own course, she will take her own trunk, just as her mother did when she left her mother, and in it she will carry different contents in the baggage of race, class, gender, and nationality.

*Critical Context*

Beginning her career as a journalist for *The New Yorker*, Kincaid offered insights into American culture. She soon gained support for her own work from the magazine's editors, who began publishing her fiction in installments. *Annie John*, Kincaid's first novel, followed her collection of short stories *At the Bottom of the River* (1983) and provided a broader context for those related autobiographical stories that are told from an adult point of view. Her novel *Lucy* (1990) introduced new characters and continued the autobiographical dimension of Kincaid's observations in the United States. Between novels, she published *A Small Place* (1988), an extended essay addressed to white tourists in Antigua and reporting on the economic and social exploitation inflicted by the continuing colonial attitudes toward the island and its native residents.

*Annie John* is one of several novels that bear witness to the newly rising status of West Indian writing. Such established West Indian writers as poet and playwright Derek Walcott (winner of the 1992 Nobel Prize in Literature), novelists V. S. Naipaul,

Wilson Harris, Samuel Selvon, Roger Mais, and Earl Lovelace, and poets Martin Carter, Edward Kamu Braithwaite, Dennis Scott, and Merwyn Morris are commanding increasing critical attention; Kincaid thus is among a new generation of West Indians who are contributing to the formation of a distinctive literary tradition.

*Bibliography*
Dutton, Wendy. "Merge and Separate: Jamaica Kincaid's Fiction." *World Literature Today* 63 (Summer, 1989): 406-410. Dutton discusses the relationship between autobiographical elements in *At the Bottom of the River* and *Annie John*. She analyzes the tension between mother and daughter as not only generational in origin, but also as the suppression of Ma Chess's role in curing Annie.
Ismond, Patricia. "Jamaica Kincaid: 'First They Must Be Children.' " *World Literature Written in English* 28 (Autumn, 1988): 336-341. Tracing the struggle between mother and daughter, Ismond regards their conflict as the classic confrontation between self and other. She views Annie as a kind of innate child-trickster figure whose efforts to escape her mother's influence lead them both ultimately to the need for reunion.
Murdoch, H. Adlai. "Severing the (M)other Connection: The Representation of Cultural Identity in Jamaica Kincaid's *Annie John*." *Callaloo* 13 (Spring, 1990): 325-340. Using psychoanalytic theories, Murdoch explores the Oedipal sources of Annie's rebellion, linking the girl's need for independence with the West Indian need for a distinct identity apart from that of the colonial period. In unraveling the analogies between parental-child conflicts and the colonial subject's experience of oppression, Murdoch defines several key oppositions throughout the novel.
Perry, Donna. "Initiation in Jamaica Kincaid's *Annie John*." In *Caribbean Women Writers: Essays from the First International Conference*, edited by Selwyn R. Cudjoe. Wellesley, Mass.: Calaloux Publications, 1990. Perry discusses storytelling traditions in the West Indies, seeing Annie's narrative as participatory in the matrilineal relationships that are grounded in those traditions. She also explores the role of obeah in shaping Annie's cure from her experience of dissociation.
Timothy, Helen Pyne. "Adolescent Rebellion and Gender Relations in *At the Bottom of the River* and *Annie John*." In *Caribbean Women Writers: Essays from the First International Conference*, edited by Selwyn R. Cudjoe. Wellesley, Mass.: Calaloux Publications, 1990. A thorough close reading of the novel. Timothy's analysis combines psychological, aesthetic and cultural approaches in her assertion that Caribbean sexual repression elicits Annie's rebellion.

*Michael Loudon*

# ANYWHERE BUT HERE

*Author:* Mona Simpson (1957-    )
*Type of plot:* Bildungsroman
*Time of plot:* Primarily the 1960's and the 1970's
*Locale:* Bay City, Wisconsin, and Los Angeles, California
*First published:* 1986

> *Principal characters:*
> ANN, the main narrator, the youngest of the four women whose lives are the novel's focus
> ADELE, Ann's mother, an emotionally charged person whose behavior ranges from eccentric to unstable
> CAROL, Adele's older sister, who narrates several sections of the novel
> LILLIAN, Carol's mother, who shelters Ann when Adele cannot properly care for her

*The Novel*

*Anywhere but Here* is the fictionalized saga of an American family. Three generations of women take turns narrating chapters of a personal and cultural history that spans the years between the turn of the twentieth century and the beginning of the 1980's. The novel's nine parts do not proceed chronologically. The speakers relate events as they recall them, each adding detail and emotion to one another's stories.

The first batch of memories is delivered by Ann, beginning with her infuriated mother's practice of stopping the car on the roads of the family's native Wisconsin and the highways that lead to California and forcing her daughter out of the car. After driving out of sight, Adele usually returns minutes later, often with an ice-cream cone as a peace offering. What brings Adele and Ann to a strip of desert highway near the California border, and later to the posh Bel-Air Hotel, is a trail of men that includes Ted Diamond, a skating instructor with whom Adele buys a house in a Wisconsin suburb. A secret plan to flee Wisconsin for Los Angeles, where Ann can have a career in television, a dream her mother has always encouraged, is disrupted by Adele's marriage to Ted. When life in Wisconsin finally becomes too unpleasant, Adele and twelve-year-old Ann load up an almost-new Lincoln Continental they can ill afford and begin the journey West.

Ann pauses, and her grandmother begins to speak. Lillian narrates the events of her life, from girlhood in a large Catholic family to a sexual encounter with and marriage to Art in the early years of the twentieth century. Carol is born shortly thereafter, and Adele is born years later, at the beginning of the Great Depression. Lillian continues to describe the family tree: Carol marries Jimmy Measey, a local Bay City man, after she returns from World War II; they have two sons, Hal and Benny. Adele marries an Egyptian community-college professor named Hisham; Ann is her only child.

When Ann again takes up the narration, she is recalling the difficult first days spent with her mother in California. Ann and Adele establish a tense and lonely existence, finding themselves short of friends and money. Adele works in the Los Angeles school system, and Ann attends a lower school that will lead her to the prestigious Beverly Hills High School. At this point, Ann digresses, turning to memories of her father. She sees Hisham only twice after he leaves Adele. Returning to life in California, Ann tells of Adele's fruitless affair with Lonnie Tishman, a shiftless, perhaps dangerous land developer. After breaking off with him, Adele begins seeing a dentist whose daughter is in Ann's class. She deludes herself into thinking that Dr. Spritzer will be their salvation.

Carol remembers some good times when her boys and her niece were young children. She can even recall one pleasant trip she took with Adele when the sisters were girls. Yet she also tells the story of Hal's troubled teenage years. After returning from Vietnam, Hal becomes addicted to drugs and is arrested. Lillian has her first of several strokes when she sees Hal on the news. As painful as these memories are, Carol hints, her recollections of Benny are much harder to live with.

Ann thinks back on her life in Wisconsin, particularly her attachment to Benny. She tells the story of returning to Bay City with her mother for her cousin's funeral when Carol's youngest son is killed in a car crash. Ann then returns to the California years and a time when Adele's life is ruled by an obsession with her therapist, Dr. Hawthorne. Hawthorne does not share Adele's interest, and when the frustration overwhelms her, Adele attacks Ann, who decides, this time, to fight back and knocks her mother to the floor. Unable to separate from her fantasy, Adele orders a wedding gown. Left to her own devices while her mother schemes, Ann manages to land the television acting role Adele had always wanted for her. She uses the money and fame from her television career to enter Brown University; she leaves her mother and status-conscious Southern California, not expecting to return any time soon.

The women finish their stories. Carol tells of her slow recovery form Benny's death, her mother's death, Jimmy's heart attack, and her own cancer. Ann describes her college years, a time of independence and emotional fulfillment. When she finally returns to California, her mother seems more stable. Adele has the last word, articulating a developing cosmic belief in the oneness of all things and looking back with pride on her decision to leave Wisconsin and rear her daughter in California.

*The Characters*

Ann is a skillful storyteller. Her sensitivity to minute details and sensations is the result of a life spent watching out for Adele's volatile moods and actions. Hers is the literary voice of the novel, even though it is her mother who claims to be writing a book. Ann has a lyrical descriptive style and represents her emotions in intriguing metaphors. Her imagination has grown powerful because it is her method of escape from and defense against Adele.

Ann portrays herself as a victim of Adele's insanity. Traumatic events such as being abandoned along the roadside and having her mother threaten suicide have conditioned Ann to fear the very thing that would relieve her—separating from Adele. This love/hate relationship twists the young Ann. She exhibits signs of sexual confusion, manipulating other children into posing for nude photographs, and of moral uncertainty, growing accustomed to dishonesty, and even theft, as a survival mechanism. Ann does survive, however, and after escaping to college in the East, she begins to straighten herself out and experience personal fulfillment. She also develops an ability to appreciate her mother's unique and impressive traits and to forgive the mistreatment she suffered as a child.

Adele is capable of both compassion and cruelty. She is an unpredictable force that can suddenly change the lives of those around her. Her energy drives the novel. Although in her chaotic younger years Adele causes Ann to suffer humiliations and disappointments, the reader is given a different impression of Adele in the book's last chapter. Carol tells Ann she finally gets along with Adele, and Ann, returning from years of living on her own, is able to share a tender moment with her mother. The frightening image of an enraged, malevolent bully is replaced by the serene voice of a woman who has pacified herself with ancient as well as New Age philosophies. Adele has also repaired the self-esteem she had lacked in the days when, of she and her daughter, it was she who seemed the neediest, the most like a child.

Lillian speaks only once, and the reader comes to know her more through Ann's vision than through her own words. She provides her granddaughter with an unregulated supply of emotional and material security until Adele takes Ann to California. Ann's memory of her grandmother is idyllic. Lillian, unlike Adele, is a stoic. She is a source of calm in the novel, having endured a life of calamity without becoming warped. Her strokes mark a new period in the family history, a time when events have become so extreme that even Lillian cannot withstand their debilitating effect.

Carol is a source of compassion and tolerance even though her own life has been full of privation and tragedy. When she refuses to have a tumor in her breast treated, she is stubbornly holding onto a symbol of the pain and loss that define her. Her monologues describe her efforts to resist martyrdom and make peace with her own memories. Carol's moderate success contributes to the novel's theme of recovery.

*Themes and Meanings*

The lives of middle-class American women in the twentieth century is the predominant focus of *Anywhere but Here*. Recurring themes illustrate the differences and similarities between the three generations of speakers. All the women in the novel discuss their memories of food and, often in connection with food, the appearance of their bodies. Their experiences with sex and partnership illustrate a change in American values. Lillian, who comes of age in the 1920's, marries the first man with whom she is intimate and does not remarry after Art's death. Carol has many flings before returning home from the war and settling down with Jimmy. Adele marries twice during the 1960's and has a series of boyfriends in San Francisco. Whatever the social circumstances, the novel suggests, the issues of love and sex are complicated and painful ones. For Ann, sexual identity is a problem. Several upsetting episodes from childhood still trouble her as she hesitantly explores her physical desires during her high-school years. Later, after leaving California, Ann describes a rewarding romantic relationship. She is learning to experience love without the fear of destruction by which it has always been accompanied.

Ann's college years are her period of recovery from the wounds of life with her mother. Along with the turmoil each woman experiences come periods of calm and often healing. There are many physical recoveries in the novel. As a boy, Benny is in and out of hospital emergency rooms, but he never slows down until the day he dies on the road. Hal recovers from drug addiction, Jimmy from heart disease, and Carol from breast cancer. Carol and Jimmy's recovery from the loss of Benny, achieved through a lawsuit against the father of the boy who drove the car in which their son was killed, allows them to place blame and put their memory of the tragedy to rest. It also enables them to make their lives more comfortable, bringing the money for a swimming pool and other home improvements. Simpson provides a profound description of the ironic combination of physical and emotional compensation available through the legal system and the insurance industry.

Adele's recuperation is also based on both physical and spiritual well being. She is calmed by "all these various philosophies," by the New Age ambition to heal oneself. On the other hand, as Ann discovers, her stability is guaranteed by an immaculate new car, a stash of antiques, and a plentiful supply of clean, stylish clothes. Neither Adele nor Ann truly begins to revive until their poisonous relationship is all but ended by Ann's leaving home.

*Anywhere but Here* is an intense study of character, but the depiction of society is detailed and realistic as well. Changes in the American cultural scene and value system are carefully marked. The then-steady increase in the middle-class standard of living is comically apparent in Jimmy's anxious anticipation of a late 1950's Christmas morning. A material value system grips Adele. She often substitutes things, possessions, for emotional needs. The war in Vietnam and the social upheaval of the late 1960's is a heavy presence in the novel. Close-knit neighborhoods are sadly altered by the absence of young men who have died and by those who, as Carol's son Hal puts it, are never the same when they return. The economic hard times of the 1970's are felt by Adele and Ann, who cannot afford the social climb they are attempting. Deprived of innocence, abandoned or betrayed by those whom she had no choice but to trust, her mother and father, Ann grows up cynical and guarded. She wears the scars of the post-Vietnam era.

*Critical Context*

Portions of *Anywhere but Here* originally appeared in literary magazines. The novel, a bestseller, reached a wider audience. It joined a growing movement in literary and psychological writing devoted to the exploration of personality in relation to upbringing. Mona Simpson depicts what might by now be recognized as a dysfunctional family. She is also aware of the culture of healing, the self-affirmation manuals and recovery programs, to which many turn for redemption.

Domestic fiction has examined the erosion of the ideal of the nuclear family and attempted to account for the increasing number of real families headed by women living without men. In exploring such themes, *Anywhere but Here* is related to contemporary works such as Sue Miller's *The Good Mother* (1987) and Ann Tyler's *Dinner at the Homesick Restaurant* (1982). Simpson's focus on the theme of storytelling also relates to the technique of oral history, the gathering of personal narratives, which has become a prominent aspect of women's historical writing. Simpson is also the author of a second novel, *The Lost Father* (1992).

*Bibliography*

Beevor, Antony. "Heading West." *The Times Literary Supplement*, June 26, 1987, 698. This enthusiastic reading of the novel identifies Simpson as a member of the "hyper-realist" school of fiction. Beevor appreciates Simpson's attention to detail, finding the depiction of the paradoxes of American culture fascinating. He assures the English reader that *Anywhere but Here* is a special, not a typical, example of the great American novel.

Flower, Dean. "Anywhere but Here." *Hudson Review* 40 (Summer, 1987): 321. Hudson takes the title of his review of several contemporary novels from his personal favorite. He compares Simpson's novel to, among other works, *A Summons to Memphis* (1986) by Peter Taylor.

Heller, Dana A. "Shifting Gears: Transmission and Flight in Mona Simpson's *Anywhere but Here*." *University of Hartford Studies in Literature* 21 (1989): 37-44. The theme of escape is a concern of this study. Heller also focuses on mother-daughter relationships and on the nature of desire in the novel.

Morse, Deborah Denenholz. "The Difficult Journey Home: Mona Simpson's *Anywhere but Here*." In *Mother Puzzles: Daughters and Mothers in Contemporary American Literature*, edited by Mickey Pearlman. New York: Greenwood Press, 1989. Morse's essay is an exploration of themes in the novel from a literary point of view. She discusses the mythic importance of the issue of flight and the search for home, evoking the biblical story of Eden. Morse also deals frankly with the issue of Ann's sexual development.

Schreiber, Le Anne. "In Thrall to a Lethal Mother." *The New York Times Book Review* 92 (January 11, 1987): 7. This review speculates on the reader's reactions to the novel's characters and narrative structure. Schreiber predicts a feeling of frustration in response to the psychological turmoil depicted.

*Nick David Smart*

# AT WEDDINGS AND WAKES

*Author:* Alice McDermott (1953-    )
*Type of plot:* Psychological realism
*Time of plot:* The 1960's
*Locale:* Brooklyn and suburban Long Island, New York
*First published:* 1992

Principal characters:
ROBERT,
MARGARET, and
MARYANNE, the children, focal characters from whose memories the
    story is told
LUCY TOWNE DAILEY, the children's mother, apparently unhappy in her
    choice of a husband and the place where she lives
BOB DAILY, Lucy's husband, the children's father, who learns to live
    among the Towne women
MOMMA TOWNE, Lucy's stepmother, who married her sister's husband
    and cared for her children
MAY TOWNE, one of Lucy's three sisters, a former nun
AGNES TOWNE, another sister, a business woman with cultivated tastes
VERONICA TOWNE, the fourth sister, an "unfortunate" one, a "stayathome"
DONALD TOWNE, Momma's son, spoiled as a child and later disowned by
    his mother because of his drinking
FRED, a middle-aged mailman who marries May

*The Novel*

Momma Towne ruled the roost when she received it from her sister, who died in her fourth childbirth leaving an infant, Veronica, and three other little girls—Lucy, May, and Agnes. Perhaps Momma gathers the children closely to her because she feels guilty about taking a ready-made family from a dead sister. Perhaps she feels remorse from being angered by the killing hand of God after she waited seven years in Ireland for the chance to come to her sister in the United States. Perhaps the guilt is the result of her deliberate and successful attempt to tempt her sister's husband into marriage not by attracting him physically but by seducing him with arguments, substituting mindplay for foreplay. When she finally has a child of her own, a son, she spoils him; while he is still a young man, she dismisses him from her house and from herself so thoroughly that he appears, hat in hand, only at weddings and wakes.

Lucy is the only one of the girls who marries and leaves home, but she is so closely tied to her stepmother and her stepmother's house that she makes arduous and frequent visits home in the summer bringing her three children. Twice a week, they make the journey from their house in Long Island, which is ten blocks from the nearest bus stop. The bus takes them past the cemetery, the churches, and out of suburbia, where they have to transfer to another bus in a crowded multiethnic neighborhood. Once there, they proceed to the subway station, where surroundings seem to the children even more bizarre. They take a train that rushes them through Queens and on to Brooklyn, then transfer to another train. The children notice their mother's confidence growing until, finally again in her old neighborhood, she settles from a hurried to a relaxed pace, sending the message that she is again at home.

Waiting for Lucy and her children are the aunts. May left a convent because she had come to realize that she loved the life of a nun too much to think of it as devotion, duty, or sacrifice. May returns to her stepmother's house and settles into the routine of caring for Momma and looking forward to the visits of Lucy's children. Veronica, the youngest of the sisters, is always at home, her face still disfigured by early skin problems, sipping cocktails that have become her nourishment. Agnes, a career woman, though able to leave the house to work as an executive secretary and to separate herself by means of her finely tuned tastes, is a stern and brittle woman.

Together, stepmother and sisters indulge in ritual complaints. Lucy is foremost in her never-ending litany of vague protests against the man she married, who dutifully drives to Brooklyn after work to fetch his family home. In the house of his mother-in-law, he performs for Momma the rites of a businessman, and he speaks politely and gently over cocktails and dinner to each of the sisters who have waited for his arrival.

Another of the ritualistic journeys that Lucy, Bob, and children take once a year is the two-week vacation, always to a similar place but never the same one. The destination is always a place with green trees, stretches of beach, and the smell of the sea, a place where Bob hopes to instill in his children a sense of wonder and beauty.

Interspersed with daily living are the weddings and the wakes, occasions that give rise to immense gatherings of family and friends in the Irish community where the Townes live. The most splendid wedding is that of May, who one day almost literally runs into Fred, the mailman, who is new to the neighborhood. Small chats become conversations, and friendly dates lead to commitments. All are happy save Momma, who insists that Fred cannot husband his resources, since the roses he sends to May in the first part of the month become daisies by the end of the month.

The children's memories of the family's joy in the wedding is allowed to overshadow, for a time, their memory of May's inexplicable death four days after her wedding; their knowledge of mortality is buried for a while as the happy event is recounted. The high point is the discovery that Fred can dance with extraordinarily nimble feet, his joy bringing life to the dance floor in song after song, couple after couple, until the dance floor is filled with a living celebration of marriage that is only later to be turned into a wake.

*The Characters*

In *At Weddings and Wakes*, McDermott filters what is known and discovered through the minds of the Towne-Daily children, most often through a composite consciousness that seems to mesh with the point of view of the author. Sometimes a particular child is chosen as a focal point, and readers are thus able to distinguish between the boy, for example, and his sisters. Robert, well-behaved and introverted, is an exemplary altar boy who rises in the mornings in time to attend early mass. He is a good boy, the priest says, prompt, courteous, with pressed cassock and shined shoes. When his sister Margaret decides to emulate his behavior and go to early mass herself, Robert is glad for her company and seems pleased to point out to her things that give him pleasure—pinkish clouds left in the sky, a last star, a hedge filled with sparrows in the morning dew. Try as she might, however, Margaret is unable to match her brother's generosity and selflessness. The gladioli that she finds in the cemetery and identifies as her own treasure, separate from her brother's, have to be a special gift, the child thinks, perhaps an offering to her teacher, Miss Joan. The flowers, the child thinks, would transform the teacher from ugly duckling to blushing bride gliding across a dance floor in the arms of a new husband. Margaret's joy turns to shame and humiliation, however, when Miss Joan spurns the flowers, which came from the dirt of a freshly dug grave.

Maryanne has a similar experience with a teacher, Sister Miriam Joseph, who, unlike Miss Joan, is tall, dark, and beautiful. Filled with love for Sister Miriam Joseph and trying to impress her, Maryanne tells her teacher about Aunt May, who died four days after her marriage and who had once been a nun. What happened to Aunt May becomes a sign of foreboding for Sister Miriam Joseph, and she dismisses Maryanne, relegating her back to the group, indistinguishable from the other children. In her mouth, the nun holds gum that replaces saliva caused by an illness that will, before long, kill her.

The particular point of view chosen by the author provides the magical aura that pervades the text. Entrance into the minds of the children and incidents surrounding the children not only help define their individual characters but also act to reinforce themes and images. These occur and recur until a reader becomes aware that beside every birth is a death, beside every child is an adult facing perhaps an early knowledge of death, and behind every wedding is a wake.

Since the view of every character and situation is somewhat skewed by its refraction in the consciousness of the children, every character and situation seems transformed from the usual to the unique, from the spiritless and timid to the heroic, from the commonplace to the incredible. For example, Bob Dailey, who is the subject of his wife's complaints when she is within the bosom of her family, is in the children's eyes hero and benefactor, the driver of the automobile that carries them home and to and from their annual vacations. Rather than being made angry by the constant complaints of the women of the Towne family, Bob understands that his wife's family provides for him the routine of daily life, the constant recognition that beneath all who are alive is an undercurrent of the lives of the dead.

*Themes and Meanings*

What is most striking about *At Weddings and Wakes* is its extraordinary tonal shadings: Every scene is a mixture of past and present, resonant of a future not yet experienced. In every present is a reverberation of other times and places; in every echo of joy or grief are re-echoes of past and future sounds and colorations of exaltation and wretchedness. Momma's joy in the birth of her own child, a beautiful boy, parallels her pleasure in hearing the sound of the baby Veronica in the belly of her sister—who would soon die at childbirth, leading to a despair similar to the one Momma experienced when she disowned her son John, grown to young manhood as an unredeemed and unrepentant alcoholic.

At no point in the novel does McDermott break point of view to explain actions or consequences. Meaning derives altogether from character and scene. A reader must be able to locate the replications, the echoes and re-echoes, the juxtapositions and parallels that find the characters all dancing on graves. The overall montage turns family lore into universal myth.

*Critical Context*

At *Weddings and Wakes* is Alice McDermott's third published novel, following *That Night* (1987) and *A Bigamist's Daughter* (1982). Though her novels have similar themes, they are startlingly different from one another. Some critics hailed *A Bigamist's Daughter* as an excellent first novel that begins as satire of authors who seek a vanity press and moves skillfully to an analysis of the protagonist herself, who is editor-in-chief of the vanity press. Gradually, the editor's cynicism turns to acceptance of women like herself who spend their time waiting for husbands and fathers to arrive. *That Night*, like *At Weddings and Wakes*, is about growing up in the 1960's, but McDermott's penchant for the evocative and ambiguous is stronger in her second novel, in which prose captures time, place, and social status in a heightened poetic style.

*Bibliography*

Baumann, Paul. "Imperishable Identities." *Commonweal* 119 (May 22, 1992): 15-16. Baumann describes the cluttered Towne apartment in Brooklyn as a place where many spirits, evoked by matriarch Momma and the laments of her daughters, need to be appeased. Baumann points out that Momma's litany of loss underlies even her pronouncement that mailman Fred cannot husband his resources. Momma's characterization of Fred in terms of money made and spent is echoed in the idea that May's death is the inevitable outcome of the couple's meeting, love, and marriage, since happiness must be paid for in a "currency of loss."

Donavin, Denise. Review of *At Weddings and Wakes*, by Alice McDermott. *Booklist* 88 (March 1, 1992): 1197. Remarks that the brightest spot in the novel is Aunt May and concludes that her death does not overshadow her life. Donavin sums up the novel as charming, pensive fiction.

Klinkenborg, Verlyn. "Grief That Lasts Forever." *The New York Times Book Review* 97 (April 12, 1992): 3. In one of the more complete reviews following the publication of *At Weddings and Wakes*, Klinkenberg characterizes the novel as the present memorialized, accomplished by a primary focus through the children, who collectively and individually underline the ambiguities and reverberations inherent in the book's themes. The continual laments of the Towne women become instant memories, extant in the past and the present and projected into the future. Klinkenborg is also one of the few reviewers who comments on McDermott's writing style, which employs formal and phrasal patterns that have a harmony of their own.

McDermott, Alice. Interview by Wendy Smith. *Publishers Weekly* 239 (March 30, 1992): 85-86. McDermott discusses her life and work, with particular reference to *At Weddings and Wakes*.

Smolowe, Jill. "Dancing on Graves." *Time* 139 (April 20, 1992): 96. Smolowe argues that McDermott's third novel secures her reputation as a storyteller of great talent. The world of *At Weddings and Wakes* is haunted, Smolowe says, conjured from the dead to the living in the same way that the vitality of the Towne-Dailey children offsets the demise of parts of the family. The children, Smolowe states, offer a "life-affirming lesson" that overcomes the family's despair.

*Mary Rohrberger*

# THE BARRACKS THIEF

*Author:* Tobias Wolff (1945-    )
*Type of plot:* Moral
*Time of plot:* The mid-1960's to the mid-1970's
*Locale:* Seattle, Washington, and Fort Bragg, North Carolina
*First published:* 1984

> *Principal characters:*
> PHILIP BISHOP, a young paratrooper from Seattle
> KEITH BISHOP, his younger brother
> GUY BISHOP, their father
> LEWIS, a paratrooper from Kentucky
> HUBBARD, another paratrooper

*The Novel*

Tobias Wolff's novella-length *The Barracks Thief* reads more like a long short story than a novel. Consisting of seven brief chapters, it seems at first to be a simple and unassuming story with little or no thematic significance; however, as is often the case with novellas, the more one thinks about the work, the more psychologically and morally complex becomes this exploration of the motivations of three inarticulate young men caught up in the demands of masculinity.

Although the story begins with the teenage brothers Keith and Philip Bishop's reactions to their father's desertion of the family for another woman—Keith runs off to be a hippie, while Philip joins the Army—the central focus is on Philip's relationship with Lewis and Hubbard, two other young and inexperienced paratroopers who are waiting at Fort Bragg, North Carolina, to be shipped to Vietnam. Because the book is in some ways Lewis' story as well as Philip's, Wolff shifts the point of view a number of times. The first chapter describes the father's desertion, Keith's running away from home, and Philip's joining the Army from a third-person-omniscient point of view. In the next three chapters, however, the point of view abruptly shifts to Philip himself, who tells of his initial experiences in the Army.

This second section presents a central episode in the story. Philip, Lewis, and Hubbard—outsiders to the other, older men, most of whom have already served together in Vietnam—are assigned to guard an ammunition dump on the Fourth of July. Lewis plays the stereotyped role of the Kentucky redneck, and he brags about his prowess with women; Hubbard complains about Army life and longs to be back home with his friends; Philip remains, as he does throughout the book, uncommitted and noncommittal. It is a long, boring day until a deputy sheriff shows up and asks the soldiers to leave the ammo dump because of a brush fire heading their way. Lewis, acting out of either braggadocio or a simplistic sense of duty, refuses to go and threatens to shoot the deputy if he tries to force them to desert their post. When the wind changes and the danger is eliminated, the three soldiers, bound together in a masculine sense of camaraderie, feel that they have proven themselves to be real men.

In chapter 5, the focus of the novel shifts to Lewis; however, because he is less articulate than Philip, his story is told by the omniscient narrator in the present tense. Lewis' experiences focus on abortive sexual encounters. While hitchhiking into town, he is picked up by a male schoolteacher who puts calamine lotion on his injured hand. The homosexual suggestions of the scene are made quite clear by the omniscient narrator, but Lewis seems to have only an inchoate awareness of the significance of the event. When he gets to town, he awkwardly picks up a prostitute, but when he does not have enough money to pay for her services, she forces him to leave at the point of a knife.

The next day, Lewis steals wallets from other men in the barracks and returns to the prostitute. Following a violent sexual encounter, Lewis tells the girl that he loves her; thinking that he is mocking her, she drives him out with the knife again. After stealing another wallet and breaking the owner's nose when he is almost caught, Lewis finds a letter in the wallet that identifies the owner as Hubbard. When Lewis is discovered to be the "barracks thief," the point of view of the novel shifts back to Philip, who tells of a "blanket party" in which the men beat up Lewis. Hubbard will have nothing to do with the beating; Philip watches but does nothing to prevent it.

The final four-page chapter of the novel, told from the point of view of Philip after the war, ties up the loose ends: Lewis gets a dishonorable discharge, Hubbard deserts and goes to Canada, and Philip's brother Keith returns home and gets a job as a security guard. Philip himself goes to Vietnam and then returns home to become what he calls a "conscientious, careful, responsible" man, "addicted to comfort, with an eye for the safe course." He sometimes wishes that the fire had set off the ammunition dump and that he, Hubbard, and Lewis had been blown up in a blast that made the earth shake. He thinks, "It would have been something."

## The Characters

*The Barracks Thief* is radically split in its character focus. On the one hand, it is Philip's novel, for it both begins and ends with his situation, and much of it is told from his point of view. On the other hand, Lewis is the barracks thief of the title, and it is his inner conflict about his image as a man that constitutes the central conflict of the novel. Because both Philip and Lewis seem more acted upon than acting, however, the reader does not learn much about either of them. Because the novel has something to do with Philip's experience of male bonding and betrayal, his personality frames the novel. The story begins with Philip's father breaking up the family and his brother running away, and it ends with Philip becoming a "good man"—a role he both accepts and chafes against.

Lewis is a more "interesting" character, although he seems almost incapable of complex thought. His motivations are central to the novel: He is the one who refuses to leave his post at the ammunition dump (an episode that establishes the theme of male bonding in the novel), and he is the barracks thief of the title (which destroys that bonding). On the one hand, Lewis is a simple stereotype, a dumb redneck who boasts and tries to prove himself as a man but who only ends up looking foolish and ineffectual. On the other hand, there is something centrally compelling about his problematical experiences with his comrades at the ammunition dump, with the teacher who rubs lotion on his swollen hand, and with the prostitute whom he says he loves. He cannot easily be dismissed as either simply stupid or simply mentally disturbed, for he seems to embody some of the problems surrounding the novel's central theme—men trying to be men in a world governed by stereotyped masculine roles.

*Themes and Meanings*

*The Barracks Thief* is an elusive novel, a rare work that seems so simple as to be inconsequential, yet so suggestive as to be profound. First of all, it is a man's story; the only woman in the novel is the prostitute—the classic object of desire, good for nothing else but the sexual pleasure of the male, but at the same time a menacing figure, refusing to be loved and threatening the male with the emasculating knife. Wolff's novel is about the kinds of things that concern men when they are together as men. Because Philip, Lewis, and Hubbard are treated as if they were sissies or children by the more experienced soldiers, they need something to prove themselves to be men—which in this context means confronting danger, facing down opponents, being sexually powerful. Thus, the ironic heart of the novel is that when the three men actually face danger at the ammunition dump, it is no danger at all. As Philip says, "Nothing happens." Moreover, the very sense of camaraderie created by the confrontation is violated by Lewis' need to satisfy the prostitute in the only way he can—with money that he steals from his barracks buddies.

Male bonding, which is at the very center of this novel, is a subject so easily open to ridicule that it is a tribute to Wolff's skill as a writer that he can successfully explore the many complexities of being a male in a male world with such subtlety. As is typical of examples of the short-story or novella forms, every event in the story is motivated by its central theme. The opening episodes focus on the loss of Philip's father as a role model and his rejection of his own role as his brother's keeper. Particularly symbolic is a scene in which the father tries to give Philip a folding bicycle as a graduation present, telling him that with it he will never be without transportation. When the father pitches over the handlebars and lies tangled up with the bike, he calls to his son, "I can't move. Give me a hand." Philip, however, turns away, and he joins the Army the next morning.

The theme of male bonding crystalizes with the ammunition dump scene; like everything else in this novel, however, the event is problematical and inconclusive. Lewis feels that he must explicitly follow his orders to shoot anyone who dares to put a hand on the fence surrounding the dump, but it is a foolish, quixotic act that defies reason and common sense. The fact that the three men feel mysteriously bonded because they have faced danger together thus is made to appear childish and trivial.

The scene with Lewis and the male schoolteacher suggests the inherent homosexual nature of any male bonding. As the teacher rubs cooling lotion on Lewis' painful hands, both Lewis and the teacher close their eyes and lose themselves in the experience, forgetting their sense of "being absolutely alone"; the image of both their hands joined with fingers interlaced is a central one of inchoate male longing for union. Thus, when Lewis clumsily tries to pick up the prostitute, and she angrily asks him what he wants, the answer is not simply that he wants sex. In addition to wanting to prove himself as a man, Lewis desires something from the woman similar to what he felt with the teacher. This is not to say that Lewis is a latent homosexual, but rather that he wants what all men want—to be at one with someone else. Wolff seems to suggest here that although that sometimes may be easier with another man than with a woman, it is never easy with anyone.

Lewis' theft of a wallet that turns out to be Hubbard's further emphasizes the difficulty of male bonding in any genuine way, especially in light of the demands of women. When the rest of the men join together to beat Lewis up, a false kind of macho bonding based on violence completely disrupts any hope of genuine male union based on love and trust. As the men wait for Lewis, they "goof around," do a bump and grind, tell dirty jokes, and talk about torture. Just before they put the blanket over Lewis' head, Philip sees his face full of humiliation and fear. He says it is the face he saw on Vietnamese he interrogated later during the war and the face that has become his brother's face through all of his troubles.

This is the climactic moment and thematic center of a complex work that deals with the difficulty of being a man in a man's world, with the problematical nature of male bonding, and with the basic human desire to unite with someone, whether it be a brother or an enemy. The novel ends with Philip looking back over the events with a sense of helplessness about what has happened to Lewis, Hubbard, and himself. He says that Hubbard never set out to be a deserter any more than Lewis set out to become a barracks thief, and he puzzles over what could have been the cause of these actions. He says that he did not set out to be what he has become, a conscientious, responsible man who mows his lawn and is good to his wife. Although he is grateful for what he has become, he has moments when he remembers what it was like to be a reckless man with reckless friends. Imagining the ammunition dump exploding, destroying all three of them, he thinks, "It would have been something." This final statement provides closure to the central theme of the novel: whether being a man means being brave and living life dangerously or whether it means being responsible and living life comfortably. To say that the former would have been "something" is not the same as saying the latter is "nothing." In *The Barracks Thief*, however, Wolff has created a compelling novel that explores the basic complexity of this choice.

### Critical Context

*The Barracks Thief* is Tobias Wolff's first novel. Its brevity and highly unified thematic focus are reminders that he is first and foremost a master of the short story. His first book, the collection of stories *In the Garden of the North American Martyrs* (1981), was one of the most highly acclaimed short-story collections of the 1980's. After *The Barracks Thief* was published, his third book was another collection of stories, *Back in the World* (1985). *The Barracks Thief* initially received little attention from critics. When the book won the PEN/Faulkner Award for the most distinguished work of American fiction, however, critics began to take the book more seriously as a complex work of fiction.

*Bibliography*
Allen, Bruce. "Name Book Year's Best." *The Christian Science Monitor* 77 (June 7, 1985): B7. Calls the work a powerful treatment of antagonisms and apprehensions of youth, intensified by war. Compares Wolff with Ernest Hemingway in his creation of abbreviated and understated scenes. Suggests that so many longings and fears are packed into such a short book that readers will finish it hardly believing that they and its characters have been through so much.
Campbell, Don. "The Barracks Thief." *Los Angeles Times Book Review*, July 29, 1984, 8. Emphasizes the brush with danger in the ammunition dump scene in the novel, arguing that it marks the three men forever. Praises the book for its sharp focus on fears, uncertainties, tangled loyalties, and instincts for betrayal of the three central characters.
Dubus, Andre. "The Barracks Thief." *America* 151 (September 1, 1984): 109. An enthusiastic review. Points out that the story focuses primarily on the complex motivations and desires of the three central characters. Compares the book to Joseph Conrad's *The Nigger of the "Narcissus"* (1897) in its dramatization of the isolation of men joined together by male work.
Kendrick, Walter. "Men with Rifles." *The New York Times Book Review* 90 (June 2, 1985): 42. Says the story presents a bleak world short on joy and long on suffering. Notes that Wolff does not editorialize in the novel but leaves the reader to decide whether it is better to die spectacularly or to live out a life in safe conventionality. What dignity the characters have is based on their telling their own story without apology or complaint.
Simpson, Mona. "The Morality of Everyday Life." *The New Republic* 193 (December 9, 1985): 37-38. Calls the novel a small-scale yet intense moral drama typical of Wolff's earlier short stories. Notes the identification between Lewis and Philip, who somehow feels guilty for Lewis' acts. Points out the irony of the story's being told by a "good man" who is neither victim nor perpetrator and the only one of the three main characters who goes to Vietnam.

*Charles E. May*

# BASTARD OUT OF CAROLINA

*Author:* Dorothy Allison (1924-     )
*Type of plot:* Domestic realism
*Time of plot:* The 1950's and 1960's
*Locale:* Greenville County, South Carolina
*First published:* 1992

### Principal characters:

RUTH ANNE (BONE) BOATWRIGHT, the narrator, a strong-minded little girl, the "bastard" of the title

ANNEY BOATWRIGHT PARSONS WADDELL, her mother, a waitress

REESE PARSONS, Bone's younger sister, Anney's child by her first husband

GLEN WADDELL, Anney's second husband, a troubled, insecure, and violent man

GRANNY BOATWRIGHT, Anney's mother, the matriarch of a large family

RAYLENE BOATWRIGHT, Anney's unmarried sister, who becomes Bone's protector

EARLE (BLACK EARLE) BOATWRIGHT, Anney's favorite uncle

## The Novel

*Bastard Out of Carolina* is the story of a young South Carolina girl's childhood, which, though blighted by illegitimacy, poverty, and her stepfather's abuse, is made bearable by the love of her extended family and even by the love of the mother who seemed to have abandoned her.

The novel is organized chronologically, taking the narrator, Ruth Anne Boatwright, or "Bone," from birth to her thirteenth year. While her own experiences provide the narrative thread for *Bastard Out of Carolina*, much of the book's thematic content can be found in incidents that Bone does not witness but that are related to her by other characters such as her grandmother, the intrepid Granny Boatwright. These stories, many of them from the past, most of them about the members of her own family, become very important to Bone. She absorbs them and reflects on them, making them as much a part of her own world as the events in which she is personally involved.

From the beginning, Bone has problems with identity. She is born while her mother, Anney Boatwright, is still unconscious after being in an automobile accident. Since the relatives do not list a father on the birth certificate, Bone is officially classified as "illegitimate."

Despite this unfortunate beginning, for a time Bone's life goes smoothly. Anney marries a sweet-tempered man, Lyle Parsons, and soon Bone has a little sister, Reese Parsons. Then Lyle is killed in an accident, leaving Anney, at nineteen, a widow with two children to support.

While she is working as a waitress, Anney meets Glen Waddell. Even though her family warns her that Glen has a nasty temper, Anney is lonely, and she marries him.

From the first, Glen seems to dislike Bone. While he and the two children are sitting in a hospital parking lot waiting for Anney to have his baby, Glen puts Bone on his lap and molests her. From that time on, she fears and distrusts him.

After their baby dies at birth and Glen learns that Anney can have no more children, he seems to become even more violent than before. Because of his hot temper, he loses one job after another. Unable to pay their rent, the family is constantly moving, and the children are often hungry. The only bright spot in Bone's life is her visits to the Boatwrights. Despite the fact that Glen sneers at them as "poor white trash," it is from them, especially from her favorite uncle, Earle Boatwright, that Anney gets the affection and the approval that she lacks at home.

When Bone is ten, Glen starts finding excuses for beating her. Because she does not want her mother to be hurt, Bone pretends that nothing is wrong. When a medical examination reveals the extent of Bone's past injuries, however, Anney realizes that she must either leave Glen or somehow keep Bone away from him. Since Anney still loves Glen and feels peculiarly protective toward him, she starts finding other places for Bone to stay.

Bone's first refuge is the home of one of her mother's sisters who is dying of cancer. Despite the circumstances, her months here are among the happiest of her childhood. As she listens to the stories told by her aunt and by her Uncle Earl, Bone realizes what it is to be a Boatwright woman. As Uncle Earle explains, the women in his family are so strong and so stubborn that they can conquer any man they meet.

When Bone is no longer needed by her aunt, she finds another consolation. After experiencing a religious conversion at a revival, she starts traveling to gospel music performances with a classmate, Shannon Pearl, and her parents, who are in the business. Once Bone realizes that the performers are more interested in liquor and lechery than in religion, however, she decides that Jesus and country music will not solve the problems in her life.

Because she bears her abuse so stoically and even lies when her relatives ask questions about "Daddy Glen," Bone is almost thirteen before the Boatwrights finally learn the truth. When they do, her three uncles beat Glen so badly that he ends up in the hospital. Glen, however, is still not finished with Bone. Finding her alone, he beats her until she is almost insensible and then rapes her. Just then, Anney walks in. At first she is furious, and she attacks Glen; then, typically, when he begins to whine and sob, she takes him in her arms to comfort him.

After she gets out of the hospital, Bone goes to live with her unmarried aunt Raylene Boatwright, a wise and kind woman who tries to explain Anney's kind of love by telling about an experience of her own. By the time Anney turns up to tell Bone that she must stand by Glen, her daughter is able to forgive her. Bone knows that this is goodbye; Anney is going to join Glen in some distant place where her brothers cannot find him. Oddly, Bone feels a certain pride in her mother; in her strength, she has shown herself a true Boatwright woman, like Raylene and, in fact, like Bone herself.

## The Characters

As the narrator of the novel as well as the protagonist, Bone is recalling past events. The fact that she can see humor in the peculiar circumstances of her birth, her raid on Woolworth's, and her venture into religion indicates that by the time she tells her story, Bone has recovered her zest for life. Yet it is clear that at the time it occurred, Glen's abuse warped her personality. Not only was she forced to detach her mind from her body so that she could endure the beatings, but in guarding her secret, she also had to withdraw from the people who loved her. Bone describes how through all of this she clung to her sense of identity, so that, once freed from Glen and from her own rage, she could once again love life.

Anney is a pretty, tender-hearted woman whose flaws are generally perceived as virtues. It is her irrational optimism that first propels her into marriage to Glen and then keeps her believing that he and his luck will change. It is her tenderness toward the weak that makes it impossible for her to turn Glen away. Ironically, though Anney lacks clearsightedness, she does, like all the other Boatwright women, have strength.

Glen, the villain of the story, is incapable of love and rules his life by his own needs. Because he has been rejected by his own family, he needs Anney's love; because he sees Bone as a rival for her mother's affection, he needs to destroy her. Although Allison makes his motivations clear, by the time one sees Glen covered with Bone's blood and whining to Anney, it is difficult not to wish Bone's uncles good luck.

Granny Boatwright, the matriarch of the Boatwright family, has many admirable qualities: toughness, resiliency, and affection for her offspring. By excusing the irresponsibility of men, however, Granny helps to perpetuate a social system that suppresses even the strongest of women.

Raylene Boatwright, a loving and perceptive woman, finally provides Bone with the maternal affection and protection she needs. Raylene is also important in the healing process, which is just beginning as the book ends. Having seen the woman she loved forced to choose between her child and her lover, Raylene can help Bone to understand her mother's conflicts and thus to forgive her.

Earle is the most fully developed of Anney's three brothers. Called "Black Earle" because of his black, curly hair and his devilish charm, he attracts women effortlessly. Like his brothers, Earle is the stereotypical good old boy, with all the vices of the type, but he can also be kind and gentle. Although his good qualities were not enough to hold his wife, they do make him Bone's favorite uncle.

## Themes and Meanings

On the most obvious level, *Bastard Out of Carolina* is a story of child abuse, movingly told from the point of view of the victim. More profoundly, it is an examination of gender roles among lower-class Southern whites of the 1950's and 1960's.

The Boatwrights define masculinity in terms of certain activities and attitudes. When a real man is not fixing a car, driving his truck, or going hunting, he will be getting drunk, whoring, and fighting. Admittedly, because of his mechanical skills, he is a valued worker, and because he has a sense of honor, he is loyal to a fault, especially to the members of his own family.

Trouble arises only when a man like Glen, who is already considered a loser by the standards of his own prosperous family, also fails as a good old boy in the Boatwright tradition, or when a woman in this culture rebels against her role as an attractive, baby-bearing work animal. Glen's insecurity turns into anger; his outlet is an action that any Boatwright would reject, the abuse of a child. With women, it is a matter of rejecting a role. Refusing to accept the excuse for infidelity, that "a man has his needs," Earle's wife leaves him, taking his children, and Alma Boatwright Yarnell eventually goes crazy and destroys everything in her house. While she is growing up, Bone feels ambivalent about gender roles; on one hand, she admires and imitates her boy cousins, even dressing like them; on the other hand, she also enjoys being with the women of the family, especially when they describe triumphs over their men. At the end of the novel, she identifies with the strong Boatwright women, specifically Raylene and Anney; however, after Bone's experience with Glen, it is difficult to imagine her ever again permitting any man to wield power over her.

*Critical Context*

Although *Bastard Out of Carolina* is Dorothy Allison's first novel, it was preceded by a book of short stories, *Trash* (1988). Both that collection and this novel contain somewhat fictionalized versions of the author's own life story. Yet as Allison has noted, real life is "meaner" than fiction. She herself was not as strong as Bone, Allison has commented, nor did she have Bone's chance to escape.

It is not Allison's treatment of child abuse, however, that has most interested critics. While they find the account of Bone's response to her ordeal both psychologically valid and deeply moving, Allison's most impressive achievement, they agree, is her accurate and sympathetic description of a social class that has generally been described in unflattering terms, as "crackers," "rednecks," or "white trash."

With *The Hamlet* (1940), William Faulkner began his trilogy about a family of poor whites named Snopes, whose dominant characteristics are dishonesty, disloyalty, bigotry, and the total lack of an ethical or moral code. Because they are so aggressive and so numerous, Faulkner shows them steadily rising to political and economic power in the South. In Harper Lee's Pulitzer Prize-winning novel *To Kill a Mockingbird* (1960), the antagonist of the idealistic lawyer Atticus Finch is the unsavory Bob Ewell, who constructs a set of lies that get an innocent black man killed rather than admit that his love-starved daughter has made sexual advances to a black.

Both Lee, with her poor but upright Cunningham family, and Faulkner, in *As I Lay Dying* (1930), did point out that there is a difference between merely being poor and being "trashy." Until recently, however, Southern fiction writers tended to concentrate their interest on the gentry, upwardly mobile business owners, and blacks, while they reserved the poor whites for their lynch mobs. It is, of course, purely coincidental that Bobbie Ann Mason's acclaimed novel *Spence and Lila* (1988) and Dorothy Allison's collection *Trash* were published in the same year; however, the date does indicate how short a time has passed since Southern writers began to substitute a realistic picture of the Southern working poor for the contemptuous stereotypes that had prevailed for so long. Because of its insights and its high literary quality, *Bastard Out of Carolina* is an extremely important novel.

*Bibliography*

Allen, Kimberly G. Review of *Bastard Out of Carolina*, by Dorothy Allison. *Library Journal* 117 (March 1, 1992): 116. Sees the focus of the story as the Boatwrights, "a proud and closeknit clan." Praises Allison for her "rich sense of family." Allen also mentions the author's accuracy and sensitivity in revealing the feelings of a sexually abused child.

Garrett, George. "No Wonder People Got Crazy as They Grew Up." *The New York Times Book Review*, July 5, 1992, 3. A highly favorable review by a critic who is himself a much-admired Southern writer. Points to the skill with which Allison incorporates so many details, episodes, and stories into a unified whole. She avoids the dangers of "cuteness" inherent in a Southern setting as well as the sentimentalizing or sociologizing that often tempt those writing about the poor. Perhaps her most impressive achievement is in the use of language, which rings true and yet is as lyrical as a gospel song.

Harris, Gale. "Ashamed and Glorified." *Belles Lettres* 8 (Spring, 1993): 4-6. Assesses the novel as an "American classic." One of the major themes of the work is pride, which in excess, as often with the Boatwright men, can be destructive, but which sometimes, as in the case of Bone, is all that enables one to endure. Another theme is human vulnerability, as seen in the universal need for love. Praises Allison's descriptive prose, her "emotional intensity and honesty," and her "complex and compassionate" characterization.

Hawthorne, Mary. "Born of Ignorance." *The Times Literary Supplement*, August 14, 1992, 18. Sees the main subject of the novel as the "complexity of cruelty," the product of poverty, "social inequity," and "the psychosis of the family." The defects of *Bastard Out of Carolina* include a lack of unity, excessive "wisecracking bonhomie" on the part of the Boatwrights, and sometimes, particularly in the case of Glen, unconvincing characterization. The book, however, is vivid, compelling, and emotionally honest.

Young, Elizabeth. "Trash Tales." *New Statesman* 234 (January 8, 1993): 41-42. Allison's aim is to portray accurately a social class "that has been neglected and misunderstood by other novelists." Because of her "force and accuracy," she is more successful than such notable writers as Bobbie Ann Mason and Carolyn Chute. Young also admires her clean style, which, though avoiding dialect, has captured the "rhythms of Southern speech."

*Rosemary M. Canfield Reisman*

# THE BEAN TREES

*Author:* Barbara Kingsolver (1955-    )
*Type of plot:* Bildungsroman
*Time of plot:* The 1980's
*Locale:* Principally Tucson, Arizona
*First published:* 1988

> *Principal characters:*
> TAYLOR GREER, a young woman who heads west to "get away" and ends
>     up accepting the responsibility of rearing a child
> TURTLE, a two-year-old Indian girl
> LOU ANN RUIZ, a woman with whom Taylor and Turtle make a home
> MATTIE, the proprietor of a used-tire shop
> ESTEVAN, a Central American refugee
> ESPERANZA, Estevan's wife, also a refugee

*The Novel*

The Bean Trees is the story of a spirited young woman who leaves her rural Kentucky home to head west and ends up forming a nontraditional family. Her new family works largely because of the simple goodwill of those involved and because of their mutual need to survive through difficult personal times. Shortly after Marietta Greer (who changes her name to Taylor once she gets on the road) sets out from Kentucky, she acquires an abused child, whom she takes in at first almost begrudgingly, but with increasing warmth and good humor. She settles in Tucson, Arizona, where she develops a friendship and creates a home with another single mother and her son, learning cooperation and responsibility in the process.

When Taylor leaves her mother and her rural Kentucky home, she is seeking only adventure. Taylor has lived a rather uneventful life. She grew up without a father, and there were few opportunities for her. Her mother worked as a cleaning lady in rich people's homes. During high school, Taylor got a job as a lab assistant at the local hospital, but several years after high school, that, too, seemed to be a dead end. When she managed to save up enough money to buy a car, she bought a 1955 Volkswagen and headed west in an open, adventuresome mood.

Having never been out of Kentucky before, she has no real destination and determines to travel until her car gives out. She is not, however, prepared for what lies in store. Stopping at a small roadside restaurant in Oklahoma for something to eat, Taylor is surprised when a woman insistently pushes a baby through the open window of her car, then gets into a truck. Only when Taylor unwraps the baby at a motel many miles later does she learn anything at all about the child. The baby is a girl, and Taylor sees evidence that the baby has been abused. Even though in her work at the hospital she had seen a corpse and a woman with a gunshot wound, Taylor is so astonished by the bruises on the baby that she doubles up in pain on the bathroom floor.

The Indian child appears to Taylor to be slightly more than a year old. She does not speak, nor does she walk. What she does do is cling to Taylor or to anything she can get her hands on. For this reason, Taylor calls her Turtle, like the mud turtle she had studied in her high-school science class.

After working through the Christmas holidays at the motel, Taylor is ready to continue on. By the time she arrives in Tucson, Arizona, she has two flat tires and not enough money for new ones. She likes Tucson, however, so the city seems to Taylor like a good place to settle down until she can earn a little money. By chance, Taylor gets her car into a small tire-repair establishment called Jesus Is Christ Used Tires. A widow named Mattie befriends Taylor and ultimately offers Taylor a job.

To find a place to live, Taylor answers an advertisement in the newspaper. Lou Ann Ruiz, who has advertised for a housemate, is also from Kentucky, and the two young women strike up an immediate friendship. Lou Ann is looking for someone to share expenses because her husband had left her while she was pregnant with their first child. She has a little money from his disability insurance, and occasionally he sends her a check. She and Taylor work out fairly good living arrangements: Lou Ann stays home with her baby, Dwayne Ray, and Turtle, and Taylor works for the tire business nearby.

Much of the interest of *The Bean Trees* involves the growing relationship between Lou Ann and Taylor. Although they are very different in personality and outlook and are thrown together by circumstances and need, they discover strength in each other; they are complementary personalities. Slowly and unconsciously, the group becomes a family, committed to one another and compassionate about one anothers' weaknesses.

Taylor's relationship with Mattie also develops into a friendship that opens the door to a wider world. Mattie is involved in the sanctuary movement, helping Central American refugees flee their native lands. Through Mattie, Taylor meets Estevan and Esperanza, and gradually she learns of hardship and sacrifice that go beyond anything she had ever seen in Kentucky.

After a trip to a local physician, Taylor learns that Turtle's abuse was even worse than she had surmised; the child has suffered many broken bones. X-rays also show that Turtle is probably about three years old, considerably older than she acts or appears. The physician diagnoses Turtle's condition as failure to thrive, although it is clear that Turtle is developing in the home environment Taylor has provided for her.

When the state becomes aware that Taylor has no legal claim to Turtle, Taylor begins to think she has to do something to keep Turtle. She decides to make a return visit to Oklahoma to try to find Turtle's relatives and get them to appoint her Turtle's legal guardian. She also volunteers to transport Estevan and Esperanza to a church in Oklahoma, because their situation is becoming precarious in Tucson.

In a trip that is both scary and funny, the Guatemalans and Taylor and Turtle succeed in accomplishing a legal adoption for Turtle and finding another safe haven for Estevan and Esperanza. They also learn about love, loss, respect, and the true meaning of "family."

*The Characters*

Taylor Greer, the main character, enlists the warm wishes of the reader immediately through her open, honest narration. She quickly lets the reader into her middle-American background. With her rural Kentucky regionalisms and dialect, she is open and sincere. She has a good sense of humor and can laugh at herself as well as at others and at the comedy of human life. As both the narrator and the main character, she carries the story of growing into responsibility and love. She learns her own ignorance and political naïveté, and while her goodheartedness and compassion for others cannot protect her from pain, they reinforce her moral fiber, which gives her the courage to do right. She did not seek the responsibility of a child, but she accepts what fate seems to throw in her path.

Turtle, the child, is seen gradually to emerge from the cocoon of silence and withdrawal with which she surrounds herself, presumably as a result of the abuse she has suffered. She is the catalyst for Taylor's discovery of responsibility, commitment, and love.

Lou Ann Ruiz is at first only Taylor's housemate, but gradually the two develop a relationship that is strong, supportive, and mutually beneficial. Lou Ann constantly belittles herself—about her appearance, her capabilities, and her potential. Yet despite desertion by her husband, she slowly gains some self-confidence and is able to take a job in a salsa factory. Obsessed with the safety of her baby, Dwayne Ray, she nevertheless understands that even the best of mothers cannot protect her child from all the world's sources of harm, a fact she points out to Taylor when Turtle is accosted by a stranger. Lou Ann helps Taylor to understand her responsibility for Turtle, encouraging her to take steps to avoid Turtle's being taken as a ward of the State of Arizona. Like Taylor, she speaks in a Kentucky dialect that is wholesome, warm, and rich. Although Lou Ann notices that similarity almost immediately, it takes both Lou Ann and Taylor some time to acknowledge the even deeper sources of compatibility between them.

Estevan, a Central American who has come into the United States illegally, is a well-educated, sensitive man whose life accidentally intersects with Taylor's. Through Estevan, Taylor learns about political atrocities elsewhere and about physical and emotional torture that might cause one to flee one's country. Estevan recognizes Taylor's naïveté and only gradually, over time, tells her of his past. Despite his loneliness, he remains faithful to his wife, even though he must perceive that Taylor has fallen in love with him.

Esperanza, Estevan's wife, is much more withdrawn than her husband. In hopes of getting Estevan and Esperanza's cooperation in naming the members of their teacher's union, political enemies kidnapped their only child, Ismene. Esperanza has difficulty coping with this loss, and at one point takes aspirin in a suicide attempt. During the trip to Oklahoma, she becomes very attached to Turtle, and Turtle to her. Only when she voluntarily poses as Turtle's real mother and signs legal papers giving up custody to Taylor does she seem finally to work through her grief over the loss of Ismene.

## Themes and Meanings

The novel is about the struggles of American life for the vast number of people for whom the rags-to-riches dream is never realized. This is the real America, the America of unskilled labor, low levels of education, and limited access to the perks of American society. Yet in Kingsolver's novel there is no bitterness, no petty jealousy or envy, no crime, merely an easy acceptance of the way things are and an appreciation of life's good parts.

The novel is also about growing up. While the device of the journey has often been used to focus such a theme, Taylor's growing up comes not so much as a result of her experiences traveling as a result of her attempts to deal with the new and unexpected responsibility of a needy child. Taylor must learn how to be a mother—how to provide for Turtle's physical needs and, even more important, how to provide for Turtle's emotional needs. Slowly, she becomes committed to satisfying those needs, to being a real parent for Turtle.

Another theme of the novel is women's strength. All the major characters are women, and they form a community of support for one another. They accept one another's weaknesses, helping one another to change what can be changed and to work around what cannot. This is a story of women who are not empowered in any way but who nevertheless have the will, the spirit, and the commitment to find the resources within themselves to do right individually.

## Critical Context

*The Bean Trees*, Barbara Kingsolver's first novel, was greeted with critical acclaim. Following a chronological structure, with past episodes related only as memories, the story moves swiftly along by virtue of the charm and spirit of its main character. Structure and style reinforce the pedestrian atmosphere of the novel, where no miracles happen except those that happen everyday—finding the strength of love, discovering commitment, and feeling that one belongs somewhere. The comedy of humanity plays itself out with a warmth and reverence that are a pleasure to read.

Kingsolver's favorite themes of family and relationships also appear in her other work. *Homeland and Other Stories* (1989) was published in the year following *The Bean Trees* and carried on the earlier book's fresh and hopeful outlook. *Animal Dreams* (1990) expressed Kingsolver's concerns for humanity and the environment. *Pigs in Heaven*, published in 1993, was a sequel to *The Bean Trees*. *Holding the Line: Women in the Great Arizona Mine Strike of 1983* (1989), a work of nonfiction, revealed Kingsolver's continuing interest in human rights and women's issues. Many critics have praised Kingsolver's fiction as "poetic"; not surprisingly, she has published poetry in a number of magazines and in a collection.

## Bibliography

Butler, Jack. "She Hung the Moon and Plugged in All the Stars." *The New York Times Book Review*, April 10, 1988, 15. A good essay that praises Kingsolver's style, pointing out her success in both dialogue and description. Butler also notes that language is one of the subthemes of the novel, linking Lou Ann and Taylor through their Kentucky dialect, Estevan through his work as an English teacher, and Turtle as a child learning to speak. Butler points out, however, that the novel seems to lose "immediacy" near its end, with the characters becoming almost too good and the plot perhaps overly contrived.

FitzGerald, Karen. "A Major New Talent." *Ms.* 17 (April, 1988): 28. In this apprecia-
tive review, FitzGerald puts Kingsolver in the context of contemporary feminists writing about friendship. In Kingsolver's fiction, however, as opposed to the nonfiction of other feminists, a reader comes to feel the power of women's relationships and their ability to provide a haven in which the women can blossom.

Lyall, Sarah. "Termites Are Interesting But Books Sell Better." *The New York Times*, September 1, 1993, C1. A lengthy, informal profile of Kingsolver.

See, Lisa. "Barbara Kingsolver." *Publishers Weekly* 237 (August 31, 1990): 46-47. This biographical account talks about Kingsolver's major and recurring themes— the environment, Native Americans, U.S. involvement in Central America, parental relationships, and women's control of their own lives. See refers to *Animal Dreams*, *Homeland*, and *Holding the Line* as well as to *The Bean Trees*. See notes that Kingsolver is committed to examining political issues but that her main goal as a writer is to entertain the reader; perhaps as a second goal, she clings to the belief that her writing can change the world.

*Paula Kopacz*

# BEARHEART
## The Heirship Chronicles

*Author:* Gerald Vizenor (1934-    )
*Type of plot:* Apocalyptic satire
*Time of plot:* The end of the world
*Locale:* The central United States
*First published: Darkness in Saint Louis Bearheart,* 1978; 2d edition titled *Bearheart: The Heirship Chronicles,* 1990

*Principal characters:*

PROUDE CEDARFAIR, the last leader of the cedar nation, he is forced into exile with his wife, Rosina

BIGFOOT (also known as BENOIT SAINT PLUMERO and DOUBLE SAINT), a trickster with great sexual appetites

BELLADONNA, a mixed-blood obsessed with her Indianness

BISHOP OMAX PARASIMO, a cleric who has been providing shelter for tribal mixed-bloods

SIR CECIL STAPLES (the Evil Gambler), the "monarch of unleaded gasoline"

*The Novel*

*Bearheart: The Heirship Chronicles* is an unorthodox narrative. A work of mixed genres, the book incorporates materials from the indigenous and mainstream literary traditions. The novel follows the traditional framework of the emergence myth, which involves the cyclical destruction and creation of the world; an integral part of the myth is the survival and renewal of the tribe through migration. Because of its experimental techniques and language, however, *Bearheart* has also been associated with postmodernism.

The novel opens with a preface, entitled "Letter to the Reader," by Saint Louis Bearheart, a bear-spirit who hovers above the cabinets of files of tribal histories in a government building. Invaded by a sense of darkness (hence the title of the first edition), he turns into the fictional author of "The Heirship Chronicles: Proude Cedarfair and the Cultural Word Wars," a futuristic narrative about the flight of Proude and his wife from the cedar nation, his adventures with a group of followers, and the achievement of his vision quest. The "pilgrimage" represents a migration from "the third world" to the fourth, and hence alludes to American Indian myths of emergence and the end of the world. The narrative is replete with hyperbolic and incredible events and details (including cannibalism and graphic acts of sex and violence) that are simultaneously shocking and amusing.

"The Heirship Chronicles" begins with the encroachment of whites upon the "cedar circus" around Migis Sandridge, a sacred site. Proude Cedarfair, the last in a line of tribal leaders, resists white exploitation of the remaining trees during an energy crisis.

His cabin is burned down; he and his wife Rosina, together with seven clown crows, go into exile.

At the Scapehouse on Callus Road, they visit a commune of thirteen women poets. Bigfoot (Benoit Saint Plumero), a trickster who resides there, is the object of these women's desire. With Bigfoot, Proude and Rosina continue with their journey in a rare silver cabriolet that the women have given them. Along the way, they pick up Belladonna, but soon their car is ripped apart by racist killers of drunk Indians. Walking along the abandoned interstate, the pilgrims chance upon various characters who join them or harass them. Among the new recruits are Bishop Omax Parasimo and the people he has been sheltering; these include Inawa Biwide, an orphan, and Lilith Mae Farrier, a former teacher who is in love with two boxers.

A major challege confronts the pilgrims at What Cheer in the middle of Iowa, where Sir Cecil Staples, the "monarch of unleaded gasoline," reigns. Victimized as an abducted child before becoming the Evil Gambler, he relishes killing his adversaries. He challenges the circus pilgrims to play word games; he defeats Lilith Mae, but he loses to Proude and is tortured to death.

The pilgrims come to Dumfries, which is populated by disfigured victims who are crippled or suffering from skin cancer. Out of goodwill, one pilgrim does a striptease for them. They masturbate as they watch and, lusting after her body, eventually dismember her. In another episode, at the Witch Hunt Restaurant, where meals made from body parts of ordinary humans and "witches" are served, one pilgrim attempts to rescue a woman who is a victim of the witch hunt. While the pilgrim (dressed as a woman) starts copulating with her, he is killed by the "food fascist." His head is chopped off and propped up on a stick, which the pilgrims retrieve and bury.

Belladonna also runs into trouble. As a mixed-blood conceived during the standoff at Wounded Knee, she takes pride in being a Native American. Yet she is also undone by her narcissism when she gives a clichéd speech at a community the residents of which are opposed to fixed ideas. After she has rejected their challenges of her Native American identity, they stop asking questions, applaud her speech, and reward her with a poisoned cookie for her "terminal creed." As she dies, Proude cuts open her womb (her pregnancy is a result of her rape by whites), takes out the fetuses of twins, and buries the three ceremonially.

As the pilgrims enter Oklahoma, they obtain the help of the Luminous Augur to cross the Canadian River. To climb over the hills without being hit by thunder, they also seek the help of the Master Stranger, who charges food for his service. Bishop Parasimo, who has replaced the tribute of food with bark, is struck dead by lightning. The other pilgrims then arrive at New Liberty, where they catch a freedom train headed for Santa Fe. The train, operated by a regime of five veterans known as the "pentarchical pensioners," turns out to be a prison. The pilgrims are branded and given an inquisition; during the ordeal, the pensioners put out Inawa Biwide's eyes.

It is not clear whether what happens next is a vision or a continuation of the journey, but the pilgrims reach a pueblo near the Jemez River, where they meet two sacred clowns waving wooden penises. Aroused by their ritual, Bigfoot grabs Rosina and makes her perform oral sex on him. Out of nowhere, one of the women poets appears and strangles him. Leaving Rosina behind, Proude and Inawa Biwide move on into the barren mountains toward Wanaki Pueblo Bonito, the ancient place of vision bears. Around the time of the winter solstice, the two have a vision of a giant bear, which tells them to enter the fourth world as bears.

## The Characters

As a mixed-genre narrative, *Bearheart* contains an assortment of characters who are given different levels of aesthetic treatment. While some characters are portrayed more elaborately than others, none is truly rounded in the realistic sense. Many embody certain traits exemplifying ideas with mythical, allegorical, allusive, or satirical significance.

The most prominent character, Proude Cedarfair, is portrayed not only as a medicine man and a shaman, but also as a repository and transmitter of tribal wisdom and values. Ultimately, he attains the stature of a culture hero in his quest to become a bear, a motif common in Native American mythology and literature. His gamble with Sir Cecil Staples is reminiscent of cosmic struggles in Anishinabe myths. Apart from cultural and mythical heroism, Proude is also endowed with a strong sense of humanism—which can be seen, for example, when he tries to save Lilith Mae, or when he cuts open Belladonna's womb in order to give her and her twins a proper burial.

At the other end of the spectrum, Sir Cecil Staples stands out as an archetype of evil. Even so, such a character exhibits certain complexities. For all of his Satanism, he also serves as an agent of social satire; his tremendous power to annihilate is derived from his ability to hoard unleaded gasoline, which he then uses as a lure to his victims, who in fact gamble with him with the full knowledge of the consequences. Furthermore, a psychological basis for his deeds is also provided in the novel. As one of thirteen abducted children raised in a big-rig trailer constantly on the road, and having developed deformities after being subjected to repeated dousings of pesticides, he is a victim turned victimizer, a person poisoned by a pathological and dysfunctional society.

Artistically and thematically, Bigfoot is the most interesting character. An embodiment of the sacred and the profane, he is both a buffoon and a hero whose carnivalistic and disruptive playfulness nevertheless contributes to the general cause of his band. Amusing and scandalous, he is particularly significant as a character because of the comic vision he brings to bear on the pilgrims' quest for tribal survival and renewal. His sexual dalliance (or assault, depending on the perspective) with Cedarfair's wife, though perplexing, suggests that one of his major functions is to interact with the reader—as, for example, by challenging any sense of complacency that might have developed in the reading process.

A mixture of the tribal hero, the antisocial, and the trickster is manifest in many of the other characters or character groups; such a mixture often turns out to be a formula for a certain kind of wisdom essential to the survival and renewal of the pilgrims.

Belladonna, who takes tremendous pride in her Indian heritage because she is the offspring of a militant Indian and a sympathetic white woman, serves as an illustration of Vizenor's argument against the invention of the "Indian." Hence, according to the overall schema of the quest, the Breeders and Hunters at the Great Wall of Orion, who applaud Belladonna's hackneyed speech but poison her for her "terminal creed," are also purveyors of truths rather than merely the adversaries of the pilgrims. In fact, the rivalry between the pilgrims and their persecutors can be seen in terms of such a play, or dialogue, involving a spectrum of characters and character traits.

*Themes and Meanings*

The titles of the novel's two editions suggest that its major thematic concerns are the "darkness" in Saint Louis Bearheart and Bearheart's "heirship chronicles"; the preface, which sets up a metafictional frame, also serves as an exposition of the titles. The novel can be understood as a historian's statement, in the form of an imaginative narrative derived from tribal archives ("chronicles"), about the predicament of American Indians ("darkness"), the sources of their problems, and the solutions. "Darkness," understood psychologically, also stresses the sense of destiny, with hints of a radical response (which Vizenor implies in his use of the term "word war"). "Heirship," though not necessarily without ironic implications, also refers to predicament and destiny, but the term's emphasis appears to be on survival and renewal. The name of the fictional narrator, "Bearheart" or "St. Louis Bearheart," who claims that the bear is in his heart, alludes to the tribal myth of bear-becoming.

According to the novel's sociomythical framework, the bear-becoming of Cedarfair is a response to the historical disaster that has annihilated American Indians, their original habitats, their meager reservations ("circus"), their culture, and their identity. The ongoing oppression is further aggravated by the ecological and energy crises that Western civilization has brought upon whites and Native Americans alike. The grim, apocalyptic reality of impoverished existence and general extinction causes the characters to refer to the book's setting—the central United States—as the "third world." The quest of the pilgrims, which begins at the point where the "third world" is being destroyed, comes to a conclusion around the winter solstice, when the rebirth of the year and the creation of the fourth world coincide. The bear-becoming of Cedarfair and Inawa Biwide is an integral part of this regenerative process, an index of which is the state of powerful balance achieved in the identification of the human and the animal.

Vizenor's professed views about American Indians, Amerian culture, and aesthetics often shed light on specific themes such as the "invention" of Indians, the problem of "terminal creeds," and the comic vision of trickster figures. Critical of the term "Indian" as a label applied by whites, Vizenor often warns against the label's perpetuation of identity problems for Native Americans. Fixations on certain ideas, known as "terminal creeds" in his terminology, are akin to terminal diseases in the sense that they are stifling rather than productive. In dealing with these issues, the tribal trickster is the most effective in upsetting stereotypes about American Indians as noble savages with values readily exploitable and consumable by whites, and in introducing elements of play and chance to disrupt the complacency associated with fixed ideas. As a "word-war" narrative, *Bearheart* in general is a dramatization of these positions.

## Critical Context

As a mixed-blood Anishinabe who grew up in Minnesota off the reservation, Vizenor had a traumatic childhood (the murder of his father is unresolved) and acquired a varied education before beginning his writing career. Biographical information about the author shows that *Bearheart* is more than a fantasy; rather, it is a piece of fiction that reverberates with the totality of the author's personal, professional, academic, tribal, and American experiences. Vizenor's use of the trickster as a privileged figure within a narrative text employing techniques and devices suggestive of "trickstery" is closely tied to beliefs derived from those experiences.

*Bearheart,* like many of Vizenor's other works, challenges assumptions about Native Americans and their literature. At the most radical level, it refutes the notion of "Indians" and seeks to undermine the structure of thinking that sets up the "Indianness" of tribal people as the containable Other of Western civilization. Because such a challenge also applies to Indians who pride themselves on their Indianness, the book stands out as an unorthodox text with a special message for Native American readers and authors. Nevertheless, *Bearheart* is paradigmatically Native American in its efforts to confront the internal colonialism of America and to affirm the vital spirit of tribal traditions at a higher level of consciousness. On this higher level, the Indian ends where the tribal mixed-blood begins.

Because *Bearheart* draws its inspiration from tribal myths, it can be associated with the body of work created by authors such as James Welch, N. Scott Momaday, Leslie Marmon Silko, and Louise Erdrich. In addition, however, the novel is also full of allusions to such canonical works of the Western tradition as the poems of Geoffrey Chaucer. Furthermore, Vizenor's academic and scholarly expertise has contributed to the book's distinctly philosophical, postmodern, and poststructuralist outlook. Thanks to his balancing—though not necessarily reconciling—of insights from Native American, European, and possibly Asian sources, Vizenor has created a fluid text with abundant possibilities for interpretation.

## Bibliography

Bruchac, Joseph. *Survival This Way: Interviews with American Indian Poets.* Tucson: University of Arizona Press, 1987. Contains "Follow the Trickroutes: An Interview with Gerald Vizenor," in which the author discusses his career and his use of history in his writing.

Hochbruck, Wolfgang. "Breaking Away: The Novels of Gerald Vizenor." World Literature Today 66, no. 2 (Spring, 1992): 274-278. An overview of Vizenor's fiction, focusing on its unorthodox and disruptive elements.

Martin, Calvin, ed. *The American Indian and the Problem of History.* New York: Oxford University Press, 1987. Discusses historical revisionism and its central place in Native American literature. Views Vizenor as a skilled practitioner of revisionism.

Ruoff, A. LaVonne Brown. "Woodland Word Warrior: An Introduction to the Works of Gerald Vizenor." *MELUS* 13, no. 1-2 (Spring-Summer 1986): 13-43. Comprehensive review of major works by Vizenor, with a useful bibliography.

Vizenor, Gerald, ed. *Narrative Chance: Postmodern Discourse on Native American Indian Literature*. Albuquerque: University of New Mexico Press, 1989. Contains highly relevant essays, including " 'Ecstatic Strategies': Gerald Vizenor's *Darkness in Saint Louis Bearheart*," by Louis Owen, "The Trickster Novel," by Alan Velie, and "Trickster Discourse: Comic Holotropes and Language Games," by Vizenor.

*Balance Chow*

# BECAUSE IT IS BITTER,
# AND BECAUSE IT IS MY HEART

*Author:* Joyce Carol Oates (1938-    )
*Type of plot:* Psychological realism
*Time of plot:* The 1950's and the early 1960's
*Locale:* A small town in western New York State
*First published:* 1990

> *Principal characters:*
> LITTLE RED GARLOCK, a poor white delinquent
> IRIS COURTNEY, a bright, lower-middle-class teenage white girl
> PERSIA COURTNEY, Iris' alcoholic mother
> DUKE COURTNEY, Iris' gambler father
> JINX FAIRCHILD, an African American teenager and star of the high-school basketball team
> MR. and MRS. SAVAGE, a wealthy and cultured college professor and his wife
> ALAN SAVAGE, their son

*The Novel*

Because It Is Bitter, and Because It Is My Heart is divided into three parts and an epilogue. With the exception of the omniscient perspective of part 1, the narrative is presented from the third-person point of view, allowing Oates to explore the perspectives of many different characters.

Because It Is Bitter, and Because It Is My Heart explores the impact of race and class on the formation of identity in America. Oates uses four families to illustrate this: the poor white Garlocks, the struggling black Fairchilds, the ambitious working-class Courtneys, and the upper-class Savages. All the individual characters are placed within the larger context of their families and social class.

The novel begins in 1956 with the discovery of the corpse of Little Red Garlock, the demented son of a poor white family. After this discovery, the novel begins its large second section, moving back three years in time to 1953. This crucial section concerns the relationship between Iris Courtney, a white working-class teenager, and Jinx Fairchild, a black teenager and star basketball player. It is Jinx who accidentally murders Little Red. In defending Iris against this repulsive sexual bully, Jinx finds himself committing a violent act that forges a secretive and powerful bond with Iris.

Iris Courtney is the central consciousness of the novel. Ambitious and bright, Iris is seeking to overcome the obstacles presented to her by her social class and by her alcoholic mother, Persia, and her gambler father, Duke. After the murder, Iris develops an erotic attachment to Jinx; she continues her obsession with him even after he breaks off their relationship. This is a side of herself that she keeps hidden from the outside world.

It is Jinx who carries the lion's share of guilt. The overheated quarrel that ends with the murder of Little Red has a serious effect on Jinx. Although he is never caught, the crime destroys his hopes and dreams. He cannot trust the white community of Hammond to give him a fair trial, because he knows that as a black man he has no presumption of innocence. Jinx begins to keep up his guard, to feel alienated from the white world that once seemed to promise him great opportunities. His guilt feelings lead to a breakdown of his personality, and he develops a troubled and self-destructive side. This leads to an "accident" on the basketball court that ruins his career as an athlete; readers understand that this accident is an unconscious self-punishment. After the accident, Jinx must quit school and basketball and give up the dream of a college scholarship that was to be his bridge to the successful white world. He marries, works at a low-level job, and eventually is sent to Vietnam, where he will die, both self-defeated and defeated by the rigidities of the racist Hammond community.

The third section of the novel begins in 1962. Iris is in radically altered circumstances. Gone is the tragic world of Hammond, along with her guilty attachment to Jinx and her ties to her dissolute mother and her distant and feckless father. Iris has reinvented herself. This third section introduces its final representative American family, the Savages. They are not part of the grubby world of Hammond but belong to the upper crust of Syracuse, where Iris is attending the university. Using her strength, her intellect, and a single-minded ruthlessness, Iris has moved up the social and economic ladder into success and well-being. This section demonstrates the distance Iris has traveled from her origins. She is to marry Alan Savage, the patrician son of the cultivated, wealthy Savages, and she is determined to forget the past, which she keeps largely hidden from her new family. At the end of the novel, Iris models her bridal gown in front of the mirror and smirks, "Do you think I'll look the part?" These final lines tell readers that Iris has constructed a persona that does not reflect her true self and that this duplicity has made her bitter and cynical. Her cool façade belies the secrets of her troubled past. Although she, unlike Jinx, has successfully crossed over into the affluent white America, Iris does not find fulfillment.

*The Characters*

Little Red Garlock, a violent and possibly retarded young man, is the product of Hammond's underclass. He has been badly brought up by his racist mother, whose life is one of squalor and mental instability.

Duke Courtney has an addictive personality over which he has little control. Duke's name suggests his identity as a "sporting gent" and inveterate gambler. This identity eventually takes precedence over his responsibilities as a husband and father.

Persia Courtney, the wife of Duke, was once a "golden girl" but has fallen on hard times. Persia is a free spirit whose name evokes the Orient, which in the Western imagination also links her to the irrational and the unconscious. She carries an aura of the erotic and the exotic, but she is often intoxicated, and she eventually succumbs to insanity and alcohol. Oates uses Persia to comment on Iris' identity—there is a "Persia" side to her character. Mother and daughter both become involved with a black man; both are drawn toward forbidden love and out-of-bounds behavior.

Iris Courtney is the daughter of Duke and Persia. There are two sides to her personality. On the surface, she is a high achiever and a good girl; underneath is an overheated world of fear and desire. She papers over this side of herself with an agreeable persona. As a result, she becomes increasingly false and duplicitous; her outer being does not bear any resemblance to her inner self. Her name is deployed ironically; she is not the fragile flower she appears to be. Her name also suggests that she is the eye or "I" of the novel, and may indicate an autobiographical core.

Jinx Fairchild is a black teenager who has a chance to make it in the respectable white world. His name is a basketball nickname, but it is also a metaphor for his unlucky life. Like Iris, Jinx undergoes a fragmentation of his identity, developing a secret side filled with turbulent and inchoate feelings. Trusting and idealistic as a youth, he becomes increasingly bitter and cynical.

Mr. Savage, a cultured, intellectual college professor, exudes social confidence and an elite liberalism that does little to mitigate the social and economic inequalities of the country.

Mrs. Savage, his wife, is a kind and handsome woman who presides over a beautiful home and fine family. She virtually adopts Iris and becomes like a second mother to her. For all of the family's civility, however, the name Savage suggests that underneath their beautiful home and high-minded values is a social dominance that wages class war on the less privileged members of American society. The name suggests that this family represents the "savage inequalities" in American life.

Alan Savage, the weak but agreeable son of the Savages, is a secretive young man who may be homosexual. It is clear that Alan has denied his desires in order to assume an image in line with his family's wishes. One might say that his instincts and desires have been "savagely" repressed; like Iris, he has a hidden side of his nature that he attempts to repudiate.

*Themes and Meanings*

Oates's main purpose is to depict the impact of race and class in America. The tragedy of Jinx Fairchild suggests that while the black man can use the narrow venue of sports as a way to achieve the American Dream, he is still largely disenfranchised. Race and class have also formed the character of Iris Courtney. Her increasingly erotic relationship with Jinx must be kept secret; in addition, the status of Jinx as a forbidden love seems to intensify her feelings. Iris cannot have a relationship with Jinx that is not premised on the racism of her society.

While Iris does not have the barriers of race to prevent her from rising in the world, her success is a betrayal of her class and of herself. The idyllic life of the Savages contrasts in an almost grotesque way with the novel's previous scenes of turmoil and tragedy. For all their charm, the Savages preside over an America of injustice and inequality. By making sure the Savages do not appear until the final section of the novel, Oates demonstrates their separation from the rest of America. It is Iris who has the eyes to see that America is "two nations." Although she looks as if she is one of the elite, her roots are in the working-class town of Hammond, home of the "other" America. Yet the sense of liberation and security Iris enjoys has come at a cost. The Savages, like a test case from Sigmund Freud's analysis of civilization and its discontents, in which desire is renounced in exchange for social and economic security.

Eroticism is another strong theme in *Because It Is Bitter, and Because It Is My Heart*, depicted as the forbidden sexual spark between Iris and Jinx. This transgressive sexuality also establishes a sense of fear and danger. Iris' most genuine sexual feelings—those for Jinx—have been thwarted and denied, so that her erotic desires are contained within a roiling inner life. The socialization of women in America, Oates suggests, requires the development of a sexual identity of either the "good girl" or the "bad girl." Iris must suppress her sexual feelings if she is to maintain her respectability. The character of Iris illustrates the theme of sexuality, repression, and gender in contemporary American life.

Violence pervades Oates's vision of race, class, and gender in America. The inequities of race and class in Hammond inevitably lead to conflict and aggression. In addition to examining the social causes of violence, Oates also suggests that an unstable streak in the American character marks all but the most educated and secure classes.

Finally, Oates looks at the meaning of success and failure in American life. Jinx dies a bitter man because he has been cheated out of the American Dream; Iris, conversely, is bitter because her success is purchased at the price of her real identity. Whether a success or a failure, no character in the novel is not thwarted and diminished by the social and psychological forces that shape American society.

*Critical Context*

*Because It Is Bitter, and Because It Is My Heart* continues Oates's return to the psychological realism of her earlier fiction. After a series of historical novels that deployed the techniques of the Magical Realists, Oates returned to the familiar contemporary terrain of upstate New York and to her usual explorations of the social and psychological issues that confront postwar America. This novel is of a piece with the two novels closely preceding it, *Marya* (1986) and *You Must Remember This* (1987). All three concern the psychological development of a gifted young woman who overcomes a troubled small-town 1950's youth.

*Because It Is Bitter, and Because It Is My Heart*, like the highly acclaimed *You Must Remember This*, explores the world of sports in contemporary America, especially the way in which the sports world is a gateway to success for the underprivileged male. Both novels also deal with forbidden love and offer a revisionist reading of the 1950's as a decade that was not so much a celebration of the American Dream as a realization of its worst nightmares. As with all of Oates's work, the human personality is depicted as a seething cauldron of excitations; these surges of emotion create an atmosphere of intensity and passion that comments on the intemperate side of the American character. The typical "Oatesian" personality is overwhelmed by fears and wishes only partially understood. One can detect the influences of William Faulkner, Flannery O'Connor, and D. H. Lawrence in this presentation of the self.

A popular and prolific writer, Oates has been publishing novels, essays, stories, poems, and plays continuously since 1963. The two most-discussed aspects of her work are its quantity and its propensity for violence. Oates attributes these concerns about excess to a wish to limit her creative potential as a woman. Although her recent work suggests elements of autobiography, moreover, Oates maintains that her writing is not confessional but rather representative of the social and psychological issues that make up the American experience. In this regard, Oates is a good example of what she has called the "visionary" novelist, who writes not for herself or out of her own experience but as a medium for the lives of those around her.

*Bibliography*
Gates, Henry Louis. "Murder, She Wrote." *The Nation* 251 (July 2, 1990): 27. While he singles out Oates's rendering of racial resentment, Gates maintains that "the real spine of the book may be in its brilliant depiction of downward mobility, the painful fragility of the Courtneys' standing in the world."

Johnson, Greg. *Understanding Joyce Carol Oates*. Columbia: University of South Carolina Press, 1987. Johnson sees Oates as a writer with a broad and sweeping vision of contemporary America. Discusses her deployment of gothic strategies and her ability to explore intense psychological states.

Milazzo, Lee, ed. *Conversations with Joyce Carol Oates*. Jackson: University Press of Mississippi, 1989. Interviews discuss Oates's writing habits, issues of violence and productivity, and the artist as the conscience of society.

Storace, Patricia. "A Home Is Not a Fist." *The New York Review of Books* 37 (August 16, 1990): 22. Praises Oates's ability to interlace the various lives and families in her novel, but complains that she is not able to "rouse her interest in a character unless the character is in crisis." Approves of her description of social life and her sense of "history refracted through fiction."

Wesley, Marilyn C. *Refusal and Transgression in Joyce Carol Oates' Fiction*. Westport, Conn.: Greenwood Press, 1993. A feminist appreciation of Oates that emphasizes the "gendered psychological experience" of Oates's heroines. Using the ideas of Fredric Jameson, Wesley explores Oates's picture of the family as a patriarchal system of power. She also adds some useful remarks about Jinx Fairchild as "transgressive other."

*Margaret Boe Birns*

# THE BEET QUEEN

*Author:* Louise Erdrich (1954-     )
*Type of plot:* Family
*Time of plot:* 1932-1972
*Locale:* The small town of Argus, North Dakota
*First published:* 1986

> *Principal characters:*
> MARY ADARE, the protagonist, who possesses magical powers, interprets signs, and tells fortunes
> KARL ADARE, Mary's brother, a weak and wandering soul
> SITA KOZKA, Mary's cousin, the daughter of Mary's Aunt Fritzie and Uncle Peter
> CELESTINE JAMES, Sita Kozka's best friend, who becomes Mary's best friend and employee
> DOT ADARE, the Beet Queen of the title, the daughter of Karl Adare and Celestine James
> WALLACE PFEF, a prominent citizen who becomes Karl Adare's lover and Dot Adare's "uncle"

## The Novel

*The Beet Queen* narrates the adventures of several characters of mixed Native American and European background from Louise Erdrich's first novel, *Love Medicine* (1985), as they interact with Mary and Karl Adare. The novel illuminates the lives of these characters over a forty-year period.

*The Beet Queen*'s sixteen chapters fall into four parts. Most are recounted by a single character; some are told by several characters. The chapters include short scenes sketched by an omniscient narrator who seems more detached than the characters. Each chapter is dated to give the reader some sense of time, but the chapters are not chronological in the traditional sense. Told and retold by different characters, the events repeat, circle, overlap, and digress.

Erdrich centers her novel on the adventures of Mary Adare, whose father is dead and whose mother abandons her and her two brothers at a fair by flying off with a stunt aviator. After the baby brother is snatched by a recently bereaved father, eleven-year-old Mary and her older brother, Karl, take a freight train to see their Aunt Fritzie and her husband, Uncle Pete, who are butchers in Argus, North Dakota. On arrival, Karl is mysteriously drawn to a flowering tree, where he is attacked by a dog; he escapes by running back to the train and leaving town. Mary plods on to the butcher shop and is taken in by her aunt and uncle, although their daughter, Sita, resents her presence.

Mary shares Sita's room, wears her clothes, steals Sita's best friend, Celestine, and performs a miracle at their school. Sita, a pretty, vain, self-centered girl, longs to have her own apartment in the big city and become a model. When Fritzie develops lung trouble and she and Pete move to Arizona, Sita moves to Fargo to seek her fortune. Mary, who has been working at the butcher shop all along, hires Celestine to help her and continues to run it successfully.

Karl Adare, a traveling salesman of various sleazy products, comes to Argus to visit Mary and perhaps Wallace Pfef, with whom he has had a homosexual encounter at a crop and livestock convention in Minneapolis. He arrives at the butcher shop when Mary is out and meets Celestine, ripe for her first romantic adventure. Overcome with lust, they entangle in a brief coupling that astonishes them both. Karl then sells Celestine a knife from his sample case and vanishes, but he turns up two weeks later at Celestine's house. Still filled with ideas of popular romance, Celestine leads him upstairs to her bedroom. This time, Karl stays. After two months, Celestine asks him to leave because of Mary's disapproval and her own independent spirit. Unwillingly, he goes, but as a parting shot, he informs Celestine that she is pregnant with his baby.

Karl next visits his cousin, Sita, who has divorced her first husband and is now married to Louis, a county health inspector. Because of the divorce, Sita has lapsed from the Catholic church that was a mainstay of her life and is in precarious mental health. When Karl gives her a Bible that has Celestine's name in it, the unbalanced Sita calls the police before breaking down completely.

Celestine sets out for the hospital in a blizzard one night when she is about to have her baby, and she crashes her Buick into Wallace Pfef's fence. He takes her in and delivers the healthy baby according to Celestine's instructions. In gratitude, she names the girl Wallacette Darlene, but Mary nicknames the child "Dot," which sticks. Celestine brings the baby with her to the butcher shop every day, and Mary becomes attached to the child. Over the years, Mary constantly meddles in her niece's life, causing tension between Mary and Celestine. They squabble constantly.

Dot grows up a sturdy, strong-willed young woman, feisty, fearless, and angry. As Wallace Pfef says, "They loved Dot too much, and for that sin she made them miserable." Yet Wallace loves her almost as much and acts as foolishly. He arranges an eighteenth birthday party for Dot that turns into a comic fiasco, but his crowning folly is to arrange a beet festival and rig the votes so that "Wallacette" is elected Beet Queen.

In a stunning finale, Dot discovers what Wallace has done. Before she can be crowned queen, she runs from the royal platform to an adjoining field, where a plane awaits the moment to take off and write "Queen Wallacette" across the sky. After a terrifying flight, the pilot returns Dot to the field, where she finds the grandstand deserted but for her mother, awaiting her and brimming with love.

## The Characters

Mary's odd nature defies her ordinary appearance. As a child, she performs a miracle, falling on the school playground ice and leaving a "manifestation" that is interpreted by the nuns as the face of Jesus. Mary sees only Karl's face in the imprint, while Celestine sees nothing at all. Mary's power to tell fortunes and foresee the future arouses fear in some of the other characters. Sita's mental illness and Dot's bad temper are blamed on her. Even the clothes she wears, tasselled turbans and wild prints, contribute to her oddness. Like other characters in the book, Mary does not develop over time but becomes more deeply what she is.

Karl would seem to be a weak, irresponsible man by his actions. He abandons Mary when they are children, he moves in and out of Wallace's house according to whim, and he changes jobs frequently. It is Celestine who asks him to leave when she is pregnant, however, and he agrees to the formality of a marriage after the baby is born. The way he is presented depends upon which character is speaking at any given time. He is frequently associated with Christian images, and sometimes with Satanic ones. When he visits Sita, she sees him sinking into the soft grass beneath her garden chairs until he is swallowed up by earth. Karl refers to himself as a "poor fool," and he may represent the fool of the tarot cards that Mary reads. He is the most ambiguous figure in the novel.

Celestine, who is half Chippewa, is a wonderful creation whose large size influences the way she sees the world and the way the world sees her. Orphaned early and reared by an older sister, Celestine develops a strong, independent spirit that stands her in good stead in dealing with the powerful Adares. She is Mary's only friend.

Dot Adare, the child of Celestine and Karl, inadvertently unites the major characters. She is an aggressive child, "as big as most children twice her age, strong and spoiled" when she enters first grade, and she grows into a wild, spiteful teenager. Still, she brings love and joy into the lives of Celestine, Mary, and "uncle" Wallace. Even Karl, her absentee father, returns to Argus for the crowning of the Beet Queen because of a sweet memory associated with his daughter.

Wallace Pfef discovers he is homosexual in his first sexual encounter with Karl Adare, and he is smitten for life. Karl sums him up: "He'd do anything to please me, but didn't have the nerve to please himself." Wallace brings this same fawning devotion to his relationship with Dot, who treats him as disdainfully as she treats everyone. Yet there is a very different side to Wallace. He is active in the Argus Chamber of Commerce, the Sugar Beet Promoters, the Optimists, the Knights of Columbus, and other civic organizations. A major force in bringing the dependable cash crop, beets, to the area, he is thoroughly sensible in all things but love.

*Themes and Meanings*

*The Beet Queen* deals primarily with marginal people who live socially and culturally displaced lives. This marginality is a source of both strength and grief for Erdrich's characters. Wallace Pfef, an outstanding civic leader, is marginal as a homosexual in a small, Midwestern town and in his role as substitute father to Dot Adare. Yet it is precisely his love for Karl and Dot that provides his greatest joy and pain. In addition to being socially marginal, Erdrich's characters are culturally marginal; they live under codes of both Christianity and archetypal myths.

The families in *The Beet Queen* are also marginal. Although the novel might be seen as a family saga portraying three generations, the plot suggests that there are many nonbiological ties that link people. Mary grows up with her Aunt Fritzie, who prefers

Mary to her own daughter, Sita. Celestine, who is Karl's wife, spends much more time with Wallace, who often plays the role of husband. Celestine's relationship with Mary is also ambiguous. While the two women are close friends by choice, it is not until Celestine bears Mary's niece that confrontations arise. These complex, mixed roles produce gaps in the clear line of relationships that inform traditional family sagas and are suggestive of tribal kinship systems.

Erdrich's method of characterization emphasizes this conflict between nuclear family and tribal codes. Mary, Karl, Celestine, and Dot are not defined by traditional European family roles. There are no "main" characters. Only in his or her own narration is each character central; otherwise, the character exists on the margin of someone else's life. Some critics have suggested that these sometimes conflicting narrations reflect an American Indian concept of individuality independent of personal psychology. Characters are sometimes associated with the natural elements, air, water, earth, and fire. The Adare family is clearly related to the element air when Karl and Mary's mother abandons them and her new baby by flying away with a stunt pilot. Years later, the one postcard Mary ever sends her mother depicts an aerial view of Argus, as if she is still circling overhead. The mother's flight is mirrored at the end of the novel when Dot flies off with a skywriter to escape the humiliation of her arranged victory as Beet Queen. Karl also escapes his early humiliation with a transient by leaping straight out of a moving boxcar into the night air.

Although these blended voices never produce an individual hero, a sense of the whole community seems to replace it. The structure of the narrative is formal and the voices are complementary, so that the major characters together create the protagonist. In the last scene, when Dot has descended to Earth after her precipitous flight and has returned home with her mother, she and Celestine lie in bed in their separate rooms. Each feels the rush of wind and hears the first drops of rain that will break the drought Argus has suffered for months. With that fresh breath of air, the reader rejoices not only for Dot and Celestine but for the entire community as well.

*Critical Context*

Louise Erdrich, of German American and Chippewa descent, was already a highly acclaimed writer when *The Beet Queen* appeared. Her 1984 collection of poetry *Jacklight* had won high praise. In that same year, her first noel, *Love Medicine*, received the National Book Critics Circle best fiction award, the Sue Kaufman Prize for best first novel, and many other awards. The second volume of her planned quartet of novels, *The Beet Queen*, came out two years later; it was followed by a third, *Tracks*, in 1988.

Erdrich's novels are all circular rather than linear, and several of the characters reappear, although new ones are also introduced. Each book stands alone as a novel but each gains from a reading of the others, since a reader familiar with the series is better able to trace the tangled relationships of the characters. In a broad sense, the novels chronicle the struggles of Native Americans to survive and maintain their fragmented and mixed culture.

Erdrich's work can be seen as part of a flowering of Native American literature that goes back to 1969, when N. Scott Momaday won the Pulitzer Prize for *A House Made of Dawn*. Erdrich herself attributes this new literature to the generally improved conditions among Native Americans, and she describes herself as one who has benefited from Bureau of Indian Affairs money and education. Majoring in English and creative writing at Dartmouth, she later received her master's degree from the writing program at The Johns Hopkins University. Although she mentions William Faulkner as an influence, the whole literary canon has left its traces on her work. One important connection with Faulkner is her strong sense of place, which for her is the plains area of North Dakota—a region that is as much a presence in her novels as are her characters.

*Bibliography*
Banks, Russell. "Border Country." *The Nation* 243 (November 1, 1986): 460-462. Banks reviews *The Beet Queen* and finds it an almost perfect example of classical comedy. Mary Adare is described as "one of the most memorable women in recent American fiction." The novel is compared favorably with recent books of similar style.
Rainwater, Catherine. "Reading Between Worlds: Narrativity in the Fiction of Louise Erdrich." *American Literature* 62 (September, 1990): 405-422. Rainwater examines the various conflicting messages in Erdrich's first three novels, with emphasis on the structure of time. The article concludes that a guiding concept in Erdrich's work is that "the world takes on the shape of the stories we tell."
Towery, Margie. "Continuity and Connection: Characters in Louise Erdrich's Fiction." *American Indian Culture and Research Journal* 16 (1992): 99-122. Traces the genealogy of various characters in three of Erdrich's novels and shows that not all of the narrators are reliable. Other kinds of connections between characters are discussed, such as the presence of tattoos, the games they enjoy, and even their favorite foods. Extremely useful for understanding the connections between Erdrich's novels.
Wickenden, Dorothy. "Off the Reservation." *The New Republic* 195 (October 6, 1986): 46-48. Praises *The Beet Queen* for Erdrich's prose style, her "poetic turns," and her "observant eye." Yet Wickenden points out the problems that arise when a novel is told in a series of extraordinary scenes rather than an evolving plot, and she finds the climactic scene at the Beet Festival contrived. The overall tone is positive.
Wong, Hertha D. "An Interview with Louise Erdrich and Michael Dorris." *North Dakota Quarterly* 55 (Winter, 1987): 196-218. Wong conducts a comprehensive interview. Erdrich and her husband talk about the origins of their work, their method of working together, their domestic life, and other topics. They discuss *The Beet Queen* and *Love Medicine* as well as Dorris' novel *A Yellow Raft in Blue Water* (1987).

*Sheila Golburgh Johnson*

# THE BELLAROSA CONNECTION

*Author:* Saul Bellow (1915-    )
*Type of plot:* Psychological realism
*Time of plot:* 1959 to the 1980's
*Locale:* Principally Jerusalem
*First published:* 1989

> *Principal characters:*
> SORELLA FONSTEIN, an imposing woman who is the center of the action
> HARRY FONSTEIN, Sorella's husband, the man whose life story is the source of both plot and theme
> BILLY ROSE, an impresario whom Sorella seeks out
> THE NARRATOR, the storyteller whose memories shape the meaning of the novel

*The Novel*

One of Saul Bellow's shorter works, *The Bellarosa Connection* tells the story of a wife's persistence in gaining an interview with impresario Billy Rose, who was responsible—through his anonymous underground railroad—for saving from the Nazis a number of Jews, Harry Fonstein among them, by bringing them to America. The narrator, a distant relative of the Fonsteins, remembers being told Harry's history.

Harry Fonstein has made his way to Italy in fleeing the Nazis, but in Rome, he is arrested and faces deportation to a concentration camp. A representative from the American impresario Billy Rose—whom the Italians called "Bellarosa"—arranges for Harry's prison door to be left open and for him to be met by a car, given false papers, and put on a ship bound for America.

In New York, Harry learns English and studies refrigeration and heating. He sails to Havana and is employed as a "legman" tracking down other Jews whose surviving relatives are looking for them. A few years later, he meets Sorella, an American girl from New Jersey. Back in America, married to Sorella, Harry works hard, studies diligently, and becomes rich.

Harry harbors a desire to meet Billy Rose, his benefactor. For years, Harry had sent Billy numerous letters, but Rose had never acknowledged them. Harry had been turned aside at Billy's office and had been snubbed by Rose in New York's famous Sardi's restaurant. Harry, though, had never given up his desire simply to thank his savior.

All this the narrator has recounted as prelude to his personal involvement with the Fonsteins. Himself now prosperous and on the eve of his retirement as head of the Philadelphia-based Mnemosyne Institute, which he has directed for forty years, the narrator meets the Fonsteins in Jerusalem, where they are vacationing. He is particularly impressed with Sorella, whom he had remembered as a huge woman whose bulk of body was matched only by her tenacity of will and the solidity of her convictions. Over tea on the terrace of the King David Hotel, Sorella continues the story of the "Bellarosa connection."

She had decided personally to take up Harry's cause, to force Billy at least to meet the man whom he had refused even to acknowledge. To this end, she explains, she had tracked down the agent whom Billy Rose had sent to meet Harry on Ellis Island. The agent, a Mrs. Hamet, had been a frustrated actress and had probably loved Billy. She was living miserably when Sorella found her and the two struck up a kind of bond, each sympathetic to the other's needs. Old and dying, Hamet tells Sorella of a journal she has been keeping, a record of Billy's "comings and goings" and of his scandalous behavior. The journal is now in Sorella's possession, and the narrator is convinced that Sorella intends to use it in some way.

A few days later, Billy Rose arrives in Jerusalem to donate a sculpture garden. The narrator now realizes that Sorella intends to confront Billy and to blackmail him with the journal. This confrontation, the central scene in the book, takes place in Billy's suite in the hotel. In spite of Billy's crudeness and his attempts to disavow any relationship with Harry, Sorella successfully intimidates him into believing that she will expose Billy's excesses to the press unless he acknowledges Harry. Billy becomes irate, mean, insulting, and dehumanizing. At this point, Sorella flings the journal at Rose and leaves.

The narrator does not see the Fonsteins again. Thirty years later, alone in his Philadelphia mansion, beset by loneliness and bad dreams, he receives a telephone request from a rabbi seeking information about the Fonsteins for a man claiming to be a relative. The narrator makes a phone call or two and learns that the Fonsteins' only son has become a failed gambler in Las Vegas. The Fonsteins themselves are dead, killed in an automobile accident. He has recorded their story as a kind of memorial.

*The Characters*

Sorella Fonstein, the central figure in the novel, is a woman of great intelligence. Her bulk and her plainness serve, to the narrator, as physical emblems of her inner strength and dignity. Unlike some other women portrayed in Bellow's novels, Sorella is a "tiger wife" of admirable force and humanity. She does not subdue Harry with the force of her character but acts as his liberator, one who understands his need for respect beyond the middle-class values of success. She has impressed the narrator with her persistence and her wit. She takes on the role of the Furies to Billy Rose's conscience, forcing him to acknowledge what his personal crudity and selfishness seek to conceal. Like the Furies of ancient Greek myth, Sorella is unbending, inexorable. There is nothing of self-consciousness, nothing of personal vanity in her campaign. It is deliberate, direct, and natural, like a life force.

Though his is the story that forms the central focus of the book, Harry Fonstein is, ironically, not the central character nor even a minor one. Though his rags-to-riches narrative is summarized early in the novel, Harry himself is a pointedly shadowy figure, existing on the periphery of the action. He has little dialogue, no movement, no real physical presence. Harry is, in fact, an abiding presence as a concept, a point of reference from which Sorella and the narrator develop their own courses of action.

Billy Rose, the half-real, half-fictional "villain" of the piece, is the most puzzling of the group. His crudity, selfishness, and hypocrisy, his blatant egotism, and his human cruelty are highlighted all the more by his one seemingly genuine act of altruism, the underground railroad. Billy seems threatened by his connection with Harry. He shows no pity, no admiration, no feelings of any kind. As a showman, Rose is more concerned with his public image than his private life; his disavowal of his "connection" is his way of sealing the crack in his public image, a crack through which his emotional, moral life might reveal itself.

After Sorella, the narrator is the most compelling character. A case may be made, in fact, that he is the central figure, since the events and their meaning are filtered through his observations and his memory. The narrator is both historian and judge. As he recalls the story, he admires Sorella and damns Billy Rose as he fully understands the real meaning of the connection. Additionally, he understands his own connection: He is the means through which the Fonstein-Rose story lives on, and the meaning of the story reverberates through his memory to the world at large.

*Themes and Meanings*

For the narrator, as for the reader, the meaning of the Fonstein-Billy Rose story— the real "Bellarosa connection"—is not just the need for the recognition of one man's responsibility to another but the human need to recognize the value, the importance, the overarching supremacy of moral kinship. What, indeed, Sorella is seeking, what Billy Rose attempts to conceal, what the narrator ultimately comprehends, is that all the participants in life's drama are connected by chains forged of the spirit and the mind. Billy's act of secret generosity has liberated Harry from physical death but has, ironically, snared Billy himself in a kind of spiritual bondage by which Billy has become connected to Harry the Jew and Harry the human being. The private Billy Rose has come into conflict with the public persona. Billy has become his brother's keeper and must recognize his kinship and his responsibility.

The narrative structure is more supple than it first appears. Though the action is related second-hand, as it were, events and conversations spanning thirty years are seen through the narrator's memory and clarified by his insights. The narrator's own working motto is "memory is life"; his position as president of a memory institute in Philadelphia (the city of brotherly love) gives him credibility as a judge and validates his observations that "God doesn't forget" and that human beings must not forget their vital connections with one another.

Finally, a lesser theme emerges near the conclusion, when the narrator learns that the Fonsteins' son has become a Las Vegas gambler. Whereas the Fonstein-Rose story gained significance in the holy city of Jerusalem, the direct descendent of the Fonsteins, son Gilbert (not a "Jewish" name) has taken his place in America's most secular city. Las Vegas has become the new Jerusalem. The question implied by the narrator is whether the new generation of Jews, American-bred, will survive with its values intact or if it will go the way of Gilbert Fonstein—or, perhaps, of Billy Rose.

*Critical Context*

The *Bellarosa Connection* can serve as a good introduction to Bellow's works. Despite its brevity, the book treats major themes of human compassion and kinship that have engaged Bellow during his long career as a writer. The characters, though not as fully drawn as in earlier, more ambitious novels, are suggestive of the fine portrayals of heroes and villains that fill Bellow's books. Billy Rose, for example, is a kind of antithesis to Tommy Wilhelm in *Seize the Day* (1956), fleeing the demands of humanity that Tommy is seeking to validate. He is also in the tradition of such Bellovian villains as Dr. Adler in *Seize the Day* and the fast-talking con-man Einhorn in *The Adventures of Augie March* (1953), unfeeling men who never come into contact with their humanity.

*Bibliography*

Braham, Jeanne. *A Sort of Columbus*. Athens: University of Georgia, 1984. Examines Bellow's novels as centering on the theme of discovery. The central characters seek to understand their spiritual conflict within an American context. Bellow's works thus sit squarely in the American literary tradition; his heroes pursue a personal vision tempered by, yet transcending, the American experience.

Clayton, John J. *Saul Bellow: In Defense of Man*. 2d ed. Bloomington: Indiana University Press, 1979. Traces the affirmation implicit in Bellow's work. Examines Bellow's characters as alienated and paranoid, yet acting in such a way as to reject alienation and to affirm the brotherhood of man. Clayton insists that Bellow is a psychological novelist first and a moral spokesman second.

Newman, Judie. *Saul Bellow and History*. New York: St. Martin's Press, 1984. An interesting study, concentrating on the five "major" novels from *The Adventures of Augie March* (1953) to *Humboldt's Gift* (1975). Provides an introduction summarizing critical opinions on Bellow's religious and psychological views of life. Newman's thesis is that Bellow is a novelist concerned with the effect of history and specific time on the actions of the protagonist.

Pifer, Ellen. *Saul Bellow Against the Grain*. Philadelphia: University of Pennsylvania Press, 1990. Argues that each of Bellow's heroes is in conflict with himself. The conflict between reason and religion ends with the hero's affirmation of a metaphysical or intuitive truth. Bellow's novels thus "go against the grain" of traditional realism and are radical in their "questioning of accepted notions of reality."

Trachtenberg, Stanley, comp. *Critical Essays on Saul Bellow*. Boston: G. K. Hall, 1979. A compendium of the most significant critical essays about Bellow and his work. Beginning with the novels of the 1940's and 1950's, the reviews and articles discuss Bellow's heroes as seekers and doubters and treat some of the author's main themes. The article on Herzog as a latter-day Odysseus is particularly insightful.

*Edward A. Fiorelli*

# BELOVED

*Author:* Toni Morrison (1931-    )
*Type of plot:* Historical realism
*Time of plot:* 1873-1874
*Locale:* Near Cincinnati, Ohio
*First published:* 1987

*Principal characters:*
SETHE, a fugitive slave who tries to kill her children to keep them from being recaptured
DENVER, the daughter to whom Sethe gave birth during her escape
BELOVED, the daughter Sethe killed, now come back in bodily form as a twenty-year-old woman
PAUL D., a former slave whose arrival precipitates major changes
BABY SUGGS, Sethe's mother-in-law

*The Novel*

*Beloved* takes its central incident from the true account of a runaway slave that Toni Morrison read in an 1856 newspaper. The slave, Margaret Garner, escaped to Cincinnati to her mother-in-law's house; shortly afterward, as the slaveowner who tracked her down was about to capture her, she killed one of her children and attempted to kill the others rather than have them returned to slavery. In *Beloved*, the woman is named Sethe, and the story starts eighteen years after the killing. Through flashbacks, multiple viewpoints, and accumulated fragments of thoughts and information, the novel powerfully expands not only to show the infinite horrors of slavery but also to show how the physical and psychological realities of the past inevitably shape the present.

If the events portrayed in the novel were told bluntly in chronological order, what happens in each character's life might well seem too strong or too sensational for the reader to absorb, just as the events have confounded and conflicted the characters themselves. The present of the novel is 1873 and 1874. Sethe and Denver are living in the Ohio house where Baby Suggs had provided refuge during their escape from slavery, first for the children sent ahead and then for Sethe and the newborn Denver.

Sethe had escaped from Sweet Home, a farm in Kentucky, and the cruelty of the slavemaster, Schoolteacher. Aided by a white girl, Amy Denver, an indentured servant heading north, Sethe gives birth to a premature baby in a leaky, abandoned boat on the Ohio River; Sethe names the child Denver. Only a month later, Schoolteacher comes riding up to the house where the family is hiding to recapture his "legal property." Sethe grabs her children and takes them into the woodshed, where she slashes the troat of the first at hand and tries to kill the others before she is stopped. After she spends time in jail, Sethe returns to the Ohio house, but she refuses to say she made the wrong choice in attempting to kill her children rather than allow them to be returned to slavery.

Sethe's two sons run away when they are still boys, and Baby Suggs dies. Mother and daughter are cut off from the community of other African Americans; Sethe goes out only to her job as a cook, and Denver does not leave the house at all. Yet they are not alone: The novel begins by noting that the house "was spiteful. Full of baby's venom." The poison is the spirit of the murdered baby, whom no one talks about but whom no one, especially Sethe, can forget.

When Paul D. comes to the house after his own eighteen years of hardship since they were all slaves at Sweet Home, he seems to manage to drive the ghost away. What happens, however, is that the spirit is incarnated, made flesh. Just at the moment when Paul D., Sethe, and Denver come back from seeing a traveling sideshow and are feeling some hope of happiness, they find a mysterious young woman sitting outside the house waiting for them. She says that her name is Beloved, which was the one word on the baby's tombstone. Denver eagerly latches on to her as the sister she never knew; later, Sethe decides that the woman is in fact her daughter come back to life, now the age she would have been, to give Sethe a chance to explain why she had to kill her.

Beloved becomes the focus for all activity. She seduces Paul D. and nearly drives him away, and he does leave when he learns that Sethe had killed her child. Alone in the house, Sethe, Denver, and Beloved develop an increasingly desperate fixation on one another as they pursue their pasts. It is Denver who is finally able to break out of the obsession, and she goes to the only other house she knows, that of Lady Jones. The community responds to this reaching out, and the family's neighbors supply them with food. The novel ends when the white owner of the house comes riding up and Sethe tries to attack him, as though reliving the coming of Schoolteacher eighteen years earlier. This time, though, she lashes out at the oppressor, not at her child. The spell is broken. Beloved disappears, and Paul D. returns, Denver is able to go forth, and the community is supportive. Sethe, if never able to forget, is able to accept herself, and life can go on.

*The Characters*

Sethe is the only female slave at Sweet Home. She marries Halle (though not in a legal ceremony) and is pregnant with their fourth child when she is assaulted by Schoolteacher and his nephews. She escapes and, with the help of Amy Denver, gives birth to the baby she names Denver on the boundary between slave Kentucky and free Ohio. Freedom, though, does not exist for fugitive slaves, and Schoolteacher tracks them down. As the novel opens, Sethe is in the Ohio house with Denver and the ghost that plays tricks on them. Paul D. arrives, bringing hope but also conflict.

Denver likes to hear the story of her perilous birth, but no one talks about the strangeness at the house. At Lady Jones's school, Nelson Lord, a boy there, tells Denver that her mother had killed Denver's sister. The information is too traumatic for Denver to bear. Denver is eighteen when Paul D. comes. When Beloved appears soon afterward, Denver feels possessive and protective of the sister she had never known. Eventually, though, she sees that she must protect Sethe from Beloved's vengeance. By the end of the novel, Denver is functioning in the community and is no longer isolated.

Beloved is assumed to be the dead baby come back to life. No one knows where she comes from or where she goes at the end of the book. Her thoughts are those of a preverbal child, and she craves sweets and food. She becomes fat, bloated, perhaps pregnant after seducing Paul D. Beloved's presence forces confrontation with the past—or, perhaps, it is because Sethe and the others are facing the past that Beloved materializes. In terms of characterization, she is an original, an imaginative creation from black folklore and a product of Magical Realism, in which the impossible is often presented as real. Beloved can also be considered a metaphorical exploration of the psychology of slavery and of Sethe's psychological problems in dealing with her past.

Paul D. is the only one of the five "Sweet Home men" who manages to survive, even after he is recaptured and sold in chains, with a bit in his mouth. When he comes to the Ohio house, he chases away the spirit that haunts Sethe and Denver, but the ghost then materializes, and he is unable to make her leave or to resist her sexual seduction. He betrays Sethe by judging her when he learns that Sethe had killed her child; after Beloved is driven away, though, Paul D. can admit his own limitations, and he reunites with Sethe.

Baby Suggs is old and crippled by the time her son Halle can earn freedom for her. She becomes a matriarch in the local black community, preaching that the community's members must love themselves and one another. She blames whites for all the troubles her people face. Yet it is the action of her daughter-in-law, Sethe, and the resulting shunning by the community that makes her finally give up struggling. She retires to her bed, interested only in looking at bits of color. Her death leaves Sethe and Denver together in the house.

*Themes and Meanings*

*Beloved* dramatizes the atrocities inflicted upon the "Sixty Million and more" of the dedication page, those who were killed on the slave ships as well as those who were slaves in America. Every African American character in the novel illustrates the difficulties faced by any victimized group or person, and the white characters show how oppression affects the oppressor as well.

The account of a slave baby murdered by its mother is "not a story to pass on," Morrison writes at the end of the novel, but the book is a tribute to those who did not have a chance to survive, to be named, to tell their own story. Sethe's own mother had killed some of her infants—those fathered by white rapists. When Beloved appears, transcending the grave, she forces memories ("re-memory") of pain, horror, and loss. Beloved represents the memories that haunt Sethe, but Beloved herself can be said to be haunted, driven to materialize and attack that which killed her. No one is free from the past.

*Beloved* is thus not only about institutionalized discrimination but also about the interior life of individuals, and it becomes universal in its emphasis on the struggles with one's personal history as well as with cultural history. Much of the focus is on the ways slavery affected women in relation to motherhood and family, specifically the ways it denied women the right to their own children. Morrison uses a variety of literary techniques and narrative viewpoints to make the reader feel and understand the "unspeakable." She uses colloquial dialogue and a wealth of folklore, myth, and literary allusions. The characters circle back to the same worrisome memories over and over, clarifying and adding details, so they and the reader come to believe and understand. Many images recur: blood, milk, food, water, colors, names, trees, clothing.

The novel is also about love, endurance, and community. A striking example of this is when the Sweet Home slave Sixo is burned alive but cries out "Seven-o!" in joyful defiance because he knows that his woman is pregnant with their child. Paul D. has been tortured, but he can eventually allow himself to feel love. The community members shun Sethe, but they understand her urge to stop supplying victims to white supremacy, and they rally to expel Beloved at the end.

The novel insists on the importance of individual responsibility as well as on the collective need to eliminate social and legal discrimination. Like most great literature, *Beloved* speaks to the hope that humanity will become more humane, will replace cruelty with compassion.

*Critical Context*

*Beloved* received considerable favorable attention when it was first published. The noted Canadian writer Margaret Atwood, for example, wrote in *The New York Times* that the novel shows Morrison as "a pre-eminent American novelist" whose "versatility and technical and emotional range appears to know no bounds."

The novel, though, became a source of controversy when it was nominated for but failed to receive either the National Book Award or the National Book Critics Circle Award. The January 24, 1988, edition of *The New York Times Book Review* carried a tribute to Morrison signed by forty-eight prominent African American writers and literary critics urging that Morrison be given greater recognition, stating that she had "advanced the moral and artistic standards by which we must measure the daring and the love of our national imagination and our collective intelligence as a people." *Beloved* was awarded the Pulitzer Prize in fiction later in 1988 and also received the Robert F. Kennedy Award.

Morrison had published four distinguished novels prior to *Beloved*. All concern the struggles of African Americans. *The Bluest Eye* (1969) is the story of a girl who wants to change her brown eyes to blue so that she will be accepted by the dominant society, but the consequences are tragic. *Sula* (1973) shows two young women who face both racism and sexism in their small town. *Song of Solomon* (1977) traces a young man's struggles for self-identity; this novel received the National Book Critics Circle Award for fiction. *Tar Baby* (1981) also deals with race relations in the contemporary world.

After *Beloved*, Morrison published *Jazz* (1992), a novel set in Harlem in 1926. The story revolves around Violet and Joe Trace, and vignettes from different episodes of their lives show horrors in which they participate but cannot understand. Morrison has also written a drama, *Dreaming Emmett* (1986), and several essays on literature and writing, including *Playing in the Dark: Whiteness and the Literary Imagination* (1992). In 1993, her many achievements were recognized with the Nobel Prize in Literature.

*Bibliography*

Bloom, Harold, ed. *Toni Morrison*. New York: Chelsea House, 1990. A collection of reprinted essays on Morrison's fiction, including Roger Sale's "Toni Morrison's *Beloved*" and Marilyn Sanders Mobley's "A Different Remembering: Memory, History, and Meaning in Toni Morrison's *Beloved*." Also includes an essay by Morrison, "Unspeakable Things Unspoken: The Afro-American Presence in American Literature," which situates *Beloved* in terms of other American novels.

Harris, Trudier. *Fiction and Folklore: The Novels of Toni Morrison*. Knoxville: University of Tennessee Press, 1991. Discusses *Beloved* in connection with folklore and images of slave life. Particularly focuses on the process of storytelling.

Otten, Terry. *The Crime of Innocence in the Fiction of Toni Morrison*. Columbia: University of Missouri Press, 1989. Gives a short analytical chapter for each novel. Of *Beloved*, notes that Morrison describes white cruelty and the pervasive ability of a depraved system to corrupt the perpetuators as well as the victims, but that Morrison also insists on personal responsibility. Sethe's killing of her child is judged to be "understandable but not excusable."

Rigney, Barbara Hill. *The Voices of Toni Morrison*. Columbus: Ohio State University Press, 1991. Discusses Morrison's novels in various contexts. Asserts that Morrison "presents a mirror to the larger culture as well as to the African American culture" as she creates a mystical and musical text. Notes that much of Morrison's focus is on language and signification, self and identity, history and myth.

Samuels, Wilfred D., and Clenora Hudson-Weems. *Toni Morrison*. Boston: Twayne, 1990. Calling Morrison a "major figure of our national literature," the authors provide commentary on the individual novels, a chronology of Morrison's life, and an extensive bibliography. Chapter 6 examines the way the story of *Beloved* is developed. Comments that the novel, which was six years in the making, is a culmination and crystalization of Morrison's themes and is "a masterpiece."

Wyatt, Jean. "Giving Body to the Word: The Maternal Symbolic in Toni Morrison's *Beloved*." *PMLA* 108 (May, 1993): 474-488. Using feminist and psycholinguistic theories, Wyatt says that *Beloved* puts into words experiences seldom included in novels. Traces language and symbolism in the novel in relation to these and other topics. States that Morrison shows that the social dimensions are always reflected in, or the "doubles" of, personal lives.

*Lois A. Marchino*

# BILLY BATHGATE

*Author:* E. L. Doctorow (1931-    )
*Type of plot:* Adventure
*Time of plot:* The 1930's
*Locale:* New York City and upstate New York
*First published:* 1989

> *Principal characters:*
> BILLY BATHGATE, the novel's hero
> DUTCH SCHULTZ, Billy's gangster employer
> BO WEINBERG, a Schultz gang member murdered by Schultz
> ABBADABBA BERMAN, Schultz's accountant
> DREW PRESTON, Weinberg's girl, who becomes Schultz's and Billy's lover

*The Novel*

*Billy Bathgate* centers on the career of the notorious gangster Dutch Schultz as told through the sympathetic voice of his fifteen-year-old acolyte, Billy Bathgate. Schultz represents to Billy a way of getting out of the slums, of distinguishing himself as an important figure by joining a powerful and much-feared organization. Indeed, the novel begins with a breathless rendition of a punishment favored by gangsters: the disposal of a rival by encasing his feet in cement and drowning him. The victim is Bo Weinberg, once a trusted Schultz associate, now a man condemned for betraying his boss.

Billy vividly portrays both the cruelty and the courage of these men. Bo is defiant to the last, refusing to abase himself or show any fear. Schultz is ruthless but respectful, conceding Bo's talents, and even admitting that Bo can get the best of him in their arguments. Bo has always had a way with words, Schultz wryly admits.

Although Schultz's violence is repugnant—he physically smashes a man into a pulp—his very irrationality makes him appealing; that is, he is not a calculating, evil man but rather an impulsive, poorly educated one who has learned how to dominate a brutally competitive world. He has his code of honor, and he demands loyalty, which, except for Bo, he commands. This is also why he can win over Drew Preston, Bo's girl. She is not awed by the gangsters, but she is stimulated by him, because he is such a contrast to her society husband and to the world of wealth that masks its evil behind good manners. Schultz may be abrupt, crude, and awkward, but he is also direct and plainspoken. Like his expressions of violence, his expressions of love are unfettered and robust, so that there is a thrilling quality to his masculinity.

Schultz, though, is in trouble, because the government has brought a case against him for tax evasion. His solution is to cultivate the upstate New York community where the trial will be held. Exhibiting himself as a public benefactor, Schultz and his lawyers craft a persona that predisposes the jury to look favorably on him as an individual abused by a government vendetta.

While Schultz busies himself with his defense, he assigns to Billy the task of escorting Drew Preston in public. Billy quickly falls in love with her, and she reciprocates his tender feelings, though both are aware that they court discovery by Schultz, which would mean their murder. Billy's affair with Preston is part of his maturation, of his becoming his own man, although he never forsakes his loyalty to the gang, which has become his second family.

Schultz's great strength is also his great weakness. By making all of his business revolve around him, he fails to see how crime is becoming organized and corporate. His way of doing business is almost feudal—depending almost entirely on violence and on the loyalty of subordinates—and he has no grasp of how to put together an organization that can compete with the combinations of power being amassed by the government and by his rival, Lucky Luciano. Schultz wants to personalize everything, so that it all evolves out of his own ego. That ego is unstable, however; on impulse, he kills an uncooperative colleague in an Onondaga hotel.

Members of Schultz's gang—particularly his accountant, Abbadabba Berman—sense that the old ways of doing things are nearly finished. Weinberg's defection is only the beginning of events that put Schultz on the defensive and that culminate in his gangland murder near the end of the novel. Berman tries to convince Schultz to do business in the new way, to recognize that he is part of a larger crime network, but Schultz can think only in terms of his own ambitions and calls off plans to amalgamate with Lucky Luciano and other gangsters. In compensation, perhaps, for Schultz's inability to adapt to new times, Berman turns to Billy, making him an apprentice and lavishing attention on the boy. Berman plies Billy with advice and gives him assignments that build his confidence and extend his knowledge of the business.

Through Berman and Preston, Billy gains perspective on Schultz. Preston, Billy finds, has her own sort of power and sense of ease. When she tires of Schultz, she simply leaves him, conveying to Billy the impression that Schultz's charisma has its limits. Billy never dares to think of actually leaving the gang, but he keeps his own counsel and is prepared to take care of himself when Schultz is murdered. At the death scene, in which Schultz, Berman, and Irving have been shot, Billy learns from Berman the combination of the safe where Schultz has stashed much of his loot. Evasive about his subsequent career, Billy intimates at the end of the novel that he has indeed amassed the Dutchman's fortune, but he does not vouchsafe what he will do with it.

## The Characters

Dutch Schultz is a remarkable fictional achievement, largely because his spare dialogue so accurately reflects his view of the world. He uses words bluntly to say exactly what he means and what he wants. His style is to have no style, so to speak, no barrier of words that coat or deflect his true intentions. His aim is to amass power, and power is an all-encompassing reality for him, making possible not only his reputation as a gangster but his success as a lover. He would seem less impressive were it not for Billy's faithful recording of his words without editorializing. Schultz would probably appear to an adult as merely a thug, as someone not quite grown up who cannot control his impulses. For the adolescent Billy, however, the gangster appeals for precisely such reasons: Schultz has not trimmed his character to fit the normal world; he has not shaped up to suit society's dictates.

Billy is equally well realized as a character. He is a fascinating mixture of Tom Sawyer and Huckleberry Finn. On the one hand, he has Huck's outlaw mentality; Billy will be educated by his adventures, by pursuing the raffish world outside the classroom and the home. He has a mother, but he is—practically speaking—an orphan, and must acquire an identity by adopting the ways of Schultz's world. He does not share his boss's appetite for violence, but he does not flinch at it either, accepting it as part of the bargain for his apprenticeship in crime. On the other hand, Billy has some of Tom's romanticism, of his desire to act like a noble knight in the service of a lady. He is attracted to rules and codes in a way that Huck is not, though Billy has none of Tom's insufferable smugness about what he knows from reading books. Billy's feelings are always fresh and firsthand.

Abbadabba Berman, Schultz's accountant, senses that Billy is both a loyal member of the gang and possessed of a personality that stands apart from it as well. That is why he confides to Billy that the old days of gangstering are about finished and that the methods of crime will have to match the subtle methods of legitimate business. Billy is the future, Berman realizes, and he tries to speed Billy's realization of that fact.

Drew Preston is not as complicated as Billy. She is essentially passive—a bored, beautiful woman, fascinated with the gangster's energy and touched by Billy's tenderness. She has little within herself on which to rely, and she depends on others to provide the excitement that makes her otherwise useless life meaningful. She is there also to woo Billy away from his exclusive devotion to Schultz, making Billy think of his own needs and desires.

Although Bo Weinberg disappears after the first pages of the novel, his presence is felt throughout the narrative, for in killing Bo, Schultz ensures his own destruction. Bo tells Schultz home truths that Schultz cannot bear to hear or to confront. Bo, in fact, is a smarter, more handsome version of Schultz. He tells Schultz, for example, that the more he has done for him, the less Schultz has counted on him, even though Bo has looked upon Schultz as a brother. This implication that Schultz's execution of Bo is fratricidal suggests that Schultz is dooming his own organization by eliminating his best partner.

*Themes and Meanings*

As the title suggests, the main focus of the novel is the education of Billy Bathgate. In this fast-paced adventure novel, which takes quick tours of the Bronx, upstate New York, Saratoga, and the docks of Manhattan, Doctorow supplies the color and the feel of the 1930's. As Billy prospers and gets to know these different worlds, he finds it impossible to return as he was to his old neighborhood. He is immediately perceived as a different person. He dresses differently, carries himself differently, and has a consciousness of a world that extends far beyond the Bathgate Avenue from which he derives his assumed name. Billy becomes, in other words, a self-invented figure, transcending his origins not only in the actions he narrates but in his very language, which is at once colloquial and formal, a blend of popular and sophisticated vocabulary that precisely captures the boy and the man who has become the narrator of this novel. In this quintessential American story, Doctorow has managed yet another stunning version of the hero's quest for identity and success.

For Billy survives the wreck of Schultz's gang and, like Herman Melville's Ishmael, lives to tell the tale. Billy hides Schultz's fortune, goes back to school, graduates from an Ivy League college, and becomes an Army officer in World War II and later a business entrepreneur—an inconceivable career in Dutch Schultz's world.

Billy is also like Melville's Ishmael in that he tells his story from the point of view of an outcast peculiarly attuned to the conventions of society that exclude him. In Depression-era America, it is very difficult for a poor boy from the Bronx to make a career for himself, and the novel makes clear that Billy is the product of certain social conditions—particularly of an economy that has no place for him unless he makes one for himself in the underworld. What is extraordinary, of course, is that his early life of crime prepares him for a position in society that is perfectly legal and respectable. Doctorow thus seems to be suggesting that the attributes that make Billy successful among criminals are not so different from the qualities needed for achievement in a law-abiding society.

In presenting Schultz and Billy in such a complex light, Doctorow seems to call into question hard and fast distinctions between right and wrong. At the very least, his novel's study of human character situates morality in an ambiguous realm, informed not merely by the personalities of his characters but by how they interact with their environment and, more specifically, with a capitalistic culture in which individuals, except for those in the privileged classes, must fight hard to earn and to maintain their status.

*Critical Context*

E. L. Doctorow is a political novelist concerned with those stories, myths, public figures, and literary and historical forms that have shaped public consciousness. Even when his subject is not overtly political—as in his first novel, *Welcome to Hard Times* (1960)—he chooses the genre of the Western to comment upon the American sense of crime and justice. Knowing that the Western has often been the vehicle for the celebration of American individualism and morality, Doctorow purposely writes a fable-like novel in which he questions the American faith in fairness and democracy. He accomplishes the same purpose by turning to the genre of the gangster novel in *Billy Bathgate*. The reality of American history has been much grimmer than its literature or its popular entertainment has acknowledged, and Doctorow's fiction shows again and again an America whose myths do not square with its history.

In most of Doctorow's work there is a tension between a naïve, childlike point of view and an older, ironic, detached perspective. In *Ragtime* (1975), the narrator seems simultaneously to be a little boy and his older self, both witnessing and remembering the past. *World's Fair* (1986) and *Billy Bathgate* seem more conventional than these earlier novels, for they are told from the standpoint of mature men reviewing their youth. Yet both novels unfold with such immediacy that they appear to be taking place as their narrators reminisce.

E. L. Doctorow has shown himself to be a master stylist, a shrewd commentator on popular genres and political themes who maintains a strong sense of narrative and storytelling. Indeed, his work should be viewed as a major evocation and critique of the American mythos and a brilliant creation of new American fables. His experiments with point of view and with the relationship between history and fiction have marked him as a major innovator in contemporary fiction.

*Bibliography*
Harter, Carol C., and James R. Thompson. *E. L. Doctorow*. Boston: Twayne, 1990. A study of Doctorow's major fiction up to *World's Fair*. Contains a chronology, a chapter on his biography, separate chapters on the novels, notes and references, and a selected bibliography. A succinct introductory study.
Levine, Paul. *E. L. Doctorow*. New York: Methuen, 1985. The first full-length study of the novelist's career. Levine provides sound and often insightful readings of individual novels as well as substantial discussions of the recurring themes in the fiction: politics, the nature of fiction and history, and Doctorow's critique of the American Dream. A useful bibliography and a discussion of film adaptations of Doctorow's work make this a comprehensive study.
Parks, John G. *E. L. Doctorow*. New York: Continuum, 1991. Includes an excellent chapter on *Billy Bathgate*, situating the novel in the context of Doctorow's career. A remarkable introductory study that includes discussion of Doctorow's major and minor work, a chronology, notes, bibliography, and a chapter on his biography.
Strout, Cushing. "Historizing Fiction and Fictionalizing History: The Case of E. L. Doctorow." *Prospects* 5 (1980): 423-437. A detailed analysis of the strengths and limitations of Doctorow's handling of fiction and history. Should be read in conjunction with Barbara Foley's article "From U.S.A. to *Ragtime*: Notes on the Forms of Historical Consciousness in Modern Fiction," included in Richard Trenner's *E. L. Doctorow: Essays and Conversations* (1983).
Trenner, Richard, ed. *E. L. Doctorow: Essays and Conversations*. Princeton, N.J.: Ontario Review Press, 1983. Yields valuable biographical and critical insights into the novelist's work. Includes several of his important essays as well as articles by others about his fiction, which are well chosen to reflect the range of critical opinion on Doctorow, the variety of his themes and techniques, and the historical background required to read his novels.
Weber, Bruce. "E. L. Doctorow: Myth Maker." *The New York Times Magazine*, October 20, 1985, 25-26, 42-43, 74-77. Primarily useful as an overview of the novelist's life and career, with special emphasis on *World's Fair* and on the growth of his reputation. This profile emphasizes Doctorow's growing importance in contemporary fiction.

*Carl Rollyson*

# BLACK WATER

*Author:* Joyce Carol Oates (1938-    )
*Type of plot:* Psychological realism
*Time of plot:* The afternoon and early evening of July 4, 1991
*Locale:* Grayling Island, Maine
*First published:* 1992

> *Principal characters:*
> KELLY (ELIZABETH ANNE) KELLEHER, a sexually insecure twenty-six-year-old magazine writer living in Boston
> THE SENATOR, a powerful, fiftyish Massachusetts politician who meets Kelly at a Fourth of July party
> BUFFY ST. JOHN, Kelly's closest friend, who is giving the party
> RAY ANNICK, Buffy's lover, a friend of the Senator

*The Novel*

*Black Water* is a fictional tragedy that refuses to abandon its origins in American political history. "The Senator," the powerful fifty-something politician whose name is never given beyond his title, arrives at a Fourth of July party hosted by Buffy St. John at her parents' home on Grayling Island, a twenty-minute ferry ride from Boothbay Harbor, Maine. During the course of this afternoon, which he spends talking, drinking, and playing tennis with the younger people gathered at the party, he captivates Kelly Kelleher, and the two of them leave late that evening to catch the last ferry off the island, to have dinner in Boothbay Harbor and, presumably, to spend the night at the motel where the Senator is staying.

Yet something goes terribly wrong. The drunken senator misses the ferry road and ends up on a narrow and abandoned track. Kelly says, "I think we're lost, Senator," but it is finally Kelly who is lost. In the rush to catch the ferry, the rented car skids off the road and plunges into the deceptively deep Indian Creek. The car overturns in the water; the Senator escapes by scrambling over Kelly, who, pinned in the car with broken bones, slowly drowns. The Senator stumbles several miles to call his friend Ray Annick back at the party for help; the accident, he yells into the phone, was the girl's fault.

The events follow closely the July, 1969, incident at Chappaquiddick, Massachusetts, when thirty-seven-year-old Senator Ted Kennedy left the scene of a similar accident and Mary Jo Kopechne was drowned. The major difference is time; while the model occurred decades earlier, Joyce Carol Oates brings this incident up to the present. Still, readers are witnessing a fictional version of recent political, but very personal, history.

Although Kennedy is never named, many other political players are; The Senator, for example, is described as "eleven years younger than George Bush." Oates uses undigested political history, discussing the 1988 presidential campaign and its attendant controversies in detail, and she has the Senator tell the younger people around him that "the Gulf War has given your generation a tragic idea of war and of diplomacy: the delusion that war is relatively easy, and diplomacy *is* war, the most expedient of options."

The short, 154-page novel is broken into two parts and thirty-two chapters. Part 1 opens with a chapter that gives the core action of the book:

> The rented Toyota, driven with such impatient exuberance by The Senator, was speeding along the unpaved unnamed road, taking the turns in giddy skidding slides, and then, with no warning, somehow the car had gone off the road and had overturned in black rushing water, listing to its passenger's side, rapidly sinking.
> *Am I going to die?—like this?*

The following chapters alternate between descriptions of the accident, the Senator's escape, Kelly's slow drowning, earlier incidents in the day (a tennis match, their first kiss, his suggestion that she join his staff) and in her young life (snippets of scenes with her parents, with Buffy at Brown University, with her earlier lover). Much of the action is described from somewhere within Kelly's fractured head; increasingly in part 2, readers get her fantasies of escape and rescue; the first sentence of part 2, for example, reads: "He was gone but would come back to save her." Almost as a refrain in the novel, Oates repeats that the water is rising: "As the black water filled her lungs, and she died." This prose has an intense, poetic quality characteristic of Oates at her best; the entire chapter 10, for example, consists of one two-page sentence that provides both momentum to the story and tension to the writing. Metaphors of loss of sight and direction, moreover, reverberate through the short novel.

It is a tribute to the power of this writing that, though the outcome of this story is certain, Oates makes it exciting. In fact, like Ambrose Bierce's famous short story "An Occurrence at Owl Creek Bridge"—in which readers watch a convicted Confederate spy escape only to realize that it was all a dream in the seconds before he was hung—Oates builds the hope that in this version of history, at least, the innocent young woman may in the end escape.

### The Characters

The model of the Kennedy character is only thinly disguised. While he does not have brothers, The Senator is otherwise easy to recognize: Described as separated from his wife of thirty years, he is a man with a "diminutive first name" and "an old-style liberal Democrat out of the 1960s, a Great Society man with a stubborn and zealous dedication to social reform" who "had been among the three leading candidates for the Democratic presidential nomination in 1988."

The center of the novel, however, is less the powerful senator and contemporary political history than Kelly Kelleher, a naïve young woman who is the innocent but willing victim of The Senator's political and sexual power. Ironically, Kelly wrote her senior honor's thesis at Brown on The Senator, and her collegiate idealism still thrives: She not only writes articles now on such issues as capital punishment for the liberal

*Citizens' Inquiry* but she also teaches two nights a week in a literacy program in inner-city Boston. Kelly is a young woman with a history of acne but not much else; she will not talk about her one lover ("G_____"), and she has regularly starved herself as self-punishment for her imagined failures. The child of a rich suburban New York City family, she ends up at the bottom of a creek with a fractured skull and broken kneecap, trapped in a slowly sinking car and abandoned by the man to whom she has been so powerfully drawn. The real tragedy in *Black Water* is hers. She is another in a long string of familiar Oates characters: single women who lack confidence in themselves and security in their sexuality and who are thus easy prey for more powerful males. Kelly even thinks that "the black water was her fault." Oates implies that one source of Kelly's problem is the Kelleher family in Westchester, which gave her all the material things she needed, but few of the emotional. A clue in the novel is the refrain, "You know you're somebody's little girl don't you?" The implication is that the adult woman has never been able to grow satisfactorily beyond that unhealthy childhood line.

*Themes and Meanings*

*Black Water* is really a novella; it is only three times as long as "Where Are You Going, Where Have You Been?," for example, one of Oates's many well-known short stories. Like that story, or her longer *Because It Is Bitter, and Because It Is My Heart* (1990), *Black Water* explores the theme of what could be called "Death and the Maiden" (the original title for "Where Are You Going, Where Have You Been?"). In work after work, Oates has probed this situation of the naïve young woman seduced by some powerful, almost demonic male figure. In "How I Contemplated the World from the Detroit House of Corrections and Began My Life Over Again," another regularly anthologized Oates story, the villain is a seductive young drug addict. In "Where Are You Going, Where Have You Been?," it is Arnold Friend (or "an old fiend," a thinly veiled representation of the Devil) who lures Connie to her death.

In *Black Water*, the antagonist is much more lifelike and fleshy—but just as evil. Selfish and greedy, The Senator thinks of nothing but trying to save himself. In the end, he has, but another Oates heroine has drowned in the waters of male power and selfishness. Again and again, Kelly thinks of The Senator's charisma, "his manly power," as she is drawn to his presence that afternoon, and when he moves closer to her, she is lost.

This is not, however, merely another story of an older man misusing a younger woman. In one short paragraph, Oates defines two central concerns of her book: "Politics, the negotiating of power. Eros, the negotiating of power." Readers witness both kinds of negotiation here; they are, she implies, two parts of the same violent American culture, and The Senator, in his charm and power, abuses both.

*Critical Context*

Increasingly in American writing in the last decades of the twentieth century, the line between fiction and nonfiction has been harder and harder to find. Nonfiction writers such as Hunter S. Thompson and Gay Talese have invaded the territory of the fictionists and appropriated most of their weapons. Conversely, novelists such as E. L. Doctorow and Kurt Vonnegut, Jr., have felt perfectly justified in placing their fictional characters in real worlds peopled by historical figures. As Doctorow has remarked, there are no longer separate categories of fiction and nonfiction today, only narrative.

In *Black Water*, Joyce Carol Oates enters this tradition. There is no denying that the basis for the action in her novella is recent political history, specifically the events at Chappaquiddick. What Oates has accomplished is to make that history taut with terror in the retelling. Yet in dredging up this tragedy, Oates has made little attempt to disguise its origins, and the reader can only feel a kind of vague discomfort; the history is too recent, the players all too alive—or dead. Doctorow's *Ragtime* (1975), in contrast, uses historical personages at the turn of the century to flesh out the tale; Susan Sontag's more recent *The Volcano Lover* (1992) is a historical romance set in the late eighteenth century. For the first time, Oates is using living people as the foundation for her fiction, and it is unsettling.

Oates has always posed questions with uneasy answers, however, and it is thus relatively simple to place *Black Water* in the context of her literary career. Like many earlier novels and short stories, *Black Water* delineates American culture not only from its violent outside but from the troubled inside as well. Reviewing *Because It Is Bitter, and Because It Is My Heart*, critic Henry Louis Gates, Jr., commented that "a future archeologist equipped only with her *oeuvre* could easily piece together the whole of postwar America." That description applies to *Black Water* as well—not merely the actual American social history, the misuse of political power, but also the psychological truths. *Black Water* continues the excavation Oates has been doing for thirty years, at a different site, and perhaps with different tools, but bringing up the same truthful artifacts of American life. Few novelists have done as much.

*Bibliography*
Bausch, Richard. "Her Thoughts While Drowning." Review of *Black Water*, by Joyce Carol Oates. *The New York Times Book Review*, May 10, 1992, 1, 29. Praises *Black Water* as "taut, powerfully imagined and beautifully written." Compares the novel to ancient Greek tragedies in its use of a chorus and its pervasive irony.
Creighton, Joanne V. *Joyce Carol Oates: Novels of the Middle Years*. New York: Twayne, 1992. A discussion of fifteen Oates novels written between 1977 and 1990. In *American Appetites* (1989) and *Because It Is Bitter, and Because It Is My Heart*, Creighton comments, "The American dream is fractured by an unintentional killing; in both, violence is an upwelling of tension, breaking through the civil games of society and the conscious control of character; in both, appetites remain unfulfilled."
Robinson, Sally. "Heat and Cold: Recent Fiction by Joyce Carol Oates." *Michigan Quarterly Review* 31 (Summer, 1992): 400-414. Robinson observes that Oates has always "specialized in a narrative technique that intrudes upon the private pains and pleasures—but mostly pains—of Others. Her narratives often explore the dynamics

of a voyeurism in which subject and object confront one another across a gulf of social difference."

Seaman, Donna. Review of *Black Water*, by Joyce Carol Oates. *Booklist* 88 (February 15, 1992): 1066. Comments that the novel displays Oates's "penchant for morbidity and command of suspense" and shows her "at her most facile and provocative."

Wesley, Marilyn C. "The Transgressive Other in Joyce Carol Oates's Recent Fiction." *Critique* 33 (Summer, 1992): 255-262. Wesley sees a dialectic in Oates's fiction, a "superimposition of a narrative leveled against the text itself to decenter the social codes through which it is organized."

*David Peck*

# BLESS ME, ULTIMA

*Author:* Rudolfo A. Anaya (1937-    )
*Type of plot: Bildungsroman*
*Time of plot:* 1943
*Locale:* Guadalupe, New Mexico
*First published:* 1972

>   *Principal characters:*
>   Antonio Márez y Luna, the novel's seven-year-old protagonist
>   Ultima, an aged *curandera* (healer) who teaches Antonio to navigate in
>     a complex spiritual and social universe
>   Tenorio Trementina, an evil wizard who seeks to destroy Ultima
>   Narcisco, the town drunk

*The Novel*

In *Bless Me, Ultima*, Rudolfo A. Anaya draws upon memories of his childhood in Pastura, New Mexico, during World War II to present one year in the life of seven-year-old Antonio Márez y Luna. Events in the novel are interspersed with allegorical dreams and are recounted from the perspective of an older Antonio. During this pivotal year, Antonio experiences the abrupt return of his three brothers from the battlefields of World War II and their subsequent departures, three senseless, violent deaths, his first year of school, and his first communion.

Antonio's maturation begins with the arrival of Ultima, a *curandera*, or healer, with whom he shares a mystical bond. Shortly before her arrival, Antonio dreams of his own birth. In the dream, his mother's brothers, the Lunas, bless him with offerings of fruit and claim him as a "man of the people," perhaps even a priest. Into this dream scene, however, enter his father's brothers, the Márezes. They arrive on horseback, shouting and shooting, laughing and drinking; they smash the fruit, wipe away the earth with which the Lunas have blessed Antonio, and claim him for the Márezes. When he awakes, he intuits that Ultima, present at his birth, is also connected to his future.

Following Ultima's arrival, Antonio encounters an increasingly complex social universe. His father is summoned to join a vigilante group that is searching for a traumatized veteran, Lupito, who shot and killed the local sheriff during a psychotic episode. Antonio secretly follows the vigilantes and watches as Lupito, still deranged, is killed by the angry crowd despite the pleas of the town drunk, Narcisco.

Antonio starts school and weathers a difficult transition from Spanish to English in an environment in which divisions between town and country and Chicano and Anglo culture fix students within a complex hierarchy of prestige. Outside school, Antonio becomes embroiled in a growing conflict between Tenorio and Ultima. Their feud begins when Ultima travels to the village of the Lunas to cure Antonio's Uncle Lucas, who has been cursed by Tenorio's daughters. Before healing Lucas, Ultima visits

Tenorio's saloon to inform him of her plans. In a classic Western-style showdown, Ultima walks down the main street of El Puerto to confront Tenorio and advise him to order his daughters to remove their curse. Tenorio denies their involvement. After Lucas is healed, Tenorio's three daughters sicken and die.

Tenorio seeks revenge against Ultima, reviling her as a witch. Since Ultima rectifies situations that even priests cannot, even those she has healed fear to protect her. Initially, Tenorio arrives at the Márez y Luna home with a drunken lynch mob. Ultima is defended by Narciso and by Antonio's father, who prove that Ultima is not a witch by applying an accepted folk standard: Ultima can pass through a door that is protected by the sign of the cross.

When Tenorio plans a second attack, Narciso braves a snowstorm in search of Antonio's brother, Andrew. Andrew, the last of Antonio's older brothers to remain in Guadalupe, frequents Rosie's, a local brothel. Narciso, silently followed by Antonio, begs Andrew to warn Ultima. Antonio is shocked and horrified to witness his brother at Rosie's door. Like the rest of the family, Antonio has denied Andrew's daily visits to Rosie's. Now, as Antonio watches, Andrew refuses to leave Rosie's to spare the aged Narciso a journey through a raging blizzard. As Narciso struggles on, Tenorio appears in his path. Antonio witnesses as the men struggle, and shots echo in the air. Moments later, Antonio holds the dying Narciso and, at his request, hears his last confession. Narciso dies at peace; Antonio returns home delirious with fever. In the dreams that follow, he repeatedly shouts out the story of how Tenorio killed Narciso. Antonio reflects that he had to tell the story to purge the fever, foreshadowing that he will be a writer rather than a priest.

Tenorio finally destroys Ultima, but at the cost of his own life. He kills Ultima's owl, a magical creature to which she is sympathetically connected. As Tenorio takes aim at Antonio, however, Antonio's Uncle Pedro shoots Tenorio, an act that redeems the Lunas' earlier failure to protect Ultima. Antonio is with her as she dies. He buries her owl in a juniper, following her instructions; he reflects that "Ultima was really buried here. Tonight."

*The Characters*

Antonio rapidly wins the reader's sympathies by identifying with underdogs, fighting back against bullies, and seeking satisfactory explanations for the suffering he sees around him. The reader also sympathizes with Antonio's blind spots, especially his nagging guilt in response to tragic events beyond his control. Antonio's hunger for justice and his spiritual insight legitimatize him as a born leader and a suitable object for the competing attentions of the Lunas and the Márezes. An emphasis on Antonio's mysterious future as the subject of adult competition, more-over, involves the reader in the question of Antonio's vocation. Gradually, the reader senses that Antonio would be unduly restricted in any of the roles the adults in his life urge upon him. Yet he cannot follow in Ultima's footsteps, since Ultima is to be, as her name implies, the last of her kind. Antonio's fate is not explicitly resolved, but the first-person narrator's perspective as an elder Antonio recounting his own childhood experiences suggests that, as a writer, Antonio will play a role similar to that of the traditional *curandera*: an intuitive, empathetic outsider serving the community without owing allegiance to any institution within it.

Ultima is an aged *curandera* healer from Antonio's mother's village who stays with his family in her final year of life. Ultima's healing powers, her position at the margins of her community, the false accusations made against her, her betrayal by those she has saved, her death, and, in a sense, her resurrection (in the memory and art of Antonio) all identify her as a type of Christ. Textual evocations of the Virgin of Guadalupe as a moon goddess, however, also emphasize the impact of indigenous belief systems on Christianity in Latin America. Ultima's symbolic power is derived in part from her position as one who is unfairly accused, whose own followers forsake or betray her, but who speaks mildly and wisely in her own defense and submits lovingly and calmly to death in the name of life. On the other hand, this familiar story is used to validate a healer who is, ultimately, a non-Christian figure; by extension the story critiques the ways in which European Christian colonizers persecuted indigenous peoples much as the Roman Empire persecuted Jesus.

Narcisco resembles numerous mythical figures, including he Greek Dionysus, the European pre-Christian Green Man, and elements of these figures that merged into European figurations of Christ in his connections to wine, growth, and rebirth. Narcisco spends many of his mornings sleeping off hangovers in the local jail. Yet when Antonio sees Narcisco's fairy-tale cottage with its superabundant gardens, he realizes that the mysterious, hidden side of Narcisco's "excess," which manifests publicly as drunken, disorderly behavior, is earthly abundance. In giving his life to preserve Ultima's, Narcisco further fulfills the role of a Dionysian earth-god. Like the earth itself, Narcisco dies in winter, but in his final words, Narcisco affirms that he is part of a larger pattern of life, death, and rebirth. Like Ultima's, Narcisco's character emphasizes pre-Christian, contradictory elements within the European tradition that has influenced Chicano culture. His fate, like Ultima's, reenacts the violence that is done to such complex figures when they are reduced to romantic figures of absolute good or evil.

### Themes and Meanings

*Bless Me, Ultima* thematically juxtaposes two moral systems. In the novel, the transcendent, binary ethics characteristic of Christianity and European high culture are juxtaposed against an immanent, nondualist ethos characteristic of the European folk tradition and of most pre-conquest religions in the Americas. Antonio struggles to resolve contradictions between the two traditions, especially in his allegorical dreams. A movement back and forth between figures from the Chicano oral tradition (such as the Virgin of Guadalupe, la Llorona, and the *curandera* tradition), and romantic figures such as Tenorio, the evil wizard whose horse is trained to kill, heightens a central asymmetry between Ultima's earth magic and Tenorio's transcendent wizardry. Tenorio and his daughters are classically evil; the daughters' performance of a conventional Black Mass in which they physically copulate with the devil clearly aligns them with romantic notions of absolute, ahistorical evil. The Church and its rituals, on the other hand, are securely identified with a transcendent, if sometimes distant and inscrutable, good that is, alas, often distorted beyond all recognition by its adherents. A set of characters who seem to draw their energies from pre-Christian, folkloric traditions, however, fall outside the romantic good/evil dichotomy altogether. Narcisco, Cico, and Samuel worship an earth deity called the Golden Carp. Antonio experiences the mystical "presence" of a river when he gathers herbs with Ultima. These characters, especially Ultima herself, all derive from a distinctly different narrative tradition and therefore operate according to different rules.

The novel's romantic perspective evaluates characters according to their ultimate allegiance to the forces of good or evil. Even Antonio's brother, Andrew, is relegated to the realm of evil in a dream in which Antonio sees him ensnared in the seething hair of a prostitute. Whenever this romantic good/evil dichotomy comes into contact with Ultima, however, the system breaks down. Particularly notable for its ambiguity is the episode in which, in order to prove that she is not a witch, Ultima passes through a doorframe in which needles blessed with holy water have formed the shape of a cross. Following the test, Antonio notices that the needles have fallen to the floor. In this episode, Ultima appears as a spiritual force outside the jurisdiction of Christianity. The hybridized folk religion that Ultima embodies emphasizes and celebrates the bicultural oral roots of Chicano culture.

*Critical Context*

*Bless Me, Ultima* is the best-selling and arguably the most popular Chicano literary work ever. The novel received the second annual Quinto Sol national Chicano literary award in 1971. The novel has been critically celebrated, probably in part owing to Anaya's "universalization" of Chicano experience through the use of mythical archetypes. The two novels that followed it, *Heart of Aztlán* and *Tortuga*, depict the struggles of the Chicano working class and have received less critical attention.

Although Anaya is one of the generation of writers whose work is associated with the Chicano movement of the mid-1960s, *Bless Me, Ultima* is frequently treated by movement writers and critics as a deviation, a distraction, or even as a betrayal. The novel's treatment of "universal" themes appealed to a number of critics who cared little about Chicano civil rights; some critics within the movement observed that the novel's fantastic, romantic depictions of a pastoral Chicano boyhood permitted such critics to ignore uncomfortable political questions. Chicano writers, critics, and activists who wanted to get racism and exploitation onto the national agenda were, perhaps inevitably, offended by Anaya's romanticization of rural poverty, his glossing over of the Spanish-speaking Antonio's disorientation and humiliation in an English-only and overtly racist classroom, and his representation of some migrant farmworkers as enthusiastically embracing this life as well-suited to the wanderlust they inherited from their vaquero progenitors.

*Bless Me, Ultima* does, however, incorporate the colonial and contemporary historical and social relations that it was accused of omitting. The fault of the novel's idealized, apolitical reception surely lies at least partly with a liberal white readership that focused on elements in the novel that were comfortable and familiar while ignoring or dismissing other aspects of the book. Antonio is, after all, only seven, and his ignorance concerning the origins of injustice is excusable. Rudolfo Anaya may have trusted his adult readers to think more carefully and reason more critically.

*Bibliography*

Bruce-Novoa, Juan D. *Chicano Authors: Inquiry by Interviews.* Austin: University of Texas Press, 1980. Contains a lengthy interview with Anaya. Gives valuable details concerning Anaya's background, his development as a writer, and his views concerning literature, politics, and the role of "the universal" in *Bless Me, Ultima*.

Calderón, Héctor. "Rudolfo Anaya's *Bless Me, Ultima*: A Chicano Romance of the Southwest." *Critica* 1 (1986): 21-47. Calderón asserts that *Bless Me, Ultima* is a romance rather than a novel. He also calls attention to the book's synthesis of diverse cultural materials and its projection of "ideals and wish-fulfillment fantasy" onto the figures that result from this synthesis.

Dasenbrock, Reed Way. "Forms of Biculturalism in Southwestern Literature: The Work of Rudolfo Anaya and Leslie Marmon Silko." *Genre* 21 (Fall, 1988): 307-320. Assesses *Bless Me, Ultima* and Silko's *Ceremony* as bicultural texts. Argues that readers of such texts tend to privilege one portion of a writer's total cultural universe at the expense of others.

Salvídar, Ramón. "Romance, the Fantastic, and the Representation of History in Rudolfo A. Anaya and Ron Arias." In *Chicano Narrative: The Dialectics of Difference.* Madison: University of Wisconsin Press, 1990. Argues that *Bless Me, Ultima* is unique among Chicano literary productions in its repression of the political into the realm of the unconscious. Salvídar's readings of the novel brilliantly reconstruct the social and political scaffolding that shapes events within the narrative. Contains a useful overview of critical debates.

Sanders, Scott P. "Southwestern Gothic: Alienation, Integration, and Rebirth in the Works of Richard Shelton, Rudolfo Anaya, and Leslie Silko." *Weber Studies: An Interdisciplinary Humanities Journal* 4 (Fall, 1987): 36-53. Sanders explores the fantastic in Anaya's work as a form of gothicism emerging in response to Southwestern history. Out of a culture's misunderstanding of its own past, Sanders argues, gothic forms representing repressed historical elements emerge.

*Margot Gayle Backus*

# BLESS THE BEASTS AND CHILDREN

*Author:* Glendon Swarthout (1918-    )
*Type of plot:* Adventure
*Time of plot:* The late 1960's
*Locale:* Arizona
*First published:* 1970

> *Principal characters:*
> COTTON, the fifteen-year-old leader of a group of "misfits" who have been deposited at Box Canyon Boys Camp
> GOODENOW, a bed wetter and crybaby who threatens suicide until Cotton accepts him
> LALLY 2, the youngest of the group, who can find solace at home only in the company of imaginary creatures he calls Ooms
> LALLY 1, the older brother of Lally 2, violently jealous and given to screaming temper tantrums
> TEFT, a boy who hates all authority and the patriarchal world in which he lives
> SHECKER, the son of a loud and tasteless but famous comic

*The Novel*

   *Bless the Beasts and Children* is one of Glendon Swarthout's most successful novels, though it is often thought of as a book for adolescents as well as about adolescents. The novel tells the story of a group of boys who turn from sniveling, cowardly behavior to heroic action in order to rescue a herd of buffalo. Terribly troubled, the boys have been "made strange" or "paranoid" by their parents, who are representative of an American culture that shapes its citizens according to cultural ideals of wealth and power for men and beauty for women, ideals that conflict with society's professed values.

   As the novel opens, Cotton and his group have obviously suffered major traumas that have thrown them into regressive patterns of behavior. Even Cotton, the most nearly normal of the group, is disturbed by a terrible nightmare. He dreams that he and his group are animals penned together and released, only to face the gunfire of a line of humans who stand in front of a line of vehicles. As the shots reach their targets, several of the boys, imaged in the dream as animals, fall heavily and yield brilliant red blood. Cotton, snorting and battering object after object, is maddened by his frustration and fear. At the climax of the dream, Cotton recognizes the face of the human firing at him, and the boy's heart is shattered because the face is that of his mother. The imagined death pulls Cotton from the nightmare, and he finds himself bathed in sweat and recalling an episode in which the boys' counselor had forced them to witness the slaughter of a herd of buffalo. The boys, who had identified with the animals, were horrified by the event. When Cotton discovers that one of his group,

Lally 2, has disappeared, he wakes the others, and they all know where Lally 2 went. Moreover, they know they have to join him, to somehow find their way back to the scene of the "crime" that had so outraged and frightened them. The rest of the novel follows the boys on a fantastic mission to save a group of animals and themselves from sure destruction.

As the story progresses, exposition about the boys and their past behaviors accompanies the action, thus making credible the growth to manhood achieved by each member of the group and manifested in their present actions. Cotton recognizes this growth when he insists, at the beginning of their pilgrimage, that he will not assume authority and that what they will do will be decided by the vote of the whole group.

Though he does not impose his will on the others, he does lead, as a sergeant would the men in his battalion on a guerrilla operation. Cotton leads by doing, by showing himself as strong as his oppressors, by refusing to give up even in what appear to be impossible circumstances. In this behavior, Cotton is the tragic hero, strong enough to fight the gods but doomed to personal failure.

Overall, however, this novel is no tragedy. Cotton leads the boys to victory. In the face of setback after setback, they regroup, change plans, and set their hearts on eventually accomplishing their objective: Symbolically, to return the chamber pot (the symbol of the lowest group of boys at the camp) and gain the buffalo head with horns and beard (the symbol of the skill and power of the beast).

Unable to take a truck from the camp grounds—because starting the motor would awaken the other campers and because they cannot push the heavy truck up a sandy incline—they abandon the truck and concoct another plan. They saddle horses and ride into town, where they find another vehicle to "borrow" and later return. As they face each succeeding obstacle and surmount it, the boys more and more identify with the heroes of every American adventure story, which they summarize as "some men with guns going somewhere, to do something dangerous" for the good of the land and the people.

Sometimes, in moments of danger, when they come to the point of disintegration, they form a circle, get into a huddle, and hug one another, heads touching. In this bonding exercise, they confirm their being. In each episode that gets them closer to their destination, each of the boys says or does something to keep the group going or to save them from obvious mistakes.

Their destination is a corral holding thirty buffalo that are destined to be shot in an annual three-day "hunt" staged by the Arizona Fish and Game Department. The purpose of the hunt is to thin the herd to maintain the proper ratio of the animals to their habitat. The people who come to the animal slaughter are not called "hunters" but "shooters," because there is no sport or need involved. Before long, the event takes on all the characteristics of a blood orgy; it is, moreover, metaphoric of Americans killing their own totem animals, mythic creatures encapsulating much past history.

Already, sixty buffalo have been killed, but the boys have come to free the animals, and free them they do. Though Cotton is killed in the effort, the buffalo run free. The rest of the boys respond; they feel songs in their toes, poetry in their hearts, and tingling in their fingertips, because they know they have made a significant step to liberating themselves also.

## The Characters

Characterization is achieved in *Bless the Beasts and Children* by several means. Flashbacks, set in italics, are relevant to one boy at a time, giving each boy's history and providing a picture of a sick psyche brought on by neglect of basic human needs. In each case, the boys are castoffs, children of parents too busy with their own affairs to really care about the well-being of their own sons. Stephen and Billy Lally, for example, are shown in one flashback competing for the affection of their parents, who bribe each of the boys with a gift and then fly off to winter in Morocco. Another example shows Laurence Teft III trying to get the attention of his parents by stealing money from his mother and driving off in his father's big car, only to collide with two other cars. Instead of speaking to his son, the father locks his cars away, and Teft simply steals a neighbor's car.

The author also illustrates the boys' characteristic behavior in interactions with others, as when Cotton decides that, since he is the oldest and most normal of the group, he needs to take control. Cotton thus hunts about in his footlocker and finds some army tags that jingle when he puts them on; he pulls out an electric razor and runs it over his face, though he has no need to shave; and, finally, he pulls out four tiny bottles of whiskey, takes a drink, and then lights a cigar—actions enough to mark him as the leader he sets out to be.

Lastly, Swarthout sometimes delineates his characters through direct exposition by the commenting narrator or by entry into the mind of a character or an animal. The careful identification of the boys with the animals helps to cast the boys' mission in an heroic mode and gives the plight of the animals considerable urgency, an urgency reflected in the death of Cotton at the end of the novel.

## Themes and Meanings

In *Bless the Beasts and Children*, Glendon Swarthout laments the passing of a time when ideals were clear and morality unambiguous; when men were men, and boys became men by imitating their fathers; when buffalo were allowed to roam the plains and were killed only when there was a need for food, and when these magnificent animals represented for the citizens of the United States a primal innocence and a noble and praiseworthy past. The six boys, as much misfits in their society as buffalo are in the last half of the twentieth century, act out of a sense of unambiguous morality and clear ideals. The boys thus become representative of what humans can still aspire to if they can see their selfish behavior for what it is, recognize their lust for power and possessions, and once again bond together in a common course for the greater good.

Cotton's death places him into the archetypal role of tragic hero. He battles forces bigger than he is, and though he is doomed to defeat, his death is cathartic, freeing his followers from their bondage. In this action, Cotton becomes also a kind of savior of his people: "They made a splendid thunder. It pulled down temples. It smote the ears of gnats and governments. It caused an impious planet to slip a cog. It must have been heard in heaven." In the end, the misfits triumph. Though they are frightened and all in tears, they are able to jeer at their elders: "Yah! Yah! Yah!"

### Critical Context

Glendon Swarthout has won several awards, including the National Society of Arts and Letters Gold Medal. *Bless the Beasts and Children* is generally considered to be his best work. A prolific novelist, short-story writer, and dramatist, Swarthout has also had several of his novels, including *Bless the Beasts and Children*, made into films. Perhaps the best-known of these is the 1976 film *The Shootist* (starring John Wayne).

Most of Swarthout's fiction can be said to be social commentary on what he identifies to be the ills of American society. In his first novel, *Willow Run* (1943), he tackles the subject of the manufacture of bombers; in *Loveland* (1968), a young man struggles against depression. *They Came to Cordura* (1958) is about bravery and cowardice and how people behave under great stress. *Where the Boys Are* (1960) is a comic novel set in Fort Lauderdale at the time when thousands of teenagers descend into Florida during spring break.

Criticism on the body of Swarthout's work is about equally divided. Some critics argue that the linearity of his plots and his frequent appeals to sentiment, sometimes approaching the maudlin, greatly mar his novels. Others, however, have found Swarthout's appeal to absolute values and past ideals to be a welcome relief from much modern fiction.

### Bibliography

Conner, John W. Review of *Bless the Beasts and Children*, by Glendon Swarthout. *English Journal* 61 (January, 1972): 139. The reviewer points to the book's use of archetypal patterns and situations as well as exuberance and wit. Praises Swarthout for retaining a hold on the general populace and not relying on the avant garde.

Garfield, Brian. Review of *Bless the Beasts and Children*, by Glendon Swarthout. *Harper's Magazine* 240 (April, 1970): 107. Garfield calls *Bless the Beasts and Children* a compassionate and compelling drama about six adolescents who start out on a quest for "redemption, pride and justice." The novel, Garfield says, is one superb example of what happens "when a writer's craft is equal to the grandeur of his theme."

Schickel, Richard. Review of *Bless the Beasts and Children*, by Glendon Swarthout. *Saturday Review* 53 (May 2, 1970): 29. Although Schickel calls the novel an exciting adventure story, he is careful to make the point that the novel uses adolescents as major characters but is not for adolescents. The death of Cotton, Schickel believes, is necessary, because the author needed an event of such magnitude to underline the proportions of the change in the characters.

*Mary Rohrberger*

# BLOOD MERIDIAN
## Or, The Evening Redness in the West

*Author:* Cormac McCarthy (1933-      )
*Type of plot:* Western
*Time of plot:* The mid-1800's
*Locale:* The Southwestern United States and Northern Mexico
*First published:* 1985

> *Principal characters:*
> THE KID, the unnamed protagonist, who joins a band of professional scalp
> hunters
> CAPTAIN JOHN JOEL GLANTON, the leader of the band
> JUDGE HOLDEN, his mysterious, almost supernatural second-in-command
> TOBIN, the kid's closest companion, a former priest who has become a
> scalper
> ANGEL TRIAS, the governor of the Mexican state of Chihuahua, who hires
> the scalpers
> TOADVINE, DAVID BROWN, BATHCAT, GRANNYRAT, and BLACK JOHN
> JACKSON, members of the band

*The Novel*

Based on historical events and actual personages, *Blood Meridian: Or, The Evening Redness in the West* recounts the exploits of a brutal band of professional scalp hunters who, employed by local governments in the American Southwest and in Mexico, murder Indians for bounty. The novel emphasizes the violent manner in which "civilization" is imposed on a savage land and thus challenges accepted notions concerning Manifest Destiny and the settling of the West.

McCarthy's protagonist is "the kid," an unnamed boy who runs away from home in Tennessee and heads west, arriving in Nacogdoches, Texas, in 1849. Although only sixteen years old, the kid is an experienced fighter, a survivor in a vicious world. Moving on to Bexar, Texas, he is offered a position with a Captain White, who is leading an expedition into Sonora, Mexico. White argues that the Mexicans are a degenerate race, deserving of conquest, and that the land is godless and needful of salvation. White proves to be mad, but the kid accompanies the group. After days in the desert, they are attacked and slaughtered by a Comanche war party; the kid is among the few survivors of the exceedingly brutal massacre. Finally reaching a town, he is arrested by the local authorities and sent with other remnants of the group to Chihuahua City, where they are put to work cleaning filth from gutters in the street.

Into Chihuahua City rides a party of professional scalp hunters, led by Captain John Joel Glanton, with the monstrous, mysterious Judge Holden as second-in-command. Holden arranges freedom for those prisoners who wish to join the scalpers, and the kid takes the offer. Glanton has been hired by Angel Trias, governor of the state of Chihuahua, to eradicate Indians in the vicinity; the fee set is one hundred dollars for each scalp brought in. Thus, the small gang of men sets out into the Mexican territory, searching for prey. Roving through the wild land, the scalp hunters find and slaughter stray groups of Apaches—men, women, and children—in addition to occasional Mexicans whose scalps might pass for Indian. A war party then catches their trail and pursues them in a series of skirmishes back to Chihuahua City, where they collect their money and proceed to take over the town in drunken riot. From that point, they ride from city to city, bringing violence, death, and horror with them wherever they go.

In Jesus Maria, Mexico, the citizens of the town turn against the rampaging gang, kill several of them, and force them to flee. They are soon hired by the governor of Sonora and again set out on their bloody business, murdering almost without distinction whatever unlucky wayfarer they encounter. Glanton's gang is then attacked and chased by Mexican soldiers under the command of General Elias; several of the band are killed, and the survivors are forced to draw arrows to determine who will have horses to ride through the desert. The kid is one of those who escape, and after a torturous journey arrives in the town of Santa Cruz, where he again joins Glanton.

The gang goes on to Tucson, losing more men on the way, and then heads for California, taking with them new recruits, including an idiot boy kept in a cage. Reaching the Colorado River, they take over a ferry crossing, killing a number of Yuma Indians in the process and enslaving others to work for them. Finally the Yumas rebel, attack the scalp hunters and massacre most of them, including Glanton himself. The kid, although wounded in the leg, again escapes and later meets other survivors in the desert. There he is encouraged by Tobin, a former priest, to kill Judge Holden—who, Tobin insists, will kill them if the kid does not. The kid, however, is unwilling to ambush the judge. He and Tobin are later rescued from certain death in the desert by a wandering band of Dieguenos Indians and find their way to San Diego, where they are imprisoned. It is now 1850; the kid has been with Glanton's gang for less than a year.

The last chapters of the book jump forward twenty-eight years, during which time the kid—now known as "the man"—has wandered, an outcast, through the West. He has tried to renounce killing, though he is sometimes forced into it. In 1878, he enters Fort Griffin, Texas, once the main supply point for buffalo hides but now a veritable boneyard, on the brink of extinction. There he once again meets the judge, unchanged over the years, and there he is apparently killed by the judge in an outhouse behind the saloon, his death horrible enough to frighten even the most hardened witnesses of violence in that dark and brutal land. The book ends with the judge dancing in a celebration of death.

*The Characters*

The kid is the novel's primary protagonist, although, like Ishmael in *Moby Dick: Or, The Whale* (Herman Melville's 1851 classic, echoed throughout *Blood Meridian*), he disappears for considerable periods in the narrative. Although he is almost instinctively capable of violence and appears to be undisturbed by the brutality of the life he pursues, McCarthy sets him apart from the other men of Glanton's gang. The reader is never given insight into the kid's thoughts; he must be judged solely by his actions and occasional statements. Nevertheless, the book does dramatize its concept of moral struggle through the kid. Judge Holden chooses him as disciple or victim from the first time he sees him, and their final encounter, though delayed for almost thirty years, is, according to the judge, predetermined. In the judge's words, only the kid, of all the group, holds back from giving himself fully to the act of bloodletting. Throughout, the kid performs acts of minor mercy, which the other members of the group refuse to do. Yet he is never able to confront the judge. After the massacre at Yuma Crossing, the kid seems increasingly haunted, finally sated with murder and gore. Still, when the judge approaches him in the Fort Griffin saloon, the kid, now the man, continues to hold back, refusing either to join the judge or stand against him. His subsequent death seems a consequence of his failure to make a choice.

Judge Holden is the most intriguing, fascinating, and horrifying of this appalling band of killers. Based on a historical figure, he is well over six feet tall, monstrous in build, and completely hairless. Yet the judge seems almost supernatural, invested with marvelous powers and knowledge, which makes his numerous acts of carnage all the more terrible. Indeed, McCarthy strongly suggests that Judge Holden embodies a greater evil than the other men of the band, that he is, in fact, demonic, a "sootysouled rascal" who waits to snare the lives and hearts of those who, like the kid, live ambivalent lives. The judge is aptly titled, for he does render verdicts and enacts punishments. Larger than life, he espouses a philosophy of the world that reduces existence to war and exacts violence and death, but he himself seems beyond death, an eternal figure in a desolate and bloody land.

John Joel Glanton comes from historical record, his exploits as a scalp hunter and outlaw profiteer found in dozens of accounts of the Old West. McCarthy's version of Glanton accords in detail with these accounts. Glanton is, in McCarthy's telling, a mad captain pursuing the Indian as Ahab does the white whale. Glanton's madness, though, is different from that of Captain White, the leader of the expedition into Mexico described in the early parts of the novel. Glanton is shrewd, a tough and hardbitten soldier. His murderous chase of the Indian has metaphysical overtones, as if he, like Ahab, is demanding that God reveal itself. Although the judge is second in command to him, Glanton seems at times manipulated by Holden; in his times of raving, only the judge can calm and quiet him. Glanton faces his death without fear, spitting in the presence of his killer and challenging, "Hack away you mean red nigger."

Of the other members of the gang, several stand out. Tobin, the former priest, is a paradoxical figure who speaks of the presence of God but participates in the most awful atrocities. He acts as moral adviser to the kid, warning him from the judge and advising him in the matter of survival. Toadvine, a horse thief whose ears have been cropped and forehead branded in punishment, is one of the first men the kid meets in Texas; they engage in a brutal fight in the mud outside a saloon but later become companions in Glanton's gang. Although Toadvine survives the Yuma Crossing massacre, he is later hanged in San Diego along with David Brown, another scalper. John Jackson is the one identified black member of the gang. Shortly after the kid joins

Glanton's gang, this Jackson kills a white member, also named John Jackson, for his racial slurs; the black Jackson is the first to die in the Yuma Crossing massacre. Although most of the scalp hunters are identified by name and personality, they are largely secondary, although distinctly drawn, characters in the novel.

*Themes and Meanings*

*Blood Meridian* can be read on a number of levels. Although far too graphic and relentless to be considered an adventure novel, it is nevertheless a compelling narrative, full of fights, escapes, mysteries, and astonishments. McCarthy is masterful at creating a believable picture of the Old West in his expert physical description of landscape, his full and detailed knowledge of place and people, and his ability to reveal character through dialogue. The novel is also fascinating for its historical re-creation of a time and way of life generally romanticized or glossed over. Indeed, *Blood Meridian* may be read as revisionist history, a much truer picture of what the settling of the West was all about. McCarthy's research into the time is everywhere evident; his authority gives the story a sense of authenticity that compels belief. There are no heroes in McCarthy's tale, nor does he glorify or excuse or even explain either whites or Indians. Each acts according to needs and desires that seem almost atavistic, and the constant violence is presented as a necessity in such a rough and barbaric world.

The novel, however, is primarily a philosophical exploration of the nature of evil and the significance of moral choice. While most of the characters, including the kid, are not introspective, two figures stand in debate with one another. Judge Holden is the primary exponent of the violence of life. There is no mystery in the world, the judge argues; all things simply are. War, then, is the only "holy" act, the only true game, for only in combat, in the taking of another life, does man prove his existence. If a higher will exists, combat becomes proof of that will, for in battle one must survive and one die, and the battle itself forces a decision to be made by the greater power. Holden argues that all things are preordained and that there is no ultimate escaping from destiny. Thus, he faults the kid for failing to give himself totally to his destiny, to the act of blood, and he accuses him of having a "flawed place" in his soul that retains "some corner of clemency for the heathen."

Tobin, the former priest, speaks for the other side. He argues for the existence of a knowing God, for individual free will and choice. He warns the kid away from the judge early in the novel, and near the end he urges the kid to face the judge, to kill him and the evil he embodies before Holden kills them. The kid has three chances to do so, but each time he refuses. Although he then wanders for twenty-eight years, the kid cannot escape the judge's decree. "Was it always your idea . . . that if you did not speak you would not be recognized?" the judge asks him shortly before he takes his life. It apparently is the kid's failure to take a stand that brings him to his terrible end.

*Critical Context*

In 1980, McCarthy moved from his home state of Tennessee to El Paso, Texas, where he wrote *Blood Meridian*. It was his fifth novel and the first set outside Tennessee. The first four (*The Orchard Keeper*, 1965; *Outer Dark*, 1968; *Child of God*, 1974; and *Suttree*, 1979) do, nevertheless, anticipate the themes, characters, and moral concerns found in *Blood Meridian*. McCarthy now appears to have taken the Southwest as his primary setting. His *All the Pretty Horses* (1992) also takes place in Texas and Mexico, although it is set a hundred years later than *Blood Meridian*. Its protagonist, John Grady Cole, is another sixteen-year-old boy setting out to make his way in a violent world, but John Grady is a stronger, more principled character than the kid, and his choices give the reader hope for his future.

*Blood Meridian* was not a commercially successful novel at the time of publication, although it did receive a number of very appreciative reviews. It is, however, now ranked by many as McCarthy's masterpiece. After many years of writing in obscurity, McCarthy achieved both popular and critical success with *All the Pretty Horses*, which won the National Book Award and the National Critics' Circle Award for fiction and was a finalist for the Pulitzer Prize. *All the Pretty Horses* is the first volume in a proposed "Border Trilogy," and it seems certain that McCarthy's reputation will continue to grow with each new work.

*Bibliography*
Bell, Vereen M. *The Achievement of Cormac McCarthy*. Baton Rouge: Louisiana State University Press, 1988. The first book-length study of McCarthy's work through *Blood Meridian*. "The Metaphysics of Violence: *Blood Meridian*" is the last chapter in the book and compares the novel to *Moby Dick* and Joseph Conrad's *Heart of Darkness* (1899) as a study of evil. Bell views McCarthy as primarily a nihilist.
Daugherty, Leo. "Gravers False and True: *Blood Meridian* as Gnostic Tragedy." *Southern Quarterly* 30 (Summer, 1992): 122-133. Argues that gnostic thought is central to McCarthy's work, especially *Blood Meridian*. There is a good god somewhere in the universe, but he is separated from the world, which is ruled by "archons" who establish their own form of justice and rule. Judge Holden, Daugherty maintains, is such an archon.
James, Caryn. "Is Everybody Dead Around Here?" *The New York Times Book Review*, April 28, 1985, 31. A mixed review of *Blood Meridian* that praises McCarthy's originality but decries the novel's "stylistically dazzling but facile conclusion."
Sepich, John Emil. *Notes on "Blood Meridian."* Louisville, Ky.: Bellarmine College Press, 1993. An expanded and revised version of Sepich's master's thesis. An exhaustive study of possible historical and literary sources for *Blood Meridian*.
Shaviro, Steven. " 'The Very Life of the Darkness': A Reading of *Blood Meridian*." *The Southern Quarterly* 30 (Summer, 1992): 119-129. Shaviro maintains that although *Blood Meridian* is primarily about death, dying, and destruction, there is nevertheless a vitality and even a joy and comedy in the presentation. He considers McCarthy "our greatest living author."

*Edwin T. Arnold*

# BONE

*Author:* Fae Myenne Ng (1956-    )
*Type of plot:* Family
*Time of plot:* The 1960's to the 1990's
*Locale:* San Francisco, California
*First published:* 1993

> *Principal characters:*
> LEILA LEONG, the narrator of the story, the oldest of three Chinese American sisters
> ONA LEONG, the second sister, who has committed suicide before the present action of the novel
> NINA LEONG, the third sister, who works for a travel agency in New York
> MAH LEONG, the girls' mother, the owner of a children's shop
> LEON LEONG, the father to the three girls, second husband to Mah, and biological father of Ona and Nina
> MASON LOUIE, Leila's lover and, later, husband
> TOMMIE HORN, the owner of a sweatshop, who becomes Mah's lover during her marriage to Leon

## The Novel

Fae Ng's novel *Bone* chronicles the fictional history of a family of Chinese immigrants living in San Francisco's Chinatown from the 1960's to the 1990's. The main characters are three sisters, American by birth and environment, struggling to make their ways to peace as persons, women, and Chinese Americans. The central event of the story is the death of the second daughter, Ona, who has recently killed herself by jumping from the thirteenth floor of a building while on drugs.

The novel itself is divided into fourteen chapters, all simply but beautifully written and all narrated by the older sister Leila, to whom the story belongs most. It is she who tells and retells, from different though not contradictory perspectives, the story of her family and of her sister's suicide. Most of the action is in the present, yet Leila's memory frequently wanders to past events that are recounted in detail.

The book begins at some point after the recent death of Ona. Leila has just returned from New York, where she has married Mason Louie, another Chinese American from San Francisco, without her parents' permission or foreknowledge. She is seeking Leon Leong, her stepfather, to inform him of the marriage; oddly, it is not her mother whom she wishes to tell.

Events of the family's history are not given in chronological order. Particular events are referred to in conversation or are recorded in the narrator's mind as she revisits those parts of the family's struggles in America that are important to her. Leila provides various interpretations and gives the perspectives of others in the family.

Leila's best and most meaningful relationship is with her stepfather, who somehow comes to represent America itself. Leila, who is employed by the local school system as a "community relations expert," does succeed in coming to terms with herself, her family, her Chinese ancestry, and her American identity.

As Leila reports her marriage to other family members, the events of their respective lives are told in turn. This organizational method provides the structure of the novel.

Leon's story is given first. He is a collector of junk, a repairman who is always undertaking projects that are never finished. Moreover, he signs on to ships as a crew employee and disappears for weeks and months at a time with little or no explanation. When he learns that his wife has been unfaithful to him, he removes himself from the house for some indefinite but extended period until the three daughters somehow succeed in getting him to return. Leon is guilt-ridden for having promised to return the bones of his father to China for burial—a promise he has never been able to keep, because of financial difficulties and the lack of direction in his life.

Mah is in many respects a good mother. On the other hand, she is always too busy at work to be a perfect mother, and she is seemingly handicapped by language and her Chinese way of thinking. Victimized by Leila's father, her first husband, who had deserted her with the child, Mah makes a second marriage with Leon and becomes unfaithful to him. When Ona kills herself, she blames her own adultery for the death.

Ona's story is one of disillusion. She has been in love with Osvaldo, whose father enters a business venture with Leon that fails. Consequently, the two men fall out as friends, and Leon forbids Ona to marry her young lover. After an abortion that she keeps secret from everyone except Leila, Ona kills herself while on drugs.

Only Nina seems to have some degree of happiness and security, perhaps because she has moved herself to New York, where she lives independent of her family. As such, she remains something of an outsider to the family, and she does not wish to return to Chinatown for her sister's funeral.

In the middle of the novel, the family visits the Chinese cemetery where Grandfather Leong (Leon's father) is buried. Unable to locate his grave and irritated by a caretaker who denies them access because it is not visiting hours, the family does succeed in learning what has happened to Grandfather Leong's bones. They have been cremated without the knowledge or permission of the family, and they can now never be recovered or returned to China.

Following this event, Leila relates the immediate responses of friends and others after Ona's death. All members of the family want to be left alone in their grief, so that they can alternately blame themselves and then other family members for the suicide. There is plenty of guilt to go around: Leon blames himself for forbidding her marriage to Osvaldo; Mah blames herself for her adultery; Leila blames herself for not trying to talk to her sister; and Nina blames herself for being absent and in New York.

The characters are never truly reconciled to their own feelings of guilt, nor do they really come to find peace within themselves. The novel concludes, however, with Leila's realization that the family's problems and, in particular, Ona's suicide, are not because the family members are transplanted Chinese. Leon's assertion that "The heart never travels" concludes the novel and is doubtless its most meaningful theme and occurrence. Yet Ng's point is that the heart never travels from home (now America), not China.

## The Characters

Leila Leong is the central character of the novel and the person whose story is being told. She has problems in coming to terms with her identity because of her Chinese heritage, yet she lives and succeeds as a third-generation American who can speak little or no Chinese and who has no real or functional identity with her heritage. Ng develops this main character primarily by revealing Leila's thoughts; indeed, most of her actions are of little consequence. Leila's story is one of self-discovery, a matter of growing up as a person and growing into an awareness of the American she has been since birth.

Readers learn of Ona Leong only from the recollections of others. Ng relates on the first page of the novel that this middle sister has killed herself. Slowly, through hints, memories, and half-memories of other characters, the reasons for her actions are revealed, if not explained. Ona kills herself because she is the daughter most assimilated into American culture; she is the one who has the fewest problems as an American and, therefore, the most problems as a Chinese American. Her abortion and forbidden affair with Osvaldo, like her drug use, are only symptomatic of what is wrong with her character.

The youngest sister, Nina, tries to escape all the family's problems by changing her geography. A job and apartment in New York accomplish this, and as a tour guide for a travel agency, she actually leads tours to China. There, she feels as out of place as the other American tourists, though she can speak enough Chinese to succeed at her employment. Nina, like the other sisters, has no problems with such things as preferring American to Chinese foods, but she cannot live in Chinatown, or even close to it, as the other family members choose to do.

The mother, Mah, experiences more real problems with cultural assimilation than the other characters. She agonizes both for and over the past; she claims it and its customs and traditions when it is to her advantage, but readily denies or ignores these on choice. Her reaction to Leila's marriage to Mason demonstrates the point. She disapproves the marriage and therefore uses Chinese language and traditions to make Leila feel guilty.

Leon, as stepfather to Leila, serves to symbolize America, the "stepfather" of the three girls. As such, he often embodies characteristics that are not good. He can never hold down a good job; he perpetually has trouble with his business schemes; he disappears for long periods of time without explanation; he is not a good husband to his wife; and he is not a good representative of the old China. He has been unable to return his father's bones home for burial.

Mason Louie, the young mechanic with whom Leila lives, then loves, then marries, is already Americanized: He repairs foreign cars, occasionally uses drugs, and is generally at peace with himself as a man, mechanic, and husband. He helps Leon to get out of trouble on several occasions, and he will have a typical relationship with his mother-in-law in the American fashion.

Tommie Horn, as owner of a sweatshop in which Mah works, had been a candidate to marry Mah, but Leon asked her first. Tommie embodies the worst of all that was true about life in China. He is a ruthless slave-driver who at once takes care of Mah and her daughters and uses them whenever he needs to get his business orders filled hurriedly.

## Themes and Meanings

Most centrally, the novel is a story of ethnic assimilation; the realization of the main character is that the transformation has already occurred. Leila learns that she is and has always been an American. The extent to which this Americanism is defined by her Chinese heritage is the real question.

Basically, the problems that confront the Leong family are not, at least in the present, caused by their ethnicity or race. For the three girls, at least, their problems are those of most young women. They are concerned with life, love, happiness, perhaps marriage if it is convenient, and careers. The social problems around them, issues such as drugs and abortion, are not unique to them, and they experience and cope with such matters as do Americans of other ethnic descent.

It is Leon, rather than Leila, who voices Ng's themes. At the beginning of the novel he asserts that "it's time that makes a family, not just blood." His comment applies generally to the Leong family and specifically to his relationship to Leila. Through the years, these two characters come to love each other more than they do those to whom they are related by blood. Ng's point is that enough time in America will assuredly make the bonds stronger to this country than the blood ties to those of China. As the novel progresses, characters accept or reject this idea, both in terms of the family and homeland, to their own benefit or detriment.

The central symbol of the novel is indicated by its title. What is the "bone" of contention here? And whose "bone" is it, anyway? Are the family's problems rooted in Chinese ancestry, heritage, and tradition, or in their perhaps misplaced and dis-placed lives as Americans? Regardless, the question is rendered irrelevant in the central scene in the cemetery. Grandfather Leong's bones are unidentifiable and will never be located. The past is lost to eternity. There is no bone, though there once was.

## Critical Context

*Bone* is Fae Ng's first novel. Published in 1993, it is a poignant statement about cultural assimilation of ethnic groups, particularly Asian Americans, into the Ameri-can way of life. The characters and events in the novel demonstrate that the process in the 1990's is not what it has been for various immigrant groups, particularly Asians, in the past. Barriers caused by language and education are not what they were even as recently as the 1960's and 1970's. As the characters recollect their lives in America, it is undeniable that the problems of Grandfather Leong, and even of Leon himself, are not those of the three girls.

It is important that this work of fiction reads as biography. The novelist accomplishes this so as to give more credibility to her experiences and themes, which are often characteristics of earlier short stories she has published.

In its social context, *Bone* realizes that "becoming American," too, has been accelerated in today's world just as other aspects of American life. Time itself becomes the cure for all the Leong family's problems, even the death of Ona.

*Bibliography*

Brunvand, Jan Harold. *The Choking Doberman and Other "New" Urban Legends.* New York: W. W. Norton, 1984. Brunvand describes problems facing Chinese and other refugees living in large American cities. Such problems confront the Leong family.

Cheng, Lucie, et al. *Linking Our Lives: Chinese American Women of Los Angeles.* Los Angeles: Chinese Historical Society of Southern California, 1984. The authors discuss problems of Chinese women as they become Americanized in Southern California. The women of the Leong family, including the mother and three daughters, confront these obstacles.

Fessler, Loren W., ed. *Chinese in America: Stereotyped Past, Changing Present.* New York: Vantage Press, 1983. Contributors write critically about the Chinese experience in America, spelling out the differences confronting Chinese historically (such as those confronting Leon and Mah Leong) and those confronting the next generation (the three daughters).

Kim, Elaine H., with Janice Otani. *With Silk Wings: Asian American Women at Work.* San Francisco: Asian Women United of California, 1983. Kim lists problems of Chinese and other Asian American women on the job market. Particularly relevant to Ng's novel are the depictions of women in a sweatshop such as the one in which Mah Leong works.

Knoll, Tricia. *Becoming Americans: Asian Sojourners, Immigrants, and Refugees in the Western United States.* Portland, Oreg.: Coast to Coast Books, 1982. Knoll describes the problems and circumstances of numerous Asian immigrant groups throughout the Western United States, including the Chinese in San Francisco.

Tsai, Shih-shan Henry. *The Chinese Experience in America.* Bloomington: Indiana University Press, 1986. Tsai gives a broad outline, replete with numerous details, about problems of cultural assimilation of the Chinese in America. The book is recent enough to take up problems of present-day first- and second-generation Chinese immigrants.

*Carl Singleton*

# THE BONFIRE OF THE VANITIES

*Author:* Tom Wolfe (Thomas Kennerly Wolfe, Jr., 1930-    )
*Type of plot:* Social realism
*Time of plot:* The 1980's
*Locale:* New York City
*First published:* 1987

> *Principal characters:*
> SHERMAN McCOY, a bond salesman who considers himself a "Master of
> the Universe" but who is going broke on an annual income of a million
> dollars
> JUDY McCOY, Sherman's fading wife, who loves to spend her husband's
> money and fancies herself an interior decorator
> MARIA RUSKIN, Sherman's Southern-born mistress, the unfaithful wife of
> an elderly multimillionaire
> PETER FALLOW, an alcoholic English reporter for a New York scandal
> sheet
> LAWRENCE KRAMER, the ambitious assistant district attorney in Sher-
> man's first trial for reckless endangerment
> THOMAS KILLIAN, Sherman's streetwise defense attorney
> JUDGE MYRON KOVITSKY, a feisty judge who presides over Sherman's
> first trial
> REVEREND REGINALD BACON, a black minister with dubious credentials
> who exploits black unrest for profit

*The Novel*

In *The Bonfire of the Vanities*, an upper-middle-class white Wall Street investment
banker who thinks he is on top of the world discovers that his fragile world is in
imminent danger of destruction from within. At age thirty-eight, Sherman McCoy is
near the peak of his career. He is married and has one young daughter whom he loves
but rarely sees because of his hectic double life. In addition to being absorbed in
business, he maintains an adulterous relationship with a sexy blonde who is having
fun while waiting for her elderly multimillionaire husband to die.

One night while driving his mistress, Maria Ruskin, home, Sherman accidentally
takes a wrong turn off the expressway and finds himself in one of the poorest and most
dangerous slums of the Bronx. After finding his way back to the expressway, he
discovers that the on-ramp is blocked with rubbish, and when he gets out to clear a
path, he sees two black youths approaching with obviously sinister intentions. Maria,
in panic, slides behind the wheel and calls for him to jump in. Backing up to get around
the barricade, she bumps one of the youths and then speeds off without looking back.

They read in the next day's newspaper that a teenager named Harold Lamb was
felled by a hit-and-run driver at that location and is hospitalized in a coma. Lamb
eventually provides a description and partial license number of the car that struck him.

An alcoholic journalist named Peter Fallow publicizes the incident in his tabloid because of its dramatic potential—a rich white man in a Mercedes-Benz knocking down a poor black youth and driving off without stopping. To further dramatize the contrast, Lamb is falsely described as a model youth and an honor student.

The police are forced to investigate because of the publicity and the public outcry fueled by the Reverend Reginald Bacon, an opportunist who blackmails wealthy liberals with threats of mob violence. When the police get around to Sherman, he breaks down and admits his involvement but does not implicate Maria.

During the rest of the novel, Sherman is processed through a cynical legal system in which he stands out conspicuously as the "Great White Defendant." The prosecution wishes to make political capital out of convicting him; the defense wishes to milk Sherman for as much money as possible. Ironically, no one really cares about the truth but only about capitalizing on the situation.

Sherman is thrown into cells with hardened criminals, most of whom are ignorant members of the underclass. Having been educated in the best schools and sheltered from the cruel realities of life, Sherman is horrified by the conditions he sees. The experience toughens him and teaches him the need to fight for himself in a ruthless, dog-eat-dog world.

Sherman quickly loses his job, because his company is afraid of adverse publicity. Without his big paychecks, he is driven to the brink of bankruptcy. He is forced to sell his expensive cooperative Park Avenue apartment, but the proceeds are tied up in a civil suit by Lamb's mother and a real-estate broker. Maria Ruskin refuses to corroborate Sherman's account of the hit-and-run incident or to admit she was driving on the night in question.

His first trial on a charge of reckless endangerment is thrown out of court by Judge Kovitsky, an old-time jurist who still believes in due process and refuses to bow to mob or media pressure. Sherman's second trial ends with a hung jury. In the meantime, Lamb dies, and Sherman is indicted for manslaughter; he faces a possible sentence of up to twenty-five years. At the end of the novel, Sherman has been reduced to poverty and has become a sort of urban guerrilla, fighting the justice system and the ignorant masses who have been whipped into frenzy by a demagogue and a corrupt newspaper.

*The Characters*

Characterization is Wolfe's Achilles heel, and his weakness in this aspect of fiction writing might explain why he had never tried to write a novel before. He has been criticized for creating characters who are stereotypes or caricatures. Throughout his career, Wolfe has been known as a social satirist, and this venture into fiction writing did not represent a radical change in technique. His previous writings, which were all important contributions to the school of the "New Journalism," focused on human foibles. In this novel, he was more anxious to point out the foibles of social classes than to attempt to invent three-dimensional characters.

Sherman represents the upwardly mobile, well-educated upper-middle-class capitalists who bring billions of dollars flowing into New York City and thereby attract hordes of "have-nots." His wife represents all the spoiled, selfish women who are married to the Sherman McCoys. Judy is sexually frustrated because her husband has turned his affections to a younger woman, and she consequently expends her energies on extravagant purchases that keep them chronically in debt.

Maria Ruskin has been criticized for being nothing more than a stereotypical "dumb blonde." She has been given a thick Southern accent to make her stand out as a character. She is just as selfish, spoiled, and bitchy as Sherman's wife, but she is quite a few years younger.

Peter Fallow is lazy and incompetent, an alcoholic and a freeloader, but he has good manners and valuable social connections. He has no conscience about what he writes for his trashy tabloid, and his editor will accept anything that can be printed without getting the paper sued for libel.

The Reverend Reginald Bacon is a self-appointed African American "leader" who stirs up trouble for what amounts to nothing more than blackmail. White liberals donate money to his various causes to keep him and his followers pacified, and much of the money finds its way into Bacon's own pockets.

The only character in the novel who develops is Sherman McCoy himself. His character change, however, is a little too radical to be plausible. He changes from a spoiled, elitist Yale University graduate into an urban guerrilla fighting a lone battle against hopeless odds.

Wolfe's forte is not characterization but rather his penetrating social intelligence, which typically finds expression in satire. The other characters in the novel can be read as New York types, and it has often been suggested that *The Bonfire of the Vanities* is a romàn a clef, with such characters as Fallow and Bacon representing people known to insiders if not to the general reader.

Thomas Killian and Lawrence Kramer are stereotypical New York lawyers. The police officials are also stereotypes who could have come out of any police television drama. *The Bonfire of the Vanities* is strongly reminiscent of Theodore Dreiser's *An American Tragedy* (1925), a masterpiece in the realist genre that Wolfe admires. Like the men involved in apprehending, prosecuting, and defending Clyde Griffiths in Dreiser's novel, Wolfe's representatives of law and order care nothing about morality or truth; all they care about is how they might benefit from a publicity bonanza.

There is not a single admirable character in the book. Wolfe portrays all humans as greedy, selfish, narrow-minded, and often sadistic. He treats the lower classes with utter contempt, but he has little regard for the upper classes either.

*Themes and Meanings*

Tom Wolfe received a Ph.D. from elite Yale University in American Studies, demonstrating his erudition as well as his focus of interest. The ideas that form the foundation of his novel can be traced to many sources.

In his 1989 essay "Stalking the Billion-Footed Beast: A Literary Manifesto for the New Social Novel," Wolfe stated that his "immediate model was Thackeray's *Vanity Fair*" (1847-1848). William Thackeray's novel is a satirical portrait of the greedy, selfish, unscrupulous inhabitants of nineteenth century London. In the essay, Wolfe observed that his main objective was to paint a comparable picture of modern New York City, in all of its grandeur and squalor and with all of its ethnic diversity:

> New York and practically every other large city in the United States are undergoing a profound change. The fourth great wave of immigrants—this one from Asia, North Africa, Latin America, and the Caribbean—is now pouring in. Within ten years political power in most major American cities will have passed to the nonwhite majorities.

Wolfe's novel is essentially a story about how the white power structure is losing out to this new, nonwhite social force. Whites are losing the privileged position they have always taken for granted and will have to learn, like Sherman McCoy, to compete vigorously for their share of the good life that America has to offer.

Wolfe, like Thackeray, professes to be amused by the spectacle he presents; however, Wolfe's mocking tone conceals an underlying concern about the future of the city he knows and loves. Like many ultraconservative thinkers, he believes that welfare payments in their various forms are insidious because they condition recipients to develop a "welfare mentality." The handouts also attract more and more needy applicants from inside and outside the country, so that affluent cities such as New York become overrun with indigent people who have nothing to contribute to a high-tech society. According to this view, liberals who advocate government and private charity are motivated not by feelings of compassion but by fear of the growing masses of discontented poor, who can use voting power or violence to confiscate property. Some leaders, like Wolfe's Reverend Bacon, orchestrate such violence for their own political and financial benefit.

There is a fatalistic thread running throughout Wolfe's novel. He believes that the white ruling class in America is doomed to be engulfed by a rising tide of have-nots who do not sympathize with the ideals upon which the country was founded. His novel echoes such pessimistic books as Jose Ortega y Gasset's *La rebelión de las masas* (1930; *The Revolt of the Masses*, 1931), in which the brilliant Spanish philosopher stated that Western civilization was threatened by a "vertical invasion of the barbarians."

*Critical Context*

Wolfe paints a picture of America's biggest, richest city in the late twentieth century. Like all the major cities of America, New York is suffering form unprecedented social unrest. The white upper classes who have run things since before the American Revolution are retreating into enclaves as the cities become flooded with poor, nonwhite immigrants from other countries and from American farmlands, where mechanization is making their labor superfluous. Many of these newcomers remain unemployed because they have no marketable skills. They become a drain on the welfare system, and government subsidies are one of the attractions that draw more and more such people to the big cities.

In many American cities, the white majority is turning into a white minority. Political power is passing from whites to nonwhites because the one thing the nonwhites possess is their voting power. Some charismatic leaders in the minority communities take advantage of unrest to obtain power and profit.

Human greed and selfishness are not monopolized by any single race. Affluent whites are so obsessed with enriching themselves that they are content to buy time with government handouts while surrounding themselves with barred windows, watchdogs, electronic protection devices, and private armies of security guards. The underprivileged nonwhites are conditioned to develop a passive-aggressive attitude— the so-called welfare mentality—demanding more and more bribes in the form of welfare payments, food stamps, subsidized housing, and other benefits as the price for not engaging in open revolution. Wolfe has been accused of exaggerating the situation and deliberately falsifying the facts to make his case more dramatic. Whether readers agree with him or not is likely to depend on their political perspectives.

*Bibliography*

Black, George. "The Far-Right Stuff." *The New Statesman* 115 (February 12, 1988): 31. An extremely negative review of *The Bonfire of the Vanities*. Black accuses Wolfe of distorting the truth about the underprivileged residents of the Bronx. He calls the book "a set piece for cartoon characters."

Scura, Dorothy M., ed. *Conversations with Tom Wolfe*. Jackson: University Press of Mississippi, 1990. Interviews with Wolfe by many different individuals, including Bill Moyers and William F. Buckley, Jr., arranged chronologically from 1966 to 1989. Contain many references to *The Bonfire of the Vanities*. Reveal Wolfe's multifaceted personality as social critic, self-promoter, and serious author.

Shomette, Doug, ed. *The Critical Response to Tom Wolfe*. Westport, Conn.: Greenwood Press, 1992. A collection of essays, both positive and negative, on books published by Wolfe up to 1990. This excellent reference source contains incisive essays on *The Bonfire of the Vanities*. Also contains a Chronology of important events in Wolfe's life and a generous bibliography.

Vigilante, Richard. "The Truth About Tom Wolfe." *The National Review* 39 (December 18, 1987): 46-48. An enthusiastic review of *The Bonfire of the Vanities* reflecting ultraconservative views. Vigilante calls Wolfe the most important writer of his generation. He predicts that because of Wolfe's example, "the social-realist novel will soon re-emerge as an accepted and perhaps dominant force on the serious-fiction scene."

Wolfe, Tom. "Stalking the Billion-Footed Beast: A Literary Manifesto for the New Social Novel." *Harper's Magazine* 279 (November, 1989): 45-56. In this landmark essay written shortly after publication of *The Bonfire of the Vanities*, Wolfe proposes that American writers return to the tradition of realism. He describes the characteristics of realism and criticizes contemporary fiction writers for neglecting the panorama of modern life in favor of cryptic subjectivism and frivolous experimentalism. As he gleefully anticipated, his essay provoked a storm of controversy.

*Bill Delaney*

# BORN BROTHERS

*Author:* Larry Woiwode (1941-    )
*Type of plot:* Psychological realism
*Time of plot:* The 1940's through the 1980's
*Locale:* North Dakota, Illinois, and New York City
*First published:* 1988

> *Principal characters:*
> CHARLES NEUMILLER, one of two brothers
> JEROME NEUMILLER, the other brother, a year older than Charles
> MARTIN NEUMILLER, their father, a teacher
> ALPHA NEUMILLER, their mother
> KATHERINE NEUMILLER, Charles's wife

*The Novel*

Based on Larry Woiwode's own life, *Born Brothers* reveals the inside of Charles Neumiller's mind as he remembers, rearranges, and finds meaning in events from his past. These memories appear as short, poetic fragments told in the first person and in present tense, with often-abrupt shifts in place and time. Letters, journals, poems, and scripts provide some information; they also serve as prompts that stimulate the thinking of a much older Charles who thinks about making ready for death.

*Born Brothers* is divided into seven sections. The main story line, mostly in chronological order, follows Charles from his earliest childhood memories to a suicide attempt when he is in his mid-thirties. Interspersed throughout the book are memories of the time when Charles, then in his early twenties, lived in a hotel called the Chesro in New York. He describes this as a "pilgrimage" and a "retreat." Occasionally, an older Charles, one who has survived the suicide attempt, appears. This Charles no longer drinks, is a caring husband and father, and has become a devout Christian who says that religious principles have turned his life around.

The book opens with a letter written in 1964 by Jerome, then a medical student in Chicago, to Charles, who is trying to break into acting in New York. Jerome announces that he is planning to visit Charles. An older Charles says that the sight of this letter triggers memories of that time. A brief image of his suicide attempt surfaces, and then his memories go back to his early childhood in Hyatt, North Dakota, where his father is a teacher.

Early childhood is the happiest time for Charles. Jerome is only a year older; they look like twins, are dressed like twins, and do everything together. Although they have a growing number of siblings, they pay little attention to them. Their father is a devout Catholic, and the boys attend St. Mary Margaret Elementary School and serve as altar boys. Charles's heroes are Dr. Rex Morgan and Joe Louis. He imagines he would like to be a doctor, but he also discovers his talent for acting, an activity that his mother, whom he loves dearly, encourages.

Childhood holds some painful memories also. His mother, afraid he will turn out badly, punishes him severely and often. The older Charles, who has a four-year-old son, comments that children spend much of their time grieving. Charles also develops an early awareness of death when he almost dies from pneumonia.

The summer after Charles completes the third grade, the Neumiller family moves to Illinois, where Martin has been promised a teaching job. After they move, everything goes wrong. The teaching job falls through, the family cannot find a place to live and must stay with Martin's parents in their partially finished house, and Alpha is pregnant again with her sixth child. Martin goes to work for his brother's construction company, and the family moves into a converted gas station. Alpha loses the child, then succumbs to a kidney disorder and dies.

Their mother dead and their father lost in his own grief, Jerome and Charles are adrift. When a classmate taunts Charles because he has no mother, Charles challenges him to a boxing match with Jerome to be the referee. Although the fight ends in a standoff, Jerome, trying to be fair, declares the other boy to be the winner. Charles, betrayed and devastated, attacks Jerome. Charles shoplifts candy from the local store and eventually involves Jerome in the misdeed. They eat too much, read a lot, and try various hobbies. As a young adolescent, Charles becomes interested in a girl named Dewey. She encourages his attentions for a time but then rejects him for another boy.

Eventually, Martin obtains a teaching job, and the boys become interested in high-school activities such as basketball and speech. Martin develops acute appendicitis and almost dies, and Jerome and Charles drive to the nearby town to visit him. On the way home, Jerome, suddenly possessed by the need to speed, loses control of the car, and it crashes into a marker in the cemetery. Both of Charles's legs are badly broken; they do not heal easily or quickly. Charles becomes involved with a girl, Bobbie, and Jerome becomes attached to her friend. The boys are increasingly obsessed with sexual exploration, and they find it increasingly difficult to reconcile these feelings with the admonitions of the priest. Bobbie pushes Charles into having intercourse, but Charles fails even to have an orgasm. Disappointment, guilt, and a fear of being trapped cause him to break off the relationship.

In high school, Jerome participates in speech and drama, but after taking care of Charles and his father, he considers going into medicine. Charles, who has always wanted to be a doctor, becomes interested in speech and drama. After his first year of college, Jerome does switch his major to premedical studies, while Charles enrolls in speech and theater. Although they are roommates again, Charles feels that their paths have crossed and that they are moving away from each other. Charles stops going to church altogether when he hears that the campus priest buys a new Cadillac every year while ignoring all the problems in the world.

Charles meets Rick Purkeet, an upperclassman who is also involved in theater and who also lost his mother at an early age. Rick makes homosexual advances toward Charles. Charles feels some attraction to Rick, who seems to be a kindred spirit, but he resists Rick's advances. One night, after getting drunk on Rick's liquor, Charles threatens to kill himself.

Charles meets Jill through the college theater. They consummate their relationship, and Charles assumes that she will want to marry him. Jill, however, breaks off with him when she gets involved with a fraternity man. At one point, with no money, no girlfriend, and no hope, Charles contemplates suicide again. At a graduation party for Jerome, Charles discovers Jill kissing Jerome; he loses control, hits Jill, becomes hysterical, and decides to leave for California. Jerome assures him that he and others do care about him, and Charles decides to stay.

Jerome goes on to medical school, while Charles, still in college, meets a fair-haired, blue-eyed woman named Katherine and falls in love. Her father hopes to break them up, so he sends Katherine to school elsewhere. Charles decides to go to New York to try his luck at acting; it is during this time that he stays at the Chesro.

After this, the main narrative line moves ahead rapidly. Charles and Katherine are married, and Jerome marries Julie, a black woman who teaches English. There are references to Charles's new show, which is doing well. Both marriages are having problems. Charles and Katherine have a daughter, Becky. Jerome tells Charles that their father has cancer, and two years later, Jerome tells Charles that the cancer has reappeared. In the fall of 1975, Martin goes to New Mexico, where Jerome is living, and Charles, separated from Katherine, goes to help take care of him. This Charles tries not to drink and reads the Bible.

Martin dies in March of 1976. At the funeral, Katherine and Charles try living together again, but Charles must go to North Dakota to take part in a bicentennial celebration. Unable to handle the stress, he starts drinking. Most of the trip is a drunken blur, and he apparently sleeps with Jerome's childhood friend. Back in Illinois, he immediately confesses to Katherine. Feeling that he has failed both personally and professionally, increasingly obsessed with thoughts of guilt and death, Charles slashes his wrists and is carried away in an ambulance. He gives a signal to start a recording. The last thing to appear is a poem in which Charles tells his brother to remember their life in North Dakota and their experience there, because the bond between them is formed by their memories of each other.

*Themes and Meanings*

The importance of memory is the main theme of *Born Brothers*. Events themselves are less important than what Charles remembers about them and what connections he makes among them. Through this process, he discerns a pattern, an emotional frame-work that enables him to function and gives him the will to go on living.

Some memories evoke feelings of grief, loss, or guilt; others create a sense of being connected to family members who care. Often, the two types are juxtaposed. Immediately after Charles remembers his mother's funeral, there is a radio script in which he tells about the birth of his son. The last section, called "Last Light," ends with his suicide attempt, but it begins with Charles walking over the farm in North Dakota to which he and his family have moved, thinking about the ways in which he has changed, changes that will allow him to survive.

At the worst of times, Charles seeks death as a release from his painful memories.

Once, when remembering his suicide attempt, Charles says that the death of his mother left him so unattached to life that he could sever that cord. The memories of his family forge ties, however; Charles, through this process of remembering, maintains and reinforces those ties.

The relationship between Jerome and Charles is the most important one. They are like yin and yang, two parts of a whole. Charles wants to be a doctor but ends up in speech and theater. Jerome wants to study speech and theater but studies medicine. Charles marries Katherine, a woman who reminds him of Jerome, fair-haired with the same blue eyes; Jerome marries Julie, a woman like Charles, dark and skillful with words.

No one can comfort Charles as Jerome does. The book opens with Charles remembering his anticipation of Jerome's visit to New York, a visit that has a healing effect on him. Fragments about this visit appear throughout the book. At the end of the book, when Charles is overcome with feelings of guilt and failure, he remembers frantically trying to get to the place where he was to meet Jerome. No one can hurt him as Jerome can, either. Charles is devastated when Jerome sides with the boy who had been taunting him. Jerome is driving the car when Charles is badly injured. These incidents seem almost self-destructive.

Although the relationship between Charles and Jerome is most important, the pattern existed before they were born, and it changes as they grow older. Jerome, named for their mother's favorite brother, who died young, is more like their mother. Charles, named for his father's father, is more like their father. When Charles looks at Jerome, he sees his mother's eyes and her concern. When he looks in the mirror, he sees his father. As the years pass, they go in opposite directions, and Jerome cannot help Charles through the crisis that leads to his suicide attempt. Charles realizes that only Katherine, who reminds him of Jerome, can help him through to the "other side."

The older Charles who has survived the suicide attempt has put his life together. His religious belief based on the study of scripture has formed a new connection with God and other believers. He has moved back to North Dakota, to the land he associates with his mother, thus reestablishing that connection. He has a son who reminds him so much of Jerome that he sometimes thinks of him as a brother rather than as a son. The process of remembering helps him to understand the pattern of his past life and the new pattern that has been woven, one that allows him to survive.

*Critical Context*

*Born Brothers* is Larry Woiwode's fourth novel, the second to deal with the Neumiller family. The first, *Beyond the Bedroom Wall: A Family Album* (1970), was nominated for both the National Book Award and the National Book Critics Circle Award. It includes many of the same characters and covers many of the same events, but it is told from different perspectives by several members of the family. Memory is an important theme in this book also; as its subtitle suggests, it is like a series of snapshots. It stops before Charles experiences the crisis that leads to his suicide attempt, however, and readers do not see how his life has changed. Because the older and wiser character of Charles appears in *Born Brothers*, the overall impression is much different.

Several parts of *Beyond the Bedroom Wall* were originally published as short stories, many of which appeared in *The New Yorker*. Several of these, plus three more written between 1982 and 1989, have been published in their original form in a book called *The Neumiller Stories* (1989).

*Bibliography*
Field, Michele. "Larry Woiwode." *Publishers Weekly* 234 (August 5, 1988); 67-68. Includes biographical information relevant to stories about the Neumiller family and discusses the background of the writing of *Born Brothers*.
Freise, Kathy. "Home Again on the Prairie." *North Dakota Horizons* 23 (Summer, 1993): 19-23. Details Woiwode's connections with the state and its role in his books dealing with the Neumiller family.
Scheick, William J. "Memory in Larry Woiwode's Novels." *North Dakota Quarterly* 53, no. 3 (1985): 29-40. Scheick discusses the importance of memory in three of Woiwode's novels, *What I'm Going to Do, I Think* (1969), *Beyond the Bedroom Wall*, and *Poppa John* (1981). He identifies two types of memories, those that make a character feel guilt and long for death and those that develop a sense of connection to one's family. The ability to order these allows Woiwode's characters to achieve a balance between them.
Woiwode, Larry. "Homeplace, Heaven or Hell." *Renascence* 44, no. 1 (1991): 3-16. Woiwode discusses the problem of being considered merely a regional writer because he writes about the Midwest. He says that all writers must write about some place, and only geographical chauvinism makes one place better than another. The author also asserts that the main duty of a Christian writer is to write the truth, which means to write about a place in precise detail.
_____ . Interview by Ed Block, Jr. *Renascence* 44, no. 1 (1991): 17-30. Woiwode explains his views on the lack of genuine emotion and standards in much modern fiction. He explains his spiritual conversion and his reasons for moving back to North Dakota. The fragmentation and discontinuity in the structure of *Born Brothers* are used, Woiwode says, because he wants readers to experience the inside of the central character's mind and his struggle.

*Eunice Pedersen Johnston*

# BRENDAN

*Author:* Frederick Buechner (1926-    )
*Type of plot:* Historical
*Time of plot:* The sixth century
*Locale:* Ireland, Wales, and the North Atlantic Ocean
*First published:* 1987

> *Principal characters:*
> BRENDAN, the book's protagonist, an Irish cleric and voyager, the alleged
>     discoverer of the New World
> FINN, the book's narrator, Brendan's faithful companion
> ERC, the bishop responsible for Brendan's education and upbringing
> CROSAN, one of Brendan's crew members
> COLMAN, a powerful poet who converts to Christianity and takes up the
>     monastic life
> ITA, an abbess, Brendan's educator
> BRIGID, a saint, Brendan's inspiration

*The Novel*

Although it is set in the sixth century and features many of the historical personages who gave significant impetus to the learning, building, and evangelizing that distinguished the onset of Christianity in Ireland, *Brendan* is less a historical novel than a meditation on the profound simplicities of the religious faith. It takes as its focus the remarkable career of Saint Brendan and through it represents the spirit of the age. The period is depicted as one in which the human mind was more liable to be overwhelmed by the proximity of God's presence in the world and when the world of creation impressed itself more immediately and strikingly on the senses of those who lived in it.

As the historical note at the end of the novel makes clear, the protagonist Brendan is noteworthy for a number of different reasons. The fact that he was a saint is one obvious reason for his significance. He was also an important churchman, and he founded the monastic settlement of Clonfert, a name that survives in contemporary Ireland as that of a Catholic diocese. Yet these achievements, relevant as they are to an appreciation of the reality of the protagonist's context, pale in comparison to Brendan's legendary status. From at least the tenth century onward, Brendan's name has been synonymous with voyages of discovery.

Two of these voyages are recounted in the novel, the first by Brendan himself in what is in effect a ship's log. Nothing more than extremely localized geographical locations and climatic conditions are provided in this clearly incomplete narrative of the journey. Internal evidence suggests that the coast of Iceland is sighted. Of much greater importance is the second voyage, an account of which is provided by the novel's narrator, Finn. The second voyage locates the other world of pre-Christian

Irish mythology, Tír-na-Nog, a name that means "the land of eternal youth." This landfall is not only Brendan's apotheosis as a navigator but is also the basis of his historical status as a legendary figure among whose exploits is said to be the discovery of America.

Exciting as these journeys are, however, the author carefully insinuates that these are simply a means to an end. They are simply spectacular and risky phases in a career that is replete with restlessness and dedication, and the novel itself is conceived as a biography of Brendan by his lifelong companion, Finn. For that reason, the voyages are not seen as the climax of Brendan's career; rather, they vie for significance with other episodes that have an explicit historical dimension. These episodes include the establishment of Brendan's monastic settlement at Clonfert and his trip to Wales in later life. The visit to Wales culminates with Brendan's involvement with the internal politics of Camelot and features a cameo appearance from King Artor, as he is called.

Yet while the historical element of Brendan's career is unavoidable, *Brendan* does not dwell on it. The background to the protagonist's life is economically sketched, but no effort is made to provide a comprehensive picture of the emergence and consolidation of Christianity in Ireland, of the religion's relationship with the religions it supplanted, or of the complex territorial and juridical issues that formed a constant undercurrent of turbulence in the politics of clan life in ancient Ireland. Such omissions make all the more plausible the intimate view of Brendan's career that Finn's narrative provides. The overall effect of the omissions is to emphasize the novelty and interest of Brendan, so that the view of him that ultimately emerges is of a personage who is representative of more elusive and awe-inspiring facets of humanity than those that typify a given historical period.

The novel's concentration on these facets is clearly indebted to the author's theological training and influenced by his well-known theological writings. The end that Brendan's life is understood to serve is that of maintaining a sense of spiritual wonder, an almost palpable awareness of the greatness of God's creation. Such an emphasis is maintained primarily by the impressive spiritedness and color of the novel's style. At times, the style is virtually a pastiche of the simplicity, sensoriness, and delight in detail that may be found in both the lyric poetry of early Christian Ireland and in the ornamented gospels such as the Book of Kells. A judicious sprinkling of Magical Realism also contributes to the establishment of the novel's remote and poorly documented environment. This perspective does not merely assist in underlining the element of wonder that runs throughout *Brendan*; it also makes acceptable the various miraculous events with which Brendan is involved that provide him with the basic credentials for sainthood. These events heighten and crystalize the undogmatic faith in, and commitment to, the divine dimension to the mortal lot by means of which the world of *Brendan* maintains an even keel.

*The Characters*

In *Brendan*, the protagonist's nautical attainments constituting the heart of the story are not presented as great feats of heroism in Brendan's mind. He does not see them as a means of spreading the gospel, nor—unlike in other stories about his contemporaries who leave Ireland—are they a punishment. Instead, they are presented as expressions of Brendan's naïve, foolhardy, God-seeking personality. Despite his education, Brendan remains essentially simple. His clerical eminence, established by his monastic foundation at Clonfert, is not synonymous with the secular power that abbots and other high-ranking members of the hierarchy possessed in those times. On the contrary, Brendan makes his way in ignorance and in poverty, with a humble, unassuming, and rather doubt-laden cast of mind.

Although Brendan is equipped with the power to work miracles and is able to apply that power opportunely in moments of danger, it is his humility that attracts adherents. Finn, in particular, provides a clear perspective on the combination of uncertainty and devotion that are continually at odds within Brendan. Unlike Brendan, Finn is not a cleric. He is more worldly, as his marriage and paternity suggest, and though he is touched by the wonder of the Christian message, he is less driven to experience the glory of it than is Brendan. Finn is clearly conceived as a foil to the protagonist, and his greater steadiness and narrower psychological range show Brendan in bolder relief than would be possible under more conventional narrative circumstances. The fact that Finn survives Brendan acts as a reminder that Finn embodies the less spectacular, more down-to-earth fate of the common man.

Most of the other characters may be thought of in terms of the contrast between Finn and Brendan, particularly when that contrast is seen as a complement rather than as a polarity. The combination of the mundane and the spiritual is located in the two conversion episodes in which Brendan is involved. Crosan, the court jester at the court of the High Kings at Cashel, is attracted to Brendan because of his mundanity. On the other hand, the bard Mac Lennin joins his fortunes to Brendan's on the basis of the latter's spiritual appeal. Not surprisingly, Mac Lennin eventually establishes his own monastic settlement. Even the most notable of the clerics whom Brendan encounters, such as Ita and Brigid, possess an earthiness through which their spiritual passions are articulated. This is particularly true of the vivid and volatile Brigid, with whose zeal and vigor Brendan's adventures make a stimulating comparison.

The characters' sexuality is one of the most consistent ways in which their earthiness is expressed, and their lack of prudery about sexual and other natural functions is one of the basic means by which they are revealed to be at home with themselves in the natural world. It is that sense of home, expressed in terms of self-possession, which is brought into critical focus through Brendan's character. He is the one who goes to extreme lengths in order to prove his worthiness to feel at home. By doing so, he demonstrates the relevance of the issues that his searching commitment represents.

*Themes and Meanings*

It is in the light of Brendan as at once the least assured and most courageous of the novel's characters that his voyages are to be perceived. They are presented not as remarkable feats of navigation but as practical manifestations of the mystery of faith. On his first voyage, Brendan deems it as reasonable to be guided by the sea-birds as to take commonsensical navigational decisions. His second voyage in search of the Other World is even more obviously a test of faith. More important, however, it is a provocative resolution of the test, offering a sense of reward that it is impossible to translate back into the struggle of the mortal lot.

The spectacular validation of Brendan's commitment that the discovery of Tír-na-Nog provides comes in forms that parody the solemnity that matters of holiness usually generate. Brendan reaches an eschatological epiphany—only to find it to be a combination of a zoo, a circus, and a paradise along the lines depicted by Paul Gauguin in his paintings of Tahiti. This discovery is not something Brendan can understand. The reader sees what Brendan himself finds difficult: that it is the journey and not the arrival that matters. The extent to which Brendan remains blind to this truism suggests that part of the author's intention is to portray his protagonist as a version of that traditional archetype of unworldliness, the Holy Fool.

Brendan's lack of conceptual awareness of the questing spirit within him is offset by his physical embodiment of it. There is nothing he can do to allay the promptings of his ardent and restless nature, and by accepting this fact of his life, he too finds his way in the world. The emphasis throughout *Brendan* of the physical as a manifestation of the spiritual is a persuasive means of integrating the characters with their environment. By showing how the characters themselves find such an integration natural, the novel reveals humanity's appreciation and awareness of creation. The sense of duality and alienation that modern humankind has been alleged to feel, and the so-called death of God that is frequently held to be responsible for this feeling, are counteracted here by the strength of faith that the characters are capable of generating.

The dangers of sentimentalizing the human condition of the remote and colorful characters who make plausible the world of *Brendan* are obvious. A work dealing with the issues addressed in *Brendan* could easily take the form of a simple-minded sermon on the spiritual purity of early Christian Ireland, viewing its inhabitants as people living in a land flowing with milk and honey whose lives consist of a paean of praise to everything that lives. For this reason, the harshness of life, the menace of the weather, the physical difficulties even of travel by land are vividly portrayed. The effect is that the novel, rather than being a homily, is something of a hymn to the possibilities of spiritual enlightenment and to the struggle that must necessarily attend the pursuit of anything so complex.

*Critical Context*

It is possible to see *Brendan* in a number of literary, cultural, and religious contexts. One of these is the literary tradition to which the life of Saint Brendan the navigator has given rise. The founding work of this tradition, the Latin work *Navigatio Sancti Brendani* (c. 900; the voyage of Saint Brendan), became one of the most popular legends of an age that saw the appearance of many such works and was widely known in various languages throughout Europe. Widespread awareness of this work is a reflection of the missionary presence of Irish clerics in Europe during the early medieval period. This historical fact is glanced at in *Brendan* by the inclusion among the protagonist's intimates of a character named Malo, whose name is commemorated in the noted French resort of St. Malo.

In addition, *Navigatio Sancti Brendani* belongs to the medieval Irish genre known as the *imrann*, or tales of journeys to other worlds. The genre still has imaginative appeal. The modern Irish poet Paul Muldoon has written poems within the loosely defined specifications of the *imrann*, and Seamus Heaney, the best-known Irish poet of the postwar period, has included a poem, "The Disappearing Island," inspired by an incident in Brendan's voyages in his collection *The Haw Lantern* (1987).

Frederick Buechner's reputation as a novelist who addresses important theological issues has been highly regarded since his first novel, *A Long Day's Dying* (1950). In his early work, he located his concerns in contemporary settings. A more imaginatively free treatment of these concerns is what distinguishes novels such as *Brendan* and *Godric* (1980), the life of a twelfth century saint. In addition, his work has gained from his theological writings, which not only seek to disseminate the Christian vision, as in *Telling the Truth: The Gospel as Tragedy, Comedy, and Fairy Tale* (1977), but also meditate on its wonder, relevance, and appeal. The confluence of the various traditions in *Brendan* suggests the continuing fascination of the sense of disturbing renewal that is such a dramatic component of the Christian message.

*Bibliography*

Anderson, Chris. "The Very Style of Faith: Frederick Buechner as Homilist and Essayist." *Christianity and Literature* 38 (Winter, 1989): 7-21. Focuses on Buechner's nonfiction, but with many insights that make the full purpose and interest of his fiction more accessible.

Davies, Marie-Helene. *Laughter in a Genevan Gown: The Works of Frederick Buechner, 1970-1980*. Grand Rapids, Mich.: Eerdmans, 1983. The most comprehensive introduction to the life and work of Frederick Buechner, locating both author and works in the context of their religious background. A useful orientation for a reading of *Brendan*.

Nelson, Rudolph L. " 'The Doors of Perception': Mystical Experience in Buechner's Fiction." *Southwest Review* 68 (Summer, 1983): 266-273. Stresses the visionary element in Buechner's work and how it assists in the articulation of his fiction's overall point of view. A sense of the position of *Brendan* in the development of Buechner's imaginative output may be inferred.

O'Faolain, Julia. "St. Patrick Monkeys Around." *The New York Times Book Review* 92 (August 9, 1987): 15. A sympathetic review, informative and appreciative of the novel's excursion into the world of Celtic Christianity.

Severin, Timothy. *The Brendan Voyage*. New York: McGraw-Hill, 1978. An account of a detailed reconstruction of Saint Brendan's alleged voyage to America, using the same kind of vessel and the same apparent route.

*George O'Brien*

# THE BRICK PEOPLE

*Author:* Alejandro Morales (1944-    )
*Type of plot:* Historical realism
*Time of plot:* The 1890's to the 1940's
*Locale:* Southern California
*First published:* 1988

Principal characters:
OCTAVIO REVUELTAS, a worker in the Simons brickyard
NANA DE LEÓN REVUELTAS, a strong worker, mother, and wife
WALTER SIMONS, the son of the brick company's founder
MALAQUIAS DE LEÓN, one of the first workers to arrive at the newly built brickyard
ROSENDO GUERRERO, the worker who lays out the plan of the original brickyard
ARTURO REVUELTAS, the eldest son of Octavio and Nana

*The Novel*

Based in part on the actual experiences of the author's parents (to whom the book is dedicated), *The Brick People* is the story of several generations of Anglo and Chicano/Mexicano families and their interactions in Southern California in the first half of the twentieth century. The principal clans are the Simons and the Revueltas families, representing the capitalist and working classes respectively.

The novel begins in 1892, with Rosendo Guerrero laying out the ground plan for the original Simons brickyard in Pasadena, California. The coordinates of the plan are based on an Aztec mandala, suggesting that the legacy of the indigenous cultures of the region lie buried under the ground. This idea is reinforced by the figure of Doña Eulalia, who identifies with an ancient oak tree and who turns into millions of brown insects upon her death.

Joseph Simons, the eldest son of Reuben Simons, the brick-making dynasty's founder, makes every attempt to keep his workers complacent. One of his greatest concerns is the worldwide increase in radical unionism. When a mass grave of Chinese workers is found on the brickyard grounds, Joseph notifies the authorities and orders that the bodies be burned so as to preclude any labor unrest. Joseph's relationship with his younger brother Walter is strained at best; he finds Walter to be arrogant and at odds with his own political views. A third brother, Orin Elmer, is a physical and intellectual weakling who is unable to participate in the family business.

Walter Simons is an "enlightened capitalist" who seeks to understand Mexican culture in order to make better use of his workers. On the suggestion of Rosendo Guerrero, Walter undertakes a fact-finding trip to Mexico, where he experiences firsthand the daily workings of U.S. imperialism under the dictator Porfirio Díaz. In the state of Chihuahua, he confers with William Randolph Hearst and other California businesspeople and witnesses the abuses of the hacienda system, including a massacre of peasants by government forces.

Upon Walter's return, the Simons company begins construction on a new brickyard in the Los Angeles suburb of Montebello. In the wake of the San Francisco earthquake of 1906, demands for building materials increase dramatically; the Simons business expands at an incredible rate. Rosendo decides to promote one of his workers, Gonzalo Pedroza, to the status of foreman. Gonzalo will become one of the most powerful and hated figures at the brickyard. The arrival of Malaquias de León and his family marks a significant moment in the history of the brickyard, for it coincides with the Mexican Revolution of 1910, the tremendous rise in immigration to the United States, and the dissemination of socialist and communist ideology throughout the Southwest. Orin Elmer's death (and the consumption of his body by brown insects) marks an end to the initial stage of the narrative.

The tension between the Simons brothers, Joseph and Walter, is aggravated when the two compete for economic control of the family assets. Walter's decision to build a home in Los Angeles essentially makes him an absentee owner at the Montebello brickyard, where recently arrived workers from Mexico are becoming more politicized. The departure of Malaquias de León coincides with the increased importance of Octavio Revueltas, who marries Malaquias' daughter, Nana, in 1926. The stock-market crash of 1929 and the resulting Depression worsen economic conditions for the entire country. Some of the Simons workers (with Octavio as their leader) establish contact with various union organizers, despite harassment from the Simons family and the foreman Gonzalo Pedroza. The Long Beach earthquake of 1933 marks the symbolic end of the boom in the brick industry, since newer and more reliable building materials have been invented.

The Simons workers finally walk out, but the strike is broken with use of poor African American workers. The Simons workers break ranks, some of them return to work, other are reduced to desperation and cynicism. The events of World War II overshadow whatever problems had existed previously: Mexican Americans serve proudly in the U.S. military, Japanese Americans are interned, the Zoot Suit riots (in which Anglo sailors attacked Chicanos) break out in Los Angeles, and Simons workers leave the brickyard to take jobs in wartime industries. Once outside the walls of the yard, Mexican families experience racial discrimination with regard to housing and bank loans. The Revueltas family is forced to move back to the home of Octavio's parents. News arrives of Walter Simons' death by choking on brown insects.

The final chapter consists of Octavio's memories of his family's original journey north from Mexico. The novel ends on an optimistic note: The Revueltas family is building a new home and moving ever so tentatively into the middle class.

*The Characters*

Octavio is a complex character who gambles compulsively and who is often absent from his family, yet he commands the respect of most readers for his sense of social justice and his dedication to his children. He functions as the radicalized worker who decides to fight the exploitation to which he has been subjected, and he provides an opportunity for the reader to learn something about the multiethnic unions that existed in Southern California throughout the 1920's and 1930's. Octavio is the first-generation immigrant whose children will live better than he did thanks in large part to their parents' hard work.

As a child, Nana de León Revueltas experiences discrimination because of her family's poverty; at one point, she meets and identifies with an African American baseball player. Once married to Octavio, she provides a solid base for her family even as she struggles to better their living conditions by making contacts outside the closed circle of Simons workers. In many ways, she is a proto-feminist character who insists upon equal status with her husband, though always within the limits of traditional Mexican values.

Walter Simons inherits a family business from wealthy parents. Unlike his brother Joseph, Walter attempts to understand Mexican culture, not because he is socially progressive but because he wants to know how to better manage his workers. He believes that if the brickyard satisfies the basic needs of the workers and their families, the threat of unionism and strikes will not arise. As a representative of "benign capitalism," Walter is the ideological foil to Octavio Revueltas and the union movement.

Malaquias de León is a precursor to Octavio's radicalism in that he is the first character who challenges the arrangement at the brickyard and decides to leave its confines in order to seek economic independence.

Rosendo Guerrero functions as a vehicle for the indigenous elements of Chicano/Mexicano culture. He is in touch with the ancient traditions and myths that periodically assert themselves over and against the rationalization of society by capitalism and Anglo puritanism.

Arturo Revueltas represents the younger generation in the novel, already anglicized to a certain extent and less familiar with Mexican traditions. His difficulty with language learning typifies the problems of all children of non-English-speaking immigrants, yet the novel presents bilingualism itself as a gift.

*Themes and Meanings*

The novel is a fictional treatment of Chicano/Mexicano history, specifically the periods immediately before, during, and after the Mexican Revolution. *The Brick People* represents for the reader Chicano involvement in a series of key historical events, ranging from the Díaz dictatorship in Mexico, to the Mexican Revolution, to the Great Depression, to successful and unsuccessful strikes organized by Mexican, Japanese, and Filipino farm workers in the 1930's, to World War II. The novel's historical sweep is grounded in the everyday lives of engaging and lifelike characters.

The text is structured upon the relationship between the Simons and Revueltas families. If the Simons family represents (on a small scale) the powerful U.S. industrialist class and, by extension, capital itself, the Revueltas family (the name means "uprisings" in Spanish) symbolizes the Chicano/Mexicano working class whose interests are necessarily opposed to those of their bosses. In addition to this political subtext, the novel incorporates images of nature (insects, earthquakes, serpents) and American Indian societies (Aztec deities, the mandala) that suggest that there are more powerful forces at work than the dominant Anglo culture may be equipped to recognize. The recurring image of the brown insects may be linked to the Chicano people in general (as it has in other works of Chicano literature)—the despised yet persistent "cockroach people" who survive against all odds.

In the character of Nana, the novel constructs a model for Chicanas that incorporates specific values of traditional Mexican society even as it breaks with certain limitations placed on women. The entire question of gender is an important undercurrent throughout the text.

By linking the important issues of class, gender, and ethnicity within the frame of a historical novel, *The Brick People* provides readers with a fascinating account of a particularly rich episode of Chicano history.

*Critical Context*

*The Brick People*, Alejandro Morales' fourth novel, is undoubtedly his most personal in that it is a fictionalized account of his parents' life. Unlike his earlier texts, which often have a fragmented structure, *The Brick People* is organized as a relatively straightforward historical novel; it follows the chronology of the early twentieth century with references to key events such as the Great Depression and World War II. The combination of historical fact and elements of fantasy places the novel in the Magical Realist tradition of contemporary Latin American literature associated with Alejo Carpentier, Gabriel García Márquez, and others.

Morales was one of the first Chicano novelists at a time (the late 1970's) when Chicano literature was not yet accepted as an important area of American studies. Chicano texts were not included in the curriculum of major universities; Chicano writers and scholars in many English and Spanish departments were greeted with outright hostility. In a real sense, Morales' role in the U.S. academy was to be one of the founders of an emergent discipline. By the time *The Brick People* appeared (written entirely in English), Chicano literature enjoyed an international readership and academic respectability, and Morales was counted among the most influential Chicano critics and writers of fiction.

*Bibliography*

Gonzales-Berry, Erlinda. "Alejandro Morales." In *Chicano Literature: A Reference Guide*, edited by Julio A. Martínez and Francisco A. Lomelí. Westport, Conn.: Greenwood Press, 1985. Contains important biographical information as well as interesting details of the publishing history of Morales' first two novels.

Hernández, Roberto E. "*The Brick People.*" *Vista Magazine* (November 27, 1988): 14. Short summary of the novel with special attention paid to the characters Nana and Octavio Revueltas. Hernández, a history teacher at Miami-Dade Community College, is troubled by Morales' "fascination with the grotesque." Nevertheless, he recommends: *"The Brick People* should be read by Americans of all walks of life, but it will strike a familiar note in those of us who came to North America in the hope of finding more than one alternative to life."

Kaganoff, Penny. *"The Brick People." Publishers Weekly* 233 (June 3, 1988): 79. A brief review that identifies Morales as a "Mexican" writer. The author concludes: "In the hopeful but unsentimental novel, amid the red dust of the brickyards and periodic earthquakes of California . . . the Mexicans struggle to find acceptance and to claim their adopted land as their own."

Morales, Alejandro. Interview by Yves Charles Grandjeat and Alfonso Rodríguez. *Confluencia* 7 (Fall, 1991): 109-114. Morales talks about his interest in history, the construction of Chicano identity, and the social responsibility of the writer. His remarks on *The Brick People* are especially interesting.

Waldron, John V. "Uncovering History in the 'Post Modern Condition': (Re)writing the Past, (Re)righting Ourselves in Alejandro Morales' *The Brick People." Confluencia* 7 (Spring, 1992): 99. A somewhat confusing application of contemporary literary theory to *The Brick People.*

*George Mariscal*

# BROWN GIRL, BROWNSTONES

*Author:* Paule Marshall (1929-     )
*Type of plot:* Bildungsroman
*Time of plot:* 1939 to the late 1940's
*Locale:* Brooklyn, New York
*First published:* 1959

> *Principal characters:*
> SELINA BOYCE, the protagonist, the bright and talented daughter of immigrants from Barbados
> SILLA BOYCE, Selina's mother, a hard-edged immigrant woman determined to get ahead
> DEIGHTON BOYCE, Selina's father and Silla's husband, a dreamer who drifts from one would-be profession to another
> INA BOYCE, Selina's sister, who is browbeaten by Silla into submission
> BERYL CHALLENOR, Selina's best friend when she is young
> CLIVE SPRINGER, a Barbadian World War II veteran with whom Selina has an affair
> RACHEL FINE, a dancer who encourages Selina to dance in a public recital

*The Novel*

Written as an attempt by Paule Marshall to reflect on her own life, *Brown Girl, Brownstones* is an autobiographically based novel about a young black woman growing up among the Barbadian immigrant community of Brooklyn in the 1940's. From the beginning, *Brown Girl, Brownstones* is a novel about the conflicting set of values represented by Deighton and Silla Boyce, with Selina, their daughter and the novel's main character, caught in the middle. On one side is Deighton Boyce, idle because he lacks the drive and discipline to embrace a culture and its materialistic values that he knows devalue him. Deighton studies to become an accountant, but never becomes one; he studies to learn to play the trumpet, but never performs. Opposing him is Silla Boyce, who embraces a hard-edged, penny-conscious immigrant ethic. Silla is determined to do what it takes to own land and get ahead materially. Though Selina identifies explicitly with her father throughout much of the novel, she slowly comes to realize that her deeper affinities are to her mother.

At the novel's start, Selina is ten, but she is described by the narrator as possessing a manner seemingly wise beyond her years, with eyes "too old . . . in their centers." When her father unexpectedly inherits a two-acre plot of land, he begins dreaming of moving back to Barbados. Silla, who has no intention of returning to her homeland and who resents her husband's dreaming as much as his idleness, plots to have the land sold.

The first two short sections of *Brown Girl, Brownstones*, "A Long Day and a Long Night" and "Pastorale," establish the close relationship between Selina and her father, the emerging similarities between Selina and her mother, and the frequently unstated attraction and respect between Silla and Deighton that underlies their fighting. The third section, "The War," covers the years of World War II, years when the conflict between Silla and Deighton erupts into a domestic war.

After Deighton is notified that he has inherited land, Silla plans to have the land sold behind his back. She succeeds, but because the check is issued in Deighton's name, she cannot stop him from getting access to the "nine hundred odd dollars" payment for the land, all of which he spends on gifts for himself and his family in a single extravagant shopping binge. For a short time, he gets a job working at a factory, but an accident sends him to the hospital, where he finds newspapers printed by a religious sect led by a man called Father Peace. Quickly accepting the gospel of this organization, he becomes a devoted follower, and when he is released from the hospital, he spends most of his time praying to Father Peace or attending meetings. Eventually, he moves out to live and work in a coffee shop run by the Father Peace group. In retaliation, Silla has him arrested for desertion, and he is deported back to Barbados on a ship. On the day World War II ends, however, a message arrives saying that Deighton jumped or fell overboard in sight of land and drowned.

In the fourth section, "Selina," Selina's own personal growth and conflicts become the agents of change and chaos in her family. Now on the verge of entering college, she begins this part of the novel in an extended state of grief over her father's death. Blaming Silla for Deighton's death and unwilling to accept her mother's values, Selina nevertheless goes with her mother to attend a meeting of the Barbadian Association, a group devoted to upward social mobility for Barbadian immigrants. Selina, though, storms out of the meeting condemning the association as "narrow-minded," "selfish," and "pitiful." She is followed out of the meeting by Clive Springer, a Barbadian former soldier and would-be artist. After a night of wandering together, the two make love on a park bench.

Clive and Selina continue to have a clandestine relationship, and Selina plots to get back into the good graces of the Barbadian Association. She hopes to win a scholarship the group is offering, but she wants to use the money to live with Clive. Fooling the members of the association proves to be easy, and she does indeed win the scholarship. Before the check is actually awarded, however, Selina and Clive argue over Clive's relationship with his mother. Selina realizes that Clive would never leave his mother, and she is also forced to reexamine her own values. Coming to the conclusion that she has no right to behave with such contempt toward the members of the association, she publicly declines to accept the scholarship money, and she admits that she had been trying to manipulate the association for reasons she no longer respects. She also realizes that although she has always wanted to identify with her father, she has always been much more like her mother in spirit. At the end, though the mother and daughter fight once more over Selina's plans to go to Barbados for at least a little while, Silla implicitly gives her daughter her approval and her blessing by accepting Selina as a woman every bit as strong as Silla herself is.

## The Characters

Selina Boyce is very much the central character of *Brown Girl, Brownstones*. Even though the novel also offers glimpses into the lives of many members of the Barbadian community and details the struggle between Silla and Deighton Boyce over power and values, these other people are seen from Selina's perspective. The novel's central consideration is the influence of various people and forces on Selina's development. Additionally, although Selina is occasionally described from a third-person-omniscient point of view, the majority of the novel is told from a third-person-limited point of view that describes what Selina perceives and how she reacts.

At the novel's beginning, Selina is still an adolescent girl, but she is respected by her parents not only for being headstrong but also for being in many respects the emotional center of her family. As the conflict between her parents develops, Selina explicitly tries to identify with her father; however, she is in fact more similar to her mother. Both love Deighton Boyce and seek his love in return, but neither knows how to deal with his unhappiness or seeming aimlessness. After her father's death, she falls in love with Clive Springer, a man who, like Deighton, is an idle dreamer. Selina's plans to leave with Clive and save him from his family and his own withdrawal make her relationship to Clive seem remarkably like Silla's relationship to Deighton. Clive, like Deighton, is willing to be controlled by a woman of stronger will but is not willing or able to change. Selina finally recognizes that she cannot control Clive, and she abandons her hopes for the two of them, planning instead to travel to Barbados alone.

Silla and Deighton represent opposing viewpoints of the immigrant's plight in America. Silla focuses primarily on the possibilities of land ownership and wealth her adopted society offers; Deighton sees primarily the cost of living in America as a West Indian immigrant and treats the benefits contemptuously. Though their positions are squarely opposed to one another, and they battle openly, they are each also aware of the extent to which they need the other. Deighton needs Silla for material, daily survival, and Silla needs Deighton for his sense of life and wonder.

Clive is, like Deighton, a dreamer and a would-be artist. Though Clive is more intellectual by nature than Deighton, he is no more effective, and he is just as dependent on strong-willed women—his mother and Selina—as Deighton was before his death.

Selina's friend and classmate, Rachel Fine, is one of the few developed white characters in the novel, and to a large extent, she represents the community of art and artists to Selina. Her friendship and encouragement of Selina's dancing provide Selina with exactly the type of encouragement Selina could not find in the Barbadian Association. When another white woman blithely insults Selina's skin color and accent after a dance recital, however, Selina begins to realize that she cannot simply replace her Barbadian community with an artistic community. This understanding supports Selina's decision to travel to Barbados to search for values.

## Themes and Meanings

It is typical for a *Bildungsroman* to focus on the growth and education of a young person. In depicting a protagonist's maturation and acceptance or rejection of social values, the novelist can hold those values themselves up to inspection. This is certainly true of *Brown Girl, Brownstones*.

Selina, like her father and like Clive, intuitively rejects the impulse to get ahead at any cost, an impulse best represented by her mother and by the Barbadian Association. What she cannot simply reject, however, is the strength and direction of character that allows Silla to work long hours at menial wages to support and improve the lot of her family. Despite Silla's flaws, Selina respects her as a strong woman.

So long as Deighton is besieged daily by Silla and is struggling to find a sense of self-respect not founded upon the assimilationist and materialist values of Silla and the Barbadian Association, Selina can use his lonely anguish as the focus of her own anger and uncertainty. Thus, Selina supports her father throughout much of the novel because he so clearly needs her emotional support, whereas Silla does not seem to.

After Deighton's death, Selina faces the task of resolving for herself the conflict of values that was always embodied by the struggle between Silla and Deighton. It is in the spirit of resolving these issues that she attends her first meeting of the Barbadian Association. Yet because of her anger toward Silla and the members of the association for their treatment of Deighton, and because of her continued rejection of the association's values, she storms out of the first meeting. Clive, who intercepts her as she leaves, proves to share her reservations about the values of the association.

When Selina begins her affair with Clive, she does not appreciate how closely she is reenacting the attitudes and roles of her mother. Like Silla, Selina manipulates those around her, especially her mother, the association, and Clive. Her mother and the association—both of whom recognize Selina as a potential leader and want her to succeed—prove to be remarkably easy to manipulate. Clive, who is weaker willed than either Silla or Selina, proves to be as difficult for Selina to manipulate as Deighton was for Silla.

When Selina, after a successful dance recital, is humiliated by a white woman (who compares Selina to a housekeeper she once hired and asks Selina to say something in her charming West Indian accent), Selina begins to see the members of the association in a new light. Recognizing not only that they have had to struggle throughout their working lives in America with such racial discrimination, but also that they have been strong enough to protect her generation from some of the most searing aspects of racism, Selina realizes that she cannot simply reject the members of the association. Because she still cannot accept their values, she decides that she must travel back to Barbados, searching for values that might be predicated on more than a desire for, or a rejection of, assimilation into the culture of mainstream America.

*Critical Context*

The critic Barbara Christian has pointed out that before the publication of *Brown Girl, Brownstones*, there were very few novels written by black women focusing on the interior life of a black woman. The two most notable precedents to *Brown Girl, Brownstones* are Zora Neale Hurston's *Their Eyes Were Watching God* (1937) and

Gwendolyn Brooks' *Maud Martha* (1953), neither of which was widely known when Marshall was writing her first novel. Against such a context of silence about black women's inner lives, Paule Marshall's coming-of-age story can be read as a demand that the voices of black female writers be recognized as culturally significant.

Yet because it appeared in the midst of the civil rights era and immediately prior to the 1960's, Marshall's inquiry into social values by a young person can also be read as a prelude to and an affirmation of a social upheaval that was then forming. Like many of the college activists of the 1960's, Selina is a young person challenging her community over its values and simultaneously searching for her own values.

Although it was favorably reviewed when it first appeared, *Brown Girl, Brownstones* was widely neglected for many years. Even as the works of Toni Morrison and Alice Walker during the 1970's created a widespread interest in the works of black women writers, interest in Marshall's first novel remained relatively sparse. The appearance of Barbara Christian's landmark study: *Black Women Writers: The Development of a Tradition, 1892-1976* in 1980 and the republication of *Brown Girl, Brownstones* by the Feminist Press in 1981 helped to rekindle interest in the book. With the publication of two well-received novels, *Praisesong for the Widow* (1983) and *Daughters* (1991), Marshall's reputation continued to grow. With the growth of her literary reputation has come the critical recognition of her first novel, not only as a worthy coming-of-age tale but also as a pivotal text in the development of twentieth century African American literature.

*Bibliography*
Christian, Barbara. *Black Women Novelists: The Development of a Tradition, 1892-1976*. Westport, Conn.: Greenwood Press, 1980. In a landmark critical study of black women writers, Christian praises Marshall as a consummate sculptor of character. Christian particularly praises Marshall's ability to dispense with stereotypes and present multidimensional characters who have a complex relationship to history and culture.
Christol, Hélène. "Paule Marshall's Bajan Women in *Brown Girl, Brownstones*." In *Women and War: The Changing Status of American Women from the 1930's to the 1950's*, edited by Maria Diedrich and Dorothea Fischer-Hormung. Providence, R. I.: Berg, 1990. An excellent essay that focuses especially on the mother-daughter relationship between Selina and Silla. Notes that despite the frequent fighting, theirs is the most constructive relationship in the book.
Evans, Mari, ed. *Black Women Writers (1950-1980): A Critical Evaluation*. Garden City, N.Y.: Anchor Press/Doubleday, 1983. This extensive collection of essays by and about black women writers contains two essays about Marshall's works. Eugenia Collier's article focuses on the tendency for characters in Marshall's novels to develop from divided selves into fully integrated whole selves. John McCluskey's essay explores the interplay of social and personal forces in Marshall's fiction.
Pettis, Joyce. "A *MELUS* Interview: Paule Marshall." *MELUS* 17 (Winter, 1991-

1992): 117-129. In this interview, Marshall talks about the genesis of several of her works, including *Brown Girl, Brownstones*.

Washington, Mary Helen. Afterword to *Brown Girl, Brownstones*, by Paule Marshall. 1959. Reprint. Old Westbury, N.Y.: Feminist Press, 1981. A brief but thoughtful exploration of the themes embodied in *Brown Girl, Brownstones*. Provides a helpful glimpse of the social context in which Marshall's novel was produced and the effects of this context on the novel itself.

*Thomas Cassidy*

# THE BURDEN OF PROOF

*Author:* Scott Turow (1949-    )
*Type of plot:* Suspense
*Time of plot:* The 1980's
*Locale:* Kindle County, a fictitious Midwestern American locale
*First published:* 1990

> *Principal characters:*
> ALEJANDRO "SANDY" STERN, a brilliant trial attorney originally from Argentina
> CLARA STERN, Stern's constant, reticent wife of thirty-one years, who commits suicide
> DIXON HARTNELL, a financial speculator who is Stern's client and his brother-in-law
> SONIA "SONNY" KLONSKY, the federal prosecutor investigating the government's case against Hartnell

*The Novel*

Based in part on the experience Scott Turow gained while working as a white-collar criminal defense counsel in Chicago, Illinois, *The Burden of Proof* employs a plot involving suicide and insider trading to explore the psyche of its protagonist, Sandy Stern. Narrated in the third person, *The Burden of Proof* consists of fifty chapters and is divided into three parts. Throughout the book, the reader shares Stern's point of view. Although Turow uses flashbacks to illuminate Stern's relationship with his wife, on the whole the plot advances in a linear fashion.

*The Burden of Proof* opens in a somewhat unorthodox fashion for a mystery, however, revealing in its first chapter that the pivotal event of the book, Clara Stern's suicide, has already taken place before the action commences. As the book opens, Stern, who has just returned from a business trip, discovers his wife's body slumped in the driver's seat of her Cadillac in the garage, dead of asphyxiation. Stern, like his children and everyone else, has difficulty coming to terms with the apparent suicide of his upright, reserved, seemingly content wife. That Clara's death was not accidental is confirmed when Stern finds a note in her handwriting that says, "Can you forgive me?" This enigmatic clue as to the reasons for her suicide is quickly followed by other equally ambiguous discoveries: Shortly before she killed herself, Clara wrote a check to an unknown payee that reduced almost to nothing Stern's prospective share of her estate, and prior to her death, she had been taking medication for a venereal disease.

The scant evidence Clara leaves behind strongly suggests a desire to punish her husband. As the understated Stern tells a police officer investigating the suicide, "Lieutenant, it should be evident that I failed to observe something I should have." In order to unravel the mystery of Clara's death, Stern must look to his own interior landscape.

The outside world quickly intrudes, however, when Stern's brother-in-law (his beloved sister's husband), Dixon Hartnell, the owner of a commodities brokerage house and apparently Stern's most significant client, is charged with illegal trading. The normally proactive, manipulative, and unprincipled Hartnell seems uncharacteristically disinterested in defending himself against the extremely serious federal charges he faces. Because the case against Hartnell implicates Stern's son-in-law, John, an employee of Hartnell's firm, Stern is forced to take an unusually active role in ferreting out the recalcitrant facts that will explain the extent of Hartnell's involvement in criminal activity.

Owing, perhaps, to his preoccupation with Clara's death, Stern fails to observe until late in the book that there is a connection between his wife's suicide and the troubles at Hartnell's firm, Maison Dixon. Hartnell's unwillingness to be forthcoming with his attorney about the former results from his involvement with the latter; gradually, Stern realizes that although his brother-in-law is innocent of charges of insider trading, he is the one who gave Clara an incurable, if comparatively innocuous, case of herpes. It is Stern's ambitious but injudicious son-in-law who carried out the illegal trades. Clara had attempted to save him, and her daughter, by drawing on money earmarked for Stern and by extracting a promise from Hartnell that he would take the blame for John's actions. In the wake of Clara's suicide—occasioned, at least in part, by her belief that the recurring nature of her disease would force her to reveal her infidelity to her husband—the typically unscrupulous Hartnell displays his own brand of honor by keeping his word to her.

While pursuing the dual mysteries that confront him, Stern must also struggle with his own part in Clara's death. He is forced to come to terms with his failures as a husband and a father—failures that stem in large measure from his commitment to his demanding legal practice. Along the way, he finds a kind of salvation in a touching, although unconsummated, love affair with the pregnant, married, former cancer patient Sonny Klonsky, who is prosecuting the government's case against Hartnell. He does not end up with Sonny, but it is largely through her agency that he comes to forgive Clara and himself, ending his story as it began some five hundred pages earlier, where it is first revealed that "full of resolve and a measure of hope, he would marry again."

## The Characters

Alejandro Stern is very much an outsider, a reserved, formal man, an Argentinean immigrant and a Jew, on whom the nickname "Sandy" sits not a little uncomfortably. Turow further distances the reader from his main character by using a third-person narrator who, although sharing Stern's point of view, frequently refers to Stern as "Mr. Alejandro Stern." Such techniques go some way toward explaining Stern's predicament in *The Burden of Proof*, his alienation from his family, his incomprehension in the face of his wife's suicide. Unfortunately, these techniques sometimes also make Stern incomprehensible to the reader, so that the mystery at the heart of the novel— why did Clara kill herself?—is never entirely resolved. Clara Stern committed suicide because of the consequences of her anger at her husband. Because the novel's focus on him is not always sharp, the causes of his wife's destructive behavior are themselves blurred.

In contrast, the portrait of Stern's antagonist, Dixon Hartnell, is vividly drawn. Here, as in John Milton's epic *Paradise Lost* (1667), the hero's opposite number is more energetic and attractive than those on the side of the angels. Indeed, Hartnell is portrayed in terms that make him out to be the devil in disguise. Toward the end of the novel, when his sins have been revealed, Hartnell tells his brother-in-law, "I've always wanted to do what other people wouldn't," to which Stern replies, "I believe that is called evil, Dixon." Although Hartnell bears the most conspicuous responsibility for Clara's death and almost manages to destroy the rest of Stern's family, he is hard to damn entirely. Stern's attitude toward Hartnell is finally disapproving but indulgent: Hartnell may be corrupt and manipulative, but he is charming and daring and—perhaps most important—uxorious. He is clearly everything that Stern is not.

The two main female characters in *The Burden of Proof* are a similar study in contrasts. Clara, like her husband, remains elusive, a kind of vacant center around which the plot revolves. This sense of absence results in part from the fact that she is dead before the novel begins. Even after Turow attempts to bring her back to life in flashbacks, however, she remains more an embodiment of principle than a human being. As Hartnell says when searching for an explanation of why he seduced her, "She was a woman to admire."

Sonny Klonsky, on the other hand, is only too mortal. A fortyish victim of breast cancer, she is also, when Stern becomes involved with her, unhappily married and pregnant with her first child. Yet Sonny is remarkably self-aware and self-possessed, and although she has far more excuses for instability than the genteel, monied Clara, she is the survivor. Doubtless it is these qualities that make her so attractive for Stern, who loves not so much the look of this younger woman as the wisdom she incorporates.

## Themes and Meanings

Sandy Stern first made his appearance as the protagonist's defense counsel in Turow's best-selling novel *Presumed Innocent* in 1987. As Turow has described the genesis of *The Burden of Proof*, it seems to have grown almost entirely out of his meditations on Stern's character:

> I had carried around with me for years this image of a guy in his mid-fifties who was getting married again. . . . Then one afternoon . . . I realized that character is Stern. I had felt bad about letting go of Stern after *Presumed Innocent*, because you don't see much inside of him in that book. I was interested in what really goes on inside this man with his exotic background and his reserved, formal exterior.

Indeed, *The Burden of Proof* is largely devoted to explorations of Stern's and other characters' psyches. While the book clearly qualifies as a mystery, it is a mystery with a difference: Not only is the victim dead from the outset, but the reasons for her death are not the obvious ones. Certainly there is enough of the usual greed and lust to propel the plot forward—the clues to Clara's death are an uncashed check for $850,000 and a prescription for medication used to combat venereal disease—but in order to discover their connection to his wife's suicide, Stern must investigate his own soul and the untold ways in which he had failed in his marriage.

*The Burden of Proof*, with its opening emphasis on Stern's marriages, is all about family, which Turow calls the "magic circle where the law ends." Clara Mittler, with her inherited wealth and good manners and her successful lawyer father, had been Stern's ticket to acceptance and success in America. In pursuing his career as a trial attorney, however, Stern seems to have lost, if not his soul, certainly his ties to his wife and children. When her youngest child left for college, Clara, seemingly desperate for human contact, finally surrendered to Hartnell's blandishments after years of putting him off. Stern did not take notice of his wife's despair, then or later. Neither did he seem to make time to develop relationships with his three children.

Stern's one strong bond is to his sister Silvia, on whom he lavishes all the courtly protectiveness and affection he possesses. Their relationship seems as ineffaceable as the Latin accent that marks Stern's speech even after decades of exile from Argentina. By such means, Turow manages to suggest at once Stern's singularity and his potential for redemption and reintegration. Finally, Stern is able to make his peace with his first wife's death and—after another death in the family, that of his old nemesis, Hartnell— marry again, thus closing the magic circle.

*Critical Context*

*The Burden of Proof* is Scott Turow's third book and second novel. After teaching creative writing at Stanford University and receiving his master's degree there in 1974, and before beginning law school at Harvard University in 1975, Turow obtained a contract for a nonfiction account of his first year of legal studies. *One L*, published in 1977, just before Turow began his final year of law school, proved to be both a critical and popular success.

After receiving his law degree, Turow worked for eight years in the U.S. Attorney's Office in Chicago, during which time he wrote his first novel. *Presumed Innocent*, published in 1987, made headlines before it appeared, largely because of the record sums of money connected with it. Turow received an advance of two hundred thousand dollars from Farrar, Straus & Giroux, the largest the publisher had ever paid for a first novel. Warner Bros. paid three million dollars for paperback rights, the highest price ever paid for reprint rights to a first novel, and film rights were sold to director Sydney Pollack for one million dollars. The hardback version stayed on best-seller lists for forty-four weeks, the paperback edition for twenty-nine weeks.

Before the publication of *Presumed Innocent*, Turow had accepted a position at a major Chicago law firm, where he worked half time while writing *The Burden of Proof*. Like its predecessor, Turow's second novel quickly became a best-seller. A third novel, *Pleading Guilty*, appeared in 1993.

Although all of Turow's works, even *One L*, are fraught with mystery, his heroes' respective moral dilemmas make his books memorable. It is the philosophical quandaries his lawyer-heroes face—those forcing them to choose between their obligation as officers of the court to uphold the "truth" and their responsibilities toward their families—that lend Turow's novels resonance.

Turow's storybook success as a writer revived the genre of the legal thriller, which has grown to accommodate lawyer-novelists such as John Grisham, whose 1991 novel *The Firm* dominated best-seller lists much as *Presumed Innocent* had done a few years earlier. Still, *Presumed Innocent* remains the standard against which the products of these other writers—and those of Turow himself—are judged. Reviews of *The Burden of Proof* were not as uniformly favorable as they had been for its predecessor. The strength of both books, however, is that they are told from the vantage point of a lawyer obsessed not so much with solving a mystery as with discovering the truth of his own involvement in an ambiguous death. The insight into the equivocal nature of morality, which seems to grow out of Turow's dual existence as a lawyer and a writer, is clearly the greatest strength of his books, helping them to rise above the conventions of their genre.

*Bibliography*

Dalton, Katherine. "Power of Attorney." *Harper's Bazaar* 123 (June, 1990): 38-39. Briefly reviews the novel, comparing it with *Presumed Innocent*. Chiefly, rehearses Turow's biography, emphasizing the phenomenal success of Turow's first novel.

Feeney, Joseph J. "Recent Fiction: The Burden of Proof." *America* 163 (October 13, 1990): 250. A highly respectful review, finding in Turow's novel an exploration of the conventions of Greek tragedy. Feeney also does a good job of analyzing Turow's style.

Gray, Paul. "Burden of Success." *Time* 135 (June 11, 1990): 68-72. Cover story on Turow, including excerpts from interviews with the author, emphasizing his biography. Reviews both *The Burden of Proof* and the film version of *Presumed Innocent*. Turow's second novel is praised for its substantial themes as well as its entertainment value.

Grisham, John. "The Rise of the Legal Thriller: Why Lawyers Are Throwing the Book at Us." *The New York Times Book Review*, October 18, 1992, 33. Locates the revival of the genre in *Presumed Innocent*, the success of which has prompted other lawyers to write about their exploits. Evaluates other contributions to the genre.

Maas, Peter. "And Scott Turow's New Mystery." *The New York Times Book Review*, June 3, 1990, 1. Compares Turow's second novel unfavorably with his first. Maas finds the pace slow, Stern poorly developed, and the book's themes overblown.

*Lisa Paddock*

# CATHERINE CARMIER

*Author:* Ernest J. Gaines (1933-      )
*Type of plot:* Historical realism
*Time of plot:* The early 1960's
*Locale:* The former slave quarter on a plantation in rural Louisiana
*First published:* 1964

>   *Principal characters:*
>      JACKSON BRADLEY, a young, educated black man determined to break
>         with his Louisiana heritage
>      BROTHER, Jackson's friend from his youth
>      RAOUL CARMIER, a proud Creole sharecropper, father to Catherine
>      CATHERINE CARMIER, Raoul's oldest daughter and main support, who
>         falls in love with Jackson
>      CHARLOTTE MOSES, Jackson's aunt and patroness
>      DELLA (JOHNSON) CARMIER, Raoul's estranged wife
>      LILLIAN CARMIER, Raoul's youngest daughter, alienated from her parents
>      MARY LOUISE, Jackson's former girlfriend
>      MADAME BAYONNE, Jackson's confidante and former teacher

*The Novel*

   There is a strong autobiographical strain in *Catherine Carmier*. Like the novel's
protagonist, Jackson Bradley, Gaines moved to California to get a decent education
and a stronger foothold on a better life than he could find at home, in the poor rural
area around New Roads, Louisiana, which, fictionalized, is the novel's setting. He
also faced a similar personal dilemma, whether to return home to teach or to seek a
more promising life elsewhere.

   By the time he finished *Catherine Carmier*, Gaines knew that writing was his life's
work, but Jackson, his fictional counterpart, has no such vision of the future. He
knows only that he cannot sacrifice himself to the seemingly futile task of trying to
educate children whose futures he perceives as singularly bleak.

   The novel is divided into three parts, each made up of several short chapters.
Throughout, Gaines uses a third-person-omniscient narrative technique, but he primarily limits forays into the thoughts of characters to those of Jackson and his
romantic nemesis, Catherine. The work also develops two distinct but parallel lines
of action. The first, dealing with Jackson's decision to leave Louisiana, centers on
Jackson and his Aunt Charlotte; the second focuses on the intense but ultimately
ill-fated love affair of Jackson and Catherine.

   Part 1 starts with the imminent arrival of Jackson on a bus from New Orleans. He
is to be met by his old friend Brother, who is introduced in the opening scene.
Catherine Carmier also waits for the same bus, which, coincidentally, carries home
Lillian, her younger sister. Thus Jackson has a brief encounter with Catherine,
revealing at the outset that there is a magnetism between them; however, they do not

begin their affair until midway through the novel.

It quickly becomes obvious that Jackson cannot find his bearings in the world of his childhood. His relationships with Brother, his former girlfriend, Mary Louise, and especially his Aunt Charlotte, although polite, are strained. Jackson knows that he cannot relate to Charlotte's church circle, but he dreads telling her the truth, that he must leave again. At a party thrown to celebrate his return, he feels more like an unwanted intruder than the guest of honor. Only Madame Bayonne, his former teacher, senses that Jackson cannot stay, and she quickly becomes his mother confessor.

Jackson's alienation is paralleled by Lillian's in the dysfunctional Carmier household. Taught to hate what her mother represents, she, too, longs to leave. She stays on, however, held by complex motives, including sibling jealousy mingled with a desire to free her sister from her unhealthy dependence on Raoul.

In part 2, Jackson and Catherine begin their affair, and Jackson tells Charlotte the truth about his plans, a revelation that almost kills her. It is her culminating disappointment in Jackson, foreshadowed by earlier revelations that he had quit going to church and had begun drinking and playing cards. Only after the Reverend Armstrong shows her that her possessiveness is destructively selfish does Charlotte forgive Jackson.

Meanwhile, the furtive, mercurial relationship between Jackson and Catherine is sexually consummated in a few stolen hours of love. Jackson cannot openly woo Catherine because her father tolerates no rivals, not even those of his own kind, Creoles of mixed racial heritage. Torn between her father and Jackson, Catherine goes through a ritual of self-loathing, marked by complex love-hate feelings for Jackson. For a time, she manages to break off the relationship, incurring Jackson's frustration and anger, even his accusation that her relationship with her father is incestuous.

In the last part of the novel, the love affair takes its final, implacable turn. Lillian secretively sends Jackson a note telling him that Catherine will be at a dance in Bayonne and urging him to go there. Jackson finds Catherine and takes her from the dance back to her house. They plan to run off together, but Raoul, cued by two black informants paid by Raoul's Cajun enemies, rushes to stop them. He and Jackson fight, and Raoul is beaten. Ironically, however, in defeat Raoul triumphs over Jackson, for Catherine at last realizes that she cannot leave her father. Jackson is once more left alone, to search for a meaningful identity that to the novel's end eludes him.

*The Characters*

Jackson is a character cut adrift from his roots, seeking to find himself. His education has put his earlier life in a sophisticated perspective that distances him from his former friends, and he resists a sympathetic engagement in their community from fears of being dragged down into a miasma of despair. He plans to leave, to continue the search for self in a world that has already scarred him with some racial bitterness. Before leaving, however, he must confront two strong adversaries.

The first is Aunt Charlotte. She has spun a moral web from which Jefferson must free himself at the cost of seeming to be a selfish ingrate. She is his patroness, and although he loves her, he knows he must disappoint her. She is a simple, strong-willed woman with a deep, abiding faith, and it is her goodness and moral rectitude that make Jefferson feel like an apostate in his darker moments. She is also the first adversary in Jackson's personal rite of passage.

The other iron-willed character is Raoul Carmier, Jackson's rival for Catherine's love and loyalty. He represents a very different sort of challenge. A proud, unyielding man, Raoul is also an imposing blocking figure. He dominates his world, made narrow by his hatred for whites and blacks alike. He treats his wife, Della, like a household servant, elevating Catherine, his favorite, to surrogate spouse. For her part, Catherine is drawn to Raoul's strength, while he, from selfish designs, has cut her off from any sort of mature relationship with other men.

In some ways Raoul is admirable. He is a hard worker who, unlike most black sharecroppers, refuses to give up the struggle against the Cajuns who have slowly displaced the blacks on the plantation's land. To survive against them, he must work long hours, plowing his fields with mules because he is too poor to afford motorized equipment. Yet there is also something ruthless and sinister about Raoul, and by the end of the novel, it is intimated that he had killed Mark, Della's son, born from a brief extramarital liaison with a black man. Strangely, it is only when he reveals his guilt that Della is once more drawn to him.

Catherine's relationship with her father hints of latent incest, but it is never expressed in overt behavior. Like her mother, she has had an amatory adventure with another man, a Creole farmer, who fathered her child, Nelson. The farmer, however, was run off by Raoul, and until her affair with Jackson, she has had no other man in her life except her father. Despite her enchanting good looks and strong passion, she is content to be her father's companion. So imbued is she with loyalty to Raoul that her love for Jackson is accompanied by feelings of guilt, betrayal, and self-hatred. At the end, Jackson is simply unable to overcome these conflicting emotions and loses the enigmatic Catherine to Raoul.

*Themes and Meanings*

*Catherine Carmier* investigates complex human relationships that in part evolve from the particular time and place in which the novel is set. Of primary importance is the racial heritage of the principal characters, for it weighs heavily on the lives of all of them, and especially on their sense of belonging and commitment.

For Aunt Charlotte, custom bound, commitment is to be found in service to the community, to the folk, accomplished principally by bringing everyone into the greater family, represented by the church. It seems a time-honored maternal mission that accepts self-sacrifice as a communal virtue, and it is strong among persecuted peoples, who, as individuals, are powerless to shape their own destinies. For the black, rural Louisiana matron living in the early 1960's, that life could offer a quiet, abiding dignity, as it does for Charlotte.

For Jackson, however, it offers only a dead end. Keenly observant, Jackson sees that Aunt Charlotte's self-sacrifice leads only to the ignominy of an obscure grave. Furthermore, he knows that what little the blacks of the quarter possess is being lost to aggressive Cajun farmers, and he wants no role in that collapsing, suffocating world. He knows that he must seek hope and personal fulfillment elsewhere.

In its subtle way, *Catherine Carmier* offers a strong indictment of racism, which has an important negative impact on the lives of all the characters and is at least the indirect cause of much misery. Although it is an oppressive cross that Jackson bitterly bears, its chief victim is Raoul Carmier. He is a man wedged between the black and white races who, because he can identify with neither, despises both. His angry, erosive intolerance weighs heavily on his family and all but destroys it. His estrangement from Della had begun because she, a mulatto who does not share his hatred for blacks, had tried to befriend the inhabitants of the quarter, and she is finally driven by the resulting desperate loneliness into the brief affair with Mark's father. After Mark's birth, she becomes a non-person in her own house, although she does give birth to another daughter, Lillian, who is Raoul's child.

Lillian becomes the unwanted, outcast child, sent away to be reared by relatives. Deprived of parental love, she is emotionally scarred with spite, even hatred, for both her mother and father. Raoul hardly acknowledges her, caring only for Catherine and the land. Lillian's resentment leads to her attempts to promote the relationship between Catherine and Jackson, which, she knows, can destroy her father. Bigotry is thus a poison that runs deep in the Carmier family well. It is also a fundamental and insidious fact of life for all the main characters in the novel, and at least the indirect source of most of their troubles.

*Critical Context*

*Catherine Carmier* was Gaines's first novel. Although it was not a critical success, it revealed the author's unquestioned skill as raconteur and established the fictional locus that he used in succeeding works. In all of his published fiction, Gaines has dealt with poor blacks in the same locale in rural Louisiana, a former slave quarter on a plantation near the town of Bayonne, places adapted from the author's boyhood home. Typically, for Gaines's black characters, that idyllic world is slowly but relentlessly disintegrating.

In *Catherine Carmier*, he also introduces central characters who appear in one guise or another in many of his later works. One is the fatherless son, alienated from his heritage and searching for a new identity and sense of self-worth. For example, Grant Wiggins, in *A Lesson Before Dying* (1993), is in many ways Jackson's resurrected *Doppelgänger*. A second major character is the childless black matron who, like Aunt Charlotte, serves both as the young man's foster parent and benefactress and as a strong defender of the community and the Christian faith. Her counterpart in *A Lesson Before Dying* is Tante Lou, who, like Charlotte, is both the protagonist's aunt and his moral conscience. In a somewhat different guise, she also appears as the title character of *The Autobiography of Miss Jane Pittman* (1971), Gaines's most famous work.

Although Gaines would later experiment with other narrative voices and techniques, in *Catherine Carmier* he uses a plain, direct, and simple style that he has never abandoned. The folk idiom and cadences of real speech, for which he has a finely tuned ear, he exploits extremely well, making his characters both intriguing and convincing. Apparent, too, is the author's sympathetic engagement in his characters' plights, his kind, fundamental empathy, a quality that marks all of his works and attenuates the bitterness of those who suffer from poverty entrenched in racial discrimination. With his very first novel, Gaines seemed to have learned that a gentle, cajoling humanism can be a much more powerful force than a strident, divisive, and message-heavy diatribe. In *Catherine Carmier* and succeeding novels, whether his characters are black, white, or racially mixed, he asks only that readers understand, not side with, applaud, or condemn them.

*Bibliography*
Babb, Valerie Melissa. *Ernest Gaines*. Boston: Twayne, 1991. A major critical intro-
    duction to Gaines, with a chronology and bibliography. Chapter 3, "Et in Arcadia
    Ego: The Declining Pastoral of *Catherine Carmier*," discusses the novel's pastoral
    elements, its parallels to Ivan Turgenev's *Ottsy i deti* (1862; *Fathers and Sons*,
    1867), and the racial background of its characters, especially the Creole heritage
    and its influence on Raoul Carmier.
Bryant, Jerry H. "Ernest J. Gaines: Change, Growth, and History." *The Southern
    Review* 10 (1974): 851-864. Tracks Gaines's artistic growth between *Catherine
    Carmier* and *The Autobiography of Miss Jane Pittman*. Argues that the first novel,
    although it established Gaines's storytelling skills, was stylistically flawed.
Davis, Thadious. "Headlands and Quarters." *Callaloo* 7 (Spring/Summer, 1984):
    1-13. Helpful for understanding the interplay between racial heritage and Gaines's
    fictional locale, especially in *Catherine Carmier*. Views the old slave quarters as "a
    microcosm of society" under a "strain of transition." Identifies three evolving
    patterns—encounters, replacements, and death juxtaposed with beauty—that "pro-
    vide immediate access to the action, themes and symbols" of the novel.
Hicks, Jack. "To Make These Bones Live: History and Community in Ernest Gaines'
    Fiction." *Black American Literature Forum* 11, no. 1 (1977): 9-19. Places *Cather-
    ine Carmier* in the perspective of Gaines's work through 1971, arguing that the
    author became increasingly concerned with black history and the black community.
    Includes a good thumbnail explication of the novel and argues that it is "informed
    by a view of personal and racial history as a prison, a tomb, from which Jackson
    Bradley can never quite escape."
Rowell, Charles H. "The Quarters: Ernest Gaines and the Sense of Place." *The
    Southern Review* 21 (Summer, 1985): 733-750. A helpful analysis of Gaines's use
    of place for thematic and symbolic purposes in *Catherine Carmier* and other works.
Stoelting, Winifred L. "Human Dignity and Pride in the Novels of Ernest Gaines."
    *College Language Association Journal* 14 (1971): 340-358. Discusses a "code of
    independence" providing dignity and pride for characters who, like Jackson
    Bradley and Raoul Carmier, must face change over which they have no control.

*John W. Fiero*

# CEREMONY

*Author:* Leslie Marmon Silko (1948-    )
*Type of plot:* Psychological realism
*Time of plot:* The post-World War II era
*Locale:* The American Southwest and Mexico
*First published:* 1977

Principal characters:

TAYO, a mixed-blood Laguna Pueblo Indian who returns from World
War II to the pueblo mentally and spiritually ill

ROCKY, Tayo's half-brother, a full-blood Laguna, who is killed in World
War II

JOSIAH, Tayo's uncle, whose death while Tayo and Rocky are at war
precipitates Tayo's breakdown

AUNTIE, Tayo's aunt, who rears him after his mother's death

BETONIE, a Navajo medicine man

EMO, the leader of a group of decorated war veterans who pose as Tayo's
friends but work against him

TS'EH, a young woman whose love reorients Tayo toward the natural
world

TS'ITS'TSI'NAKO (THOUGHT-WOMAN), a Laguna Indian divinity in whose
thought the novel occurs

*The Novel*

In *Ceremony*, Tayo has returned from World War II with a condition that Western
medicine would call battle fatigue, although that diagnosis does not account for its
origin in his nature as an Indian fighting a "white" war. His malady is precipitated by
an incident that haunts him: During the war, he was ordered to help execute a group
of Japanese prisoners. The resemblance between Japanese and Laguna faces makes
him think that one of the Japanese is his Uncle Josiah, and while he cannot fire his
weapon, he believes that he has watched the execution of his beloved uncle. Shortly
afterward, his half-brother Rocky, whom Tayo has been sent by Auntie to protect, dies
in battle, and Tayo's cumulative failure destroys his sense of self.

Western drugs and shock therapy cannot rid Tayo of the illusion of Josiah as the
Japanese soldier, largely because such methods treat the individual as the bearer of
illness in isolation from his society. Tayo's malady is part of the larger evil that afflicts
the pueblo: its inextricable complication with Western civilization, language, and
lifestyles. With his family already fragmented by conflicting allegiances, and with the
pueblo afflicted by a drought that traditional ceremonies have not relieved, Tayo, in
order to support the family, decides to retrieve the herd of cattle that his Uncle Josiah
had bought.

The cattle's recovery comes as part of his recovery. After a traditional ceremony fails to cure him, Tayo heads south after the cattle and finds himself in Gallup, where his mother had lived as a prostitute and had borne Tayo. There, he finds Betonie, a Navajo medicine man, whose ceremonies deal with the situation of the Indian in relation to the dominant white culture. Betonie's version of the scalp ceremony works; it reorients Tayo toward his Indian nature, and Betonie gives Tayo an astrological sign by which he can track the cattle as a completion of the ceremony.

Tayo finds the cattle, which have been stolen by a white rancher and confined by a larger fence, along which they have beaten a path in search of escape. Tayo cuts the fence to free them, and though he is apprehended by the ranchers, he escapes and continues searching. He finds the cattle with Ts'eh and her animal-spirit husband, who have corralled the cattle in a dry river bed. Tayo's developing love for the woman is the mode of his return to his own humanity, and in light of that he lives with her a life far closer to that of pre-Western contact.

His isolation, however, has caused both the legal and tribal authorities, as well as his fellow Laguna veterans, to believe he has gone mad or wild and to hunt him. Emo and his group come close to apprehending him, but when they fail, the group ritually kills Harley, a member of the group who appears to have let Tayo escape. Tayo witnesses the killing. In a crisis over whether to intervene in order to save Harley, his closest friend, Tayo realizes the extent of the evil that has caused his malady and that has afflicted his family and people.

At the end of the novel, Tayo rejoins the pueblo and tells his story to a group of elders led by Ku'oosh. It is a ceremonial telling of the story, entering the larger story of the pueblo. Emo and his group are lost in alcohol, and Emo kills Pinkie, another veteran, in a drunken fit, then runs off to California. The family is rejoined, the ceremonies have succeeded, and Silko offers the novel to the sunrise, the evil of the times having been returned to the dark from which it had come.

*The Characters*

Silko's characters make sense of their experience and participate in the novel's action essentially from their position relative to the two competing cultural milieus, traditional Laguna and white America. As the main character, Tayo has the greatest struggle, both relative to Laguna ways and to the dominant white society. His progress in the novel is best seen as a form of cultural synthesis and survival, a difficult, life-determining struggle.

For the older Laguna people, especially Tayo's old Grandma and for Ku'oosh, the traditional ways endure despite the intrusions of white America. For the next generation, including Tayo's mother, her sister Auntie, and Uncle Josiah, white culture has extended further into the conduct of their lives, breaking down their traditional roles. For the youngest adults—including Tayo, Rocky, Robert, Emo, and the other veterans—the white world presents the most dangerously unsettling threats to their survival as a people.

Old Grandma, within whose authority Auntie attempts to act as matriarch, begins and closes the main action of Tayo's healing when she first declares that he needs a medicine man and places all of his and the family's troubles in the context of the ongoing story of the pueblo. Her daughter, Auntie, challenges the idea of bringing in the medicine man, largely because of Tayo's mixed blood and because her Christianity casts doubt on traditional spiritual powers. Only at the end of the novel does Auntie accept Tayo fully; she begins to talk to him as she had spoken to her full-blood children, incorporating him in the traditional way that forms the discursive and narrative fabric of Laguna culture.

Rocky serves as a foil for Tayo. Preferred over Tayo by Auntie as her own full-blood son, Rocky nevertheless is enamored of white culture. He studies hard, wants to be a football star, and enlists in the Army to serve his country, at the expense of helping Josiah maintain the family. Auntie allows Tayo to enlist only in order to protect Rocky. When Josiah is deciding to buy the Mexican cattle, Rocky contends that the cattle do not meet the specifications in the manuals on cattle-raising and that white scientists know more than Indians about cattle. His adoption of white values leads him to war and to his death.

Tayo wants to live as a Laguna, but Auntie, the war, and its scars prevent him. The progress of Tayo's cure is marked by stages in which he moves from the illness caused by his involvement in the war (and by his serving destructive elements in the alien white culture) and toward a productive involvement in the family and pueblo. His task is to recover the cattle, assuming Josiah's providential role, and to be reoriented through ceremony and its enabling effects to recover a traditional relation to the land and people.

*Themes and Meanings*

*Ceremony* opens with three poems that place the novel in the continuously creating mind of Ts'its'tsi'nako, or Thought-Woman, one of the Laguna deities. The context of the novel as a Laguna story and as ceremony is created in the poem's three voices in order to counter the destructive forces that threaten the pueblo at large and Tayo in particular. The novel examines the continuity and viability of Native American culture in the context of the white world. Pueblo culture will survive, Silko implies, by adapting to changing circumstances. Silko avoids placing all blame for the problems afflicting the Laguna characters on white America; the "witchery" encompasses both white and Native American peoples. Tayo's illness is portrayed not in Western terms, as an individual disease, but in terms of Laguna's more encompassing pathology, as loss of harmony throughout the natural and spiritual world.

The context of Tayo's malady as part of the larger evil afflicting the pueblo is enlarged by the drought and by the fragmentation of his family. His mother, for example, was a victim of Indian dependence on the dominant culture for sustenance and for self-image. She loses her integrity by prostituting herself to white men, an activity that she entered as a way of validating her being and body within the zone of Indian/white contact. Tayo is a product of her violations, and because his father is unknown (and white), Auntie keeps him at a formal distance from herself and her son Rocky. Their Laguna family is thus afflicted, in part by Auntie's reaction to Tayo's mixed blood, and in part by Auntie's Christianity, the source of her intolerance. Auntie is frustrated in her traditional role as matriarch, first by failing to reintegrate her sister into the family and later by refusing to accept her sister's son fully.

Josiah attempts to preserve the family through the drought by buying a herd of hardy Mexican cattle, which in their endurance are a figure of the indigenous culture itself. The cattle refuse to be kept and repeatedly break fences and attempt to return to Mexico. In the main action of the novel's present time, Tayo sets off to recover the cattle, attempting to fulfill Josiah's plan for sustaining the family.

*Critical Context*

Because of her own Indian and white ancestry, Silko is interested in the position of the mixed-blood Indian in relation to the tribe and in the survival and adaptability of tribal culture, particularly the importance of stories and storytelling. Her book *Story-teller* (1981) is an autobiographical account of her education in Laguna stories.

Part of her assertion of tribal culture is the inclusion of traditional stories of spirit beings; these stories are included in *Ceremony* as poems that interrupt the narrative and provide alternate ways of viewing the action. The episodic poems place the action within the mythic and ritualistic modes of Laguna thought and create a dialogue between the novel's historic and mythic elements, unifying its spiritual and secular worlds. Her technique appears as a postmodern gesture of breaking down the realistic conventions of the novel in order to reveal a deeper significance, rendered as a firmly Laguna context in which the conflicts that the characters undergo are repetitions of spiritual crises embedded in myth. The story of Pa'caya'nyi, for example, is told in nine episodes as explanation and solution for the drought. While Tayo in his illness believes that he caused the drought by cursing the rain after Rocky's death, the Navajo medicine man Betonie says that the true cause is an evil that has been in the world a long time. Betonie's ceremony is parallel to the ceremony required in the myth, but the modern medicine man must incorporate new elements to defeat the new circumstances of the ancient witchery. Silko's writing of the novel is her version of such a renewed ceremony.

*Bibliography*

Allen, Paula Gunn. "The Feminine Landscape of Leslie Marmon Silko's *Ceremony*." In *Studies in American Indian Literature*, edited by Paula Gunn Allen. New York: Modern Language Association of America, 1983. Allen divides men and women characters into those who do or do not "live in harmony . . . with the earth spirit": that is, those allied with the feminine principle of Thought-Woman (the creativity of earth and her children) and those "inimical to all that lives, creates, and nurtures." She reads Tayo's healing as the result of the ceremony's reuniting of land and person.

Hailey, David E., Jr. "The Visual Elegance of Ts'its'tsi'nako and the Other Invisible Characters in *Ceremony*." *Wicazo Sa Review* 6 (Fall, 1990): 1-6. Hailey emphasizes that Silko's novel gives the reader the means to read it and that part of her art is in the shaping of the poems to configure various creatures and mythological beings in a directly visual way. Her graphics, he contends, enrich the "conceptual life" of the invisible characters, reinforcing their presence throughout the text.

Hoilman, Dennis R. "'A World Made of Stories': An Interpretation of Leslie Silko's *Ceremony.*" *South Dakota Review* 17, no. 4 (1979): 54-66. Hoilman studies Silko's strategies as an American Indian writer addressing a non-Indian audience that lacks the necessary cultural background to understand her world. He argues that the mythic and ritualistic poems answer the need for Laguna contexts while creating difficulties of their own, which are resolvable by seeing the novel as setting in motion the curative ceremony it describes. The essay speculates profitably on relations between the poems and the narrative and assesses the book's value for the non-Indian reader (as an introduction to Indian ways of seeing) and for the Indian reader (as an "affirmation of allegiance to the old ways" that also "suggests a healing ceremony for the future").

Seyersted, Per. *Leslie Marmon Silko*. Boise, Idaho: Boise State University, 1980. An excellent monograph introduction to Silko's biography, short fiction, and essays as well as to *Ceremony*. Summarizes Laguna pueblo history by way of contextualizing Silko's family, which has been prominent in Laguna governance, and her upbringing. Seyersted's reading of *Ceremony* is a fine recapitulation of the novel's historical and cultural contexts.

Slowick, Mary. "Henry James, Meet Spider Woman: A Study of Narrative Form in Leslie Silko's *Ceremony.*" *The North Dakota Quarterly* 57 (Spring, 1989): 104-120. Slowick reads *Ceremony* in the tradition of Latin American Magical Realism, mainly citing statements by Gabriel García Márquez. She traces the intersection of "primitive and realist" stories and of the "magic" and the "real." Her argument would be better built on parallels with Miguel Asturias' *Hombres de maíz* (1949; *Men of Maize*, 1975), in which Asturias used Magical Realism to portray the consciousness of Mayan characters and used conventional realism to depict other characters.

*Robert Bensen*

# CHINA BOY

*Author:* Gus Lee
*Type of plot: Bildungsroman*
*Time of plot:* The early 1950's
*Locale:* San Francisco, California
*First published:* 1991

Principal characters:

KAI TING, the only American-born member of the Ting family
DAI-LI TING (MAH-MEE), Kai's mother, who dies before he is seven
COLONEL T. K. TING, Kai's father, now a banker in civilian life
EDNA MCGURK TING, the Philadelphia society woman who becomes Kai's stepmother
TONY BARRAZA, a former professional boxer and one of Kai's boxing coaches
UNCLE SHIM, an old friend of the Ting family and Kai's calligraphy teacher
TOUSSAINT LARUE, Kai's best friend

*The Novel*

*China Boy* is the story of Kai Ting, the American-born son of a refugee Shanghainese family. Ending an odyssey across both friendly and unfriendly terrain, the Ting family finally settles in San Francisco.

*China Boy* opens with Kai's retelling of how his family—including his mother, father, and three elder sisters—fled the civil war in China, and how they came to be situated in San Francisco, specifically in the Panhandle, a tough, largely poor neighborhood. It is in this "concrete crucible" that Kai does his growing up.

The almost six-year-old Kai is his mother's favorite child and only son, and she pins large hopes upon him. Kai's sisters are all considerably older than he is, and he assumes the natural position of coddled youngest child. His world revolves around his mother, whose passion, charisma, and overabiding sense of family weave for young Kai a protective cocoon. In fact, until he starts school, Kai has little sense of the world outside the Tings' home. He has even less sense of other children his age and what it will take to cross the boundary between the protection of family and the dangers of a world populated with hostile strangers.

Tragically for Kai, his mother dies. While he could previously rush home from the schoolyard and the streets of the Panhandle to the security of home, Kai is now robbed of the balance from that reality. To compound matters, his father marries Edna McGurk, who steps into her new role of stepmother with reluctance but nevertheless with draconian ideas about how to rear suddenly inherited children. From an almost idyllic existence of Chinese food, ancestral stories, the Shanghainese dialect—or "Songhai"—and the loving, doting presence of Mah-mee, Kai is propelled, within the space of months, into a subsistence that is circumscribed by a relentlessly cruel stepmother, a strictly enforced new tongue, and the still-new experience of the tough streets of the Panhandle.

As "China Boy" in his predominantly black neighborhood, Kai immediately becomes the easiest target of boyish aggression and plain meanness. His tiny frame does not help him, and neither do his nearsightedness and his inability to communicate in the language of the street. His stepmother locks him out of the house until dinnertime, and Kai has no recourse but to live his daylight hours among his street-seasoned peers. Kai is constantly beaten up, but he does manage to make two friends. One is Toussaint LaRue, and the other is Toussaint's mother. Mrs. LaRue represents for Kai the mother and all the mothering that he has lost.

After a particularly vicious attack on Kai, his father decides to enroll him at the Young Men's Christian Association (YMCA) with the hope that Kai will receive some instruction in self-defense. At the YMCA, Kai's eyes are opened to yet another new world. It is a world of aggression-driven boys, but in this environment, there are also grown men who take the time to help channel the aggression toward worthwhile ends. Puny, scared, ill-treated and starved, Kai learns to box. He also learns to trust, especially in his coaches. Over the months, their collective instruction and their belief in their smallest student begins to show results. Kai puts on weight; Tony Barraza, the boxing coach, sees to it that the stepmother-starved Kai is fed in the YMCA cafeteria. Kai is soon able to step into the ring in his beginner's class and last three rounds with an opponent. He is far from being able to beat the street bullies, but he is gaining a sense of self and what he can accomplish. He also makes friends, and his English improves.

Despite his blossoming at the YMCA, Kai is quickly brought down to earth in an encounter with the meanest neighborhood bully. Kai is once again badly beaten up. At the same time, his home situation does not improve. His father is invariably away on business, Edna is unbearably cruel, and his sisters can do little to help him. On top of that, he is stricken with the realization that his memory of his mother is fast fading.

With his YMCA mentors behind him, and with the arrival from his sister, Megan, of a photograph of his mother as extra moral support, Kai faces the street bully again in a do-or-die effort. Kai again takes brutal punishment, but this time he gives as good as he gets. His triumph gives him the much-needed first step toward a credible place in his neighborhood. He has won the first, the most important, battle of his seven years.

*The Characters*

Dai-li Ting, Kai's "Mah-mee," appears only in the beginning of the book. Yet her presence is an important one, for it is primarily through her that Kai has a sense of who he is, who his ancestors are. She speaks her native Songhai with Kai and his sisters and instills in them the value of family togetherness, of a cultural past that is now remote but that can nevertheless be reenacted in some semblance in their now-American lives. Dai-li Ting is vivacious, unpredictable, idiosyncratic, passionate, and she loves her only son fiercely. She is the anchor in Kai's world, and her brief appearance in the novel only serves to underscore his loss when she dies of cancer. With her death, Kai is stripped not only of love and protection but also of the most palpable reminder of his ancestral roots.

Colonel Ting is Kai's military-hero father, now a bank officer in civilian America. He abhors the degeneration in his homeland that led finally to civil war, and he is concerned primarily with becoming and being American. He is taciturn, rigid, and an iconoclast among the Chinese community in San Francisco because of his disavowal of most things Chinese. To his son, he is distant and unapproachable, and his presence does nothing to soften the blow of Mah-mee's death. Colonel Ting is the typically uncommunicative father, and it seems that the best he can do for his son is to enroll him at the YMCA, thus giving Kai over to a group of surrogate fathers.

Edna McGurk, the second Mrs. Ting, is more than Kai's tormentor. Unbearably intolerant and cruel, and unable or unwilling to reach out to her stepchildren, Edna is also Kai's constant reminder that she is not Mah-mee, that everything Mah-mee represented should be consigned to a forgettable past. Edna's cruelty to her stepchildren dramatizes Kai's bereavement and his lonely, unprotected status.

Tony Barraza is Kai's favorite coach at the YMCA. A former boxer, he now devotes his time to the molding of young bodies and minds, and as he takes Kai under his wing, he is the surrogate parent that Kai so badly craves. He offers Kai guidance, friendship, and a chance to make something of an impossibly deprived childhood.

Uncle Shim is a reminder of happier days for Kai, for this old family friend, who is Kai's calligraphy teacher, was a constant visitor when Mah-mee was alive. Together with Mah-mee, Uncle Shim represents the connectedness to Kai's cultural heritage. His visits become infrequent as a result of Edna's desire to purge all things "Asiatic" from the Ting household, but Kai manages to track him down. The meeting between Uncle Shim and Tony Barraza in the YMCA cafeteria brings together the two separate worlds represented by the two men. While Tony is the American personification of action and street smarts, Uncle Shim is the personification of Chinese tradition, passivity, and the philosophizing of life's unexplainable cruelties.

Toussaint LaRue, or "Toos," is Kai's only friend among his neighborhood peers. Toos makes the overture of befriending Kai, the "ratshitchinkface" alien; his kindness is a gritty act in the Panhandle. Toos's moral strength is grounded in the strong bond between him and his mother, and he becomes Kai's street teacher and steadfast friend.

*Themes and Meanings*

*China Boy* is a *Bildungsroman*, or rite-of-passage story. Although the novel covers only approximately one-and-a-half years of Kai's life, it depicts a pivotal point in his growing, a time of great change and uncertainty out of which he will gather strength and survive or to which he will succumb. With the death of his mother, the physical and emotional distance of his father, the cruelty of his stepmother, and the everyday violence that he faces on his neighborhood streets, Kai is plunged into a seemingly inescapable dungeon. To escape, Kai has to draw on the very last dregs of a personal integrity—the somehow unquenchable resilience of a seven-year-old—in order to salvage a childhood gone awry. Facing violence both within and without his home, Kai nevertheless soldiers along, and despite incredible odds neutralizes the neighborhood bully in the defining battle of his short life. This culminating act signals a breakthrough for Kai, and the novel leaves the reader with the hope that with one battle won, Kai is set to win others and, ultimately, to win the long war of his childhood.

The novel is also about displacement, about the suspension between two clearly defined, seemingly irreconcilable cultures. The culture represented by Kai's mother and Uncle Shim seems, with Mah-mee's death, to slip away with each day. Kai, speaking a five-year-old's broken "Songhai," is the flotsam from that culture. The reality of a relentlessly alien culture is all around him, but without its language, without recognizable points of reference to help him in his transition, Kai is in danger of becoming both a refugee from one culture and an unwanted stranger in another.

Ultimately, though, the novel is about the possibility of reconciliations: between past and present, between ethnicity and nationality, between passivity and action. There is time for Kai to recollect the lost pieces of his past in order to give direction and purpose to his present. Confronted by racism both at home and on the streets, Kai is befriended and aided by individuals who recognize the inherent stranger in themselves and who see in Kai only the human quality of need. Physically and emotionally brutalized by both his stepmother and the neighborhood boys, Kai is unable to retaliate. His understanding of "yuing chi," or karma, seems to feed his childish fatalism. With the bodybuilding and mind-building at the YMCA, however, Kai seems finally to be able both to assert himself and to preserve his integrity. In the novel's epilogue, Kai confronts his stepmother at their doorway. He has just survived his fight with the bully, and his clothes are drenched with blood. Edna is concerned only that he has rung the doorbell too early and that she will once again have to bleach the blood—the Asiatic blood—out of his clothes. As a recognition of his past and present, of his ethnicity, of his action, of his new self, Kai tells her, "You are not my Mah-mee! . . . I ain't fo' yo' pickin-on, no mo'!"

*Critical Context*

*China Boy* is Lee's first novel. It is at least semiautobiographical; like Kai, Lee himself is the only American-born member and only son of an immigrant Shanghai family. Also like Kai, Lee has a stepmother, whom he credits with having taught him English.

*China Boy* was published in 1991, in the midst of heightened literary activity among Chinese Americans and among Asian Americans in general. The book also arrived in the midst of continued debate in the Asian American literary community. Some Asian American writers, notably playwright Frank Chin, claim that much Asian American writing panders to white imagination and represents a self-orientalizing. Others, including novelists Maxine Hong Kingston and Amy Tan, insist that the integrity of Chinese American writing demands that the myths and half-truths that have been perpetuated in the name of "things oriental" still need to be addressed. In any case, *China Boy* draws as much from the "child-meets-world" American tradition of Mark Twain, Ernest Hemingway, Harper Lee, and Carson McCullers as it does from the redefining, ever-evolving American tradition represented by the continuum of Han Suyin, Jade Snow Wong, Louis Chu, and Kingston.

*Bibliography*
Kim, Elaine H. *Asian American Literature: An Introduction to the Writings and Their Social Context*. Philadelphia: Temple University Press, 1982. Kim's work is a seminal one, the first scholarly, full-length study of Asian American literature. The approach is chronological, providing a much-needed context for the discussion. Includes an extensive bibliography referencing both Asian American literature and Anglo-American portrayals of Asians and Asian Americans.
Lee, Joann Faung Jean. *Asian American Experiences in the United States: Oral Histories of First to Fourth Generation Americans from China, the Philippines, Japan, India, the Pacific Islands, Vietnam, and Cambodia*. Jefferson, N.C.: McFarland, 1991. Lee amasses oral histories of Asian Americans across class, age, and geographical lines. The accounts are lively and frank, and together underscore the diverse nature of being Asian American. See especially "Growing Up in Mississippi," Sam Sue's account of growing up as a second-generation Chinese American marginalized by both whites and blacks.
Simpson, Janice C., and Pico Iyer. "Fresh Voices Above the Noisy Din." *Time* 137 (June 3, 1991): 66-67. Analyzes *China Boy* in the context of other works by contemporary Chinese American novelists, including Amy Tan, David Wong Louie, and Gish Jen.
Tsai, Shih-Shan Henry. *The Chinese Experience in America*. Bloomington: Indiana University Press, 1986. A well-documented account of the history of Chinese in the United States. Includes photographs, maps, drawings, and social and historical data; also included is a bibliography that covers works pertinent to Chinese American history and sociology.

*Pat M Wong*

# THE CHOSEN PLACE, THE TIMELESS PEOPLE

*Author:* Paule Marshall (1929-　　)
*Type of plot:* Historical realism
*Time of plot:* Unspecified; probably the 1960's
*Locale:* Bournehills, a fictional West Indian island
*First published:* 1969

> *Principal characters:*
> MERLE KINBONA, a mulatta Bournehills native who returns to the island from her studies in England
> LEESY WALKES, an old island prophetess
> VERE WALKES, Leesy's nephew, who returns to Bournehills from the United States
> ALLEN FUSO, an American researcher of Irish-Italian descent
> SAUL AMRON, a Jewish American anthropologist and director of the Bournehills project
> HARRIET AMRON, Saul's wife, a white Anglo-Saxon Protestant heiress from Philadelphia
> LYLE HUTSON, a senator in the legislature of the island and member of the power elite

*The Novel*

Through her experiences as an American of Barbadian heritage, Paule Marshall embodies the cultural dichotomy that provides the major tension in much of her fiction, including *The Chosen Place, the Timeless People.* This novel, exploring the means through which an individual comes to identify with a group, moves beyond the individual. It examines the problems facing many Third World countries in their struggle to establish a national identity.

The novel is divided into four books, each individual title representing one aspect of the connection between the individual and the group. The first book, "Heirs and Descendants," introduces the societal strata of Bourne Island, so determined by its colonial past, and introduces as well the newcomers who believe they have come to change that past. The aging Jewish American anthropologist, Saul Amron, travels with his wealthy Philadelphian wife, Harriet, and a research associate, Allen Fuso, to Bournehills to study its primitive agricultural community and educate its people. They are part of the multimillion dollar development scheme of a major U.S. foundation. Saul's plan is to carry out a careful anthropological survey of the district before applying his findings to the community's development. As the researchers are quickly warned, other attempts to change the beautiful yet rugged island have failed. Particularly uncooperative have been the poor workers who have frustrated the civil servants of the island.

In book 1, the Amrons meet Merle Kinbona, a tense and eccentric middle-aged mulatta native who frightens Saul and Harriet with her seemingly disconnected chatter and boldness. Merle returns to the island from her studies in England after she receives news that her father is dying. Her purpose is to put her life in order, to make a fresh start, and the novel opens with her still consumed with her London experiences.

The second book, "Bournehills," focuses on the land itself. The community of Bournehills, a remote section of Bourne Island, is a Caribbean island clearly patterned after Barbados. The island itself, as seen from the air, is one of a group of small islands that look like stepping-stones linking North and South America. Bourne Island, however, is slightly out of line, more to the east, facing the Atlantic Ocean. It seems in its geographical position to link the New World with Africa. Despite the world's apparent abuse and then abandonment of them, the people of Bournehills hold on to their traditions as a means of sustenance and as a mark of their existence.

The third and fourth books, "Carnival" and "Whitsun," are named after ritual times of the year and hence point to both continuity and change. While the carnival is going on, Merle and Saul reveal the most intimate details of their past to each other. They also agree to become lovers. Merle reveals that her father was a wealthy white landowner who, though he did not claim her as a child, furnished her with funds to study in England. While in London, she was active in politics, led a bohemian life, and became the kept woman of a wealthy and jaded British woman. To escape the clutches of the woman and the decadence of the life she was leading, Merle married a Ugandan student and eventually gave birth to a daughter. Bitter after Merle's sudden break, the woman took revenge by informing Merle's husband about her past. Shocked and disappointed, he left Merle and took the child to East Africa with him.

Saul reveals that early in his career he deserted a Peruvian public-health nurse who had become his mistress. His first wife, a survivor of the Nazi concentration camps, died of a miscarriage while out on field work with him in Honduras. His guilt for this incident had kept him out of field work altogether until he met Harriet, who was recently divorced.

At the end of the novel, in the "Whitsun" section, Merle, Saul, and Allen Fuso are clearly the survivors. Merle decides to seek her daughter, though not necessarily a resolution to her marriage, in East Africa. Alone after Harriet's death, Saul continues to fight for the rights of the oppressed, though from behind a desk in the United States for an indeterminate period of time. Allen remains in Bournehills, although he is never able to participate in the life of the community completely.

*The Characters*

Saul and Harriet Amron are part of Marshall's purpose to provide a comment on the American role in developing countries. While much is heard about the project, very little is seen of it being worked out in practice. Saul functions as a sympathetic observer. He is a committed intellectual who has worked all of his life in underdeveloped countries and has acquired a pragmatic confidence in his ability to understand and improve them. Saul has the wisdom to learn patiently about the habits and needs of the peasants of the island and about the rhythms of the land and life there. It is his patience that earns him the respect he needs to proceed with his mission. Eventually, it becomes clear that he might not understand the island and its people as much as he had thought. As one of his last acts on the island, Saul helps to put together an organization of workers. Though he is not able to see the union fully launched, there is the strong prospect that it will continue after he has left the island.

Through his involvement with Merle, Saul Amron comes to understand the relationship between the native and the colonial government. He stands up for the islanders' rights and tries to help them overcome their economic difficulties. Saul's position in the novel is ironic; although he is a representative of the white patriarchy, he is also, as a Jew, a member of a group that historically has been victimized. This irony is broadened following the revelation that his wife, Harriet, is heir to a shipping company that was actively involved in the slave trade.

Harriet functions in the novel as the quintessential white Anglo-Saxon Protestant. Harriet, who was instrumental in getting her husband the Bournehills assignment, promises to keep out of his way on the expedition, but she subtly tries to control him. As his experience in Bournehills takes him further from her emotionally, she is threatened. Knowledge of his brief affair with Merle spurs her to have him transferred back to America. He breaks with his wife, cut off from the work that has become so vital to him, and she commits suicide.

Merle Kinbona functions as the voice of a voiceless people, the people of Bournehills. While she is the daughter of a mulatto and a black woman, she makes no attempt, unlike other islanders, to present herself as anything but black. The author draws a link between Merle's acceptance of her blackness and her refusal to deny Bournehills. She is fiercely committed to the island and its people, although she is personally rootless. Merle knits the entire cast together: the Americans, the middle-class professionals from the capital, the plantation overseers, and the ordinary people of Bournehills.

Although Merle's affair with Saul precipitates Harriet's suicide, the relationship has also begun to allow Merle to confront her past and, like Saul, to accept her flawed nature. Merle's and Saul's self-acceptance is linked with their acknowledgment of exploitation and what must be done to change society in order to end exploitation.

Leesy Walkes, the old island prophetess and native of Bournehills, is the voice of tradition. She clings to the traditional rhythms of the land and fears the coming of the technological age.

Vere Walkes, Leesy's nephew, leaves Bournehills to go to the United States in an attempt to make a success of his life, only to return a failure. Yet his mechanical talent is apparent when he rebuilds a battered old car that people had believed would never run again. Tragically, this talented young man has identified his goals in terms of technology instead of people, and it is this love for machines that destroys him: He is killed in a car race, as his aunt had known he would be. It is the capitalist world that destroys Vere; the car was built in Germany and designed in America. He is represented as a tragic victim of capitalist technology.

Allen Fuso, an American researcher, is an outsider to Bournehills. During the course of the novel, he comes to recognize his homosexual identity.

Lyle Hutson, a successful barrister, senator in the legislature of the island, and member of the power elite, has been born poor and black. He won a scholarship to the elite boys' secondary school in town and had later gone on to study in England. He had been somewhat radical in his youth, proclaiming socialism and revolution. Once he returned to the island and married into a prominent family, however, he spoke for change in more moderate terms. He had started building his future on the spoils of the past. His house is symbolic and public witness to his cultural betrayal.

## Themes and Meanings

*The Chosen Place, the Timeless People* is a novel about neocolonialism and the reverberation of past actions in the present. Yet the novel is not a political tract; rather, it carefully explores the ways in which people's relationships are critical to the historical process. The book demonstrates that there is an ongoing interaction between the apparently faceless forces of society and the choices human beings make. The parts of the novel reflect that interaction. The novel also emphasizes the connection between character and context, while extending that connection beyond gender or racial indicators to include an entire people and their land.

The novel turns on its epigraph, a saying from the Tiv people of West Africa: "Once a great wrong has been done, it never dies. People speak the words of peace, but their hearts do not forgive. Generations perform ceremonies of reconciliation but there is no end." The theme is that of the complex series of interactions between the oppressed and their oppressors; its truth is that half measures cannot substantially change those interactions.

Finally, the novel portrays history as an active, creative, and moral process composed by human beings. According to Marshall, individuals and whole cultures decide upon the moral nature of an act, a series of acts, a history. In this novel, Marshall brings together the two themes that are most central to her work: the importance of truly confronting the past, both in personal and historical terms, and the necessity of reversing the present order.

## Critical Context

In its analysis of characters who are inseparable from their particular culture, and in its insistence on the intersections of the past and present, *The Chosen Place, the Timeless People* is a culmination of Marshall's earlier work. Marshall moves from a localized setting in which she focuses primarily on one character or one family to the entire sociocultural fabric of Bournehills as a prototypical Third World country. Her scope is considerably larger than in her previous works, yet the people of this novel are psychologically related to characters in her earlier novels and stories. *The Chosen Place, the Timeless People*, in its characters, themes and techniques, creates a coherent universe of Marshall's work. Marshall has matured as a writer in this novel, but her vision has not changed dramatically; rather, her emphasis moves from the way that the world affects an individual psyche to the way that many psyches create a world.

Marshall's presentation of a black woman as a major actor in the social, political, and cultural issues of her society can be compared to Alice Walker's depiction of the title character in her novel *Meridian* (1976). Both Merle and Meridian are new literary characters in African American women's novels, complex women struggling to understand themselves as black and female. In seeking their own identity, they find that they must pursue major social transformation. They are female literary characters of a social and political depth seldom seen in African American literature. In developing a character such as Merle Kinbona within the context of her particular society, Marshall announced the major theme of African American women's fiction of the 1970's, in which black women were being presented both as complex, developing persons and as active participants in the sociopolitical world.

*The Chosen Place, the Timeless People* has been praised for examining the problems facing many Third World countries in their struggle to establish a national identity. In this novel, black culture in the Western Hemisphere is linked with its African past and the promise of the future. Marshall proposes that the hope for the future lies in borrowing this past and using it as the basis for unified action and power.

*Bibliography*
Brock, Sabine. "Transcending the 'Loophole of Retreat': Paule Marshall's Placing of Female Generations." *Callaloo* 10 (Winter, 1987): 79-90. Maintains that Marshall's fiction emphasizes the black woman's search for space, both physical and emotional, within the white patriarchy.
Christian, Barbara. "Sculpture and Space: The Interdependency of Character and Culture in the Novels of Paule Marshall." In *Black Women Novelists*. Westport, Conn.: Greenwood Press, 1980. Explores the author's use of culture, folklore, and environment as a means of creating character.
Skerrett, Joseph T., Jr. "Paule Marshall and the Crisis of Middle Years: *The Chosen Place, the Timeless People*." *Callaloo* 6 (Spring-Summer, 1983): 68-73. Discusses *The Chosen Place, the Timeless People* as a novel about time, the crisis of old age, and generativity.
Spillers, Hortense J. "Chosen Place, Timeless People: Some Figurations on the New World." In *Conjuring: Black Women, Fiction, and Literary Tradition*, edited by Marjorie Pryse and Hortense J. Spillers. Bloomington: Indiana University Press, 1985. Asserts that a proper interpretation of *The Chosen Place, the Timeless People* must account for Marshall's use of history, myth, ontology, and ritual.
Stoelting, Winifred L. "Time Past and Time Present: The Search for Viable Links in *The Chosen Place, the Timeless People*, by Paule Marshall." *College Language Association Journal* 16 (September, 1972): 60-71. Maintains that healing of fragmented selves, rediscovery of lost identity, and repairing of bridges of communication between people who share a common heritage is possible only through an honest confrontation with the past.

*Genevieve Slomski*

# THE CIDER HOUSE RULES

*Author:* John Irving (1942-    )
*Type of plot:* Social realism
*Time of plot:* The 1880's to 1900; the 1920's to the 1950's
*Locale:* Maine
*First published:* 1985

> *Principal characters:*
> WILBUR LARCH, an obstetrician and abortionist who directs the St. Cloud's orphanage
> HOMER WELLS, an orphan, Dr. Larch's surrogate son
> CANDY WORTHINGTON (née KENDALL), Homer's closest friend, the love of his life and mother of their son, Angel Wells
> WALLY WORTHINGTON, Candy's husband, the son of a privileged couple
> MELONY (MELODY), an unadoptable, perpetually angry orphan
> OLIVE WORTHINGTON, Wally's mother, a wealthy, sensible, decent woman
> RAYMOND KENDALL, Candy's father, a master mechanic
> ANGEL WELLS, Homer and Candy's son
> ARTHUR ROSE, the chief of a crew of African American orchard workers

*The Novel*

Written as a tribute to the decency and dedication of the most impressive practitioners of the medical profession, *The Cider House Rules* is a multigenerational chronicle covering the life of Wilbur Larch, who as a young doctor is drawn by compassion and judgment to forge a career as an obstetrician and abortionist. Accepting an appointment as the director of St. Cloud's, an isolated, under-equipped orphanage in Maine, Larch struggles with the moral questions, medical challenges, and social difficulties involved in helping desperate, frightened, and usually penurious women whose pregnancies require, in his estimation, either termination or an expert, comfortable birth. His acceptance of the obligations involved in providing a proper home, either within or beyond the orphanage, for the children he delivers is the burden and blessing of his long life as a man who, in the spirit of the practical New Englander, wants to be of use to humanity.

Larch moves almost incidentally toward his life's work through a series of circumstances arising from accidents of timing and his upbringing. Once settled at St. Cloud's, he commits himself completely to his task as healer and symbolic father to an extended family of life's victims. His own experiences with social hypocrisy and human frailty have convinced him that social conventions are often detrimental to people's most fundamental needs, but his choices to work beyond the legalities of society are guided by a moral compass that is set firmly in accordance with a higher law. Surrounded by faithful, adoring associates—Nurse Angela, Nurse Edna, and Mrs.

Grogan—Larch struggles with the nearly impossible task of giving every orphan an opportunity to find a family built on love and respect.

The obstacles he faces are epitomized by his attempts to train Homer Wells, an orphan who can never completely settle into a life beyond the orphanage, to be his successor and the carrier of his legacy of care and encouragement. While Larch knows instinctively that Homer, like himself, will find his truest satisfaction in service at St. Cloud's, he understands that Homer must discover this for himself. The central narrative design of the novel thus follows Homer's progress into the world and his eventual return to his ultimate "home." Homer has returned to the orphanage three times between his birth in about 1920 and the time immediately before the United States enters World War II. At that time, he is invited to spend the summer at the home of Wally Worthington, who has journeyed to St. Cloud's with his girlfriend, Candy Kendall, to terminate her pregnancy. Wally and Candy live in Heart's Haven, an attractive town on the Maine coast, and as Homer enters their life of optimism, confidence, prosperity, and unreflective happiness, his somber outlook is altered by his first real opportunity to live as a member of a successful, privileged family. His friendship with Wally and Candy is immediately complicated, however, by his almost instantaneous, overwhelming romantic attraction for Candy, who is similarly attracted to him. Since both of them also "love" Wally, a complex, ongoing situation of permanent emotional turmoil is initiated.

When Wally joins the Air Force, Homer and Candy become lovers, conceiving a child they decide to keep but pretend they have adopted as an orphan. Wally's plane is shot down over Burma, and although there is no word of his fate, his family and friends continue to have intimations of his survival. Angel Wells is born with both parents uncertain how to proceed, so they choose to follow Homer's doubt-ridden strategy to "wait and see." In a parallel plot, Dr. Larch has been continuing with his work at St. Cloud's but has been forced into a defensive posture by officious trustees. In a brief idyll that concludes when Wally writes from India about his escape, Homer and Candy, with their son, live and work at St. Cloud's. Wally returns home, paralyzed and sterile but as cheerful and amiable as before. Wally's father dies from Alzheimer's disease, and Homer and Candy move to the Worthington family orchard at Heart's Haven, where Homer becomes the superintendent of the business. Angel Wells is reared by three parents after Candy and Wally are married.

There is a significant shift in narrative perspective as the novel moves forward sixteen years to the mid-1950's. From an unfolding present-tense construction, the narrative changes to a mixture of the past recollected while the present emerges as a kind of projected future already recorded (as in sentences beginning "Wally and Candy would . . ."). Homer decides that the entire truth of his relationship with Candy must be disclosed. Angel Wells falls in love with the daughter of Mr. Rose, the lethal, defensively psychotic chief of the migrant apple workers. Wally remains cheerful and accepting, and when Dr. Larch dies in his nineties, Homer finally returns to St. Cloud's in the identity of "Dr. Fuzzy Stone," a fictitious creation of Larch's designed to ease Homer into the role he was destined to fill. When the body of a woman known only as Melony arrives at the hospital, Homer recognizes an old acquaintance from his youth who has haunted his existence through the years. Their reunion in the orphanage completes the cycle of birth-search-renewal-ripeness that describes the pattern of the life of Wilbur Larch, the secular saint who is the God/Father of all the orphans.

*The Characters*

John Irving has said that he wanted in *The Cider House Rules* to write about a person he "absolutely" admired. Therefore, Wilbur Larch is presented in terms designed to bring the reader extremely close to the character, making his actions admirable, his moral decisions beyond the motives of personal pleasure, his personality extremely congenial, and his human complexity sufficiently realistic so that he does not become a simplistic hero. There is a comfortable quality about Larch, in spite of his rage against brutality and mendacity, that begins with his extraordinary warmth and decency—his genuine, heartfelt caring for human suffering, the vital capacity to share the pain of his patients that all doctors should possess.

The groundwork for the advancing action that covers nearly a century is the introduction of the social conditions that shape Larch as a youth and young medical student. The only other character who is treated with anything like the same thoroughness is Homer Wells, Larch's surrogate son, an orphan never officially adopted but a member of Larch's "family" at St. Cloud's. Like Larch, Homer is observed practically from birth, the social circumstances of his upbringing both within and outside St. Cloud's serving to form him. Larch's desire to see him as a worthy successor operates both as a source of strength and as an obstacle to his development as an individual. Irving illustrates the affinities and similarities of the two men as well as the single-minded intelligence that causes Homer to differ from Larch: He prefers not to use his medical skills to perform abortions, even though he agrees with Larch's philosophical and ideological arguments.

As the narrative course follows Homer away from and back to St. Cloud's in a pattern of growth and consolidation, Irving employs the primary methods available to an omniscient narrator. Dr. Larch and Homer Wells are seen in active engagement with the world, and their characters are revealed through their singular styles of expression. Most significant, they are examined in detail from a psychoanalytical perspective that permits the reader to follow the processes of their conscious (and subconscious) minds. Irving is not hesitant to explain motive and preference or to show both men in reflective moments that deepen experience. Aside from the woman known only as Melony (a corruption of Melody)—who is described as always angry, an example of the darker impulses brought out by loneliness and mistreatment—the remaining characters are presented essentially from the outside. Even Candy, who with Melony takes a crucial role in Homer's life as the polar opposites of sexual involvement, does not have an extensive separate existence away from her connection to the track of Homer's narrative. The other interesting characters are sharply sketched and convincing in their actions, but they tend to be personifications of particular human inclinations (Ray Kendall is a master machinist; Meany Hyde is always jovial) rather than fully realized depictions.

## Themes and Meanings

In an interview shortly after *The Cider House Rules* was published, Irving stated, "It is a book with a polemic." In accordance with George Orwell's dictum that "All art is propaganda but not all propaganda is art," however, Irving has utilized two of the dominant modes of the novelist's art to frame his argument. The more prominent is Irving's debt (and homage) to Charles Dickens, whose conception of the novel as an arena for the exploration of dynamic social issues is apparent in the manner in which *The Cider House Rules* uses institutional rigidity, the tyranny of class consciousness, and the redemptive faculties of the extended family as focal points for its examination of the controversy surrounding abortion rights. The other, less familiar mode has its origins in the eighteenth century concern for the "Man of Feeling" featured in the work of such writers as Henry Fielding and Lawrence Sterne, whose protagonists acted out of a fusion of emotion and intellect that emphasized the heart (or passions) as important measures of moral justice. The two modes are joined throughout the narrative, as the decisions and choices Larch and Wells make are presented as the consequences of their formative contacts with American society. Neither man begins with any specific agenda other than a feeling for human suffering and a desire to alleviate it. Larch arrives at his chosen profession through his eye-opening experiences with women who are helpless and frightened. Wells, in his search for an independent identity, is always aware of the isolation of an orphan and the need to establish some kind of contact with other people. Since both men accept that the finest kind of career is "to be of use," the manner in which they can use their skills—technical and personal—is the subject of internal debate, spirited dialogue, and, at times, direct proclamations of conviction. It is in these moments that the novel fulfills Irving's description of a polemic, but it is the intensity of the genre, not its familiar form, that is applicable in this case.

While both Larch and Wells as "admirable" characters are expressions of Irving's own ideas, the novel is not simply a brief for abortion. Both the pro-choice position and the pro-life position are amply expressed, and the ultimate choice that Larch and Wells make is based on their sense of the most humane course of action in an imperfect world. Irving envisions the practitioner of the healing arts as a person who must address the fundamental needs of the human spirit by providing care, consolation, and comfort as obligatory accompaniments to the physical and technical aspects of medicine, and he is very concerned with the terrible feelings of isolation and loneliness that overcome patients ravaged by illness. In a symbolic sense, the novel suggests that everyone is ultimately an orphan in a cosmic void, and that only human love (or divine love in human form) can rescue a lost soul. The families that are organized by love are the truest means of social salvation, and for all his foibles, "St. Larch" is an exemplar of goodness in his role as the prime organizer of a community of compassion.

*Critical Context*

*The Cider House Rules,* Irving's sixth novel in seventeen years, moves away from some of his familiar themes while deepening his interest in the family (in many forms) as a source of strength in a fractured, frightening universe. Continuing to combine elements of Magical Realism with the great traditions of the Victorian novel, Irving uses the lore of apple growing and marketing and the graphic details of medical procedures as a solid ground upon which he places the terms of a debate concerning ethical practices and essential human needs.

While the power of love and the forces of eros remain as important elements for Irving, *The Cider House Rules* is a transitional work, shifting the focus of narrative consciousness from the entropic, absurdist cosmos of *The World According to Garp* (1978) toward the realm of the miraculous, which Irving's *A Prayer for Owen Meany* (1989) would bring into prominence. Wilbur Larch, who knows when to break the rules, is guided by an intuitive faith in a higher set of rules that foreshadows the spiritual quest upon which Irving would enter in the latter book.

*Bibliography*

Burgess, Anthony. "A Novel of Obstetrics." *The Atlantic* 98 (July, 1985): 98-100. Review of *The Cider House Rules* by another prominent novelist. Burgess finds the novel's themes admirable but judges the book to be lacking in artistry.

Clemons, Walter. "Dr. Larch's Odd Orphanage." *Newsweek* 105 (May 27, 1985): 80. Clemons criticizes the book from a standard traditionalist position, citing what he claims is its lack of structure, its shallow characterizations, and its sentimentality.

DeMott, Benjamin. "Guilt and Compassion." *The New York Times Book Review* 90 (May 26, 1985): 1, 25. A balanced, subtle, probing examination of the book. Notes the novel's defects but recognizes its virtues, especially its "courage of imaginative ardor" and its straightforward storytelling.

Harter, Carol C., and James R. Thompson. *John Irving.* Boston: Twayne, 1986. A comprehensive study of Irving's career, with a solid chapter on *The Cider House Rules,* a chronology, and a useful list of notes and references.

Reilly, Edward C. *Understanding John Irving.* Columbia: University of South Carolina Press, 1991. An illuminating, clearly written study of Irving's work, with an incisive chapter on *The Cider House Rules,* which Reilly calls a "definite maturing of Irving's literary talents." Includes a brief biography and a good annotated bibliography.

*Leon Lewis*

# CITY OF NIGHT

*Author:* John Rechy (1934-    )
*Type of plot: Bildungsroman*
*Time of plot:* The 1950's
*Locale: El Paso, Texas; New York City; Los Angeles; San Francisco; New Orleans*
*First published:* 1963

> *Principal characters:*
> THE NARRATOR, a Mexican American male prostitute
> MR. KING, a man who craves love but pretends to be indifferent to people
> PETE, a New York street hustler
> THE PROFESSOR, one of the narrator's clients
> MISS DESTINY, a transvestite
> NEIL, a masochist
> JEREMY ADAMS, a "score," who offers love

## The Novel

Based in part on John Rechy's own experiences as an itinerant male prostitute in the late 1950's, *City of Night* is a powerful evocation of a nameless narrator's journey through the underside of America's urban wastelands and a haunting description of the different people he encounters there.

*City of Night* is divided into four parts, roughly equivalent to the narrator's stays in New York, Los Angeles, Hollywood, and New Orleans. It is further divided into short character sketches—named after the individuals who are described—that alternate with sections entitled "City of Night," which propel the action forward. The entire novel is a first-person narrative told by the nameless narrator-protagonist, and all actions are filtered through his consciousness.

The novel begins in El Paso, Texas, the narrator's hometown, with the death of his dog, an event that shapes his consciousness and to which he returns repeatedly throughout the novel. When the child is told that dogs cannot go to heaven, he experiences a loss of faith that is exacerbated by the fact that the dog's decaying carcass has to be reburied because of its smell.

Both parents are impoverished Mexican immigrants, and the home offers the child no escape from the mother's suffocating Catholicism and fierce, protective love and the father's increasingly erratic and threatening behavior, which often manifests itself in terrifying rituals of affection. The narrator's hatred of his father leads to both acts of rebellion and withdrawal from life. This emotional withdrawal increases his isolation so that his mirror becomes the most important object in his life; for him, it narcissistically confirms the reality of his undecayed, youthful body.

Restless after a tour of duty in the Army, the narrator hurls himself into the large cities of America, where he quickly learns to earn his livelihood as a male hustler. It is in New York that the characteristic pattern of the adult narrator's life begins. He is obsessed by a need to be with and wanted by as many people as possible. Hustling seems to be the easiest way to fulfill these desires; as a hustler, the narrator maintains a heterosexual front, although in moments of intense introspection he sees through his own self-deception. His customers, called "scores," neither expect reciprocal sexual acts, nor do they wish him to appear gay. Doing so would destroy their own sexual fantasies.

Most of the narrative provides a guided tour through different sections of the 1950's gay subculture. In the hundreds of people the narrator encounters, he detects an overpowering loneliness camouflaged by various poses of defiance. Mr. King, one of the narrator's first clients, pretends not to care about any human interaction; at the same time, though, he desperately tries to impress the narrator by dressing up for him, and during their second meeting even asks the narrator to move in with him. The Professor both disguises and articulates his feelings of hurt; he talks of love and keeps a scrapbook with pictures of his "angels," but considers himself ugly and thus forced to buy sex. Even a fellow hustler, Pete, who has spent most of his life on the streets and is supposed to be tough and uncaring, drops his mask of heterosexual masculinity with the narrator; as a result, they never speak to each other again, because they both feel that they have violated the code of their trade.

Relentlessly, the narrative continues to explore the narrator's hustling in Los Angeles, San Francisco, Chicago, and New Orleans. In between, he returns to El Paso. This city becomes a refuge for him, a retreat offering sanctuary from the life of the streets and a place to contemplate life behind the protective security of his window.

From Los Angeles to New Orleans, the narrator observes some of the more bizarre aspects of gay life, from the world of transvestites (Miss Destiny) to the sadomasochistic underground (Neil). The men who offer more than money for sex, that is, the possibility of bonding and affection, are immediately rejected. It is in New Orleans, during Mardi Gras, that the narrator encounters Jeremy Adams, a man who finally—although only briefly—breaks through most of the emotional barriers the narrator has erected. Yet even Jeremy does not succeed. Nevertheless, Mardi Gras brings about an emotional crisis of such proportions that the narrator calls a number of Catholic churches, only to be rejected by all but one, in a desperate attempt to find spiritual solace. At the end of the novel, he returns to El Paso and his window to give meaning to his life and experiences, aware that his quest is not yet over.

*The Characters*

From the beginning of the novel, the narrator gains the reader's sympathy because of his overwhelming loneliness. As a child of poor parents and a member of an ethnic minority, he is made to feel different from an early age. This difference is used by the author to create motivation in the narrator's decision to become a hustler. Despite his attempts to display no emotion toward his clients and to kill compassion in himself, he displays an understanding of those who are different, so that people confide in him. Thus he becomes for the reader an emblem of hope for humanity in an inhumane world.

Mr. King feels guilty about his sexual orientation despite his bravado announcements to the contrary. He invites the reader's pity because, much like the narrator, he pretends that he lacks compassion. This hard exterior is quickly exposed as a veneer designed to mask his devastating loneliness. He resembles most of the narrator's clients; they are neurotic because of society's rejection and persecution of their sexual orientation.

The Professor differs from Mr. King because of his intellect and command of language, which he uses to manipulate people. His failure, as it is communicated to the reader, is his inability to recognize true love. Despite his erudition and scholarly importance, he believes that he is unattractive and therefore compelled to pay for sex. The Professor, because of his sense of captivity in an inadequate body, fails to recognize that Larry, his male nurse, loves him unconditionally. Again, the Professor is portrayed as a victim of societal expectations.

Pete is one of the male hustlers whom the narrator describes at length. He is the representative of an entire group of lost young men. Like other hustlers, he is supposed to be tough and heterosexual. When the narrator and Pete spend one night together just holding hands, even this limited show of affection and emotional need is too much for both. Their roles have been compromised, and they avoid one another from then on.

Miss Destiny, a transvestite, is the most elaborately described character in the book. Her portrait is fully developed, and her regal attitude stands in stark contrast to her seedy surroundings. She is shown as more oppressed by society than Mr. King; for example, by law she is not even allowed to wear female attire. Yet she is also described as courageous, because she defies society and its laws. Ultimately, she is as lonely as the other men in the novel, left with the sinking feeling that God played a cruel trick on her.

In many ways, Neil is the most pathetic and repulsive character in the novel. He is a masochist who sees his life's mission as initiating other men into sadomasochism. His function is to show how far a human being can stray from humaneness and still talk about love.

Jeremy is the representative of those men who want more than sexual gratification from the narrator. He has overcome the intense narcissism that enslaves the narrator and thus is able to offer affection and the possibility of love. In many ways, he is one of the most fully realized characters of the novel, and he engages the reader's sympathy. His failure to win the narrator over to his point of view is painful, because the reader wants him to succeed.

*Themes and Meanings*

At the most basic level, the novel is a psychological study of the narrator and his quest for meaning in life. The makeup of his family—the mother's fierce love and the father's inexplicable hatred—seem designed to push the narrator into homosexuality, thus giving expression to a view commonly held at the time of the writing of the novel. Seen in its entirety, the novel is an elaborate investigation of the narrator's fragmented identity. Since he refuses to reveal his name throughout the narrative, he deliberately frustrates a reader's normal expectations to get to know him fully. In fact, all the more elaborately described characters the narrator encounters during his wanderings are carefully chosen to create a contrast to his murky identity. At the same time, this narrative technique allows the reader to imagine the life of a hustler. Like the narrator, the reader meets a character, is drawn into his life for a short period of time, and then as abruptly withdraws. This is underscored by the fact that the narrator attempts to create complicity between the reader and himself by addressing the reader several times directly as "you"; he seems to crave the reader's approval (or, perhaps, absolution). In the same way that the narrator assumes the role of confessor for his clients, the reader becomes the narrator's confessor (or psychologist). Thus the novel can be read as a sustained cry for help, and the comfort that is wished for comes through the telling of the tale; that is, the narrative itself can be read as part of the therapy to heal the narrator's wounded self.

The novel explores the narrator's refusal to accept death and decay. His inability to face this most basic of human conditions leads him, by his own explanation, into hustling; he has lost faith in religion, so other people's desire for his youthful body becomes a substitute for salvation. This crisis of faith is not brought to a complete and satisfying resolution, but the loneliness that the novel so eloquently investigates provides a thematic and structural unity.

Apart from toying with questions of identity, the novel critiques a social system that by law discriminates against those with a different sexual orientation. While the novel tends to fixate on the pathological nature of the people the narrator encounters, the cry against social injustice, not yet fully articulated in political and social terms, cannot be ignored.

All these ideas are tightly interwoven in a circular structure. The novel begins and ends with the narrator's memory of his dog's death and the unresolved crisis of faith that this event precipitated. After all, the anarchy the narrator senses in himself throughout the novel is nothing but the fear of sharing the dog's fate: to grow old and to die. His inability to form meaningful relationships with other people must be seen in light of this. Relationships seem futile to him, because they offer what he considers false hope: the idea of permanence. Yet since the novel ends where it began, it also offers an element of hope. The narrator has come back to where his psychological crisis started, and the reader is left with the impression that when the narrator ventures forth again from his window, he will do so with a fuller understanding of himself and even greater compassion for those people he will encounter.

*Critical Context*

*City of Night* was John Rechy's first novel, and it almost overnight became a best-seller and an underground classic. Its description of parts of the gay subculture was more honest and detailed than had been attempted by writers before. In addition, the novel's narrative framework and technical experimentation show Rechy's indebtedness to other twentieth century writers such as James Joyce and John Dos Passos.

The novel demonstrates the growth of a gay awareness, although this awareness is not yet fully evolved in the book. Through the form of the *Bildungsroman*, the novel of the development of a protagonist's character, Rechy captures the tortured life of his narrator and imbues it with dignity and meaning. The novel's protagonist and structure are also indebted to the picaresque novel. Like the picaro, a hustler lives on the fringes of the law and survives by his wit and resourcefulness.

In several subsequent works, including *Numbers* (1967), *This Day's Death* (1969), and *Rushes* (1979), Rechy continued his attempt to define gay male sexuality and identity. In all these works, questions of Latino identity were almost completely pushed aside. Although Rechy has claimed that all of his main characters are Latino, the emphasis on their ethnic, rather than sexual, identities came much later. There are few indications in *City of Night*, for example, apart from the narrator's lapsed Catholicism and his recurrent feelings of guilt, that ethnic identification is central to his self-understanding. More recently, though, Rechy has investigated questions of Latino identity in his novels *Bodies and Souls* (1983) and *The Miraculous Day of Amalia Gómez* (1991). He has also written a best-selling nonfiction work, *The Sexual Outlaw* (1977), and several plays.

*Bibliography*
Bruce-Novoa, Juan. "In Search of the Honest Outlaw: John Rechy." *Minority Voices* 3, no. 1 (1979): 37-45. Draws connections between Nietzsche's concept of Dionysian and Appolonian consciousness and the narrator of *City of Night*. Asserts that Rechy creates opposition between lived experience and withdrawn contemplation of it.
Fry, Joan. "An Interview with John Rechy." *Poets and Writers Magazine* 20 (May/June 1992): 25-36. Concentrates on style and narrative strategy. Rechy declares and wants readers to recognize that he is a Chicano writer. Also talks about his teaching and writers who have influenced him.
Giles, James R. "Religious Alienation and 'Homosexual Consciousness' in *City of Night* and *Go Tell It on the Mountain*." *College English* 36 (1974): 369-380. Analysis of the destructive role of religion in works by Rechy and James Baldwin. Reads both novels as gay fiction. Rechy is seen as the more important gay author because Baldwin emphasizes ethnic over sexual identity.
Hoffman, Stanton. "The Cities of Night: John Rechy's *City of Night* and the American Literature of Homosexuality." *Chicago Review* 17, nos. 2-3 (1964): 195-206. Compares the novel to works by James Baldwin and Gore Vidal. Argues that gay novels are too limited in their subject matter to capture the interests of a general audience, a view that was still possible in the early 1960's but that must be reconsidered in light of the later mainstreaming of gay literature.
Tatum, Charles M. "The Sexual Underworld of John Rechy." *Minority Voices* 3, no. 1 (1979): 47-52. Analysis of Rechy's first five novels. Sees the individual's attempts to free himself from all societal constraints as the unifying characteristic of these works. Asserts that this struggle reflects the reality of urban America.
Zamora, Carlos. "Odysseus in John Rechy's *City of Night*: The Epistemological

Journey." *Minority Voices* 3, no. 1 (1979): 53-62. Reads the novel as a *Bildungsro-man* in the tradition of Johann Wolfgang von Goethe and James Joyce. Identifies the quest for identity as the book's central concept. Analyzes the protagonist's journey as providing structure and unity to the book.

*Ludger Brinker*

# THE COFFIN TREE

*Author:* Wendy Law-Yone
*Type of plot:* Psychological realism
*Time of plot:* The 1960's through the mid-1970's
*Locale:* Burma, New York City, and Chicago
*First published:* 1983

> *Principal characters:*
> THE NARRATOR, a young Burmese woman whose father sends her to the
>   United States
> SHAN, the narrator's elder half-brother, who accompanies her to the
>   United States
> THE NARRATOR'S FATHER, whose brief appearances in the novel only
>   underscore his tyranny over the lives of his children
> THE INHABITANTS OF 3 EAST, a psychiatric ward to which the narrator is
>   committed after she attempts suicide

*The Novel*

The *Coffin Tree* is the story of a young Burmese woman who leaves her country, where civil war is impending, to arrive in New York City in October, 1969, along with her elder brother, Shan. Their father, a revolutionary, had been in hiding in the hills of Burma for three years, but he manages to arrange for the safe departure of his two children. In exile in America, the narrator recounts the story of her childhood in "monsoon country," the traumatic early years in New York City, the death of her brother, and the time she spends in a psychiatric ward after attempting suicide.

When *The Coffin Tree* opens, the narrator's tyrannical maternal grandmother has just died, and she is left in the care of elderly maiden aunts. Her father is absent, presumably involved in the continuing Revolution of the Hilltribes, to which he has pledged his life. Readers are introduced to the family members in the narrator's home: Auntie Lily and Auntie Rosie, whose collective primary function is to run the household; the inertia-gripped Uncle, a glutton; and the narrator's adored half-brother, Shan.

There is a military coup one day, and the narrator's father has fled to the hilly north. Although the tension is almost palpable, from the narrator's matter-of-fact description of the murder of "Prince R's" son to her recounting of her aunts' efforts to procure food at the markets, there seems to be a suspension of time and space. The day-to-day has become the glue of existence. Before, such trivial details formed the invisible backdrop to life's worthier moments; now, however, the mundane takes center stage, as if by necessity, so that sense can be made from ending up, as the aunts do, with two pairs of men's undershorts instead of sugar, salt, oil, or aspirin. Uncle's inertia turns into infectious fatalism, and the household becomes entrapped in a world explained by "must be!" Suddenly, two or three years after the coup, word comes that the narrator's father has arranged for the flight of his two children, presumably to a safer place.

The narrator and her brother arrive in New York City. Fleeing the upheaval in their homeland, it would seem to the refugees that festive, year-end New York City is the perfect haven. Instead, it is the setting for their dissolution. The traumas of flight and severance from homeland are now juxtaposed against the escalating problems of being in a strange new city. When the promised funds from Burma do not materialize, the pair face unaccustomed poverty. Humiliated and penniless, they manage to reach a journalist acquaintance of their father's, Benjamin Lane. During a year spent in the journalist's basement, the narrator and Shan reach their nadir: Clinging to their pride, they decline to have their meals with the Lanes; instead, they sneak food from the Lanes's kitchen to maintain the illusion that they are fending for themselves.

Meanwhile, Shan continues a descent from sanity. While the narrator had already wondered about her brother's storytelling flights of fancy back in Burma, it is during their years in the new country that she begins to notice distinct signs that his grasp on reality is slipping day by day. Finally, in Chicago, both siblings imprisoned by Shan's illness, Shan dies one evening from a heart attack.

The second half of the novel is about the narrator's experiences among the fellow inhabitants of 3 East, a psychiatric ward, and of the events, after Shan's death, leading to her attempted suicide. After Shan's death, the narrator drifts through the numbing routines of a job and domestic chores. When she learns of her father's death, the news paradoxically shakes her from her stupor. She has found a new purpose to her days: She will systematically direct herself toward suicide. Interspersed with these accounts are flashbacks to her childhood in Burma and memories of her brother and her father.

By the end of the novel, the narrator has left 3 East behind her. She comes to a reconciliation with, if not a resolution of, the disparate strains of her life: the ones that pull her to the "monsoon country" and the unresolvable nature of familial ties, and the ones that now bind her to the new country where she has spilled her blood. The narrator points out, with neither ecstasy nor regret, that the position she writes from is that of being alive.

*The Characters*

The narrator is a girl of fourteen when the narrative begins, and she is in her late twenties when the novel ends. She is the cloistered younger child of an upper-middle-class family in Burma, where her father is a revolutionary hero. Though cloistered, and pampered in the material sense as a result of her family's wealth, the narrator is uncared for emotionally. To her recently deceased maternal grandmother, she was a "mother killer," blamed for her mother's death in childbirth. Her aunts seem to dote on her, yet their doting seems to derive from their own sense of function rather than from the fact that the narrator is a motherless child in need of love. With her father mostly absent, the narrator's only emotional support comes from her brother, who tells her what she never tires of hearing: "You are my sister; I'll look after you." Innocent even in the turmoil of the last years in Burma, the narrator is compelled to become self-reliant and resourceful. When her brother becomes ill, she becomes his nurse, parent, and anchor to reality.

Shan, the narrator's half-brother, is ten years older than the narrator. He is the charismatic older brother of her youth who tells her stories, shows her secret places, keeps a coterie of unsavory friends, and seems to charm everyone except his father. Best of all, he is the narrator's protector. Daring and dashing in Burma, Shan is out of his element in New York City. Here he does not have the means to play prodigal son, and he has no hangers-on with whom to play. Like his sister, he is untrained for any but the most menial jobs, but while his sister diligently seeks work, he is almost reluctant to have to think about a necessary income. Shan seems to have left much of his bravado in Burma, and the chronicle of the early years in America recounts Shan's rapid disintegration. Exhibiting such classic symptoms of manic depression as paranoia, sleeplessness, and wild mood swings, Shan becomes the narrator's millstone.

If the narrator is the emotional center of the novel, her father represents the novel's emotional void. Although he appears only sporadically, his very absence becomes a telling presence in the narrator's life. In brief appearances at his home, he is nevertheless able to send his whole household into a fearful frenzy. He is a cold, calculating man, and he seems to be defined by the violence that is a part of his revolutionary work. He is a father who tries to beat the stuttering out of his son, who is remembered by the narrator for a single manifestation of fatherly love. Even in death, he plays a pivotal role in his daughter's life, pushing her toward suicide.

Most of the inhabitants of 3 East have also attempted suicide. They are a varied group, but collectively they are a reminder of the depths to which the narrator has sunk in confrontation with life's relentless demands. In their bantering and teasing and their matter-of-fact assessments of incarceration, however, they provide the necessary respite from the narrator's lonely, guilt-ridden existence.

*Themes and Meanings*

*The Coffin Tree* is a novel about betrayal. The narrator seems to have been betrayed from birth; her mother dies giving her life, giving her over, it would seem, to no one in particular. Her grandmother reminds her constantly that she is a "mother killer." Her aunts and uncle are living in her father's house not because of her but because of their own private reasons. She is most deeply betrayed, however, by the two people who matter most to her.

The narrator's father, whom she describes as "born to wield" power, was the tyrannical god of her childhood. He is usually absent, ostensibly playing his preferred role of leader of the People's Army. Only from adult retrospection does the narrator realize the general indifference her father must have felt toward her, and she comes to realize that what she knew of her father was the "official version." Her resentment finally shows: "His business was to be a father to us, his children; why else had he given us life?" Finally, she realizes that when her father had gone into hiding after the coup, there was really no danger to her or to Shan. Even her father's enemies had known that it would not have been any use to seek his surrender by threatening his children. His feelings for his children simply did not equal his devotion to his revolutionary tasks.

Shan also betrays the narrator. The narrator has grown up believing that the elder brother and protector of her childhood would always protect her, simply because she was his sister. The brother in Burma, however, is not the same person in America. Instead of protecting her, he becomes the dependent one, dependent on her to get them through the difficult situation of their exile. As he sinks deeper into an illness for which he refuses to seek help, she begins to see through his ravings and lies. As he continues to undermine her trust and belief in him, he is also betraying her memories of him—in retrospect, perhaps the stories he had told her, which had seemed large shreds of life for her to cling to, were merely products of his selfish need to alter his own reality.

The novel also deals, unavoidably, with cultural and personal displacement, with the difficult adjustments from a familiar culture to an alien one, from wealth to poverty, from blinkered naïveté to real life, with all of its visceral betrayals. The novel also chronicles a personal odyssey. The narrator literally crosses an ocean, and the ill winds that propel her to America, a hostile new land, continue to keep her wandering from obstacle to obstacle until she is eventually able to find her own personal restoration. The novel opens with the line, "Living things prefer to go on living." It is not until the last pages of the novel, when the narrator repeats the first sentence, that the reader realizes that the novel is a testament to the commodity called "life." By then, the significance of the title is evident: At first a reference to the tree that yields wood for coffins, it becomes, by novel's end, a symbol of hope, of life itself.

*Critical Context*

*The Coffin Tree* is Law-Yone's first novel. Although Law-Yone was herself born in Burma and came to the United States when she was twenty, it is not clear to what extent the novel is autobiographical. The public events alluded to in the book roughly parallel the unrest, the uprisings by ethnic minorities, and the succession of military regimes that have ruled Burma for many of the years since its independence from British India in 1948.

*The Coffin Tree* was first published in 1983, several years before a pronounced escalation in the publishing of Asian American texts by mainstream publishing houses. A paperback edition appeared in 1987; however, relatively little critical attention has been paid to the novel. Law-Yone, a book reviewer for *The Washington Post*, also published a short story set entirely in Burma in 1988.

*Bibliography*
Aung San Suu Kyi. *Freedom From Fear: And Other Writings.* New York: Penguin, 1991. A collection of writings by the winner of the 1991 Nobel Peace Prize. Aung San charts her involvement with the Burmese National League for Democracy and the tumultuous political events of the late 1980's in Burma. Provides a helpful context for Law-Yone's fiction.

Forbes, Nancy. "*The Coffin Tree.*" *The Nation* 236 (April 30, 1983): 551. Forbes notes that since *The Coffin Tree* is Law-Yone's first novel, it is "not surprising that it reads like autobiography." Forbes also states that the novel seems to be "on familiar terms with all experience, no matter how bizarre," and that Law-Yone "writes with a cool sense of incongruity."

Larson, Charles R. "Books in English From the Third World." *World Literature Today: A Literary Quarterly of the University of Oklahoma* 58 (Summer, 1984): 383-384. Larson supposes that because the "horror of the tale is simply so convincing, so dramatically total," Law-Yone's book must be autobiographical. The review makes an interesting comparison between "Americans and Europeans going crazy in exotic climes" and the converse scenario faced by the book's Asian protagonists.

Law-Yone, Wendy. "Ankle." *Grand Street* 7 (Spring, 1988): 7-24. A short story that raises a few of the themes explored in *The Coffin Tree*. The narrator is a young Burmese girl who is plunged into the company of an unsavory couple as a result of the ineffectual protection of her parents. The story has some of the pathos of *The Coffin Tree* but is much more lighthearted, almost comic, in its treatment of childhood.

*Pat M Wong*

# THE COUNTERLIFE

*Author:* Philip Roth (1933-     )
*Type of plot:* Metafictional
*Time of plot:* 1978
*Locale:* New York, New Jersey, Israel, and London
*First published:* 1986

>     *Principal characters:*
>         NATHAN ZUCKERMAN, a writer of fiction
>         HENRY ZUCKERMAN, his brother, a dentist
>         CAROL ZUCKERMAN, Henry's wife
>         MARIA, Henry's former Swiss lover
>         MARIA FRESHFIELD, Nathan's English lover and wife

*The Novel*

*The Counterlife* continues the saga of Roth's alter ego, Nathan Zuckerman, who has appeared in a number of the author's books over a two-decade period. *The Counterlife* is a highly speculative and highly playful work in the form of a novel in progress about the possibilities and hazards of fiction writing.

Asked why she enjoys Jane Austen's work so much, one of Roth's characters, a very proper Englishwoman, replies, "She simply records life truthfully, and what she has to say about life is very profound. She amuses me so much. The characters are so good." In describing what Austen's fiction is, Mrs. Freshfield unknowingly also describes what *The Counterlife* is not, at least not in any way that Mrs. Freshfield could ever understand. As comic as it is complex, *The Counterlife* consists of five narratives that, while interrelated, are not linearly developed in any conventional sense, are not resolved, either individually or together, and are often at odds with one another.

"Basel" begins with what the reader only later learns is a eulogy, written but because of its inappropriateness never delivered, by forty-four-year-old Nathan Zuckerman on the occasion of his brother Henry's death at age thirty-nine. That discovery is just the first in a bewildering series of surprises in a novel of unexpected reversals that derive—or seem to derive—from Nathan's efforts to understand his brother's death and therefore his life in the only way Nathan knows, by writing about them. (Part 4 will suggest a very different, though parallel, point of departure for *The Counterlife*'s multiple narratives.) Henry elected surgery rather than accept the impotence that is a side effect of the drug prescribed to control his heart condition. Henry, it appears, wanted to become sexually active again in order to continue his affair with his dental assistant, Wendy, an affair that is itself the result of, as well as an attenuated version of, Henry's tempestuous affair with a married Swiss woman named Maria some years before. That affair Henry has confessed to only one person, perversely enough, his brother Nathan, a novelist famous for turning family secrets into best-selling fiction. Having failed to give up his conventional life for a more satisfying, or at least exciting, counterlife in Switzerland with Maria, Henry chooses to risk death rather than give up his more perfunctory and even farcical after-hours dalliance with Wendy. This, of course, is not the version that Henry's wife Carol offers in the eulogy she delivers in Nathan's stead. Carol's Henry is a dedicated family man willing to risk his life for the sake of a complete, which is to say sexually satisfying, marriage. Whether Carol actually believes this "version" of Henry, neither Nathan nor the reader can say for sure. What is clear is that in his uncertainty, Nathan finds ample room for narrative speculation.

Stories and counter-stories, as well as counterlives, continue to proliferate in part 2, "Judea." Here Henry has survived not only surgery but also postoperative depression. He finds his cure for the latter in Israel, where he transforms himself into Hanoch, a disciple of a fanatical Zionist named Mordecai Lippman. A dismayed and desperate Carol dispatches Nathan—no longer living alone in New York but married to his very own and very English Maria—to bring Henry back to his senses and to his family. Although Nathan's mission fails, his experiences in Israel cause him to ponder more deeply and more imaginatively Henry's situation and his own, particularly as a Jewish American writer.

These speculations become the subject of the novel's next section, "Aloft." Aboard a flight from Tel Aviv to London, Nathan writes and rewrites a letter to Henry that he will never send and then ponders the letter that a friend, an Israeli journalist, gave him just before departure. His musings give way to farce when a fellow passenger dressed as a Hasidic Jew turns out to be Nathan's biggest fan. Claiming Nathan as his inspiration, Jimmy Ben-Joseph Lustig tells Nathan that he is about to hijack the plane, though he also says that he is only joking. In any case, farce gives way to nightmare when two security men thwart the plan, if it is a plan, perhaps mistaking Jimmy's joke, if it is a joke, for the real thing. Jimmy is brutally beaten, and Nathan tries, seemingly without success, to give his Kafkaesque interrogators what they want, an account of himself that they can believe.

In part 4, "Gloucestershire," however, Nathan is the one with the heart problem and the desire to live a different life. He wants to live in London with Maria, who is not yet his wife, as she already was in "Judea." Nathan desires exactly the kind of conventional life from which Henry wanted to escape in "Basel." Now it is Henry who cannot deliver the eulogy and who listens to one he knows to be false. Afterward, he goes to his brother's apartment, looking for the notebooks into which he is sure Nathan recorded Henry's confession of his affair with Maria. Though he is aware of his brother's propensity for "cannibalizing" family secrets for the sake of his fiction, Henry is still dismayed, as is the reader, though for a quite different reason, to find a manuscript labeled "Draft #2" which appears to be parts 1, 2, 3, and 5 of *The Counterlife*. Furious, Henry removes the incriminating sections and dumps them in a garbage bin at a rest stop along the Jersey Turnpike. At this point, the chapter switches form and point of view a second time. In an interview with a "restless soul," presumably Nathan's ghost, Maria discusses her visit to Nathan's apartment and her decision to leave the manuscript as she found it, even though doing so will surely jeopardize her marriage. As the ghost shrewdly realizes, that may be the reason Maria leaves the manuscript intact, allowing it to do what she is too timid to.

Yet in "Christendom," Nathan, like Henry in "Judea," is back again, in London, following what is now described as a "quiet flight" (perhaps, therefore, with no attempted hijacking) from Israel. Maria is now, as she was in part 2, his wife. Nathan's brief stay in Israel has, however, changed him, sensitizing (or perhaps oversensitizing) him to anti-Semitism, English style. At the restaurant to which he has taken Maria to celebrate her twenty-eighth birthday, Nathan sniffs anti-Semitism in another diner's rather loud complaint about a foul smell. Well aware of her own mother's anti-Semitism, Maria tries to calm Nathan; failing, she decides that perhaps a Jew and a Christian cannot live happily ever after. Alone at the house they are having renovated but have not yet occupied, Nathan wonders whether Maria may be gone for good, a possibility that Nathan, ever the novelist, quickly sees in narrative terms. First, he imagines her farewell note, in which she says she cannot endure "a lifetime of never knowing whether you're fooling," existing as nothing more than a character in some ongoing fiction of his devising. He then imagines his reply, which ends, as the novel does, "It may be as you say that this is no life, but use your enchanting, enrapturing brains: this life is as close to life as you, and I, and our child can ever hope to come."

*The Characters*

In his family and educational background as well as his career as a novelist, Nathan Zuckerman is clearly Philip Roth's self-confessed "front man," alter ego, and all round ventriloquist's dummy. Rejecting the role of "family id," Zuckerman is perhaps most like Roth in the sense that Roth described himself in a 1984 interview as being "like somebody who is trying vividly to transform himself out of himself and into his vividly transforming heroes. I am like somebody who spends all day writing." What makes it especially difficult, even risky, to discuss Nathan or indeed any of the *The Counterlife*'s characters with any degree of certainty is that they exist in several ontological and narrative states consecutively and at times concurrently. They are in a sense at once real (if the reader follows Coleridge's advice and suspends disbelief, as most novels allow and require) and doubly fictitious (insofar as they are both Zuckerman's and Roth's creations). Although no less "real" or compelling than the characters in the novels of Jane Austen that Maria's mother, Mrs. Freshfield, admires, they are far more elusive and problematic, for it is impossible to determine just where the facts of their lives leave off and Zuckerman's as well as their own fictions begin. Henry, for example, seems entirely in character when he defends himself as one who lives with the facts, unlike Nathan who, fearing real life, spends his life trying to alter them from the safety of his study. But the Henry who makes this claim is, or may be, already as much a character in Nathan's fiction and/or his own mind as he is in Roth's novel.

On the one hand, the novel's characters, including Nathan, are presented in quasi-allegorical fashion. Nathan "is" the family id, Henry is the successful professional firmly grounded in the reality principle (alternately the younger brother envious of what he takes to be Nathan's irresponsible life of sexual excess). Mordecai Lippman is Zionism, and Maria is cast as "famous English insouciance" to Nathan's equally famous and equally allegorical "Jewish intensity." On the other hand, since, as Nathan claims, "playacting . . . may be the only authentic thing we ever do," the characters seem far less stable than their allegorical meanings will allow and therefore far more open to the transformational possibilities that *The Counterlife* explores and exploits so comically and provocatively. Nathan is thus both the diaspora Jew and defender of the faith, depending on which country and in what chapter he happens to be at the time. With his Swiss mistress, Henry nearly overcomes his upper-middle-class inhibitions. Similarly, with his very English lover/wife, writer of "fluent cliches and fluffy ephemera for silly magazines," Nathan, author of the aptly titled novel *Carnovsky*, expresses a very different kind of desire, "to give up the artificial fiction of being myself for the genuine, satisfying falseness of being somebody else." All the while Nathan remains a writer, not distant from his work in the Joycean mode of a god paring his fingernails but implicated in it, obsessed with the problematic relation of life and art, with, as Nathan, or "Nathan," puts it, "the kind of stories that people turn life into, the kind of lives that people turn stories into."

### Themes and Meanings

"But the *might-have-been* is but boggy ground to build on," notes the narrator of Herman Melville's *Billy Budd, Foretopman* (1924). "The might-have-been," however, is the very stuff on which Zuckerman and Roth build their various counterlives and counter-books. A simple "what if" yields a proliferation of narrative deductions and permutational possibilities in a text that manages to delight and disorient in equal measure. Along the way, biographical facts become metaphorical structures: Bypass surgery becomes a system of narrative bypasses, blocked arteries turn into blocked stories, and impotence, infidelity, and promiscuity become textual as well as sexual facts of life in a novel that invites "polymorphous perversity" while resisting "simple penetration." As with the cryonics mentioned in "Basel," so with Roth's entire novel: "Anything is possible," including the resurrection of the dead. In "Judea," in "a world of bare beginnings," Henry begins again, a rugged self for a rugged landscape.

Every significant character in *The Counterlife* exists in multiple versions, not just written and rewritten, but read and reread, interpreted and reinterpreted, as the line separating actual events from imagined ones blurs, both becoming the raw materials for Nathan's nonstop "narrative factory." In effect, the novel reproduces Roth's usual compositional process: eighteen months or so spent writing in an effort to find his subject, followed by six months writing the more or less final draft. Where *The Counterlife* differs from Roth's earlier work is in its foregrounding of the compositional process by incorporating material, as it were, from the initial eighteen-month groping stage, material normally consigned to the wastebasket or file cabinet. In doing so, Roth makes *The Counterlife* into his most playful yet also most serious, extensive, and provocative meditation on what critic Bernard Rodgers has called "the enigma of identity" in relation to "the conflicts between life and art, the writer and his creations, reality and fiction." Typical of Roth's approach to writing as a form of "problem solving," *The Counterlife* is, in Paul Gray's words, "a metaphysical thriller" about "the elusive nature of truth"—or, as Nathan imagines Maria saying rather accusingly, about Nathan's "preoccupation with irresolvable conflict." Thus, the novel plays the pastoral impulse in its various guises (including and especially Mrs. Freshfield's) against the entanglements and contradictions of its five parts.

*Critical Context*

Honored with a National Book Critics Circle Award, *The Counterlife*, Roth's thirteenth book of fiction, continues and further complicates the story of the author's most extensively portrayed and ambiguously angled alter ego. Nathan Zuckerman first appears as the main character in two stories by Peter Tarnopol, the main character in Roth's *My Life as a Man* (1974); Tarnopol writes the stories as a form of therapy following a disastrous marriage clearly modeled on Roth's own. From the role of protagonist in stories within a story, Nathan becomes a hero in his own right in *The Ghost Writer* (1979), *Zuckerman Unbound* (1981), and *The Anatomy Lesson* (1983). The publication of all three Zuckerman novels in a single volume punningly titled *Zuckerman Bound* (1985), however, seemed to indicate that Roth was done with Zuckerman.

*The Counterlife* shows that he was not, shows that Zuckerman the sexually insatiable (as many of his readers believe him to be) is also Zuckerman the narratively indestructible and inexhaustible. The entire Zuckerman saga deals in fictional form with many of the same issues Roth felt compelled to address following the negative remarks made chiefly by Jewish readers and critics about *Goodbye, Columbus* (1959) and more especially *Portnoy's Complaint* (1969), books that Roth rightly claimed were neither anti-Semitic nor unambiguously autobiographical except to the most literal-minded readers. Roth's most direct responses to their charges are to be found in *Reading Myself and Others* (1975) and in the numerous interviews he has, often warily, given. In Zuckerman, Roth has found a way to deal with these same issues in a more imaginatively complex way, turning ad hominem misreadings to narrative advantage. Zuckerman figures importantly in *The Facts: A Novelist's Autobiography* (1988), more briefly in the novel *Deception* (1990), and more briefly still in *Operation Shylock: A Confession* (1993). In all these works, *The Counterlife* in particular, questions of simple autobiographical identity and equivalence dissolve in Roth's dizzying and provocative brand of performance art, his seemingly endless variations on the theme of metamorphosis.

*Bibliography*

Halio, Jay L. *Philip Roth Revisited*. New York: Twayne, 1992. In this updating of Bernard Rodgers' *Philip Roth* (1978) in the same Twayne's United States Authors series, Halio discusses all of Roth's books through *Deception*, emphasizing plot summary. A brief but useful bibliography is included.

Lyons, Bonnie. "'Jew on the Brain' in 'Wrathful Phillipics.'" *Studies in American Jewish Literature* 8 (Fall, 1989): 186-195. Lyons reads *The Counterlife* in relation to the other Zuckerman writings. She concludes that the novel's strength derives from Roth's handling of the variety of Jewish identities.

Searles, George J., ed. *Conversations with Philip Roth*. Jackson: University Press of Mississippi, 1992. Reprints thirty-eight interviews with Roth. Extended discussions of *The Counterlife* appear in the interviews by Mervyn Rothstein, Paul Gray, Alvin Sanoff, Katherine Weber, and Hermione Lee. Includes a brief introduction and a useful chronology.

Shechner, Mark. "Zuckerman's Travels." In *The Conversion of the Jews and Other Essays*. New York: St. Martin's Press, 1990. Shechner argues that the importance of *The Counterlife* derives from its combination of "theatrical lightness" and "historical density." Shechner's essay should be read in connection with his lengthier discussion of Roth's earlier work in *After the Revolution: Studies in the Contemporary Jewish American Imagination* (1987).

Shostak, Debra. "'This Obsessive Reinvention of the Real': Speculative Narrative in Philip Roth's *The Counterlife*." *Modern Fiction Studies* 37 (Summer, 1991): 197-215. Shostak reads the novel as a "speculative" fiction about "the sources, meaning, and power of narrative" and about the self as narrative. Roth's "commitment to—and redefinition of—the 'real'" enables him to transcend "the implicit nihilism and anxiety of the postmodern decentered or indefinite self."

*Robert A. Morace*

# THE CUTTER

*Author:* Virgil Suarez (1962-    )
*Type of plot:* Bildungsroman
*Time of plot:* 1969
*Locale:* Cuba and the United States
*First published:* 1991

*Principal characters:*

> JULIAN CAMPOS, a twenty-year-old university student who seeks an "exit notice" from the Cuban government
> BERNARDA DEL RIO, Julian's grandmother
> CARMINA, Julian's housekeeper and friend
> BLANCAROSA CALDERON, the woman who betrays Julian and his friends
> SILVIA, Julian's neighbor and fellow escapee
> OFELIA, Silvia's daughter

## The Novel

*The Cutter* is the story of a young man's desperate attempt to leave what he believes to be a repressive Communist regime in Cuba. The novel is divided into five sections that mark the stages of Julian's journey away from Cuba: "The Notice," "The Fields," "The Operation," "The Shore," and "The Refuge." The story is told from the point of view of an omniscient third-person narrator.

The book begins when protagonist Julian Campos is twenty years old. Julian is a university student who has recently returned to Havana after having completed his years of mandatory military service in the Young Pioneers. Julian drifts off into the "freedom of sleep" only to be abruptly awakened by his ailing grandmother, Bernarda Del Rio, who informs Julian that someone is at the door. The visitor is a government official who hands Julian a telegram from the Ministry of the Interior. Julian has been waiting to leave Cuba ever since his parents received an "exit notice" five years earlier. Julian resents the fact that his parents left him behind. Although Elena and Ernesto, Julian's parents, wanted to take their son with them to the United States, the authorities at the airport demanded that they leave Julian in Cuba or forfeit the privilege of leaving the country themselves.

Although Julian is disenchanted with the government in Cuba, he still believes that the legal system works. He is therefore convinced that if he goes through the proper bureaucratic channels, he will be rewarded with an exit notice from the Ministry of the Interior. Heartened by the receipt of the telegram, Julian plans a new life in the United States for himself and his grandmother, but it is not to be. Julian is told that he must do additional "voluntary work" if he wants to leave Cuba.

In the second section, "The Fields," Julian spends months cutting cane for Cuba's "Ten-Million-Ton Sugarcane Program." The work is slave labor, and Julian and his coworkers are mistreated. The men arise early and work all day, regardless of weather conditions. The workers receive substandard food, live in overcrowded housing, and are monitored by characters reminiscent of cruel overseers on Southern plantations before the Civil War. This section of the novel depicts Cuba at its worst, leading the reader to understand why Julian is compelled to leave the country. Julian grows increasingly despondent about his prospects for leaving Cuba, particularly when he receives the belated news of his grandmother's death.

When Julian is finally released from the fields and permitted to go home, he realizes that he will never receive an exit notice. He learns from Ofelia, his neighbor, that she and her mother, Silvia, are planning to escape. In the third section, "The Operation," Julian joins them in this quest. Blancarosa Calderon, Julian's former classmate, is a key figure in the escape plan and offers her assistance to Silvia, Ofelia, and Julian. Julian and his friends discover too late that Blancarosa works for the government. She betrays the group of escapees, resulting in the deaths of Silvia and Ofelia. Julian, however, survives. "The Shore," the novel's fourth section, describes his continued move toward the United States and freedom.

In the novel's final section, "The Refuge," Julian reaches the United States. In contrast to most of the Cuban characters, those in the United States are kind to him and are eager to help him adjust to his new country. Padre Marcelo, the priest at the Catholic Refugee Center, finds Julian a temporary job at a small cafe in Miami. Julian clearly enjoys his newfound freedom, and he contemplates the possibility of seeing his parents again. The section implies that the story will have a happy ending. Although Julian appears reluctant to search for his parents, the novel ends with a suggestion that ultimately he will find refuge with them.

## The Characters

Julian, the major character, captures the sympathy of the reader at the beginning of the book. He longs for freedom and attempts to attain it legally, but he eventually realizes that he will never be allowed to leave Cuba. Although Julian's parents were deeply distressed about having to leave their son behind when they left the country, they made the choice to leave. Despite Julian's own desperation to leave Cuba, he never forgives his parents for leaving for the United States without him. Julian is a good, responsible young man. He cares deeply for his ailing grandmother Bernarda and for Carmina, Bernarda's housekeeper and nursemaid. Julian tries to do what is right and obtain his freedom legally, but he suffers for his efforts. The novel suggests that there is no justice in Communist Cuba for *gusanos*, those people who refuse to join the Communist Party.

Bernarda, Julian's grandmother, represents that group of people who believed in the system but became disillusioned after the repressive government began to retaliate against those who opposed the revolution. Julian's father, Ernesto, was such a man. After Ernesto was imprisoned for organizing "antirevolutionary activities," Bernarda renounced Cuba and the revolution. She longed for a reunion with her son in the United States.

Carmina, Bernarda's faithful housekeeper and friend, nurses Julian's grandmother until she dies, then takes care of Julian after his return from the work camp. Although

Carmina sympathizes with Julian's desire to leave Cuba and assists him in his efforts, she refuses to leave Cuba. It is her home, and Carmina suggests that she has a kind of freedom there.

Nicanor is in charge of *El Comite*, "the community watchdog." He is the only major black character. He is a widower who lost his pregnant wife in a fire ten years before the action of the novel. Before the revolution, Nicanor was unemployed. He refuses a chance to flee Cuba after the revolution, vowing to attain a position in which he is powerful enough to "get even" for his wife's death. Nicanor watches Julian carefully and suspects, near the end of the novel, that Julian plans to leave Cuba illegally. Nicanor represents the repressive, ruthless government. He is clearly responsible for thwarting Julian's attempts to leave Cuba legally.

Blancarosa Calderon inspires no sympathy, for she betrays her friends. Although government officials and party sympathizers call Julian a *gusano*, a traitor, it is clear that Blancarosa is the only traitor in the novel: She deliberately deceives those who entrust their lives to her.

Ofelia, Silvia's daughter and Julian's neighbor, tells Julian about the planned escape. Ofelia believes herself to be in love with Julian and is jealous of Blancarosa, toward whom Julian seems to have some romantic inclinations. Fermin, Ofelia's father, goes to the cane fields with Julian. He and Julian spend time together in the camp jail cell. At the camp, Fermin is caught buying *aguardiente*, an illegal alcoholic drink. Fermin, who drinks to ease his frustration, tells Julian, while they are in detention, that he wants to die drunk. Fermin dies mysteriously, apparently getting his wish. Silvia and Ofelia are told that Fermin suffered a fatal heart attack.

*Themes and Meanings*

*The Cutter* is a scathing critique of the Communist government in Cuba. The events in the novel take place after Fidel Castro's revolution. The novel takes a vehemently anti-Communist position, with the repressiveness and evil of Communism as a recurrent theme. Other themes surround the dominant political one. The novel concerns the desire for personal freedom and independence, but it is also about the loss of innocence and of the belief that if one does the right thing, good will necessarily be the end result.

Julian moves from an attitude of hopeful skepticism to despair and rebellion, and he comes to understand, by the end of the novel, the value of freedom. Despite his ambivalence about his parents' abandonment of him, it seems clear that Julian and his parents will not only meet again, but they will also reunite as family.

The struggle between the forces of good and evil is clear throughout the novel. Julian, his grandmother, and his friends are representations of good, as are the opponents of Castro's regime. The democratic society of the United States, which Julian strives to join, stands in stark contrast to the repressive regime of Cuba, which he seeks to escape. Blancarosa and members of the Communist Party are the forces of evil. They are unredeemable, uniformly corrupt, and cruel.

The themes of escape and exile take curious twists. Escape becomes a necessity, and exile becomes a relief. Julian feels no ambivalence about leaving his native soil. Once in the United States, he has no fond memories of Cuba and no longing to return. His associates that "home" with pain and misery. The plot of the novel is rather simple, and its messages are clear: Communism is bad, escape from it is essential, and freedom is worth any price.

*Critical Context*

The Cutter, Virgil Suarez's second novel, is his attempt to come to grips with his native Cuba and reflects his bitterness toward the country from which he and his parents were exiles. Suarez's own family left Cuba in 1970, about the time at which this novel is set. Suarez is unrelenting in his criticism of the Cuban government and of Castro's Cuba as a harsh, repressive, and cruel place where a semblance of freedom exists only for those ruthless characters who follow the Party line. He has no favorable character to speak for or represent the government.

What seems conspicuously absent from the novel, as it is often found in works by writers from the Caribbean, is a detailed description of the island itself. Cuba is a beautiful island, but Suarez chooses not to depict that natural beauty, indicative of his treatment of the entire life and culture of the island. Suarez's portrayal of Cuba is perhaps too harsh and the novel itself too preachy and melodramatic. It is, however, obviously heartfelt.

Suarez's first novel, *Latin Jazz* (1989), was not favorably received and was relatively unsuccessful. *The Cutter* has had a similar fate.

*Bibliography*

Kaganoff, Penny. Review of *The Cutter*, by Virgil Suarez. *Publishers Weekly* 238 (January 4, 1991): 67. This brief review summarizes the plot of the novel, stating that it shows how ordinary people can be driven to undertake extraordinary risks.

Krist, Gary. "Other Voices, Other Rooms." *The Hudson Review* 45 (Spring, 1992): 144-146. Krist discusses Suarez as representing the changing face of American literature, as an author previously "unheard and unpublished." Krist suggests that the subject of *The Cutter* is revenge and that the novel is "tainted by politics."

*Los Angeles Times Book Review*. Review of *The Cutter*, by Virgil Suarez. March 31, 1991, 6. Praises the novel as ambitious. Notes that the third-person, present-tense narration creates both distance and immediacy.

Robertson, Deb. Review of *The Cutter*, by Virgil Suarez. *Booklist* 87 (December 1, 1990): 718. A brief review giving a plot summary. Calls the book a reminder that oppression is not dead. The book retains its power by avoiding indignation and self-righteousness on the part of the author.

Stavans, Ilan. "The Cutter." *The New York Times Book Review*, April 14, 1991, 20. In an unfavorable review, Stavans accuses Suarez of being a "dirty realist" who writes in "cold, unornamented, Hemingwayesque style." Stavans says that Suarez's characters are cartoon-like stereotypes and that the novel itself is melodramatic.

*Margaret Kent Bass*

# THE DARK HALF

*Author:* Stephen King (1947-    )
*Type of plot:* Horror
*Time of plot:* 1960-1989
*Locale:* New Jersey and Maine
*First published:* 1989

> *Principal characters:*
> THAD BEAUMONT, a novelist and English professor
> GEORGE STARK, Thad's pseudonymous alter ego
> ELIZABETH ("LIZ") BEAUMONT, Thad's wife
> SHERIFF ALAN PANGBORN, Castle Rock's sheriff and Thad's ally
> DR. HUGH PRITCHARD, a physician who performed Thad's strange operation
> FREDERICK CLAWSON, Thad's former literary agent
> RICK COWLEY, Thad's literary agent
> HOMER GAMACHE, the first murder victim
> RAWLIE DELESSEPS, one of Thad's colleagues

## The Novel

Following fifteen previous Stephen King horror novels, including the immensely popular *Carrie* (1974), *'Salem's Lot* (1975), and *The Shining* (1977), *The Dark Half* exploits fictions within fiction and paranormal phenomena that mystify and terrorize a cast of plausible characters.

Thad Beaumont, the protagonist, has been a successful novelist whose most popular works were written under the pseudonym "George Stark." Writing as Stark, Beaumont created a fearsome embodiment of evil, a ruthless, robotlike killer named Alexis Machine. The gruesome fictional horrors perpetrated by Machine were responsible for Beaumont/Stark's sales and literary notoriety.

Trouble begins, however, when Beaumont determines to abandon his Stark pseudonym and decides to write serious works under his own name. From the moment of this decision, he is incapacitated by writer's block. He even suspects that he can write successfully only as Stark. Meanwhile, Beaumont's former agent, the sleazy Frederick Clawson, reveals to *People* magazine that Stark is Beaumont, a fact that Beaumont acknowledges in an interview that culminates in the mock burial of George Stark and Beaumont's confirmation that Stark's career has terminated. A fiction or not, Stark refuses to stay buried in his mock grave. Ghoullike, he emerges and launches a campaign of terror and grisly murders among Beaumont's associates and loved ones. The objective of his brutal rampage is to force Beaumont formally to resurrect him and to recommence writing, this time under Stark's direction. Confused, menaced, and terrorized by a Stark who may or may not be a monster of his own creation, Beaumont is plunged into a seemingly endless nightmare as he tries to gain credibility with his wife, his friends, and the sheriff and to cope with and then subdue Stark.

Mystery, suspense, and plausibility are lent to this scenario by King's recital in *The Dark Half*'s prologue of a critical event in Thad Beaumont's childhood. Troubled by the sound and vision of birds and wracked by headaches, the precocious Thad undergoes surgery for removal of a brain tumor. Within Thad's brain, the surgeon discovers, and removes, living portions of Thad's twin, who had been cannibalized by Thad when the two were fetuses.

King paces his plot through three parts that together encompass twenty-six chapters plus an epilogue. Following the essential information about Beaumont's childhood operation in the prologue, part 1 convincingly sketches Thad's domestic situation in Castle Rock, Maine, and introduces the major characters. The consequences of Thad's writing block and his *People* interview, the mock burial of George Stark, the emergence of something from Stark's "grave," and Castle Rock's grisly murders (the first victim, Homer Gamache, is beaten to death with his own prosthetic arm), open the mystery and raise questions that beguile the reader throughout the book. Is George Stark real? Is the whole story a dream? Is Thad schizophrenic, paranormal, or simply mentally unbalanced? On what grounds can credibility be lent to Thad's suspicions or to George Stark's "return"? What is Stark's game?

In part 2, Stark takes charge of events, conducting a series of calculatedly horrific murders the purpose of which is to terrorize Thad into writing once more as Stark. At the same time, Thad wrestles with doubts about his own stability; he also tries to retain his wife's understanding and win Sheriff Pangborn as an ally. Part 2 closes with the relentless Stark closing in on Thad by abducting his wife and twins.

In part 3, the tables turn against Stark. Without fully comprehending the paranormal events associated with this monster, Sheriff Pangborn nevertheless competently and wholeheartedly joins Thad in efforts to thwart Stark. Events climax with Stark, his hostages, Thad, and the sheriff testing wits in the Beaumont household. Stark's defeat and the Beaumont's liberation come by means of increasingly ubiquitous sparrows, King's "psychopomps" (those who conduct the living to the dead), which blanket the landscape and then whirl the dying Stark into space and oblivion. As a finale, Sheriff Pangborn and Thad ignite Stark's automobile and then crash it into the Beaumont house, destroying the home so that the whole bizarre tale can be obscured by a mundane house fire and thus be rendered comprehensible to Castle Rock's natives.

King's characters gain dimension through both words and actions, but with the exception of Stark, they achieve three-dimensionality only briefly. Thad is thus convincing when confronting his authorial problems or rather cynically exploiting his *People* interview. Stark is effective and believable, but only as a symbol. Rawlie DeLesseps, Thad's English department colleague, though a relatively minor figure in moving the action, comes through successfully because of his quirky professorial manner. Dr. Pritchard speaks and behaves like a believable surgeon. Stark's victims—and they are numerous—react plausibly during their last moments of terror. Like Thad's detestable literary agent Frederick Clawson, however, most of the victims were no great bargains for civilization in the first place.

*The Characters*

King is accomplished in the production of credible characters in familiar domestic and small-town settings. One of the hallmarks of his composition is his ability to draw readers into the normal routines and trials of middle American households. These familiar settings are essential backdrops against which the author then casts grotesque and fantastic events. As King's protagonist, Thad Beaumont evokes sympathy from the outset. His struggle with writer's block is almost a cliché. Readers wonder whether Beaumont has created and fallen victim to his literary alter ego, George Stark, a Frankenstein. Thad, though, is neither mad nor hallucinating. He is a good and decent man who unintentionally opens the door to evil, an evil that springs from his own creativity and actions, an evil that victimizes him, his family, and his acquaintances and that therefore must be fought.

Liz Beaumont, Thad's wife, is a somewhat passive, two-dimensional loving soul. She is worried about her husband, but until the latter stages of the book, she is uncomprehending about Thad's personal struggle with Stark. She manifests some resolve and initiative when Stark takes her and her twins hostage, but she functions chiefly as a gauge of the normal.

As Thad becomes ensnared in the irrationalities that surround Stark's reality, Sheriff Alan Pangborn serves as the rational counterfoil to Thad's suspicions about who and what Stark is. Pangborn is the reader's solid if unimaginative alter ego. He is at first mystified and professionally skeptical about Thad, suspecting his innocence, his explanations, and his emotional stability. Eventually, however, he becomes Thad's essential ally.

George Stark is the embodiment of evil, and he has most of the literary accoutrements required to make him appear diabolical. He is calculating, cold-blooded, ruthless, and maniacal. In his supposed reality, he hails from Oxford, Mississippi, and he is replete with a hokey Southern charm and menacing redneck speech. Inevitably, he is more interesting than the Thad Beaumont who ostensibly created him, and he provides the drama that gives life to *The Dark Half*. Stark's own authorial creation, Alexis Machine, lives up to his name as a vicious killer from whom Stark borrows words and symbols of his evil as well as the techniques that he employs in his slaughterings.

Stark's numerous murder victims are convincing in their last moments of confusion and terror; however, they tend to be either rather stupid innocents, or like the agent Clawson, unpleasant. King's characters nevertheless always maintain enough substance to rush his story along.

*Themes and Meanings*

*The Dark Half* is a sensational, wordy, and not well-resolved tale of conflict between King's vision of what middle America regards as good and what can always be cataloged as evil. King gives substance to this struggle by revealing the troubling doubts, often moral ones, that evolve within his protagonist. The scene of this contest, as in other King books, is a small town, in this instance the fictional Castle Rock,

Maine. The setting is deliberately conservative, a family-oriented small-town repository of solid American values. The world outside Castle Rock, is one to which many of King's characters are viscerally opposed. They fear and dislike the technocratic-managerial culture engulfing them, and they view its future in apocalyptic terms. Stark and Alexis Machine, as manifest pillars of destruction, are sufficient evidence of this.

All *The Dark Half*'s principal characters consequently are disparaging observers of big cities and big-city types. Thus New York is backhanded several times as the Maggoty Old Apple—a prejudice widely shared. The female photographer who comes to Castle Rock to manage George Stark's mock burial is likewise derided, while sensationalist and tawdry *People* magazine, readers are told, has its year-round nest in New York. The Washington, D.C. characters fare no better; they include Dobie Eberhart, a loud, avaricious prostitute who caters to senior politicians, and Thad's former literary agent, a low-rung corporate lawyer, blackmailer, and "creepazoid." Even *The Dark Half*'s conclusion is foreboding. One of the sparrows draws Thad's blood—a sign, he believes, that for having fooled with the afterlife he will soon have to pay a price.

*The Dark Half* thus continues King's themes that humankind is trapped and confused in a chaotic universe and is further victimized by failures to conquer the evil ladled from its own cultural brew. To the extent that King wrote the book to entertain, he succeeded once again. Still, the crafting of this tale perhaps does not warrant the utter suspension of readers' disbelief.

*Critical Context*

Since the mid-1970's, Stephen King has ranked among the most popular of American authors. Many academic and literary critics likewise rank him among the country's best writers. His readership reaches into the tens of millions, and he has fed its appetites with new books (as well as their film versions, articles, and written conversations) almost every year. His canon ranges far more widely than can be inferred from *The Dark Half*, encompassing science fiction, elements of legends, myths, tragedy, the political and historical, and every imaginable aspect of the gothic, macabre, and horror genres. His capacity to mine and recast materials from all these areas attests an assiduously acquired mastery as well as to his unique perceptiveness and immense enthusiasm for his work. His genius for fascinating and drawing in his readers is palpable. A self-described "guru of the ordinary," he beguiles with replications of commonplace dialogue, feelings, sights, and experiences, the better to stretch imaginations, to shock, or to horrify.

Critics note that *The Dark Half*, with its play upon pseudonymous authors—King and his earlier pseudonymous self, Richard Bachman, whose "death" King cites in the author's note, and Beaumont and George Stark—represents the liberation (and improvement) of King's writing. As Bachman, King struggled to get things out of his system, wrestled with himself, and experimented. Creatively, Bachman may have made King possible, and in that sense *The Dark Half* may be interpreted as autobiographical. Perhaps King's anxieties make possible his rapport with an anxiety-ridden American culture that nurtures self-destruction.

## Bibliography

Collings, Michael R. *The Stephen King Phenomenon*. Mercer Island, Washington: Starmont House, 1987. One of the author's many books on King and his works. An interesting, clearly written estimate of King's influences on American literature, film, and American culture. Scholarly in substance, but written for laymen.

Magistrale, Tony. *Landscape of Fear: Stephen King's American Gothic*. Bowling Green, Ohio: Bowling Green State University Popular Press, 1988. Expertly links King to the gothic tradition of which he is a master and to major themes in American literature as explored by William Faulkner, Mark Twain, Edgar Allan Poe, and Nathaniel Hawthorne.

_____. *The Moral Voyages of Stephen King*. San Bernardino, Calif.: Borgo Press, 1989. A clear, substantive analysis of King's continuing interest in interactions of good and evil. The author also deals with other recurrent themes in King's novels: the individual search for identity, self-destructiveness, social decay, and psychological imbalances.

_____. *Stephen King: The Second Decade, "Danse Macabre" to "The Dark Half."* New York: Twayne, 1992. A companion volume to Joseph Reino's (cited below), this is jargon-free scholarship written for an intelligent popular audience. Critical, but very appreciative of King as a major writer. Views King as a trenchant commentator on an America that sees tawdry weaknesses and menace in the American Dream. Opens with an informative King interview. Cross-analyzes thirteen King novels. Useful chronology and maps of settings.

Reino, Joseph. *Stephen King: The First Decade, "Carrie" to "Pet Sematary."* Boston: Twayne, 1988. Well-informed, clearly presented analysis in Twayne's series on major American writers. Though invaluable, it does not deal with King's revelatory writings as Richard Bachman. Less effective in defining King's indebtedness to Western literary traditions.

*Clifton K. Yearley*

# DAVITA'S HARP

*Author:* Chaim Potok (1929-    )
*Type of plot:* Psychological realism
*Time of plot:* The 1930's
*Locale:* New York City
*First published:* 1985

*Principal characters:*

ILANA DAVITA CHANDAL, the narrator, a young girl trying to find her own place amid the traditions to which she is exposed

CHANNAH CHANDAL, Davita's mother, a Polish Jew who flees her homeland for New York

MICHAEL CHANDAL, Davita's father, a Gentile from Maine who works as a liberal journalist

JAKOB DAW, a school friend of Channah and later a well-known left-wing writer

SARAH CHANDAL, Michael's sister, a nurse and Christian missionary

EZRA DINN, Channah's cousin, an Orthodox Jew

DAVID DINN, Ezra's son and Davita's friend

*The Novel*

The novels of Chaim Potok typically concern themselves with conflicts between worldviews, usually as represented by the American Orthodox Jewish tradition and aspects of the secular world. *Davita's Harp* is the story of a girl's search for balance—between practicality and idealism, between the inner self and the outer environment. Davita's parents are intelligent people who have rejected their respective religions and become passionately dedicated to Communism. Davita describes in detail the Communist Party meetings that the Chandals hold in a succession of tenement apartments, apartments that they are regularly forced to leave by unsympathetic landlords.

Amid the instability of Davita's physical environment, two objects stay constant: a picture on her parents' bedroom wall of three white horses, and a door harp hung on the front door of whatever apartment they call home. Davita looks at the picture often, feeling that she is almost able to enter into the scene. She also loves to listen to the sounds of the harp whenever the door is opened or closed. To Davita, it rings the gentlest and sweetest of tones.

Eight-year-old Davita, a precocious child with a rich inner life, is growing up in turbulent times. Her main outer influence is her parents' politics. She often falls asleep at night to the sound of impassioned voices talking about dialectic materialism, tools of production, capitalists, Benito Mussolini, and Adolf Hitler. Although her parents do not talk about the religions they have abandoned, Davita learns about them both. She learns about Christianity from her aunt, Sarah Chandal; she learns about Orthodox Judaism from her neighbors, the Helfmans, and from Ezra and David Dinn. She learns about the power of the imagination from Jakob Daw, a noted leftist writer and family friend. Jakob tells Davita about the search for truth; the images he uses in his stories come from deep within his heart and lodge at a correspondingly deep level within Davita's own.

Eventually, Michael's newspaper sends him to cover the war in Spain, Channah becomes absorbed in Party activities, and Davita is left essentially on her own. She follows the Helfmans to the local synagogue and starts to attend regular services there. During his second tour in Spain, Michael is caught in the bombing of Guernica, where he is killed trying to help a wounded nun. Davita feels a deep emptiness and starts to say Kaddish for her father, a prayer she knows David Dinn said daily for eleven months after his mother died. Females do not usually say Kaddish, and Davita creates quite a stir.

Jakob Daw comes again to visit, and Davita finds some relief in his presence. He tells her a story about a little black bird struggling against the wind; the bird eventually finds safety inside the sweet music of the door harp. One day when out rowing in the park, however, Davita goes deeply into her sadness with a strange detachment, watching herself stand up and step quietly out of the boat. Out of contact with the world, Davita goes with Aunt Sarah to recover in the family farmhouse in Maine. When she returns to New York, she transfers to the synagogue school to be closer to her friends Ruthie Helfman and David Dinn. Davita is happier there than in public school, but she is growing up and thinking deeply about her relationship to what she sees around her—things familial, political, religious, and sexual. When Davita goes with her class to see the Pablo Picasso painting *Guernica*, she again experiences a sense of detachment from her surroundings. She flies up and enters into the painting, taking from it a little gray bird, which she puts into the door harp for safe-keeping.

Channah's dreams for Communism are eventually shattered, and she collapses from both physical and emotional exhaustion. To recover, she too goes with Sarah to the farmhouse in Maine, and Davita stays with the Helfmans, becoming more and more involved with their Orthodox ways. When Channah returns, she and Ezra decide to marry. Although Davita misses her father and Uncle Jakob (who has also died), she now has a strong family life, and she is an excellent student.

When Davita is graduated from the eighth grade, it is expected that she will receive the Akiva Award for highest academic average. The school directors cannot accept that the first-place graduate is female, however, and they give the award to a boy. Davita feels betrayed and incensed, realizing with great pain what her mother, her father, and her Uncle Jakob before her had learned—how a single event can change the course of a person's life. Yet the inner life that had caused Davita so much anguish in the past now comes to her aid.

Lying on her bed, she suddenly finds herself inside the door harp, sitting between the black bird of Jakob and the gray bird of *Guernica*. The birds fly the harp, with Davita inside, to the Maine farmhouse, where Davita sees her father, Aunt Sarah, and Uncle Jakob and receives their blessing. The novel ends on an open note, as Davita— still bitter from the experience—returns to her family and welcomes a new baby sister.

"Enjoy your childhood," she whispers to Rachel. "They'll take it away from you soon enough." Davita, though, also starts to tell Rachel a strange story that does not have an ending, "a story about two birds and some horses on a beach far away."

## The Characters

Although Potok is a traditional writer who believes in the primacy of plot, some of his characters seem to stand more for views that Potok wants to put forth than as people integral to the storyline. This is especially true of Channah and Michael Chandal, who seem most substantial when they are espousing the primacy of human rights and their commitment to Communism as a means to create an international community. As characters, however, they tend to blend into the background in the novel.

The same kind of one-dimensionality is suggested by Sarah Chandal and Ezra Dinn. Although the actions of both are important to the story line, their primary usefulness—especially Dinn's—seems to be as spokespeople for the Christian and Orthodox perspectives that Potok wants to detail. The characters of Ruthie Helfman and David Dinn also serve to present religious information, but because they are in closer contact with the day-to-day musings of Davita—the most fully developed character in the novel—they seem more real somehow.

Davita is the character on whom the novel rests. Her acute perceptions carry the reader along as she tries to make sense of the world around her and as she comes to rely more and more on what she finds within. In the first chapter, the reader learns that Davita is telling the story as she looks back in time. This at least partially accounts for her ways of thinking and speaking, for Davita's perceptions in the novel are not those of a typical child. The accumulated wisdom that overlays her observations may create a sense of incongruity for some readers.

Some critics have suggested that Potok's attempt to speak through a female persona is less successful than his characterization of male narrators. Potok includes intimate female scenes here; for example, Davita sees Channah, in her loneliness, exploring her body in front of a mirror, and Davita is shown experiencing her first menstrual period. Such scenes, however, seem less alive than the richly woven, detailed scenes in the synagogue.

The most profound and thought-provoking characters, Davita and Jakob Daw, reflect themselves in visions and stories. The sense of individual definition that they exude is less a separation from others than a deep familiarity with their own inner lives. To get closer to Jakob Daw, the reader has to descend into the stories he tells to Davita. In Jakob, political or religious views do not overshadow his essential humanity, and his character is the touchstone by which Davita—and probably the reader—will be oriented. With orientation comes understanding, and Davita is the vehicle of integration in the novel. She pulls together what is best in all the characters and their belief systems. Although she has been damaged by both politics and religion, Davita is left with a strong sense of worthiness and leaves her convictions about the art of living with the reader.

## Themes and Meanings

Potok situates most of his novels within the context of American Jewish life in the first half of the twentieth century, and Orthodox Judaism is certainly a central focus in *Davita's Harp*. Because Potok goes deeply into the particulars to locate what is universal in human experience, however, his readership is not restricted. *Davita's Harp* is set against a background of Christianity as well as Judaism, and it also investigates political issues as Potok deals with what he considers to be the central social problem of the twentieth century: how people confront ideas that are different from their own.

Potok structures his novels carefully and tends to set up the central metaphor of each in an early scene. This time, the metaphor is the door harp, which plays gentle, sweet music. The harp has been a constant in Davita's peripatetic life, yet it is a dynamic symbol. The harp is strong enough to accept outer influences: In fact, it becomes a haven for the bird of Uncle Jakob's story, the bird that Davita liberates from *Guernica*, and eventually even Davita herself. Though the harp is solid and stationary, it becomes the means through which Davita can fly outside the limitations of time and space: to the Maine farmhouse to give her aborted graduation speech; to a reunion with her deceased father and uncle; and to a greater understanding and healing of spirit. The metaphor underscores the central theme in *Davita's Harp*: the inexhaustible power of the human imagination, which is able to create its own reality.

Davita's gender is not incidental to the novel. Potok focuses on the interaction between her intellectual promise and the possibilities for a female scholar to expand within the existing Orthodox tradition. It is clear that Davita's potential—and, by implication, other women's—will not be realized. She is excluded from saying prayers, and she is denied the academic prize she earns. Even after coming to terms with the situation, Davita says that she is planning to attend a public high school—a very good one—in the fall.

Potok, however, is an optimistic writer who has faith in human nature. He believes that there is meaning and order in the universe and that people should search for truth. At one point, Uncle Jakob tells Davita to be sure to wear her glasses, because it is important to see clearly. This seems to be Potok's intention with the novel, to help himself and his readers see through surface values. He portrays the intellect as necessary and practical, not merely as an abstract faculty. He also suggests that the intellect, which gives rise to outer action, is guided by something profound and universal. Davita has a strong sense of this inner knowingness, and as the novel's sole voice, she will nourish it in readers. Looking within to gain a more expanded perspective on outer circumstance is the process, Potok suggests. He also suggests that the stories people bring forth in order to communicate the truths they find inside help to take everyone closer to realizing the wholeness of spirit that is the human birthright.

## Critical Context

In his novels, Potok returns again and again to conflicts between American Orthodox Judaism and secular perspectives on psychology, cultural values, and the arts, speaking largely out of his own experience. As a rabbi, Chaim Potok stands out among important Jewish American writers. Although consistently critical of the ultra-Orthodox position, Potok is fully committed to Judaism and presents its complexities in his work. Although similar in theme and setting to most of Potok's fiction, *Davita's Harp* is the first novel he has written from the female perspective.

Potok has been criticized by fundamentalists for his portrayal of the Orthodox tradition. In *Davita's Harp*, some of these critics focused on the Akiva Award situation, declaring that such injustice could never happen. Potok countered by explaining that Davita's experience was based on something that actually occurred to his wife when she was thirteen. Because of her gender, his wife was refused the class valedictory, Potok says, and the hurt stayed with her. In 1986, Potok said that he planned to write again of Davita, picking her up in midlife as a feminist writer who feels compelled to leave the Orthodox tradition. Thus, Davita's introduction provides a means for Potok to investigate an issue that is shaking religions to their core in the late twentieth century: the desire of women to take active and meaningful roles.

Potok is generally classified as a Jewish American writer. He prefers, however, to be known as an American writer who focuses on a small and particular American world. Potok creates worlds in his fiction through which readers—Jews and non-Jews alike—can locate aspects of their own subjectivity, expanding their understanding of themselves and appreciating the underlying interconnectedness of human experience. Potok has extended Jewish American writing by moving religion from the sidelines, where it is found in many novels, to the center of his work. Although Potok's style has been criticized, he is nevertheless recognized as an impressive writer who has made an important contribution to American literature.

*Bibliography*
Abramson, Edward A. *Chaim Potok*. Boston: Twayne, 1986. This full-length study traces Potok's ideas through the recurring themes in his work. Includes full chapters on Potok's first five novels, but *Davita's Harp* is dealt with in less detail. Also includes a chronology, a bibliographical chapter, and a bibliography of primary and secondary sources.

Kauvar, Elaine. "An Interview with Chaim Potok." *Contemporary Literature* 27 (Fall, 1986): 291-317. This rich, thought-provoking article focuses on themes that run through Potok's novels. Because the interview was conducted as *Davita's Harp* was being published, Kauvar refers to the book repeatedly. Potok is articulate, and his remarks will help readers to penetrate more deeply into the philosophical underpinnings of his work.

Potok, Chaim. "The Culture Highways We Travel." *Religion and Literature* 19 (Summer, 1987): 1-10. This material was originally presented as a lecture at The University of Notre Dame. Potok speaks candidly. He discusses how his characters become caught between two conflicting universes that they love.

True, Warren. "Potok and Joyce: The Artist and His Culture." *Studies in American Jewish Literature* 2 (1982): 181-190. In several interviews, Potok has mentioned the strong influence of James Joyce on his work. In this article, True compares Joyce's Stephen (from the 1916 novel *A Portrait of the Artist as a Young Man*) with Potok's Asher Lev. True looks at both characters as they feel the pain of being different.

Walden, Daniel, ed. *Studies in American Jewish Literature* 4 (1985): 1-120. This issue devoted to Potok includes articles investigating both his life experiences and his written work. Includes an overview of critical response to Potok's works, an interview, and a bibliographical essay. Of particular interest may be Joan Del Fattore's article, "Women as Scholars in Chaim Potok's Novels."

*Jean C. Fulton*

# DEAR DIEGO

*Author:* Elena Poniatowska (1933-    )
*Type of plot:* Romance
*Time of plot:* The 1920's and 1935
*Locale:* Paris, France, and Mexico City, Mexico
*First published: Querido Diego, te abraza Quiela*, 1978 (English translation, 1986)

Principal characters:
    ANGELINA BELOFF (QUIELA), a Russian painter in love with the Mexican
    painter Diego Rivera
    DIEGO RIVERA, a famous Mexican painter

*The Novel*

Dear Diego is based on one chapter of Bertram Wolfe's *The Fabulous Life of Diego Rivera* (1963). The novel is a fictionalized portrayal of Quiela (the Russian painter Angelina Beloff) as a broken-hearted lover waiting for the well-known painter Diego Rivera to send for her from Mexico City.

*Dear Diego* is divided into twelve love letters dated from October 19, 1921, through July 22, 1922—nine months in which Quiela, in spite of her desperation and longing for her lover, creates her own work as an illustrator for the Parisian magazine *Floreal*. By painting in nine months exactly, she affirms her identity through the art that Diego Rivera represents for her. The letters are followed by a brief narrative at the end of the book.

The book begins as Quiela is waiting for her lover. She expects him to send for her, but toward the end of the novel she realizes that he does not need her anymore. On one level, the narrative is about one woman in love with someone who does not want her; at the same time, it is about the aesthetic process of painting without the influence of her lover, a process that makes Quiela a newborn woman at the end.

The plot of the novel is fairly straightforward: Angelina Beloff (Quiela), a Russian painter in Paris, falls in love with the Mexican painter Diego Rivera. They live together for ten years. Diego Rivera goes back to Mexico in order to participate in the new beginning of his country after the Mexican revolution, and he forgets about her. Although he sends some money for Quiela, he never answers any of her letters. Quiela (the nickname Rivera gave her) writes him several times about how much she loves him and how important his ideas about painting have been for her. In a sense, he becomes a mentor for her. These episodes are brought out in Quiela's letters. The short concluding narrative describes Quiela's trip to Mexico in 1935, thirteen years after she has stopped writing. She does not look for Rivera, but she runs into him at a theater in Mexico City. He does not recognize her. The incident can be interpreted in two ways: Either Rivera has forgotten her to the point that he does not even recognize her, or, alternatively, the woman he sees is no longer the heartbroken lover of Paris but a new Angelina Beloff, an artist who has her own life and art and who does not need him any more.

*The Characters*

Angelina Beloff captures the sympathy of the reader. She represents women artists of the 1920's; she is struggling for her place in modern art. From Pablo Picasso, she learns about the possibilities of playing with lines instead of copying directly from reality. At first, she paints representationally, gradually moving to embrace the abstract style of cubism. This shift in Quiela's aesthetic coincides with her increasing emotional distance from Diego Rivera. In a way, being alone in Paris helps her to achieve a self-affirmation in her art.

Diego Rivera, the lover for whom Quiela cries and the famous painter who is developing a new Mexican art, is a womanizer who takes up with the Mexican painter Frida Kahlo while Quiela still waits for him in Paris. Rivera is portrayed through the writings of Quiela, and readers do not really have any account of him directly. This fact limits the appreciation of his actions and makes the reader accuse him of neglecting his lover all alone by herself in Paris. One possible interpretation of these actions could be that he is letting her alone so that she can grow as an artist and develop without depending on him. This interpretation, however, is not the best one; rather, Rivera stands for the macho male who thinks that women cannot live without him.

*Themes and Meanings*

The novel is a feminist outline of the oppression in which women live when they love too much. Quiela waits endlessly for someone she knows is not coming back. The fact that the novel deals with two artists gives the work implications about art and love that extend beyond the melodramatic discourse of the letters and Quiela's process of forgetting about Diego.

During the nine months covered by the letters, Beloff tells her whole story. She has been an independent woman who has developed her technique as a painter as the only real center of her life. She grew up in Russia; her father was an important influence in her life because he always insisted that she have a profession. As an independent woman at the beginning of the twentieth century, she is something of a pioneer and role model, even though her longing for Diego makes her appear weak. In her letters, she expresses the anger and the mixed emotions she feels toward Diego, but she eventually realizes that she has to find her center again; significantly, it takes nine months for her to be reborn. Life will not stop for this woman just because Diego Rivera does not want her.

In Quiela's last letter, the tone changes completely. She writes to Rivera for the last time and tells him about her already finished illustrations for the Parisian magazine *Floreal*. Her artistic work is done; she has recuperated with dignity. It is not until 1935, when she goes to Mexico, that she again comes into contact with Rivera; even then, she does not seek him out. (According to Bertram Wolfe's biography of Rivera, Beloff did in fact contact him in Mexico City because she needed his signature in order to sell some of his paintings that belonged to her. In the novel, this scene is not even mentioned; Poniatowska's version of the story is more dramatic, since Rivera does not recognize Beloff when they finally run into each other.)

The novel is also about the fascination of Angelina Beloff with anything Mexican. Colors are important also, especially gray and blue. Gray is her color before Diego's eyes, and blue is the bright color in which Diego describes her. Gray is Europe for Diego, and blue is Mexico.

### Critical Context

*Dear Diego* is a testimonial work of fiction in the Latin American tradition of the *novela testimonio* (testimonial novel) developed by the Cuban author Miguel Barnet with his famous *Biografía de un cimarrón* (1966; *The Autobiography of a Runaway Slave*, 1966). The most important element in this kind of literature is the use of a "witness" to provide the writer with the basic monologue in which the character tells his or her story. In *Dear Diego*, the "witness" is the chapter dedicated to Quiela by Bertram Wolfe in his biography of Rivera. Poniatowska read Wolfe's biography and from this material developed the story line of her novel; she thus created a work in which it is the written word itself that acts as the "witness" of the story. The basic monologue is derived not from an interview with Angelina Beloff herself but from research on Beloff done by Poniatowska. The final monologue presented by the narrator is the collection of letters. In this respect, the novel does not follow the testimonial fiction structure of the first voice telling the story. In *Dear Diego*, the letters to Diego Rivera from Angelina Beloff constitutes the narrative discourse.

### Bibliography

Berry, John. "Invention, Convention, an Autobiography in Elena Poniatowska's *Querido Diego, te abraza Quiela*." *Confluencia* 3 (Summer, 1988): 47-56. Berry analyzes Poniatowska's technique of writing the twelve letters to Diego Rivera. He concludes that *Dear Diego* is neither a testimonial narrative nor an autobiography but contains elements of both. Berry considers the novel to represent a break with existing literary conventions.

Gold, Janet. "Feminine Space and the Discourse of Silence: Yolanda Oreamuno, Elena Poniatowska, and Luisa Valenzuela." In *In the Feminine Mode: Essays on Hispanic Women Writers*, edited by Noël Valis and Carol Maier. Lewisburg, Pa.: Bucknell University Press, 1990. A postmodern reading of Poniatowska's short story "La felicidad" that places her writing in the context of other works by Hispanic women.

Lagos, Maria-Ines. "Elena Poniatowska." In *Modern Latin-American Fiction Writers*. Vol. 113 in *Dictionary of Literary Biography*, edited by Matthew J. Bruccoli. Detroit: Gale Research, 1992. A good overview that includes a brief biography of Poniatowska and discusses her fiction, journalism, and criticism. Lagos focuses on the relationship between history and fiction in *Dear Diego* and argues against criticism of Poniatowska's creation of a weak, submissive female protagonist.

Paul, Marcella L. "Letters and Desire: The Function of Marks on Paper in Elena Poniatowska's *Querido Diego, te abraza Quiela*." In *Continental, Latin American, and Francophone Women Writers,* edited by Ginette Adamson and Eunice Myers. Lanham, Md.: University Press of America, 1990. Paul analyzes Poniatowska's Quiela as an exploration of language as a means of communication that fails when it is not an expression of the self.

Poniatowska, Elena. Interview by Susana Conde. *Belles Lettres* 7 (Winter, 1992): 41-45. Poniatowska discusses her characters, themes, and style and comments on the effects of gender on writing.

*Daniel Torres*

# DEAR RAFE

*Author:* Rolando Hinojosa (1929-    )
*Type of plot:* Social realism
*Time of plot:* The mid-1950's to the early 1960's
*Locale:* The Rio Grande Valley of southern Texas
*First published: Mi querido Rafa,* 1981 (English translation and revision, 1985)

>   *Principal characters:*
>   JEHU (JAY) MALACARA, the chief loan officer at Klail City First National
>       Bank and a cousin to Rafe Buenrostro, to whom Jehu writes letters
>   NODDY PERKINS, the owner of Klail City First National Bank and political
>       boss in Belken County
>   IRA ESCOBAR, a petty politician
>   BECKY CALDWELL-ESCOBAR, the wife of Ira Escobar, a secret lover of
>       Jehu, and a political socialite
>   SAMMIE JO PERKINS-COOKE, the daughter of Noddy Perkins and a secret
>       lover of Jehu Malacara

*The Novel*

   *Dear Rafe* is based on Rolando Hinojosa's vivid experiences in the Rio Grande
Valley of South Texas from 1929 to 1946 as well as on his knowledge of the Korean
War. *Dear Rafe* is a fictionalized portrayal of the area's white power brokers and their
attempts to control the economy in the lower Rio Grande Valley.

   *Dear Rafe* is divided into two parts, forming a total of forty-seven chapters and a
conclusion. The first part consists of twenty-three chapters made up of Jehu Malacara's letters to Rafe Buenrostro. The second part is made up of twenty-four chapters
that deal mainly with speculation on Jehu Malacara's mysterious departure from Klail
City First National Bank in Belken County.

   The book begins with Jehu's letters to his cousin Rafe, who is recovering in Belken
County War Memorial Veteran's Hospital from wounds incurred during the Korean
War. Both are now employed; Rafe, although convalescing, is an attorney and a
lieutenant of detectives in the district attorney's office in Belken County, while Jehu
is the chief loan officer of the Klail City First National Bank. Jehu tells Rafe of the
political activities going on in the valley. He focuses on the subtle games played by
the area power brokers, mainly Noddy Perkins and Ira Escobar. Jehu is indirectly
involved in various political power plays, for he not only knows who is manipulating
whom but is also in charge of money being lent to selected businesses that are
subsequently taken over by Klail City First National Bank. During these socioeconomic and political fracases, Jehu becomes involved with two women, the beautiful
Becky, the Mexican American wife of Ira Escobar, and the younger Sammie Jo, the
spoiled daughter of Noddy Perkins. Ira is so caught up in his quest to be county
commissioner—giving his undivided attention and services to Noddy, who can and

does make his ambitions a reality—that he is not aware of his wife's love affair with Jehu. Sammie Jo, who has been married before and who is known to be promiscuous, is also having an affair with Jehu, perhaps because she is being neglected by her husband, Sidney. Sidney is having a homosexual relationship with a high-ranking state official, Hap Bayliss, who is also controlled by Sammie Jo's father, Noddy. During this time, Jehu is also dating, off and on, Olivia (Ollie) San Esteban, an aspiring pharmacist in Klail City.

There are also two important minor characters in the novel. Morse Terry eventually takes Hap's position as a Texas state representative. Terry, once a successful real-estate broker, let a big land deal fall into the hands of a group of Mexican Americans, an economic and political faux pas that caused him to fall from grace with the white power brokers, especially Noddy Perkins. The price he had to pay was to become a politician who would be controlled by Noddy. Viola Barragan is a powerful white figure in the real-estate business in Belken County and also a key figure in Jehu's rise to a prestigious role in the Klail City First National Bank's money-lending sector, an upward move unusual for a Mexican American. She is also Jehu's firm supporter, regardless of his political and personal activities.

In the latter portion of the series of letters to Rafe, the reader is led to believe that Jehu gets so tired of the underhanded ploys of the white power brokers, especially Noddy, that he resigns his position as head loan officer at the Klail City First National Bank and also breaks off his relationships with Becky and Sammie Jo—especially since he has good reason to believe that Noddy has found out that he has been having an illicit affair with Noddy's daughter. Hence Jehu goes back to his ever-faithful Ollie, who, it is believed, sells her part in a drugstore business to her brother so as to pursue a medical degree at the University of Texas at Austin. Jehu goes with her to give her his full support.

Part 2 is based on interviews with various characters in Belken County. The unnamed interviewer is trying to determine why Jehu Malacara left his post at Klail City First National Bank; hence, what follows is speculation on the part of several characters who are either only briefly mentioned in part 1 or who have not been heard of before. Each of the chapters in part 2 begins with a brief descriptive background on each character. Most of the time, these characters speak to Galindo, who serves as the author's listener. The characters give their views as to why Jehu Malacara left the Klail City First National Bank, with a few opinions about Jehu's relationships with Becky and Sammie Jo included.

"A Penultimate Note" brings the novel to its basic closure. A few following paragraphs, included under the heading "Brass Tacks Are Best; They Last Longer," include speculation by most of the Klail City Mexican Americans as to the guilt of Jehu. As in part 2, there are voices that speculate as to Jehu's whereabouts—and so the novel ends.

*The Characters*

Jehu, the Mexican American loan officer, captures the attention of the reader at the beginning of the novel. He is a shrewd character who learns how to survive the socioeconomic pressures placed upon him by white power brokers, who try to coerce him into selling out his people. Jehu, however, discloses the power brokers' intentions and their efforts to control both the economy and the politics of the valley. Despite Jehu's efforts to serve as a role model for his people, his sense of honesty and fair play cause him to leave his post at the bank; he is thus a failure in the eyes of most of the local Mexican American population.

Noddy is the chief power broker; he is not only the owner of Klail City First National Bank but also political boss of Belken County. From the beginning of the book, the reader gains a dislike for this underhanded character. Noddy controls most money transactions, especially in the real-estate industry in the Valley. "St. Noddy" also manipulates the social lives and careers of susceptible whites and Mexican Americans. The one person he cannot control is Jehu Malacara.

Ira Escobar is a Mexican American petty politician who also works for the Klail City First National Bank. Yet his lack of knowledge of politics leaves him vulnerable to use in others' power plays. He is so naïve a character that he never realizes that his wife is having an affair with Jehu or that his people think of him as a sellout. Through Ira's actions, the author is able to convey to the reader what is not appropriate sociopolitical behavior in the eyes of the Mexican American community. The reader dislikes Ira and sees Jehu as a champion for the values of Mexican Americans in Texas.

Becky Escobar is Ira's wife. She is a pretty Mexican American woman who desires to break into the social ranks of the area's Anglo women. A clever woman with a taste for the fine arts, she is an essentially moral person, but she has a weakness for the attention of the handsome Jehu. Through her, Jehu learns of the political role that her husband plays in Noddy's schemes. He also comes to understand the importance of Ira's family in the politics of the area's Mexican Americans.

Sammie Jo Perkins is Noddy's daughter. She is a spoiled upper-crust woman, and her actions first capture the reader's attention. Sammie Jo likes to spend time at her father's ranch, a place of security from the negative effects of her unsuccessful marriages. She falls for the alluring Jehu; this affair is her way of getting attention from her husband. Although her relationship with Jehu is not discovered by her father, he causes it to end. This illicit relationship represents a forbidden crossing of Anglo-Mexican social lines. Through his association with Sammie Jo, Jehu learns about Noddy's devious real-estate and political activities.

*Themes and Meanings*

The novel is an astute critique of the questionable tactics used by power brokers to control the socioeconomic and political lives of Mexican Americans in the Rio Grande Valley, of which Belken County is a microcosm. The events of the book reflect the real source of conflict between Anglo Texans and Texas Mexicans, the latter of whom have been politically controlled since Texas became a state. The novel symbolizes the plight of Texas Mexicans who are subjected to the political dictates of Anglo

Texan power brokers and who are socially segregated from Anglo Americans.

The novel is also about growing up Mexican American, about honor, loyalty, bravery, and love. The chronicles of the Texas Mexicans who work and live in the valley represent a lifestyle that is a cross between Anglo and Mexican society, from a sociological and political perspective. The young people will grow up, go to war for their country, and come back to the valley with little change in their socioeconomic and political status, which means that they will fulfill the roles that Texas Anglo society has designed for them. There will be few surprises, for only a few Mexican Americans will ever be accepted as equals in the ranks of Anglo Texan society. This sense of inequity pervades the novel; growing up Mexican American means coming to terms with this reality, trying to conform to the dictates of Anglo society while still maintaining a cultural identity. The educated Mexican Americans accept leadership roles to challenge their people's subjugation; the moment they need help, however, their elders turn on them, breaking whatever cohesion existed between the older generation and the changing new breed of upward-bound valley Mexican Americans.

*Critical Context*

*Dear Rafe*, Hinojosa's first attempt to use the epistolary form, earned wide recognition. The epistolary novel has not been much used in the twentieth century, but Hinojosa's work champions this literary form. Furthermore, Hinojosa avoids using formal English. When making reference to local things, he uses elliptical expressions; for example, he shortens words (writer is shortened to "wri," for example). These usages can be confusing to the reader at first; however, Hinojosa employs these stylistic devices so cleverly that the reader is soon able to figure out their meaning. This approach has helped to earn Hinojosa a reputation as the writer of the understatement.

*Bibliography*

Passty, J. N. "*Dear Rafe.*" *Choice* 23 (January, 1986): 742. Passty emphasizes Jehu Malacara's and Rafe Buenrostro's roles in the Mexican American effort to restore "lost" lands to the descendants of the Mexican families that onced owned them.

Salazar-Parr, Carmen. "La Chicana in Literature." In *Chicano Studies: A Multidisciplinary Approach*, edited by Eugene E. Garcia, Francisco A. Lomelí, and Isidro D. Ortiz. New York: Teachers College Press, 1984. Useful in order to appreciate fully Hinojosa's female characters. Salazar-Parr states that the reader must realize "that the mistresses and prostitutes do not necessarily symbolize 'bad' women in Chicano literature."

Saldívar, José David, ed. *The Rolando Hinojosa Reader: Essays Historical and Critical*. Houston: Arte Público Press, 1985. A helpful overview of Hinojosa's career.

Tatum, Charles M. "Rolando Hinojosa-Smith." In *Chicano Writers*, edited by Francisco A. Lomelí and Carl R. Shirley. Vol. 82 in *Dictionary of Literary Biography*, edited by Matthew J. Bruccoli. Detroit: Gale Research, 1989. Tatum analyzes six novels and one scholarly book by Hinojosa and also provides the reader with a biographical sketch. Notes that Hinojosa intends each of his works to form a part of a lifelong novel that he calls "Klail City Death Trip." *Dear Rafe* is part of this fictional world.

_____ . *"Dear Rafe." Hispania* 69 (September, 1986): 560-561. Notes that the principal difference between *Dear Rafe* and Hinojosa's prior novels is this work focuses on Anglo financial and political manipulations. Observes that the reader is given a bird's-eye view of financial and political life in the Rio Grande Valley.

*Silvester Brito*

# THE DEATH OF BERNADETTE LEFTHAND

*Author:* Ronald B. Querry (1943-    )
*Type of plot:* Detective and mystery
*Time of plot:* 1990's
*Locale:* New Mexico and Arizona
*First published:* 1993

> *Principal characters:*
> BERNADETTE LEFTHAND, a part Jicarilla Apache and part Taos Pueblo
> Indian, a beautiful dancer, wife, and mother
> GRACIE LEFTHAND, Bernadette's admiring younger sister, narrator of
> most of the book's action
> ANDERSON GEORGE, Bernadette's husband, a Navajo rodeo bronco buster
> TOM GEORGE, Anderson's quiet brother
> EMMETT TAKE HORSE, a crippled Navajo, a onetime suitor of Bernadette
> STARR STUBBS, a friend and employer of Bernadette, narrator of some of
> the book's action

*The Novel*

Bernadette Lefthand's death is the first incident reported by her shocked and grieving sister, Gracie. The girls' father and Gracie at first assume that Bernadette's death had come as the result of an automobile accident, a common cause of death among young Indians. It turns out, however, that she has been brutally murdered and that the police are looking for Bernadette's husband, Anderson George.

The heart of the novel is the story of Bernadette's life on the Jicarilla Apache reservation centered around Dulce, in northern New Mexico. She has always been a beautiful and popular girl, and as a teenager she emerged as a champion dancer at powwows held throughout the Southwest. As a student at the Indian school in Santa Fe, she fell in love with a handsome young Navajo named Anderson George. After graduation, the two married, and Bernadette gave birth to a baby boy.

Gracie Lefthand's account of her sister's life focuses on many of the trips the two girls took with Anderson and his brother Tom. They visited their late mother's sister in the Taos pueblo and enjoyed a strong sense of family warmth with their aunt and her family. With the George brothers, they went to rodeos on the Navajo reservation, and after one such adventure had a memorable stay at an old but newly refurbished hotel in Gallup. The four young people also visited a friend of Bernadette on the Hopi reservation, where during a festival they were again made to feel part of a family despite the age-old enmity between the Hopi and the Navajo.

The sense of Bernadette as a special person is underlined in the sections of the novel narrated by Starr Stubbs. Starr is the wife of a popular country singer who has built a large home near Dulce as a place to recover from the stresses of his concert tours. Starr no longer accompanies her husband on the road, and she has hired Bernadette as a kind of housekeeper, in part to have someone to talk to. In a short time, she has come to admire Bernadette as much as Gracie does. Starr provides an important perspective, since she is well read in matters having to do with Indians and is a sympathetic commentator on their problems. Despite her good intentions, however, she is unable truly to understand her Indian friends.

During the early part of the novel, there are occasional brief third-person narratives in which an unnamed character seeks out a Navajo witch for instruction. The menacing note in these sections becomes more pronounced when it becomes clear that the apprentice witch is Emmett Take Horse. A onetime contemporary of Bernadette at the Indian school, he had been a successful jockey in the informal Navajo horse races until an accident had left him disfigured and crippled. He resents the handsome Anderson George as well as Bernadette, who had rejected him as a suitor.

After a benefit powwow in Dulce at which Bernadette has been honored, she is bludgeoned to death. Emmett has tried to use witchcraft to influence the increasingly drunken Anderson George to kill Bernadette, but in the end, Emmett has killed her himself, arranging matters so that Anderson appears to be guilty. Consumed by remorse, half convinced that he had committed the murder, Anderson hangs himself in the jail cell where he is being held. Gracie is left to rear Bernadette's infant son.

## The Characters

Bernadette Lefthand is the only fully drawn character. In one sense, despite its title, the novel is more about her life than her death. She is seen, by her sister and by Starr Stubbs, as almost faultless, a gifted and beautiful young woman who succeeds as a mother as well as she had succeeded as a dancer at powwows. She is kind to her sister and a welcome companion to Starr, providing the white woman with important insights into Indian life and customs. She seems to show that even in depressed economic conditions, considerable joy and satisfaction are possible for at least some young Indians.

Anderson George is a more complex character. As a teenager, he has stood out from others in his group; he is handsome and almost as talented at rodeo riding as Bernadette is as a dancer. As a young adult, however, Anderson is less satisfied with his life than is his wife. Despite having won the beautiful Bernadette, he follows what the book presents as a typical Indian pattern in relying more and more on alcohol to soften the hard edges of his life. Partly as a result of his increasingly frequent drunkenness, he becomes less and less successful in the rodeos and comes more and more under the baleful influence of Emmett Take Horse. In the end, he is too far gone in drunkenness to realize that, despite appearances, he has not murdered his wife.

The most interesting character is Emmett Take Horse. He makes a deliberate choice of evil in seeking out the old witch who teaches him the ways of witchcraft, but he seems to lose faith in the power of his magic. He decides finally not to rely on the spell he has cast on Anderson George to accomplish Bernadette's death; instead he kills her himself and arranges for the blame to fall on Anderson.

Of the other characters, Starr Stubbs receives the most attention, although her character is not developed at length. Instead, she is used to represent whites who have goodwill toward Indians but who, despite book knowledge and the best of intentions, cannot truly understand the ways and the hardships of Indian life. Tom George is a sober foil to his more glamorous brother; Gracie, similarly, is the younger sister so admiring of Bernadette that she has little personality of her own.

*Themes and Meanings*

Ron Querry presents a somewhat less dismal picture of life for young Indians than have other recent writers dealing with similar material. Most of the experiences of the Lefthand sisters are relatively pleasant. They travel often: to powwows where Bernadette is a fancy dancer, to Taos to visit their mother's sister and bask in warm family feelings, to rodeos on the Navajo reservation, and to see friends on Hopi land. When her son is born, Bernadette finds in her enjoyment of motherhood a distraction from her concern over Anderson George's increasing reliance on alcohol and his developing friendship with Emmett Take Horse.

At the same time, Querry does not ignore or minimize the problems faced by his characters. Bernadette and Anderson both have to face the reality that however enjoyable their lives have been as teenagers, no matter how much admiration they have won for their skills, there is little hope of rewarding careers for them as adults. Starr Stubbs offers employment to both of them (she hires Anderson to look after her horses) and friendship to Bernadette, but she cannot change the basic conditions of their lives. Life on the Jicarilla lands around Dulce offers no more opportunity for rewarding employment than does life on the Navajo reservation, where more than half of the adults are unemployed.

Still, other novels dealing with similar material, including James Welch's *Winter in the Blood* (1974) and Leslie Marmon Silko's *Ceremony* (1977), have focused more intensely on the depressing aspects of contemporary Indian life and on the dependence on alcohol of many adults on the reservations of the Southwest. Querry is more interested than these writers in the significance of the survival of witchcraft among the Navajo, although in the end he leaves open the question of whether the methods of witchcraft have genuine effects on their targets.

*Critical Context*

Ron Querry's first novel is an important addition to the growing literature by and about Native Americans. The recent flood of such fiction was begun in 1969 with N. Scott Momaday's Pulitzer Prize-winning novel *House Made of Dawn*. Querry, whose background is Choctaw, has chosen to place the action of his novel among Jicarilla Apache, Navajo, Hopi, and Pueblo Indians (he has also, it should be noted, chosen to use the term "Indian" throughout *The Death of Bernadette Lefthand*). He takes pains to include explanations of the ceremonies and customs of his characters, as if Gracie were speaking to non-Indians during her narratives. At some points, this material is not closely integrated into the action of the novel, perhaps because it is not part of Querry's own background.

*The Death of Bernadette Lefthand* takes the form of a conventional mystery novel, in which almost everything is known from the beginning except the identity of the murderer. In combining a murder mystery with Indian witchcraft, Querry works in a genre also explored by Louis Owens in *The Sharpest Sight* (1992). In dealing with life among young Indians by focusing on female characters, he is in the territory pioneered by Momaday in *The Ancient Child* (1989).

Although he deals at length with witchcraft among the Navajo, Querry seems less interested than many other Native American writers in other aspects of Indian mysticism. Silko, Owens, and Momaday, in particular, include characters who see and know more than ordinary people and write about events that are not open to easy rational explanation. Querry, on the other hand, uses the mystery and menace of the old witch to create an atmosphere of dread, but he does not clearly accept the supernatural as real. Emmett Take Horse's decision to perform the murder of Bernadette himself seems to result from a lack of confidence in magic—an attitude that may reflect a similar hesitancy on the part of the author.

*Bibliography*
Kincaid, James R. "Who Gets to Tell Their Stories?" *The New York Times Book Review*, May 3, 1992, 1, 24-29. An excellent essay dealing with recent developments in fiction by American Indian writers. Provides a context in which *The Death of Bernadette Lefthand* can be understood.
Larson, Charles R. *American Indian Fiction*. Albuquerque: University of New Mexico Press, 1978. Provides a sound introduction to the history of fiction by and about American Indians. Attention is focused on such seminal novels as James Welch's *Winter in the Blood* and Leslie Marmon Silko's *Ceremony*, both important predecessors of *The Death of Bernadette Lefthand*. Larson also recognizes the vital role played by N. Scott Momaday's *House Made of Dawn*.
*Publishers Weekly*. Review of *The Death of Bernadette Lefthand*, by Ronald B. Querry. 240 (June 28, 1993): 68. A brief but enthusiastic review. Gives special attention to Querry's skill in developing the narrative and to his sympathy for his characters.
Simson, Maria. "Native American Fiction, Memoirs Blossom into Print." *Publishers Weekly* 238 (June 7, 1991): 22-24. Deals with the emergence of books by American Indian writers on the marketplace of American publishing. Simson notes that academic publishers remain important in the publication of works by Indian writers, but that trade publishers have become increasingly interested in Native American works.

*John Muste*

# DELIA'S SONG

*Author:* Lucha Corpi (1945-    )
*Type of plot:* Bildungsroman
*Time of plot:* The late 1960's to the mid-1970's
*Locale: Berkeley and the San Francisco Bay Area in California*
*First published:* 1989

Principal characters:
   DELIA TREVINO, a Mexican American student at the University of California at Berkeley
   JEFF MORONES, a young activist at Berkeley, the ultimate winner of Delia's affections
   ROGER N. HART, alias "James Joyce," a marine biologist around whom Delia's fantasies revolve
   MATTIE JOHNSON, Delia's mentor, a sociologist and activist
   MARTA TREVINO DE CIOTTI, Delia's beloved aunt
   SAMUEL CORONA, the intellectual leader of the student revolution
   JULIO SINGER, a congo-playing poet
   SARA GONZALEZ, Delia's roommate

*The Novel*

*Delia's Song* recounts a young woman's maturation during the turbulence of student riots and civil rights movements in academic institutions during the late 1960's. The novel is divided into three sections and consists of twelve chapters.

The story begins with a flashback in an italicized passage that suggests the intensity of Delia's emotional state. The book then switches immediately into the central event of the main plot, which took place earlier in the novel's chronology. The disjointed nature of the plot requires the reader to remain attentive to cues within the narrative in order to make chronological sense of the sequence of events, but the unconventional structure is one of the novel's best features.

Delia, dressed as the Carmelite Santa Teresa and overwhelmed by suddenly erupting memories of fire, terror, and threatening predators, has an emotional blackout as she contemplates a tenacious single yellow rose hanging to its branch in November (the rose is a unifying symbol throughout the narrative). She falls, swooning, and is rescued by none other than James Joyce himself, or so it seems to the distracted Delia, who is herself not who she seems in this scene. Gathering her wits, she continues to her destination, a "Day of the Dead" costume party given by Mattie Johnson, her mentor.

The narrative then shifts to the story's chronological beginning, as a nineteen-year-old Delia is introduced to the highly charged political campus life at Berkeley. She meets Samuel, Jeff, and Sara and begins her involvement with the social movement to establish a department for Third World studies at the university. The students and idealistic activists of MASC (the Mexican American Student Confederation) are taken with Delia's mysterious but intelligent personality.

The political and sexual tensions build. The confrontation between the students and the administration culminates in a conflict with the police, the sting of tear gas, and sudden mayhem. In the midst of all the upheaval, Jeff and Delia kiss, ostensibly to divert attention from themselves as activists, but obviously with much passion. Their kiss creates a romantic connection that forms the love theme of the novel, but the could-be lovers are soon star-crossed, separated by youthful misunderstandings when Jeff, heroically carrying a wounded Delia away from the rioting, takes amiss a comment she makes. The two become increasingly sensitive, estranged, and huffy, as young lovers tend to be, and the chapter ends with Delia's pride smarting when Sara tells Delia that Jeff has requested a transfer to the Riverside campus.

The group disintegrates after the revolution, as internal and external pressures create personality conflicts and inevitable disillusionment. Samuel begins to drink heavily, and Delia, involved with an abusive lover (the most disturbing of several disappointing lovers), becomes more and more depressed, agonizing over her failures with Jeff. The main character's decline parallels the decline of the student activist group, and Delia's despair echoes the difficulty of the group's idealistic dreams.

The narrative returns to the Day of the Dead costume party, where Delia has gathered her wits enough to proceed on her journey after her fall in the first chapter. She arrives late at the party and again encounters the mysterious "James Joyce," who, like herself, is in costume. She and "Joyce" consummate their desires by making love in the backyard under the barbecue pit (a spicy reference to Delia's country of origin, its folklore, and her sexuality), after which "Joyce" gives Delia his card, encouraging her to call him; she does not.

The second major movement of the novel takes Delia away from Berkeley, away from the two men of whom she is enamored—Jeff Morones of the kiss and now "James Joyce" of the barbecue pit—to her Aunt Marta's in Monterey, California.

The history of Delia's family occupies the center of the novel and is related through conversations with Aunt Marta. Delia's growing commitment to her writing parallels her healing focus on herself and her heritage. When the lost lover Jeff appears, invited to the house by an unsuspecting Aunt Marta, the interrupted romance resumes on a stronger beat, but Delia remains unsettled because of her obsession with "James Joyce," who, it turns out, is a distant relative of Mattie's and a widower.

Delia and Jeff, however, begin a courtship and engage in a number of lover's quarrels, which serve in part to develop the novel's social criticism of sexism. Delia decides, upon receiving an invitation from Mattie, to return to Berkeley for a visit and to look up her "Joyce," the tormenting object of her fantasies since their erotic encounter.

The third section of the novel narrates Delia's return to Berkeley to say farewell to Mattie (who has decided to move to Honduras) and to meet Roger N. Hart, alias "Joyce," in order to settle the question of her attraction to him. After much indecision, she does call him. She discovers that although he is a decent and worthy man who has held her in his own mind all this while, she is not, in fact, in love with him. Thus she returns to a rather nervous Jeff, but not without first coming to terms with a lifetime of conflict through her writing.

She returns to Monterey, completes her book (one very like *Delia's Song*), shares the story and manuscript with a concerned Aunt Marta, and eventually hands the typed manuscript over to a mystified and upset Jeff, who has not understood his lover's odd behavior. The book is Delia's statement of personal liberation, saying to Jeff, in effect, "this is who I am, take me as I am or not at all." Aunt Marta questions the wisdom of such a brash and honest move, but Delia is for once certain of her actions.

*The Characters*

Delia is the title character and the consciousness through which the novel is largely filtered. A young woman—a freshman from a Mexican heritage at the University of California at Berkeley—Delia struggles to come to terms with a painful past, a confusing present, and an uncertain future. The reader is initially confused about her identity; not only is she disguised as a saint, she is lost and distraught. The opening scream of pain (one of many interjected italicized poetic passages reflecting nightmarish eruptions of memory) introduces the question that is the novel's focus: Who, really, is Delia Trevino?

That Delia has some unresolved personal pain is evident in the flashback narrative, told in italicized stream-of-consciousness passages. The flashbacks reveal the heroine's disturbance over the violent deaths of her two brothers, Sebastian and Ricardo, and indicate her conflicted relationship with her mother and father, who devalue this intelligent and sensitive girl-child.

Coming from a Mexican heritage complete with folkloristic elements (seen in images of spicy, hot foods and Catholic iconography), Delia carries internally the burden of the family's hopes, even when those hopes have been dashed by the loss of her brothers. She carries these turbulent feelings with her to college, but she remains distant, taciturn. She becomes, therefore, an attractive mystery to her influential professor, Mattie Johnson, and to the group of students to which Mattie introduces her.

This group, all members of the activist MASC, consists of Samuel Corona, who becomes Delia's confidant; Julio Singer, a conga-playing poet; Sara Gonzalez, her roommate; and Jeff Morones. None of these characters is highly developed, although Jeff, who is the foil for Delia's maturation, begins to take on some three-dimensional qualities near the end of the book.

Jeff is a young, idealistic, and sensitive young man, one whom Delia cannot understand at all (largely because she is in conflict within herself). Jeff seems baffling to Delia as he leaves Berkeley, feeling himself shunned, as does she, and drops out of her life.

When Jeff appears in the novel again, he is a successful young man who has pursued his love of horses, his love of poetry, and a career. He represents for Delia forces with which she must come to terms in her own life and culture, forces that will devalue her intellect, her sexuality, and her culture, but forces that, nevertheless, are as loving as they are insensitive. Jeff has matured by the time he appears on Aunt Marta's doorstep, but the reader does not participate in this young man's sudden maturation, although the reader learns that Jeff's father has died. Jeff's character is told rather than shown, and as such remains rather flat.

Mattie Johnson, Delia's mentor and eventual friend, is a more fully developed character than Jeff. She is present during Delia's growing-up process, serving as wise woman, academic adviser, and sometimes pal. Mattie is an activist, a professor, and the intellectual core around which the group of students gathers as the story is unfolded. Mattie's role in the novel is essential, because she is the character who holds most of the themes together as well as the character through which most of the others connect (except for Aunt Marta, who is the answering "wise woman" figure in Monterey). Significantly, when Mattie leaves Berkeley to pursue her socialist ideals in Honduras, Delia finally completes her initiation into womanhood, rejecting her fantasy lover, returning to full selfhood and her true love, Jeff.

*Themes and Meanings*

*Delia's Song* describes the political, sexual, and emotional tensions characterizing America in the late 1960's and early 1970's. Divided into three major sections, *Delia's Song* outlines the pain and excitement of this turbulent period through the experiences of its eponymous principal character, Delia, as she emerges from naïveté into a new social and sexual maturity.

The events of Corpi's first novel are strongly autobiographical, echoing a young Mexican American woman's quest for literary respect, sexual identity and equality, an academic degree, and a fulfilling love during the political transformations of late-1960's California. One of the most effective social themes of *Delia's Song* is the disturbing reality of sexism as it is experienced in Chicano culture. Delia must struggle against her own family's limiting attitudes as well as those of her colleagues. Her two brothers, both dead (one shot as a soldier in Vietnam, the other killed by a drug overdose), receive the affections of their mother that Delia desires and deserves. The deepest expression of her struggle for sexual and intellectual identity takes place in herself, as she moves from being an idealistic girl carrying many resentments along with much low self-esteem into a fully developed artist, academic, and partner in love.

The narrative structure suggests a field of awareness rather than a linear, historical sequence of events. Dreams, flashbacks, sprinkles of family history, and memories all interrupt the plot. Stream-of-consciousness flashbacks, vignettes of dream imagery, bits of journal entries, family oral histories, and even newspaper clippings are used as narrative elements. The entire story is presented in a limited-omniscient point of view, filtered principally through the emotions and mind of Delia, but taking liberties by revealing the inner thoughts of other characters as well.

The structure of the novel presents one of the main themes: that life happens all at once, at the level of consciousness, and has meaning to the degree that people have awareness of it. Delia's life makes sense only when looked at as an entire fabric, not as a series of logically related events.

The three sections create a circular narrative structure, suggesting the heroic "monomyth" typical of James Joyce's work. This structure takes the heroine from her fall into illusion and experience, into an incubation period leading to severe soul-searching, and finally returning her to the initial locale, Berkeley, so that she can be released from the past and rejoin her first love as a fully individualized woman.

With the presence of Joyce felt from the first pages, both in the technique of stream-of-consciousness narration and the actual appearance of "James Joyce," a costumed man who lifts Delia from a dizzying fall, *Delia's Song* traces the cyclical heroic path in its three main sections. After the first "fall" when Delia meets "Joyce" in the first pages of the novel, Delia continues her heroine's journey through an initiation into academia, life, and sexuality to her three-part return: her return to her true love, Jeff; her "return" to campus, to Mattie's, and to her fantasy; and finally her "return" to a sense of wholeness, a sense of selfhood, which is what the journey is all about. Her journey back to Berkeley completes the heroine's quest cycle, allowing her to complete the novel she has been writing, to understand the difference between the illusory lover and the real one, and to resolve the inner tensions that have kept her distant and tormented.

As the novel ends, readers are promised that the truth has set Delia free, that Jeff will understand her evasive and erratic behavior, and that Delia's heroic quest has ended at last with a Joycean "yes," uniting her with not only her lover but also, more important, with an enduring sense of her own worth as a woman and as a writer.

*Critical Context*

*Delia's Song* is the first published novel of a well-established poet, but it is not a strong work. Lucha Corpi has gained critical acclaim for her *Palabras de mediodía/Noon Words* (1980) and is well respected as a poet and fiction writer, with works appearing in numerous journals. Yet *Delia's Song*, while fascinating in its efforts, fails to live up to Corpi's artistic reputation.

*Delia's Song* has much to recommend it, but as a fully grown, full-blown novel, it fails. One senses that it may have been hastily written, if gathered over three decades; one senses that the author may have been purging a past as much as creating a work of art. These speculations come to mind because the characters stay, for the most part, flat and undeveloped, even though the characterization of Delia does compel attention and respect.

The psychological complexity of Delia—even though she never quite becomes a flawed, endearing, human being—holds the key to the novel's contribution to modern literature. The importance of the novel is its celebration of the intellect and sexuality of a Mexican (and, by extension, any) woman. In the description of Delia's self-doubt, her tormenting concern about her talents, and her erratic (sometimes saintly, sometimes sexy) personal development, the novel indicates the jagged inner life of any young woman with a mind trying to maintain integrity in a world that is given to devaluing her.

*Bibliography*
Brinson-Pineda, Barbara. "Poets on Poetry: Dialogue with Lucha Corpi." *Prisma* 1, no. 1 (1979): 4-9. Interview with Corpi about her poetry and her dominating social themes of women's oppression and liberation.
Curiel, Barbara Brinson. "Lucha Corpi." In *Chicano Writers: First Series*, edited by Francisco A. Lomelí and Carl R. Shirley. Vol. 82 in *Dictionary of Literary Biography*. Detroit: Gale Research, 1989. Discusses Corpi's poetry at length and gives more critical attention to her short stories than to her first novel. Notes that "Corpi's recent fiction is characterized by its portraits of women in untenable situations who choose a course of action and who follow it, often with tragic consequences."
*Publishers Weekly*. Review of *Delia's Song*, by Lucha Corpi. 234 (November 4, 1988): 80. Condemns *Delia's Song* as an over-romanticized, poorly told tale of a "one-dimensional" heroine whose "decisions seem glib." Asserts that "the conflicts in the central character are so superficially explored that her efforts to resolve them are ultimately of little interest."
Sanchez, Marta Ester. *Contemporary Chicana Poetry: A Critical Approach to an Emerging Literature*. Berkeley: University of California Press, 1985. Acknowledges Corpi's outstanding literary reputation. Written before publication of *Delia's Song*.
Vallejos, Tomás. "Chicano/a Writing: Social Insights." *American Book Review* 11 (January-February, 1990): 13. Discusses the virtues and flaws of Corpi's first novel, noting that she has unsuccessfully attempted to transfer her fine poetic voice to the genre of fiction. Argues that the strong points of *Delia's Song* are its technically well-wrought narrative structure, the interest generated by the use of Delia's nightmares, and the account of the political events in Berkeley.

*Joyce Ann Hancock*

# DELIVERANCE

*Author:* James Dickey (1923-     )
*Type of plot:* Adventure
*Time of plot:* September, about 1960
*Locale:* Rural northeast Georgia
*First published:* 1970

*Principal characters:*
ED GENTRY, the vice president of an advertising firm
LEWIS MEDLOCK, a survivalist and physical-fitness buff
DREW BALLINGER, a sales supervisor for a soft-drink company
BOBBY TRIPPE, a gregarious mutual-fund salesman and bachelor
UNNAMED MOUNTAIN MEN, a menace to the four canoeists
MARTHA GENTRY, Ed's wife of fifteen years
GEORGE HOLLEY, an employee of Ed's with artistic ambitions
THE GRINERS, two rustic brothers who agree to drive the canoeists' cars
    from Oree to Aintry
BULLARD, a sheriff who investigates what happened on the river
QUEEN, a deputy sheriff who suspects Ed's involvement in the disappear-
    ance of his brother-in-law

*The Novel*
   *Deliverance* tells the story of four middle-class men who set out in two canoes for
a September weekend of deliverance from their suburban routines. Autumn, middle
age, and the damming of the wild Cahulawassee River are imminent, as Ed Gentry,
Lewis Medlock, Drew Ballinger, and Bobby Trippe seize the opportunity for an
outdoors adventure while they still can. Driving to rugged northeast Georgia, they
arrange for a couple of coarse mechanics to drive their cars to where they plan to land.
The four men launch their canoes in Oree and intend to paddle as far as Aintry. The
outing turns out to be a deadly ordeal that tests each of the participants.
   The narrator is Ed, recollecting that fateful weekend from the vantage point of ten
years after the events. He recalls the four men's euphoria during their first day on the
idyllic river. In the early morning, Ed botches an attempt to hunt a deer with his bow
and arrow. Later, after becoming separated from Lewis and Drew, Ed and inept Bobby
pause from their journey at an apparently peaceful stretch of riverbank. They are
accosted and assaulted by two brutal mountain men. Bobby is raped, and Ed is about
to be abused when Lewis shows up and sends an arrow through the chest of one of the
attackers. The other runs away.
   The four men must now decide what to do with the corpse. Arguing on behalf of
reason and the rule of law, Drew insists that they must report the incident to the
authorities and rely on the justice of their case. Lewis, however, insists that they are
the only law in the wilderness. Convinced that they would not receive a fair trial in

this backwoods region, the other two men side with Lewis. The men bury the body where it would not be found and resume their journey, in a much more somber mood.

The river becomes turbulent, and the men are thrown out of their canoes and into the rapids. Drew is killed, perhaps by a bullet shot from the cliffs overhead. Lewis' leg is badly broken, and with Bobby still traumatized by the sexual assault, Ed has to take responsibility for getting the three surviving adventurers back to civilization. Fearful that an armed mountain man is still lurking above waiting to pick them off, they spend the evening camped beneath the cliffs.

Ed climbs, slowly and laboriously, to the summit in order to confront whoever might have shot Drew and might still be intent on ambushing the others. In the very early morning, perched in a tree, Ed sights a mountain man and shoots him with an arrow. The action causes Ed to fall out of the tree and onto an extra arrow, wounding himself in the side. The other man is dead, though Ed cannot be certain that he is indeed the second mountain man who ran away when Lewis interrupted the assault on the riverbank. He cannot even be certain that the man he killed has done or intended any harm to any of them. When Ed examines Drew's body, it is impossible to determine whether he died from a bullet wound. Fearful of legal consequences, Ed and Bobby submerge the bodies of both Drew and the mountain man in the river.

When Ed, Bobby, and Lewis at last arrive in Aintry, Lewis is hospitalized, and all three are interrogated by a suspicious sheriff. Each corroborates the others' claim that what happened to Drew out on the river was a terrible accident and that nothing else untoward occurred. Sheriff Bullard is skeptical, especially since his deputy Queen's brother-in-law is missing, but lacking any evidence of foul play, he has to let the three men go free. Ed takes the responsibility of informing Drew's bitter widow of her husband's unnecessary death. Returning to his own home, he is himself transformed. Memories of their outing on the river haunt and inspire a revivified Ed.

*The Characters*

In Ed Gentry, Lewis Medlock, Drew Ballinger, and Bobby Trippe, Dickey provides a compelling variety of responses to the ordeal of life wrenched from the anesthetics of convention. Ed's is the heightened consciousness through which all the experiences are filtered. Married to the nurturing Martha for fifteen years, Ed admits to being a "slider," to having learned to take life on its easiest terms. He is content with being merely vice president of his advertising firm, and repressing his own artistic aspirations, he envies George Holley, a talented employee who attempts to rise above the mediocrity of commercial design. Yet a lurking discontent impels Ed toward the river, toward an experience that will change his life by forcing him to reexamine it. The same impulse is also probably responsible for his friendship with Lewis.

Though married and the father of three children, Lewis is a survivalist and partisan of physical fitness. He scorns the physical and psychological lethargy into which he has seen men of his background slide, and he regards the river expedition as a denial of the middle-class values that businessmen such as Drew and Bobby represent. While Bobby is the most complacent, the most dependent on creature comforts and facile routines, and therefore the least equipped to cope with crisis, Lewis is closest to being what Dickey, in a 1979 essay, called "The Energized Man"—"the man who functions with not, say, fifteen per cent of his faculties . . . but ideally, with a hundred per cent, a veritable A-bomb among the animated spectres of the modern world." Yet for all his admiration of Lewis' rugged self-reliance, it is Ed who learns the important lesson of transcending individualism.

While Lewis subscribes to the pastoral myth of a benevolent nature, Ed is more skeptical; he is convinced that "there is always something wrong with people in the country." The Griners and the other rural people encountered by the four suburban men enable Dickey to examine the concept of the "noble savage," Jean-Jacques Rousseau's contention that humans are inherently benevolent but are corrupted by society. Ed becomes convinced that, free of the civilizing influence of human community, natural man is a brute, capable of the violence that is indeed inflicted on the group. It is true that the crude Griner brothers end up keeping their promise to deliver the men's cars and that the rural folk in Aintry prove extremely hospitable to the physically and psychically wounded survivors. The mountain men who attack Ed and Bobby seem naturally degenerate, however, and once beyond the constraints of civilization, Ed himself proves capable of inflicting violence.

As the chronicle of a traumatic weekend recollected in the tranquillity of a ten years' distance, *Deliverance* emphasizes the extent to which it has been a conversion experience for Ed, delivering him from ennui and reconciling him to his existence as a modern suburban man. He remains troubled by his memories and tormented by guilt over Drew's death and over the possibility that he murdered an innocent man. Ed's narrative is an attempt at verbal exorcism and self-justification. Returning again to the canoe trip, Ed hopes at last to attain deliverance.

*Themes and Meanings*

In its exploration of the individual man tested by the frontier elements, *Deliverance* perpetuates the legacy of classic American fiction. Yet the novel is also very much a product of the turbulence, violence, and apocalyptic mood of the late 1960's. In a 1976 interview, Dickey himself explained the novel's success thus: "I wrote the right book at the right time."

That time was one of widespread skepticism over the continuing validity of institutions and traditions. Dickey removes his four protagonists from their comfortable social setting and places them in the wilderness in order to test their individual resources and to probe the premises of modern civilization. What begins as a pleasant weekend outing for four middle-class and middle-aged men soon forces each to confront fundamental issues about a life he has been taking for granted.

*Deliverance* is also an expression of environmental concerns. Civilization is encroaching even on the remote Georgia wilderness in which Ed, Lewis, Drew, and Bobby go canoeing. They encounter the jetsam of urban life floating along the most accessible parts of the river, and even its most primitive parts will soon be conquered by a dam. Their adventure one autumn weekend represents a desperate last chance:

for each mortal man individually and for the vanishing environment.

*Deliverance* is a variation on and an ambivalent response to the pastoral myth, a persistent belief in the elemental purity of a life lived in harmony with nature and a Romantic rejection of the city as necessarily corrupt. Survivalists, like Lewis and many contemporaries who saw nuclear holocaust as inevitable, insisted on the need to be prepared to turn to a simpler, more self-reliant way of life than that to which a technological, commercial mass society was accustomed.

Dickey's novel is a parable of control, of the degree to which any person can take charge of his or her own life; it is significant that the four men rendezvous to begin their trip at a place called Will's Plaza Shopping Center, as if to underscore their ordeal as a test of will. It is also, as the title suggests, a deliverance. In Lewis's eventual reintegration into the human community, moreover, the experience is a deliverance precisely from self-control, from the bleak tyranny of the autonomous self. "Deliverance" is a theological term connoting salvation of the isolated sinner through humble acceptance of divine grace. Yet in Ed's relationship with his wife, Dickey also explicitly relates the concept of deliverance to sexuality, to its implied recognition of the importance of the other, of the limits of self-possession.

*Critical Context*

*Deliverance* was the first novel by Dickey, a prominent poet. Later Dickey novels have included *Alnilam* (1987) and *To the White Sea* (1993). Although initial reviews were negative, *Deliverance* became a huge commercial success, as did a critically acclaimed 1972 film adaptation. Already admired by connoisseurs of poetry, Dickey, who made a cameo appearance in the film as Sheriff Bullard, became a familiar public figure.

Though the novel was attacked on publication for allegedly glorifying violence and for ignoring urgent social issues, *Deliverance* has come to be regarded as an important work of fiction by a writer who is much more sophisticated than his public image of boozer and brawler would admit. The novel possesses clear affinities to such Dickey poems as "On the Coosawattee," "The Owl King," "Fog Envelops the Animals," and "The Vegetable King." The book can profitably be studied as an extension of the author's work in poetry; it has also introduced large numbers of readers to an author they might never have encountered as a poet.

*Deliverance* shares with much of Dickey's poetry a preoccupation with defining the individual (invariably male) by challenging him against the violence of the natural world. The novel reflects Dickey's characteristic cult of experience, as well as that of much of the rest of American literature, concentrating as it does on an individual man's ambivalence toward civilization and toward the company of women. The testing of the self through violent encounter with the wilderness echoes William Faulkner's "The Bear" (1942), Herman Melville's *Moby Dick: Or, The Whale* (1851), and James Fenimore Cooper's Leatherstocking Tales.

Though at the outset of the story Ed has been married for fifteen years, he refers to the experience as having transformed him from a boy into a man. *Deliverance* is thus reminiscent of such other coming-of-age narratives as Mark Twain's *The Adventures of Huckleberry Finn* (1884), Stephen Crane's *The Red Badge of Courage: An Episode of the American Civil War* (1895), and J. D. Salinger's *The Catcher in the Rye* (1951). William Golding's *Lord of the Flies* (1954) likewise combines the initiation of a child into the adult world with an exploration of the theme of the noble savage, of the fundamental qualities of a human being outside the influence of civilization.

Fyodor Dostoevski's *Zapiski iz podpolya* (1864; *Notes from the Underground*, 1918) and Joseph Conrad's *Heart of Darkness* (1899) are also likely precedents. Like *Deliverance*, both are first-person attempts to penetrate beneath the social veneer to the essential identity of a solitary human being. Both project an unflattering view of human nature, and, like Dickey's powerful novel, raise questions about reliability and the ethics of lying.

*Bibliography*
Baughman, Ronald. *Understanding James Dickey*. Columbia: University of South Carolina Press, 1985. An accessible guide to Dickey's life and work that argues that the key to understanding him is to read him as a poet of the self. Chapter 6 discusses *Deliverance* as a demonstration of the theme of renewal, of how Dickey and his characters transform themselves.
Bloom, Harold, ed. *James Dickey*. New York: Chelsea House, 1987. Includes an introduction, nine essays, and a chronology. In "*Deliverance*: Initiation and Possibility," Linda Wagner examines the novel's careful structure and documents its debt to *Huckleberry Finn*.
Calhoun, Richard J., ed. *James Dickey: The Expansive Imagination*. De Land, Florida: Everett/Edwards, 1973. Includes an interview with Dickey and fourteen essays, mostly on his poetry. In "James Dickey's *Deliverance*: Darkness Visible," Daniel B. Marin analyzes the sharp narrative focus by which Dickey articulates the emergence of a dark, repressed truth.
Calhoun, Richard J., and Robert W. Hill. *James Dickey*. Boston: Twayne, 1983. A book-length overview of Dickey's career that provides a critical introduction to his most important works. Chapter 7 summarizes the plot of *Deliverance* and discusses the negative reactions of its first reviewers.
Doughtie, Edward. "Art and Nature in *Deliverance*." *Southwest Review* 64 (Spring, 1979): 167-180. Doughtie examines the dichotomy between art and nature in *Deliverance*. He argues that Dickey presents art as a necessary mediator between nature—external and internal—and modern urban civilization.
Endel, Peggy Goodman. "Dickey, Dante, and the Demonic." *American Literature* 60 (December, 1988): 611-625. Endel reads *Deliverance* as the story of a midlife crisis told from the Augustinian narrative stance of a new man describing his old, dead self. The novel, she contends, illustrates human change through grace.

*Steven G. Kellman*

# DESSA ROSE

*Author:* Sherley Anne Williams (1944-        )
*Type of plot:* Historical realism
*Time of plot:* The late 1840's
*Locale:* Alabama, primarily the large, isolated northern farm of Sutton's Glen
*First published:* 1986

### Principal characters

DESSA ROSE, an escaped field slave condemned to die for her involvement in a coffle uprising

KAINE, Dessa's enslaved husband, murdered for striking his master

ADAM NEHEMIAH (MR. NEMI), a social-climbing white Kentuckian who is commencing a book on slave rebellions

RUFEL (RUTH ELIZABETH CARSON SUTTON), a deserted plantation mistress who harbors runaway slaves

BERTIE (FITZALBERT SUTTON), Rufel's absent husband, a riverboat gambler

NATHAN, Dessa's cofflemate and Rufel's lover

ROSE, Dessa's mother

DORCAS, Rufel's mammy

HARKER, the leader of the Glen slaves, who courts Dessa

## The Novel

Williams writes in her author's note that *Dessa Rose* is in part the fictionalization of two real antebellum events: the revolt of a slave coffle, ferociously instigated by a pregnant black captive, and a report of a Southern white woman who defies social dicta and dares to safeguard fugitive slaves. As the novel reinvents these historical incidents, it accomplishes two objectives. It exonerates the slaves from literary and historical stereotypes of blacks as victims, beasts, infants, and opportunists. Moreover, the novel explores the complex communal, familial, and interracial networks that functioned in—and in resistance to—the institution of slavery.

*Dessa Rose* is divided into a brief prologue, three middle sections of two chapters each, and a short epilogue. The prologue revives Dessa's past, lost love. Of nearly identical length, the epilogue replaces Dessa's memory of lost passion with a present moment of her loving and being loved in freedom. In the first two midsections, flashbacks alternate with third-person narration. Black and white, female and male, enslaved and freeborn—all these voices meander through the sections. The voices interweave in a mix of private recollection, public dialogue, interior examination, and interpersonal engagement.

The first section inaugurates a cycle of escape, recapture, and escape that subsequent sections repeat. Pregnant and ragged, Dessa lies shackled and silent in the cellar of an Alabama sheriff's farm. She has committed the slave's two most heinous transgressions: She has attacked and killed white men, and she has helped in a slave revolt.

Love lures Dessa to murder, and hatred nearly snatches her from life. Her master, Terrell Vaugham, smashes the beloved banjo of her husband Kaine, the father of Dessa's unborn child. Heartbroken, Kaine attacks Vaugham and dies in the struggle. Dessa then avenges Kaine's death by attacking Vaugham, and she is punished by sale to a slave trader who is passing through with his human merchandise. Even in this misery, Dessa and others on this coffle manage to slip their chains, surprising and killing all guards and dealers but one, and driving this man to madness. Yet escape proves brief. The rebels are ambushed by bounty hunters. After childbirth, Dessa will hang for her insurgency.

Confined to a root cellar for the duration of her pregnancy, Dessa is an object of notoriety and fascination to both whites and blacks. To author Adam Nehemiah, this drooping "darky" is the savage centerpiece of his forthcoming volume on slave rebellion, and he sees her as the engine to propel him into the elite inner sancta of slaveholding gentry. To the slaves who glimpse Dessa as they arrive with food or replace her slop jar, she is the proud "debil woman," a votive of African authority whose fearlessness and self-determination they discreetly emulate. These differences in perceptions of Dessa highlight both a white culture of domination, one that misapprehends the docility and surrogacy of the slaves, and a slave culture that instigates gestures and meanings in defiance of oppression.

Several of Dessa's comrades from the coffle return to rescue her. They deposit her in the safety of Sutton's Glen, a backwoods farm owned by Rufel, who turns blind eyes to the fugitives flocking there for refuge. Tucked among the cotton fields, slave and mistress cultivate animosity. For example, when Harker, a former cofflemate, broaches an idea for gaining freedom that must involve Rufel, Dessa initially rejects the plan. She balks at owing the liberty of herself and her little boy to a white woman. To Dessa, Rufel epitomizes every infliction and indecency that whites heap upon slaves: their arrogance, inhumanity, hypocrisy, and greed; their disloyalty and capriciousness; their self-elected mastery of another race.

Harker's plan, however, is too crucial for Dessa to dismiss. From town to town, Rufel exhibits a wagonload of the Glen's most valuable slaves. With Dessa as mammy and nursemaid, Rufel sells the slaves, only to have them escape their captors and rejoin the group at some predesignated rendezvous. The scheme nearly unravels when Adam Nehemiah recognizes Dessa and persuades the local sheriff to confiscate her. Playing flustered lady and flabbergasted maid to the hilt, Rufel and Dessa discredit Nemi and secure her release. The group divide their money and separate for points west and north. That the last two chapters are written in the first person underscores the freedom that Dessa and her cohorts achieve.

*The Characters*

Dessa and Rufel are significantly parallel. Both have names that suggest homelessness: "Odessa" implies an odyssey, and "Ruth" calls to mind the loyal but exiled kinswoman of the Old Testament. Like Dessa's Kaine, Rufel shares a star-crossed love: Nathan, the leader of the coffle uprising, simultaneously assumes skilled administration of the farm and acquires an amorous section of her bed. Dessa gives birth to a son she names Desmond Kaine (Mony); Rufel nurses an infant daughter. Dessa mourns her lost mother; similarly, Rufel grieves for the mammy who loved her more palpably than did her own distant biological mother. Finally, both women struggle to exhume, acknowledge, and exterminate feelings of abandonment by loved ones. For Dessa, this encompasses family members "sold away" to purchase racehorses, livestock, and other trophies. For Rufel, these feelings center upon her husband Bertie, whose sporadic and shortening visits to the Glen point to his addiction to gambling.

Though both women express differences caused by chasms of race and power, both eventually acknowledge these differences, bridge them, and appreciate each other as intimates and individual beings. This forwards the novel's suggestion that physical liberation from oppression is accomplished by mental liberation from self-destructive images and toxic memories.

Kaine and Adam Nehemiah are another matched pair. Their names, from the fractured family of Genesis (Adam, the first man, and his murdering son Cain), ironically suggest the ruptured bonds between blacks and whites in enslavement. Through their art, the characters underscore the futility that underlies obsession with loss: Kaine the musician constructs his banjo to remember an African past that he himself, allegedly fathered by a white man, never has nor will experience; Nemi the author forges his books on enslavement to gain entrance into an aristocracy that presently gives him faint respect. Both projects are silenced, Kaine's when he is murdered; Nemi's when Dessa's second escape leaves him ragged and raging in the street. The two men's struggles with personal histories of rejection and loss function as a metaphor for the fabricated histories that decline the dimensions—and dictate the decline—of slavery.

Ironically, the men's common muse is Dessa. Dessa's rebellion revives prospects of a lucrative sale of Nemi's book, yet he relates to her as a nemesis. He inscribes her in his notes as a beast of woolly hair, impulsive temper, primitive expression, and devious intent. Kaine, on the other hand, sings and speaks to Dessa to demonstrate that she feels love and pain deeply. These relationships convey the complex impact of enslavement on black women. Nathan, Harker, and the community of other black men have been demeaned by enslavement. They favor light-skinned women and occasionally describe black women as mules. Yet the men do resist self-deprecatory images of enslavement. Tenaciously rebelling against the division and dehumanization of slave families, they offer themselves as surrogate fathers, brothers, and husbands, and they assert themselves as leaders and tacticians in the struggle for emancipation.

*Themes and Meanings*

That the slaves do resist commodification is one theme the novel critiques. With neither rationale nor explanation, masters can buy, sell, overwork, and murder slaves simply because these are their property. A mistress such as Rufel can brag of her mammy, but she need not remember that mammy's name or acknowledge that mammy's black family. This is an objecthood that slaves counteract by assertive renaming, as when Dessa rejects the nickname "Button," which Rufel attempts to give to Dessa's son. In another example of naming as resistance, the slaves derisively rename whites and reclaim their own perspectives of life in enslavement. "Miz Ruint" is the name the Glen slaves comically christen Rufel for bungling her marriage and beginning a romance with a slave.

Ultimately, slaveholders are bestialized by their system of bondage. While the slaves' communities privilege industry and respect of authority, in white communities, anarchy rampages. So-called good masters discourage religion among enslaved populations, and the fields and kitchens swell with the light-skinned faces of their bastard children. Supposedly stern sheriffs are shamelessly seduced by the winks of wicked women. Finally, as even the slaves sardonically recognize, the language of the masters is often worse than that of their supposed inferiors.

The mistress' complicity in enslavement is also scrutinized in the novel. Rufel, for example, suspects that Bertie beats slaves, but she hesitates to confront him. Her powers are compromised by her complete legal and social subordination to her husband. Her family may be the source of her husband's wealth, and she may take charge of the farming while her absent spouse frequents steamboats, casinos, and whorehouses. Nevertheless, just as the slave must obey the slaveholder without question, so, too, must the mistress utterly submit her will to the master's prerogative. For the mistress and the mammy, rape and the fear of rape suppress women's powers and stamp them in their limited place.

"You have seen how a man is made a slave," reads the epigraph to the novel's first section, from *Narrative of the Life of Frederick Douglass, An American Slave* (1845). Language is the principal means of enslavement. More than even the whipping scars that waffle Dessa's thighs, language underscores slavery's project to erase black self-esteem; and language elevates the slaves to stand as authors of their own dignity. Thus the book's first sections, in which Dessa struggles from captivity, are entitled "Darky" and "Wench," names that whites would apply to black women. On the other hand, the final section, which signals Dessa's entrance to freedom, is entitled "Negresse," after the enslaved women of Haiti who liberated themselves. Dessa herself suspends white control when she attaches Rose, her enslaved mother's name, to her own.

*Critical Context*

*Dessa Rose*, Sherley Williams' first novel, was published in a post-1970's wave of revisionist fiction about slavery. For its focus on the sufferings and the resistance of the enslaved, substantiated by meticulous research and spoken from a black viewpoint, the novel stands with such lionized works as Charles Johnson's *Middle Passage* (1990), Toni Morrison's *Beloved* (1987), Caryl Phillips' *Cambridge* (1991), and Margaret Walker's *Jubilee* (1966). Dessa's tale evolved both from an earlier work that told the story from Nehemiah's perspective and from the critical response to William

Styron's *The Confessions of Nat Turner* (1967), a best-selling novel that came under fire for neglecting the strengths of slave communities and underestimating the potency of black expressive traditions.

Like the characters who populate it, the novel looks behind and forward in relationship to Williams' wide-ranging artistic productions. Beginning her career with poetry—her first collection, *The Peacock Poems* (1975), was nominated for a National Book Award—Williams has cultivated the themes of community, spirituality, love, leadership, and resistance that demarcate *Dessa Rose*. The oppositional gazes and surreptitious glances that blinker transactions among the novel's slaves and slaveholders are looks that anticipate Williams' sojourns into cinema and drama, which include an Emmy Award-winning reading of her poetry.

*Bibliography*

Christian, Barbara. "'Somebody Forgot to Tell Somebody Something': African-American Women's Historical Novels." In *Wild Women in the Whirlwind: Afra-American Culture and the Contemporary Literary Renaissance*, edited by Joanne M. Braxton and Andrée Nicola McLaughlin. New Brunswick, N.J.: Rutgers University Press, 1990. Christian distinguishes the novel from nineteenth century slave narratives and pre-1960's historical fiction, particularly in its privileging of vernacular language and folk culture and its distancing from documentary sources.

Davis, Mary Kemp. "Everybody Knows Her Name: The Recovery of the Past in Sherley Anne Williams's *Dessa Rose*." *Callaloo* 12 (Summer, 1989): 544-558. An outstanding essay that examines naming in the novel as an act of "signifying" upon slaveholders, both to retaliate against spurious treatments of slavery by white authors and to commemorate the rebellion and resistance of enslaved black women.

Goldman, Ann E. " 'I Made the Ink': (Literary) Production and Reproduction in *Dessa Rose* and *Beloved*." *Feminist Studies* 16 (Summer, 1990): 313-330. Discusses both novels as asserting the exploitation of enslaved women's bodies and attempting simultaneously to repossess these bodies for ownership by black women. Both the protagonists within the texts and the texts themselves claim literary production, speech, and maternity as means of fighting commodification and erasure.

Henderson, Mae. "(W)riting 'The Work' and Working the Rites." *Black American Literature Forum* 23 (Winter, 1989): 631-660. Provides an excellent introduction to the context and techniques of *Dessa Rose*. Analyzes Williams' work as a critique of the methods of white male literary mediators and a comment on enslavement in historically authentic discourse. Evaluates subversive discursive strategies, the slaves' vernacular, and discourse of domination.

Jordan, Shirley M. *Broken Silences: Interviews with Black and White Women Writers*. New Brunswick, N.J.: Rutgers University Press, 1993. Williams considers the sexuality, humanity, and heroism of her characters and the novel's relationship to the women's movement, African American literacy, and literary critics.

McDowell, Deborah E. "Negotiating Between Tenses: Witnessing Slavery After Freedom—*Dessa Rose*." In *Slavery and the Literary Imagination*, edited by Deborah E. McDowell and Arnold Rampersad. Baltimore: The Johns Hopkins University Press, 1989. Proposes Dessa's cycles of enslavement and escape as symbolic of both the liberating and confining aspects of language. Alternately named and misnamed, Dessa complicates and disrupts assumptions about race, gender, literacy, truth, memory, power, and possibility.

Moody, Joycelyn K. "Ripping Away the Veil of Slavery: Literacy, Communal Love, and Self-Esteem in Three Slave Women's Narratives." *Black American Literature Forum* 24 (Winter, 1990): 633-648. Discusses themes of *Dessa Rose, Beloved,* and Harriet Jacobs' *Incidents in the Life of a Slave Girl* (1861). While Jacobs' antebellum narrative emphasizes literacy and community, the twentieth century works stress the empowering potential of both community and romantic love. All three theorize supportive community networks as essential precursors to individual self-esteem.

*Barbara McCaskill*

# THE DEVIL IN TEXAS

*Author:* Aristeo Brito (1942-    )
*Type of plot:* Magical realism
*Time of plot:* The 1850's to the 1970's
*Locale:* The Texas-Mexico border towns of Presidio and Ojinaga and the surrounding
area
*First published: El diablo en Texas,* 1976 (English translation, 1990)

>   *Principal characters:*
>   BEN LYNCH (DON BENITO), a powerful, wealthy Anglo landowner
>   FRANCISCO URANGA (DON PANCHO), a journalist and lawyer who resists
>       the injustices he sees perpetuated upon the Chicano population
>   ROSARIO (URANGA LYNCH), Francisco's sister, who marries Ben Lynch
>   (TÍA) PAZ, Francisco's wife
>   REYES and
>   JESÚS URANGA, Don Pancho's sons
>   JOSÉ, SR., the son of Reyes Uranga, married to Marcela
>   JOSÉ, JR., who "speaks" from Marcela's womb and returns to Presidio
>       when his father is dying

*The Novel*

   No plot, as such, exists in this short novel, but the activities of the two main families
named in the work may be traced through some one hundred twenty years (1853-
1970). The book begins with a prologue, told in the stream-of-consciousness technique, which sets the stage for the following narrative, told from multiple points of
view. The next three parts, "Presidio 1883," "Presidio 1942," and "Presidio 1970,"
illustrate the conflict between Anglos, represented by the Lynch lineage, and Mexicans (who eventually become Mexican Americans, or Chicanos), represented by the
Uranga family. The action throughout the book takes place in the border towns of
Presidio, Texas, and Ojinaga, Mexico, on each side of the Rio Grande. No main
character, except perhaps the Devil, is introduced in the prologue, but the barrenness
and desolation of far west Texas, which will be the locus for years of conflict between
the neighboring communities, is emphasized. Since Aristeo Brito was reared in this
same environment of antagonism and conflict and, as an adult, returned "home" to
research the book, many similarities between the author's life and the narrative
appear.

   "Presidio 1883" details the Anglo domination of the area, introducing Ben Lynch
(Don Benito), whose wealth and influence enable him to threaten, cajole, or cheat the
Mexicans. He is powerful and has the strong arm of the Texas Rangers on his side
whenever there is a conflict between him and the Mexicans he employs. At one point,
he discovers a ring of horse thieves and proceeds to host a party to which they are
given a special invitation. Much to their surprise, the thieves are summarily slaugh-

tered. The only person willing to stand up to Don Benito is Francisco Uranga, a lawyer and journalist who encourages the Mexican Americans to resist oppression; at one point, Francisco becomes a representative for the Mexican government. His efforts are in vain: One of his sons (Jesús) is ambushed and drowned in the Rio Grande one night; another becomes a part of a subversive band of roaming outlaws. His own sister Rosario marries Ben Lynch, the devil incarnate. Throughout this part of the book, incidents detail the misfortune and abuse experienced by the Chicanos. One such incident is the death of a twelve-year-old who dies as a result of a lung disorder contracted while working long hours in the mines. Descriptions of several key locations, symbolic as well as real, are provided in "Presidio 1883": a cave situated deep in the Santa Cruz Mountains, a train station, a fort where devils and spirits roam at night telling their sad life stories and where tourists are taken (for a fee). In addition to the human characters from the two main families, the Devil in many disguises appears in this section of the book.

In "Presidio 1942," life continues much the same, although the Texas Rangers are replaced by the Border Patrol and some farm laborers, such as Teléforo and his son Chale, acquire a degree of professional status. Because these Hispanics have the responsibility of controlling the undocumented workers, their position in the social hierarchy is somewhat enhanced. Life in the little agrarian community continues to be boring and depraved. The young people who do not flee to a better existence somewhere else in Texas spend their time as shiftless bums in bars or brothels. Francisco Uranga's grandson José, a sharecropper on the land his family originally owned, abandons his home and pregnant wife in order to dodge the draft by escaping across the border. His wife Marcela dies in childbirth, but the fetus speaks fervently from the womb about social injustices perpetrated on the generations of Urangas. The surreal presence of a powerful and malignant devil continues to stalk the land.

Years later, in "Presidio 1970," José Uranga (the fetus in section two) returns to the deathbed of his father. In a fantastic dialogue with the dead man, José learns of his father's reasons for fleeing and of his experiences in prison. The plight of the Chicano has never improved, despite the passage of time and changing generations. Although he is initially bitter and resentful, the younger José decides to remain in Presidio to combat the wrongs perpetuated on his genetic and cultural fellow-sufferers.

*The Characters*

Ben Lynch, the Anglo landowner introduced in "Presidio 1883," typifies everything abusive and negative in the social system of the late nineteenth century along the Texas-Mexico border. He and others in the book are more types than fully developed characters. His motivation is greed; his ambition is acquisition of money, land, and power. He will stoop to any level to accomplish these goals. By marrying Rosario, he aims to ensure that the Mexican American population will be divided in their loyalties, because, in a perverted sort of way, he has become "family." In like manner, he takes other Chicanos into his confidence in order to undermine their traditional allegiance to one another.

Francisco Uranga will not be a pawn for the powerful Anglo landowner. He is smart enough to realize that the Mexican American population is being exploited. His publication, a small newspaper called *The Frontiersman*, eventually becomes a strong voice of protest concerning the life of the Mexicans in the Southwest. Few details concerning Francisco's daily life are provided, but his son Reyes inherits the seeds of rebellion.

Reyes Uranga is enraged when he realizes the extent to which Ben Lynch will go in his abuse. When he discovers that Lynch has ordered his brother drowned and his friends shot in cold blood, he resists in a manner different from his father, using a rifle instead of a pen. He becomes known as "Coyote" and organizes resistance against the traffic of illegal aliens back and forth across the border.

José Uranga, Reyes' son, who is married to Marcela, is important to the narrative because he represents an element of civil disobedience. His willingness to leave his pregnant wife and risk his life escaping across to Ojinaga to avoid the draft resembles his Uncle Jesús' willingness to continue to transport Mexicans across the river illegally.

Marcela Uranga, José's wife, represents the long-suffering woman in a border society. Her husband and his relatives are involved in resistance to the ruling caste, so she must face her emotional and physical problems alone. She feels pain at the thought of bringing a child into the abusive world of the Chicano worker on the borders of the southern United States. When a tall man in a Stetson hat passes by and winks at her, she is convinced that she has seen the Devil incarnate; she will not be consoled and eventually goes mad. Her death in childbirth is not an unrealistic one.

José, the unnamed fetus in "Presidio 1942," is the last of the Urangas introduced in the novel. His soliloquy from the womb represents a somewhat "genetic" knowledge of the plight of the Chicanos passed from generation to generation. He is portrayed as a semimessianic figure who returns in "Presidio 1970." His speech at that time is not with a living human, but with his dead father.

*Themes and Meanings*

*The Devil in Texas* might be described as a collage of images, dates, events and characters who people the towns of Presidio and Ojinaga. The three dates used to divide the book do more to suggest timelessness than fixed time, and the historical and spiritual journey of the Mexican Americans effected by the Treaty of Guadalupe Hidalgo in 1848 is a fractured one.

The theme of exploitation (past, present, and future) is illustrated by the life stories of the Uranga family, whose accident of birth causes them to lose lives, prestige, land, power—even human dignity. The unnamed fetus in "Presidio 1942" who returns in "Presidio 1970" may represent a sign of hope for the Chicano, because he seems to have in his blood the same resistant spirit of his ancestors, despite his earlier abandonment of the cause.

Numerous images appear and reappear: a haunted fort that is used as a tourist attraction for the few visitors who find their way to the remote land; a river that symbolizes life but also division and death; a bridge that is built more for control of traffic between the two countries than for convenience; a cave where the Devil surely lives. By far the most dominant image is that of the Devil, who takes on various guises but who, for the purposes of this social commentary, is represented by Anglos in general and Ben Lynch in particular. In fact, everything evil, painful, or in any way restrictive is credited to the power of the "Devil in Texas." Initiated in the prologue, these symbols carry more narrative momentum than do the named characters. One of the most impressive features of the text lies in its "holographic" effect: One can begin reading almost any section and experience the impact, if not the details, of the other sections.

*Critical Context*

*The Devil in Texas*, first published in Spanish in 1976, is an experiment in narrative technique in the tradition of Juan Rulfo's *Pedro Páramo* (1955) and works by such other writers as Agustín Yáñez and Carlos Fuentes, who cast their stories in a semifantastic ambiance. Brito's work differs, however, in that it defines the Chicano experience. Its Texas border setting does not restrict it to a regional audience; its powerful emotional message of alienation and powerlessness should be familiar to the "hyphenated" citizen of any race or location. Brito was one of the first to use (in the original Spanish version) Mexican Spanish, Chicano Spanish, English, and a mixture of English and Spanish in a written linguistic pattern typical of oral linguistic expressions, hence capturing the spirit of the issues together with the prosaic reality. The myriad narrative voices that tell the story also contribute to the mosaic experience of the novel.

Aristeo Brito's unique blend of fact and fiction laced with mythical and symbolic overtones transforms an apparently simple story line into a collage of images that project a powerful social message. With its rich intricacy of plot, theme, and symbolism, *The Devil in Texas* qualifies as an integral part of the canon of Chicano literature.

*Bibliography*

Eger, Ernestina N. Review of *El diablo en Texas*, by Aristeo Brito. *Latin American Literary Review* 5 (Spring-Summer, 1977): 162-165. Review of the 1976 Spanish edition. Succinctly captures the tone of each of the sections of the book and locates it in the Chicano and Mexican traditions.
Lomelí, Francisco. "Survey of Chicano Literature." *Bilingual Review* 15 (January, 1989): 135. Although Brito's work is not specifically mentioned, this journal article offers an excellent background for reading the novel.
Jiménez, Hector. Review of *The Devil in Texas*, by Aristeo Brito. *Hispanic*, November, 1990, 70. Short, concise review of the 1990 edition.
Lewis, Marvin A. "*El diablo en Texas!*: Structure and Meaning: Studies in Language and Literature of United States Hispanics." In *Contemporary Chicano Fiction: A Critical Survey*, edited by Vernon E. Lattin. Binghamton, N.Y.: Bilingual Press, 1986. A discussion of narrative technique, imagery, and symbolism.

Tatum, Charles. Introduction to *The Devil in Texas*, by Aristeo Brito. Tempe, Ariz.: Bilingual Press/Editorial Bilingüe, 1990. Offers background information on the status and change of the people living along the Rio Grande as well as biographical facts about Aristeo Brito that impact the narrative.

*Teresia Taylor*

# DISAPPEARING ACTS

*Author:* Terry McMillan (1951-     )
*Type of plot:* Romance
*Time of plot:* The 1980's
*Locale:* Brooklyn, New York
*First published:* 1989

> *Principal characters:*
> ZORA BANKS, a music teacher and aspiring singer
> FRANKLIN SWIFT, a construction worker and carpenter
> CLAUDETTE,
> PORTIA, and
> MARIE, Zora's friends and support system
> MOMS, Franklin's mother, who hates him and everything he does

*The Novel*

*Disappearing Acts* is an urban love story. The novel provides a realistic portrayal of a relationship between a black man and woman struggling to find their place in life separately and together.

*Disappearing Acts* is written in the first person. The chapters alternate between Zora and Franklin's point of view, chronicling their relationship over the course of two and a half years.

The novel begins with Franklin's monologue. He is a construction worker and carpenter who never graduated from high school; he is looking to start his own business so that he does not have to depend on white people for work. He has been hurt in relationships before and plans to remain romantically uninvolved until he gets his "foundation" set up. Zora's monologue reveals that she's also "taking a sabbatical" from the opposite sex and concentrating on her singing career. Both of them are lonely, and when they meet, it is love at first sight.

The novel moves rapidly, as does their relationship: Before long, Franklin has moved in with Zora, and they are spending most of their time together. The plot is propelled by the ups and downs of their relationship as they move from suspicion to trust, from secrets to revelations. Franklin is still married, although he has not lived with his wife in six years. Zora gets seizures, but she has not had one in four years. Each feels lucky to have found the other, and the first six chapters of the book are optimistic.

Gradually, Franklin's inability to find steady work starts to eat at him and at Zora. He ruins her birthday because he is unhappy with himself and lying to her about losing his job. Partly because Franklin does not have a job, partly because she is not ready for a baby, Zora has an abortion, a fact she tries, unsuccessfully, to hide from him. He is upset but forgives her, and she continues to support him, emotionally and financially.

The novel proceeds in an episodic fashion, as Franklin deals with his children, his inconsistent employment, his depressed sister Darlene, and his desire to hold on to Zora. Zora, in the meantime, stops seeing her friends, takes up and abandons voice lessons, has a seizure, and uses the money she has been saving for a studio session to finance their new apartment.

Things change for Zora once she discovers that she is pregnant again. She decides to keep the baby, even though she and Franklin are not married. She seems to be contented during her pregnancy, as if she is finally finding a balance for herself in the relationship. Franklin, on the other hand, grumbles about not being able to have sex and complains about Zora's weight gain. Although he does not really want a child, he thinks that having one will help him to hold on to Zora.

Eventually, though, Franklin's sense of self and empowerment deteriorate to the point where he hits Zora. She accepts his apology, but after Jeremiah is born, Franklin is out of work again, feeling even more insecure and ignored, and he starts to threaten Zora. He has no one to be angry at but himself, and the more he drinks, the more threatening he becomes. Fearing for herself and Jeremiah, Zora stays with her friend Portia and secures a restraining order against Franklin. Over the phone, she tells him to leave their apartment. Angry that she has called "the white man" on him—the worst thing she could do—Franklin leaves the apartment, but not before destroying as much as he possibly can.

Several months go by, during which time Franklin starts working again and goes back to school. Zora misses him, but she continues teaching and writing songs. The novel ends on an ambiguous note. When Franklin stops by to see her and Jeremiah, the reader is left with the impression that even though Zora is moving to Toledo, where her father and stepmother live, she and Franklin might someday reconcile.

*The Characters*

At the beginning of the novel, McMillan provides a monologue for each of the main characters, Zora and Franklin, setting them up as two people looking to better themselves. Both want success, and both are lonely but afraid of being hurt as they have been so many times before. This information, in addition to that about their class differences, foreshadows the struggle ahead.

Franklin is a construction worker and carpenter, employed sporadically throughout the novel. His spells of unemployment and his inability to get ahead depress him and often lead to heavy drinking and verbal abuse of Zora. He is angry at everyone, white people and his mother in particular; both are forces in his life that he believes hold him back and keep him from succeeding. Conflicting with this are his emotions for Zora, whom he loves and for whom he wants to provide. When he finds he cannot, he sinks further into depression and violence. McMillan retains the reader's sympathy for Franklin through his point-of-view chapters; the first-person voice gives the reader insights into both characters that would otherwise be missing. Since the novel is about the relationship, such intimacy propels it and develops both the characters equally.

Zora is college educated, and she is teaching music to junior high school students when Franklin meets her. She is ambitious; she writes her own music, plans to take voice lessons, and moves to Brooklyn in order to save money for her own piano. In short, she is everything Franklin is not. Named for the writer Zora Neale Hurston, Zora wants to be a professional singer. She also wants a relationship with the right man, however, and once she gets involved with Franklin, her plans for success take second place. Her friends complain that she never calls them anymore, and she finds herself covering for Franklin, lying about his educational background and marital status. Against her better judgment, she lets Franklin talk her into moving into a bigger apartment. This illustrates Zora's passivity and willingness to let Franklin take the lead in their relationship. In the end, she is a disappointing character: She lets herself disappear in the relationship and never fully realizes her ambition to be a singer; she settles for being a songwriter instead.

Because the novel is about their relationship and is narrated from their points of view, Zora and Franklin are the most developed characters. Their dialogue and scenes with each other propel the story. The other characters tend to be one-dimensional and function only in relation to Zora and Franklin. Moms, Franklin's mother, serves solely to explain Franklin's anger towards women. Her lack of approval and love has ruined him and his sister Darlene. Moms is unreasonable and not very believable, particularly when she throws mashed potatoes at Zora at Thanksgiving dinner.

Zora's friends function as a sounding board for her. As characters, they serve no other real purpose. Claudette is a successful lawyer, married to a doctor, with two children. She represents what everyone wants. Portia, a drifting good-time girl, ends up pregnant. She ultimately marries her lover and goes back to school. Marie is a struggling comedian with a drinking problem that may be caused by her hidden homosexuality, an issue touched on but left unexplored. By the end of the novel, she is sober and on the road to success.

*Themes and Meanings*

The novel is a fairly conventional love story, told in an unconventional structure of alternating voices. By telling the story from both Franklin's and Zora's points of view, McMillan depicts a relationship between a black man and a woman that is sympathetic and presents both as well-rounded characters. At the same time, however, she uses their story to explore larger issues of race, sex, and class in American society.

McMillan has been consistently praised for her portrayal of Franklin, which some critics claimed broke with stereotypes of black men traditionally found in African American women's writing. Franklin is at once a victim of oppression in white America and an oppressor and victimizer in his own home. Through him, McMillan shows what happens to a person who feels great anger but who has no way of venting it and ends up taking it out on those he loves. He is constantly in and out of work and cannot seem to get ahead in the white world. Yet McMillan is careful to present Franklin as more than a victim of racism; contrasted with Zora, who has a successful career and works hard for her dreams, Franklin is also seen as someone who fails to take responsibility for his own life at crucial moments.

The story is also about class differences and how these affect a relationship. Traditionally, black men have not had the same kinds of opportunities as black women, both in higher education and white-collar jobs. Although Franklin is smart, being black and undereducated closes many doors for him—a situation faced by many young black men in America. The tension this creates between Zora and Franklin is further explored from the female point of view in *Waiting to Exhale* (1992), McMillan's third novel.

The book has also been called a "postfeminist" love story because it reflects the concerns of women who are successful in their careers but who still must bear the burden of making their relationships work. In Zora and Franklin's relationship, the conflicts brought about by changing gender roles are played out. Although Franklin is unemployed, Zora does the housework and cooks when she comes home. Because he is out of work, a failure in the traditional male role of provider, he is too embarrassed to even pick their son up from day care. McMillan's use of the alternating voices shows the struggle from both sides clearly.

When *Disappearing Acts* first appeared, many critics objected to the profanity it contains. In her effort to be authentic, McMillan sprinkles her characters' dialogue with four-letter words, which tend to lose their impact as the story progresses. McMillan's style is realistic rather than lyrical, however, and the book's language reflects that. In *Disappearing Acts*, she has consciously rejected the poetic language of contemporaries such as Toni Morrison and Paule Marshall.

*Critical Context*

*Disappearing Acts* is McMillan's second novel. Her first, *Mama* (1987), attracted considerable serious critical attention. With *Disappearing Acts*, McMillan took another step away from the mainstream of African American women's literature, setting the scene for her third novel, the national bestseller *Waiting to Exhale*.

In the introduction to *Breaking Ice: An Anthology of Contemporary African-American Fiction* (1990), McMillan talks about the "New Black Aesthetic" from which she writes. Unlike the writers of the Harlem Renaissance, the 1960's, or the 1970's, for whom race and racism were a major preoccupation, McMillan and her contemporaries are writing from a place where racism is simply a fact of life, unsurprising and unchanging, and not the only source of conflict. *Disappearing Acts* reflects this position: While Franklin loses work because he is black, the central story is his relationship with Zora.

When McMillan submitted the first part of the novel to her publisher, she was asked to write the whole novel from Franklin's point of view; the editor sensed the marketing potential of a black woman writing a novel from a black man's point of view. McMillan refused; that was not the story she wanted to tell, regardless of the commercial appeal.

Additional problems came when the book was published and her former lover filed a multimillion dollar defamation suit against McMillan and her publisher, claiming that he was the basis for Franklin. He found the character unflattering and said that he was unable to find work because of it; however, the case was dismissed in April, 1990.

*Disappearing Acts* established McMillan's reputation as a writer with considerable popular appeal. The novel prefigures the issues and structure of *Waiting to Exhale*, which was also written in alternating points of view. Yet McMillan's work has not received the serious scholarly attention given to her most prominent contemporaries, Alice Walker and Toni Morrison. McMillan's work defies the contemporary African American women's literary tradition, and because of this, at least, it deserves some serious discussion.

*Bibliography*
Davis, Thulani. "Don't Worry, Be Buppie: Black Novelists Head for the Mainstream." *The Village Voice Literary Supplement* 85 (May, 1990): 26-29. Davis analyzes four books by African American novelists, including *Disappearing Acts*.
Giles, Molly. "An Interview with Terry McMillan." *Poets & Writers* 20 (November, 1992): 32-43. Giles, a writer herself, interviewed McMillan shortly before *Waiting to Exhale* was published. McMillan discusses her development as a writer and her three novels. She briefly talks about writing from a man's point of view in *Disappearing Acts*; however, the interview is more generally about McMillan's writing process and evolution.
McMillan, Terry. Introduction to *Breaking Ice: An Anthology of Contemporary African-American Fiction*, edited by Terry McMillan. New York: Penguin Books, 1990. McMillan discusses the impetus behind the anthology and changes in the African American literary tradition. Refers to the "New Black Aesthetic," a term coined by Trey Ellis.
Reid, Calvin. "Court Dismisses Libel Suit Against Penguin USA." *Publishers Weekly* 238 (April 26, 1991): 11. Brief article about the dismissal of Leonard Welch's $4.75-million defamation suit against McMillan and her publisher. Welch claimed that McMillan had based Franklin Swift on him and that, as a result of the unflattering portrait, he had been unable to find work. This dismissal "further strengthened legal protection for novelists and publishers from defamation lawsuits by people who believe themselves to be the models for unflattering fictional characters."
Smith, Wendy. "Terry McMillan." *Publishers Weekly* 239 (May 11, 1992): 50-51. McMillan discusses her publishing history. She talks about resisting pressure from her first editor to write *Disappearing Acts* only from Franklin's point of view. Provides valuable insight into the workings of publishing.

*Geeta Kothari*

# DOGEATERS

*Author:* Jessica-Tarahata Hagedorn (1949-    )
*Type of plot:* Social realism
*Time of plot:* The 1950's
*Locale:* The Philippines
*First published:* 1990

### Principal characters:

RIO GONZAGA, the narrator, ten years old as the novel begins
PUCHA GONZAGA, Rio's older cousin, a flirt and "social butterfly"
FREDDIE GONZAGA, Rio's father, a cautious man with connections
SEVERO ALACRAN, the rich and powerful "King of Coconuts," owner of
    Intercoco and Mabuhay Studios, a womanizer
"BABY" ROSARIO ALACRAN, Severo's ugly daughter, seventeen years old
    as the novel begins
GENERAL NICASIO LEDESMA, the powerful chief of armed forces and
    special intelligence, who runs "torture camps" for subversives
JOEY SANDS, a disc jockey and prostitute at the CocoRico, a sleazy bar
BOY-BOY, childhood buddy of Joey, a shower dancer at Studio 54
ORLANDO "ROMEO" ROSALES, a waiter and aspiring actor
TRINIDAD GAMBOA, a cashier and clerk, Romeo's girlfriend
LOLITA LUNA, a famous singer and actress, lover of General Ledesma and
    Severo Alacran
DAISY CONSUELO AVILA, a beauty-contest winner who becomes a guer-
    rilla
SENATOR DOMINGO AVILA, Daisy's father, an opposition leader
THE PRESIDENT, an inert and silent figure
THE FIRST LADY, a selfish, extravagant, false woman who is called "the
    Iron Butterfly" behind her back
CORA CAMACHO, a catty television reporter
CLARITA AVILA, Daisy's cousin and close friend, who becomes the guer-
    rilla called "Lydia"
RAINER, a wealthy German director who becomes Joey's lover

## The Novel

*Dogeaters* is a fragmented, fast-paced, multicharactered novel that demands extreme concentration on the reader's part. The first half of the book, entitled "Coconut
Palace," is a wild panache of seemingly unconnected narratives, beginning with the
privileged adolescent cousins Rio and Pucha Gonzaga attending films and listening
to the radio serial *Love Letters*. The plot shifts to the powerful and politically
influential Alacran household, from which oldest daughter Baby elopes. A third shift
focuses on the sordid life of Joey Sands, a drug abuser and prostitute who lives in a

seedy shack with Uncle and works in a gay bar called CocoRico. The final shift is to the lower-middle-class courtship of Romeo Rosales and Trinidad Gamboa, who meet at a theater. All Manila societies are thus represented.

Rio and Pucha get their weekly manicure and pedicure at Jojo's New Yorker, and some of the narrative threads begin to come together. It is revealed that Rio's father works for Severo Alacran, with whom he and General Nicasio Ledesma are obligated to play golf on weekends. Description of the austere life of the general's wife precedes the sordid profligacy of Joey Sands. Following an assignation between Joey and a male lover, the scene shifts to the elegant mauve bedroom of Rio's mother, where Rio watches the mutual flirtation between her mother, her cross-dressing seamstress, and her manicurist, whom Rio's father scornfully refers to collectively as "The Three (dis)Graces."

A beauty contest assembles all the politically powerful in Manila, who falsely pretend pleasantries to one another. After winning the contest, Daisy Avila lapses into deep depression, impulsively marries and then leaves a foreign playboy banker, and retreats to visit her cousin Clarita. A letter from Clarita to Daisy, cautiously sanctioning Daisy's furtive departure with a man named Santos, ends the novel's first half.

"The Song of the Bullets," the novel's second half, is filled with confusion and murder. It opens with a frustrating dream of the First Lady and then flashes to a scene in which Romeo Rosales is trying for a screen test. In town for the Manila International Film Festival, a German director named Rainer meets and courts Joey, whom he hires as companion for a week. Joey eventually steals the German's drugs and money and is an unfortunate witness to the assassination of Senator Avila.

News of the assassination reaches Baby Alacran, depressed and all but forsaken by her new husband. Romeo, on his way to meet Trinidad for lunch while contemplating the best way to break up with her, is shot in the melee that surrounds the senator's assassination, gets implicated as the senator's murderer, and is kidnapped and murdered himself. Lolita Luna begs General Ledesma to get her out of Manila; when he demurs, she contemplates a lucrative pornographic film offer. Baby's husband and several friends get high on drugs and alcohol one hot afternoon at the Monte Vista Country Club, where an allusion is made to a man who has "confessed." Suspense and intrigue heighten from here to the novel's end.

Joey, fearful for his life as a witness to the assassination, collapses in Uncle's shack. Fearing that Uncle will betray him, he kills Uncle's dog, steals what money and drugs he can find, and hides out in Boy-Boy's apartment. As General Ledesma interrogates the captured guerrilla Daisy Avila, excerpts of *Love Letters* interrupt intermittently on the radio, heightening the tension. Daisy is brutally assaulted after being shown photographs of a man (perhaps Rosales) who has been hideously murdered. The scene is alluded to in a bitingly satirical interview with the First Lady that follows, amplifying the horror.

Boy-Boy arranges for Joey to be harbored in a guerrilla camp far away in the mountains, where he becomes companion of Clarita and the released and recuperating Daisy. The lives of Rio and Pucha are brought up to date in two closing chapters, which convey news of the two marriages of Rio's brother Raul, who has become a faith healer, the death of Rio's paternal grandmother, Pucha's short-lived marriage to Boomboom Alacran, and finally Rio's sudden move to America with her mother, a painter. The novel ends with Rio's nostalgic return trip, on which she encounters abandoned buildings and ruin where her home used to be.

## The Characters

In a novel as abrasive and controversial as this, the author uses an engaging and sympathetic character, Rio Gonzaga, to hook the reader's sympathy. She is shown first at age ten, narrating a privileged middle-class girlhood in Manila; later, she is seen as a transplanted adult. The novel intersperses her story among a wide spectrum of diverse and unrelated characters to give the boisterous, noisy, and fast-paced sense of a crowded, corrupt, and decaying metropolitan center that the author both loves and hates, both feels compelled to embrace and longs to escape.

The characters and the novel are thoroughly Filipino, and obviously the reader's appreciation of the book would be heightened by knowledge of stormy Manila politics and history and familiarity with Spanish and Tagalog, the dialect spoken in the book. Non-Filipino readers may feel lost because of the hundreds of unglossed Tagalog words and phrases. These add authentic flavor, however, and the confusion that results reinforces the novel's sense of overcrowding, ruin, and even assault.

The word *alacran*, the last name of the most powerful clan in the book, means "scorpion" in Spanish, and the name "Boomboom" Alacran resembles "BongBong," the nickname of Ferdinand Marcos, Jr., son of the deposed president. The beauty pageant where Marcos met his future wife Imelda is satirized in the story of Daisy Avila. Hagedorn bitingly satirizes the extravagant, controversial, and corrupt dictatorship of Marcos in her characters the President and the First Lady.

The impact of the four-hundred-year rule of the Philippines by Spain and the forty-year colonization by the United States is symbolized by Hagedorn's references to Spanish Catholicism and American films. Religion is depicted as a stultifying and demeaning force, and Hagedorn's final word in her novel, a blasphemous parody on the Lord's Prayer, is her attempt to wrench free from imposed religious sanctions and from imposed foreign influence.

The book's characters are addicted to American-style glamour and Western entertainment. Rio has a "Rita Hayworth" mother and Rio and Pucha are first shown watching a Rock Hudson and Jane Wyman film in a Manila theater. Trinidad Gamboa dreams of Romeo Rosales proposing to her like a character in a romantic musical. Cora Camacho, "the Barbara Walters of the Philippines," interviews Senator Alacran for her television show, and a journalist named Steve interviews the First Lady. Characters dream of escape to the West: The Actress, Lolita Luna begs for it, Joey Sands tries to sell his body to get it, and Rio Gonzaga breezily accomplishes it.

Beside being driven by fantasy, the characters are driven by appetite and greed. Joey shows the seamy side of the drug and flesh trade that has made Manila a world leader in prostitution and pedophilia. Hagedorn takes pleasure in cataloging names of foods, particularly street foods, and the characters seem always to be hungry. General Ledesma is hungry for food and sex, and Lolita Luna is hungry for drugs. At the heart of the book is an all-purpose motto for the characters: "Food is the center of our ritual celebrations. . . . You can't describe a real *Pinoy* without listing what's most important to him—food, music, dancing, and love—most probably in that order."

Appetites can lead to wasteful extravagance, such as the "twelve-tiered hallucination" that is Baby Alacran's wedding cake, gluttonously consumed by the First Lady. At the other extreme is the despairing poverty of colonial oppression, illustrated by Joey's diet of powdered coffee while he hides out from authorities. Hagedorn, juxtaposing racial and national influences, feels most sympathy for the dispossessed: orphans, guerrillas, exiles, the alienated, and the suffering.

*Themes and Meanings*

*Dogeaters* is a wild ride into the underbelly of Manila society. It is also a clever tour de force that illustrates American and Spanish influence with energetic detail. One of the central themes of the novel is reality versus fantasy, and the novel poses the question of what will be revealed if pretense and deception are stripped away.

Hagedorn explodes pretense in the ruling class, bitterly satirizing the profligacy and waste of a corrupt regime. She also exposes the depravity and desperation in slum towns such as Tondo, home of Joey and Uncle. Morality on both these levels has been sacrificed, to greed in the first instance and to survival in the second. If any scenario among the many varied episodes displays human warmth and caring, it is the guerrilla contingent of Daisy and her cousin Clarita, with whom Joey finds refuge in the mountains. Removed from Manila, this community of supporters is also a long way from the aggression, deception, and depravity that are common features of city life, high and low. Joey's wasted life thus shows the possibility of transformation and resilience in exile. Rio is also hopeful in her pragmatic exile. That she and her artist mother will succeed away from Manila is assumed.

Dreams are a central feature of the novel; together with radio serials and film plots, dreams are manifestations of the fantasies in which all the characters indulge. Joey's dreams while he is transported to the mountains are forceful and terror-filled. The long dream sequence that opens the novel's second half is an obscure, sacrilegious hallucination by the First Lady, complete with appearances by Hollywood stars and the pope. Rio's recurring dream about her brother and herself as nocturnal moths drawn to a light in a deserted house ends the book.

Another unifying feature of the characters is the *tsismis* (gossip) in which they indulge. They are all as addicted to gossiping as they are to eating, to drugs, and to sex. Cora Camacho and the First Lady are the most blatant and manipulative in this. A final letter from Pucha to Rio also suggests that some facts about Pucha's life as Rio has presented it are just unfounded gossip. Excerpts from *The Metro Manila Daily*, itself a fiction, present intermittent gossip and inaccuracies.

Hagedorn's title, *Dogeaters*, has generated outcry among Filipino readers and represents her most radical statement. The term is a pejorative for Filipinos. Her novel exposes a dog-eat-dog world with canine ferocity. As Uncle tells Joey at one point, his dog eats better than they do. Trinidad and Romeo wonder casually if the barbecue on a stick that they've just purchased from a vendor might be dog meat; Romeo teasingly says that he does not mind eating dog. The title, thus, is sassy as a slap, signaling readers that the novel will audaciously break taboos and explore much that is forbidden.

*Critical Context*

*Dogeaters* is Hagedorn's third published book and her first novel. Nominated for the National Book Award, this turbulent book was received as both impudent and groundbreaking. In its fragmented format, it tests the bounds of what a novel can or should be. In content and intent, it represents the most radical of the literatures published in the early 1990's by Asian American authors.

Hagedorn's early life resembles that of one of her principal characters, Rio Gonzaga. Both grew up in Manila in comfortable circumstances in the 1950's, had an older brother, and moved to the United States as teenagers with their mother, returning to the Philippines to visit.

After several years in the San Francisco area, where she was lyricist and leader of the West Coast Gangster Choir, Hagedorn moved to New York City, where she has worked as poet, playwright, performance artist, and commentator for *Crossroads*, a syndicated weekly newsmagazine on public radio. Prior to the publication of *Dogeaters*, she wrote two collections of poems, prose, and short fiction, *Dangerous Music* (1975) and *Pet Food and Tropical Apparitions* (1981). *Danger and Beauty* (1993), the book that follows *Dogeaters*, contains early uncollected poems, material from her first two books, and a final section of previously unpublished work.

Hagedorn's frequent visits to Manila have verified for her the accuracy of her depiction of people and places. Evidence that she is trilingual (in English, Spanish, and Tagalog) surfaces in the linguistic dexterity of *Dogeaters*. In writing a nightmarish account of Manila during the Marcos years, she exposes a corrupt regime and the addictive effects of Hollywood imperialism.

*Bibliography*

d'Alpuget, Blanche. "Philippine Dream Feast." *The New York Times Book Review* 95 (March 25, 1990): 1. D'Alpuget examines *Dogeaters* from the perspective of a writer of novels set in Indonesia and Malaysia. She first concentrates on the meaning of the book's title, comments on the rich variety of character, and focuses on the notion of fantasy as a driving force. Her illumination of Philippine history is a useful gloss to events in Hagedorn's book.

Gonzalez, N. V. M. "*Dogeaters*." *Amerasia Journal* 17, no. 1 (1991): 189-192. Gonzalez, a respected and established Philippine American author, examines a radical young writer of the same ethnic background. He finds Hagedorn's troubled depiction of the Marcos years coherent and intelligent. By calling her a "virtuoso," he endorses her effort at exposing a tortured society in the throes of change.

Gordon, Jaimy. *"Dogeaters." American Book Review* 12 (November, 1990): 16. Gordon uses a wealth of rich and memorable phraseology to stress the accuracy of Hagedorn's depiction of place and character. The review is useful in its summary of the novel's two sections and in its exploration of the character of Rio. While pointing out that the numerous unglossed expressions may tire the reader, the review nevertheless flatters Hagedorn's style and method.

Hagedorn, Jessica. "On Theater and Performance." *MELUS* 16 (Fall, 1989-1990): 13-15. This short piece by the author gives useful background and context to her multimedia orientation, a perspective useful to appreciating the energy and fragmentation of *Dogeaters*. Hagedorn reveals how she has subverted and exploited Western theater and culture, a notion seminal to an intelligent reading of *Dogeaters*.

Pearlman, Mickey. "Jessica Hagedorn." In *Listen to Their Voices: Twenty Interviews with Women Who Write*. New York: W. W. Norton, 1993. Personal and professional details of Hagedorn's life are revealed in a chatty and inviting style. Pearlman intersperses quotations of Hagedorn with passages from *Dogeaters*, and her article is useful in tracing Hagedorn's influences of place, character, and history.

*Jill B. Gidmark*

# DONALD DUK

*Author:* Frank Chin (1940-     )
*Type of plot: Bildungsroman*
*Time of plot:* The 1980's
*Locale:* San Francisco, California
*First published:* 1991

> *Principal characters:*
> DONALD DUK, a twelve-year-old Chinese American boy who hates every-
> thing Chinese
> KING DUK, Donald's father, the owner of a Chinese restaurant
> UNCLE DONALD DUK, a Cantonese opera star and the old opera mentor
> of King Duk
> DAISY DUK, Donald's mother
> PENELOPE and
> VENUS, Donald's older twin sisters
> ARNOLD AZALEA, a rich white American boy, Donald's best friend and
> classmate
> MR. MEANWRIGHT, a history teacher at Donald's school
> LARRY LOUIE, an old Chinatown dance instructor from whom Donald
> takes tap-dance lessons

*The Novel*

*Donald Duk* deals with the identity crisis of a twelve-year-old Chinese American boy living in San Francisco's Chinatown. The protagonist gradually comes to discover himself and his cultural heritage through ritualistic participation in the Chinese New Year celebration and through a series of surrealistic dreams about working on the Central Pacific Railroad in 1869.

The novel contains eighteen chapters and an epilogue. Chin uses an omniscient point of view to tell the story dramatically in the present tense. He strategically blends history, myth, and folklore with the narrative discourse to explore the forging of the Chinese American identity. The narrative is animated by the sights and sounds of Chinatown.

The opening of the novel delves into the mind of the young protagonist, Donald Duk, and brings out his deep sense of cultural disorientation. He hates not only his ludicrous name but also everything Chinese, including his looks. Contemptuous of his ethnic heritage, he wants to be recognized as "American." He goes to a private school and avoids the other Chinese students there. His best friend is an all-American white boy, Arnold Azalea, and his ideal hero is the white tap-dancing film star Fred Astaire. Donald seeks to emulate Astaire by taking tap-dance lessons from Larry Louie.

Donald's father, King Duk, a famous chef who owns a Chinese restaurant, is making elaborate preparations to celebrate the Chinese New Year and to mark his son's coming of age according to Chinese tradition. He has built 108 model airplanes—named after Chinese folk heroes—which he plans to set afire and fly on the fifteenth day of celebration. He has also invited his old opera mentor, Uncle Donald Duk, to come to San Francisco to perform a Cantonese opera. He himself is preparing to play the role of Kwan Kung, Chinese god of war and literature. Donald feels embarrassed that the opera will be performed at his school also. He is ashamed of his father's Chinatown accent. He dreads the advent of Chinese New Year because of the stupid questions people ask about the quaint Chinese beliefs and customs.

Donald's friend, Arnold Azalea, who is fascinated by Chinese culture, comes to stay at their house during the New Year celebration. One night while Arnold is asleep, Donald steals one of his father's model airplanes, goes on the roof of the house, and launches it, thinking that perhaps his father will not even notice the missing model. When he returns to his apartment, Uncle Donald Duk confronts him about the missing model. Uncle Duk tells him that the model stolen by him was built in commemoration of Lee Kuey, nicknamed the Black Tornado. Uncle Duk also reveals that Donald's Chinese name is not Duk but Lee and that his great-great-grandfather was the first of the Lees to come over from China and work on the Central Pacific Railroad.

Donald's imagination is fired by the adventurous story of his immigrant forefathers, and he is mentally prepared to receive some education in his ethnic past. Chin uses the surrealistic method of dreams in which Donald is transported back into his racial unconscious and feels kinship with mythical Chinese heroes. In his dreams, he is transformed into one of the twelve hundred Chinese workers who helped build the transcontinental railroad in 1869 and set a record by laying more than ten miles of track in ten hours. Returning to the world of reality, however, he is outraged to discover that the Chinese who made railroad history were completely obliterated by their white masters; not a single photograph of the railroad's completion celebration showed a Chinese face.

The climax of the novel comes when, infuriated at white racism, Donald enters his history class and challenges the accuracy of Mr. Meanwright's version of Chinese American history. His friend Arnold produces the documentary evidence to support him. Mr. Meanwright concedes that he is caught totally unprepared. Meanwhile, in the midst of clamorous noise of gongs and drums, the costumed players of the Cantonese opera, including King Duk in the role of Kwan Kung, enter the school hall, shouting "Happy New Year." Donald grins at his history teacher, wishing him Happy New Year in Chinese.

The epilogue describes the festivities of the fifteenth day of celebration: the feast, the opera, the lantern parade, and the launching of the model airplanes. Donald participates in the parade for the first time by running in the dragon costume. He has come to terms with his cultural heritage. The Chinese New Year festival has become his symbolic rite of passage to self-esteem and self-knowledge. He has learned the important lesson that he does not have to erase his Chinese identity entirely to become an "American."

*The Characters*

The character of Donald Duk is central to Chin's vision of the Chinese American experience. Donald personifies the anguish and the disconcerting experience of a self-conscious young boy growing up straddling two cultures. His given name reflects Chin's ambivalent attitude toward Chinese American identity. On the one hand, the name suggests the derisive view many Americans have of Chinese men; on the other hand, it scoffs at the Chinese attempt to assimilate to mainstream America no matter how ridiculous the consequences.

At the beginning of the novel, the reader finds Donald to be a smart but arrogant and sharp-tongued boy who nurtures self-hatred and shows little respect for his family and neighbors. Driven by his desire for assimilation, he feels alienated from the Chinatown community and wants to reject his Chinese self. His only saving grace seems to be his sense of humor. When harassed by Chinatown gangsters, he uses humor and self-mockery as weapons to protect himself from ridicule and violence. Yet he soon realizes that it is time for him to grow up and not to act like his cartoon namesake to get out of a fight. His character undergoes a change after Uncle Donald Duk awakens in him a consciousness of his proud ethnic heritage. He realizes in the end what his father had been telling him all along: that he does not have "to give up being Chinese to be an American." Chin makes Donald both a credible character and a powerful symbol of cultural displacement in contemporary American society.

King Duk provides a sharp contrast to his son's character. He represents the old generation of Chinese immigrants who derive their identity and strength of character from adherence to the traditional way of life. Though he is an entrepreneur who runs a successful business and has outwardly adjusted to the American way of life, he keeps his ethnic culture alive by celebrating Chinese New Year with customary activities and festivities. His building of 108 model airplanes is a glorious tribute to the memory of Chinese folk heroes led by his ancestor Lee Kuey. His role-playing of Kwan Kung in the Cantonese opera is symbolic of his manhood and spiritual strength.

Uncle Donald Duk, the old Cantonese opera star after whom Donald was named, serves as a wise mentor who initiates Donald into traditional Chinese lore and immigrant history and awakens in him a sense of curiosity and pride in his ethnic past. He thus plays an important role in launching Donald on the path of self-discovery by opening up the world of dreams to his creative imagination.

The characters of Daisy Duk, Donald's mother, and his twin sisters, Penelope and Venus, remain flat and caricaturelike. They seem to exist merely to complete Donald's immediate family circle and to make small talk occasionally. Sometimes the twin sisters serve as mediators between Donald and his parents, but mostly they ridicule their mother and brother.

Arnold Azalea seems to represent the new generation of white Americans who have adjusted to the realities and demands of a multiethnic society and are willing to rectify the historical mistakes made by their ancestors.

Mr. Meanwright, the teacher of California history, is a stock type who feeds the young minds with racially identified stereotypes without questioning their validity.

The books he uses in class affirm a biased view of history reflecting white supremacy. Donald rightly calls him one of the "badly informed people."

Larry Louie, an old Chinese tap-dance instructor who tries to look like Fred Astaire but does not really want to be him, exemplifies the ambivalent nature of the Chinese American identity. Like Donald, he regards Fred Astaire as his idol, but unlike Donald, who wants to be Fred Astaire, Larry Louie maintains his Chinese identity.

*Themes and Meanings*

Since *Donald Duk* deals with themes of initiation, coming of age, and search for identity, it can be viewed as a *Bildungsroman*, a novel of growth and education. Chin focuses on the physical, emotional, and psychological development of the protagonist. At the beginning of the novel, Donald is wallowing in self-contempt. He hates his name and his Chinese looks. He even walks through Chinatown waddling like his cartoon namesake. His father instructs him to straighten his slouching shoulders to improve his physical posture. When gang members laugh at his name and try to take his pants off, he quacks in his Donald Duck voice to make them laugh to save himself from the humiliating situation. After this incident, he makes a resolve to end this childish stuff of quacking and laughing at his name to get out of trouble. The incident marks his first decisive step toward self-growth.

The next stage in Donald's road to self-discovery comes after the incident of his theft of the model airplane. His encounter with Uncle Donald Duk opens the doorway to his proud ethnic past. Donald now begins to reclaim his Chinese heritage by identifying with the Chinese immigrants in his dreams about working on the Central Pacific Railroad in 1869. Infuriated at history's neglect of Chinese achievement, he stands up to his history teacher to set the record straight. The act shows his moral courage, intellectual development, and assertion of autonomy.

Finally, his first-time participation in the New Year dragon parade signifies his acceptance of his Chinese self. The ceremony marks a symbolic rite of passage to his self-respect and identity as a Chinese American.

*Donald Duk* is also a novel with a purpose. It challenges and counters the stereotypes of Chinese American males as passive, docile, and nonassertive by reconstructing their immigrant history. The history books Donald reads at school perpetuate the stereotypes by asserting that "the Chinese in America were made passive and nonassertive by centuries of Confucian thought and Zen mysticism. . . . From their first step on American soil to the middle of the twentieth century, the timid, introverted Chinese have been helpless against the relentless victimization by aggressive, highly competitive Americans." Chin regards this view of history as a systematic attempt to emasculate the Chinese American male. In *Donald Duk*, he uses the fictional mode to dispel racially identified stereotypes and to offer a corrective view of the American experiences of Chinese immigrants.

By reconstructing history through Donald's vivid and elaborate dream sequences, Chin shows that the Chinese who came to America in the nineteenth century and built the railroads in the American West were tough, adventurous, competitive, courageous, and proud men who not only set records for track-laying but also asserted the idea of Chinese foremen for Chinese gangs and launched a successful strike for back pay. Chin's need to restore Chinese American history is well articulated by Donald's father: "You gotta keep the history yourself or lose it forever, boy. That's the mandate of heaven."

## Critical Context

*Donald Duk* was Frank Chin's first novel, though he had already established himself as a major voice in Asian American literature as the author of two critically acclaimed plays, *The Chickencoop Chinaman* (1972) and *The Year of the Dragon* (1974). He had also written a collection of short fiction, *The Chinaman Pacific and Frisco R.R. Co.* (1988), which won him the American Book Award. He is also known as one of the editors of the pioneering work *Aiiieeeee! An Anthology of Asian American Writers* (1974).

Like Chin's plays and short fiction, *Donald Duk* dramatizes the themes and conflicts that have become central to his vision of the Chinese American experience. Using a twelve-year-old Chinese American boy as the protagonist, Chin explores the problems of forging a new Chinese American identity. He also explodes ethnic stereotype as he lashes out at white historians for their distorted views of Chinese American history. Written in colloquial English, the novel follows the rhythmic patterns of spoken Cantonese, lending verisimilitude to the story.

A versatile writer, Chin has written poetry, criticism, film scripts, essays, articles, and reviews as well as plays and fiction. His work has appeared in many newspapers, magazines, and anthologies. Despite the polemical nature of his work, he is in the vanguard of the new generation of Asian American writers who are emerging from years of communal and cultural neglect and making an impact on American literature.

## Bibliography

Cheng, Scarlet. Review of *Donald Duk*, by Frank Chin. *Small Press* 9 (Spring, 1991): 87. A brief review that introduces the novel's main characters, with a glimpse of its story line.

Haven, Tom De. "He's Been Dreaming on the Railroad." *The New York Times Book Review* 96 (March 31, 1991): 9. Using illustrative detail from the novel, Haven focuses on Donald's mental makeup and his education through dreams. He praises Chin's energy and invention, but finds fault with his plot structure, narrative flow, style, and characterization.

Ho, Cathy Lang. "Taking It from Frank Chin." *San Francisco Review of Books* 16, no. 1 (1991): 31-32. Viewing *Donald Duk* as a coming-of-age novel, Ho underline's Chin's preoccupation with "the problems of a dual heritage" and contrasts his view of the Chinese American experience with that of novelist Maxine Hong Kingston. Ho praises Chin's historical research and his incorporation of Chinese folklore and mythology into the novel.

Louie, Ai-Ling. "Growing Up Asian American: A Look at Some Recent Young Adult

Novels." *Journal of Youth Services in Libraries* 6 (Winter, 1993): 115-127. Primarily written for a young adult audience, this article looks at *Donald Duk* in the context of seven other recent young-adult novels about Asian Americans. Louie points out that though the novel offers "a valid portrait of an Asian American young adult," it is "not very accessible to young adults. There are problems with style and plotting that make the book hard for young people to read."

Samarth, Manini. "Affirmations: Speaking the Self into Being." *Parnassus* 17, no. 1 (1991): 88-101. In this incisive review essay dealing with three Asian American novels, Manini treats *Donald Duk* as "Essentially a novel about the evolving *male* Chinese-American self" and shows how Chin "uses language . . . obliquely to probe his Chinese-American identity." Manini regards the novel's women characters as nothing more than "cardboard cut-out" figures who "posture lightly on the fringes of male experience."

*Chaman L. Sahni*

# DREAMING IN CUBAN

*Author:* Cristina Garcia (1958-    )
*Type of plot:* Historical
*Time of plot:* 1972-1980
*Locale:* Santa Teresa Del Mar and Havana, Cuba; New York City
*First published:* 1992

> *Principal characters:*
> CELIA DEL PINO, an old woman in Cuba, a staunch supporter of Communism
> LOURDES PUENTE, her oldest daughter, a bakery owner in New York City
> PILAR PUENTE, Lourdes' daughter
> FELICIA VILLAVERDE, Celia's second daughter
> LUZ and MILAGRO VILLAVERDE, Felicia's twin daughters
> IVANITO VILLAVERDE, Felicia's son

*The Novel*

*Dreaming in Cuban* is the story of three generations of a Cuban family, told from a variety of points of view. The story begins with Celia del Pino, an aged woman, watching the waters off the north coast of Cuba with binoculars. She is on guard, devoted to The Revolution and El Lider (Fidel Castro, who is never mentioned by name in the book).

The novel is not told in straightforward, narrative terms, although there is a clear narrative thread running through the story. The book shifts back and forth between scenes, and the narrative is told from a variety of points of view. Some of it is told in the first person by Celia, Lourdes, and Pilar, including a number of extracts from Pilar's diary. There are also numerous flashbacks to the past, mostly Celia's past.

One device that is used to re-create the past is a series of letters that Celia wrote over a period of more than two decades. All of these letters were written to Gustavo Sierra de Armas, her first lover, a Spanish lawyer. After Gustavo returned to Europe in 1935, Celia wrote to him monthly up until 1959, when the revolution succeeded and Celia became a dedicated Communist. Throughout the book, Celia speaks of The Revolution (always capitalized when Celia's point of view is espoused) in the present tense.

Felicia, Celia's second daughter, still lives in Cuba and never leaves that country; unlike her mother, however, she continuously refers to the present political state of her country as one of tyranny. Felicia is married three times, but never happily. Her first husband, Hugo Villaverde, the father of Felicia's three children, is never actually seen during the periods covered by the story, although he is alluded to a number of times. In 1966, Felicia threw a burning rag into Hugo's face, then locked herself and her children in the house.

Felicia marries her second husband, Ernesto Brito, in 1978. Ernesto dies shortly after the marriage in a grease fire. Felicia then blacks out a period of months of her life and finds herself living at an amusement park, married to Otto Cruz. He works at the amusement park and apparently found Felicia wandering aimlessly about the park. She has no memory of the marriage.

Both Celia and Felicia have spent significant periods of time in insane asylums. They also both have regular visions of Jorge Del Pino, Celia's husband, who died in a New York hospital of cancer just before the story's beginning. Lourdes and Pilar, in New York, also have recurring visions of this man. He gives all of them advice, although the advice varies according to who is having the vision. All of them are reassured that they are thinking the right thoughts and taking the right actions, even though these actions are at cross purposes.

Lourdes, Celia's oldest daughter, is a marked contrast to her mother. Lourdes lives in New York with her daughter, Pilar, and runs a bakery. About midway through the book, she opens a second bakery and names her enterprise Yankee Doodle Bakeries. She is an emerging capitalist, and she dreams of a franchise of bakeries throughout the country.

A large part of the book is told by way of Pilar's diary. Pilar brings the story full circle, in a sense. She is the most obviously American character in the book; she wears jeans and sneakers and plays bass guitar. Nevertheless, she feels much more strongly tied to her grandmother than to her mother. At one point, she gets as far as taking a bus to Miami in hope of finding a way to return to Cuba.

In this sense, *Dreaming in Cuban* is also a political story. Pilar's rebellion against her mother ironically brings her to consider atheism and to decide that Communism may not be such a bad idea. The third generation of characters is rather confused. Ivanito, the youngest child, is only thirteen at the closing of the story, and thus of all the characters is least interested in politics. The final scene in the book shows Lourdes taking the boy to Havana, giving him two hundred dollars, and telling him to get out of Cuba.

The novel ends with the last of Celia's letters, written in 1959, a few weeks after the success of the revolution. Celia celebrates this success, decides to devote the rest of her life to the cause, and thus has no further need to write letters to her former lover.

*The Characters*

Celia, the matriarch of the family, is an old woman at the outset, but she is nevertheless a strong supporter of the new ways that Fidel Castro (El Lider) has imposed upon her native country. Her religious views are somewhat ambivalent; while she is nominally a Catholic, as most people in her country are, one of the earliest scenes in the novel involves a Santeria ceremony. Celia is first seen guarding the coast of Cuba against a replay of the Bay of Pigs invasion, and she is last shown at a Santeria ceremony following the death of her daughter Felicia.

Lourdes lives at the opposite extreme. She has fled to the United States and runs a bakery in New York City. She opens a second bakery during the second section of the book and dreams of franchising a series of bakeries. Lourdes, though born in Cuba, is never seen in that country until the epilogue, when she appears at her sister's funeral.

Pilar, Lourdes' daughter, is very American; she is interested in punk rock and is attempting to become a bass player in a rock band. On the other hand, she is also very interested in Cuba, and she finds it difficult to tolerate her mother's fanatic hatred of Communism. She feels contempt for capitalist society and misses her older relatives in Cuba.

Felicia, who never leaves Cuba is extremely opposed to Communism. Like her mother, she often has visions of the deceased Jorge.

Luz and Milagro, Felicia's twin daughters, are more interested in modern life than in their mother's feelings. Milagro's words are never seen in the book. She is the younger twin (by a few minutes). Luz does express her thoughts, and those thoughts are generally negative. She thinks that her mother is crazy (Felicia does spend some time in an asylum) and that there must be a better way of dealing with things. She makes some attempts, later in life, to visit her father, who has fled to Czechoslovakia.

Ivanito is a little boy throughout the book. He is five years old as the story opens, thirteen when it closes. Ivanito is the only one of Felicia's children who clearly loves his mother. He is the only character in *Dreaming in Cuban* for whom readers feel genuine sympathy. He is torn between his love for his capitalist aunt, his anti-Communist mother, and his ancient grandmother.

*Themes and Meanings*

*Dreaming in Cuban* works on three levels. At the surface, it is a melodrama, the story of various members of a large family scattered among New York, Florida, and Cuba. This, however, is the least intense part of the story. The fact that this is a Cuban family, wherever its members may live, is central to the work.

The political level of the novel is quite close to the surface. The characters include Communists working hard for El Lider and capitalists who despise the Cuban government. The author's own political stance is never made clear. Communism is praised and criticized alternately. The major point is that the characters themselves, both those who remain in Cuba and those who emigrate to the United States, are somewhat confused. The members of the third generation, especially Pilar, are torn between a way of life in Cuba that is uncomfortable and a longing for a return "home."

The most intense part of the story, and the reason for the title, is spiritual. Cuba, as a Communist country, is supposed to be atheistic; however, spiritual values are not changed instantly by an altering of the political climate. Most Cubans in the story are Roman Catholics; only Pilar, the most American of the family and the youngest character portrayed in detail, considers atheism as a possible way of life.

Underneath Catholicism, however, lies an even older religion. The story begins and ends with rites of Santeria, an ancient religion with roots in Africa. In its Latin American form, Santeria has taken on some of the trappings of Christianity. Most notably, ancient gods are represented by Christian saints, the legacy of attempts to cover up the practice of the ancient rituals.

Despite appearances, the ancient rites are still practiced. Animals are sacrificed, and magical herbs are used as remedies for a variety of illnesses. Even the family members in New York consult Santeria priests and priestesses when they have spiritual or physical problems. Felicia, who refused to take the rites seriously while she was alive, is buried in a Santeria funeral.

Finally, many of the characters have supernatural visions. Jorge Del Pino, Celia's dead husband, appears regularly to a number of the characters, both in Cuba and in New York. The characters so visited invariably take these appearances as quite real. While there is a certain amount of insanity in the family (two of the women have been institutionalized), the supernatural seems to play a very real, seemingly rational part in everyone's lives. In some ways, Jorge actually appears as the most rational character in the novel, despite his supernatural form.

*Dreaming in Cuban*, at its deepest level, is actually a consideration of reality and the way humans perceive that reality. Dreams, waking life, supernatural visitations, and insanity are so intertwined in the narrative that it is often difficult for the reader to decide which events are actually taking place and which are imagined.

*Critical Context*

Cristina Garcia, the author of *Dreaming in Cuban*, was born in Cuba in 1958, shortly before the revolution. Her parents were among the many Cubans who emigrated to the United States following that revolution, and the author spent her childhood in New York. She has worked as a journalist for *Time* magazine; *Dreaming in Cuban* is her first work of fiction.

*Dreaming in Cuban* is not about Cuba but rather about Cubans and the strange social and spiritual attitudes that pervade Cuban society. The Communist government of Cuba retained power even after the breakup of the Soviet Union and the vanishing of support from that country. At the same time, Catholicism has remained the dominant religion, with an underpinning of ancient African rites. The seeming conflict between rational Marxism as espoused by the government and the private practice of secret rituals involving ancient magic makes Cuban society unique.

*Dreaming in Cuban* is a study in contradictions. The book opens with Celia Del Pino guarding the coast against an attack from the north; the failed Bay of Pigs invasion is still a recent memory. Yet some of her family are living in the United States. Her husband, in fact, had gone to New York for medical treatment when he discovered he had cancer; he dies there just before the opening of the story. When the family members all return to Cuba for Felicia's funeral, there is no real sign of reconciliation. The members of the New York branch of the family are still culturally tied to the land of their birth, but they have no intention of remaining in Cuba. Lourdes, the most extremely anti-Communist member of the family, ends the story by giving Ivanito, her young nephew, money to get out of Cuba.

*Bibliography*

Eder, Richard. "Cuban Revolution Tugs on Family Ties." *Los Angeles Times*, March 12, 1992, p. E10. Generally laudatory review of Garcia's novel. Eder praises

Garcia's realistic passages as "exquisite" but observes that she is sometimes "indulgent and awkward" in her use of magical elements.

Gann, L. H., and Peter J. Duignan. *The Hispanics in the United States: A History.* Boulder, Colo.: Westview Press, 1986. An overview of the history and culture of the various groups of Hispanic immigrants to the United States. Of particular interest in relation to *Dreaming in Cuban* is chapter 6, "The Cubans," which deals with the Cuban-born population of the United States.

*Kirkus Reviews.* Review of *Dreaming in Cuban*, by Cristina Garcia. 60 (January 1, 1992): 7. Brief, hostile review that claims that the novel "lacks sufficient freshness of insight to be consistently compelling."

Metraux, Alfred. *Voodoo in Haiti.* New York: Schocken Books, 1959. A factual account of the various forms of voodoo and related religions with African roots as they are practiced in Latin America and by Latin American immigrants in the United States. Despite the title, the book's discussion is not confined solely to Haiti or to voodoo. Includes a long discussion of Santeria, the religion practiced in *Dreaming in Cuban.*

Weiss, Amelia. Review of *Dreaming in Cuban*, by Cristina Garcia. *Time* 139 (March 23, 1992): 67. Rapturous commentary on the novel. States of Garcia that, "Like a priestess, in passages of beautiful island incantation, she conjures her Cuban heritage" from across the political and physical gulf separating Cuba and the United States.

*Marc Goldstein*

# EAT A BOWL OF TEA

*Author:* Louis Chu (1915-1970)
*Type of plot:* Satirical and romantic comedy
*Time of plot:* 1941-1949
*Locale:* New York City and San Francisco, California
*First published:* 1961

> *Principal characters:*
> WANG BEN LOY, a young Chinese American waiter in New York's Chinatown
> LEE MEI OI, his bride from Sunwei province, China
> WANG WAH GAY, Ben's father, who runs a gambling hall
> LEE GONG, Mei Oi's father, a retired laundry owner
> AH SONG, a bachelor playboy
> WANG CHUCK TING, Wah Gay's cousin, president of the Wang Family Association

*The Novel*

Acclaimed as the first authentic Chinese American novel, *Eat a Bowl of Tea* can be read as a romantic comedy that pokes fun at the "bachelor society" of Chinatowns in the United States during the immediate post-World War II period. The novel opens *in medias res* on a scene that tantalizes by its potential for development. The protagonist, Wang Ben Loy, a bridegroom of two months, wakes up one morning to the buzz of his doorbell in a New York Chinatown apartment. Answering his door, he finds a prostitute offering her wares to an old customer. Ben Loy has to persuade her that he is now a married man; he then rejoins his bride in bed. Meanwhile, however, his interior monologue reveals that he has recently become impotent. Chu's strategically chosen point of departure contains possibilities for a tragic or a comic development of plot, for empathy or for irony.

A flashback consisting of the ensuing eleven chapters then introduces Ben Loy's character, describes the events leading up to his marriage, and sketches in his situation and ambience. Ben Loy is a Chinese American in his twenties. He is a filial son, a good worker, but something of a sensualist. Brought up in the patriarchal family system of Confucian China, he is under the authority of his father. His father, Wah Gay, has been an émigré in the United States for almost thirty years. Starting out as a laundryman, Wah Gay is now proprietor of a gaming establishment, an improvement in prosperity, if not respectability. In 1923, Wah Gay had returned to his native Sunwei district in Kwangtung (or Guangzhou) province to marry, made sure that his wife bore him a son, then left her and his son in China for twenty-five years while he worked in New York. Ben Loy has grown up in China until the age of seventeen, when, in 1941, his father sends for him. Wah Gay puts Ben Loy to work at a relative's restaurant in the fictitious small town of Stanton, Connecticut (recognizably Stamford, Connecticut), supposedly at a safe remove from the fleshpots of New York and its Chinatown. A fellow waiter, however, soon initiates Ben Loy into the blandishments of weekends in New York City, where he quickly becomes a regular customer of prostitutes.

After two years in Connecticut, Ben Loy joins the U.S. Army during World War II, then returns to a similar lifestyle after his discharge in 1947. His parents, however, feel that Ben Loy is now of an age to marry. In his characteristically overbearing way, Wah Gay packs his son off to their native village in China, where a match has been arranged between Ben Loy and Mei Oi, daughter of Lee Gong, a longtime comrade of Wah Gay. Fortunately, Ben Loy and Mei Oi hit it off at first sight, and their wedding in China and its consummation form a joyous and sexually fulfilling event for both. The newlyweds then return to New York to start married life and a family in the New World. Another, grander wedding banquet is given in New York by Wah Gay for his Chinatown cronies; by this time, however, Ben Loy has become impotent after the first flush of nuptial bliss. His fiascoes fill Ben Loy with humiliation and guilt, while Mei Oi feels useless and unwanted and wonders how she can start a family in this new land.

Through Mei Oi's dilemma, the complication of the plot begins. The opportunity for motherhood soon presents itself to Mei Oi through the person of the Chinatown playboy, Ah Song. Ah Song ingratiates himself with Mei Oi, who, in her lovelorn situation, is seduced and enters into an affair with him. Soon Mei Oi is pregnant and passes off the expected child as Ben Loy's, much to the satisfaction of her father-in-law, her father, and a complacent Ben Loy, who does not care to question this fortunate conception.

Unfortunately, Ah Song has been sighted sneaking into Ben Loy's apartment. Soon the gossips of Chinatown are agog with news of Ben Loy's cuckoldry. Within the immediate family, Lee Gong is the first to hear of this, and he confronts his daughter, who stoutly denies all. Subsequently, Wang Chuck Ting, president of the Wang Family Association, learns of the scandal and brings this family shame to Wah Gay's attention. Wah Gay then berates Ben Loy, who in turns slaps Mei Oi. In order to flee the Chinatown gossips, the young couple at first move to Stanton, Connecticut, but they are unwelcome to their Connecticut relatives, and so they return to New York.

The novel's catastrophe occurs when Wah Gay, enraged by the family dishonor, ambushes Ah Song after a tryst with Mei Oi and slices off his left ear. Wah Gay must then hide out at a friend's New Jersey home while the police search for him following a complaint from Ah Song.

At this point, the unofficial Chinese judicial system of Chinatown intervenes and provides a resolution. Chinatown's Ping On Tong ("peace association") and the Wang Family Association agree that Ah Song ought to suffer some punishment for his adultery. They persuade Wah Gay to come out of hiding, and they compel Ah Song to drop charges against Wah Gay. Ah Song is then condemned to five years of ostracism, while Wah Gay and Lee Gong have both lost so much face that they leave New York, one for Chicago and the other for Sacramento.

In the codalike final chapters of the novel, Ben Loy and Mei Oi also leave New

York. Mei Oi is shown to be a repentantly virtuous wife as she repulses the advances of another would-be seducer lured by her beauty and her reputation. Ben Loy shows himself to be a loving and forgiving husband who is willing to accept his share of blame for his wife's having gone astray. They start their relationship anew in San Francisco, where Mei Oi bears a baby whom Ben Loy accepts as his own. In due course, Ben Loy seeks a cure for his impotence from a Chinese herbalist who makes him "eat a bowl of tea" concocted from medicinal herbs. Miraculously, this bitter medicine works. Ben Loy regains his virility, and he and Mei Oi look forward to having their next baby.

## The Characters

*Eat a Bowl of Tea* is a comic novel. It is not surprising, therefore, to find that most of the book's characters bear a resemblance to the archetypal characters of classic comedy.

Ben Loy is the individual at the center of the novel, a young Chinatown waiter who resembles such sympathetic underdog youths of classic comedy as Henry Fielding's Tom Jones and Mark Twain's Huckleberry Finn. Born and reared in a Chinese village until the age of seventeen, Ben Loy has imbibed the traditional Confucian values and is thus a filial son. As the novel opens, he is in his twenties, holds a job, has done his hitch in the Army during World War II, and is a married man, but he still regards his father with some awe. His one character flaw is his sensuality, which leads him to patronize prostitutes.

Ben Loy's father, Wah Gay, has been a sojourner in America for thirty years. He started out as a laundryman but now owns and operates a gambling establishment in New York's Chinatown. Wah Gay fits the classical comic mold of the heavy-handed parent who tyrannizes the younger generation (in this respect, he is like Huck Finn's father). He exercises a rigid, traditionally Confucian domination over Ben Loy, deciding when to transplant him from his native village to New York and determining whom he is to marry. He thus gives his son no chance to develop his own individuality or to pursue his happiness. Although Wah Gay insists that Ben Loy be a good Confucian son, he himself is not a good Confucian father, for he makes his living from gambling.

Mei Oi, Ben Loy's sympathetic bride, is an attractive young woman who loves her husband and wants to be a mother. She has grown up in her native village in China, where she has been nurtured and sheltered by her family and the societal structure of her clan. Confronted with the freedoms of New York, the impotence of her husband, and the blandishments of a sweet-talking seducer, she naïvely falls.

Lee Gong, Mei Oi's father, is a longtime friend and associate of Wah Gay's. He, too, is a Chinese émigré in the United States, and he too is cast in the mold of the overbearing parent in his dealings with Mei Oi.

Ah Song is an idling playboy who preys on Chinatown women gullible enough to give credence to his tales, in which he boasts of his wealthy connections in Canada and runs down the reputations of the women's husbands. He is a known philanderer and is treated as a contemptible villain by the men of Chinatown.

Wang Chuck Ting is the uncle of Wah Gay and elder statesman of the Wang clan in Chinatown. Wealthy and politically well-connected, he is a wheeler-dealer who can get his friends jobs, apartments, or contacts in the police department. When the enmity between Wah Gay and Ah Song threatens to spill over to the authorities beyond Chinatown, Chuck Ting steps in, in the manner of a *deus ex machina*, to contain their dispute within Chinatown. He stage-manages the Chinatown judiciary system to achieve a resolution for the novel.

Interestingly, the men who frequent the Wah Que Barber Shop make up an entity that resembles the chorus in Greek drama. At the barbershop, they exchange tidbits of gossip, comment on the doings of the principal characters, and mirror public opinion in Chinatown.

*Themes and Meanings*

*Eat a Bowl of Tea* is a satirical novel of manners that probes the mores of Chinatown society during the 1940's, and its plot can be seen to develop along the lines of a classic comedy. The movement of classic comedy is usually a progression from one kind of society to another: At the beginning, the negative characters who obstruct this progress are in charge of their society; at the end, the events in the plot that bring the hero and heroine together cause a new society to crystalize around the hero.

Indeed, the conflict in *Eat a Bowl of Tea* is one between a society of elders and a society of youth, between the tradition-bound Chinese sojourners who came to America to make money and the new Chinese Americans who are in America to stay. Ideologically, the conflict is a clash between the Confucian Chinese ethic of family hierarchy on one hand and the American Dream of the individual's right to pursue happiness and identity on the other. Wah Gay and Lee Gong, especially the former, represent the Confucian older generation, while Ben Loy and Mei Oi represent the younger generation of Chinese Americans. Wah Gay treats his son as his belonging and his responsibility, allowing Ben Loy no opportunity to develop his individuality; Wah Gay makes decisions about Ben Loy's travel, work, and marriage. Wah Gay's attitude is typical of the Confucian father who has almost unlimited powers over his children; for example, the Confucian father who killed his grown-up son would be punished only by sixty blows and a year's banishment.

Louis Chu shows us that this oppressive familial structure leads to disingenuousness and hypocrisy. For example, Wah Gay's playing the role of the provident father creates an ironic tension between his ideal image of himself and his real circumstances. For Wah Gay's means of livelihood—operating a gambling joint—is hardly an exemplary one for a model Confucian father. Ben Loy, on the other hand, must keep up appearances to conform with his father's desired image of him as a good, hard-working boy. Behind this filial façade, however, Ben Loy secretly resorts to prostitutes as a release. Thus, when Wah Gay announces his plans for Ben Loy's marriage, the latter seeks an outlet for his bottled-up emotions of frustration with the first available prostitute. The irony of his family oppression intensifies when Ben Loy's frequenting of prostitutes threatens the fruitfulness of his marriage and thus endangers the continuity of the family, ideal or not.

After the novel's catastrophe is precipitated by Wah Gay, the obstructive representatives of the older generation, Lee Gong and Wah Gay, lose their authority and disappear into self-exile. The Confucian system of family hierarchy is in retreat. The action then focuses on the now unobstructed actions of the younger generation, Ben Loy and Mei Oi, as they attempt to rebuild their marriage and their lives. They found their new sense of self and family not upon an authoritarian hierarchy but upon a loving mutuality of understanding and forgiveness. They also move from the old American East (New York) to the new American West (San Francisco). In so doing, they are following the archetypal American journey, voyaging westward to seek a second chance at happiness and self-realization on new frontiers and (in Huckleberry Finn's phrase) in "the territory" ahead.

*Critical Context*

First published in 1961, *Eat a Bowl of Tea* languished in neglect for almost two decades until a post-1960's generation of Asian American readers and scholars rediscovered it. The novel was rescued from obscurity by a university press (reprint 1979, University of Washington Press) and a commercial publisher (reprint 1986, Carol Publishing) and was made into a sensitive and entertaining 1988 film directed by Wayne Wang. Chu's book has been belatedly and securely established as a classic of Asian American literature.

*Eat a Bowl of Tea* is prized because it is the first novel by a Chinese American insider depicting Chinatown life in a realistic, unexoticized mode. To be sure, it was preceded by several novels of Chinatown life that were more popular with the American public, such as Lin Yutang's *Chinatown Family* (1948) and Chin Yang Lee's *Flower Drum Song* (1957); however, these books depicted Chinatown life in an idealized, exotic manner that tended to feed falsifying stereotypes about Chinese Americans. Chu's observation and recording of his Chinatown is, by comparison, much more authentic.

Unlike Lin and Lee, who neither lived nor worked in Chinatown, Chu's life and career was intimately bound up with Chinatown. Born in Toishan, China, Chu emigrated to America when he was only nine years old; after he was graduated from college, he became director of a New York society center, host of the radio program *Chinese Festival*, and executive secretary of Chinatown's Soo Yuen Benevolent Society.

Chu's realism is especially original in his dialogue. Chu renders the language of his Chinatown characters with such a fine ear that one can hear the cadences of Cantonese underlying the broken English and savor the authenticity of the speakers' banter and vilification. Indeed, the speeches of Chu's barbershop male gossips are at least as expressive and naturalistic as Ernest Hemingway's rendered Spanish, and the early reviewers who expected Chu's ghetto characters to speak in polite standard English or Hollywood's Charlie Chan-ese were, of course, bewildered by the book's raw, unadulterated language.

Chu's novel also mirrors with fidelity the conditions in the "bachelor society" of America's Chinatowns. This bachelor society had come into being because American immigration laws of the first half of the twentieth century largely prevented working-class Chinese from bringing wives into the United States; at the same time, miscegenation laws prevented Chinese men from marrying Americans and establishing families in America. (Wealthier, merchant-class Chinese men were allowed to bring their wives into the United States.) Thus, men such as Wah Gay and Lee Gong had to marry and leave their wives in China while working in America, enjoying connubial visits with their wives perhaps only once a decade. In the Chinatowns of that period, then, the population was overwhelmingly male, mostly "married bachelors." Hence a woman such as Mei Oi, a war bride of a Chinese American, would have been a precious rarity to the Chinatown community.

*Eat a Bowl of Tea* is a satirical and comic novel of archetypally classic construction. Choosing his raw materials from Chinese America, Louis Chu created a novel that sorts the profoundest themes in the American grain—the dream of the individual in pursuit of happiness and self-actualization, the desire that America be another Eden. *Eat a Bowl of Tea* is Louis Chu's only published novel, but he has deservedly been designated Chinese America's first novelist. He is indeed, the forerunner of such worthy Chinese American fiction writers as Frank Chin, Maxine Hong Kingston, and Amy Tan.

*Bibliography*
Chan, Jeffery. Introduction to *Eat a Bowl of Tea*, by Louis Chu. Seattle: University of Washington Press, 1979. An excellent introduction by a distinguished Chinese American scholar and short-story writer. Chan praises Louis Chu for his graphic and accurate transcription of Cantonese idiom and his keen, satirical analysis of a Chinatown in tradition from a bachelor society to a family society. Chan also includes a brief biographical account of Chu.
Chua, Cheng Lok. "Golden Mountain: Chinese Versions of the American Dream in Lin Yutang, Louis Chu, and Maxine Hong Kingston." *Ethnic Groups* 4 (1982): 33-59. A comparative treatment of Lin's *Chinatown Family*, Chu's *Eat a Bowl of Tea*, and Hong Kingston's *The Woman Warrior: Memoirs of a Girlhood Among Ghosts* (1976) and *China Men* (1980). Analyzes the differing ways in which the Chinese ideal of family conflicts with the American Dream of success, happiness, and individual identity. Chua's approach includes historical and archetypal criticism.
Gong, Ted. "Approaching Cultural Change Through Literature." *Amerasia Journal* 7 (Spring, 1980): 73-86. Traces a pattern of cultural development from Chinese to Chinese American in a study of works by Monfoon Leong, Louis Chu, and Frank Chin. Examines their common themes of father-son relationship and generational conflict. In *Eat a Bowl of Tea*, Ben Loy's sexual prowess represents his individuality, which conflicts with his father's dominance.

Hsiao, Ruth Y. "Facing the Incurable: Patriarchy in *Eat a Bowl of Tea*." In *Reading the Literatures of Asian America*, edited by Shirley Geok-lin Lim and Amy Ling. Philadelphia: Temple University Press, 1992. Hsiao's essay places Chu in a tradition of literary endeavors to debunk patriarchy. Indeed, patriarchy is the true villain of Chu's novel. Hsiao concludes, however, that Chu was unable in his own characterization to free his creative imagination from male images of women and that patriarchy remains an incurable disease of Chinese society.

Kim, Elaine H. *Asian American Literature: An Introduction to the Writings and Their Social Context*. Philadelphia: Temple University Press, 1982. Elaine Kim is the dean of Asian American literary history. Her book on Asian American literature is a groundbreaking study of the field. Chapter 4, "Portraits of Chinatown," contains a thoughtful, balanced, and illuminating discussion of the literary as well as sociological qualities of Chu's novel.

*C. L. Chua*

# EVA LUNA

*Author:* Isabel Allende (1942-    )
*Type of plot:* Magical realism
*Time of plot:* The middle and late twentieth century
*Locale:* An unnamed South American country
*First published:* 1987 (English translation, 1988)

> *Principal characters:*
> EVA LUNA, the narrator, an illiterate girl who becomes a television scriptwriter
> CONSUELO, her mother, a servant
> ROLF CARLÉ, Eva's lover, a photojournalist
> ELVIRA, a cook who rears Eva after Consuelo dies
> HUBERTO NARANJO (COMANDANTE ROGELIO), a street boy who becomes a guerrilla leader
> MELESIO (MIMÍ), Eva's friend, a female impersonator
> RIAD HALABÍ (THE TURK), a shopkeeper, Eva's benefactor
> ZULEMA, his unfaithful wife

## The Novel

*Eva Luna* is the story of a poor girl with a great gift for storytelling who, because of her indomitable spirit, manages to survive a perilous youth and become a successful television scriptwriter. The title character of the novel is also the narrator. Even when Eva herself could not have witnessed what she describes, the implication is that she is faithfully reporting what she has been told by those who were present and thus, in a sense, making those events a part of her own narrative. Since all the people mentioned affect Eva's own history, these stories are an essential part of her life.

The book begins with Eva's birth, the product of the sole sexual encounter of her parents. Her mother, Consuelo, a servant of unknown parentage, had decided to console an Indian gardener who was presumed to be dying from snakebite. When he recovered and went back to the jungle, he left Consuelo pregnant. Even though she died when Eva was only six years old, Consuelo remained an important part of her life, primarily because she told her such fascinating stories.

Allende then moves back in time to introduce Rolf Carlé, the son of Lukas Carlé, an Austrian schoolmaster. Rolf was a baby when his father went to war; during his father's absence, Rolf has made him into a hero. Unfortunately, when Lukas returns, he is so tyrannical that by comparison the Russian occupation troops seem angelic.

Although Allende does not bring Eva and Rolf together until almost the end of her novel, she continues to trace his adventures as well as hers. For example, in one chapter Eva tells about her mother's death, her employment in a household where only the cook, Elvira, treats her with kindness, and her meeting with a street boy, Huberto Naranjo, who becomes her protector. In the next, she describes Rolf's reaction when his father is murdered by his students: a feeling of guilt by association so consuming that he cannot eat and, as a result, is shipped off to kindly relatives in South America. As Eva points out, when Rolf arrives in the German settlement of La Colonia, he is not far from the place where she is growing up.

Deposited with first one employer and then another by the mad mulatto godmother who rules her life, Eva never feels secure. Nevertheless, she occasionally does exhibit her spirit. On one memorable occasion, because she is disgusted with the cabinet minister who spends every day on an ornate chamberpot that she must empty, she deliberately pours the contents over his head. Fleeing from his wrath, Eva finds her old friend Huberto, who places her in the care of a famous madam, La Señora, and her best friend, Melesio, who calls herself Mimí whenever he performs as a singer, dressed in women's clothes. Eva's life with these two of society's outcasts is supremely happy.

Unfortunately, a political uprising brings the idyll to an end. This time, Eva is rescued by Riad Halabí, called "the Turk" by the people of Agua Santa, the isolated village where he keeps a shop. A man so compassionate that he covers his unsightly harelip with a handkerchief for fear of offending his companions, Riad Halabí has a wife, Zulema, who cannot endure him. During one of Riad's absences, Eva is horrified when Zulema seduces Riad's young cousin Kamel. After Kamel realizes what he has done and runs away, the lovesick Zulema kills herself. Because she was the one to find the body, Eva is arrested, and though she is finally cleared and released, she is forced to leave the village and Riad, even though he is now as much in love with her as she is with him.

In the final section of *Eva Luna*, the lives of Eva, Mimí, Huberto, and Rolf become intertwined. Believing herself to be in love with Huberto, who is now a guerrilla leader called Comandante Rogelio, Eva becomes his mistress. Meanwhile, with Mimí's encouragement, she begins writing and selling scripts for television serials that become so popular that the authorities attempt to influence their content. In the guerrilla camp, Eva meets Rolf, now a documentary filmmaker. When Eva is told that she is in danger from the authorities, Rolf takes her to La Colonia. In that Edenic setting, Eva and Rolf discover that they have at last found the mates they have sought for so long. In time, Eva says, their love eventually wore out, or, if one prefers another ending, it lasted forever.

*The Characters*

Eva Luna is not only Allende's protagonist and narrator but also the character whom the reader comes to know best. As she tells the story of her life, Eva seems to be supremely honest. For example, she admits that she is often rebellious, but without that trait, she comments, she might not have survived. For someone who has suffered as much as she has, she is amazingly devoid of self-pity. When she recalls one of the beatings administered by her godmother, Eva simply says that the neighbors came over to stop the beating and then used salt to cure her wounds. The very fact that she does not attempt to elicit pity makes one more sympathetic to her plight. The reason

Eva can distance herself from such unhappy events, as well as from happy ones such as her days and nights of lovemaking, is that above all, she is a storyteller. Even when life betrays her, she can rewrite it in her imagination, as she probably is doing at the end of the novel when she imagines an everlasting love.

Of all the other characters in the novel, Rolf is the most complex. In one sense, he is shown as a male equivalent to Eva. Because both of them have been so mistreated as children—Eva by her godmother and her employers, Rolf by his father—their commitment to unqualified love seems almost miraculous. One must give both of them much of the credit for preserving their souls as well as their bodies. While his father was still alive, Rolf worried more about his sister than about himself, and after his father was killed, Rolf was so shocked at his own feelings that he became ill. Like Eva, Rolf refuses to turn bitter, and thus he is able to respond to kindness, in his case to the warmth of the "uncle" and "aunt" at La Colonia. Although as a photojournalist Rolf has no doubt learned to be objective, Eva's insistence that he is more rational than she may not be accurate. After all, she also mentions a time that Rolf burst into tears when he suddenly remembered one particularly miserable segment of his childhood. It is hardly unusual for the actions of a character to reveal more than a writer's or a lover's description of him.

Some of Allende's other characters, such as La Señora, Melesio/Mimí, and even the gallant Colonel Tolomeo Rodríguez, although not examined in as much detail as Eva and Rolf, are nevertheless fully formed and plausible. On the other hand, one of the principal characters, Huberto Naranjo, remains shadowy. Admittedly, the author spends considerable time explaining Huberto's conversion from vandalism to Cuban-style communism. Exactly who he is remains less clear than what he is. It may be that Allende means to use Huberto primarily to represent the macho ideal of manhood, offering protection to women but denying them equality.

In relatively minor roles, one is happy to settle for the outrageous and often hilarious caricatures that make Allende's fiction such a delight to read. The godmother with the two-headed baby, the cabinet minister on his chamberpot, the cook who sleeps in her coffin, and the two nubile sisters who initiate Rolf into erotic pleasures all contribute to the magical quality of the novel.

Any consideration of Allende's characterization must stress that this novel is presented as Eva's story, not Allende's. If, as she insists throughout, Eva is creating this novel rather than dutifully relating it, even such matters as how each of the other characters is treated reflect Eva's judgments and, in turn, reveal her character, thus giving the work still another dimension.

*Themes and Meanings*

As the niece of Chilean president Salvador Allende, who formed a representative government only to be assassinated in 1973 in a military coup that was immediately followed by a reign of terror, Isabel Allende has every reason to be preoccupied with the abuse of power. In *Eva Luna*, she consistently contrasts the heartlessness of wealthy people such as Eva's abusive *patrona* with the kindness of social outcasts such as La Señora and Mimí. During much of the novel, her characters manage to keep their distance from the sources of power. The tyrannical ruler of the nameless country, the sadistic head of the secret police, and corrupt toadies such as the cabinet minister, however, are always present in the consciousness of her characters, and they become only too real to Mimí when he is thrown into prison for leading the Revolt of the Whores and to Eva herself when she is forced to flee because of her suspected involvement with the guerrillas.

Given her own experience with repression, it is amazing that Allende manages to avoid polemics in her works. She shows that even in the darkest of times, there is always the possibility of fulfillment through love. For Eva Luna, this comes only after she has come to terms with the shock of Zulema's suicide. When, for her first time in years, she feels the pains of menstruation, Eva knows that now her body will once again permit her to function as a woman, thus making possible her total commitment to Rolf. Although this aspect of the plot of *Eva Luna* might be seen as inconsistent with the feminism that pervades Allende's fiction, one must make a distinction between accepting one's gender and admitting inferiority. Implicit in the relationship between Eva and Rolf is the rejection of the patriarchal system. The two are companions and equals.

The fact that, as a creative artist, Eva seems to possess an almost godlike power indicates how closely Allende's attitude toward her art is related to her feminism and to her politics. When Mimí sets Eva down at her typewriter to begin "dusting off memories and weaving destinies" in a world of her own creation, Eva realizes that she has "the power to determine my fate, or invent a life for myself," as well as for other characters. It is this sense of her own power that gives her the strength to disagree with General Rodríguez and finally to refuse him. When the general asserts that there is no such thing as lasting love, Eva replies as one who is in control of her own life and of her own imagination: "I also try to live my life as I would like it . . . like a novel." Thus Allende reminds readers that there is in fact no real barrier between the "real" world and the world of ideas and of idealism.

*Critical Context*

With *Eva Luna*, Isabel Allende returned to the kind of fiction that had established her reputation. Her first novel, *La casa de los espiritus* (1982; *The House of the Spirits*, 1985), was written in the tradition of Magical Realism, like the novels of Gabriel García Márquez, the noted Latin American author and Nobel laureate to whom Allende acknowledges her indebtedness. Although in *De amor y de sombra* (1984; *Of Love and Shadows*, 1987) Allende continued to explore the theme of repression and political tyranny, in form that novel was realistic or even naturalistic. Although it was an exciting story, it lacked the mysterious, enchanted, and often haunted atmosphere that readers saw again in *Eva Luna*.

Eva and Rolf appear again in *Cuentos de Eva Luna* (1990; *The Stories of Eva Luna*, 1991), a collection of twenty-three stories supposedly invented by Eva at the request of her lover. In the novel that followed, *El Plan Infinito* (1991; *The Infinite Plan*,

1993), Allende for the first time set a work in the United States. Her North American protagonist is a rootless wanderer, not unlike Eva Luna, who searches for love and justice in a world that sometimes seems to contain only brutality and betrayal.

Because of her technical virtuosity and her transcendent humanistic vision, Allende is considered to be one of the most gifted Latin American writers of the late twentieth century. Her importance is perhaps best stated in the frequently quoted words of Alexander Coleman, who wrote in *The New York Times Book Review* (May 12, 1985) that Allende was "the first woman to approach on the same scale as the others [male Latin American novelists] the tormented patriarchal world of traditional Hispanic society."

*Bibliography*
Bader, Eleanor J. "A Life Like a Dimestore Romance." *Belles Lettres: A Review of Books by Women* 4 (Winter, 1989): 5. An unfavorable review, calling the characters in *Eva Luna* a "largely unsympathetic, unlikable lot—cynical, angry, and manipulative," who therefore fail to interest the reader. Eva herself has no faith in the possibility of political change, caring only for her art. After calling the plot "confusing" and "unbelievable," Bader concludes by saying that Allende could do better than write "a life that reads like dimestore romance."
Karrer, Wolfgang. "Transformation and Transvestism in *Eva Luna* by Isabel Allende." In *Critical Approaches to Isabel Allende's Novels*, edited by Sonia Riquelme Rojas and Edna Aguirre Rehbein. New York: Peter Lang, 1991. Explains how Allende uses mythic elements from sources such as *The Arabian Nights' Entertainments* and contemporary soap operas. Karrer's discussion of the "semiotic code of clothing" throughout the novel, with its "theme of magical transformation," is particularly helpful. Even though Allende has Eva accept her gender role, much in the novel supports more radical possibilities.
Rehbein, Edna Aguirre. "The Act/Art of Narrating in *Eva Luna*." In *Critical Approaches to Isabel Allende's Novels*, edited by Sonia Riquelme Rojas and Edna Aguirre Rehbein. New York: Peter Lang, 1991. Differentiates between the multiple roles of Eva Luna as a fictional character in the "act" of narrating and as a writer interested in her "art." As the novel proceeds, Eva can be seen to develop in narrative skill. The work is a "prime example of Isabel Allende's belief in the magical power of words."
Rotella, Pilar. "Allende's *Eva Luna* and the Picaresque Tradition." In *Critical Approaches to Isabel Allende's Novels*, edited by Sonia Riquelme Rojas and Edna Aguirre Rehbein. New York: Peter Lang, 1991. Rotella discusses *Eva Luna* in terms of Allende's feminism, focusing particularly on the figure of the pícara, who traditionally uses her body as well as her brains in outwitting her opponents. Although Eva is "surprisingly passive and dependent" for a pícara, she does possess the prime qualification, "inventiveness." The admixture of romance makes *Eva Luna* even more typical of the picaresque genre.
Ryan, Alan. "Scheherazade in Chile." *The Washington Post Book World* 18 (October 9,

Masterplots II

1988): 1-2. A highly favorable review, quoting a "technically dazzling" climactic scene as an illustration of Allende's art. One major subject of *Eva Luna* is the art of storytelling, as seen in the relationship between the world in which Eva lives and the life that she invents for herself. Eva's storytelling has the power to transform real life.

*Rosemary M. Canfield Reisman*

# FACE

*Author:* Cecile Pineda (1942-      )
*Type of plot:* Psychological
*Time of plot:* The 1980's
*Locale:* Brazil
*First published:* 1985

> *Principal characters:*
> HELIO CARA, the narrator and protagonist of the novel, whose face is disfigured after a fall from a cliff
> LULA, Helio's mistress and intended wife, who leaves him after the accident
> SENHORA CARA, Helio's mother
> JULIÃO, Helio's stepfather
> LUIS and MARIO, coworkers of Helio who turn their backs on him
> CARDOSO, Helio's former boss
> GODOY, a doctor

## The Novel

*Face* chronicles one man's effort to rebuild his soul after a devastating calamity has changed his life. After a short prologue, the book is divided into two major sections. It is told in the third person through the consciousness of the major character, although there are frequent flashbacks to earlier periods in his life. In addition, the author intersperses the commentaries of doctors and other observers of the novel's action. In the struggle of Helio Cara to repair his badly deformed face, the reader envisages the persistence and resilience of the human spirit.

The book begins with Helio Cara, an ordinary barber with an ordinary life, stumbling as he is running down the rugged rocks of the poverty-ridden, shack-filled Whale Back section of the Brazilian city of Rio de Janeiro. As he makes his way down the multi-tiered levels of rock, he loses his grip and falls. Although he survives, his face is irretrievably disfigured.

Helio has difficulty remembering the incident after its occurrence. Although his life is forever changed, the exact moment of the injury is clouded by the impact of the trauma. This trauma is so total that he does not even remember any pain or have clear images of people, such as his coworkers, who were prominent in his life before the tragedy. Wearing a white handkerchief to shield his face from the scorn and mockery of others, Helio reflects on his predicament. The only individuals he perceives clearly are his mother, whom he has lost long ago to his stepfather, and his mistress, Lula, whom he suspects he will now lose after this terrible injury.

Helio recalls a time before the accident, when he was living with Lula and enjoying their romantic comradeship. He is talking idly with his mistress when a telegram comes from Rio Piedras, the remote town in the country that he had left years ago for the large, impersonal city of Rio de Janeiro. The telegram reveals that his mother is dying.

Back in the present, readers witness the attempts of doctors to treat and remedy Helio's condition. The doctors conduct themselves professionally and genuinely try to repair Helio's face. Yet their scientific discourse does not address the pain Helio feels in his soul.

Helio attempts to return to his former job as a barber. Although his superiors and coworkers are not overtly antagonistic toward him, they clearly do not wish to have him around and feel that what has happened to his face has made him, in effect, a different person. Helio remembers his former boss, Cardoso, who had taught Helio to read and had ameliorated his backwoods status, schooling him in the rudiments of urban civilization.

Helio applies to have his face rehabilitated, suffering an embarrassing moment when he goes to the window selling lottery tickets instead. His fate in life the exact opposite of a lottery winner, Helio finally locates the right place. Yet he becomes increasingly desperate when the doctors, led by an administrator named Godoy, tell him that even though the state-subsidized Brazilian health-insurance plan covers the physical, mechanical aspects of his facial rehabilitation, the aesthetic aspects are extra. In other words, if Helio wishes his face to be beautiful again, or at least as beautiful as it once had been, he will have to pay for it himself. As Helio, without a job and with his mother dead, has no money, this is an impossibility. Closed in and daunted, Helio seems defeated at every turn. Yet soon Helio, beleaguered and hounded as he is, has a first glimmer that it will have to be his own initiative, not the assistance of others, that provides his rehabilitation.

Helio relates his abandonment by Lula. Lula still loves him and does not leave him callously, but nevertheless his condition makes it impossible for their romance to continue, and Lula reluctantly severs the relationship. Continuing his odyssey with the Brazilian medical bureaucracy, Helio is admonished that he should have had his workplace issue a letter of disability immediately after the accident; without this, there is no question of full reconstruction being authorized.

Helio decides to take his life fully into his own hands and repair the face himself. Helio leaves the city and returns to the hinterlands, where he had been born. Helio finds himself disoriented by the vast difference in scale and lifestyle between city and country. He returns to his mother's shack, and he recalls the pain he had experienced after his father's death, when his mother had remarried to a man named Julião, an action that Helio had regarded as a betrayal.

Helio once again attempts to find work, but even the merchants of his hometown disdain him. Bereft of other options, he uses his last remaining money to amass supplies for the reconstruction of his face. Revealing an ingenuity in excess of what could be expected from his largely menial and deprived existence, he slowly makes his face anew. It is only when this process is near completion that he is psychologically able to recall the scene of his father's death. Helio receives a letter from Godoy; presumably, the hospital is now ready to subsidize the remainder of whatever further treatment is needed. Helio imagines encountering Lula and her new boyfriend, and he looks forward to encountering society on his own terms, his identity fully renewed.

## The Characters

Helio Cara, the hero and narrator of the book, is a young, lower-middle-class Brazilian man. Although the book shows Helio only after the accident has occurred, readers are offered glimpses of his earlier life. Helio appears to be an absolutely ordinary person; there is nothing unusual about his life at all. This changes after his face is damaged. Although the accident is a tragedy, completely destabilizing Helio's life and robbing him of all that he cherishes, it has the curious side effect of making him for the first time an unusual person.

Initially, Helio appears only unusual in his torment, as he is pushed further and further to the margins of society. As he commences his heroic quest, however, Helio is revealed as determined and capable. Although he possesses a substandard education and seems to have only a normal mentality, Helio's misfortune stimulates him to notable feats of imagination and intellect. Helio finds that he has the foresight and the competence to literally re-envisage himself, to re-create his own face, which, from the very beginning of the novel, symbolizes not just the physical lineaments of his facial features but also his inner soul, which has suffered far more severe damage. Additionally, Helio, working only from the limited amount of verbal knowledge that Cardoso has provided him, is able to read medical manuals and piece together the methods he needs to effect his face's repair, and he is able to find all the practical materials that he needs. At the beginning of the book, Helio is painfully average; at the end, he has made something inspiring and exemplary out of his own pain.

Helio is the narrative center of the book, and the only character fully revealed; all the other characters elucidate aspects of his identity. Lula, his former mistress, represents the social acceptance and validation that Helio loses after the accident. When a prospective meeting with her is pictured at the end of the novel, what is conveyed is Helio's revitalized capacity to engage with his fellow human beings. More minor characters, such as Helio's coworkers Luis and Mario, play much the same function on a diminished scale.

Cardoso is one of the few auxiliary characters pictured positively; in teaching Helio to read and initiating him into the ways of the world, he is one of the few constructive models that Helio can call upon as he begins his quest for self-healing. Godoy, the doctor, starts off as an antagonistic representative of insensitive scientific authority, but by the end of the book, he is ready to assist Helio in his effort. This can be seen as symbolizing the willingness of an indifferent society to suspend its recalcitrance toward those who are suffering after they have proved their merit, as has Helio.

Helio's mother, dead father, and stepfather Julião represent the deeper level of his childhood, which is gradually revealed in the course of the novel. The cruel death of the father and his swift replacement by the hated Julião underscore the fact that Helio's facial injury is but an overt metaphor for a kind of primal wound already inflicted upon him by this childhood trauma. Although Helio's face had been intact before the accident, his psyche was badly injured. Helio's self-healing operates on both the literal and psychological levels. This is demonstrated when he is finally able to come to grips with his father's death even as he reaches the turning point in his odyssey of facial reconstruction.

## Themes and Meanings

The themes of *Face* are, from the beginning, symbolic and metaphysical in nature. Although the Brazilian setting, as manifested in Rio de Janeiro and Rio Piedras, is scrupulously drawn, such realistic features are not of the essence in this book. There is little conventional suspense in the action; readers are aware of Helio's plight from the beginning, and there are at least hints of the course the novel will take. What is central to the novel is the examination of psychological issues of identity that Helio's experience provokes. Without a face, Helio is without an identity. Even those who once loved him cannot now recognize him, even though he is still the same person inside. The way in which Helio carries on without a face and succeeds in making himself a new one, however, implies that faces are not indices of truth and authenticity; they are essentially disguises, additions to true identity that people make in order to function socially. Helio's loss of his face calls attention to the conventional, rather than natural, origin of the selves people present to one another.

Helio's self-reconstruction is reminiscent of existential themes of isolation and arbitrary self-projection. Yet, Helio is not seen purely as a victim powerless to alter his fate. In reconstructing his face, he displays not only a will to live but also an entrepreneurial assertiveness. Not content to play the role of victim that European philosophies would assign him, Helio reacts to his situation with a committed spirit of Third World resistance. This political and ethical undertone is all the more powerful because of the novel's meticulous avoidance of obvious political themes.

## Critical Context

*Face* was Cecile Pineda's first novel. It was not, however, her first creative effort; for many years previous to the book's 1985 publication, she had been an experimental theater director in San Francisco. This theatrical background permeates the novel in many ways. To act in the theater is to play a part, to disguise one's normal self. Often, as in classical Greek and Japanese drama, this is manifested literally in the use of masks. Pineda's familiarity with drama enables her to understand how even the everyday human face both expresses and masks emotions, how it is both messenger and barrier between the self and the outer world.

Pineda has seldom written about explicitly Hispanic subjects. In both *Face* and *The Queen of the Amazon* (1992), though, she does write about the culture of Brazil. The Brazilian setting of these works enables a dialectic of the strange and the familiar whereby Pineda is able to displace issues that other Latino writers might treat naturalistically onto a more stylized and metaphysical plane. Even in novels that have no thematic relevance to Hispanic experience—such as *Frieze* (1987), a compelling work concerning a medieval Buddhist temple in the East Indies island of Java—

Pineda continues to highlight themes, such as the fortitude of the individual against all external obstacles, that occur in the rest of her work.

This emphasis on identity and self-affirmation could be read as obliquely referring to American minority experience. Both *Face* and *Frieze* are taut and parabolic works in which images and themes prevail over conventional narrative. In *The Queen of the Amazon*, though, Pineda displays a looser, more sprawling style that permits a more panoramic view of human experience.

*Bibliography*

Bruce-Novoa, Juan. "Deconstructing the Dominant Patriarchal Text: Cecile Pineda's Narratives." In *Breaking Boundaries: Latina Writing and Critical Readings*, edited by Asuncion Horno-Delgado, et al. Amherst: University of Massachusetts Press, 1989. In the first discussion of Pineda to profit from the insights of contemporary literary theory, Bruce-Novoa discusses how Pineda encourages the reader to respond creatively to the plight of the protagonist of *Face*.

Clute, John. "Stitched Up." *The Times Literary Supplement*, December 13, 1985, 1434. Clute understands the magnitude and the ambition of Pineda's themes. He emphasizes their relationship to essential issues of identity and being. He is critical, however, of what he perceives to be the bland, innocuous nature of her presentation.

Cole, Diane, "The Pick of the Crop: Five First Novels." *Ms.* 13 (April, 1985): 14-15. Pinpoints Pineda's avoidance of sentimentality with potentially pathetic and maudlin subject material. Cole also mentions the novel's complicated flashback and overvoice techniques, often slighted by other reviewers.

Colman, Cathy. Review of *Face*, by Cecile Pineda. *The New York Times Book Review*, April 28, 1985, 24. Discusses the primal terror of Helio's experience. Colman, though, faults the novel for not developing more strong central characters.

Johnson, David. "Face Value." *The Americas Review* 19 (Summer, 1991): 73-93. Johnson discusses the imagery of masking in the novel, and the ideas of authenticity and inauthenticity it raises, as a Mexican American critique of modern consumer society.

Lowenkopf, Shelley. Review of *Face*, by Cecile Pineda. *Los Angeles Times Book Review*, June 23, 1985, 2, 10. Emphasizes the stark force of the novel's story. Also intelligently discusses the influence of Pineda's stage experience on the construction of her fiction.

*Nicholas Birns*

# THE FIFTH HORSEMAN

*Author:* José Antonio Villarreal (1942-      )
*Type of plot: Bildungsroman*
*Time of plot:* 1893-1915
*Locale:* Mexico
*First published:* 1974

> *Principal characters:*
> HERACLIO INÉS, the youngest of five brothers, who becomes a horseman
>     and an officer in Pancho Villa's army
> DAVID CONTRERAS, the bastard son of Don Aurelio Becerra, owner of
>     Hacienda de la Flor
> TEODORO INÉS, Heraclio's older brother
> CARMEN BECERRA, Don Aurelio's daughter
> ANTONIO RIVERA, Heraclio's friend and bodyguard
> CELESTINO GÁMEZ, one of Villa's generals
> DOMINGO ARGUIÚ, the Spanish aristocrat who marries Carmen
> MARCELINA ORTIZ, the girl who marries Heraclio
> XOCHITL SALAMANCA, Heraclio's mistress during the Mexican Revolu-
>     tion

*The Novel*

Based in part upon the experiences of José Antonio Villarreal's father during the Mexican Revolution, *The Fifth Horseman* records the fictionalized education of Heraclio Inés as he moves from relative innocence to war-weary experience.

*The Fifth Horseman* falls into two major parts; the first is concerned with peace, while the second is concerned with war. Beginning in the middle of the action, the novel's prologue opens on June 24, 1914, showing Heraclio leading Pancho Villa's attack on Zacatecas. Thereafter, by flashback, the omniscient third-person narrator goes back to 1893, the year of Heraclio's birth, only gradually bringing the protagonist forward through various stages of development to 1911, the year in which Heraclio joins Villa for the attack on Juarez. Subsequently, Heraclio's star rises with Villa in book 2, "The Campaign" and falls in book 3, "Los Desgraciados (The Disgraced Ones)" after Villa's defeat at Celaya.

Tied by tradition to the feudal social structure of the Hacienda de la Flor, the setting for book 1, Heraclio Inés is born the fifth son to a family of semi-independent horsemen, a factor that places him above the peasantry but below Don Aurelio Becerra, the hacienda's owner. After his father dies while attempting a dangerous feat of horsemanship, Heraclio also discovers that he has been born to a code of honor, and in 1905, when he ceases to herd sheep with David Contreras in order to train as a horseman, he finds his brothers' enforcement of the code to be rigid and brutal. Refusing to let his brothers break his spirit, Heraclio resists; nevertheless, through the various trials that constitute his rites of passage, he makes himself into a master horseman, passing the final test, the ride of death, and surviving. Yet when he sees his oldest brother, Teodoro, grovel before Don Aurelio, Heraclio declares his independence and moves in with Antonio Rivera, a peasant.

Having proved his manhood in terms of the code, Heraclio next realizes the romantic side of his being by falling in love with Carmen Becerra, Don Aurelio's daughter. Disregarding the social gulf that separates them, Heraclio and Carmen plunge into a passionate relationship that is doomed to fail. Believing that love should prevail over class, Carmen reveals her affair to her mother, with the result that her parents rush her marriage to the decadent Spanish aristocrat Domingo Arguiú. Having faced facts, Heraclio knows that marriage to Carmen is impossible; still, the two lovers continue their liaison until one of Don Aurelio's administrators threatens Heraclio with violence and exposure. Heraclio reacts by killing the man, a turn of fortune that forces him to flee to the mountains. He joins a group of bandits led by Ysabel Pulido and his onetime friend David Contreras, who resents Heraclio's liaison with Carmen, his half-sister.

Under Ysabel Pulido, Heraclio and the others move north to join Celestino Gámez, a follower of Pancho Villa. When Pulido, who functions as David's spiritual father, dies and Heraclio ascends to leadership of the band, David becomes Heraclio's enemy, never forgiving the horseman for what he believes to have been the theft of his birthright. Thereafter, Antonio Rivera attempts to prevent David from killing Heraclio.

Following Villa's victory at Juarez in 1911 and the apparent end of the revolution, Heraclio returns home and marries the saintly Marcelina Ortiz. When the murder of President Francisco Madero reignites the revolution, however, Villa recalls Heraclio. In the campaigns that follow, Villa and Heraclio fight their way south with the Division of the North. In the course of this march, Heraclio meets and saves Xochitl Salamanca, a young acrobat who becomes his wartime wife and who remains with him until she dies of smallpox in the aftermath of Villa's decline. Meanwhile, David Contreras turns vicious bandit and, in an act of revenge, finds and kills Marcelina as well as Heraclio's new daughter. In the fulfillment of his code and in the absence of law, Heraclio then kills David.

After Villa's defeat at Celaya and subsequent retreat, General Gámez goes over to the enemy, an act that Heraclio sees as a betrayal of both the revolution and Mexico. Loyal to Villa and the people, Heraclio finds and executes Gámez; then, with all ties severed, he heads north toward a voluntary exile in the United States.

*The Characters*

Heraclio, the novel's protagonist, is the most important character in the work. All the other characters function in one way or another to shape Heraclio's development from naïve youth into mature man. Although he is a man of action, courageous and swift, Heraclio also thinks deeply, with the result that he develops the moral and spiritual wisdom to deal with the loss and disillusion that his life brings.

Tortured by his illegitimacy and finding only rejection where Heraclio succeeds—with Don Aurelio, Carmen, and Ysabel Pulido—David Contreras holds Heraclio responsible for his thwarted life, and his bitterness so poisons him that he becomes deadly. David represents what Heraclio might have become had he allowed his own disillusion to embitter him.

Teodoro, Heraclio's oldest brother, represents the arrogance of the paternal system under which the characters live. He teaches Heraclio the craft and code of the horseman. Heraclio learns, however, that if he is ever to become his own man, he must cast off Teodoro's authority, an authority that suppresses the man's own family only to grovel before the next-higher social class.

Rich, aristocratic, and proud, Carmen Becerra is Don Aurelio's daughter. As such, she represents a social peak to which not even a naturally superior man like Heraclio may aspire. Rather, like the mares in her father's pasture, she is marked for breeding with a blue-blooded Spaniard, the corrupt Domingo Arguiú. Nevertheless, Heraclio pursues and dominates her; in the process, she teaches Heraclio to recognize and admit the romantic side to his nature.

Marcelina Ortiz, the innocent girl who has loved Heraclio all of her life, marries the horseman following his affair with Carmen. Marcelina represents the ideal wife. In a parallel not to be missed, she comes to Heraclio bearing the same name as his dead mother; she thus stands for the continuing value of motherhood combined with the purity of wedded love. Evil, in the form of David Contreras, may destroy her, but the ideal she represents is eternal and inviolate, a continual inspiration to Heraclio.

Xochitl Salamanca, the Mayan circus performer who becomes Heraclio's wartime wife, attaches herself to him in the midst of the revolution. In Xochitl's character, Villarreal has embodied the spirit of the revolution, a spirit to which Heraclio makes passionate love. Coming into the novel with Villa's rise to power, Xochitl remains with Heraclio until she dies miserably in the epidemic that follows Villa's decline.

General Celestino Gámez, a Villista general, is possessed of vitality, strength, courage, and intellect. When Villa's fortunes collapse, though, Gámez shows his flaw by seeking his own rather than the people's good. In order to preserve his own integrity, Heraclio risks great danger to punish Gámez's betrayal, and the general dies amidst the symbols of his corruption.

Antonio Rivera, a relatively flat character, passes through the novel as an image of the steadfast friend. He gives up his own life to protect Heraclio.

Domingo Arguiú teaches Heraclio by example that blue blood is no proof against moral decadence. When he tries to corrupt Heraclio, he merely excites the horseman's contempt. Eventually, his cowardice leads to his death.

*Themes and Meanings*

Almost Homeric in scope, *The Fifth Horseman* presents an anatomy of the Mexican Revolution, its causes, its initiation, its fighting, and its results, the whole of the immense event parading before the reader through the effects it brings to bear on a few families and, in particular, the life of a single man, Heraclio Inés. Had Villarreal lived in an earlier time, he might well have attempted to write an epic on his subject; instead, he brings the full weight of his talent to bear in the creation of a unique and telling novel.

In the first half of the novel, with dramatic precision, Villarreal re-creates a picture of what life was like when Mexico still writhed in the grip of the dictator Porfirio Díaz. Under Díaz, the Mexican social structure—a social structure depicted on the Hacienda de la Flor—became stratified and static, the wealthy few ruling the many poor with a heavy authority. At its best, the system preserved a kind of hopeless, immobile order by locking each man and woman into a hereditarily determined place; at its worst, the system produced peonage, slavery, brutality, and intolerable injustice in all phases of life. Heraclio's craft as a horseman places him well above the peons but well below the landowning classes; as a result, he is afforded the opportunity of viewing both stations objectively as he advances toward manhood.

If, in the first half of the novel, Heraclio aspires to and attains a high degree of personal maturity, the novel's second half shows him continuing his moral journey, this time working his way forward toward a state of sociopolitical maturity. Born to be independent of the system, Heraclio might well have turned his back on the revolutionary wind that swept Mexico; instead, when the crisis develops, Heraclio opts for change that will produce good for the whole. When he does, he democratically casts his lot with the people.

With Francisco Madero's elevation to the presidency of Mexico, Heraclio believes that the revolution has succeeded and that the people have won. When Villa is imprisoned and Madero is assassinated, however, Heraclio quickly realizes that a few corrupt men can bring a good thing down. Thereafter, committing himself to Villa, he faces for the first time the chaos of extended war, discovering in the process that the war itself corrupts the men that make it and that the acquisition of power can quickly lead to its abuse.

By means of some fine war writing, Villarreal makes the battles of the revolution spring to life, their violent immensity acting as backdrop for Heraclio's own continuing development. For as long as Villa remains strong, hope for the revolution, hope for the people, remains alive. Yet after the battle at Celaya, where the old order unites to defeat Villa, the people's cause is essentially lost. In the period of disillusion and death that follows, Heraclio learns that the most for which he can hope is the preservation of his own integrity and a period of peace. Rather than compromise with the corrupt new forces that grip Mexico, Heraclio executes the traitor Gámez and marches north into voluntary exile. Heraclio's plan is to return to Mexico when the time is ripe in order to help rebuild his beloved country.

*Critical Context*

*The Fifth Horseman*, José Antonio Villarreal's second novel, ends chronologically where *Pocho* (1959), his first novel, begins, with the voluntary exile of its protagonist north of the border. In fact, Juan Rubio, the father of *Pocho*'s protagonist, is often thought to be a portrait of Heraclio Inés in later life; as a result, many readers have enjoyed reading the books together. Yet the novels are not mutually interdependent. *Pocho*, the first major novel in what is sometimes called Chicano literature, has enjoyed continued success since its first publication and remains a unique fictional record of the Mexican American experience. Equally independent as a work of art, *The Fifth Horseman* remains an accomplished historical novel about the Mexican Revolution; considered either as Latino or American literature, it is fully capable of holding its own high position independent of *Pocho*.

Experimental in style, *The Fifth Horseman* applies Spanish syntax to English vocabulary, bringing both a weight and dignity to the dialogue that normal Anglo-Saxon word order might not have supplied. Some have criticized Villarreal for using this technique, while others have applauded the boldness of his effort, seeing, perhaps, that in elevating the style of his novel, he also broadens the work's scope by giving it a formality of language that recalls heroic poetry.

As a historical novel, *The Fifth Horseman* finds its literary antecedents in works as diverse as *Voina i mir* (1865-1869; *War and Peace*, 1886) and *Gone with the Wind* (1936). At the same time, the special nature of Villarreal's material calls to mind two additional subgenres of North American literature. From the Mexican point of view, *The Fifth Horseman* shows a clear connection with such "novels of the revolution" as Mariano Azuela's *Los de abajo* (1916; *The Underdogs*, 1929) and Martin Luis Guzmán's *El águila y la serpiente* (1928; *The Eagle* and *The Serpent*, 1930). From a strictly American point of view, *The Fifth Horseman* seems closely related to the Western, to such novels as Owen Wister's *The Virginian* (1902) and Jack Schaefer's *Shane* (1949). Regardless of how one chooses to classify *The Fifth Horseman*, the historical nature of the novel remains dominant.

*Bibliography*
Bruce-Novoa, Juan. "José Antonio Villarreal." *Chicano Authors: Inquiry by Interview*. Austin: University of Texas Press, 1980. Reviews Villarreal's writing career and says of *The Fifth Horseman*, "The novel creates the mythological, heroic ancestor of the modern Chicano." Bruce-Novoa asks Villarreal a total of twenty-four questions about his life and work, eliciting a revealing variety of responses.
Dimicelli, Judith M. "A Chicano Twentieth-Century Book of Genesis." *Bilingual Review/Revista Bilingüe* 3 (January-April 1976): 73-77. Dimicelli's concise but thorough essay-review provides a fine appreciation of the novel. With convincing penetration, she argues that Heraclio provides an "image of the very genesis of contemporary man, for this work concerns man's involvement in political revolution and personal liberation." Aimed at the general reader, Dimicelli's essay is at its best in discussing the novel's themes.
Leal, Luis. "*The Fifth Horseman* and Its Literary Antecedents." In *The Fifth Horseman*, by José Antonio Villarreal. 2d ed. Binghamton, N.Y.: Bilingual Press/Editorial Bilingüe, 1984. Leal presents an excellent study of *The Fifth Horseman*'s literary antecedents. In addition to linking the work to American Westerns, novels of the revolution, and historical fiction in general, Leal provides a useful discussion of

Mexican fiction and nonfiction about the revolution. He also delves into literary theory, citing such critics as Octavio Paz and Carlos Fuentes in order to develop his thesis and place *The Fifth Horseman* in a tradition.

Parotti, Phillip. "Heroic Conventions in José Antonio Villarreal's *The Fifth Horseman.*" *Bilingual Review/Revista Bilingüe* 17, no. 3 (1992): 237-241. Links elements of Villarreal's technique to the epic tradition. Argues that although *The Fifth Horseman* is not an epic, Villarreal's conscious employment of some heroic conventions lends Heraclio some mythic proportions.

Tatum, Charles M. *Chicano Literature*. Boston: Twayne, 1982. Although brief, Tatum's discussion of *The Fifth Horseman* is telling. According to Tatum, the novel's women are relegated to inferior roles, and Heraclio's portrait is overdrawn. At the same time, Tatum applauds Villarreal's "realistic descriptions" of the revolution and his careful re-creation of "the social order that existed in Mexico prior to 1910."

*Phillip Parotti*

# THE FIRM

*Author:* John Grisham (1955-    )
*Type of plot:* Suspense
*Time of plot:* The 1980's or the early 1990's
*Locale:* Memphis, Tennessee, and the Gulf Coast
*First published:* 1991

> *Principal characters:*
> MITCHELL Y. MCDEERE, a star graduate of Harvard Law School hired as
>   an associate attorney by a Memphis law firm
> ABBY MCDEERE, the young wife of Mitchell, a schoolteacher
> RAY MCDEERE, Mitchell's brother, who is serving time in a Tennessee
>   penitentiary
> NATHAN LOCKE, a longtime partner in Mitchell's law firm
> OLIVER LAMBERT, the senior partner of the law firm
> AVERY TOLAR, the partner in the firm with whom Mitchell is assigned to
>   work
> DEVASHER, head of security for the law firm and liaison with the Morolto
>   family
> WAYNE TARRANCE, an FBI agent who involves Mitchell in his investiga-
>   tion of the law firm
> EDDIE LOMAX, an ex-convict turned private detective who knew
>   Mitchell's brother Ray in prison
> TAMMY HEMPHILL, Lomax's secretary and later Mitchell's coconspirator
>   in his plot against the firm

*The Novel*

Drawing upon his experiences as a native of the Deep South and as a lawyer, John
Grisham created in *The Firm* a chase and suspense adventure involving the Federal
Bureau of Investigation (FBI), the Mafia, and a young attorney coming to terms with
the reality of life in the world of big business and big money.

*The Firm* is divided into forty-one short chapters. It is written from the third-person
point of view, principally from the perspective of Mitchell McDeere; parts of the book
are told from the viewpoints of other characters.

When Mitchell McDeere completes Harvard University Law School in the top five
of three hundred graduates, he is much in demand, but no offer matches that of the
firm of Bendini, Lambert, and Locke in Memphis, Tennessee. In addition to a starting
salary of eighty thousand dollars a year, he is assured payment of his student loans, an
expensive automobile, a low-interest home loan, and incredible perks for good work.
When Mitchell and his wife Abby settle in their new house in Memphis, he is caught
up at once in preparing for the state bar exam, which he passes a few months later with
the highest score in the state.

Soon Mitchell is working twelve or more hours a day, and his home life suffers. The senior members of the firm are pleased, however, and his career seems well on its way to success, for he does not know the dangerous secret the senior partners are hiding from him and other young lawyers. The firm is a front for the Morolto Mafia family in Chicago and is involved in tax frauds and other illegal operations involving millions of dollars.

Satisfied with the firm despite the long hours, Mitchell is shocked when he is approached in a downtown restaurant by FBI agent Wayne Tarrance and told of the firm's illegal activities and Mafia connections. Several deaths of younger firm members in recent years were in fact murders, not accidents and suicides as had been reported. Tarrance endeavors to recruit Mitchell in a plan to expose the firm.

At first reluctant, even frightened, by such a dangerous scheme, Mitchell begins to become disillusioned when he discovers that both his car and his house have been bugged. Two senior members of the firm, Oliver Lambert and Nathan Locke, informed by their security agent DeVasher of taped conversations between Mitchell and his wife, are increasingly concerned about their new "star." To assure his complaince with their plans, they send him with Avery Tolar, his mentor in the firm, to Grand Cayman for business and relaxation. There, a young woman in their employ seduces Mitchell, who has previously been totally faithful to his wife.

Subsequent contacts with the FBI, both in Memphis and in Washington, and his growing suspicious about the mysterious deaths lead Mitchell to contact a private investigator, Eddie Lomax. Eddie is a friend of Ray, Mitchell's brother, who is in prison. Eddie agrees to investigate the firm, but before he comes up with any significant information, he is murdered. Mitchell resolves to divorce himself from the firm and its illegal activities, and together with Eddie's secretary and sometime lover, Tammy Hemphill, who wants revenge for Eddie's death, he conspires to outwit the firm.

While devoting ever more hours to his work, Mitchell is at the same time meeting with the FBI agent, who promises him a new life for his cooperation; Mitchell also gathers material for his own purposes. Meantime, DeVasher, increasingly suspicious, shows the young attorney compromising photographs made of him with the young woman in Grand Cayman; DeVasher threatens to send the pictures to Abby McDeere should he find any cause whatever. Though fearful that Abby will discover his infidelity, Mitchell continues in his dangerous plan. With the aid of Tammy Hemphill, he manages to photocopy confidential files from the firm and place them in storage. On Grand Cayman, Tammy seduces Avery Tolar, puts knockout drops in his drink, and steals his keys to the storage files in the firm's island condominium. Abby McDeere has secretly flown to Grand Cayman to meet Tammy, and the two copy all the incriminating files, which Tammy then takes to Nashville.

Through a plant in the FBI, the firm learns of McDeere's defection and plans his destruction, but Mitchell's scheme progresses. At his insistence, the FBI arranges for his brother Ray's escape from prison. When Mitchell receives a coded warning from the FBI that the firm knows everything, he sends a message to Abby through Tammy and flees Memphis. He and his wife rendezvous on the Gulf Coast, where they videotape many of the documents shipped to them by Tammy and plan their escape.

For days, they are pursued by both the FBI and the Morolto Mafia family before their escape arrangements are completed. Barry Abanks, a scuba instructor from Grand Cayman, and a man known only as George, himself a fugitive from the law, arrive in George's boat to pick up the McDeeres, who are armed with fake identification and the videotapes of the documents, and speed them away to the Caymans. The original documents are left in the motel for the FBI, but the McDeeres keep the videotapes as security. The novel ends with Mitchell and Abby drinking rum punch on a tropical beach and planning their future as fugitives.

*The Characters*

Mitchell McDeere, the protagonist, is an idealistic graduate of Harvard Law School at the beginning of the novel. He is something of an All-American boy, a former high-school football player who has always scored highly in whatever endeavor he undertook. He is happily married, and when he is offered the fantastic job in Memphis, his life would seem to be almost perfect. It is, however, clouded by several shadows: His widowed mother, whom he has not seen in several years, is a a waitress living with her second husband in a trailer park in Florida, and his brother Ray is serving a sentence in a Tennessee penitentiary in for killing a man in a barroom brawl. As Ray points out when his brother visits him in prison, Mitchell is the first McDeere in generations who has made something of himself.

*The Firm* is to some degree a novel of initiation, for Mitchell, something of an idealist, learns many bitter facts of life as a result of his involvement with Bendini, Lambert, and Locke. When the plot reaches its climax, he has not only outsmarted the members of the firm, the Mafia backers, and their hired gunmen, but he has also hoodwinked the FBI agent and would seem to have gained the ascendancy. He, his wife, and his brother are in possession of eight million dollars, documents to use as security, and the necessary papers for a new life and new identity. Yet questions remain: At what cost has such a seemingly idyllic existence been achieved, and what are the perils and anguish to be faced by fugitives constantly afraid of being apprehended by dangerously vindictive members of the underworld? The groundwork for making credible the change in Mitchell's character from bright and promising young attorney to conniving fugitive is laid in the early revelations concerning his dysfunctional family, particularly his brother's criminal record.

Abby McDeere is a model wife and schoolteacher, product of a wealthy and privileged background, who is very much in love with her husband. Their relationship seems ideal, although the time and energy required of Mitchell by the firm annoys her, and an increasing amount of tension develops in their marriage. She remains blissfully unaware of her husband's one-night infidelity on Grand Cayman. By the end of the novel, she is fully involved in Mitchell's nefarious schemes to outwit both the Mafia and the FBI, and become independently wealthy. The change in her character is abrupt and, if the reader is inclined to analyze it closely, hardly credible.

The senior members of the firm—Royce McKnight, Nathan Locke, and Oliver Lambert—are rather standard "crooked lawyer" stereotypes, although Locke is given somewhat more dimension because of his grim and frightening behavior. He is early described as "an ominous and evil man," and his appearance and demeanor are a foreshadowing of the dark secrets behind the firm's shiny facade. The Mafia members, Joe Morolto, Lou Lazarov, and others, are fairly standard villain types, as is DeVasher, the brutal security manager for the firm, who takes pleasure in using the "bugs" in the homes of young lawyers to monitor their sex lives.

Among the FBI agents, all are stereotyped except for Wayne Tarrance, who has certain character idiosyncrasies that distinguish him from the others. His personal habits, his comments, and his appearance all serve to make him a credible, if not fully rounded, personality. The other agents, like the Mafia members in the novel, are flat and undeveloping characters.

Tammy Hemphill, although she exhibits most of the qualities of the archetypal hardboiled secretary of the archetypal private detective, is a rather well-developed character. Married to an Elvis Presley impersonator so devoted to the singer that he has legally adopted Presley's name, she loves her boss and thus becomes involved in Mitchell's undercover scheme to outwit the firm and the FBI. Her actions are much more credible than those of Abby or even Mitchell, since she is bent on revenge for the firm's murder of Eddie Lomax.

## Themes and Meanings

*The Firm* is a typical suspense novel, ending in a hair-raising chase with the protagonist and his associates being pursued by two powerful and dangerous forces. As a typical example of this genre, *The Firm* is not overly burdened with theme or meaning, since its primary purpose is obviously to hold the attention of the reader. The novel is, in the popular parlance, a "page-turner," and thus it is not necessary nor even desirable for the author to burden the reader's mind with philosophical or moral considerations. Certainly, the actions of the protagonist have heavy ethical implications, but what the ultimate ethical statement of the novel is intended to be is difficult to say. If Mitchell and his associates had merely defeated the Mafia and escaped their murderous plans, a clear moral statement would have been evident in the novel. Yet they also outwit the FBI and escape with a large amount of cash, thus benefiting indirectly from the very illegal acts they were supposed to expose. As a consequence, the meaning to be drawn from the novel is clouded.

John Grisham's reason for turning to the suspense-chase genre for his second novel was probably a result of the failure of his first novel, *A Time to Kill: A Novel of Retribution* (1989). That book dramatized social problems, including race relations, and contained serious moral and ethical implications, but it attracted little attention from the reading public or critics. Thus Grisham apparently determined after that failure to write a book that would sell, and he did. Ironically, as a result of the phenomenal success of *The Firm*, *A Time to Kill* subsequently became a best-seller in its own right.

*Critical Context*

With *The Firm*, John Grisham established himself as one of the leading practitioners of the craft of suspense writing. He has mastered well all the trappings of the genre, including particularly the age-old battle between good guys and bad guys and the obligatory chase in which the protagonist is put into grave danger and escapes through his wit and other talents. The novel established Grisham as a popular writer, and his subsequent works, including *The Pelican Brief* (1992) and *The Client* (1993), have been eagerly awaited and have immediately become best-sellers.

There is also something of the novel of initiation in the work, since Mitchell McDeere certainly loses whatever illusions he may have concerning the ethics of the practice of law, at least law as practiced by the firm for which he works. It is clear that Mitchell is awakened to the basic corruption in certain areas of business, law, and human life in general, and that the pattern of the novel is clearly entwined with this change in him. In contrast to most disillusioned heroes, however, Mitchell ends the novel in a happy state, living in a kind of earthly paradise, even though his security may be tenuous.

*Bibliography*

Grisham, John. "The Rise of the Legal Thriller: Why Lawyers Are Throwing the Books at Us." *The New York Times Book Review* 97 (October 18, 1992): 33. Grisham analyzes the rise of the "lawyer novel," a phenomenon to which he has contributed as much as any author. He discusses the abiding fascination with the law of the reading public and how lawyers have turned to fiction in order to satisfy this interest. In addition to his own work, he considers that of other lawyers turned writers and their varying approaches.

Landner, M. "An Overnight Success—After Six Years." *Business Week*, April 19, 1992, 52. That a magazine such as *Business Week*, aimed at the commercial community, should include an article on an adventure novelist indicates clearly the extent to which Grisham has been a financial success and how that success has drawn the attention of people other than his readers. Landner traces Grisham's remarkable career as a writer who struggled for years to write a successful book.

Matthews, Thomas. "Book 'em." *Newsweek* 121 (March 15, 1993): 78-81. A review of Grisham's fourth novel. *The Client* (1993), which, like the two before it, *The Firm* and *The Pelican Brief*, immediately appeared on best-seller lists. Matthews considers this work and those that preceded it in relation to the genre of the "lawyer novel." He also analyzes the phenomenal success that made Grisham one of the most widely read American authors in the space of only three years.

*W. Kenneth Holditch*

# FISKADORO

*Author:* Denis Johnson (1949-    )
*Type of plot:* Apocalyptic
*Time of plot:* The mid-twenty-first century
*Locale:* The Florida Keys
*First published:* 1985

> *Principal characters:*
> FISKADORO HIDALGO, a young boy whose encounters with death and rebirth prepare him for the coming of a new age
> ANTHONY TERRENCE CHEUNG, a middle-aged Chinese musician who is obsessed with learning about and coming to terms with the past
> MARIE WRIGHT, Cheung's grandmother, the oldest living woman in the world

*The Novel*

In *Fiskadoro*, Denis Johnson, a poet-novelist whose apocalyptic impulse is the driving force behind much of his work, propels readers forward into a cosmos born out of the ashes of a nuclear holocaust. He brilliantly imagines a world cut off from all that remains elsewhere, a present disconnected from its past. This is a world ruled by new religions, where Quonset huts sit beside the burned-out husks of automobiles. This is a landscape scarred by fire, contaminated by radioactive waste. This is "a place ignored by authority," a society of bizarre body-maiming rituals, a culture where the god Jesus, the god Quetzalcoatl, and the god Bob Marley join hands to form a hybrid holy trinity. This is a Key West of the waking dead.

The book begins in the present tense, narrated by an unnamed first-person narrator who is looking back on "a time between civilizations" from a futuristic perspective, a telling that attempts to retrieve a lost chapter in the history of the world. The point of view soon shifts to a third-person omniscience that moves almost dreamily into the eyes and minds of the three main characters: Fiskadoro, A. T. Cheung, and the ancestral Grandmother Wright.

Fiskadoro appears carrying a briefcase, the contents of which include the pieces of a disassembled clarinet. The relationship between Fiskadoro and his musician-mentor Cheung is forged at this moment. Fiskadoro has sought out Cheung in order to learn how to play the clarinet—that magical, mysterious metal contraption passed onto him from a long line of Hidalgo fathers and sons. As director and member of a rag-tag group of musicians who call themselves the Miami Symphony Orchestra, Cheung is immediately drawn to Fiskadoro. He soon steps in and becomes a surrogate father figure for Fiskadoro after Fiskadoro's own father—a man named Jimmy Hidalgo—drowns, his body lost to the sea.

Grandmother Wright spends most of her time sitting in silence, listening to her grandson, Cheung, teach Fiskadoro simple finger scales on his clarinet. Yet some of the most powerful passages found in the novel rise up out of Grandmother Wright's unbroken silence. Just because she does not speak does not mean that she does not remember. Instead, she is constantly surrounded and bombarded by images from The End of the World, an event she personally dates at 1974: the year during which her father committed suicide, the year her mother went crazy, the year she herself escaped from Vietnam aboard a helicopter that crashed into the ocean. She was miraculously saved however, "not because her hands reached out" but because "other hands than hers reached down and saved her."

Grandmother Wright is Cheung's last and only living connection between the present and the past. He is a man obsessed with finding meaning in what happened to a place distilled by amnesia. He traces the origin of forgetting to the bombing of Nagasaki in 1945. "As the bombs fell," Cheung reflects, "already we were forgotten." Cheung does what he can to preserve the memory of a world that is both gone and forgotten. He has committed to memory such historical documents as the Declaration of Independence and the Constitution as well as the name of his first love. Cheung's pursuits are fruitless, however, for he lives in a time when survival is based on an ability to forget the past, to let go, to be born again.

Grandmother Wright holds all the secrets, but she is not alone. Fiskadoro too finds himself coming into the knowledge of the past when he wanders into the "patchwork of marsh and tangled vegetation" among a primitive culture known as the Quraysh, who worship and practice tribal ceremonies in the darkness of the swamps.

Only when Fiskadoro returns home do readers learn that he has been brainwashed into participating in a ritual of penis-bisection that would make him like other men among the swamps. His journey into darkness and back into light is a metaphorical rebirth that prepares Fiskadoro for the coming of a new civilization—an age to which the first-person narrator (who disappears early on from the novel) belongs. The narrator's futuristic voice describes Fiskadoro as "the one known to us best of all" and remarks cryptically that he was "the only one who was ready when we came."

*The Characters*

Fiskadoro, the adolescent boy, nearly thirteen, is the central figure in the novel. His story, like many stories that focus on adolescents, is a rite of passage into awareness, a coming of age into a whole new way of life. Fiskadoro is a precocious boy who does not want to be like the other men in a village made up primarily of men who fish and of women who cook the fish that the men catch. Fiskadoro thus seeks out the help of Cheung, who agrees to teach him to play the clarinet. Fiskadoro believes that music will magically pour forth from his clarinet, but this is not the case until the end, the moment when Fiskadoro is reborn.

Fiskadoro's passage into a heightened state of awareness takes him on a journey into the darkness of the swamps, where the Quraysh worship the incarnation of the god Mohammed, who has manifested himself in the guise of a two-headed snake. Among the Quraysh, Fiskadoro's transformation from a boy into a man takes on both physical and symbolic implications. When he reappears later in his village, staggering and drugged, he is truly no longer "like other men." His memory of who he is and where he has been has been completely erased. Fiskadoro is now history-less. He does not even remember his own mother. He is now ready for—and prepared to be born into—the future.

Grandmother Wright's passage out of Vietnam in 1974 parallels Fiskadoro's re-awakening into a world that is hard to call his own. She has suffered through two major holocausts—the End of the World as well as Vietnam—yet amid this suffering she has still managed to live, to keep her eyes open to witness the coming of a new civilization as it washes in, "a ship or shape"—it is not known which—in the ghostly mist. Although Grandmother Wright refuses to speak, readers are granted access to her memories from Vietnam. The flashbacks to Saigon are the richest moments in this book, and Grandmother Wright, though silent, is the character whom readers get to know most intimately. Unlike Grandmother Wright, Fiskadoro is kept at a constant distance, even though he is the protagonist. Grandmother Wright is clearly the most fully imagined, fully realized figure in the book.

Cheung is a character found floundering obsessively in his pursuit of the past, a man who lives outside his own time, aligned only with the forces of history. At a moment when he recognizes that "there's something spiritual going on here," he quickly admits, "But I don't want to learn what it is. I'm certain of this." This is the closest Cheung comes to experiencing a moment of clarity, though he resists the under-standing that could possibly follow it by turning back: back to a time that he cannot change, a time to which he does not belong. Cheung does belong to a group of like-minded men and women, all of whom cling to the artifacts of the previous civilization. Yet his journey ultimately ends in failure with the discovery that the nature and origin of forgetting was born out of the ashes of Nagasaki, a hundred years before.

*Themes and Meanings*

When Fiskadoro returns to his village, unable to remember, it is as if he is starting life brand new, like a baby. Being thus born again, Johnson suggests, is the first step toward the possibility of living, not merely surviving, in this world and in worlds to come. Fiskadoro is the future. In a world born out of the contaminated ashes of a nuclear apocalypse—an apocalypse that mirrors Fiskadoro's own self-mutilation—history loses its importance, its hold over the living. As Grandmother Wright's silence quietly articulates, remembering does nothing but render one speechless and static in the presence of unspeakable events.

The events that give rise to the novel are also left unspeakable, as if Johnson simply was not interested in the details, the political framework, leading up to the End of the World, but rather in what rises out of this horrific end. The world of *Fiskadoro*, a time referred to only as the Quarantine, is a place born out of fire and death. Yet life still exists; people live, fish, plant gardens, play music, and even find time to make love. Yet the central question remains: Which of them will be saved? Or, perhaps even more important, what does it mean to be saved? Early on in the novel, readers are told that the boy Fiskadoro was the only one "ready when we came." Johnson seems to suggest, at the novel's close, that salvation is possible only for those who suffer, who are willing to lose themselves completely in the search for knowledge and meaning.

In his previous novel, *Angels* (1983), Johnson's apocalyptic impulse played itself out in its examination of the lives of two characters who were running from themselves. Yet in *Fiskadoro*, his follow-up novel, Johnson's notion of an apocalypse is a visceral reality versus an emotional/psychological abstraction. The world of *Fiskadoro* is a place inhabited by ghosts, by visions of corpses sitting in automobiles. There are reminders everywhere of the holocaust that has separated the Florida Keys from whatever remains of the rest of the world. It seems a natural progression for a writer driven by an apocalyptic imagination to turn his talents to asking the question: So what happens after the end of the world? The answer is not pretty. Johnson's gifts as a gritty realist are not lost in his imaginings of a world blighted by atomic fallout. As the narrator from his third novel, *The Stars at Noon* (1986), says: "I wanted to know . . . the exact dimensions of Hell." Hell is measured in the pages, in the world of *Fiskadoro*.

*Critical Context*

*Fiskadoro*, Johnson's second novel, appeared in 1985, a year several other books about nuclear war by such established writers as Kurt Vonnegut and Tim O'Brien were also published. Johnson, whose debut novel, *Angels*, is firmly rooted in the real world—an America of prisons and bus stops, junkies and thieves—took a chance by choosing to follow up with what some critics would consider a work of science fiction. *Fiskadoro*, however, is a novel that transcends simple genre limitations, a book in which Johnson explores several themes that continue to recur in both his fiction and poetry: the role of forgiveness, salvation, redemption, the powers of grace. *Fiskadoro* is somewhat weighed down by its lofty, postapocalyptic dimensions, and for this reason, it is Johnson's least accessible work.

Johnson himself admits he is "not completely happy" with *Fiskadoro*; he has called the novel "too scattered." Yet the book, despite its shortcomings, is by no means a failure. Johnson's body of work—including several novels, the collection of stories *Jesus' Son* (1992), and books of poetry including *The Incognito Lounge and Other Poems* (a 1982 National Poetry Series Selection) and *The Veil* (1987)—is as impressive as that of any writer of his generation. It seems possible, even, that *Fiskadoro* might be read in a distant future as a historical artifact—a leftover piece of history— from a civilization whose ancestors were stupid enough to build atomic bombs.

*Bibliography*

Brians, Paul. Review of *Fiskadoro*, by Denis Johnson. *Bulletin of the Atomic Scientists* 42 (March, 1986): 50-53. In a discussion of several books that examine the threat or aftereffects of nuclear war, Brians praises *Fiskadoro* for its refusal to romanticize the "new primitive culture emerging out of the atomic ashes." He notes the resurgence of interest in "nuclear war fiction" by "serious" contemporary writers and credits the "posture of the Reagan Administration" for producing such a strong response from writers who might not otherwise address the issue of nuclear war.

Corwin, Phillip. "Creating a New Form in Fiction." *Commonweal* 112 (August 9, 1985): 444-445. Corwin considers *Fiskadoro* to be, despite its "grandiose pretensions," one of the few works to rise up out of the doomed pessimism of most visionary novels. What distinguishes *Fiskadoro* is "an original, visceral prose style . . . that approaches the creation a new form in fiction." Johnson's juxtaposition of the real and the surreal is judged to be the book's lasting literary achievement.

Hinson, Mark. "'From Somewhere Else': An Interview with Denis Johnson." *Apalachee Quarterly* 29/30 (1988): 100-107. In a rare interview, Johnson talks about the apocalyptic forces that lurk behind much of his work. "The whole point of *Fiskadoro*," Johnson says, "is that every day is an apocalypse." He admits that he is not wholly satisfied with *Fiskadoro*, which he says draws much of its energy from his childhood spent in Manila during the 1960's.

Hoffman, Eva. "Postapocalypse Pastoral." *The New York Times Book Review* 90 (May 26, 1985): 7. Hoffman's review is a well-fashioned overview of a book that she believes "succeeds in everything but its subject." Hoffman argues that the actual backdrop of the novel—the notion that nuclear Armageddon has occurred—is a subject "too overwhelming to be taken out of . . . historical context and serve as the pretext for allegory," that the event itself casts too big of a shadow over the otherwise subtle inventions that do in fact work within the author's imaginings.

Neville, Jill. "Fiskadoro." *The Times Literary Supplement*, May 24, 1985, 573. Although Neville admits that Johnson is a writer of "prolific gifts," she finds the novel to be problematic. "Johnson," Neville says, "makes the reader flounder inside the strangeness of his apocalyptic vision. Too much is left unexplained." What Neville considers to be "strangeness," however, might to some readers be viewed as the wildly fertile imagination of an inventive and unpredictable writer.

*Peter Markus*

# THE FLOATING WORLD

*Author:* Cynthia Kadohata (1956-    )
*Type of plot: Bildungsroman*
*Time of plot:* The 1950's
*Locale:* California, Nebraska, and Arkansas
*First published:* 1989

Principal characters:

OLIVIA ANN, the novel's protagonist, who is depicted from the ages of twelve to twenty-one

HISAE FUJIITANO (OBASAN), Olivia Ann's powerful maternal grandmother

BENJAMIN TODD, Olivia's outgoing and talkative oldest brother, four years younger than she

WALKER ROY, Olivia's quiet and brooding middle brother, five years younger

PETER EDWARD, Olivia's youngest brother, ten years younger

ISAMU, a foster parent with whom the three oldest children stay

CHARLES OSAKA (CHARLIE-O), Olivia Ann's stepfather; loud, undignified, cheerful, and optimistic

MARIKO (LAURA), Olivia Ann's moody, graceful, intellectual mother

DAVID TANIZAKI (TAN), Olivia Ann's first boyfriend

ANDY CHIN, Olivia Ann's boyfriend in Los Angeles

THE GHOST of JACK, Olivia Ann's biological father

*The Novel*

Olivia Ann's unusual 1950's adolescence is one without a permanent address; she lives in a series of motel rooms and rented houses as her father moves from job to job. Her family consists of parents, a cranky grandmother, and three younger brothers. With the exception of intermittent marital problems between her parents, the family unit offers her a stable and loving environment in an otherwise "floating" world. Obasan, her feisty grandmother, taunts and harasses her but also protects and loves her in a hardened and unorthodox way. Her younger brothers are her best friends and allies, playmates who find the constant moves an opportunity for playing games and exploring new sights.

Morning hikes and afternoon drives with Obasan are the children's routine. They encounter a threatening man at a gas station, buy apples from a field worker, and play tag outside their motel room. To avoid her grandmother's taunts and pinches, Olivia Ann locks herself in a bathroom at one point, and her grandmother tries to bribe her to come out. After Olivia finds Obasan dead on the bathroom floor, the family brings her body to Wilcox, California, to be buried next to her third husband, they then head south for Los Angeles. An accident in which a bus hits a car acquaints them with death for the second time in the same trip.

Flashbacks illuminate the characters, revealing how the three older children live with Isamu and bond in both serious and humorous ways, how Olivia gains respect for Obasan despite the pain Obasan causes her, and how she comes to develop a close relationship with Charlie-O, her stepfather. A frustrating detour to try to locate the "second father" of Olivia Ann's mother leads to aborted petty thievery on Olivia Ann's part. Later, she vows to try to be good "for a whole week."

In Gibson, Arkansas, the family rents a house and enjoys their longest stay in one place. Olivia Ann comes to realize that her mother had an affair when they lived in Oregon and that although she loves Charlie-O, she is not in love with him. Returning in the early morning after sneaking out at night for a slumber party, Olivia Ann longs to ask her mother whom she really loves. In a seminal image of the book, Olivia Ann feels as if she is floating suspended between sky and water.

Olivia Ann develops skill at card tricks as a result of to the family's long and frequent drives. In Arkansas, Charlie-O gambles a lot and loses, to the distress of his wife. At sixteen, Olivia has a job inoculating chickens in a hatchery in Missouri and meets her first boyfriend, Tan. Though the work is hard, she is attracted by the workers' toughness, tension, and mystery. Her lovemaking with Tan, and Tan's father's loss of his job, are emotional highs and lows.

Helping Tan and his family pack for a move to Indiana, Olivia feels her first twinges of longing to strike out on her own. A year later, on the verge of departing for Los Angeles, her parents give her a going-away party. For a time Walker disappears, making the family fearful and tense, but after he is located, Olivia Ann and Charlie-O enjoy early-morning coffee together. Olivia notices how vulnerable her father really is.

With her own apartment and a sales job in a lamp shop in Beverly Hills, Olivia adjusts well to life on her own. She dates Andy Chin, who wrecks cars for a living, and sees Andy alternately being wooed and abused by the insurance-fraud specialist who employs him. When Walker arrives for a visit, Olivia Ann and Andy drive him north to Oregon. The fact that he is the first family member to visit her in California reinforces the special bond they feel for each other.

The book ends with a chapter devoted to Olivia Ann's two fathers: her stepfather, Charlie-O, whom she thinks of throughout the book as her real father, and "Jack," her biological father, who was married to another woman at the time her mother conceived her. Jack's wife has asked Olivia Ann to take over Jack's vending-machine business in exchange for a small percentage of the profits, and Charlie-O accompanies her for part of the trip. Along the route, Olivia Ann sees a vision of Jack, who has died, as a ghost of about the age he would have been when he knew her mother. The spirit world thus offers an appropriate context for the ending, which can be read as a blessing upon Olivia Ann's nascent adult life.

## The Characters

This first-person narrative, a coming-of-age story, is written entirely from Olivia Ann's perspective. She serves as an honest narrator, wide-eyed and playful as an adolescent, a bit wiser but still whimsical as an adult. As the oldest child in her family, she is spunky and aggressive toward her brothers, and their image of her is often of a loud and angry person. She is vigilant and nurturing toward them even as their mother seems preoccupied. Though matter-of-fact in her description of their adventures, her curiosity and love for her brothers shine through. She is an agreeable narrator; she can laugh at herself, and she presents her world clearly, without unnecessary elaboration.

The character of Obasan dominates the early part of the book. Obasan inhibits Olivia Ann's spontaneity, but she also fiercely protects her granddaughter from threatening outsiders. Olivia Ann calls Obasan her "tormentor" in the first sentence of the book, but it is to pages of Obasan's diary that Olivia Ann goes for advice about sex, and it is to a shrine to Obasan that she respectfully yet fearfully serves rice cakes soaked in tea. Obasan is a powerful woman who smokes cigars, outlives three husbands, and engineers the marriage of Charlie-O to her daughter when her daughter is eight months pregnant. In spite of the fact that she is dead by page twenty-nine, she is the most vivid and energetic character in the novel, and her presence endures even after she is buried. Though Kadohata has been accused of being socially irresponsible in her portrait of Obasan, the author has insisted that the character of Obasan should not be taken to represent all Japanese grandmothers; nor, Kadohata has said, did she intend her novel to be a definitive expression on the Japanese American experience.

Charlie-O is one of the most sympathetic father figures in contemporary literature. Though he is the biological father of her brothers but not of Olivia Ann, Charlie-O and Olivia Ann have a stronger bond than any other two characters in the book, and he is the only father in her heart. They both share a longing to be closer to Mariko, to have Mariko be more open and forthcoming with them, but they do not let her demureness or the family's tribulations defeat them.

Olivia Ann's mother, Mariko, is a shadowy presence, remote and ethereal, existing just beyond the understanding of both Olivia Ann and Charlie-O. Charlie-O emotionally pursues her and then despairs as his wife prevaricates in her affections, unable to commit her heart to him fully. His sense of morality is stronger and more uncompromising than hers. Even in the face of Mariko's infidelity and his own temptation, he is unable to be unfaithful to his wife, a fact he reveals to Olivia Ann when he tells her that extramarital relationships are "wrong": " 'Two people get married! They get married. Period.' "

*Themes and Meanings*

The novel's title points to its central image, the floating world. The family literally "floats" from place to place without setting down firm roots. They are, therefore, more "rooted" to one another than to any place, which makes the fact of Mariko's infidelity more disturbing than Olivia Ann admits. The stable love between Olivia Ann and Charlie-O balances her mother's lukewarm bond with him, and the closeness between Olivia Ann and her siblings is unconditional. Obasan both disrupts and cements the family relationships. She is a mercurial threat, a reminder that all may not be as it seems and that stability could end at any time. Even after her death, Olivia Ann feels "itchy," as if Obasan's soul has somehow come to roost within Olivia's body.

The Japanese term for "floating world" is *ukiyo-e*, which refers to the Japanese concept of a nocturnal realm of pleasure, entertainment, and drink, and each of those descriptors functions in the novel. Evening escapades and descriptions of the night are common in the book. The book is pleasurable reading because it nostalgically describes a pleasant childhood, one abounding in good humor, love, and, for the most part, enjoyable experiences. The characters both entertain one another and experience life with wide-eyed wonder, as though things they observe are being staged merely for their delight. An episode of heavy drinking during a novelist's birthday party in Arkansas reinforces the uninhibited entertainment the guests enjoy in chasing animals.

Olivia Ann glosses the term *ukiyo* by saying that it also refers to "change and the pleasures and loneliness change brings." The family's frequent moves are the result of her father's bad luck with jobs and of her parents' dissatisfaction with their marriage. Olivia Ann is quick to emphasize that she loves traveling around, and the book traces the advantages rather than the hardships of such a nomadic life. Chapter 7 explores the idea of floating "in and out of alertness" while the family travels, reinforcing the image of suspension. They are soothed by the constant noise that the car makes, "like the breath of the sea in a shell."

The book is presented from the viewpoint of an adolescent, and the details of this perspective contribute to the pleasure of the reading. During one particularly tense poker game, Charlie-O is losing money in the living room; in the kitchen, meanwhile, Olive Ann and her brothers are blithely dividing out orange ice cubes among themselves. The ice cubes begin to melt when their mother's angry upbraiding silences the children. Though the observations mature as the novel progresses, the freshness of image remains. The vision of Jack that closes the book is effective and ethereal.

*Critical Context*

When *The Floating World* was published, most of the reviews were glowing. Cynthia Kadohata's first novel earned her comparisons to Mark Twain, Jack Kerouac, Raymond Carver, and William Faulkner. The book is autobiographical in that much of the author's early life was spent on the road with her family in Arkansas, Georgia, and Michigan before she settled in Los Angeles at the age of fifteen. She has said that she likes to travel because it helps her see ordinary things in surprising ways, and she infuses such delight and wonder into her first novel. Her novel includes a long episode set in Arkansas about workers who sort male from female chicks, a job her real-life father held after he divorced her mother.

While traveling around the country drives the plot in her first novel, Kadohata set her second novel, *In the Heart of the Valley of Love* (1992), in Los Angeles in the year 2052. The second book is the story of seventeen-year-old Francie, who arrives in "the valley of love" and stays for seven years. When she is nineteen, she is pinned against a wall when a car jumps a curb, crushing her arm. Such an accident really happened to Kadohata in Los Angeles when she was twenty-one, and the event impressed on her the unpredictability of life. Kadohata says that writing about things that have happened to her blurs the distinction between what is real and what is fiction, and she calls her second novel not so much futuristic as dreamlike.

*Bibliography*

O'Hehir, Diana. "On the Road with Grandmother's Magic." *The New York Times Book Review* 94 (July 23, 1989): 16. O'Hehir credits the character of Obasan with supplying most of the energy in *The Floating World*. The article is useful in its comment that Kadohata is writing not an ethnic history but a history that could have happened to any set of characters. O'Hehir stresses the episodic structure of the novel and Kadohata's direct and straightforward tone.

Pearlman, Mickey. "Cynthia Kadohata." In *Listen to Their Voices: Twenty Interviews with Women Who Write*. New York: W. W. Norton, 1993. Pearlman's interview analyzes Kadohata's first two novels in terms of Kadohata's own life and her ideas about writing. Pearlman discusses issues of cultural identity and queries Kadohata about what effect being a "hyphenated American" has on her writing. The interview also briefly discusses other Asian American writers.

See, Lisa. "Cynthia Kadohata." *Publishers Weekly* 239 (August 3, 1992): 48-49. Interview in which Kadohata relates incidents in her life to events in her novels. See and Kadohata discuss the process of writing as it fits into Kadohata's life. The article is especially useful for its discussion of what the character Obasan represents in *The Floating World*.

*Jill B. Gidmark*

# FOOLS CROW

*Author:* James Welch (1940-    )
*Type of plot: Bildungsroman*
*Time of plot:* 1869-1870
*Locale:* The Montana Territory
*First published:* 1986

> *Principal characters:*
> FOOLS CROW (WHITE MAN'S DOG), a young Blackfeet who comes of age
> as his tribe's existence is threatened
> FAST HORSE, a boyhood friend of Fools Crow who becomes disenchanted
> with the Blackfeet way of life
> RIDES-AT-THE-DOOR, Fools Crow's father, a Blackfeet war chief
> RED PAINT, Fools Crow's loving and devoted wife
> MIK-API, a medicine man who teaches Fools Crow

*The Novel*

    *Fools Crow* is the story of a young Blackfeet man who learns the customs of his tribe even as his people confront the destruction of their culture by the westward expansion of white settlers. The novel consists of five parts narrated in the third person by an omniscient voice.

    White Man's Dog is the oldest son of a powerful Blackfeet war chief. As the story begins, he has earned only mockery from the other members of his band, the Lone Eaters, having demonstrated no particular courage or wisdom. When White Man's Dog performs well on an expedition to steal horses from the neighboring Crow tribe, the young brave knows he has taken the first step toward manhood. His power continues to grow when Mik-api leads White Man's Dog to the mythic Raven. Raven sends the boy on a quest to rescue a wolverine caught in a steel trap. Wolverine becomes White Man's Dog's "power animal," a source of physical and spiritual strength.

    Beginning to acquire real stature, White Man's Dog learns the ways of healing from Mik-api and takes a bride, Red Paint, the daughter of Yellow Kidney, a noble warrior who disappeared on the adventure in Crow territory. Fast Horse, a boyhood friend of White Man's Dog, was also a member of the horse-taking party. When Yellow Kidney returns, badly maimed by the Crows who captured him, he tells the Lone Eaters that Fast Horse's loud boasting in Crow camp led to his capture. While Yellow Kidney speaks, the already sullen and bitter Fast Horse disappears in the night. Later, he is spotted in the gang of Owl Child, a renegade Blackfeet who lives to rob and kill the whites who advance into Indian territory to cut wood and raise cattle.

    Even though Red Paint, now pregnant, asks White Man's Dog not to go, the young man joins the war party that rides against the Crows to avenge Yellow Kidney. White Man's Dog is lucky in battle, but the members of his band think he is cunning, and they give him a new name—Fools Crow. In the autumn, after a company of soldiers rides into camp looking for Owl Child's band, Fools Crow and Red Paint go off alone into the Rocky Mountains, the "Backbone of the World," to celebrate in peace the child they will have together. While they are away, Fools Crow performs another task for Raven, killing a white man who had been slaughtering too much game. The Lone Eaters approve of Fools Crow's actions, but they warn one another against waging a war with the white settlers that they may not be able to win.

As had been feared, the coming winter brings violence. Fast Horse, who had been injured by a white rancher and returned to the Lone Eaters to be healed by Mik-api, rejoins Owl Child's gang and seeks his revenge. Fools Crow is on Fast Horse's trail, but he cannot prevent the murder of the rancher and the rape of his wife. Meanwhile, Yellow Kidney, waiting out a blizzard in a war lodge not far from where Fast Horse murdered the rancher, is shot by another white man seeking revenge. The conflict has become too much for the settlers, and the Blackfeet are asked to send all of their chiefs to a meeting with soldiers and other government officials. Rides-at-the-door, representing the Lone Eaters, listens as the Blackfeet are threatened with destruction if they should refuse to accept the invasion of their land peacefully.

When Fast Horse and Owl Child ambush a supply wagon moving through Blackfeet country, even the renegades know that the soldiers will punish innocent people in the nearby camps for their murderous actions. The signs of impending doom abound. News of a wave of smallpox sweeping the Indian camps reaches the Lone Eaters. Fast Horse discovers the body of Yellow Kidney and sends him back to his people lashed to travois poles. Nitsokan, "dream helper," visits Fools Crow and sends the warrior on a journey. Fools Crow believes this adventure will somehow enable him to help his people survive the tragedy that has befallen them.

Nitsokan leads Fools Crow to Feather Woman, an important figure in Blackfeet mythology who suffers daily for a sin she committed in ancient times. Feather Woman creates a magical skin painting that reveals to Fools Crow a vast village of Blackfeet suffering from smallpox, an army of soldiers riding against the camps, and hunting grounds empty of buffalo or any other game.

Although much of what the magic skin reveals quickly comes to pass, some of the Lone Eaters, including Fools Crow, Red Paint, and their newborn son, Butterfly, survive. The novel ends as the Lone Eaters celebrate the arrival of spring with a traditional ceremony. The buffalo have returned to the hunting ground, and Fools Crow believes that the Blackfeet have been chosen to survive.

*The Characters*

Fools Crow embodies the noblest qualities of traditional Blackfeet existence. He learns from the warrior Yellow Kidney, the medicine man Mik-api, and the chief Rides-at-the Door, his father. Fools Crow becomes courageous, loyal, and brave. Through Fools Crow, both the earthly and spiritual aspects of tribal life are illustrated. He hones his skills as a buffalo hunter and a horse-taker, and he becomes a good provider for Red Paint. At the same time, Fools Crow studies the mystical ways of healing and performs quests for spirits such as Raven and Nitsokan. He is a hero of epic proportion, literally the hope of his people.

Fast Horse, a mean, boastful young man who grows up to be a ruthless killer, shows that Blackfeet culture is not immune to the dark side of human nature. In contrast to Fools Crow, Fast Horse loses his faith in the spirits that govern the Lone Eaters and spurns the wisdom of his elders. When Fast Horse becomes a renegade, living on the run, Fools Crow meets him again and understands that there is a certain pleasure to an existence unfettered by the complex laws and beliefs of the Lone Eaters. The outlaw's life is also a solitary one, however, and the reader knows that Fast Horse will die broken and uncomforted.

Rides-at-the-door is a strong brave who has led many war parties. He is a wise and intelligent man who has learned English and understands that the U.S. government is a grave threat to all the Blackfeet bands. Rides-at-the-door, like the tribe as a whole, wrestles with a conflict between pragmatism and pride. He knows that the Lone Eaters and the other bands cannot defeat the white soldiers, but he is unwilling to surrender the land that has always been their home. In his dealings with his sons, with other chiefs, and with the whites, Rides-at-the-door struggles to find the honorable path.

Red Paint is a figure of selfless love. Her concerns are always for others. Reflecting on the various tragedies that have struck her family—the mutilation of her father by the Crows and the smallpox that infects her brothers—Red Paint knows that she would trade her own happiness with Fools Crow to restore their well-being. Red Paint's virtue is rewarded by the safe return of Fools Crow from the land of Feather Woman and by the healthy birth of Butterfly. She represents the redemptive quality of loving human relationships.

Mik-api, the Lone Eater's healer, is a keeper of the ancient ways of the Blackfeet. This is symbolized by the fact that, while other character's names are given in English, Mik-api's is always in the tribal tongue. Mik-api's character brings before the reader the issue of "medicine," a word that conveys a sense not merely of healing but also of overall power. When the novel begins, Mik-api's medicine is strong. He cures members of the tribe and, most important, helps Fools Crow to acquire power. When smallpox ravages the camp and the government continually imposes its will on the tribe, however, it becomes evident—to Mik-api, Fools Crow, and the reader—that the Blackfeet medicine has failed.

*Themes and Meanings*

*Fools Crow* is both an elaborate portrayal of the Western American Indian way of life and an effort to document the outside pressures that crippled this indigenous culture. The novel contains intricate details of the everyday events of tribal life. When Red Paint cooks or treats a skin, the reader is taught that chokecherries are used to flavor meat and that brains are rubbed into hide in order to soften it. The methods and customs of Mik-api's healing rituals and seasonal celebrations such as the Sun Dance and the Thunder Pipe ceremony are also delivered in vivid detail. Welch relies on an extremely realistic style to convey these images. This literary approach translates easily into what critics sometimes call Magical Realism (the description of supernatural events in natural terms) when the novel turns its attention to the dreams and visions that guide Fools Crow's coming of age. Having acquainted the reader with a full range of Blackfeet experiences, the novel then undertakes the difficult task of giving a balanced account of the circumstances that brought about the tribe's downfall.

This balance is achieved primarily by the contrast between the nobility of such characters as Fools Crow and Rides-at-the-door and the savagery of Owl Child and Fast Horse. When Rides-at-the-door listens to the director of Indian policy tell the Blackfeet chiefs that vital provisions promised in previous treaties will be withheld unless the tribe meets further demands, the reader's sense of justice is bound to be injured. On the other hand, when Fast Horse empties his rifle into an unsuspecting rancher's body while Owl Child rapes the man's wife, it is understood that such conduct is likely to inspire retribution. Welch selects a tone of inevitability with which to relate the tragic circumstances that culminate in a vicious massacre of women and children along the banks of the Marias River. As white settlers gradually move their cattle herds into buffalo hunting grounds and establish military outposts to protect the ranch houses that spring up in increasing numbers, even a reader unfamiliar with the history of Western settlement will sense the inevitability of bloodshed.

While the novel sensitizes the reader to an important and troublesome episode in American history, it is not a dry or unemotional text. Welch heightens the reader's interest by evoking a panoply of human impulses that cross cultural boundaries. The love between parents and children and husbands and wives contrasts with the hatred between enemies and feelings of jealousy toward more successful peers. Although Fools Crow struggles with fear, shame, and guilt, his character is strong and his luck is good. He enjoys a high degree of personal satisfaction. The themes of cultural disintegration and personal achievement are woven together when, before setting out on his quest for Feather Woman, Fools Crow asks himself, "What good is your own power when the people are suffering . . . ?" A profound discussion of the relationship between the individual and society is the ultimate achievement of the novel.

*Critical Context*

*Fools Crow* is James Welch's most critically acclaimed work of fiction. The book received many commendations, including an American Book Award. The academic community has also responded enthusiastically, finding in the novel an example of excellence in cultural criticism and literary technique.

*Fools Crow* provides historical background, a careful representation of Blackfeet customs and beliefs, crucial to the understanding of Welch's other published works, which all share the overarching theme of the plight of the Native American in contemporary society. A reader's sensitivity to the depiction of reservation life in *Winter in the Blood* (1974) or to the complex issue of assimilation discussed in *The Indian Lawyer* (1990) will be greatly enhanced by the Native American consciousness evoked in *Fools Crow*. Along with such writers as Louise Erdrich, N. Scott Momaday, and Leslie Marmon Silko, Welch has helped to make the Native American novel an important part of American fiction in the second half of the twentieth century.

*Fools Crow* is a virtuoso performance of the craft of fiction. From the suspense of Fools Crow's first horse-taking expedition to the tense negotiations between Blackfeet chiefs and government agents and the incredible pathos of the aftermath of the Marias River massacre, the novel displays a wider range of emotion than any of the author's other works of fiction. *Fools Crow* blends the narrative control of Welch's earlier novels with the lyric intensity of his collection of poems *Riding the Earthboy Forty* (1971).

*Bibliography*
Berner, Robert. "Quaternity in James Welch's *Fools Crow*." In *Entering the Nineties: The North American Experience*, edited by Thomas E. Shirer. Sault Sainte Marie, Canada: Lake Superior University Press, 1991. Berner focuses on the narrative structure of the novel. He assesses the relationship between the plotline and Welch's use of symbols.
Bovey, Seth. "Whitehorns and Blackhorns: Images of Cattle Ranching in the Novels of James Welch." *South Dakota Review* 29 (Spring, 1991): 129-139. Discusses the cultural clash between Blackfeet and white settlers from an agricultural point of view. Compares images of ranching in *Fools Crow* with the same subject in Welch's first novel, *Winter in the Blood*.
Owens, Louis. "Acts of Recovery: The American Indian Novel in the Eighties." *Western American Literature* 22 (May, 1987): 53-57. A brief discussion of *Fools Crow* in relation to works by Native American writers Louise Erdrich and Michael Dorris.
Sands, Kathleen Mullen. "Closing the Distance: Critic, Reader, and the Works of James Welch." *The Journal of the Society for the Study of Multi-Ethnic Literature of the United States* 14 (Summer, 1987): 73-85. Sands probes the theme of alienation in Native American culture. She analyzes Welch's relationship to both critical and casual readers. *Fools Crow* is discussed alongside Welch's earlier works, including his poems.
Westrum, Dexter, "James Welch's *Fools Crow*: Back to the Future." *San Jose Studies* 14 (Spring, 1988): 49-58. Dexter analyzes the novel from the point of view of cultural studies. Particular attention is given to the novel as a historical account of the massacre on the Marias.

*Nick David Smart*

# THE FOURTEEN SISTERS OF EMILIO MONTEZ O'BRIEN

*Author:* Oscar Hijuelos (1951-    )
*Type of plot:* Family
*Time of plot:* The twentieth century
*Locale:* Pennsylvania, Cuba, New York, California, and Alaska
*First published:* 1993

> *Principal characters:*
> EMILIO MONTEZ O'BRIEN, an actor and photographer, youngest child and only son of Nelson and Mariela Montez O'Brien
> MARGARITA MONTEZ O'BRIEN, the eldest O'Brien child, a Spanish teacher
> NELSON O'BRIEN, an Irish immigrant and sire to fifteen children
> KATHERINE ANNE (KATE) O'BRIEN, Nelson's sister, who dies of pneumonia soon after she and her brother settle in Pennsylvania
> MARIELA MONTEZ O'BRIEN, Nelson's wife, a Cuban immigrant and mother to fifteen children
> GLORIA MONTEZ O'BRIEN, the youngest O'Brien daughter, who is hopelessly in love with younger brother Emilio
> ISABEL MONTEZ O'BRIEN, the second O'Brien daughter, who marries a Cuban and settles in Cuba
> MARIA MONTEZ O'BRIEN, the third O'Brien daughter, a successful singer
> LESTER THOMPSON, Margarita's wealthy and abusive first husband
> BETSY MACFARLAND, Emilio's first wife, a golddigger
> JESSICA BROOKS, Emilio's beloved second wife, who is running a restaurant in Alaska when he meets her
> LESLIE HOWARD, a courtly octogenarian pilot whom Margarita meets and marries when she is ninety

## The Novel

*The Fourteen Sisters of Emilio Montez O'Brien* opens with a chart of those sisters and of Emilio in order of their dates of birth. Their story, though, begins with the migration to the United States of Nelson O'Brien, a young Irish photographer, and his sister Kate. When Kate dies of pneumonia soon after they settle in bucolic Cobbleton, Pennsylvania, a despondent Nelson goes off to Cuba to cover the Spanish-American War. In Santiago, Cuba, he meets and marries Mariela Montez and begins the large and lively family whose experiences are the subject of Oscar Hijuelos' third novel. Concentrating on Margarita, the eldest, born in 1902, and Emilio, the youngest, born in 1925, the book traces the experiences of the O'Briens throughout most of the twentieth century.

As the opening sentence proclaims, "The house in which the fourteen sisters of Emilio Montez O'Brien lived radiated femininity." That radiation is powerful enough to cause horses to throw their riders, cars to skid into ditches, and a plane to fall from the sky; Hijuelos endows his gynocratic household with Magical Realism. One of the sisters, Patricia, is even explicitly clairvoyant, adept at divining the fates of her many siblings; however, recognizing a rival to his narrative authority, Hijuelos relegates Patricia to a minor role and characterizes her as reluctant to indulge in prophecy.

Patriarch Nelson O'Brien senses himself condemned to solitude in his own crowded home, and his proficiency at generating daughters perplexes and perturbs him. He rejoices when his final, fifteenth, child turns out at last to be a son. For Emilio, surrounded and coddled by a mother and fourteen sisters, woman sets the standard.

Emilio is not born until the middle of the novel, and the focus of the first third of the book is on Margarita and her largely erotic longings. Her adolescent fantasies focus on a barnstorming pilot whose plane becomes disabled near the O'Brien house. Margarita's marriage to the wealthy Lester Thompson proves to be a disaster and, after sixteen years, ends in divorce. In later years, Margarita finds fulfillment in teaching and in travel. She becomes the lover of a Cuban she meets in Spain and later, at the age of ninety, marries a pilot named Leslie Howard. In a culmination of her adolescent dreams about the demobilized aviator who came to stay with the O'Briens so very long ago, she learns at last to fly.

As a child, Emilio is especially attached to Margarita, while sister Gloria develops an unseemly crush on him. He eventually breaks free of coddling by the female O'Briens when he enlists in the Army, serving in the infantry during fierce combat in Italy. When World War II concludes, Emilio goes to New York to make his mark as an actor. After some success on the stage, he moves to Hollywood, where, during a career that lasts five years, he makes forty-two B-films. Using the screen name Montgomery O'Brien, he becomes popular playing private investigator Lance Stewart as well as Tarzan, but he is undone by womanizing. Marriage to a manipulative fan ends in ruinous divorce, and Emilio abandons Hollywood stardom for work on an oil rig in Alaska. It is there that he meets and falls in love with Jessica Brooks. Their marriage is joyful, and Emilio is devastated when Jessica and their baby die in a fire. He eventually recovers from severe alcoholic depression to commence a new career in California as "photographer to the stars," thereby resuming the family business that first brought Mariela Montez into the Santiago studio of Nelson O'Brien.

*The Fourteen Sisters of Emilio Montez O'Brien* is an old-fashioned collation of life studies, a patient record of moments from ten decades. Photography often provides its pretext for narration. When, at various stages of their lives, Nelson, who continues with his camera work even after opening the Jewel Box Movie Theater, assembles his family for a group portrait, Hijuelos proceeds to tell the story behind the picture. After Emilio retires from work in front of a lens and himself becomes a photographer, much of the rest of the story is generated by either the new prints that Emilio produces or the old ones that he ponders.

In the novel's epigraph, Nelson explains to Emilio his preference for the archaic shuttered, folding-bellows camera that, as late as 1937, the older man still prefers to use, because it "captures not only the superficial qualities of its subjects but also, because of the time it takes to properly collect light, their feelings, as they settle on the subjects' expressions; sadness and joy and worry, with variations therein, are collected on the plate." It is a manifest parallel to Hijuelos' own device for arresting the fleeting images of existence—the sadness and joy and worry, with variations therein, experienced by each of the O'Briens. For Hijuelos, memory is photographic, if imperfect, and his storytelling is inspired by and analogous to the photographer's dream of retaining traces of light—and life—on paper.

*The Characters*

As a title, *The Fourteen Sisters of Emilio Montez O'Brien* is a misnomer, or at least misleading. With an expansive, rhapsodic style, the novel celebrates fecundity, but it does not give equal time or attention to all fourteen sisters. Emilio, though not born until more than a third of the book is finished, is the object of as much narrative interest as any of the other O'Brien offspring. The first O'Brien child is old enough to be mother to the youngest, whom she in fact suckles as an infant.

Margarita is a creature of exquisite, insatiable longing, through sexual and romantic trials that span the twentieth century. Emilio is an Olympic philanderer whose brief brush with vulgar glamour suffuses the story with melancholy over mutability. He is graced by an acquaintance with Errol Flynn and enshrined in celluloid. Rather than three-dimensional personalities, most of the other O'Briens are types, for whom a simple set of traits suffices: Helen is a beauty, Irene "ever-plump" and omnivorous, Veronica compassionate, Violeta "pleasure-bound and promiscuous."

Similarly, the non-O'Briens in the novel are foils to and extensions of the story's central figures. Lester Thompson, the wealthy sadist whom Margarita marries, is a cad who serves to test and reveal his young wife's qualities. Leslie Howard, the gentle, loving pilot she marries when she is ninety, enables the plot to circle back to Margarita's girlish dreams of erotic fulfillment with an aviator. Emilio's two wives are a comparable study in contrasts: Betsy MacFarland, who seduces him in Montana and soon traduces him in California, serves as an agent of cosmic retribution for the film star's arrogance and philandering, while Jessica Brooks, the spunky woman he meets in Alaska, illustrates the possibility of true love and its fragility.

Aside from Margarita and Emilio, Nelson O'Brien, the family patriarch, is the novel's most prominent personality. The plucky young photographer is crushed by the death of his beloved sister shortly after their immigration from Ireland. Thereafter, despite ostensible energy and cheerfulness, Nelson nurses a secret melancholy evident in occasional boozing binges and in fits of depression. He never entirely adjusts to his life in America and in a household of fifteen women.

Early in their marriage, Nelson plucks Mariela from her native Cuba and brings her back to Cobbleton, a foreign town that mystifies and terrifies her and where only one other resident, a Puerto Rican butler named Herman Garcia, speaks Spanish, the only language in which Mariela is ever comfortable. In part because most of them do not speak her language, the family takes Mariela in her role as dependable matriarch for granted. After Mariela's death, however, Margarita discovers notebooks that reveal a complex emotional life none of the O'Brien children had suspected in their mother.

Yet nothing seems lost on the narrator. Hijuelos recounts the experiences of his characters from the perspective of an omniscient storyteller who has complete access not only to the events of their lives but also to their hidden hopes, joys, and disappointments. The book's presentation of its characters is magisterial; it offers detailed, authoritative portraits of Nelson, Mariela, and their children as they develop over the decades.

### Themes and Meanings

*The Fourteen Sisters of Emilio Montez O'Brien* resumes Hijuelos' project of divulging the sordid secret that all lives are defeated by the treachery of desire. He suffuses his third novel with the melancholy of futile longing. As a B-film actor, Emilio exploits the desires of those who gaze at his bright image in darkened theaters, but his first disastrous marriage occurs when Emilio himself succumbs to the wiles of an opportunistic fan—"once again he had allowed himself to be taken in by his own desire," observes the narrator, explaining both Emilio's seduction by Betsy MacFarland and a general law of the Hijuelos universe, where characters are forever longing and never achieving satisfaction for long.

*The Fourteen Sisters of Emilio Montez O'Brien* continues Hijuelos' project of chronicling the experiences of Cuban immigrants in the United States. Cobbleton is not very hospitable to a Hispanic newcomer, and Mariela Montez is obliged to forfeit much of her native culture when she abandons Cuba and follows her new husband to Pennsylvania. The novel dramatizes the process by which her children assimilate to the dominant society, and it suggests a haunting sense of loss felt by both the immigrant generation and its offspring.

Half a dozen years later, Nelson warns his eldest daughter always to use English with him, " 'cause in this country it's been my observation that Spanish will be of little use to you, certainly useless to you as far as gainful employment and one day finding yourself a husband." Though Margarita becomes a Spanish teacher and Isabel marries a Cuban pharmacist and moves to Santiago, the youngest of the siblings learn little or none of their mother's mother tongue. Yet in the confluence of Yankee optimism and Latin fatalism, the sanguine blood does not win out. Publicly exuberant, Nelson takes to private tippling, as insulation against his chronic melancholy. Hijuelos' theme, like that of much classic American fiction, is the revenge of the past on the self-assured man.

### Critical Context

The first book published by Hijuelos after the huge critical and popular success of *The Mambo Kings Play Songs of Love* (1989), *The Fourteen Sisters of Emilio Montez O'Brien* was greeted with the attention and respect appropriate to its author's new prominence. Like Mexican Americans Sandra Cisneros and Richard Rodriguez, Hijuelos owed his public success not only to talent but to timing and a Latino identity as well. His third novel, though, is an ambitious bid to transcend the Cuban American experience. Through the offspring of an Irish father and a Cuban mother, who blend "continents of blood and memory—from Saracen to Celtic, Scythian to Phoenician, Roman to pagan Iberian, African to Dane, a thousand female and male ancestors, their histories of sorrow and joy, of devastated suffering and paradisiacal pleasures linked by the progression of the blood," it attempts to mine particular experience for universal treasure.

*Bibliography*
Birkerts, Sven. *"The Fourteen Sisters of Emilio Montez O'Brien." The New Republic* 208, (March 22, 1993): 38-41. Birkerts reviews Hijuelos' career as a symptom of multiculturalism in contemporary American culture. He finds *The Fourteen Sisters* an unlikely successor to *The Mambo Kings Play Songs of Love* in both setting and narrative perspective. Birkerts finds Hijuelos' premise unwieldy, his plot weak, and his portrayal of characters unengaging.
Fein, Esther B. "Oscar Hijuelos's Unease, Worldly and Other." *The New York Times*, April 1, 1993, p. C19. During an interview, Hijuelos states: "I consider myself a New York writer of Cuban parentage with different influences." He insists that the O'Brien genealogy is as important as the Montez one and reveals that he was influenced not only by Gabriel Garciá Márquez but also by W. B. Yeats and Flann O'Brien, whose name is echoed in the book's title.
Mallon, Thomas. "Ripening in Pennsylvania." *The New York Times Book Review* (March 7, 1993): 6. Praises the novel's bountiful details and notes its bold sexuality. Contends that Hijuelos has created a realistic family chronicle that verges on the tall tale and applauds its willingness to celebrate joy.
Simpson, Janice C. *"The Fourteen Sisters of Emilio Montez O'Brien." Time* 141, (March 29, 1993): 63-64. Notes the novel's leisurely narrative rhythm and characterizes the book as a series of vibrant snapshots. Faults the novel for its portrayal of women in a dependent and nurturing role.
Span, Paula. "View from Another Room: Writer Oscar Hijuelos, Traveling Beyond His Window with *The Fourteen Sisters.*" *The Washington Post*, March 17, 1993, p. B1. Profile of Hijuelos that discusses his eagerness to explore another America, beyond New York and masculine sensibilities, in his third novel.

*Steven G. Kellman*

# FREDDY'S BOOK

*Author:* John Gardner (1933-1982)
*Type of plot:* Novel of ideas
*Time of plot:* The 1970's and the sixteenth century
*Locale:* Madison, Wisconsin, and Sweden
*First published:* 1980

> *Principal characters:*
> JACK WINESAP, a psychohistorian and lecturer
> SVEN AGAARD, a traditional historian, an expert in Scandinavian history
> FREDDY AGAARD, Sven Agaard's reclusive, eight-foot-tall son
> GUSTAV ERIKSSON VASA, a sixteenth century Swedish nobleman, the first king of independent Sweden
> LARS-GOREN BERGQUIST, his cousin and best friend
> HANS BRASK, Bishop of Linkoping
> THE DEVIL

*The Novel*

*Freddy's Book* is a dual fiction, a contemporary story that includes a historical novel with fantastic elements. The book probes the relationships of art to life and of human beings to one another.

The first section, "Freddy," takes up roughly a quarter of the entire work and serves as an introduction to the longer second half, "Freddy's Book," which is subtitled "King Gustav and the Devil." "Freddy" not only sets up the longer section but also places it in context by introducing the themes that flow throughout the entire work.

As the book begins, Jack Winesap, a psychohistorian and popular figure on the academic lecture circuit, has just finished speaking at a college in Madison, Wisconsin, when he meets Sven Agaard, an old-line traditionalist historian who believes that Winesap's methods are dubious and their results harmful to true historical and human understanding. Winesap agrees to be Agaard's guest at the older man's home during his visit, and while he is there, the debate between the two men continues, introducing many of the themes that are developed in the second half of the book. In particular, the two historians confront such basic issues as what constitutes truth in human experience and what role language plays in relaying that truth.

During their conversation, Agaard reveals that his son, Freddy, is a "monster." At first, Winesap dismisses this as exaggeration, but he later learns that it is in some ways true. Freddy Agaard is an eight-foot-tall recluse given to intense inner reflections. He is also an artist in his own right, and later, when Winesap is alone in the bedroom Sven Agaard has provided him, Freddy slips into the room and shyly deposits a manuscript. It is entitled "King Gustav and the Devil," and it is the second half of the novel.

"Freddy's Book," as Gardner entitles the section, recounts how Gustav Eriksson Vasa, a Swedish nobleman and patriot, leads a revolt against the ruling Danes in the sixteenth century to secure independence for his country. The struggle is a violent one, marked with vicious fighting and massacres, and Gustav triumphs only because he is aided by the Devil himself. Once in power, however, Gustav is obsessed with creating what he terms a "masterpiece," a government that will prove itself worthy of the Swedish people and provide for their lasting good. To accomplish this, Gustav realizes that he must cast his ally, the Devil, out of the Swedish kingdom.

This task Gustav assigns to two very different men, his cousin and closest friend, Lars-Goren Bergquist, and Hans Brask, the elderly, disillusioned Bishop of Linkoping. Bergquist, who, like Freddy Agaard, is an eight-foot giant of a man, believes in the power and goodness of the human spirit, but he has begun to question its effectiveness in the wider world. The brilliant cleric Brask, on the other hand, has felt his own spirit become dry and hard, a victim of the power of his intellect and his ability to manipulate rhetorical language to prove any point, however little he might believe it in spirit.

Together, Lars-Goren and Bishop Brask ride north to Lapland, where the Devil has established the seat of his power. Along the way, they engage in a continual series of philosophical discussions, the sort of dialogues that are common in Gardner's writings; the disputes between Grendel and the Dragon in *Grendel* (1971) and between the Sunlight Man and Police Chief Clumly in *The Sunlight Dialogues* (1972) are further examples of these intellectual exchanges. In these debates, the participants discuss key points that concerned Gardner throughout his career, especially the role of "moral" art in society, and how such art can not only comment upon the human condition but also actually improve it.

The moment for discussion ends when Lars-Goren and Bishop Brask pierce the white, snowy vastness of Lapland to confront the Devil in his lair. Although the narrative raises the possibility that this creature is only a devil, and not the Devil of Scripture, it is a monster of immense power and cunning, able for a while to hold both men at bay. Then Bishop Brask, breaking through his own world-weariness to a fresh hope in the triumph of good over evil, distracts the beast long enough for Lars-Goren to slash the Devil's throat with a knife made of Lapp reindeer horn. The Bishop, however, dies with his adversary in the struggle, and Lars-Goren and King Gustav are left to live in a world that has paradoxically lost both primeval evil and original innocence. "History," in the modern sense of the word, has begun, and human beings are on their own.

### The Characters

Jack Winesap and Sven Agaard are, in some ways, stock characters who represent philosophical positions in an ongoing debate about language as art and entertainment versus language as a guide to the truth. As is usually the case with Gardner's fictions, however, both are also fully realized, individual human beings who have specific characters and desires. In the case of Winesap, the overriding drive is to be liked and accepted; for Agaard, to be recognized as an accomplished and honest scholar. Freddy Agaard can be seen as a synthesis of them, becoming in his writings the historian as creator, the artist who transmutes the dry facts of the archives into a re-creation of actual human beings. As an artist, he is also in some ways a "monster," an individual set apart from the normal run of humanity. "Monster," both in its strict linguistic derivation and as Gardner uses it, does not necessarily connote a sense of horror or fear but simply someone set apart by a special gift or talent to "show forth" or reveal something essential to human existence. It is in this sense that Freddy Agaard is a monster, and "King Gustav and the Devil" is his finest product of showing forth, or illustrating, the facts of the human condition.

Within the confines of that book, Gustav Eriksson Vasa, the first king of Sweden, is a man torn between idealism and realism. Determined to create an independent nation with a monarchy that will serve his people, he finds that he must temper his noble nature by accommodating the brutal realities of politics, even if this means literally accepting the Devil himself as an ally. A master of political rhetoric, better known as propaganda, Gustav consoles himself with the rationalization that the end must justify the means for the cause of the greater good. Yet throughout the narrative he must constantly fight against self-doubt and even despair.

A similar conflict confronts his cousin Lars-Goren Bergquist and the elderly Bishop of Linkoping, Hans Brask. Both men have openly sworn allegiance to what the world commonly accepts as the good—for Lars-Goren, the right of a people to be free, especially in spirit; for Brask, the revealed truths of the Christian faith—but each is tormented by the gulf between his belief and the world. Unlike Gustav, they have no convenient political excuse for their actions and must instead face their doubts on an individual level. Lars-Goren does this by retreating to the comfort of his family, while Brask uses intellectual brilliance as his prop against despair. It is only after their philosophical discussions on the ride north to face the Devil have forced a merger of sorts in the two men that either can realize that good intentions are useless without action and that intelligence, however profound, means nothing unless it serves other human beings.

*Themes and Meanings*

*Freddy's Book* explores the central themes and meanings that occupied John Gardner throughout his career as an author, especially how an individual must act in order to be a decent human being and how an artist (who is always in some fashion a "monster") can both celebrate those actions and encourage them. This is what Gardner seems to have meant in his repeated discussions of moral fiction, which are articulated in *Freddy's Book*.

Art is both artifice and reality. It re-creates the real world while creating an independent world of its own. The characters in this novel, whether they are popular lecturers such as Jack Winesap, academic historians such as Sven Agaard, or romantic visionaries such as Freddy Agaard, are engaged in the same tasks. So, however, are persons in the "real world," such as King Gustav or his all-too-human servants, Lars-Goren and Bishop Brask. Each of them, in his individual fashion, must confront and defeat devils in many forms, whether of despair, cynicism, or popular indifference. The important point, which Lars-Goren and Bishop Brask come to understand and which Freddy Agaard articulates, is to face these devils, for it is in the confrontation itself that victory lies.

### Critical Context

*Freddy's Book* was Gardner's first volume after the publication of his controversial critical volume *On Moral Fiction* (1978), which dismissed most contemporary American writing as specious and insubstantial because it refused to treat important subjects in a worthy fashion. Gardner, who had been severely attacked on a number of fronts for the views he advanced in *On Moral Fiction*, seems to have used *Freddy's Book* as a way to respond to his critics by demonstrating what moral fiction was, how it could be done, and what it should accomplish.

First, moral fiction is serious, in that it deals with important issues that confront real human beings. When Jack Winesap and Sven Agaard talk, they are not merely discussing idle academic subjects but are debating what it means to know the past and what can be learned from it. In other words, they consider what history is in its truest sense. Freddy Agaard does not write a steamy historical potboiler but a true yet imaginative re-creation of a lost world that still has powerful and lasting impact on the way people think and live now. Even the characters in "King Gustav and the Devil" are not cardboard cutouts but fully realized human beings who confront the same sorts of passions and doubts and choices with which readers must grapple every day. In short, *Freddy's Book*, while it appears to be the sort of clever "novel within a novel" artifice that Gardner roundly attacked in *On Moral Fiction*, is actually a serious, in-depth dialogue that leads toward that greater understanding that Gardner always maintained was the major, perhaps sole, purpose of the novel, indeed of all true art.

### Bibliography

Butts, Leonard. *The Novels of John Gardner.* Baton Rouge: Louisiana State University Press, 1988. A relatively brief but helpful examination of Gardner's body of work. The novels are thematically grouped, with *Freddy's Book* being compared and contrasted with the earlier *Grendel*. In his conclusion, Butts terms *Freddy's Book* one of Gardner's "lesser works."

Cowart, David. *Arches and Light: The Fiction of John Gardner.* Carbondale: Southern Illinois University Press, 1983. One of the earlier full-length appreciations of Gardner's career, this volume still has some useful insights and observations. Its chapter on *Freddy's Book*, "History as Fiction, Fiction as History," is a generally perceptive reading of the novel.

MacCurdy, Carol. "On Moral Fiction: The Embattled John Gardner." In *Thor's Hammer*, edited by Jeff Henderson. Conway: University of Central Arkansas Press, 1985. Places *Freddy's Book* in the context of Gardner's call for moral fiction that addresses the serious issues of human life in a serious fashion. MacCurdy notes how many of the issues raised in Gardner's critical volume are expressed through the characters and plot of the novel. There is an interesting and informative comparison and contrast of *Freddy's Book* to the earlier *October Light*, which also contained a novel within a novel.

McWilliams, Dean. *John Gardner*. Boston: Twayne, 1990. An excellent introductory view of Gardner's life and work, with special emphasis on *On Moral Fiction*. There is a separate chapter on *Freddy's Book*. Notes and references, a selected bibliography, and a chronology make this book extremely useful.

Morace, Robert A. "John Gardner and His Reviewers." In *Thor's Hammer*, edited by Jeff Henderson. Conway: University of Central Arkansas Press, 1985. Discusses the critical reception of *Freddy's Book*, which puzzled some reviewers unable to deal with its complexities. Others, who were disturbed by the novels' two-part structure, accused Gardner of the cleverness he had attacked in *On Moral Fiction*. Only a relatively few perceptive critics fully understood Gardner's intentions and accomplishments.

Morris, Gregory. "The Limits of Borrowing: The Matter of John Gardner's Sources." In *Thor's Hammer*, edited by Jeff Henderson. Conway: University of Central Arkansas Press, 1985. Examines in detail Gardner's use of sources, which to some of his critics comes dangerously close to plagiarism. Morris cites numerous specific borrowings in *Freddy's Book* and also discusses the use of sources in Gardner's *The Life and Times of Chaucer* (1977), which was in many ways the sort of "psychohistory" discussed in *Freddy's Book*.

_____. *A World of Order and Light: The Fiction of John Gardner*. Athens: University of Georgia Press, 1984. Dealing with *Freddy's Book* in a chapter of its own, Morris provides useful background information, especially about the sources Gardner used. Morris explains the plot clearly and lucidly. His analysis is generally coherent and sensible.

*Michael Witkoski*

# FROM THE RIVER'S EDGE

*Author:* Elizabeth Cook-Lynn (1930-        )
*Type of plot:* Historical realism
*Time of plot:* The late 1960's
*Locale:* Missouri River country near Pierre, South Dakota
*First published:* 1991

> *Principal characters:*
> JOHN TATEKEYA, a Dakotah cattleman who seeks justice after the theft of
>     forty-two head of cattle
> AURELIA, John's young lover
> ROSE TATEKEYA, John's wife
> HARVEY BIG PIPE, an old friend of John
> JASON BIG PIPE, the son of Harvey, suitor of Aurelia
> WALTER CUNNINGHAM, the district attorney
> JOSEPH NELSON III, the defense attorney

*The Novel*

With the Missouri River as a background presence, its dammed-up waters forcing change upon Native American inhabitants of the South Dakota grasslands who have lived there for generations, *From the River's Edge* juxtaposes modern progress with the Native American struggle to retain a separate culture and identity in a world of white rules and white justice.

This fictional story, related by an unseen third-person narrator, is divided into three parts. Each corresponds, in turn, to the trial, summation, and verdict of the legal proceeding to establish the innocence or guilt of an unnamed young man accused of stealing John Tatekeya's cattle.

The novel beings soon after the discovery of the theft of forty-two cattle from John's herd. John, who is in his early sixties, is taciturn and reclusive, yet he is a respected member of the Dakotah Sioux community. He seeks help from the U.S. government to locate his missing animals. After finding three of the missing herd scattered throughout the countryside, he decides to pursue justice through the courts.

In his younger days, John had been a rodeo rider, somewhat wild and reckless, and sometimes in minor scrapes with the law. Now he finds himself somewhat disconcertingly on the other side of the justice system. As John at first rides the wide prairies and grasslands searching for traces of his missing cattle, he muses about his past and about the changes brought on by the damming of the great Missouri River, including the inundation of much of his own grazing land. During his silent and reflective searches, John visits acquaintances and friends, including Harvey Big Pipe, and tries to discover not only his missing cattle but also the significance of the changes around him.

During the trial, John is misunderstood, degraded, and finally made to seem guilty of stealing his own cattle. Neither the district attorney, the judge, nor even John's own attorney show any awareness of how John perceives the proceedings or that their sense of justice is not necessarily shared by him. Through all this, John is keenly aware of what is happening, but he makes no attempt to correct the bigoted notions of those involved. He feels that such an attempt would do no good. During the trial, the district attorney attempts to discredit John through disclosure of John's previous arrests and of his extramarital affair with a younger woman, Aurelia. Through flashbacks, the origins of John's and Aurelia's relationship, and the character of Aurelia herself, are made known.

As the trial drags on, John recalls histories of his people related to him by Old Benno and handed down from figures such as Smutty Bear, Struck-by-the-Ree, and his own great-grandfather, Grey Plume. The stories are about the earliest treaties with the whites and the broken promises that followed. History seems to repeat itself as the injustice, ignorance, and intolerance continue in the supposedly enlightened era of the novel's present.

Waiting for the trial's end, John becomes increasingly disillusioned and despondent. He keeps himself occupied doing chores on his ranch, and at one point he is visited by his younger brother, Dan. Dan talks him into attending the *wacipi*, an intertribal gathering in Bismarck, North Dakota. On the way, the two share memories of some wild youthful adventures, and John recalls his marriage and reflects upon his relationship with Rose. At the gathering, John seems to regain some lost sense of himself.

As the trial concludes, so does a phase of John's life. Aurelia decides to leave him for Jason Big Pipe, who, it turns out, was an unwilling accomplice in the theft of John's cattle. She feels that she, too, has now become part of John's larger betrayal. A young white man, who is never named, is found guilty of the theft of three of John's forty-two missing cattle, and soon after is free on bail. That day, John's barn is set on fire, apparently by the boy, in retribution. As his neighbors gather to help put out the blaze, John is finally overwhelmed by the events, and he collapses. Yet the novel's final images are positive: John and Rose reach a reconciliation of sorts, and John and Harvey pass on traditions to a young boy of the tribe.

*The Characters*

John Tatekeya, the Dakotah rancher whose cattle have been stolen, at first appears enigmatic. The reader may be at a loss to understand John's seemingly indifferent behavior toward the trial. Yet what seems a puzzling lack of response on John's part may be tied to the point of the story: that the crimes committed against John, by the individual and by the system, are only the most recent in a long legacy of prejudice and contempt. In other instances, the reader readily sympathizes with John's deep feelings toward the natural world, his respect for tradition, and his sense of personal honor. In the end, John is demystified; the story reveals him as a human being with understandable problems, concerns, obligations, and faults.

Aurelia, John's lover, is a beautiful young woman torn between two worlds. On one hand, Aurelia is respectful of the ways and traditions of her people; on the other, she is defiant of the proscriptions placed upon her by some of those same traditions. Closely monitored by her tradition-minded grandmother, Aurelia is in many ways emblematic of the struggle of women in any culture to be their own persons in the modern world. Readers can sympathize with Aurelia's decision, at seventeen, to become John's secret lover; she helps readers to understand the conflicting impulses to remain true to traditional values and at the same time to break free of outmoded ones. The only fully developed female character in the novel, Aurelia may symbolize the synthesis of old values and new.

Rose Tatekeya, John's wife, is seldom seen in the story until the ending. Rose may represent traditional values of womanly behavior and the inability of many women to embrace the changes of the modern world. Yet Rose is possessed of inner strength and awareness. She knows of John's affair, and her deep hurt is revealed when it becomes open knowledge. Yet, in the ways of her people, she stands by John in the end, not speaking of her own disappointments and supportive of his own deep anguish. In a patient and understanding way, in the aftermath of the trial and the burning of John's barn, she cries with him, and she reveals her belief that John's actions were never meant to hurt her.

Jason Big Pipe, the son of John's close friend Harvey, turns out to be involved in the theft of John's cattle. He betrays John during the trial, yet in other instances he seems respectful of tribal customs. Like Aurelia, he is trying to make sense of conflicting messages. Jason has been interested in Aurelia for some time, and he makes his intentions known to her late in the story.

Walter Cunningham, the district attorney, while clumsily seeking "justice," treats John as though he were an ignorant and uneducated child. At one point, Cunningham speaks enthusiastically to John of his hobby: the study of General George Armstrong Custer, the infamous "Indian fighter" who died at Little Big Horn. Like the defense attorney Nelson, Cunningham typifies the prejudice and ignorance historically shown Native Americans by the U.S. legal system.

*Themes and Meanings*

Though the progress of the narrative is charted by means of the trial, it is also closely tied to the changes in the land brought about by the new Oahe Dam. Likewise, John's search for those who stole his cattle is part of a larger struggle to make sense of the sweeping changes multiplying around him. The focus of the narrative is therefore not primarily on either John's investigation of the theft or on the trial that follows. Rather, the narrator takes readers with John as he visits his friends and neighbors, his own thoughts, and, through his memories, the spirits of former members of the Sioux tribe. Through these journeys, John's struggle to reconcile personal history and tradition with the new values he finds in the modern world is shown.

Interspersed among John's recollections of the past, and especially his remembrances of Old Benno, are the scenes of the trial itself. In these, the author takes the opportunity to examine the continuing mistreatment of Native Americans through the

American legal system. Her tone is often moderate rather than angry, however, and her method is often to portray characters ironically. The episodes of John's testimony and cross-examination during the trial, for example, while unmistakably critical of the button-down rigidity of the justice system, show that those who represent "justice" are clearly themselves unjust. Another example is the district attorney's preoccupation with the history of Custer. Cunningham's enthusiastic lecture to John about a figure notorious for bigotry and violence demonstrates that even those charged with upholding justice and preventing prejudice may actually be perpetuating the stereotypes and injustices of the past.

Paralleling John Tatekeya's proud sense of Native American people, their relationship to the land, and their traditions is the sense of change, both cultural and technological, introduced by the rapacious American culture. The Missouri River's flow is, in a sense, the current that carries the traditions of the past to the present for John. Though the course of the river has been altered, resulting in sometimes wrenching changes to the lives of those who live along its banks, for others, like Aurelia, the river itself continues. Following the new river's edge is "effortless" for her and indicates the promise of new possibilities.

Though the novel is set in the late 1960's, there is a sense of contemporary relevance and continuing concern over the treatment of Native Americans. As well, the novel raises questions concerning Native American views of their own culture, and the reader should perceive the book's determined questioning of values from within Native American society. John Tatekeya's various journeys, Aurelia's personal discoveries, the presence of the spirits of the past, and Rose's decision to stand by her husband all reveal issues of continuing relevance.

*Critical Context*

*From the River's Edge* is the first novel-length work by author Elizabeth Cook-Lynn. She previously published two collections of poetry, *Then Badger Said This* (1983) and *Seek the House of Relatives* (1985); a collection of her short fiction, *The Power of Horses and Other Stories*, appeared in 1990. In these works as well as in various magazine, journal, and review articles, Cook-Lynn has continued writing about people and themes related to the Sioux and Lakotah/Dakotah cultures of the South Dakota region of the United States. *From the River's Edge* reflects Cook-Lynn's continuing preoccupation with teaching as well, for the story seeks to impart a message to its readers about the cultural, historical, and political realities of the American Indian.

In *From the River's Edge*, Cook-Lynn departs from the sometimes folkloric approach taken in her earlier work, with mixed results. While the story of John Tatekeya at times reaches into myth and legend for anecdotal stories related by Old Benno or Grey Plume, the narrative never achieves the synthesis for which the author seems to be aiming. Such a combination of oral traditions and modern narrative technique would seem to go along with the overall theme of culture in transition; however, the attempt may suffer from the modern narrative voice itself, which some critics view as intrusive and preachy. Also, whereas her previous work was able to convey a realistic sense of Sioux heritage through songs, dances, social customs, and family interactions, *From the River's Edge* tells more about the culture of John Tatekeya and his people than it shows, and this may be a weakness of the novel.

The author should be credited, however, with producing a story that achieves a sense of complexity in many of its characters while avoiding stereotypes. Also, the apparent intent of the novel should be praised. The story seldom bogs down in overworked examples of white injustice toward Native Americans. Such scenes are present, but these episodes are interwoven with history and tradition of the Dakotah Sioux, and the result is a fairly successful interplay between the past and present.

*Bibliography*
Bruchac, Joseph. "As a Dakotah Woman: An Interview with Elizabeth Cook-Lynn." *Survival This Way: Interviews with American Indian Poets.* Tucson: University of Arizona Press, 1987. Through his interview, Bruchac shows some of the beliefs and motivations that influence Cook-Lynn's works. Cook-Lynn comments on her identity as a poet and discusses some of the concerns that show up in her writing, including religion and male/female relationships. Useful for background information regarding the author's works.
Houston, Robert. "Stealing Cattle and a Way of Life." *The New York Times Book Review* 96 (September 8, 1991): 35. Houston sees the novel as originating from the best motives and refers positively to its complexity, but he comments that the execution is flawed. He objects to heavyhanded dialogue and confusing diction in the story and complains that the novel merely tells about incidents rather than shows them.
Jordan, Robert. Review of *From the River's Edge*, by Elizabeth Cook-Lynn. *Library Journal* 116 (May 15, 1991): 108. Jordan comments on how the novel is based upon an actual trial. He suggests that though the story is an isolated portrait of the period, its characters are multifaceted. Jordan also makes brief comparisons to other novels and to the film *Dances with Wolves* (1990).
Kino, Carol. "Old Loyalties." *The Times Literary Supplement*, October 16, 1991, 4620. Kino praises the day-to-day details of the Indian characters as honest portrayals. Kino, however, objects to Cook-Lynn's mingling of fact and fiction, noting that John Tatekeya's dialogue comes from actual court transcripts. Kino suggests that this interferes with the truth of the character.

*George Thomas Novotny*

# A GATHERING OF OLD MEN

*Author:* Ernest J. Gaines (1933-    )
*Type of plot:* Social realism
*Time of plot:* The late 1970's
*Locale:* Louisiana
*First published:* 1983

> *Principal characters:*
> MATHU, an old black man in whose yard the body of Beau Boutan, a
>     Cajun boss on the plantation, is discovered
> CANDY MARSHALL, a thirty-year-old white woman who owns the planta-
>     tion land on which Mathu and other African Americans live
> CYRIL ROBILLARD (CLATOO), the first of the old men who recognizes the
>     significance of their stand
> ROBERT LOUIS STEVENSON BANKS (CHIMLEY), the old man who gathers
>     the others together
> MATTHEW LINCOLN BROWN (MAT), one of the first old men to gather
> LOUIS ALFRED DIMOULIN (LOU DIMES), a reporter who is dating Candy
> SHERIFF MAPES, the investigating officer
> FIX BOUTAN, the patriarch of the Cajun family, famed for vigilantism
> GILBERT BOUTAN, one of Fix Boutan's sons, representative of the new
>     generation
> CHARLIE BIGGS, Mathu's godson and the actual killer of Beau Boutan

*The Novel*

    *A Gathering of Old Men* is written in the first person and is narrated by fifteen separate voices. The book tells the story of one day, one killing, and the coming-of-age of a community in Louisiana in the 1970's. Ernest Gaines, a master of first-person storytelling, creates in this work a continuous narrative seen from many very different points of view.

    At the opening of the novel, a Cajun boss, Beau Boutan, has been murdered in the Quarters, a section of an old Louisiana plantation. Suspicion naturally falls on Mathu, an elderly African American man on whose doorstep the body lies. Candy Marshall, the young white woman who owns the plantation, sends word to all the black families in the area to bring the elderly black men of the community to Mathu's home. At the same time, she declares that she herself shot Boutan. There is fear that retaliation for the killing will come either from the legitimate authority, Sheriff Mapes, or more dangerously from Fix Boutan, who is the elderly head of Beau's Cajun family, which is notorious for vigilantism.

    About eighteen old men gather at Mathu's house, each carrying a twelve-gauge shotgun that has been discharged and contains a number-five shell, thereby replicating the murder weapon. This is done at Candy Marshall's command, for Candy has taken on the role of protector. It turns out that she gets more than she bargained for.

Through the various narrative voices, readers follow simultaneously the thoughts and actions of the sheriff and his deputy, the Boutan family members, and the old African American men. It seems obvious to all the characters that despite Candy's claim, it is Mathu who is responsible for Beau's death. Tension builds as all the characters begin to converge on Mathu's house, where a standoff between Sheriff Mapes, Mathu, and Candy develops.

Candy Marshall is an untraditional plantation owner, being young, female, and on the side of the old black men rather than of the white authorities. She is incapable, however, of breaking out of the tradition of protectionism and patronage that views these elderly black men—even Mathu, who has helped to rear her and upon whom she deeply depends—as children who need to be cared for and watched over by white adults. Candy continues to give orders, even after it is clear that the men will handle the situation on their own, even after Mathu has told her that it is time for her to go home.

Meanwhile, Fix Boutan has learned of his son's death and is preparing to "fix" Mathu. Before any decisions are made, however, he has to wait for the family gathering to be complete. His son Gilbert has been notified at college and is returning home. Gilbert, a football player at Louisiana State University, has become known as half of an outstanding combination called "Salt and Pepper" because of the racial mixture of the duo. As a result, he does not harbor the bigotry of his family; he is not as eager as his father and his father's men to take matters into his own hands and go outside the law for revenge. After much debate of the matter, Fix agrees to go along with his son's wishes, at the same time disowning him.

Fix's man Luke Will and some of his cohorts refuse to abandon their vigilante ways, however, and they head off to Mathu's house. There, Charlie has returned and made his statement of guilt, first to Mathu, then in front of the others and to the sheriff. In the process, he has claimed both responsibility for his actions and his manhood. Sheriff Mapes prepares to take him in; however, by the time this is sorted out, Luke Will has arrived ready for action. Although, at Candy's bequest, the old men had all arrived with guns that had been fired and were therefore empty, they have since reloaded them in preparation for trouble with the Cajun community. Thus they are ready for Will and his thugs, and there is a shoot-out, with each of the old men fighting for his own sense of liberty and self-esteem. Sheriff Mapes is injured by Luke Will. Charlie Biggs, determined to protect his "fathers," is killed; in the ensuing gunfight, Will is also gunned down.

The novel ends with Lou Dimes reporting on the funerals of Beau and Luke in the Cajun community and of Charlie in the Quarters. Dimes also discusses the resulting investigation, which amounts to a trial of both the black and Cajun communities. Charlie and Luke, the instigators of the conflict, are both dead; the rest of the participants in the gun battle are put on probation for five years or until their deaths, whichever comes first—a reminder that these are all old men. The participants are also warned that they have lost the privilege of carrying any kind of firearm, and they are forbidden to be within ten feet of anyone who does—which, Dimes points out, is in Louisiana like telling the men never to say "Mardi Gras" or "Huey Long."

## The Characters

Mathu, an old black man more than eighty years old, is still tall and straight, a strong man who is the only African American ever to stand up to Fix Boutan. He is admired even by the sheriff, and Candy depends upon him. Mathu never says that he killed Beau, but neither will he deny it. He tells Mapes: "A man got to do what he thinks is right. . . . That's what part him from a boy." It is Mathu's influence that brings Charlie back to face up to his responsibility.

Several other of the old men stand out: Cyril Robillard, also known as Clatoo, is one of the first narrators to arrive on the scene of the murder and also the first of the old black men to realize the significance of the stand they are taking. Robert Louis Stevenson Banks, also known as Chimley, is the man who brings the gathering together. Matthew Lincoln Brown, also known as Mat, is one of the narrators; he has perhaps the deepest insight into the changes that are taking place.

Louis Alfred Dimoulin, also known as Lou Dimes, is the reporter who both is and is not a part of the community. He therefore can use his outsider's stance to observe the events.

Candy Marshall is an untraditional plantation owner. Although her sympathies are with the black community, her attitudes of patronage and protectionism place her squarely in the ranks of "good honkies" who mean well but cannot grasp that they are not necessary. She cannot understand that it is time for her to go home.

Sheriff Mapes is a racist, but he does intend to uphold the letter of the law in his community. He also learns to respect the black men who defy him, and he grows more human by the end of the novel; he is even injured trying to protect Charlie, the black man who has murdered Beau Boutan.

Fix Boutan is the patriarch of the Cajun community, noted for taking the law into his own hands and taking care of his own. Age has mellowed him somewhat, however, and he is willing to listen to his son, Gil, when Gil tells him that the time has come to leave justice to the law.

Gilbert Boutan, Fix's son, represents the new South. A Cajun college-student football player with a black friend, he needs to educate his father, despite the pain it causes.

Charlie Biggs, the murderer, kills Beau in a fit of anger. He first runs, but he returns to take responsibility and to be recognized as a man before he dies.

## Themes and Meanings

*A Gathering of Old Men* is difficult to classify; although it begins with an unsolved murder, it is much more than a mystery, and although it comments on social injustice, it is also the coming-of-age story of a whole community. Like much of Gaines's work, *A Gathering of Old Men* is concerned with the interrelatedness of human beings within a community, with the effects of bigotry and the historical fact of slavery on the relationships of people in the South, and with the ability of human beings to mature and gain wisdom and dignity no matter what their age.

In the Louisiana township where the story takes place, there are three distinct groups. The white community contains a range of people, from Sheriff Mapes, who is in a position of power that he uses according to his own discriminatory lights, to Candy, who sees herself as benevolent protector of the blacks who live on and work her land, to Lou Dimes, who is an outside observer. The members of the Cajun community, who are viewed by other whites as inferior, as a result enforce greater hardship on the blacks. The members of the African American community, who are mostly elderly or very young, struggle to survive. Yet the novel makes it clear that each community depends upon the others, and that there are connections between the groups that run deeper than they know. For example, some of the African American characters have names that obviously connect them with the Cajun community.

The clear divisions of these disparate groups are the result of historical and social forces (including slavery, discrimination, and respect for property rights) and are kept strong by bigotry, racism, and class divisions. Times are changing, however, and the balance of power begins to shift. In the novel, when the old African American men stand firm for themselves, not only must Mapes move beyond his racist enforcement of the law, but also Candy must give up her paternalism, Fix must stop his vigilantism, and the black community must take on both greater power and greater responsibility.

In Gaines's earlier *The Autobiography of Miss Jane Pittman* (1971), the title character, an elderly former slave, finally achieves her complete independence when she defies the white owner of the land on which she lives by walking past him to go to the protest in her town. Similarly, Charlie Biggs achieves his manhood by acknowledging his responsibility for the killing of Beau Bouton and refusing to run. At the same time, he refuses to be treated as a boy any longer, and he insists on being called "Mr. Biggs" by the sheriff.

*Critical Context*

In *A Gathering of Old Men*, Ernest Gaines returns to the use of the first-person narrative that was so successful in *The Autobiography of Miss Jane Pittman*; this time, however, he uses the technique in a more complex manner. Eleven black and four white narrators tell the story, each in a slightly different time and place. Many of the characters, particularly the old black men, have both given names and names by which they are known, and this fact seems to signify both the closeness of the community and the failure to recognize the men in their own right. The importance of naming stands out when Charlie demands to be called "Mr. Biggs," to be recognized as a fifty-year-old man, not a boy any longer. Like Miss Jane Pittman, Charlie must name himself to become his own person.

*A Gathering of Old Men* also echoes Richard Wright's story "The Man Who Was Almost a Man." In that short fiction, the narrator runs rather than face belittling treatment by his community, both black and white, and the responsibility for his actions; thus, he is "almost" a man. In Gaines's novel, Charlie Biggs becomes a man not by killing but by accepting responsibility for his action and demanding to be treated as a man.

Gaines combines both tragedy and comedy in his novel. During the shoot-out, some real deaths occur, but some of the action is almost slapstick in nature. The author seems to be saying that this is the human condition, to be heroic and to be silly, but the emphasis is on being fully human.

*Bibliography*

Babb, Valerie Melissa. *Ernest Gaines*. Boston: Twayne, 1991. An entry in the Twayne's United States Author's Series, this work begins with a helpful chronology and a brief biography, looks at Gaines's works in chronological order, and concludes with a selected bibliography. Includes a chapter entitled "Action and Self-Realization in *A Gathering of Old Men*" that contrasts the murder in the novel with that committed by Bigger Thomas in Richard Wright's *Native Son* (1940). Some useful interpretation.

Folks, Jeffrey J. "Ernest Gaines and the New South." *Southern Literary Journal* 24 (Fall, 1991): 32-46. Compares the treatment of the New South by Gaines and Flannery O'Connor. Points out that although both writers recognize that increased urbanization, mechanism, and materialism distort both individual identities and communal ties, neither sees the solution as fleeing. Rather, both authors argue that social and psychological needs must be met through the reassertion of primary human needs.

Gaudet, Marcia, and Carl Wooten. *Porch Talk with Ernest Gaines: Conversations on the Writer's Craft*. Baton Rouge: Louisiana State University Press, 1990. A useful collection of interviews with Gaines. Begins with an introduction, a brief biography, and a comprehensive index. The interviews are divided into subject areas; *A Gathering of Old Men* is discussed throughout the book.

Harper, Mary T. "From Sons to Fathers: Ernest Gaines' *A Gathering of Old Men*." *College Language Association Journal* 31 (March, 1988): 299-306. Harper focuses on the development of the movement of the "old men" of the community from ineffectual individuals into a group of respected father figures and role models for the younger generation. An interesting and informative work.

Rowell, Charles H. "The Quarters: Ernest Gaines and the Sense of Place." *The Southern Review* 21 (Summer, 1985): 733-750. Rowell sees the Quarters in Gaines's fiction as the central focus of Gaines's symbolic geography, the stage on which he works out his plots. Thus it becomes a microcosm in which all human aspirations, actions, and psychology can be worked out.

*Mary LeDonne Cassidy*

# THE GOOD MOTHER

*Author:* Sue Miller (1943-      )
*Type of plot:* Social realism
*Time of plot:* The 1970's
*Locale:* Primarily Cambridge, Massachusetts, with scenes in New Hampshire, Maine, Connecticut, and Chicago
*First published:* 1986

> *Principal characters:*
> ANNA DUNLAP, a musician and divorced mother
> BRIAN DUNLAP, Anna's former husband, a lawyer
> MOLLY DUNLAP, the three-year-old daughter of Brian and Anna
> LEO CUTTER, Anna's lover, an artist
> BUNNY, Anna's mother
> FRANK MCCORD, Anna's maternal grandfather, the patriarch of her mother's family
> URSULA, Anna's piano student and best friend

*The Novel*

The Good Mother is a fictional study of Anna Dunlap, a woman who has lived most of her life under the domination of someone else—first her mother, then her husband, Brian. When Anna divorces her husband and tries to build a new, more satisfactory life with her daughter, she achieves a certain brief happiness, but the price she pays is almost more than she can bear.

Anna is the first-person narrator of *The Good Mother*, which begins while Anna is in the process of divorcing Brian. The first chapter, one of fourteen, foreshadows the events of the entire book. On a retreat from the strain of her dissolving marriage, Anna rents a cottage in a small town in New Hampshire. As Anna and Molly attend a film, enjoy a café dinner, and get ready for bed, Miller's superb, realistic style evokes a close and loving relationship.

Anna receives legal papers from Brian's attorney that she must notarize and return the following day. Anna leaves Molly asleep in the car when she visits the filthy home of a reclusive notary in order to have the papers stamped. When she returns after her nightmarish experience, she finds that Molly has opened the car door to look for her and has been attacked by one of the cats that roam the property; Molly has been screaming in fright for some time. Comforting the child, Anna feels that she is not strong enough, not good enough, to rear her alone. Again and again in the novel, Anna creates a private Eden that is shattered when the larger world intrudes.

Anna's early life is told in flashbacks of her mother's family, a handsome, high-strung group of five siblings dominated by Anna's grandfather, Frank McCord. He held Bunny and his other children to an unspoken standard of achievement and bound them with his approval or disapproval.

Anna was expected to have a brilliant career as a concert pianist. After Anna attended a summer music camp for two years, however, her teacher advised Bunny not to send her again, for Anna was not "musically gifted." After that summer, Anna felt that her life as a serious person was over.

Once resettled with Molly in Cambridge, Anna finds a friend, Ursula, among her piano students, and through her finds a part-time job testing memory retention in rats at a Boston University laboratory. Molly is happily enrolled at a day-care center, and the child fills Anna's evenings with love and innocent prattle. Although she knows that her life is limited and uncertain, Anna is content until she meets Leo Cutter, a Cambridge artist whose life is as tenuous as hers. With Leo, Anna finds the sexual fulfillment that she never had with Brian; however, she carelessly permits Molly to share their bed when the child is upset. This happens several times, and once when Anna and Leo are united in intercourse.

The following summer, Molly goes to Washington, D.C., to stay with Brian and his new wife for a month. After a few weeks, Anna receives a phone call from him saying he will not return Molly and that the decision has something to do with Leo. Anna spends an agony of waiting until Leo returns from his art show in New York. She then finds out that with no prurient motives, Leo did let Molly touch his penis once, at her request, when he was emerging from the shower. Molly has told her version of the incident to Brian.

Anna is soon enmeshed in a net of lawyers, family-service officers, and psychiatrists as she fights to retain custody of Molly. Each step of the legal process heightens the tension. In his testimony in court, Leo lets himself be blamed for the sexual indiscretions, but he is inwardly furious. Anna grows wary of him, and he feels betrayed. Still, he loves Anna and tries to salvage the relationship. The conservative judge decides against Anna, and she loses custody of Molly. In her extreme grief, Anna loses all feeling for Leo, and she abruptly moves to Washington to live near her child. Anna and Molly take a long, bitter time to make peace with their losses.

After a year and a half, Molly is doing well, and she moves back to Boston with her father and his now-pregnant wife. Anna returns to Cambridge, again to be near Molly. She creates a life for herself that is a shadow of what she had wanted, but she is a survivor.

*The Characters*

Anna, the "good mother," captures the sympathy of the reader from the start. As narrator, she shares her innermost thoughts with the reader, as well as her life and the characters who inhabit it. The story is told about four years after the events, and from Anna's changing perceptions of the other characters, it is clear that she has grown wiser. Although she gains a deeper appreciation of the value of a real family, Anna is also proud of the way she has "made do" with her own circumstances. Yet the novel is ambiguous; although Anna never sinks into self-pity, conditions suggest that she is a victim.

Brian, Anna's former husband, appears to be a thoroughly decent man, but he and

Anna have a tepid relationship, and she is frigid throughout their marriage. When Brian's law firm transfers him from Boston to Washington, Anna suggests that they separate. He has an affair with another woman who later becomes his wife while his marriage with Anna is dissolving. Later, when Anna discusses Brian with her psychiatrist in preparation for the custody battle, she wonders if he is not unconsciously punishing her for hurting him. Brian's horror at the sexual indiscretions with Molly reflects the views of society at large, for he is a man who plays by the rules.

Leo, Anna's lover, represents not only the sexual fulfillment that Anna lacked in her marriage but also a passionate approach to life that nobody in Anna's circle has ever held. He is a visual artist whom Anna describes as having "recklessness of the heart." Yet he is essentially one-dimensional, a sensual, intense, gifted artist who stands outside conventional society. Although his work is overtly what matters most to him, Anna is never drawn into this important aspect of his life, nor is he interested in her music.

Molly Dunlap, Anna and Brian's daughter, is one of the triumphs of the novel. She is the most important person in Anna's life, and Anna describes her daughter's physical presence and emotional states in exquisite detail. Molly's dialogue is appropriate for a three-year-old and also a subtle indicator of what is going on in the child's mind beneath her glib chatter. She is a bright, formerly happy child who is struggling to make sense of the torn world her parents have created.

Frank McCord, Anna's grandfather and patriarch of the family, exhibits the repressive Calvinism under which Anna grew up. He is both contemptuous and manipulative. Although she struggles to retain control of her life by refusing his offer of money, she finally loses whatever pride she has when she is forced to ask him to pay for her lawyer. An arrogant, successful, self-made man, Frank McCord holds everyone to the same standards he holds for himself.

*Themes and Meanings*

While the plot of *The Good Mother* centers on who retains custody of Molly, the real adversaries are not Anna and Brian. The true struggle is between Anna's experimentation and the traditional role that society demands of a mother.

Anna leaves a marriage that is apparently no better or worse than most, even though Anna is sexually unawakened during her marriage. Brian is so good that even though he does not really understand Anna's dissatisfaction, he is generous in the terms of the divorce and offers Anna custody of Molly without a quibble. There is a suggestion that Brian and the traditions he upholds accept Anna as long as she represents some idealized version of a virgin mother. While Anna centers her life around Molly, Brian is supportive and considerate.

Anna sets the engines of retribution in motion when she steps out of her chaste role as single mother to engage in a passionate love affair with Leo. As her sexuality flowers, her character also changes; she grows less passive and more sure of herself. Brian's attitude shifts; he recognizes that Anna has become a woman he never knew. When he hears of the sexual indiscretions she has permitted with Molly, he is poised to punish her in the harshest way he can: by legally taking the child from her.

By emphasizing the warmth and closeness between Anna and Molly throughout the novel, Miller leaves no doubt in the reader's mind that the child's interests would be best served by remaining with Anna. The psychiatrist who testifies on her behalf in court also recommends that Anna retain custody. Forced to enter the world of business and law to plead her case, however, Anna is helpless. Even Leo, assured to the point of arrogance in his own art world, is portrayed as inconsequential, even laughable, in the ill-fitting jacket he borrows to meet Anna's lawyer.

On the other side is Brian, a lawyer who knows how to use the system in which Anna is an outsider. Anna and Leo are being punished for violating the rules of society. By attempting to make up their own rules, they have forfeited the protections and safeguards enjoyed by those who conform. Significantly, it is Anna who is twice punished; she loses Molly and, because of her own withdrawal, loses Leo as well.

The part-time job training rats that Anna takes while living in Cambridge is perhaps a paradigm of her own condition. She runs rats through a maze and records how many tries it takes them to complete it before they learn in which direction a reward is waiting. At the end of the novel, when Anna is in a frenzy of sorrow and tries to reach Molly in Washington, Anna also becomes lost in a maze. Throughout the novel, Anna's own history of failed attempts (piano, marriage, motherhood, love affair) takes on overtones that suggest the lives of animals who only learn by trial and error, and then not very well.

A strong feminist theme is manifest in *The Good Mother*. Anna is not talented enough to have a career as a pianist, yet neither is she quite at home in the domestic sphere. When Leo expresses some disdain for her attitude toward her work, which is not the consuming passion that his is, Anna insists that her real commitment is to Molly, and "to doing carefully and well what I do." Indeed, the only role that she seems well suited for is that of a mother. Once that is taken away from her, she is left with very little.

*Critical Context*

*The Good Mother* was Sue Miller's first novel and became a great success. It sold well, was praised in reviews, and was widely discussed. The book reflects the concerns that Miller explored further in *Family Pictures* (1990) and *For Love* (1993). Each of the novels focuses on a family in trouble and the nature of loving relationships. In her books, Miller refuses to follow the conventions of happy endings, allowing only ambiguous futures for her characters after they struggle with conflict and pain.

The popularity of *The Good Mother* perhaps stemmed from its relevance to social problems that dominated public consciousness in the 1980's. The breakup of the American family, feminist concerns regarding the place of women in society, changing roles of mothers, sexual abuse of children, the personal in conflict with the public—all are themes that contribute to the complicated world of *The Good Mother*.

Far from suggesting answers to any of these problems, however, *The Good Mother* simply follows them to their logical conclusions within the context of the plot. Anna loses everything she holds dear by the end of the novel. The only constant is her love for Molly, which she never compromises or uses even for what may be the child's own good. Some critics have suggested that the popularity of *The Good Mother* resulted because the novel played on women's fear of being left alone, yet such a conclusion seems simplistic.

In *The Good Mother*, Sue Miller staked out her territory; the country of domestic conflict, where issues of love, control, and divided loyalties strip her characters bare. In subsequent works, she has continued to explore the extreme margins of this territory with sensitivity.

*Bibliography*
Drzal, Dawn Ann. "Casualties of the Feminine Mystique." *The Antioch Review* (Fall, 1988): 450-461. A feminist analysis comparing Anna's dilemma with other fictional heroines who are neither housewives nor career women. The problem is identified as the inability to find serious work. Drzal concludes that these women lead marginal, compromised lives.
Leber, Michael. "*The Good Mother*." *Library Journal* 111 (May 15, 1986): 79. Provides a good overview of the novel for the general reader and considers some of the techniques Miller uses to create the drama and high tension of the plot. Calls Miller's first novel "a stunner."
McManus, Barbara F. "Anna and Demeter: The Myth of *The Good Mother*." In *The Anna Book*, edited by Mickey Pearlman. Westport, Conn.: Greenwood Press, 1992. McManus discusses the novel as it parallels the Greek myth of Demeter and Persephone and as it resembles Leo Tolstoy's *Anna Karenina* (1875-1877) in the heroine's struggle between erotic and maternal love. Useful to someone with a serious interest in literature.
White, Roberta. "Anna's Quotidian Love: Sue Miller's *The Good Mother*." In *Mother Puzzles*, edited by Mickey Pearlman. New York: Greenwood Press, 1989. White examines the novel in terms of the different kinds of love (and absence of it) that influence Anna's life and fortune. White concludes that Anna's "capacity to sustain her love for her child through all the challenges to it constitutes a kind of heroism. . . ." This article should prove provocative to readers who find Anna more ordinary than heroic.
Zinman, Toby Silverman. "The Good Old Days in *The Good Mother*." *Modern Fiction Studies* 34 (Autumn, 1988): 405-413. Presents a sophisticated reading of the novel that places it in the context of what Zinman calls "nihilistic nostalgia." The term loosely means a style that loots the recent past for icons and then desecrates them. Anna's longing for her grandparents' primitive summer estate is the powerful nostalgia that rules Anna's life.

*Sheila Golburgh Johnson*

# GORKY PARK

*Author:* Martin Cruz Smith (1942-  )
*Type of plot:* Detective and mystery
*Time of plot:* The 1970's
*Locale:* Moscow and New York City
*First published:* 1981

> *Principal characters:*
> ARKADY RENKO, the chief homicide investigator for the Moscow police
> department
> MAJOR PRIBLUDA, a KGB agent
> PASHA PAVLOVICH, a plainclothes detective
> ANDREI IAMSKOY, a Moscow prosecutor
> ZOYA, Arkady's wife
> IRINA ASANOVA, a film student implicated in a murder case
> JOHN OSBORNE, an American fur dealer
> WILLIAM KIRWILL, a New York City policeman investigating the murder
> of his brother

*The Novel*

   *Gorky Park* is set in the Moscow of the 1970's, during the Leonid Brezhnev era, when the Soviet Union was still intact and viewed as a major threat to the United States. The main character, Arkady Renko, is a superb homicide investigator who is confronted with a baffling case: the murder of three people in Gorky Park—an unlikely setting for such a crime because it is so public and would seem to invite immediate detection. Yet the bodies are frozen, and even more strangely, their fingertips have been removed to destroy their fingerprints and their faces have been skinned, making physical identification extremely difficult. For Arkady, most cases are simple ones: one Russian kills another in a fit of passion or in a drunken spree. Truly interesting and intricate cases—usually involving politics and affairs of state—are the province of the Komitet Gosudarstvennoi Bezopasnosti (KGB), the Soviet Union's secret police.

   Even before Arkady can investigate the scene of the crime thoroughly, he is interrupted by Major Pribluda, a KGB agent who handles the bodies roughly, thus destroying (Arkady fears) vital evidence. Yet Arkady's feelings are mixed. Although he wants to do a careful investigation, he dislikes mixing in politics and would just as soon turn over the case to the oafish Pribluda if he is going to interfere with it.

   Naturally, Arkady is curious about this bizarre crime and continues to investigate when he meets with no opposition from Pribluda. He is encouraged by his superior, the town prosecutor Andrei Iamskoy, who has enormous respect for Arkady's talent and persistence. Ice skates left at the scene lead Arkady to their owner, Irina Asanova, a beautiful film student who refuses to cooperate with Arkady's investigation but who intrigues him with her enigmatic behavior and independence.

Irina is a contrast to Arkady's wife, Zoya, a beautiful but humorless Communist Party functionary who is having an affair with one of Arkady's friends. Zoya is ambitious, and Arkady has neglected her for his work. She wants him to play the political game, for he is the son of a famous general, Josef Stalin's most trusted military man, and she is chagrined that her husband has not made the most of this privileged position to ascend the Soviet ladder of power. Arkady, however, cannot abide the corruption that would require him to kowtow to bureaucrats.

Gradually, Arkady pieces together evidence about the identity of the three murder victims—one of them a friend of Irina. Working from blood samples, teeth, and various chemical analyses, Arkady discovers that one of the victims is an American. At the same time, he makes use of a scientist who has developed a special process for reconstructing faces. He will use one of his sculpted heads to get Irina to admit that it was her friend who was killed. When he is able to link a KGB informant to the murder, Arkady has his lieutenant, Pasha, accompany the man home to acquire additional evidence. Both men, though, are murdered, and the evidence disappears—probably because the KGB is involved, Arkady suspects; he believes it is Pribluda who has murdered Arkady's detective and his informant.

In fact, as Arkady slowly realizes, it is an American businessman, John Osborne, who has been manipulating him and several other officials. Osborne is a well-connected fur dealer who has been visiting the Soviet Union since World War II. He is, Arkady finally deduces, the murderer—a man who kills for the sheer sport of it—but also a man who has decided to create his own sable market by smuggling several sables (worth more than gold) out of the country.

The novel concludes with Arkady's final confrontation with Osborne—not in Moscow, but in New York, where he and Irina, assisted by New York detective William Kirwill, track Osborne to his den of sables.

*The Characters*

Like most mystery stories, *Gorky Park* is driven by an intricate plot. It is the detective's search for the truth and his solution to the crime that create interest. Nevertheless, the novel contains many well-developed characters. Arkady is in the tradition of the stoical detective, a loner who has to figure things out for himself and is alienated from the establishment. At the same time, he is not a stock American or English character in Russian clothes. He is extraordinarily bright, but he realizes that he lacks some of the basic techniques for solving crimes that any New York City detective would have in his possession, primarily because his investigations have been relegated to routine matters. He is middle-aged, worried, and depressed over his failing marriage to Zoya. Though he eventually beds Irina, he does so with a sense of fatality, suspecting that they will not be able to stay together.

Irina is fiercely alive in her desire to leave the country. She detests Soviet life, which is why it takes her so long to discover that Osborne is not her benefactor but her enemy. For he has promised Irina and her friend that he will take them to the United

States if they collaborate in his plan to smuggle the sables, and Irina clings to the illusion that her friend has escaped the country and has not become one of the murder victims in Gorky Park.

Andrei Iamskoy and John Osborne are the most devious and complex characters in the novel. Arkady eventually learns that they met in the war and that they share an insatiable greed. Iamskoy has posed as Arkady's supporter, but his plan has been merely to keep an eye on Arkady, using his reports to gauge how close Arkady is to actually solving the crime. Arkady eventually has to kill Iamskoy in order to continue his pursuit of Osborne, the evil genius of the book, who delights in getting away with murder and with the sables, not only duping the Soviets but actually getting Federal Bureau of Investigation (FBI) agents in New York to abet his schemes by making them think that Arkady is a KGB agent.

Much less successful as a character is William Kirwill. He talks like a New York City detective, but his story about his brother, James Kirwill, who came to the Soviet Union to satisfy a missionary impulse, seems farfetched. Moreover, Kirwill's story about his family—his mother and father were Irish American Communist sympathizers—works only as a weak explanation for Kirwill's understanding of Soviet mores and the Russian language. Kirwill is a helping character, and Arkady badly needs his assistance, but Kirwill never achieves independence as a fictional creation. He is merely there to further the plot.

One of the most surprising characters is Major Pribluda. Arkady has misjudged him. He is a blundering KGB agent, but there is also a grudging sense of humanity in his character, which accounts for his refusal, at one point, to obey a direct order to kill Arkady. Pribluda is not evil, he is merely a servant of the state doing his job, and he is without the imagination to act any other way, except when his basic sense of decency is violated.

*Themes and Meanings*

In Arkady Renko, *Gorky Park* presents a man of integrity who searches for the truth. Everything in the Soviet system should tell him to compromise, to mouth Communist Party pieties, to avoid those areas of investigation that may embarrass officials or complicate relations with powerful Americans such as Osborne. Arkady could live a comfortable life, behaving like a docile bureaucrat and being rewarded with high office and various luxuries, including trips abroad. Yet, in a curious way, he is patriotic: He insists on solving the crime.

The plot of the mystery story serves the author well by emphasizing the detective's intelligence and independence. He must rely on his own wits, and he cannot afford to be flattered by his superiors. He represents, therefore, the strongest possible alternative to the collectivist police state, where individuality is devalued, indeed crushed. By definition, the detective is a nonconformist and is likely to suffer for his singularity. In order to do his job, Arkady must risk everything—his job, his home, and his family. The Soviet system is set up, in other words, precisely so that he cannot do his job.

Yet the author also shows that Arkady can find other detectives and laboratory technicians within the system who are as curious as he is and who want to determine the truth. This is why Arkady is so angry when Pasha is killed. It is not merely that he has lost a friend and colleague; it is that the very process of investigation has been threatened. What Arkady lives for has been attacked. Within the system, moreover, Arkady has his admirers, though his lone-wolf behavior makes him incapable of changing the political realities in which he must work.

There is a sadness and grayness in the system that is masked by the bravado of the Brezhnev era, when the Soviet Union seemed like a formidable empire. The society is corrupt and decaying from within, and yet the very process of corruption is so ingrained that it provides what little true dynamic there is. This accounts for Arkady's depression, his reluctance to do anything but investigate no matter what the consequences. The investigation is his only area of freedom.

A more disturbing theme is the collusion between the FBI and KGB that is introduced in the last part of the novel. Osborne is confident that his connections in both security services will do his bidding; he has been valuable to both of them, providing each agency with intelligence. It is a cynical view of the world that the novel apparently endorses, for the FBI agent is presented as approving—or at least tacitly accepting—the plan to murder Arkady in New York. That this view of the world cannot ultimately prevail, however, seems the message of the plot twist that results in the FBI agent's murder. Only a man allied to neither side—a man like Arkady—survives at the end of the novel.

*Critical Context*

*Gorky Park* was hailed as a superb thriller on publication, and it quickly became a best-seller. Critics were impressed not merely by the style and presentation of action but also by the author's astonishing knowledge of the Soviet Union. The novel gives the feel of traveling Moscow streets, of delving deeply into the government bureaucracy and everyday life. What it felt like to work in the country, to be a member of the Communist Party, to go to a party, spend a day at home—all kinds of activities are brought to life in an engaging tale of suspense.

Since the novel was published well before the end of the Cold War and the demise of the Soviet Union, Western readers also found it a novelty to be rooting for a Soviet hero. Even though Arkady is a misfit, he is a "comrade," a member of Soviet society, and he remains Soviet even when he is transported to New York. He thinks only of returning after the crime is solved, for his identity has been formed in the Soviet Union; whatever his society's faults, he must return home. This means abandoning Irina, whose dream has been to reach the United States. Arkady cannot imagine emigrating, no matter how much he loves her.

In his basic patriotism, Arkady resembles the detectives in American stories, who may be hypercritical and aloof, but who also stand for and reestablish the society's basic values. The system may be corrupt, but the detective with integrity cleanses it, if only in some small part, by solving a crime.

Arkady has become a series character, making appearances in the subsequent novels *Polar Star* (1989) and *Red Square* (1992). Although the times change, the politics differ, Arkady's weary yet resilient character remains basically the same. Like all detectives, he aims to restore order, to act as a symbol of justice, however flawed he and the system might be. His tenacity is life-affirming, no matter how disappointed he may become. He does not really expect to be happy, yet he endures.

*Bibliography*
Jacoby, Tamar. "Gorky Park." *The New Republic* 184 (May 9, 1981): 36-38. Lauds Smith's creation of a jaunty and sardonic hero who must work strenuously for his insights into crime—an unusual feature for a thriller. Praises the novel for transcending the thriller genre by seriously examining the nature of evil and what it means to be free. Argues that only the last scene—too easily resolved by a shootout—is unworthy of the novel's complexity.
Kanfer, Stefan. "Gorky Park." *Time* 117 (March 30, 1981): 81-83. Kanfer is impressed with the passion, wit, and moral resonance of the novel and calls Arkady Renko a great character. Equally impressive, Kanfer says, is the complex social context, though the novel's ending is disappointingly simplistic.
Lekachman, Robert. "Gorky Park." *The Nation* 232 (April 4, 1981): 406-407. Finds the solution to the mystery too pat and the novel's ironies too symmetrical, but notes that Smith is extraordinarily well-informed about police and security matters. Remarks that the depth of knowledge overrides other flaws, such as his weak treatment of women.
Prescott, Peter S. "Gorky Park." *Newsweek* 97 (April 6, 1981): 99. Observes that the plot verges on the bewildering, yet its very complexity enhances its realism. Compares Arkady with John le Carré's George Smiley, noting that each character has an unfaithful wife and must function in a society corrupted by an infinite cynicism.
Shevchenko, Arkady N. *Breaking with Moscow*. New York: Alfred A. Knopf, 1985. A memoir by a Soviet diplomat, United Nations bureaucrat, and self-confessed spy for the United States. His account provides a remarkable insider's view of Soviet society and Soviet-American relations that illuminates the issues and the historical context of *Gorky Park*. Like Irina Asanova, Shevchenko grew to hate the Soviet regime, and his desire to remain in America is comparable to hers.

*Carl Rollyson*

# GREEN GRASS, RUNNING WATER

*Author:* Thomas King (1943-    )
*Type of plot:* Social criticism
*Time of plot:* The 1960's to the 1980's
*Locale:* Blossom, Alberta, Canada
*First published:* 1993

> *Principal characters:*
> LIONEL RED DOG, a Blackfoot Indian
> CHARLIE LOOKING BEAR, Lionel's cousin
> ALBERTA FRANK, a professor, lover of Lionel and Charlie
> NORMA, Charlie's mother, Lionel's aunt
> ELI STANDS ALONE, Norma's brother
> KAREN, Eli's deceased wife
> BILL BURSUM, Lionel's employer, Charlie's former employer
> LATISHA, Lionel's sister, owner of the Dead Dog Café
> COYOTE, a trickster
> ROBINSON CRUSOE,
> ISHMAEL,
> THE LONE RANGER, and
> HAWKEYE, escapees from a mental hospital
> DR. HOVAUGH, a doctor in a mental hospital
> BABO, a worker in a mental hospital

*The Novel*

In *Green Grass, Running Water*, the line between reality and fantasy is blurred. The novel opens and closes with short sections devoted to Coyote, the trickster, who accounts for many of the book's inexplicable incidents.

The story then turns briefly to four characters—Robinson Crusoe, Ishmael, the Lone Ranger, and Hawkeye—all presumably Blackfoot Indians who have escaped from the mental institution in which they were confined. Their mission, with the help of Coyote, is to fix the world. These five add considerable humor to the story, but they may leave some readers baffled initially, both because it is not always clear where reality ends and fantasy begins with them and because they overstep linear time lines.

These characters present various creation stories drawn from Greek, Christian, and Native American mythologies. King's Ahdamn-First Woman story is the Adam and Eve story in contemporary garb; the first two humans on earth eat both fried chicken and the Edenic apple. Young Man Walking On Water (King's version of Christ) articulates King's beliefs about the conflict between the Indian culture and the dominant white culture—a major reason for his having written this novel—when he proffers his interpretation of Christian rules: "the first rule is that no one can help me. The second rule is that no one can tell me anything. Third, no one is allowed to be in two places at once. Except me."

The essence of *Green Grass, Running Water* is that a know-it-all white culture has intruded insensitively—sometimes dangerously, usually stupidly—upon the folkways of Native American cultures, which have conserved a land and a way of life by means that make environmental sense. These folkways are misunderstood and disrespected by those in nominal power, who refuse to observe longstanding treaties. Such people do not respect native festivals such as the Sun Dance, which they try to photograph—behavior that is an insult to the Indians.

On the fantastic level, Coyote helps the Blackfoot by using his trickster powers to thwart much of what the white people wish to do in order to, in their terms, advance civilization. Coyote and the escapees from the mental institution collaborate on fixing the world.

Two major structural challenges faced King in *Green Grass, Running Water*. First, he needed to mix mythology with reality, a quintessential ingredient in his revisionist history of his subjects. He achieved this end by using the Coyote trickster and his cronies to handle the mythic content of the novel; in so doing, the author infused the book with considerable humor. Second, he had to find a way to interweave eight interrelated yet individual stories.

King approaches this structural task by writing in short segments, sometimes a few lines, sometimes three or four pages, occasionally, but rarely, longer. Within the longer, more linear segments, King successfully experiments with a device that provides readers with necessary background. A segment may begin in the here and now, but the second paragraph will be a reflection on some past event; the third will continue the presentation of the here and now, the fourth will take up the presentation of the past event, and so forth to the end of the segment.

King handles this complicated structure deftly; reading these segments is neither confusing nor annoying. King frequently ends his paragraphs with cliffhanger sentences. One hates to leave a here and now paragraph and retreat to the past, but a few lines later, the here and now takes over again. This style provides King's narrative with a unique forward momentum.

Two major story lines dominate King's novel: Alberta's desire to become pregnant and Eli's struggle to keep the government from taking his mother's property. Nearly everything else in the novel stems from these two basic lines of development. When King departs from one story line to move into another, readers remain oriented, because each story line is connected to one or both of the main stories King is developing. Although five or six segments may be interposed between two elements of one of King's main narrative threads, it is never difficult to pick up that thread when King resumes telling that part of the story.

Two events bring the novel to its resolution. First, Alberta gets her wish. She becomes pregnant, but by neither Lionel nor Charlie. Then, an earthquake hits the area around Blossom, destroying the dam that Eli has been fighting and, in the process, returning the tribal waterway to its rightful owners and drowning Eli. Both events are Coyote's doing. The trickster has prevailed.

*The Characters*

The central figure in *Green Grass, Running Water* is Lionel Red Dog, who as a youth had a promising future that, through a series of misadventures not of his own doing, was foreclosed to him. During a trip to Salt Lake City to read a professional paper for a colleague in the Department of Indian Affairs, which employed him, Lionel was unwittingly drawn into an Indian activist group, and he landed in jail.

When he returned to Blossom, he was fired. His conviction made it difficult for him to get another job. Finally, Bill Bursum, the white owner of a local store, offered to hire Lionel to replace his cousin Charlie, who had left Bill's employ to attend law school. Twenty years later, Lionel is still at work in the store; he is Bill's best salesman, but he has never had a salary increase. Bill Bursum's story is closely connected to Lionel's.

The same is true of Charlie's story. Charlie, having completed law school, is a Porsche-driving success, employed by Duplessis International Associates, the construction firm commissioned to dam a tribal river. When the dam is finally destroyed, Duplessis, no longer needing its token Indian, fires Charlie.

Alberta Frank is a college professor in Calgary who, realizing that her biological clock is running down, wants desperately to have a baby but has no desire to have a husband. She engages in simultaneous affairs with Charlie and Lionel, and her story is intricately tied to theirs.

Norma is Lionel and Latisha's aunt and Eli Stand Alone's sister. Latisha, owner of the Dead Dog Café, is a successful businessperson who was married to George Morningstar, a good-looking, immature, unsuccessful white man from Ohio, who has left his wife and children.

Eli left the reservation some thirty years earlier to attend the University of Toronto. He married Karen, a white woman, and has spent his life teaching literature at the university. He and Karen returned to Blossom once before their marriage and attended the Sun Dance. Karen always wanted to attend another Sun Dance, but more than two decades later, recovering from cancer, she is killed in an automobile accident, never having been able to realize her wish.

Eli, learning through Norma of his mother's death some weeks after its occurrence, returns to Blossom to find that the tribal river has been dammed and that a power plant is about to be put into operation. He retires and becomes a man with a mission. When the dam is opened, the house that Eli and Norma's mother built with her own hands will be washed away. Eli exercises every legal remedy available to prevent the dam from becoming operative. He defies the government agency and Duplessis International Associates that have built the dam.

Clifford Sifton, who works for the builders of the dam, comes daily to ask Eli officially to leave. Eli daily refuses, also officially. He and Sifton become friends. Eli gives Sifton coffee; Sifton brings Eli books. Because of Eli's stubbornness, people, including Bill Bursum, who have bought property on what will be the lakefront created by the dam are kept from developing that property.

Straddling the line between the real and the fantastic are Dr. Hovaugh, a psychiatrist at a mental hospital, and Babo, who works in the hospital. Four of their patients have escaped. These four are delusional, and their association with Coyote brings out the mythical elements in the story.

## Themes and Meanings

Thomas King lives with a foot in two worlds, the Native American world that is part of his heritage and the world of the white society of which he is fundamentally a part despite his Cherokee lineage. He understands both worlds well. He writes in *Green Grass, Running Water*, as he did in his first novel, *Medicine River* (1990), with a greater sympathy for the underdog society than for the dominant society.

*Green Grass, Running Water* directs its social commentary to current topics, including the feminist cause. Alberta is a liberated woman, bright, well-educated, and financially independent. She wants motherhood but denies any necessary connection between motherhood and marriage. She is a nurturing sort, more drawn to Lionel than to Charlie because Lionel is the less successful of the two, the one who needs nurturing. This, however, does not make Alberta want to marry him.

Throughout the novel, white society transgresses upon the native culture in ways both small and large. The small transgressions occur in insensitive acts: for example, a white tourist happens upon the Sun Dance and begins photographing it. Even worse, George, who is married to Latisha, a successful, independent Native American, wants to photograph the Sun Dance and, in an abortive reunion with Latisha, makes slighting remarks about her culture—something that Eli's white wife, Karen, never did.

In one heartbreaking vignette, King tells of how Alberta's parents, Ada and Amos, drove south to the United States to participate in a sacred tribal dance with relatives. At the border, they encountered arrogant customs agents who forced them to unpack their car. When the agents discovered their tribal costumes, they spread them on the asphalt and then, because the costumes were decorated with eagle feathers, confiscated them.

After considerable negotiation, the costumes were returned in plastic garbage bags with the feathers broken. The return of the costumes could not make amends for what had happened. The initial insult at the border, which results in Amos' arrest, was horrible. To have the costumes defiled as they were was an added insult. The greatest insult, however, was that the border agents robbed Alberta's parents of their dignity.

Among the larger affronts the Blackfoots suffered from white society was the building of the dam and its plans to operate a power plant and develop a recreational area on tribal land. Eli Stands Alone has left his people and gone to Toronto, seemingly forsaking his forebears. On the surface, he has repudiated his heritage.

King shows, however, that in the end, Eli cannot forsake his past. He returns to the house his mother built and, using knowledge and self-confidence he gained in the white world, he obstructs the operation of the dam for years. He keeps the project in limbo until, through the intervention of the trickster, nature reclaims the project.

In this novel, a symbiosis exists between the two societies King depicts. Among the ills the natives face is that their young people leave the reserve (King's preferred term for a reservation) and go out into the broader world beyond. They never really leave home, however, and when they return, they do so better equipped to defeat those who would suppress native culture.

*Critical Context*

*Green Grass, Running Water* was written at a time when considerable attention was being paid to Native American history. Advances in knowledge have resulted in considerable revisions of American history, which had largely been written from the perspective of a white establishment dominated by people with Western European outlooks.

The Columbus quincentenary in 1992 became, rather than a celebration of the discovery of the New World, a year of strident questioning. People asked such questions as, "How does one discover a world that has already been settled for centuries and that has a culture in many ways as advanced as that in Europe?" The Inca, the Aztec, and the Mayan Indians were exceptionally advanced in mathematics and such related areas of physics as astronomy. In the fields of art and architecture, these cultures had produced works of great sophistication.

Another prominent Native American novelist, Gerald Vizenor, addressed such questions in *Bearheart: The Heirship Chronicles* (1990) and *The Heirs of Columbus* (1991); he, like King, emphasized the trickster tradition. King is artistically dependent on this tradition in *Green Grass, Running Water*, using it to bring about the dual resolution of his novel.

King addresses a number of compelling social concerns in this novel. He presents independent, self-possessed women quite capable of functioning productively without men. Alberta Frank and Latisha Morningstar are prototypical modern women. They are too busy to march in parades or burn bras in public protests, but they forge ahead as contributing members of society, with minds of their own. They have no qualms about defying convention. They fit well into the context of women's liberation.

King is also concerned with the contemporary problem of the flight of young Native Americans to cities. He seems even more concerned, however, about what happens to someone like Lionel, who remains in Blossom in a dead-end job, accepting his fate all too willingly even though he has for two decades harbored vague, at times unrealistic, plans for continuing his education.

*Bibliography*

Bencivenga, Jim. "*Medicine River*." *The Christian Science Monitor*, October 3, 1990, 13. This eight-hundred-word review of King's first novel is appreciative. It contains insights that suggest the course King's work will likely take. Bencivenga has an intelligent understanding of King.

Butler, Jack. "*Medicine River*." *The New York Times Book Review* 95 (September 23, 1990): 29. Butler comments on one of King's concerns, which recurs in *Green Grass, Running Water*: the photographing of Indian artifacts and ceremonies. He commends King for the subtle ending of *Medicine River* and appreciates the deftness with which King "counters stereotypes."

King, Thomas. "Borders." *World Literature Today* 66 (Spring, 1992): 269-273. The first appearance of a portion of *Green Grass, Running Water* in print. The magazine contains a short biographical piece along with a prepublication excerpt from the novel. A brief but useful estimate of the author.

McManus, James. "Has Red Dog Gone White?" *The New York Times Book Review* 98 (July 25, 1993): 21. McManus comments on King's control of the diverse stories developed in *Green Grass, Running Water*. He calls the book "ambitious and funny" but criticizes King for spending too much time developing some of the book's less interesting characters.

Weaver, Jace. "Thomas King." *Publishers Weekly* 240 (March 8, 1993): 56-57. The fullest biographical overview of Thomas King; includes an interview that focuses on *Green Grass, Running Water*. Stresses the comic imagination with which the book is infused.

*R. Baird Shuman*

# GRIEVER
## An American Monkey King in China

*Author:* Gerald Vizenor (1934-    )
*Type of plot:* Neorealism
*Time of plot:* The early 1980's
*Locale:* Tianjin and Beijing, China; Minnesota
*First published:* 1987

> *Principal characters:*
> GRIEVER DE HOCUS, an American "crossbreed" teaching in China
> EGAS ZHANG, the director of the foreign affairs bureau
> HESTER HUA DAN, Zhang's daughter
> KANGMEI, Zhang's stepdaughter, sired by an American
> SHITOU, a Chinese shaman who crushes stone
> CHINA BROWNE, Griever's friend in America
> MATTEO RICCI, Griever's symbolic rooster

*The Novel*

Early in *Griever: An American Monkey King in China*, Gerald Vizenor informs his readers that "imagination is the real world, all the rest is bad television." Four pages later, he reinforces this contention, which is essential to an understanding of what Vizenor hopes to accomplish artistically: Imagination, he writes "is what burns in humans. We are not methods to be discovered, we are not freeze-dried methodologies. We remember dreams, never data, at the wild end." As *Griever* alternates between reality and fantasy, between consciousness and the dream world, readers need to remember these early admonitions. They have direct artistic import and, in light of Vizenor's subject, penetrating political implications.

Based on several months of language teaching that Vizenor and his wife did in post-Maoist Tianjin, China, *Griever* continually moves between documentable history and overt fantasy. This is one of the few novels that provides readers with a bibliography of historical sources in its final pages.

One might call *Griever* a nonfiction novel, a term applied by critics to such works as Truman Capote's *In Cold Blood* (1966). Yet Vizenor, unlike Capote, departs unapologetically from his facts, intermixing reveries with consciousness; he thereby creates a fantastic tale that borrows from his traditions as a "crossbreed" Chippewa, and he links these traditions, particularly that of the trickster, to similar traditions in Chinese legend.

*Griever* is essentially a tale about its protagonist's experiences in China during the period leading up to the Tiananmen Square uprising. Vizenor does not relate these experiences linearly but rather focuses on Griever de Hocus, a trickster whose last name suggests the sort of role he plays. As the novel develops, Griever becomes more and more outrageous, sneering at the bureaucracy, outwitting it at every turn, usually in highly humorous episodes that suggest the lighthearted effectiveness of tricksters— always humorous characters—in the Native American tradition.

Griever's first major move in this direction is heterodox but not openly defiant of China's structured official bureaucracy: On his first day in Tianjin, when he observes a butcher slaughtering chickens in the open market, he puts a handful of Chinese money on the butcher's blood-covered slaughtering block to buy all the chickens he can. When the accommodating butcher seeks to slaughter Griever's chickens for him, Griever protests that he wants them alive.

Having made this point, he then releases them, and they flutter off—except for one rooster, a handsome cock with orange wattles whom Griever names Matteo Ricci. Matteo figures prominently and symbolically throughout the rest of novel. The slaughter also foreshadows much more shocking slaughters on which Vizenor reports later in the book: the brutal, inhuman torture and slaying of the Lazarist Sisters of Saint Vincent de Paul in 1982, and an execution caravan, in which two trucks carrying prisoners drive their captives slowly through the streets to their executions—which, in a fanciful turn in the story, do not occur. The prisoners, like the chickens Griever buys, somehow escape their fate.

Egas Zhang is Griever's first official contact in China. Egas meets Griever at the airport and takes him to the guest house that he will share with a ragtag group of seven other teachers, some of whom—notably Carnegie Morgan and Colin Marport Gloome—are symbolically named. Egas Zhang has reared two daughters, Hester Hua Dan and Kangmei. Kangmei, however, is not his child; Egas hates her. Kangmei issued from a liaison between Egas' wife and an American who, through a series of mischances, became stateless and finally died in an earthquake that killed three hundred thousand people in Tianjin.

Kangmei has blonde hair that she usually hides under a scarf. Her stepfather is despotic. He has spies who observe the people around him and report their activities. Egas finally drowns Hester Hua Dan and her daughter, his grandchild, in the pond behind the guest house during the carnival. Kangmei escapes to Macao with Griever in an ultralight airplane that he has assembled.

Griever enacts a final vengeance in his last meeting with the detested Egas Zhang. Egas has continually prodded Griever to give him bear paws, gall bladders, and other aphrodisiacs. Shortly before his escape to Macao, Griever offers Egas a concoction that the depraved man accepts hungrily. This potion, however, contains estrogen, which in a short time will give Egas pendulous breasts and the high voice of a woman. He will go through life "walking and talking like a mutant hermaphrodite."

## The Characters

Griever de Hocus, an autobiographical character, is a bright, well-educated cross-breed Chippewa Indian half a world away from his Minnesota roots. In Tianjin, he teaches English. Vizenor constructs in Griever the traditional trickster of native American legend, a figure that occurs in most of his writing. Griever is mischievous but resolute in his defiance of despotism. He prefers to outwit rather than outfight his opponents. Griever almost singlehandedly creates the action that propels the novel. He is an omniscient third-person narrator as well as the perpetrator of all the book's crucial events.

Egas Zhang is the slippery villain. He is the quintessential bureaucrat, an obedient man devoid of independent values or principles. He appears accommodating, but behind this façade, his xenophobia lurks. This xenophobia is heightened by his knowledge that his wife conceived a child by an American who had lost his citizenship. She insisted on delivering this child, Kangmei, and Egas had to rear Kangmei as his own despite her blonde hair, a badge of illegitimacy. History repeats itself when Egas' own daughter, Hester Hua Dan, becomes pregnant after an encounter with Griever, who is Egas' virtual opposite in every fundamental respect.

China Browne is the friend back home. She is a sounding board to whom Griever writes regularly. Letters to her begin and end the book, creating a frame for the novel.

Kangmei, Egas Zhang's stepdaughter, becomes Griever's lover and his companion on his flight out of China to Macao. The trip takes several days in the ultralight aluminum plane, propelled by a snowmobile motor, that Griever has assembled. Kangmei is caught between two cultures and has lived a life of rejection. Is she in love, or is she simply desperate for a better life? Vizenor does not reveal her real motives.

Shitou is a shaman who crushes stone with his bare hands. He has many of the mystical attributes of both the shaman and the trickster in Native American legend. By allowing him to figure prominently throughout the novel, Vizenor holds the mirror to the folklore of two cultures separated by half a world but sharing comparable beliefs about the supernatural, preconscious state.

Matteo Ricci, although a rooster rather than a human, occupies a prominent place in the novel. Rescued from the chicken slaughter, his freedom (and survival) purchased with a few pieces of paper money, Matteo accompanies Griever everywhere, even to the auspicious opening of Maxim de Beijing's. Griever's rescue of Matteo is a reenactment of his rescue of frogs from a science experiment when he was a schoolboy and also is a foreshadowing of the freeing of the prisoners from the execution caravan. The essence of these rescues provides a veiled statement about the rights of all living things.

Hester Hua Dan, the dutiful daughter of Egas Zhang, is a translator. She bears the shame of an illegitimate pregnancy in a country where, according to Vizenor's repeated mantras, one child is all that is permitted. Hester could escape with Griever, but she is so used to conforming to her father's authority that she stays in Tianjin and is murdered.

*Themes and Meanings*

Skillfully juxtaposing himself between two worlds, the Native American culture from which he sprang and the post-Maoist culture with which he became involved as a language teacher in China, Vizenor discovers common threads that unite the two. He does not and cannot, nevertheless, blind himself to the excesses of the Chinese government, to the cruel control of every aspect of human existence with which the government concerns itself. Opposition is squelched summarily, frequently by the execution of dissidents, and a hypocritical, puritanical bureaucracy deals with moral turpitude in equally unforgiving ways.

Griever's rooster, Matteo Ricci, serves as an alarm clock to the residents in the guest house of the language institute. Vizenor wonders, however, whether such an alarm clock is needed: The beginning of each day is heralded by blasts from loudspeakers that play the propagandistic anthem "The East Is Red," which is broadcast throughout China every morning as the sun slowly appears on the distant horizon.

Late one night in Tianjin, however, Griever steals from the guest house, climbs on a bamboo ladder to a broken window in the security-tight administration building, and patches his own tape into the recording of the song to which one-fifth of the world's population awakens every morning. In that section of Tianjin, "The East Is Red" is replaced that morning by the rousing strains of John Philip Sousa's "The Stars and Stripes Forever" and the U.S. Marine hymn.

Egas Zhang officiously storms the guest house in an attempt to find out how this atrocity has happened. Griever, having stolen back into his quarters, answers the knock on his door like any just-awakening person working methodically through his morning ablutions. The exchange between him and Egas is one of the most humorous in the book, but it also shows the trickster at work outwitting the methodical, unimaginative bureaucrat. Griever is equally skillful in retrieving his ultralight airplane from the bureaucrats at the customs office, who try to extract two thousand dollars duty from him before giving him his property.

In these encounters, Griever, as a representative of Western society, demonstrates how futile are governmental attempts to subjugate human beings. The themes of individual freedom and individual accomplishment underlie nearly every major episode in the novel.

As the narrative progresses, Griever becomes increasingly flippant and outrageous. Toward the book's end, when he is sitting on the ground viewing a propagandistic film with one of his language students, the student asks Griever if, in his country, there are vicious mosquitoes like the ones that are at the moment sucking the blood from Griever's veins. Griever replies that American mosquitoes own television sets; he then goes on to expose the student to obscenities that do not appear in the innocent boy's English-Chinese dictionary. Finally, Griever makes the student blush by asking him if there are any sex scenes in the film the two are about to see.

Some students watch the film from behind a large white sheet that is strung up for use as a projecting screen. Griever notes how those behind the screen see blurred images, reversals, more romantic impressions than the ones seen by those who look at the film from the front. This observation suggests the duality of vision of the entire novel, the two perspectives of which Griever, now on the reverse side of his usual venue, is fast becoming aware.

*Griever* sets intelligent wit against bureaucratic gravity, and in the conflict it is wit, in the best trickster tradition, that triumphs. "Wit" in the trickster sense becomes synonymous with individual freedom and inner personal satisfaction, things of which totalitarian regimes rob their citizenry.

*Critical Context*

Set in the period immediately prior to the uprising in Beijing's Tiananmen Square, *Griever* deals with China's internal political conflicts. The books reveals that the Chinese acknowledge the need for international trade that will attract Western dollars, yet the nation is mired in an oxcart society in which change, while inevitable, will not be orderly.

Here is a society in which people shoot rats for meat and for the skins to be fashioned into shoes. In sharp contrast to this sort of economy is a boom in Beijing that sees the opening of Maxim's, a restaurant where lunch will cost the equivalent of what an average worker earns in four months.

With considerable irony, Vizenor writes that people are discouraged from drinking distilled spirits when they eat dog meat because to do so is thought to cause hemorrhoids. He goes on to say, however, that this is a small price to pay for the consumption of a devoted pet. Such biting ironies are typical of this book and of Vizenor's other novels, some of which share characters from *Griever*.

It is not easy to compare Vizenor's writing to that of his contemporaries. His approach and style are unique. At times, because of his frequent temporal and geographical shifts, his writing reminds one of J. R. R. Tolkien's or of Lewis Carroll's, although Vizenor is by no means derivative. The fantasy world he constructs reminds one of these two authors, yet Vizenor's work also exudes the mysticism of Native American tradition.

*Bibliography*

Bowers, Neal, and Charles P. Silet. "An Interview with Gerald Vizenor." *MELUS* 8 (1981): 43. A brief interview. Vizenor discusses the trickster tradition and his use of it. Among the earliest Vizenor interviews.

Bruchac, Joseph, ed. *Survival This Way: Interviews with American Indian Poets.* Tucson: University of Arizona Press, 1987. Vizenor reflects on his career as a writer. He notes his uses of history in his writing. Interesting juxtaposition of Vizenor with other Native American writers.

Hochbruck, Wolfgang. "Breaking Away: The Novels of Gerald Vizenor." *World Literature Today* 66 (Spring, 1992): 274-278. Succinct but penetrating. Hochbruck has a comprehensive view of Vizenor's fiction. Shows how Vizenor bolts from literary conventions.

Martin, Calvin, ed. *The American Indian and the Problem of History.* New York: Oxford University Press, 1987. Demonstrates how revisionist history is at the heart of much Native American writing. Places Vizenor high among those who use history in imaginative and sometimes fanciful ways. One of the more balanced discussions of Vizenor.

Vizenor, Gerald. "Trickster Discourse." *American Indian Quarterly* 14 (Summer,

1990): 277-287. Vizenor defines and explains the trickster tradition. He also discusses postmodernism. His conceptual grasp of current critical theory is apparent.

*R. Baird Shuman*

# GRINGOS

*Author:* Charles Portis (1933-    )
*Type of plot:* Adventure
*Time of plot:* The early 1990's, in the season of Christmas and the New Year
*Locale:* Mérida, the capital of the state of Yucatán, Mexico
*First published:* 1991

> *Principal characters:*
> JIMMY BURNS, a freelance teamster, tracer of lost persons, and onetime dealer in illicit Mayan artifacts
> REFUGIO BAUTISTA OSORIO, Jimmy's stalwart friend and Mexican counterpart, a jack-of-all-trades
> RUDY KURLE, an investigator of extraterrestrial visitations
> LOUISE KURL, Rudy's wife and assistant, a helpful woman with a degree in human dynamics
> DAN, an overage hippie and leader of a dangerous band of outcasts
> DOC RICHARD FLANDIN, a self-styled expert on Mayan culture
> FRAU ALMA KOBOLD, the invalid widow of a talented but neglected photographer of Mayan temples

*The Novel*

*Gringos* is, as its title suggests, a novel about expatriate Americans in Mexico. It is an adventure story, as Portis' novels sometimes are, and the account of a quest, as Portis' novels almost always are.

The protagonist and narrator is Jimmy Burns, a native of Shreveport, Louisiana, a former Marine military policeman who is both a teamster and a tracer of lost persons. Jimmy resides in a small hotel, the Posada Fausto, in Mérida, in the Yucatán peninsula. Frau Alma Kobold, the wheelchair-ridden, chain-smoking widow of an archaeological photographer, is a fellow resident for whom Jimmy often acts as errand boy. Mérida has a large community of gringos (Americans) who comprise a comic gallery of soldiers of fortune, eccentrics, and misfits.

Jimmy gets what he believes to be a routine job hauling supplies to an archaeological site. While working on his truck in preparation for the trip, he is menaced by a gang of hippies calling themselves the Jumping Jacks. They are led by an aging biker, Dan, whose two lieutenants are toughs with shaved heads and vacant eyes. Other Jumping Jacks are Beany Girl, a tall woman who horrifies Jimmy by urinating in front of everyone, and Red, a girl hardly more than a child. Jimmy later learns that Red is LaJoye Mishell Teeter of Perry, Florida, a runaway for whose return a two thousand dollar reward has been offered. Jimmy faces the hippies down with a shotgun and disables their rattletrap station wagon, but they later escape. During the encounter, Jimmy has learned that the Jumping Jacks are on a quest: They are seeking the inaccessible City of Dawn and a mystical leader known as El Mago.

On his run to the archaeological site, Jimmy meets Rudy Kurle and allows the latter to tag along with him. Jimmy stops to conduct some business with Refugio Bautista Osorio, an old friend with whom he will later team up in a search to which the middle third of the novel is devoted. Rudy is also searching for the City of Dawn, which he believes to be a landing site for visitors from outer space. He takes voluminous notes, and although he is secretive about the information he possesses, he peppers Jimmy with pseudoscientific babble about flying-saucer landings around the world. The archaeological expedition breaks up when its leader, Dr. Henry Ritchie, unexpectedly dies of a fever. Jimmy finds two of Dr. Ritchie's assistants, college students named Gail and Denise, suddenly on his hands. Rudy wanders off down the river and does not come back. At this point, the novel becomes the story of Jimmy's quest for the City of Dawn, where he believes he may find both Rudy Kurle and LaJoye Mishell Teeter.

Doc Richard Flandin has studied Mayan ruins for many years and is writing a book which, he says, will put all the posturing university professors in their place. He announces that he is dying of prostate cancer and will accompany Jimmy and Refugio on their trip downriver as a kind of defiant final gesture. Denise returns to the United States, but Gail joins the new expedition and takes up with Doc Flandin, who immediately replaces the deceased Dr. Ritchie as her affectionate tutor. Ramos, a pugnacious dog, completes the company.

Along the way, the group discovers a shriveled body floating in the river; the corpse is that of a tiny, hairy old man with huge feet. Refugio calls him a *chaneque*, a small woodland creature of mysterious origin. Others in the party think he may be a howler monkey. The expedition discovers that the City of Dawn is Likín, a hilltop ruin across the river in Guatemala, and that hippies and flying-saucer seekers have gathered there from all over North America to await the appearance of El Mago. Jimmy, Refugio, and Ramos cross the river and eventually confront Dan and his two lieutenants atop a Mayan temple in a driving rainstorm. Dan refuses to give up the girl or a Mexican boy he has kidnapped since their previous encounter. In a brief but violent scene, Jimmy shoots Dan to death, and Refugio does the same to the henchmen. Rudy then reappears, unharmed and in high spirits.

The Mexican boy is returned to his relations and LaJoye Mishell Teeter to her father. Doc Flandin no longer speaks of dying. Instead, he returns to work on his book with Gail as his assistant and confidante. Rudy carries the pygmoid corpse away in a trombone case and embarks upon a lecture tour on which he represents the *chaneque* as an unfortunate visitor from the stars. Frau Kobold is dying, and Jimmy learns that she is responsible for the debacle at the City of Dawn. She wrote an anonymous letter to a flying-saucer newsletter prophesying the appearance of El Mago at Likín, which she and her husband had visited and photographed many years earlier. Emmett, an expatriate friend, dies and bequeaths his trailer, the Mobile Star, to Jimmy. Louise Kurle reveals that she is Rudy's sister; Rudy had presented her as his wife because he wished to prevent unwanted advances by the gringos of Mérida. Louise nurses Jimmy through a siege of dengue fever, and they then get married. Finally, Eli Withering, an old temple-robbing colleague, pays a visit. Freda, his new live-in girlfriend, turns out to be Beany Girl, much cleaned up and made up. Gallantly, Jimmy does not expose her.

## The Characters

Charles Portis' protagonists are usually gentle, naïve fellows who drift artlessly through an absurd, often savage world. Since Portis' fictional world is a comic one, the characters' very innocence serves as their shield and as a comfort to the reader. Jimmy Burns, however, resembles Mattie Ross and Rooster Cogburn—the central characters in Portis' second novel, *True Grit* (1968)—far more than he does the author's other protagonists.

Jimmy is self-sufficient, competent (he can repair a clutch and perform other equally esoteric mechanical tasks), resourceful, brave, and loyal. He was a military policeman in the Marine Corps and saw combat in Korea. He is unaffected and approachable. He is extremely tolerant of others, but he does have his own code of conduct. For example, during his first encounter with the Jumping Jacks, he seems less offended by their insults and threats than by Beany Girl's act of immodest urination. There are certain things, he thinks, that no decent woman will do, and that is one of them. Of course, Jimmy has his blind spots and shortcomings. It is so difficult for him to make a commitment to a member of the opposite sex that Louise Kurle, who experiences no such difficulties, finally transfers the matter of marriage from his to her own capable hands.

Although by no means one-dimensional, the other characters—as in Portis' earlier fiction—are generally ruled by some particular obsession or eccentricity. Doc Flandin takes a perverse delight in the neglect with which the academic Mayanists treat his work and theories. Frau Kobold feeds upon her own bitterness and resentment. She and her late husband, Oskar, once appeared in a Fox Movietone Newsreel, but that was many years ago. She dislikes Doc Flandin because he considers himself a scorned outsider while, in her judgment, he lives like a king. Jimmy learns the depth of her bitterness only after her death. For many years, he has been receiving anonymous hate letters. It turns out that despite—or, perhaps, because of—his many kindnesses toward her, Frau Kobold was their author.

Rudy Kurle finds evidence of extraterrestrial visitation all around him, but he is loath to share his notes with any other investigator. His sister, Louise, is a social worker without portfolio; it is simply her nature to help people. Dan, an ex-convict, is a former member of a motorcycle gang and a white supremacist group; he represents the dangers of charisma in a time when emotion is too seldom leavened with thought. Jimmy characterizes Beany Girl and LaJoye Mishell Teeter (Red) as girls who too easily get into cars with strangers.

Refugio Bautista Osorio is the Latin personality, the explicit contrast to all the gringos of the book. He is the revered head of the family and has a fine son, Manolo, who is just approaching manhood. Refugio is a shrewd businessman who delights in haggling with Jimmy. He boasts that his name appears on many leaves of Doc Flandin's book and that he will someday be famous. He fights bravely, and lethally, at Jimmy's side in the battle against the murderous hippies. Thereafter, Refugio will date all occurrences as either before or after the time he and Jimmy killed the "pagans."

*Themes and Meanings*

*Gringos* is the story of a mission to free a silly adolescent girl from the influences of an evil, deranged man, partly for pecuniary and partly for humane reasons. The mission concludes in a bloody gun battle. *Gringos* is also a spoof of the flying-saucer mania and the New Age silliness so prevalent in America during the last decades of the twentieth century. The novel is also a perceptive, though understated, commentary on the clash between North American and Latin American cultures. Finally, it is a study, simultaneously wry and sympathetic, of a community composed of outcasts.

All the gringos in the novel have come to Mexico in search of something—wealth, fame, enlightenment, sanctuary from the law or alimony payments or some past disgrace. The quest is the motif around which all of Portis' novels are constructed.

Another consistent element in Portis' novels is their tone of tolerance and undemonstrative compassion. Following the success of *True Grit*, Portis was sometimes compared to Mark Twain because of the subject matter, the setting, and the humor of the book. The comparison is not very apt. While the angry, bitter Twain is a descendant of Juvenal and Jonathan Swift, Portis is from the line of Geoffrey Chaucer, Miguel de Cervantes, and William Shakespeare—writers who could satirize human beings and institutions, yet retain an affection for them. *Gringos* glows with affection for the flotsam and jetsam who congregate at Shep's bar in Mérida. For example, at Emmett's funeral, Harold Bolus sings "Let Me Be Your Salty Dog," a lively bluegrass number. The effect is ludicrously inappropriate, but Harold means well. He thinks, mistakenly, that the song was Emmett's favorite.

Portis' protagonists survive, and sometimes thrive, by means of their common sense, while others who pretend to greater wisdom flop about like a fish on the shore. These characters are nonintellectual, not anti-intellectual. Jimmy, who is also the narrator, never disparages the skewed learning of Doc Flandin and Rudy Kurle, even when they patronize him. He simply chooses to live according to a folk wisdom more appropriate to himself. After Rudy has given a long discourse on flying-saucer landings and their significance, Jimmy declares—to himself, not to Rudy—that he is a geocentrist. He means this spiritually rather than astronomically. He will, to use Voltaire's phrase, cultivate his garden.

It seems proper to invoke the name of Voltaire, since *Gringos* is reminiscent of *Candide* (1759) in several ways. Like the latter, the former is a rambling, episodic comic tale with a picaresque hero. Characters appear, disappear, and reappear, often in another guise. The hero winds up far from his home in Caddo Parish, Louisiana, but he has overcome adversity thanks to his resolve, his common sense, and his innate humanity.

*Critical Context*

*Gringos*, said one reviewer at the time of its publication, would be hard to categorize. Would it be found on the bookstore shelves under adventure, humor, or general fiction? *Gringos* is not the first Portis novel to resist classification. *Norwood* (1966) and *The Dog of the South* (1979) are clearly comic novels. The protagonists, Norwood Pratt and Ray Midge, are innocents. Like Don Quixote, each man inhabits a world of his own creation as he conducts his quest. *True Grit*, on the other hand, blurs the generic lines. It has been called a Western, and that designation was no doubt reinforced by the successful film adaptation starring John Wayne. Yet anyone reading *True Grit* immediately realizes that "Western" is too limited a term to describe the book. *Masters of Atlantis* (1985), Portis' fourth and quirkiest novel, has been found shelved under the heading of science fiction. Yet whatever *Masters of Atlantis* is—and that is not easy to say—it is not science fiction.

Portis is a regional writer, in the sense that his novels are either set in the South or feature Southern protagonists (like Jimmy Burns in *Gringos*). He is a master of the dialect of the Arklatex, Jimmy's native soil. His novels, however, have much more than a regional appeal. Portis is not an experimenter in fiction. He uses traditional forms, and although his plots are loosely constructed, his scenes are written with precision and economy. In *Gringos*, he once again proves that he is a major comic writer by displaying the wit, the unpretentious charm, and the affirmative qualities that have won him a loyal readership.

*Bibliography*

Houston, Robert. "Weirdos in a Strange Land." *The New York Times Book Review*, January 20, 1991, 7, 9. Houston praises *Gringos* as a true depiction of Mexico and its American expatriates and states that the book is driven by Portis' love for his characters and for Mexico. Even though his focus may occasionally blur and his plot wander, Portis always furnishes his reader with delight.

Jones, Malcolm, Jr. "Happy Motoring in Mexico: Charles Portis's Wonderful High-test Hi-jinks." *Newsweek* 17 (February 11, 1991): 60-61. Jones remarks on the literary establishment's neglect of Portis' work and the probable reasons. He discusses the deft alternation between aimlessness and purposefulness in the narrative. Finally, he asserts that this is the author's most inward-turning book, one in which the comedy rests upon a bedrock of melancholy.

Michaud, Charles. Review of *Gringos*, by Charles Portis. *Library Journal* 116 (January, 1991): 155. The reviewer notes, as have many others, that most of the book's characters are on some kind of quest. The author spoofs these often ridiculous quests but also portrays a world that can turn suddenly deadly. The reviewer concludes that readers who delighted in *True Grit* and *The Dog of the South* will not be disappointed in *Gringos*.

Steinberg, Sybil. Review of *Gringos*, by Charles Portis. *Publishers Weekly* 237 (October 26, 1990): 56. Steinberg concentrates primarily upon identifying the book's characters in this largely unfavorable review. She finds a tiresome sameness to Portis' uprooted Americans. Further, Steinberg argues that, despite its wild and woolly nature, the story does not really go anywhere.

Wolfe, Tom. *The New Journalism.* New York: Harper & Row, 1973. In 1960, Portis joined the *New York Herald Tribune*, where he worked with Jimmy Breslin, Dick Schaap, and Wolfe, practitioners of the "new journalism." Portis eventually was named London correspondent, one of the paper's choicest assignments. Wolfe comments upon Portis' days at the newspaper in the early pages of his book.

*Patrick Adcock*

# A HERO AIN'T NOTHIN' BUT A SANDWICH

*Author:* Alice Childress (1920-      )
*Type of plot:* Social realism
*Time of plot:* The 1960's
*Locale:* New York City
*First published:* 1973

> *Principal characters:*
> BENJIE JOHNSON, a thirteen-year-old African American boy
> ROSE JOHNSON (CRAIG), his mother
> BUTLER CRAIG, Rose's boyfriend
> JIMMY-LEE POWELL, Benjie's best friend
> MRS. RANSOM BELL, Benjie's highly religious grandmother
> NIGERIA GREENE, an African American teacher at Benjie's school
> BERNARD COHEN, a white teacher at Benjie's school

## The Novel

Providing a realistic portrait of a young boy becoming a drug addict in the inner city of New York, *A Hero Ain't Nothin' but a Sandwich* suggests that there are no simple answers to the problems of addiction, poverty, and crime. *A Hero Ain't Nothin' but a Sandwich* is told as a series of brief monologues. Presented in a "documentary" style, the novel depicts each of the main characters telling his or her story in turn. This approach serves both to reinforce the novel's graphic realism and to illustrate the complexity of the problems that it addresses. All the novel's characters are distinct individuals, offering their own explanations for Benjie's problems, justifying their own actions, and, at times, impugning the motives of others. By telling her story in this way, Childress is able to strip away her characters' self-deceptions and balance every plausible accusation against an equally plausible countercharge.

The novel begins with Benjie's description of his neighborhood. It is a dismal place: Poverty and drugs are everywhere; rampant crime makes young and old alike afraid to leave their homes; most families have been torn apart by divorce or death. It is important for the reader to see Benjie's world through this character's own eyes and to develop sympathy for him at the very beginning of the novel. If Childress did not structure the plot in this way, the reader might be tempted to dismiss Benjie as merely a thief and an addict. As the author suggests, however, Benjie's situation is quite complicated. While he is, admittedly, a drug user, he also has a number of admirable qualities that make him a likable character.

In the second monologue, Butler Craig indicates that Benjie's use of drugs is more extensive than Benjie has indicated. Butler mentions that Benjie is now "into stealin" and has sold items belonging to his own family in order to support his habit. Though Butler does not condone Benjie's behavior, he does express genuine affection for the boy.

One by one, all the characters interpret Benjie's problem in terms of their own relationship to him. Jimmy-Lee Powell reflects upon the close friendship that he and Benjie once had; he regrets that Benjie's use of heroin has caused a gulf to form between them. Benjie's grandmother feels that the use of drugs can only be cured through prayer and intense religious faith. Nigeria Greene, one of Benjie's teachers, sees addiction as resulting from the oppression imposed by whites upon all African Americans. Benjie's mother is saddened by her son's inability to speak openly about his problem; at the same time, she reveals her own inability to convey her true feelings to Benjie.

All the characters grasp some part of Benjie's situation, but none of them sees it in its entirety. Childress wants the reader to understand that many factors have caused Benjie to experiment with drugs. While he cannot solve his problems until he admits his own responsibility, the poverty and violence of his neighborhood have also been a major factor in making drugs available to him.

When Benjie arrives at school one day obviously under the influence of drugs, Nigeria Greene and Bernard Cohen set aside their personal differences in order to help the boy. They take Benjie to the principal of the school and arrange for Benjie to enter a drug-treatment program. This quick action brings about a temporary improvement in Benjie's situation. Nevertheless, Benjie still finds it difficult to accept Butler as a replacement for his natural father. He regards Butler as a failure and treats him with contempt. The two of them quarrel, and Benjie again begins to think about buying heroin. Finding no money in the house, he pawns Butler's only overcoat and suit. This theft proves to be the last straw for Butler. He leaves Rose and moves into a different apartment in the same building. This decision deprives Benjie of one of the few male role models from whom he could have learned.

A short while later, Butler suddenly feels that he is not alone in his new apartment. As he looks around, he catches sight of Benjie stealing yet again. Benjie panics and goes to the roof in an attempt to cross over to the next building. When Benjie slips, Butler grabs him and saves his life. This heroic action and the drug-related death of one of his friends lead Benjie to ask for help in solving his problem.

One night when Benjie cannot sleep and is again tempted to buy heroin, he writes "BUTLER IS MY FATHER" over and over on a sheet of paper, waiting for the craving to pass. He places this paper in the pocket of Butler's new suit but, on the following day, attempts to retrieve it. Though Butler never mentions it, he has taken the paper, and Benjie knows that he must have read it. He realizes that Butler is "cool," the hero for whom he had long been hoping.

The novel ends ambiguously, as Butler waits for Benjie to report to his new drug-treatment center. Benjie is late, and the reader is led to wonder whether Benjie has succumbed yet again to the drugs that have almost killed him. Childress herself provides no answers, and readers are left to draw their own conclusions.

## The Characters

Benjie Johnson, though only thirteen, is old before his time. Having witnessed intense poverty, he gives the impression of being cynical, hard-hearted and indifferent. Yet Benjie's attitude serves only to hide more tender feelings. Inside, he longs for someone to look up to and fantasizes about the great things that he would like to do.

Benjie's pride is both his undoing and his potential salvation. The pride of showing off has led Benjie to use drugs in the first place. As Nigeria Greene repeatedly says, however, if African Americans developed a genuine pride in the history of their people, they would not allow others to destroy them through addiction.

Butler Craig proves to be the hero in whom Benjie had long ago ceased to believe. As Butler says late in the novel, true heroes are not the rich; they are ordinary people who work day after day to support their families. Butler is also capable of more traditional forms of heroism: He risks injury in order to save Benjie's life and, in his youth, stood up to a racist when everyone else had been afraid.

Benjie's grandmother, Mrs. Ransom Bell, is one of the most complex characters of the novel. At first appearing to be merely a religious zealot, Mrs. Bell gradually reveals herself to be capable of real tenderness. Mrs. Bell had once been a shake dancer (a performer who shook to a musical accompaniment). Though she now condemns her earlier life as immoral, she still takes pride in her skill. In one of the most joyful scenes in the novel, Benjie and Butler persuade Mrs. Bell to show them the dancing for which she had once been famous.

Nigeria Greene is a black nationalist who, without any sense of irony, wears tailor-made English suits. He is fervent in his desire to teach seventh-graders the part of their history that is missing from the school's textbooks. Though often self-righteous, Mr. Greene (dubbed "Africa" by his students) has excellent intentions and is the first one who acts to save Benjie from addiction.

Bernard Cohen is, on the surface, Nigeria Greene's nemesis. In reality, however, the two teachers are working for the same goals. Mr. Cohen cares about the education of his students and is appalled by the quality of their earlier education. Although he wants his African American students to know their own history, he does not believe that this should be all they learn. He attempts to teach black culture in a larger context, improving the skills that his students will need in order to succeed in the world. Mr. Cohen's sincerity is proven by his unwillingness to be transferred to another school even though he could earn more money there.

*Themes and Meanings*

While *A Hero Ain't Nothin' but a Sandwich* does not glamorize theft or drug use, it does suggest that Benjie's problems are not entirely of his own making. Benjie's addiction has resulted both from his own poor choices and from the limited options that society has offered him. Childress reserves some of the harshest passages of the novel for the social workers who blame everything that Benjie has done on his "environment" and, in so doing, fail to help him. *A Hero Ain't Nothin' but a Sandwich* suggests that, while a person's problems may indeed be the result of poverty or injustice, it is up to each individual to take responsibility for his or her own life.

The title of the novel reflects Benjie's cynicism and his belief that, in the modern world, heroism is no longer possible. Benjie learns, however, that real heroes are not those who are perfect. The heroes of the modern world are people such as Butler Craig who may be flawed and have troubles of their own. Real heroes are those who are willing to help others even when they themselves have nothing to gain.

In many ways, all of the people who surround Benjie share at least some of this heroism. Mr. Cohen and Mr. Greene overcome their personal differences in an effort to save Benjie from drugs. Benjie's mother risks her own relationship with Butler Craig because of her devotion to her son. Even Jimmie-Lee Powell and the school's principal would help if only they knew what to do. Nevertheless, Childress does not present these characters as stereotypical heroes. Like Benjie, all the characters have their own individual "addictions": For Butler, it is jazz and his "name-brand bottle that can be tasted now and then"; for Mrs. Bell, it is religion; for Mr. Greene, it is politics. The temptation toward addiction, Childress suggests, is universal. The true hero (or perhaps the true adult) does not, however, permit this temptation to destroy what would otherwise be a productive and meaningful life.

*Critical Context*

Alice Childress is a playwright and director as well as a novelist. In 1956, Childress' play *Trouble in Mind* received an Obie Award as the year's best off-Broadway production. The author's theatrical experience had an important effect upon *A Hero Ain't Nothin' but a Sandwich*. Rather than telling her story through a mixture of narrative and dialogue, Childress relied upon a series of dramatic vignettes to build her novel layer by layer. Each character's point of view serves to change the reader's perspective toward Benjie and his addiction. Like the audience of a play, the readers of this novel see the action not through the eyes of a single individual but through the collective experience of a large number of characters.

The graphic realism of *A Hero Ain't Nothin' but a Sandwich* surprised many readers when the novel first appeared. Although intended for a teenaged audience, the novel contains obscenities, racial epithets, slang, and explicit references to violence and drug use. Childress' intention was not to shock her readers but to permit them to see the world through Benjie's eyes. While Benjie is only thirteen years old, he lives in constant fear of being murdered, robbed, or raped. He has been exposed to suffering more severe than that known by many adults. It should not be surprising, therefore, that Benjie temporarily succumbs to the troubles that surround him. The challenge facing Benjie is how to escape from a life that seems doomed to failure.

The novel's frequent use of dialect (such as "chile" for "child" and "letrit" for "electricity") and slang (including "skag" for "heroin," "cop" for "steal," and "jive" for "phony") places the work in the same general tradition as Mark Twain's *The Adventures of Huckleberry Finn* (1884) and J. D. Salinger's *The Catcher in the Rye* (1951). Like those novels, *A Hero Ain't Nothin' but a Sandwich* uses nonstandard speech in order to create an atmosphere of realism and to underscore the socioeconomic class of its main characters.

*A Hero Ain't Nothin' but a Sandwich* also bears similarities to *The Adventures of*

*Huckleberry Finn* and *The Catcher in the Rye* in other ways. Childress herself has noted that *A Hero Ain't Nothin' but a Sandwich* was the first novel since *The Catcher in the Rye* to be banned from high-school libraries in Savannah, Georgia. Moreover, this novel, like its predecessors, is a combination of *Bildungsroman* (a coming-of-age novel) and social commentary. It presents a flawed central character who quickly gains the readers' sympathy and, by the end of the novel, their understanding.

*Bibliography*

Baker, Augusta. "The Black Experience in Children's Books: An Introductory Essay." *Bulletin of the New York Public Library* 75 (March, 1971): 143-146. This article will help the reader to understand the resistance that Childress' novel received when it first appeared. Published two years before *A Hero Ain't Nothin' but a Sandwich*, Baker's essay defines what many critics believed to be an "appropriate" depiction of black children in literature. Baker's recommendations are almost antithetical to Childress' characterization of Benjie Johnson. For example, Baker argues that black characters in children's fiction should not use dialect, profanity, or racial epithets.

Childress, Alice. "A Candle in a Gale Wind." In *Black Women Writers, 1950-1980: A Critical Evaluation*, edited by Mari Evans. Garden City, N.Y.: Anchor Press/ Doubleday, 1983. An extremely useful discussion by the author herself of her attitudes toward writing and the major factors that influenced her works. Childress mentions that she resists the urge to write about "accomplishers," preferring instead to deal with "those who come in second . . . or not at all." Childress also describes the way in which her work in the theater has influenced characterization in her novels.

Hay, Samuel A. "Alice Childress' Dramatic Structure." In *Black Women Writers, 1950-1980: A Critical Evaluation*, edited by Mari Evans. Garden City, N.Y.: Anchor Press/Doubleday, 1983. Hay describes Childress' process of creating a plot through the presentation of information in succeeding episodes. According to Hay, the plots of Childress' works tend to be rather simple; it is only on the level of characterization and motivation that complexity is achieved.

Killens, John O. "The Literary Genius of Alice Childress." In *Black Women Writers, 1950-1980: A Critical Evaluation*, edited by Mari Evans. Garden City, N.Y.: Anchor Press/Doubleday, 1983. Killens discusses Childress' use of humor and satire as weapons against prejudice. Though Killens focuses primarily on Childress' plays, he uses *A Hero Ain't Nothin' but a Sandwich* as an example of the author's ability to construct "awesomely beautiful and powerful moments" in her works. Killens notes the frequent appearance in Childress' works of the themes of struggle and the need for African Americans to love their own people.

*Jeffrey L. Buller*

# HIGH COTTON

*Author:* Darryl Pinckney (1953-    )
*Type of plot: Bildungsroman*
*Time of plot:* The 1960's to the 1980's
*Locale:* The "Old Country" (the South, especially the Savannah River area), India-
napolis, New York City, London, and Paris
*First published:* 1992

> *Principal characters:*
> THE UNNAMED NARRATOR, a young, reluctant member of the black elite
> in search of his identity
> THE NARRATOR'S FAMILY, his parents and two sisters
> GRANDFATHER EUSTACE, an old-style black intellectual whose influence
> the narrator cannot escape
> THE BEIGE STEPGRANDMOTHER, Grandfather Eustace's second wife
> AUNT CLARA, the narrator's great-aunt, matriarch of Opelika, Alabama
> HANS HANSEN, the narrator's best friend during high school
> DJUNA BARNES, an aging writer for whom the narrator does odd jobs
> MAURICE, the assistant managing editor of a publishing company where
> the narrator works
> THE POWER BITCH, the secretary of the publishing company's managing
> editor
> VIRTEA, head of the publishing company's Black Caucus

*The Novel*

Narrated in the first person by an unnamed protagonist whose story spans three
decades, *High Cotton* seems obviously autobiographical, at least in broad outline.
Like the novel's protagonist, Darryl Pinckney is the product of an elite black family.
His grandfather was graduated from Brown and Harvard universities and was a
minister. Pinckney too grew up in Indianapolis, was graduated from Columbia
University, and worked for a New York publishing house, and he too has puzzled over
the nature of black identity in America.

Yet how far the novel's anecdotal details agree with the author's life is another
matter. The author was selective, both to be discreet and to make his points—around
which he perhaps felt free to embroider and invent, since he presented his work as
fiction.

The novel's main story line traces the development of the young protagonist. It
begins with his boyhood in Indianapolis during the era of the Civil Rights movement.
As a child, the narrator gets mixed messages about his blackness: He is told that he is
"just as good as anyone else out there," but he still notices that some people "moved
away from you at the movies." For him, one of "the Also Chosen," the future beckons,
but still the past oppresses via the "collective power" of numerous older relatives who,
heavy with their knowledge, "enlisted the departed" to their cause.

Most prominent among the "old timers" is Grandfather Eustace, proud that he belongs to the black aristocracy, "a sort of dusky peerage with their degrees, professions, and good marriages among their own kind." Grandfather Eustace is anxious to pass on his proud heritage to the narrator. Looking back, however, the narrator confesses that "I spent much of my life running from him, centripetal fashion, because he was, to me, just a poor old darky."

The narrator and his grandfather, however, agree about the narrator's neighborhood. After one visit with the narrator's family, Grandfather Eustace refuses to return to their rundown house, which he says is "on the wrong side of Indianapolis." The block has biting dogs, disreputable neighbors, and Buzzy, a twelve-year-old bully who throws bottles at passing cars and spouts Black Power slogans. Tormented by Buzzy, the bookish protagonist retreats into Anglophilic fantasies, imagining his home as the British Isles and himself as various British worthies.

Life opens up for the protagonist when his family moves to a predominately white suburb, right across from a country club. His grandfather coaches him on how to survive white classrooms, but happily he suffers "no traumas of any kind." Instead, he becomes popular with his white classmates and teachers, and his best friend, Hans Hansen, is white. He has trouble only with black classmates, who call him "Dr. Thomas" or "Tom."

The protagonist briefly joins the revolutionary Heirs of Malcolm, but he hardly seems committed (in a comic twist, Hans Hansen drives him to the group's meetings in a sports car). He appears to join to satisfy his curiosity and his black critics and to reap "the social satisfactions of being a Black Power advocate in a suburban high school." All in all, the protagonist seems well launched on a predictable life course. Thereafter, he enjoys "the paradise of integration" throughout high school, a trip to London, college at Columbia University, life in New York City, and a trip to Paris.

He seems willing to forget his blackness or to wear it lightly, as convenient—if the world will let him; however, the world does not. Despite his ease with the predominately white world, it constantly reminds him of his blackness, which it sometimes defines in rude and stereotypical terms—for example, when Djuna Barnes insults him, when taxis do not stop for him, and when white women speed up their walks ahead of him. Other blacks, too, will not let him forget. One of these is his grandfather, who lives on in New York City and eventually dies in an Indianapolis nursing home.

The death of his grandfather compels the narrator to make a pilgrimage to the "Old Country," Georgia. There, along the banks of the Savannah and Ogeechee Rivers, in Augusta, in family graveyards, and in the Thankful Baptist Church, the narrator finally confronts his black heritage. The novel ends with his profound and moving meditation on that heritage, the suffering it has involved, and the meaning of being black in America.

*The Characters*

*High Cotton* is replete with interesting characters, some developed only in brief sketches, others at more length. They are described directly, through the eyes of the narrator, who is marvelously observant and witty.

The narrator is characterized indirectly, primarily through his allusive language and wry tone. Otherwise, he is prone to be coy rather than confessional, at least about some aspects of his life. For example, readers learn nothing about his love life; in fact, the word "neuter" might best describe him, since the only principle he seems to represent is opportunism. He seems to have no strong commitments to any values or persons, including himself. Rather, he is in the process of finding himself, undergoing a prolonged adolescence supported by indulgent parents who send him checks even after he is graduated from college.

Once the narrator gets into a confessional mode, however, no one can be harder on himself. He acknowledges that for most of his life he has been "out of it," that his indifference to the "old-timers" and the heritage they represent was "like a camou-flage maneuver, a prolongation of the adolescent lament that I wasn't real but everyone else was. . . ." He finally accepts his "responsibility to help my people, to honor the race." In this sense, the whole book is a confession, an expiation, a modern rime of the ancient mariner (now become the black artist as a young man).

Many of the other characters are the protagonist's relatives, particularly the old-timers, who fill in the sense of the black past and are lovable for their crankiness and personality. Each offers his or her record of suffering and response. Among these are Aunt Clara, who practically owns a small Southern town, and Uncle Castor, who found his outlet in jazz. Chief among the old-timers is Grandfather Eustace, who recognizes much of himself in the young narrator. Like the narrator, Grandfather Eustace is a highly intelligent man who endured a long adolescence and several trial careers before he found his calling. Unhappily, in the present Grandfather Eustace is "the emperor of out-of-it."

Via other characters, the narrator surveys contemporary black life, from the Civil Rights and Black Power movements through equal opportunity and affirmative action. He gives a brief but charming portrayal of his parents, who take him to a civil rights march in chapter 1 and in the final chapter gently tweak him for not attending National Association for the Advancement of Colored People (NAACP) conventions. A hilarious segment of the novel satirizes the Black Power movement, represented by Sister Egba and her followers in the Heirs of Malcolm. The publishing house where the narrator works contains another interesting collection of characters, including Big Boss, Little Boss, and the Power Bitch. After pressure from the Black Caucus, the bosses promote Maurice to assistant managing editor, but his new position only turns him into a glorified security guard "obliged to spy on employees." His story demonstrates how equal opportunity and affirmative action have not brought an end to suffering and the need to respond.

### Themes and Meanings

As the book's range of characters shows, the meaning of being black in America has both not changed and changed tremendously over the generations. The African American experience has always involved suffering, but the degree and nature of that suffering have varied; hence, responses that once seemed valid eventually grow out of date. Thinking of the old-timers, the narrator realizes that he "would never know what they knew"; in the same way, Grandfather Eustace "considered it good form not to talk to us about the hardships he had witnessed," and his grandfather, in turn, "had thought it wise not to speak too truthfully about his years in bondage." Grandfather Eustace's suffering "from being black at a time when everyone was white" and his fusty idea of a black aristocracy date him as "a terrible snob," while the revolutionary poses and rhetoric of the Heirs of Malcolm render them comic.

In particular, *High Cotton* seems to portray the morning after the Civil Rights movement, critiquing with cold realism both low expectations and high hopes. These mixed messages are suggested by the demonstration that the young narrator attends; to him, it is merely confusing and anticlimactic, a spectacle gawked at by white spectators. Grandfather Eustace calls such marches " 'Congo' lines," but then the whole movement occurs without his permission. He is even disappointed that his grandson suffers no traumas in white schools. Apparently some people, both black and white, were surprised by and unprepared for the gains of the Civil Rights movement. On the other hand, in others the movement might have inspired inflated hopes that were subsequently dashed or unrealized.

The narrator seems to critique such hopes, even fantasies, by applying the outrageous term "the Also Chosen" to blacks. Most reviewers took the term (which implicitly juxtaposes blacks with Old Testament Jews, God's "Chosen People") to allude to the "Talented Tenth," W. E. B. Du Bois' term for the best and brightest African Americans. Grandfather Eustace would doubtless agree with such a usage, but the narrator also applies the term to his generation, the first born under the dispensation of the Civil Rights movement: "Perhaps the old-timers were right to insist that we, the Also Chosen, live wholly in the future," he speculates.

The Civil Rights movement was an undeniable high point in African American history, but how does one prepare for the inevitable letdown? The narrator concludes the book with a lament for a vanished time:

> Even now I grieve for what has been betrayed. I see the splendor of the mornings and hear how glad the songs were, back in the days when the Supreme Court was my Lourdes, and am beyond consolation. The spirit didn't lie down and die, but it's been here and gone, been here and gone.

*Critical Context*

*High Cotton* is a significant contribution to the discussion of race in America, providing a balance in several ways. For one, the novel calls attention to an often overlooked segment of African American society, a literate black middle class that has been established for generations. For another, it examines black identity as a complex concept that has changed over time and that is fraught with ambiguity. For still another, it stresses the weight of African American history on the present: "The past gets longer and longer," the author notes. Finally, the book injects honesty into a public discussion almost stifled by stereotypes, clichés, ignorance, hypocrisy, and political correctness. Pinckney seems to take delight in opening up the discussion by revealing shibboleths and flinging around "bad" words (he refers to Harlem, for example, as "Valley of the Shines").

In *High Cotton*, his first novel, Pinckney already has a successful voice, a voice that is shocking, erudite, entertaining, and distinctive. Prior to publishing the novel, he developed the voice by writing essays on African American literature for *The New York Review of Books*. So what if his narration in *High Cotton* does resemble a string of essays and anecdotes loosely tied together? This narration too seems to be part of his distinctive style.

*Bibliography*
Als, Hilton. "Word!" *The Nation* 254 (May 18, 1992): 667-670. Describes Pinckney as a writer who is interested in words rather than in promoting an agenda. In his criticism, Als writes, Pinckney explores black authors as writers "whose blackness, politics and flesh and blood made history through their language." In *High Cotton*, Als claims, language is the key to the narrator's search for identity, since it gives him "the voice needed to write his name in the field of existence."
Bell, Pearl K. "Fiction Chronicle." *Partisan Review* 59 (Spring, 1992): 282-295. Bell praises Pinckney as an "astute and independent-minded critic of black literature" who is not "intimidated by orthodox pieties about race and gender." Similarly, the narrator of *High Cotton* is described as "in search of authenticity but distrustful of enthusiasm and wary of commitment." Thus, the hard-won revelation that he finally experiences is "fiercely honest."
Fein, Esther B. "A Writer, But Not a Black Everyman." *The New York Times*, April 9, 1992, pp. C17, C26. This article, based on an interview with Pinckney, notes parallels between him and the narrator of *High Cotton*. Mostly, however, the article records his desire not to be tagged as representative of any one class, race, or group. Rather, "he wants his book to be testimony not only of his race but of his devotion to literature as well."
Stuart, Andrea. "Invisible Man." *New Statesman and Society* 5 (August 14, 1992): 38. Stuart finds *High Cotton* impressive technically but lacking in human qualities. She asks, "What is a black identity when poverty and deprivation play no part in your equation?" She describes the narrator as a nonentity ("the original invisible man"), dubs the book "a curiously chilly experience," and wonders whether the author "has a heart at all."
White, Edmund. Review of *High Cotton*. *The New York Times Book Review* 97 (February 2, 1992): 3. White applauds *High Cotton* as "the considered achievement of a seasoned mind." In particular, he praises Pinckney for writing about race without succumbing to "a puerile 'political correctness' [that] imposes hypocrisy on most writers. . . ." Instead, Pinckney "has dared to treat his theme with excruciating honesty" and "total freedom from restraint."

*Harold Branam*

# HOMEBASE

*Author:* Shawn Wong (1949-    )
*Type of plot: Bildungsroman*
*Time of plot:* The 1950's and the 1960's
*Locale:* Guam and the Western United States
*First published:* 1979

> *Principal characters:*
> RAINSFORD CHAN, a young fourth-generation Chinese American
> BOBBY CHAN, Rainsford's father, an engineer who dies when Rainsford is seven
> RAINSFORD'S MOTHER, the owner of a flower shop, who dies when Rainsford is fifteen
> RAINSFORD'S GRANDFATHER, the man after whom Rainsford is named
> RAINSFORD'S GREAT-GRANDFATHER, the first immigrant in the family, a man who helped build railroads in the American West
> RAINSFORD'S UNCLE, a medical doctor with whom Rainsford lives after his mother's death
> RAINSFORD'S AUNT, manager and owner of a children's shop
> RAINSFORD'S "DREAM-BRIDE," an important creation of Rainsford's mind

*The Novel*

  *Homebase* is a novel about fifteen-year-old Rainsford Chan, a fourth-generation Chinese American struggling to establish his identity both as a person and as an American. The central events of his life, and the ones with which the narrative is most concerned, are the deaths of his father (when Rainsford is seven years old) and of his mother (when he is fifteen).

  The novel is divided into five chapters, each of which has a generous number of what might be called "speculative flashbacks." Rainsford never knew his grandfather or great-grandfather, and he knew his father only slightly before his death. These "speculative flashbacks," which actual make up most of the work, are founded both in reality and in imagination; Rainsford does have some factual information about his grandfather and great-grandfather in the form of letters, documents, and a few family stories and legends that have come down to him. He enlarges upon these to discover and define meaning for his own existence.

  Wong begins the novel by giving the basic facts of Rainsford's present circumstances and family history. The reader learns immediately of several important events in the young narrator's life: Rainsford is fifteen years old, and both of his parents are dead. The narrator is pursuing the lives of his family members, especially those of his grandfather and great-grandfather. He tells us that he cannot speak Chinese, but he remembers his own father teaching him "Home on the Range," buying him Superman T-shirts, and taking him to see World War II films. Although his grandfather and great-grandfather are never given names, they become central to the story, and it is through them and through Rainsford's imagined history of their lives that he comes to terms with his own identity. Much of the opening section is a history, mostly contrived by Rainsford, of his great-grandfather's life while helping to build railroads in Nevada and Wyoming.

In the second chapter, Rainsford writes a letter to his father, who has been dead some eight years. The letter is an attempt by the young teenager to establish a relation with someone not present so that he can go on with his life as a complete individual, with a heritage and self-understanding. The other major event of this chapter is Rainsford's recollection of his father's death; a poignant story is told of the young boy ironing his father's shirts on the night his mother comes home to report his father's death. Readers also learn that two years after his father's death, his mother had taken a lover in order to try to escape some of her own pain from the loss; the attempt is not successful, but it has no negative effects on Rainsford himself.

Rainsford's mother dies when he is fifteen, and the youth goes to live with his uncle, a medical doctor, and his aunt, who runs a children's store. It is important in the third chapter that his relatives treat him well, basically by leaving him alone and providing for him. Rainsford assumes many characteristics of his uncle, such as a taste in clothes and personal habits, and has good experiences in high school. He lives with these relatives for three years.

In the fourth chapter, Rainsford's main activity is to drive around in his car, thinking about himself, his past, and his family members—all now dead except for his aunt and uncle, who function successfully as parents primarily by leaving him alone. On one of these night trips, he sees a passing train and begins to speculate about and to recall his great-grandfather's experiences while working on the railroads in the 1860's. Just as important, however, is his creation of a "dream-bride," a fifteen-year-old girl who will, so he thinks, help him to firmly find himself and become, at last, an American by identity as well as residence.

The grandfather is the main character in the last chapter. Rainsford meets a Navajo Indian who has Chinese blood and is able to inform him of his own name—and, therefore, of his own identity. Rainsford Chan had been named, so he always knew, after a place in California ("Chan" is the Chinese word for California). Rainsford has never been able to find a Rainsford, California, and so has felt that his own identity is incomplete; he has had no knowledge of who or what he actually is. In the last pages of the novel, his search for self is successfully concluded: Rainsford learns that the land itself (that is, America) is his ancestry.

*The Characters*

Rainsford Chan, the narrator and main character of the novel, reveals the process of his struggle for identity as he lets the reader know his thoughts. His development occurs rather quickly as readers realize, rather instantly, that he is "American" in every way. Only Rainsford himself is unaware of this. Moreover, as he tells of events and episodes in his family history, it is clear that other family members before him have already made the transition. Rainsford's struggle and characterization is understood by the reader not so much through his actions (he does little more than drive around in his car at night, and he seldom engages in conversation) as through his thoughts about the past.

Rainsford's father is dead, and they never knew each other as adults. Fixed only and eternally in memory, the father nevertheless exerts tremendous influence on the youth. "Bobby," which is a mispronunciation of "Daddy" by Rainsford as a toddler, is the only character in the work to have a name (except Rainsford himself). Bobby, it is recalled, had spent much time with Rainsford when he was young; the things the child remembers all reflect the father's overt intention to Americanize his son. Through teaching him American games, songs, and traditions, the father effectually denies the Chinese heritage of the family.

Of all these unnamed, dead characters, Rainsford's grandfather is perhaps of most importance. Again, the reader, like the narrator himself, knows little of the grandfather's actual life. Perhaps the most significant fact is that the grandfather had once returned to China but then returned to the United States. At the end of the work, Rainsford's discovery that he had been named after Angel Island in San Francisco Bay—the place where his grandfather had been processed by immigration officials upon his return to the United States—fixes permanently Rainsford's identity as a person and as an American.

The characterization of Rainsford's great-grandfather, who could not speak English and was subjected to prejudice and discrimination of which Rainsford knows nothing, at least by experience, stands in contrast to Rainsford's own life. Even though the fourth-generation American can speculate about his great-grandfather's life, he has nothing in common with him. Rainsford is a stranger in Chinatown, going there out of curiosity like Americans of other racial groups. Rainsford had grown up drinking milkshakes and eating french fries.

Rainsford's aunt and uncle, childless themselves, become his parents after his mother's death. Like other characters in the novel, they are stationary; however, they are different in that they are alive. Primarily, they serve as role models for young Rainsford, who evidently is on his way to acquiring the usual prerequisites of the American Dream after he comes to peace with himself. As successful Americans themselves, the aunt and uncle, though never denying their Chinese heritage, race, and ancestry, live lives in which these things are functionally not important. They live in an upper-middle-class neighborhood near the beach, drive sports cars, and go jogging, for example.

Rainsford's mother is similarly characterized. She, too, is dead from the beginning of the work, and so never changes. Readers learn that she is very proud of her son and favors him with an extreme amount of attention both at home and at the flower shop she owns and manages after her husband's death. Rainsford takes great delight that when "American" customers order "Oriental" bouquets, it is he, Rainsford, who designs them—and does so with absolutely no knowledge of what they are or might look like.

The final character of any consequence is not only dead but also nonexistent. Rainsford imagines a "dream-bride," a girl of some fifteen years of age who could somehow make his life complete. He envisions a trip with her in the American Midwest, knowing only that somehow such a creature would establish his own worth as an individual. The "dream-bride," of course, turns out to be America herself.

### Themes and Meanings

Rainsford Chan's story is one of finding himself. He must determine his identity and meaning as a person, a man, and an American. Of these three, only the second one (that is, his identity as a man) presents few problems; remarkably, he experiences less of this struggle than a reader might lend plausibility. He is athletic and likes girls, cars, war films, hamburgers, and milkshakes; hence, there is rather an absence of problems.

His struggle to find himself as a person revolves mostly around the fact that his parents are dead. This works in the novel not as a Freudian formula; rather, it serves as a way for the novelist to emphasize that Rainsford's background and heritage—even his parentage—are dead. His realizations are never quite made from an existential context, and yet he does discover and define meaning from within the self.

It is the problem of his identity as an American that is of most concern to the novelist and reader. Slowly, Rainsford learns that he is and always has been American, that the problems surrounding him because of his biological ethnicity are not only irrelevant but nonexistent. Wong emphasizes this most especially in the "speculative flashback" technique he uses in telling the stories of Rainsford's parents, father, grandfather, and great-grandfather. All of their experiences as Chinese stand in direct, perhaps even stark, contrast to those of the young narrator. Rainsford's problems are never their problems; indeed, it often seems that Rainsford's struggle, though valid, meaningful, and beautifully rendered, is something of a luxury, a self-indulgence. This fact does not undercut the severity or the importance of his struggle; rather, it emphasizes the totality of his loss of Chinese identity and role as a mainstream American.

Wong uses several epic conventions in his work. The trip that Rainsford takes with his family from Berkeley to New York and back, as well as the few years in Guam, are reminiscent of the journey made by Odysseus. Too, his call to his forefathers to help him find meaning in life has more in common with prayer to the Muses than it does with traditional Asian, worship or reverence for ancestors. Moreover, his car becomes something of a weapon in his internal war. These connections are never overt, but such occurrences make young Rainsford's existence and experiences somewhat akin to those of Odysseus.

### Critical Context

*Homebase*, written at the end of the 1970's, is an important statement about the role of Asian Americans in the United States at the time. The author explains minority "mainstreaming" for such Chinese immigrants, but his message applies just as meaningfully to immigrants of other races and nationalities. Such minority fiction was coming into vogue for the first time during this period, following some rather huge publication successes of the 1960's in which books by minority authors became truly important for the first time. Wong writes of a time when newly arrived immigrants could not survive in America without first giving up their history, heritage, and past. He emphasizes this most centrally in the novel by distinguishing between "Chinese" and "Chinaman." Rainsford Chan is by birth "Chinese"—he becomes a "Chinaman" (and therefore an object of discrimination and prejudice) only when he goes to Chinatown. As ethnic fiction, *Homebase* makes its statement clearly through its title: America, not China, is Rainsford Chan's home base. China can never be more to him than other homelands can be to other Americans, virtually all of whom are descended from immigrants.

*Bibliography*
Gong, Ted. "Approaching Cultural Change Through Literature: From Chinese to Chinese American." *Amerasia Journal* 7 (Spring, 1980): 73-86. Gong delineates the processes of acculturation common to all Chinese immigrants. A reading of Gong's study validates the credibility of Rainsford Chan's experiences.
Hom, Marlon K. "A Case of Mutual Exclusion: Portrayals by Immigrant and American-born Chinese of Each Other in Literature." *Amerasia Journal* 10 (Fall/Winter, 1984): 29-45. Hom's article, while discussing works written both in English and in Chinese, elucidates various problems between Chinese and American cultures. Helpful in understanding Rainsford Chan's entrapment in middle territory between the two cultures.
Kazin, Alfred. *A Writer's America: Landscape in Literature.* New York: Alfred A. Knopf, 1988. Two chapters of this book discuss the landscape of the American West, which is central to Rainsford Chan's discovery of self and identity. These include chapter 3, which has information about the lands where Chan's forefathers worked on the American railroad, and chapter 6, which explains the role of California in the American identity, something learned by the main character.
Spencer, Benjamin T. *Patterns of Nationality.* New York: Burt Franklin, 1981. Part 1 of this text, entitled "The Nature of Nationality," spells out particular changes experienced by various ethnic groups arriving in the United States. The author addresses problems that occur when "continuity" and "change" confront various groups of new arrivals.
Yu, Connie Young. "Rediscovered Voices: Chinese Immigrants and Angel Island." *Amerasia Journal* 4, no. 2 (1977): 123-139. Yu discusses in some length the experiences of Chinese immigrants arriving in the United States to be processed for residency through government officials at Angel Island. Such experiences were lived through by both Rainsford Chan's great-grandfather and grandfather.

*Carl Singleton*

# THE HOUR OF THE STAR

*Author:* Clarice Lispector (1925-1977)
*Type of plot:* Social realism
*Time of plot:* The 1970's
*Locale:* Rio de Janeiro, Brazil
*First published: A Hora da Estrela,* 1977 (English translation, 1986)

*Principal characters:*
> RODRIGO S. M., the narrator, who struggles to write the story of Macabéa
> MACABÉA, a young girl from the northeast of Brazil who has migrated to
> Rio de Janeiro, where she works as a typist
> OLÍMPICO DE JESUS MOREIRA CHAVES, Macabéa's boyfriend, a thug from
> the northeast
> GLÓRIA, Macabéa's office mate
> MADAME CARLOTA, a fortune-teller whom Macabéa visits

*The Novel*

In *The Hour of the Star,* Clarice Lispector creates a male narrator, Rodrigo S. M., to write the story of a young Brazilian girl who has recently moved to Rio de Janeiro. The narrator has caught sight of this young girl on the street. She is nothing special; the slums of Rio de Janeiro are filled with thousands like her, shopgirls and office workers sharing one-room flats, invisible and superfluous, silent in the clamor of the city.

The first quarter of the book is taken up with Rodrigo's ruminations on why and how he is writing the story of this young girl. He declares that her story must be told by a man, for a woman would feel too much sympathy and end up in tears. The story must be told simply and with humility, for it is about the unremarkable adventures and the shadowy existence of a young girl trying to survive in a hostile city. Rodrigo feels the need to identify with his subject, so he decides to share her condition as closely as possible by wearing threadbare clothes, suffering from lack of sleep, neglecting to shave, giving up sex and football, avoiding human contact, and immersing himself in nothingness. He envisions this identification with his protagonist as a quest for transfiguration and his "ultimate materialization into an object. Perhaps I might even acquire the sweet tones of the flute and become entwined in a creeper vine."

After describing the disastrous physical appearance of the girl, Rodrigo briefly rehearses her early history. She was born, suffering from rickets, in the backwoods of Alagoas, where her parents died of typhoid when she was two years old. Later she was sent to Maceio to live with her maiden aunt. The aunt, determined to keep the girl from becoming a prostitute, enjoyed thrashing her niece at the slightest provocation or no provocation at all. The child never knew exactly why she was being punished. The only education she experienced beyond three years of primary school was a short typing course, which gave her enough confidence to seek a position as a typist in Rio de Janeiro.

At the a moment Rodrigo's story intrudes into her life, the girl is about to be fired. Her work is hopeless—full of typing errors and blotched with dirty spots. Yet her polite apology for the trouble she has caused inspires her boss to modify his dismissal into a warning. The girl retreats to the lavatory to try to recover her composure. When she looks into the tarnished mirror, her reflection seems to have disappeared; her connection to even her own existence is as fragile and tenuous as is Rodrigo's commitment to identifying her. It is nearly halfway through the text before he even allows her a name.

One day, the girl garners enough courage to take time off from work. She exults in her freedom: the luxury of having the room to herself, of indulging in a cup of instant coffee borrowed from her landlady. She dances around the room and contemplates herself in the mirror. It is a moment of sheer happiness and contentment. On the next day, the seventh of May, a rainy day, she meets her first boyfriend; they immediately recognize each other as northeasterners, and he asks her to go for a walk. He also inquires her name, and for the first time in the text the girl is identified:

—Macabéa.
—Maca — what?
—Béa, she was forced to repeat.
—Gosh, it sounds like the name of a disease . . . a skin disease.

Macabéa explains that her name was a result of a vow her mother had made to the Virgin of Sorrows.

Although the meetings of Macabéa and Olímpico are rain-drenched, their relationship is parched. Conversation is strained, for what little Macabéa has to offer is scorned as foolish or nonsensical by Olímpico. She costs him nothing; the only thing he treats her to is a cup of coffee, to which he allows her to add milk if it does not cost extra. The one kindness he has shown her is an offer to get her a job in the metal factory if she is fired. The high point of the relationship occurs one day when Olímpico decides to show off his strength to Macabéa by lifting her above his head with one hand. Macabéa feels that she is flying—until Olímpico's strength gives way, and he drops her into the mud. Not long after, he drops her entirely. Olímpico has become enamored of Macabéa's workmate, Glória.

Maternally sympathetic to Macabéa, Glória recommends a doctor to her when she is feeling unwell and lends her money to consult a fortune-teller who has the power to break bad spells. The doctor diagnoses Macabéa as suffering the preliminary stages of pulmonary tuberculosis, but the words mean nothing to her. He is appalled by her diet of hot dogs and cola and advises her to eat spaghetti whenever possible. Macabéa has never heard of the dish. As for the fortune-teller, Macabéa accepts the loan, asks for time off from her job, and takes a taxi to see Madame Carlota.

The fortune-teller cuts the cards to read Macabéa's fortune and immediately exclaims over the terrible life that Macabéa has led; then she sees a further misfortune—the loss of her job. Turning another card, though, brings a life change. All of

Macabéa's misfortunes will be reversed: her boyfriend will return and ask her to marry him, and her employer will change his mind about firing her. A handsome foreigner named Hans will fall madly in love with her and shower her with unimagined luxuries. Macabéa is astounded; she embraces Madame Carlota and kisses her on the cheek. She leaves the fortune-teller's house in a daze. When she steps off the curb, she is struck by a hit-and-run driver in a yellow Mercedes.

The narrator observes Macabéa, who is lying on the pavement bleeding, and wonders about her death. Macabéa gathers herself into a fetal embrace and utters her final words: "As for the future." The narrator lights a cigarette and goes home, remembering that people die.

### The Characters

Rodrigo S. M., the self-declared narrator of the novel, is the voice of self-consciousness, in counterpoint to Macabéa's almost total lack of self-consciousness. He observes the oblivion of his protagonist, and by writing her story goads her into a kind of self-knowledge. The question of the narrative voice in this novel is complex, for Clarice Lispector's own voice is also heard. At times, the reader hears her directly; at times, she can be detected behind or through Rodrigo's words; at times, she seems to be speaking through Macabéa; and at times, her silence is as expressive as her voice.

In the naming of Macabéa and Olímpico, Lispector reveals her ironic playfulness. The Maccabees were a family of Jewish patriots and rulers in the second and first centuries B.C. who led the Jewish people in their struggle for freedom against Syrian rule. Their recapture of the Temple in Jerusalem is marked by the Jewish festival of Hanukkah. The triumphs, power, and fame of the Maccabees are in direct contrast to their namesake's poverty, vulnerability, and obscurity. Olímpico, of course, suggests Mount Olympus and the Olympic Games—the classical spirit of Greek competition. Olímpico competes, but he does it furtively and criminally. He is an accomplished petty thief and is proud of his secret murder of a rival.

Lispector seems to have created Macabéa as a primitive alter-ego. Like Lispector, Macabéa comes from the northeast of Brazil, and like Lispector, she is a creature of spirit. Lispector, though, was a highly educated woman of the world, the wife of a diplomat, the recipient of a law degree, a journalist, and a highly regarded writer of experimental fiction. Macabéa is an empty vessel, so devoid of a place in the world that the only fortune that she can experience is the divine bestowal of a fleeting state of grace.

Olímpico embodies masculine worldliness and ambition. He is concerned with "important things," while Macabéa only notices "unimportant things." She is impressionable where he is impervious to anything he does not understand. What he does understand is the power of blood and the life force, which are embodied for him in the figure of Glória.

Glória represents the survivor. While she lacks any higher self-awareness, she has mastered the skills of survival. She knows how to use her sexual charms and is capable of handling a clerical position. While she is not troubled by the finer points of conscience, she is capable of a kind of maternal compassion.

*Themes and Meanings*

*The Hour of the Star* begins and ends with passages that prominently feature the word "yes." The "yes" at the beginning of the book is acquiescence to life: "Everything in the world began with a yes. One molecule said yes to another molecule and life was born." The "yes" at the close of the book is an acceptance of death:

> Dear God, only now am I remembering that people die. Does that include me?
> Don't forget, in the meantime, that this is the season for strawberries. Yes.

Yet even this acceptance of death is interrupted with the insistence that one enjoy life for as long as it offers itself. Lispector died of cancer in the same year that *The Hour of the Star* was published. She characterizes death, "my favorite character in this story," as the ultimate encounter with oneself.

Death and rebirth and metamorphoses are intimately linked in this twisted fairy tale of a Cinderella whose only transformation into the princess happens at the moment of her death. Lispector hangs Macabéa's story on the frame of the fairy tale, with a wicked stepmother (the aunt), an uncaring father (the boss), a traitorous stepsister (Glória), a false suitor (Olímpico), and a fairy godmother (Madame Carlota). Yet the prince that Madame Carlota promises is only an illusion—at most, he is the driver of the Mercedes that runs Macabéa down. The storyteller cannot conjure a happy ending for this poor girl from the northeast.

Reality intrudes. On one level, Lispector is exposing the cruelty and difficulties faced by those who have been forced to emigrate from the hinterlands of Brazil into the cities. Northeast Brazil is the poorest region of a country that, though blessed with natural resources, has not been able to devise a system in which wealth can be distributed in any equitable way. Macabéa and Olímpico, products of the impoverished northeast, present the faces of the victim and the violent—both are devoid of any "civilizing" culture. Olímpico will fight his way into a marginally bourgeois existence, probably by marrying Glória and joining her father in the butchery business. Macabéa hungers for bits of knowledge; she collects advertisements and listens to the culture capsules presented on the radio. This knowledge, though, seems only to alienate her even further from the urban pathways of modern Rio de Janeiro. Her instinctual being does not accord with official reality.

*Critical Context*

*The Hour of the Star* was the last book that Clarice Lispector published during her lifetime. She wrote it at the same time as she was writing *Um Sopra de Vida* (1978; a breath of life), a confessional novel bordering on lyrical poetry. *The Hour of the Star* is unique among Lispector's novels in that it deals with contemporary social and political problems in Brazil.

Lispector is best known for moving Brazilian fiction away from regional preoccupations. Like her Argentine contemporary Jorge Luis Borges, she was more concerned as a writer with such major twentieth century literary preoccupations as existentialism, the *nouveau roman*, and linguistic experimentation. Her prose is highly imagistic, and her protagonists develop more through their interaction with everyday objects than through the action of the plot. In rhythmically developed epiphanies reminiscent of James Joyce and Virginia Woolf, her characters gradually come to an awareness of the isolation and ephemerality of their individual existences. Lispector is one of the early voices of female consciousness in Latin American literature; her protagonists are generally middle-class urban women attempting to find a place in the contemporary world.

*The Hour of the Star* shares many of these themes and stylistic qualities with such earlier works as *Laços de Família* (1960; *Family Ties*, 1972) and *Maçã no Escuro* (1961; *The Apple in the Dark*, 1967), but Lispector's focus on the devastating effects of poverty in contemporary Brazil marked the first time that her very real social concerns (as revealed in her newspaper columns and elsewhere) were addressed in her fiction. Lispector's early death, a day before her fifty-second birthday, silenced one of Latin America's most experimental and original voices.

*Bibliography*
Cixous, Hélène. "The Author in Truth." In *"Coming to Writing" and Other Essays*, edited by Deborah Jenson. Cambridge, Mass.: Harvard University Press, 1991. Cixous meditates upon *The Hour of the Star* as Lispector's final work: "a text like a discreet psalm, a song of thanksgiving to death." She posits that in Macabéa, Lispector has created the ultimate "other," her own "personal stranger."
_____ . *"The Hour of the Star*: How Does One Desire Wealth or Poverty?" In *Reading with Clarice Lispector*, edited and translated by Verena Andermatt Conley. Minneapolis: University of Minnesota Press, 1990. A collection of seminar lectures given by Cixous between 1980 and 1985. Cixous describes *The Hour of the Star* as "a text on poverty that is not poor." She asserts that Lispector is exploring the question of the ultimate identity and equality of worth of all human beings.
Fitz, Earl E. *Clarice Lispector*. Boston: Twayne, 1985. Provides an excellent introduction to Lispector's life and works. A good bibliography up to the year 1985 is also provided.
Lindstrom, Naomi. "Clarice Lispector." In *Women's Voice in Latin American Literature*. Washington, D.C.: Three Continents Press, 1989. Includes discussion of the major themes in Lispector's works and her use of various narrative techniques. Useful in setting *The Hour of the Star* within the context of Lispector's other work.
Peixoto, Marta. "Rape and Textual Violence in Clarice Lispector." In *Rape and Representation*, edited by Lynn A. Higgins and Brenda R. Silver. New York: Columbia University Press, 1991. Examines the techniques by which Lispector writes the victim's experience in three short stories and in *The Hour of the Star*. Notes that in *The Hour of the Star*, Lispector reveals the complicity of the narrator,

the author, and the reader in the suffering of Macabéa.

Pontiero, Giovanni. Afterword to *The Hour of the Star*, by Clarice Lispector. Translated by Giovanni Pontiero. Manchester, England: Carcanet, 1986. Pontiero discusses how Lispector's nostalgia for her childhood home, Recife in the northeastern Brazilian state of Pernambuco, was the genesis of this book. He is also concerned with Lispector's investigation of the psychological consequences of poverty as revealed in the character of Macabéa.

*Jane Anderson Jones*

# THE HOUSE OF THE SPIRITS

*Author:* Isabel Allende (1942-    )
*Type of plot:* Historical realism
*Time of plot:* The turn of the century to the 1970's
*Locale:* An unnamed South American country
*First published: La Casa de los espiritus,* 1982 (English translation, 1985)

> *Principal characters:*
> CLARA DEL VALLE TRUEBA, the daughter of a wealthy aristocratic family
> ESTEBAN TRUEBA, Clara's husband, the son of an impoverished middle-class family who acquires immense wealth and power
> ALBA TRUEBA, Clara and Esteban's granddaughter, who narrates the story

*The Novel*

*The House of the Spirits* follows three generations of three families, each of which represents a social class with its particular culture and political outlook. This historical fiction is based on Isabel Allende's own childhood growing up in Chile, her family and relatives, and her experiences as a journalist covering her country's political turmoil.

*The House of the Spirits* is narrated by Clara's granddaughter Alba, who is piecing together her family's past using the numerous notebooks that her grandmother had written throughout her life and incorporating her grandfather Esteban's memoirs.

The book begins when Clara is a young child; although she lives in luxury and is pampered by her family, she stands out as the protagonist and an individual with special qualities. She can communicate with the hereafter, she can foretell events, and most important, she can sense injustice and corruption. She can foresee that Esteban will seek to marry her after the mysterious death of his fiancée, her sister Rosa. Clara knows that she does not love him, but she senses that her duty to others resides with this marriage. This duty begins when they visit Esteban's country estate, Tres Marías, where poverty and neglect of the peasant class are visible to Clara. She knows that Esteban has illegitimate children through one family, the Garcías, and this important relationship enters into the Truebas' lives throughout the novel. From now on, Clara will alternate between living in the reality of the here and now—attending to her family and helping others—and her escape world, where she communes with spiritual forces that allow her to see what is unjust and duplicitous about the real world.

Throughout her marriage to Esteban and the birth of three children, Blanca and the twins Nicólas and Jaime, Clara represents a better tomorrow, a promising and equal society for her country that is not possible now—hence her magical qualities. Esteban becomes a powerful senator and an influential conservative politician who fights against the social reform and political democracy represented by new voices of liberalism and economic equality. He works secretly with other patriarchal figures and foreign governments to overthrow the socialist candidate for president, Isabel

Allende's nonfictional uncle by marriage, Salvador Allende, who was president of Chile from 1970 to 1973, when a coup overthrew his government.

The concluding chapters cover the coup and its aftermath. A reign of terror occupies the imaginary country, a parallel to the historical events in Chile. In the novel, Alba is kidnapped and tortured by the right-wing military, but she is able to return home and be united again with her grandfather. Her memories and close alliance with her deceased grandmother Clara enable her to overcome the terror and the suffering; because Alba shares many of the magical properties of her grandmother, she can "hear" Clara's voice and feel her presence in prison. Alba is motivated by Clara to write down her story so it will not be forgotten. Alba represents the future, a time when the country and its people will be at peace with one another and can forgive one another. Alba does not wish for revenge on her enemies, for they are all related and will survive only with the help of one another; she has learned this from Clara. It is Clara's notebooks, along with her memory, that are responsible for Alba's recovery and understanding of the three families that form her past.

*The Characters*

Clara, the protagonist, symbolizes the good and the humanity in people. Her magical qualities make her stand out as a figurative embodiment of a clearer and purer imitation of reality; her name connotes clarity, openmindedness, and insight, and she weaves throughout the text in life and in death as an essential figure of striving and hope. Clara's momentary escapes from the world highlight the irrational nature of the real world, with its corruptions and injustices. A phrase repeated throughout the text—"But reality was different"—emphasizes this and underscores that the better, more humane world of Clara does not yet exist. Clara is the only character who by her very fictional nature can be a hero in this mad historical arena. She is outside this "real" time and place, and the reader is intended to learn from her example.

Esteban represents an entire class whose loyalty is to the conventions of the past, with its strict hierarchal rules and prescribed behaviors. Because of this, Esteban's character does not undergo change; even when he recognizes that the new military government is not an answer to the country's problems, he still looks back to the days when his social class controlled the government and economic resources. He will never admit to mistakes, and this is his failure and the origin of his sorrow. Esteban's words and actions transmit what he represents, for he is quick to anger, temperamental, and emotional, and he has no insight for other ways of seeing. Unlike Clara, he has no respect for individual qualities but always reacts to the codes of society; he ignores his children out of wedlock, and this disinheritance of history is why he is condemned by the novel. He loses his identity when he breaks the links between generations that should always be preserved.

The García family occupies an important role in the novel; like Clara and Esteban, the Garcías represent a social class and way of life. The Garcías constitute the farm-labor population and the urban poor; the family's ancestry is a mix of indigenous South Americans and European immigrants. They have been oppressed for centuries because of who they are, and their role in the text is pivotal. Pedro Segundo is Esteban's right-hand man on the estate; he loathes Esteban, but he represents the older generation, who serve their social superiors well and do not attempt to alter the status quo. His son, Pedro Tercero, symbolizes the younger generation who see things differently; he is a labor organizer of landless people who have been chained to the estate. Pedro's life is interrelated with Clara's and Esteban's lives by his lifelong love relationship with their daughter Blanca, and it is this dissolving of class lines that signals the author's aspirations for the future and positive change for the country. Their daughter, Alba, therefore embodies the emergent democratic perspective that has too frequently been denied for Chile and other Latin American countries.

## Themes and Meanings

*The House of the Spirits* presents the reader with a multiplicity of meanings. First, the Latin American worldview recognizes reality as wearing many faces; it is understood that there are truths above and below the surface. Part of this recognition stems from a political reality in Latin America that has manipulated and distorted the life of the individual. The reader sees this in the discrepancy of wealth and status that defines each character. Only a privileged few, like the del Valles, lead a life of comfort; their opulence is satirically portrayed early in the novel, particularly in regard to their feasts and their leisure. In contrast, even the dwindling middle classes have a difficult time, as shown by the poverty and distress of Esteban Trueba's mother and his sister, Férula. The urban slums are also described in realistic detail; Isabel Allende's purpose is to document this pervasive tragedy, evident in not only Chile but many other countries as well.

Another meaning of the text is an explication of history; Allende presents the coup and the political events of the 1970's not as isolated, unconnected incidents but as developments with roots far back in the social structure of the country. By encompassing an expansive temporal span and following several families through the generations, Allende gives substance and meaning to what happened; as the past is brought forward and kept alive, the forces of history are made visible. By preserving the memory and the past, the truth will not disappear. The importance of Clara's notebooks and Alba's memoir reflect this; both women respect history and the role of memory in their lives. The women's writings then, like the text itself, illustrate the significance of knowing the past and not forgetting it as Esteban has done. The novel, like history, is not organized and logical; it cannot be confined by dates and times, and it is contingent upon innumerable factors. The historical novel presents the dynamics of social organisms over time in a condensed version that illuminates things that might otherwise be invisible. Allende forcefully reminds her readers of the interconnections between the past and the future as well as those between fiction and nonfiction.

A third meaning of the text is philosophical; the author anticipates a more peaceful and egalitarian tomorrow not only for the citizens of Chile but also for all Latin America. This is evident throughout the novel; as time unfolds, racial and class barriers disintegrate through marriage and the forming of new relationships. The three main family groups become intermingled in a perceptible development in the author's quest for harmony and change. Clara's son Jaime becomes a doctor and lives among the poor, Blanca marries Pedro and moves to Canada, and Alba's boyfriend Miguel is not from her social class or political background. Clara becomes best friends with Pedro Segundo after an earthquake that foreshadows the fall of this feudal system. Even Esteban must form unusual alliances with people outside his political doctrine to seek assistance for Alba. The novel concludes with Alba's optimism, forgiveness, and expectations for her unborn child in a literary beginning that the author believes will have parallels in reality.

*Critical Context*

*The House of the Spirits* is an important contribution to contemporary Latin American fiction. Isabel Allende's individual mixture of realism and Magical Realism places the novel firmly in the classical and recent traditions of Spanish-language writers who innovatively respond to the myriad realities of their countries with a complex use of realism on the written page. Latin American novels frequently borrow events, characters, and features from one another in a related, continuing chronicle of the cyclical Latin American reality. Julio Cortázar, Carlos Fuentes, Gabriel García Márquez, and Mario Vargas Llosa periodically refer to one another's fiction. Isabel Allende too retropes some of the characteristics of García Márquez's historical fiction *Cien años de soledad* (1967; *One Hundred Years of Solitude*, 1970). This parodic homage, in the use of repeated time and names, is also a unique aspect of the novel and one that expands its literary horizons.

*The House of the Spirits* is Isabel Allende's first novel, and its readability has made a significant impact on readers who have not been familiar with Latin American literature or history. In particular, the idiosyncratic character of Clara and the close female connections that she sustains with her daughter and granddaughter have ensured the book's prominence in autobiographical and testimonial literature as well as in gender and feminist studies. Additionally, an interest in metafiction is evident in the work; Allende's use of multiple layers of time, reality, and storytelling combine to form a provocative and interesting literary product that also forms alliances and relationships with other contemporary Latin American texts.

*Bibliography*

Adams, Robert M. "The Story Isn't Over." *The New York Review of Books* 32 (July 18, 1985): 20-21. A narrative overview for readers with an interest in the fundamental thematics and background of the novel. Asserts that *The House of the Spirits*, with its emphasis on detail and a building "toward an explanation of [its] own existence," embodies a return to the traditions of storytelling.

Allende, Isabel. "The Spirits Were Willing." In *Lives on the Line: The Testimony of Contemporary Latin American Authors*, edited by Doris Meyer. Berkeley: University of California Press, 1988. This wonderful essay by Allende discusses the origins and process of writing the novel; it is also relevant to scholars interested in the craft of fiction writing. Allende's political motivation is outlined, and she describes the coup and its aftermath, which motivated her to write this first novel: "All of us who write and are fortunate enough to be published should assume the commitment of serving the cause of freedom and justice."

Antoni, Robert. "Parody or Piracy: The Relationship of *The House of the Spirits* to *One Hundred Years of Solitude*." *Latin American Literary Review* 16 (July-December, 1988): 16-28. Antoni discusses Allende's unconscious parodying of García Márquez using a variety of formal features. His intention is to illustrate how Allende ultimately presents her own effective voice. This intelligent article is persuasive in its examination of narrative voices in both novels.

Earle, Peter G. "Literature as Survival: Allende's *The House of the Spirits*." *Contemporary Literature* 28 (Winter, 1987): 543-554. Focuses on the nonfictional reality behind textual events. There are astute interpretations of the principal characters, particularly Clara, Blanca, and Alba, who "embody historical awareness and intuitive understanding." A readable and fine introduction to the text.

Magnarelli, Sharon. "Framing Power in Luisa Valenzuela's *Cola de lagartija* and Isabel Allende's *Casa de los espiritus*." In *Splintering Darkness: Latin American Women Writers in Search of Themselves*, edited by Lucía Guerra Cunningham. Pittsburgh: Latin American Literary Review Press, 1990. In this provocative critique, Magnarelli shows how Allende revises conventional notions of the male-centered narrative. Her emphasis is on Esteban's framing by the female voice and on his continuing struggle to maintain his patriarchal power. The directing narrations of Clara and Alba, however, undercut and transform historical as well as fictional traditions.

*Jane H. Babson*

# THE HOUSE ON MANGO STREET

*Author:* Sandra Cisneros (1954-        )
*Type of plot:* Bildungsroman
*Time of plot:* The mid-1960's
*Locale:* A Latino neighborhood in Chicago
*First published:* 1984

> *Principal characters:*
> ESPERANZA CORDERO, a young girl growing up in a Latino quarter of
>     Chicago
> ALICIA, a college girl who rejects tradition and her father's attempts to
>     confine her
> SALLY, a beautiful girl who goes out with boys and whose father beats her
> MAGDALENA (NENNY) CORDERO, Esperanza's younger sister
> LUCY, a quiet neighbor girl from Texas, Esperanza's friend
> RACHEL, Lucy's little sister

*The Novel*

Based on Sandra Cisneros' experiences growing up in a Latino neighborhood of Chicago, *The House on Mango Street* is the story of a girl's search for identity as she comes of age. The narrative covers one crucial year in her life. Esperanza Cordero, a young Chicana, is ethnically Mexican and culturally Mexican American. As the first-person narrator of the stories, she describes herself, her neighbors, their dreams, and what goes on around Mango Street. In the process, she gains an understanding of herself and of her true identity.

Cisneros has described the forty-six short vignettes that make up the novel as crosses between poems and short stories. The tiny chapters are intensely lyrical, written in prose that is highly charged with metaphor. Each section has a title, and each could stand alone as an autonomous piece, like a prose poem. Esperanza's voice, however, unifies the narrative. Her quest for identity and purpose shapes the plot, which is otherwise loosely defined.

Esperanza describes her family's house on Mango Street as a "sad" little house with a swollen door and no yard or trees. The red bricks are crumbling, and everyone shares a bedroom. It is not the house she imagined her family would have when they moved. She feels as ashamed of the new house as she felt of the old apartment, the one where Mother Superior pointed to the boarded upstairs window and said "You live *there*?" Her parents say this house is temporary, but Esperanza knows better. She dreams of having her own house someday.

Esperanza describes her world with a child's innocence, although her innocence is beginning to fade. She is approaching puberty and the longings and confusion it brings. Moreover, she is an astute observer of the world around her, especially of adults and their actions. She intuits human nature and seems to understand well the emotions her friends, family, and neighbors are feeling.

In the first few sections of the novel, she introduces her family by describing their hair. She introduces the neighbor girls, Lucy and Rachel, in a giddy account of the afternoon they met and shared a new used bicycle. She offers sketches of her neighbors Meme, Louie, Marin, Davey the Baby, and Rosa Vargas, a woman with so many children she does not know what to do. She also describes Alicia, a determined college student who wakes up with the "tortilla star" every morning to pack lunchboxes and who is trying to go to college despite all the duties she has had to shoulder for her siblings since her mother's death. She is portrayed as worn but strong, afraid only of the mice she sees at night and of her dictatorial father.

Midway through the novel, the narrative begins to explore Esperanza's adolescence more closely. Her descriptions and ruminations are emotional, sometimes troubled, sometimes exuberant. She tries on different attitudes and personae. One day Esperanza, her little sister Nenny, Lucy, and Rachel try on old high heels. The grocery man shouts indignantly that high heels are dangerous on little girls, and then a bum tries to bribe the well-heeled girls for a kiss. They run away frightened. No one complains, Esperanza says, when Lucy's mother throws the old shoes in the trash. In this vignette and others such as "Hips," "Geraldo No Last Name," "Sire," and "Four Skinny Trees," Esperanza tests her nascent sexuality, marvels at her body's changes, and savors the emotions of a first crush. In "The First Job," Esperanza is fooled by an elderly man who takes advantage of her trust and naïveté. He grabs her and kisses her in the lunchroom.

Sally, a beautiful, flirtatious girl, strongly influences Esperanza. Sally, it seems to her, knows how to express her sexuality. Esperanza calls herself the ugly daughter whom nobody comes for, so naturally she is smitten by Sally's self-assurance and by the fact that boys adore her. Emulating Sally, though, does not work for Esperanza. In "The Monkey Garden," she is humiliated when she tries to save Sally from a group of boys only to find that Sally does not desire to be rescued. Sally's betrayal becomes complete when she disappears at a carnival and leaves Esperanza alone unprotected. That night, Esperanza is sexually molested by a boy who says only, "I love you Spanish girl." Later episodes focus on Sally's beatings by her father and her attempt to escape by marrying a traveling salesman. Of course, this marriage entraps Sally in a different kind of prison.

As Esperanza matures, her interest in self-identity grows stronger. Of course, Latino society limits young women to certain roles. Marriage is acceptable. Esperanza, though, vows not to "grow up tame like the others." She calls marriage a ball and chain. She does not wish to inherit her grandmother's place at the window, where the old woman sat and sighed sadly as she watched the world go by. Esperanza inherited her grandmother's name, but she does not want her circumstances.

Alicia serves as Esperanza's mentor. Kind, older, and supportive, she teaches her protégé that a woman can pursue her dreams despite male domination. Alicia tells Esperanza that she is Mango Street, like it or not; that no matter where she finally finds her own house, she will come back home to Mango Street again. In the end, Esperanza acknowledges this crucial tie, saying that what she remembers most is the sad red house that "I belong but do not belong to." The stories she tells release her from and also tie her to her past and her community. She vows to return, to rescue the women to whom the book is dedicated. She will accomplish this by handing down their stories to others.

*The Characters*

Esperanza is the story's narrator, and the world of Mango Street is filtered through her sensibility. Her youth makes her a reliable narrator, in the sense that the reader can believe her observations to be honest and unexaggerated. As narrator, she provides the reader with a dual plot: One is the story of her own search for identity, a story about creativity and what it means to become an artist; the other is the story of her Latino neighborhood. The humor, joys, frustrations, and desperation Esperanza describes in the women's stories create a mosaic of Latina life.

Alicia, the persevering college student, is a portrait of a young woman who may win out against the odds. Yet life takes its toll on her. Responsible for taking care of her brothers and sisters after her mother's death, and doing so under the constant pressure and scrutiny of her domineering father, she nevertheless makes time to study; she rides the bus for hours a day to get to and from classes. She is a positive role model who may serve to make the reader aware of the poverty and social barriers women of the underclass must overcome.

Sally, the beautiful girl who gives herself to boys, provides a contrast to Alicia. Her presence also adds tension to the story of Esperanza's search for identity. Esperanza must deal with the conflicting urges she feels when confronted with Sally's lipstick, nylons, beauty, and apparent popularity, in comparison to Alicia's quiet life of household duties and college study. Esperanza says she wants to be like Sally and tries to imitate her, but finally she realizes that Alicia has made better choices. Alicia and Sally share similarities in their lives at home—domineering fathers want to confine them—but they deal with their problems and frustrations differently. Sally flees her father by eloping with a marshmallow salesman, but her new husband and her new home also confine her. The narrative suggests that her husband beats her, just as her father did. Sally's lack of self-esteem is a foil for Alicia's quiet dignity.

Guadalupe, Elenita, and the Three Sisters at the party are characters who help to convey how women of the previous generation have coped with their roles and their lives. They are also spiritual guides for Esperanza, who instinctively recognizes their wisdom and appreciates what they preserve of the Mexican culture. They are members of a sisterhood, so to speak, into which Esperanza will someday seek initiation.

Nenny's importance lies in her age. She is Esperanza's little sister, and her youth and naïveté remind the narrator (and the reader) that no one can go back in time. Nenny's presence recalls the theme of dual vision—Esperanza's puberty means simultaneous allegiance to youth and adulthood, like her dual allegiance to Mexican and American culture.

Rachel and Lucy, Esperanza's young friends, are not so crucial to the novel thematically, but they do serve to remind the reader that Esperanza is still a child. They are part of her childhood world, the world she leaves when she is reporting her observations of the harsh adult world.

## Themes and Meanings

Esperanza's descriptions focus on the women she knows. Since she is a young adolescent, theirs is a world she will soon be expected to join. Her portraits reveal how women's lives are made difficult by the men who dominate them. Often her perspective, which can be both childish and mature, points to the ways that society at large oppresses Latin Americans. The Latina women Esperanza talks about thus bear a double yoke. Living in a strongly patriarchal society, often in fear of violence, they find their choices for survival and self-expression limited. Meanwhile, many suffer along with their men from all the problems of living in poverty. Their burden is the fate the narrator wants to escape.

Esperanza repeatedly insists, sometimes whimsically, sometimes desperately, that she must have a house of her own somehow. She is also intent on becoming a writer. The two needs are intertwined, and they eventually become inseparable in the narrative. Her two wishes, to be a writer and to own her own house, are her prerequisites to freedom and self-identity. How artistic creation strengthens identity and provides dignity is an important theme.

Esperanza often thinks aloud about her identity, in subconscious or naïve ways. She is Chicana, or Mexican American, and she is Mexican by parentage. This dual identity leads her to perceive two possibilities in everything she encounters. One fundamental example is her name: in English it means "hope"; in Spanish it means "too many letters," sadness, and waiting. She says she would like to create a new name for herself. Ezperanza wants to re-create herself from scratch and create the house, too, that will reflect and define her. The house may symbolize the book of her stories that she wants to write.

The house she imagines and describes becomes her symbol for freedom and artistic expression. It also ties her to her community, the anchor of her identity and the source of her stories. In the end, she says that she will leave Mango Street with her books and papers but will come back for those she left behind, meaning that she will not abandon her roots.

Cisneros' careful treatment of Esperanza's narratives, especially in her use of English phrasings that reflect Spanish idioms, allows her to share some nuances of the Mexican American culture that she cherishes. She has Esperanza describe with pride and tenderness the strong ties families and neighbors keep, especially the bonds between women. Yet she is also a strong critic of sexual and physical violence, an endemic problem in Esperanza's neighborhood and, by extension, in Latino society in general.

## Critical Context

*The House on Mango Street* falls between genres. It could be considered a series of prose poems, a chain of vignettes, or a set of short stories unified by the narrator's voice and identity. The chapters were written as a series of stories one might open at any point, so that each might be appreciated as a single piece or as a part of the whole. The novel is not linear but moves from one event to another, often revisiting settings and characters in much the same way a young girl's conversation or inner thoughts might skip from story to story or person to person by association or some other trigger of memory.

After *The House on Mango Street*, her first book, Cisneros published *Woman Hollering Creek, and Other Stories* (1991) and *My Wicked, Wicked Ways* (1992), a volume of poetry. These works also explore the themes of feminism, biculturalism, family violence, artistic creativity, and personal identity. All of Cisneros' work offers insights into what it means to be a Latino in the United States.

*Bibliography*
Cisneros, Sandra. "Sandra Cisneros." In *Interviews with Writers of the Post-Colonial World*, edited by Feroza Jussawalla and Reed Way Dasenbrock. Jackson: University Press of Mississippi, 1992. Cisneros discusses the genesis of her first novel, her use of voices, the effect bilingualism has on her writing, her life in Texas, her parents' lives, feminism, her favorite writers, and her novel in progress
de Valdes, Maria Elena. "In Search of Identity in Cisneros's *The House on Mango Street*." *Canadian Review of American Studies* 23 (Fall, 1992): 55-72. The author systematically charts the stages of Esperanza's search for identity, emphasizing along the way how the narrator's quest is complicated by her "double marginalization."
Kolmar, Wendy K. "Dialectics of Connectedness: Supernatural Elements in Novels by Bambara, Cisneros, Grahn, and Erdrich." In *Haunting the House of Fiction: Feminist Perspectives on Ghost Stories by American Women*, edited by Lynette Carpenter and Wendy K. Kolmar. Knoxville: University of Tennessee Press, 1991. Kolmar discusses the theme of the dual experience. Esperanza's ability to live in two worlds allows her to see the supernatural as natural, to recognize Mango Street as the fertile source for her stories, and to carry with her the voices of women she will knit together into "a vision of interconnectedness."
McCracken, Ellen. "Sandra Cisneros' *The House on Mango Street*: Community-Oriented Introspection and the Demystification of Patriarchal Violence." In *Breaking Boundaries: Latina Writing and Critical Readings*, edited by Asuncion Horno-Delgado et al. Amherst: University of Massachusetts Press, 1989. Taking a feminist perspective, McCracken finds that the novel criticizes capitalistic and patriarchal social structures that oppress Latin women. McCracken insists that texts such as Cisneros' are undervalued by academics and excluded from the American literary canon because they do not "speak the same language" acceptable to academia.
Olivares, Julian. "Sandra Cisneros' *The House on Mango Street* and the Poetics of Space." In *Chicana Creativity and Criticism: Charting New Frontiers in American Literature*, edited by Maria Hererra-Sobek and Helena Maria Viramontes. Houston:

Arte Público Press, 1988. Olivares argues that the house motif represents Cisneros'
"house of story-telling" and that the narrative charts a young writer coming into her
own as artist.

*JoAnn Balingit*

# I, THE SUPREME

*Author:* Augusto Roa Bastos (1917-      )
*Type of plot:* Historical
*Time of plot:* 1800-1840
*Locale:* Asunción, Paraguay
*First published: Yo, el Supremo*, 1974 (English translation, 1986)

> *Principal characters:*
> José Gaspar Rodríguez de Francia (Dr. Francia), the champion of
> Paraguayan independence from Spain and the new country's first
> dictator
> Policarpo Patiño, the dictator's naïve confidential secretary
> Juan Parish Robertson, an English adventurer and representative of
> British interests in the region
> Pilar the Black, the dictator's trusted personal valet and general ser-
> vant
> General Manuel Belgrano, an Argentine general sent first to annex
> Paraguay by force, then to negotiate an alliance through diplomacy
> Antonio Manuel Correia da Camara, a Brazilian envoy sent to
> negotiate an alliance
> Bernardo Velazco, the colonial governor of the province of Paraguay,
> enemy and detractor of Francia
> Sultan, the dictator's republican dog, both companion and critic

*The Novel*

*I, the Supreme* offers a fictionalized account of the key events and motives behind
the nineteenth century dictatorship of Gaspar Rodríguez de Francia (also known as
Dr. Francia), who governed in Paraguay from 1814 until his death in 1840. In the
novel, Augusto Roa Bastos presents a revision of the accepted interpretations of this
period in history, analyzing not only the lingering effects on Paraguay but also the
traditional notions of historical writing as the repository of objective truth.

Although *I, the Supreme* is considered a novel, it exhibits few of the traditional
characteristics of the genre. There is, in fact, no sense of logical continuity that could
constitute a plot, and no single voice that could be considered to narrate events.
Indeed, the book is essentially a juxtaposition of different, and frequently contradictory, conversations, monologues, myths, journal entries, circulars, letters, historical
documents, footnotes, and anonymous commentaries, all brought together by an
unidentified, ostensibly impartial "compiler." This compiler, who replaces both the
traditional narrator and the concept of the author, selects, orders and presents the
diverse fragments that comprise *I, the Supreme*. While the novel is predominantly
fictional, many of the incorporated texts are taken from authentic historical sources,
the value and veracity of which the reader is forced to judge as the novel unfolds.

Besides rejecting the traditional notions of narrator and narrative plot, the novel also eliminates the concept of chronological time. Past, present, and future all merge into a sense of permanent timelessness. The fictional dictator discusses his death and burial as if it were already past, and he argues with historians not yet born and texts not yet written. At other times, two events occurring at vastly different times are telescoped into one moment and presented as simultaneous. This eternal present is emphasized by the insertion of a variety of both European and native Paraguayan myths into historical events as if they were part of the reality being narrated. As a result, the novel offers no progression but rather functions within the timeless dimension of myth.

Insofar as the events of *I, the Supreme* can be said to be located in space and time, the majority of the text is set in the dictator's office and personal quarters in the national palace during the last few months of his life. The novel begins with the appearance on the door of the main cathedral in Asunción of a lampooned dictatorial decree condemning the dictator to death, dismemberment, and oblivion. The outraged Francia, now isolated, ill, and both politically and physically powerless, defends himself and his policies against the judgment of posterity. The rest of the novel consists of this defense before the judge, represented by the reader. Francia's only companion in this enterprise is his naïve personal secretary, Policarpo Patiño, who serves primarily as a scribe taking dictation and as an audience for the dictator's lengthy ramblings and self-justifications. The central action of the text revolves around their extended discussions and arguments on a variety of topics, ranging from real and imagined events to philosophy, writing, and language. A large portion of this dialogue is devoted to the dictation of a "Perpetual Circular," in which Francia recounts his version of events and his ideas on the nation and power. The dialogue and dictation are continuously interrupted by excerpts from the dictator's personal diary, which provide a more intimate self-analysis and critique. Interspersed with this, the reader frequently encounters documents written by the dictator's contemporaries and by future historians; these documents serve as points of departure for further debate between the dictator, his secretary, and his conscience. In this way, all the major events in the novel are narrated, either by the two main characters or by the different historians and historical documents quoted.

Eventually, as the fictional Francia approaches death and the novel becomes increasingly fragmented, the voices of denunciation become stronger and more heavily judgmental. Conversely, the dictator's defense gradually disintegrates until it joins with the detractors and emerges as a self-condemnation. The novel ends abruptly in incoherence, in the middle of a sentence, which corresponds presumably to Francia's physical demise. The "compiler" does provide a curious postmortem to the novel, however, in the form of an appendix of documents that attempt to pinpoint the final resting place of the dictator's bones. The results of the scientific investigation, like those of the novel itself, are inconclusive and only serve to underscore the unsatisfactory nature of any written text. The reader is left with a sense of incompletion and the awareness that the issues presented are left unresolved. In this way, *I, the Supreme* is deliberately open-ended so that the debate can continue in the reader's mind.

*The Characters*

Gaspar Rodríguez de Francia (Dr. Francia) is clearly the central figure of *I, the Supreme*. He is merely a voice in the text, an essence rather than concrete presence; he is never described physically. This essence, however, is extremely ambiguous, since it is formed from the different points of view in the novel. Ultimately, he emerges as a lonely, impotent, isolated, sick old man on his deathbed, raging to hang onto the power he formerly possessed and to justify his actions for posterity. The only power left to him is that of speech, and he attempts to use it to manipulate the reader's attitudes in the novel. Unfortunately, he becomes trapped in his own contradictions and dies frustrated and unredeemed by history.

Policarpo Patiño is the dictator's naïve personal secretary and constant companion. Like Francia, he is a disembodied voice in the text, portrayed as ignorant, simple-minded, extremely credulous, and superstitious. He serves as a kind of Sancho Panza to the dictator's philosophical Don Quixote, a foil for his constant ramblings, self-justifications, and desire to "dictate."

Juan Parish Robertson is a fictionalized reconstruction of a historical character. Presented through the dictator's eyes, he represents everything that is negative about British colonialism, specifically the desire to make a fortune at the expense of the inferior colonials. An entrepreneurial adventurer, he is portrayed as weak and hypocritical, and he eventually betrays the dictator who had befriended him and his brother, Roberto. Upon their return to England, the two brothers write a scathing attack on their former benefactor, disguised as an account of their voyage and entitled *Letters from Paraguay*. The inclusion of excerpts in the text serves in the construction of the dictator's ambiguity.

Pilar the Black is the dictator's trusted personal valet, general servant, and food taster. He eventually betrays his master and is put to death for treason. Curiously, there are two vastly different versions of his betrayal given: In one, he attempts to usurp Francia's identity and power; in the other, he steals from the government stores to provide money for his Indian mistress. Neither account is verified, and the conclusion is left to the reader. His presence and subsequent torture and death serve to contradict the dictator's self-image as benevolent despot.

General Manuel Belgrano, the Argentine general who attacked Paraguay in an attempt to annex it, appears as an illusory dream character. Viewed as an honest and idealistic man who withdrew his troops when he realized that the Paraguayans did not want to be "liberated," he later becomes a friend of the dictator when he comes to negotiate an alliance between their two countries.

Antonio Manoel Correia da Camara is presented as a hypocritical, self-serving, and deceitful Brazilian envoy sent to trick Francia into ceding Paraguayan border territory. Like Belgrano, he is presented as if in a dream, and it is never made clear whether his presence is real or imagined.

Bernardo Velazco is the royalist governor of Paraguay prior to its independence from Spain. One of Francia's principal enemies, he is strongly against the formation of a republican state and liberal ideals. He appears in the text through both the dictator's narration and excerpts of his letters. Nicknamed "Bel-Asshole," he is portrayed as hypocritical and untrustworthy.

Sultan is the dictator's remarkable dog, who appears at the end of the novel as an accusatory alter-ego, revealing the dictator's essential contradictions and self-deceptions as he slips into death.

*Themes and Meanings*

*I, the Supreme* offers a complex interweaving of several themes equally important to the comprehension of the novel. The text is a reexamination of the nineteenth century dictatorship of the historical Francia, a figure of primary importance whose ambiguous presence continues to haunt Paraguay more than a century and a half after his death. Revered as the "Karai Guasu" ("great white father") and hated as the instigator of the infamous Paraguayan Reign of Terror, Francia still lives in the imagination of the nation. Roa Bastos challenges these images through the juxtaposition of documentary "fact" and novelistic "fiction," in what he himself calls a "transhistory" or an analysis of the validity of the historical interpretations of that period. This means that he does not attempt to rewrite history so much as to demonstrate the shortcomings of historiography (the historians' task to write the "truth" of history) as a scientific process. The fictional Francia continually argues in self-defense against his historians, revealing their political and emotional biases. This theme is directly embodied in the split of the character into "I" and "HE," an important opposition that permeates the novel. The "I" represents the dictator as human being, while the "HE" symbolizes the image of Francia that has been perpetuated in history books.

Since much of the novel deals with the historical dictatorship of Francia, there emerges a second theme that is also very important: the theme of absolute power. One of the major criticisms that historians have leveled at the "founding father" of Paraguay is that he became obsessed with the notion of power and set himself up as the supreme and perpetual dictator, the absolute controlling authority, of the newly formed republic. *I, the Supreme* deals directly with this issue; the incorporated documents and characters debate the concepts of democratic versus despotic governments as well as the origins, and dangers, of power itself. In particular, Roa Bastos plays the dictator's ideals of democracy against the reality that was achieved under his rule, revealing his inconsistencies and ultimate self-betrayal.

The historical background of the novel also serves as a point of departure for the author's examination of the boundaries between reality and fiction, another major theme in the text. The constant debate between authentic and fictional documents, as well as between real and imagined events, demonstrates to the reader that reality is difficult to identify and define. In fact, *I, the Supreme* questions the very notion of what constitutes truth and reality, and whether such things as absolute truth or absolute reality exist. The argument between historical reality and the limitations of historical interpretation exposes at the same time the fact that any written text will, of necessity, be fiction, since it is a product of the biases, preconceptions, and even ignorance of the author.

This leads to the central theme of the novel: the impossibility of language to communicate reality. As the dictator examines his life and argues with his historical interpretations, he realizes that any attempt to convey meaning through words (either written or oral) is doomed to failure, since there is always a gap between the event and the account, as between any object and the word used to express that object. As *I, the Supreme* draws to a close, there is an increasing sense of frustration as Francia's speech becomes disjointed and incoherent and, in the middle of a sentence, finally ceases altogether. Since language is fundamentally unreliable, only silence can remain.

*Critical Context*

*I, the Supreme* is Roa Bastos' second novel and his most widely acclaimed work. The author spent much of his life writing short stories and screenplays as well as an earlier novel, *Hijo de hombre* (1960; *Son of Man*, 1965), but this work clearly represents his artistic maturity.

Although it is contemporary to the major works of the Latin American "Boom" era of the 1960's and 1970's, it is not usually analyzed within that context. Instead, it is generally included within the tradition of the "dictator novel" that began in the 1930's with the publication of *Tirano Banderas* (1926; *The Tyrant*, 1929) by the Spanish author Ramón del Valle-Inclán and *El señor presidente* (1946; *The President*, 1963) by the Guatemalan author Miguel Ángel Asturias. This genre focuses on the social, political, and even psychological consequences of dictatorship and its mechanisms for maintaining power, a phenomenon that, unfortunately, has been prevalent in Latin America since the wars of independence at the beginning of the nineteenth century.

Many critics have considered *I, the Supreme* to be the culmination of this genre, along with two other novels in the same category that were published almost simultaneously: *El recurso del método* (1974; *Reasons of State*, 1976) by Alejo Carpentier and *El otoño del patriarca* (1975; *The Autumn of the Patriarch*, 1975) by Gabriel García Márquez. All three novels reject the traditional technique of portraying the dictator as an almost mythical, dehumanized monster constructed by an external point of view and look instead at the internal conflicts of the dictator as a human being. Roa Bastos' creation presents the most radical departure from earlier models. While García Márquez and Carpentier generate a composite or hybrid image of the dictator based on characteristics of actual historical figures from different eras and areas, *I, the Supreme* does exactly the reverse: It begins with one single historical figure (Francia) and presents him through a series of fragmented and contradictory perspectives.

In many ways, this work could be considered a precursor of the postmodern novel in Latin America. Roa Bastos' experimentations with literary techniques (fragmentation of both space and time; elimination of narrative voice, global structure, and plot; incongruous juxtaposition of a variety of texts and textual styles) work continually to challenge and deconstruct the reader's assumptions and expectations, not only with regard to the book's subject, the historical dictator, but even in terms of the written text itself and the borders between fiction and reality.

In the years since the publication of *I, the Supreme*, Roa Bastos has also established himself as an essayist on a broad range of topics, from his own writing techniques to the sociopolitical and linguistic realities of modern Paraguay. His third novel, *Vigilia del Almirante* (1992; the vigil of the admiral) continues his exploration of the realm of historical revisionism with a reconstruction of Christopher Columbus' voyage in 1492 and affirms Roa Bastos' place in the Latin American literary canon.

## Bibliography

Da Rosa, Doris C. "*Yo, el Supremo* and Augusto Roa Bastos' Search for the Future of Paraguay." *Discurso Literario* 1 (Spring, 1984): 169-176. Examines the novel as a historical revision of Francia's regime but not as an unqualified justification. Maintains that the historical perspective of the text reflects contemporary circumstances and problems of Paraguay. Offers the conclusion that the nationalist pursuits of the nineteenth century dictator portrayed in *I, the Supreme* provide a model for modern-day Paraguayan nationalists.

Foster, David William. *Augusto Roa Bastos*. Boston: Twayne, 1978. Solid introduction to Roa Bastos and his works, with a chronology and bibliography. Chapter 5, "*Yo, el Supremo*: The Curse of Writing," provides insights into the novel's narrative techniques and themes, especially the fundamental opposition between fiction and historical text. Concludes with a discussion on the elaboration of myth and the demythification of meaning in language.

King, John. "*Yo, el Supremo*: Dictatorship and Writing in Latin America." *Comparison* 7 (Spring, 1978): 98-107. Analyzes the correlation between "dictating" and writing in the novel. For King, the dictator, like any author, appropriates and controls history through his narrative, "dictating" a privileged version of the events through manipulation of language. King concludes that the attempt fails because "every text is the absorption and transformation of other texts" and is therefore not absolute; moreover, there is a gap between the original dictation and resulting script that serves only to generate errors in the intended message. Thus the dictator's text ultimately "questions the very nature of history and discourse."

Martin, Gerald. "*Yo, el Supremo*: The Dictator and His Script." *Forum for Modern Language Studies* 15 (April, 1979): 169-183. In this Marxist analysis of the novel, Martin argues that Roa Bastos both reexamines the historical reality of Francia and projects an implied critique of the Latin American "New Novel." Asserts that Roa Bastos exposes writing as a hopelessly one-dimensional form of power that is inadequate to the communication of meaning. Concludes that the novel offers a unique interpenetration of literary and political ideologies, "fusing 'literary revolution' with 'revolutionary literature.' "

Ugalde, Sharon Keefe. "Binarisms in *Yo, el Supremo*." *Hispanic Journal* 2 (Fall, 1980): 69-77. An excellent analysis of the polar oppositions and contradictions that form the structural and thematic basis of the novel. Examines in particular the mythological polarities and concludes that Roa Bastos deliberately rejects resolution of contradictions.

*D. Jan Mennell*

# IN THE HEART OF THE VALLEY OF LOVE

*Author:* Cynthia Kadohata (1956-    )
*Type of plot:* Science fiction
*Time of plot:* 2052
*Locale:* Southern California
*First published:* 1992

> *Principal characters:*
> FRANCIE, the narrator and protagonist of the novel, a nineteen-year-old Japanese American
> AUNTIE ANNIE, Francie's aunt, who takes care of her niece after her parents die
> ROHN JEFFERSON, a boyfriend of Auntie Annie who disappears abruptly after his arrest
> MARK TRANG, a student at a Los Angeles community college who becomes Francie's boyfriend
> JEWEL, a student at the college who is in her late thirties
> HANK and EMMY, Jewel's parents
> MATT BURROUGHS, a fellow student of Francie, Mark, and Jewel who is accused of murder
> CARL, a tattooist and a friend of Mark

*The Novel*

In the Heart of the Valley of Love is set in a future Southern California of the mid-twenty-first century. It centers on the experiences of Francie, a young Japanese American girl of that time, and her family and friends. The story is told in the first person and is divided into sixteen short chapters.

In the Heart of the Valley of Love begins with the narrator and protagonist, Francie, driving through the Mojave Desert in the company of her Auntie Annie, who has taken care of her since the death of her parents. With them is Annie's boyfriend, Rohn. On their way to the desert, they had been stopped by a highway patrolman, but Rohn had bribed the officer to let them go. Despite this incident, the three people in the car are having a good time as they speed eastward. In the scarcity of this projected twenty-first century, such necessities of life as water are jealously hoarded and dearly priced. When Rohn is offered an opportunity by an enigmatic man named Max the Magician to buy some water, he agrees with alacrity. The entire water purchase, though, is a trick played by the authorities, with Max as either tool or dupe. Rohn is arrested and carted off to an unknown locale. Even though Auntie Annie is far senior to her in years, Francie feels a responsibility to take care of her aunt in the wake of Rohn's disappearance. Having weathered many travails during her life, Francie sees herself as supremely adaptable.

Francie reflects on the death of her parents. They had known that they were dying and had been understandably bitter. This bitterness, however, was laced with bursts of sincere optimism. The memory of her parents' courage lends Francie the strength to persevere even after the upsetting episode of Rohn's kidnapping.

Francie enrolls in a local two-year college that serves primarily the underprivileged classes. Here, she develops a circle of friends for the first time since she had moved to California from Chicago in her early teenage years. Among these is Mark Trang, a fellow student who becomes her boyfriend, and Jewel, an older woman who becomes the unofficial leader of the group. Jewel is involved in an abusive relationship with a real-estate agent named Teddy. When Teddy is arrested, Jewel, accompanied by Francie, bails him out.

Francie works part-time in a law office, but her primary efforts are concentrated upon school, especially her work on the school newspaper. She realizes that, because of the class stratification in twenty-first century America, she will never be permitted to be a member of the social elite, who are isolated in heavily garrisoned "richtowns." She is nevertheless determined to make the best of her life. Her relationship with Mark deepens as they realize that they share many experiences, beliefs, and values. Mark and Francie go together to visit Jewel's parents, Hank and Emmy. Hank recounts a time in his long-ago childhood, in the year 2000, when he had walked with his father to a secluded arroyo unblemished by the overpopulation and technology rampant even then in the region. He wonders why his father had taken him there.

Mark and Francie go to be tattooed by Carl, a friend of Mark. For the couple, it is a kind of ceremony, a ritual of self-affirmation against the prescriptive norms of society. They become involved in trying to help Matt Burroughs, a fellow student accused of murder. They attend a rally on his behalf, and Francie becomes close to Matt's mother, Madeline, after interviewing her for the school paper. Matt, however, betrays all of his supporters by skipping bail; he may also have killed his mother. Francie and Mark also become involved in trying to expose a school administrator, James Goodman, who is soliciting prostitutes from among the students. When Goodman kills himself, however, they decide not to publish the evidence they have.

Rohn has not returned, but Auntie Annie still holds out hope. Francie agrees, especially because the riots that overtake Los Angeles after the June primaries mean that petty criminals such as Rohn are no longer such a major concern. Jewel is still tantalized by the secret of her grandfather's arroyo, and Mark and Francie accompany her on an expedition there. Their excavations yield a box that reveals that Jewel's grandfather had once loved a woman name Maria, though he had not left his wife for her. Jewel takes the rings that had belonged to her grandfather and Maria; she writes her own name on a piece of paper and puts it in the box as a substitute. Mark and Francie follow suit, writing not only their own names but those of all of their friends and relatives. Not only have they gotten in touch with the past, they have staked their own place in history as they prepare for their future.

*The Characters*

Francie, the heroine and narrator of the book, is a nineteen-year-old Japanese

American woman. The story is told through the prism of her first-person awareness and recounts the development of her social and cultural attitudes. In using a young narrator to describe a strange future universe, Kadohata gains the advantage of being able to have her character assume the novelties of the future rather than convey them to the reader in a didactic manner. Francie spent her childhood in Chicago but moved to Los Angeles in her early teenage years. Her parents died prematurely, leaving her in the care of her Auntie Annie. At first confused by the complexities of adult life and by the bleak circumstances of her own life, Francie matures in the course of the novel. In contrast to the older women in the book, Auntie Annie and Jewel, Francie does not let the obstacles posed by the persistent misogyny of her society stand in her way. Through her work on the school newspaper, her romance with Mark, and her other friendships and loyalties, she develops a strength that enables her to face courageously the difficult social problems that exert so much pressure upon her.

Auntie Annie, Francie's aunt, is desolated by the disappearance of Rohn. Somewhat hapless and vulnerable at times, she nevertheless is a stabilizing influence on her niece.

Rohn Jefferson, Annie's boyfriend, gets on the wrong side of the law simply by trying to provide for his family. His arrest reflects the social turmoil and dislocation that pervade the novel.

Mark Trang, Francie's boyfriend, is her principal ally in navigating the intricacies of the depressing world of Los Angeles in 2052. Humorous, independent, and determined, he helps Francie to elucidate her own values, thus assisting in making them clear to the reader as well.

Jewel, an older woman and fellow student of Mark and Francie, possesses a maturity and a set of life experiences that aid Mark and Francie in establishing their adult identities. A good influence on others, she is less fortunate in her own personal life, which is dominated by her seemingly permanent relationship with the bullying Teddy.

Hank and Emmy, Jewel's parents, present the distant past—in other words, the late twentieth century. The arroyo mentioned by Hank to his daughter provides the scene for the inspiring denouement of the book.

Matt Burroughs, a young man accused of murder, betrays those who trust him. He shows that even though the Los Angeles of 2052 is an unjust society, not all those deemed criminals are basically innocent men like Rohn; for some, the punishment is merited by the crime. There is still personal evil as well as a broader social corruption.

Carl, Mark's tattooist friend, is a kind of unofficial priest. His tattooing of Francie and Mark becomes a ceremonial, metaphoric acknowledgment of their commitment to each other.

*Themes and Meanings*

*In the Heart of the Valley of Love* uses science-fiction conventions and a future setting to discuss concerns very much of the time of its writing. In the recessionary 1990's, California, long the utopian embodiment of the American Dream, was afflicted with an unfamiliar sense of limitation and despair. Kadohata's California of sixty years hence is an extrapolation of the trends perceived as dominating the California of the author's present. The scarcity of resources, the sharp division between the privileged inhabitants from the "richtowns" and the benighted urban proletariat, and the potential of authoritarian solutions to problems of social unrest are but the most prominent of the cultural factors operating in the world of *In the Heart of the Valley of Love.* A good primer on the sociology behind Kadohata's world, especially in the division between a technologically advanced elite and an underprivileged lower class, is Mike Davis' *City of Quartz* (1990), a meditation on the economics and culture of the Los Angeles of the author's day.

Kadohata is one of a number of writers interested in a future Southern California setting. The most visible of these manifestations is in the "cyberpunk" school of science fiction, which tends to emphasize the depersonalizing effects of hegemonic corporate and media power while stressing that the future will not lead to the kind of radical or redemptive transformation traditionally heralded by science fiction. Kadohata's hypothetical Southern California, though, is sharply different from that of cyberpunk. Kadohata's female protagonist is quite a change from cyberpunk's typical hardboiled male heroes. Cyperpunk has also been accused of stressing degrading and obvious caricatures of Asian and Asian American people. Both Francie and Mark are Asian American, and both are pictured affirmatively, as visionaries who will help to change their society for the better.

This sense of affirmation is not exclusively ethnic in stripe. Like the characters in Kim Stanley Robinson's *The Gold Coast* (1988), Kadohata's protagonists are in search of some sort of moral center upon which they can premise their young lives so they will not end in the despair of previous generations. The scene at the secluded arroyo, even though in dramatic terms it is more significant to Jewel than to the two main characters, is crucial in this respect. Here, Francie and Mark make a kind of covenant with their own future, storing their own just-established identities in the receptacle that for so long had symbolized a dead man's long-lost love. In inscribing themselves onto the past, they are carving out an identity for themselves in eternity.

Kadohata recognizes the perils that the future may hold, but she does not yield to cynicism or despair. In this, she echoes the convictions set forth in Carolyn See's courageous and transformative novels *Golden Days* (1987) and *Making History* (1991). Kadohata, like See, stares into a terrifying future and views it as full of hope.

*Critical Context*

Cynthia Kadohata's first novel, *The Floating World*, was published to broad acclaim in 1989. That novel was an autobiographical work tracing the experiences of a young Japanese American girl growing up in the America of the 1950's. Although the title is taken from a famous Japanese art style of the eighteenth and nineteenth centuries, the novel is thoroughly American in setting and orientation. Many of the motifs and details—the long, exhilarating drives through desert terrain, the observant sensibility of a young girl who acts as the narrator—will be familiar to readers of *In the Heart of the Valley of Love*. Whereas *The Floating World* is set in the past and appeals to the nostalgia in readers, however, Kadohata's second novel is set many decades in the future and appeals to readers' sense of speculation and wonder.

Ethnic writers in America are often expected to restrict their subject matter and themes. Portrayal of established minority communities is common; less frequent is a searching look at how those communities might be transformed and catalyzed by the America of the future. Kadohata's turn to science fiction marks her as a writer not content simply to write according to conventional formulae that will automatically garner her good reviews. Kadohata aims for a more genuine imaginative freedom; it is this imaginative willpower that makes her one of America's most promising writers.

*Bibliography*
Blackford, Staige D. Review of *In the Heart of the Valley of Love*, by Cynthia Kadohata. *Virginia Quarterly Review* 69 (January, 1993): SS21. Discusses the social and chronological setting of the novel, laying particular emphasis on the depiction of scarcity and poverty in the future Southern California.
Li, Cherry W. Review of *In the Heart of the Valley of Love*, by Cynthia Kadohata. *Library Journal* 117 (June 15, 1992): 102. Centers upon Kadohata's depiction of an engaging young Asian American heroine. Also discusses Kadohata's panoramic vision of a future society.
Quick, Barbara. Review of *In the Heart of the Valley of Love*. *The New York Times Book Review*, August 30, 1992, 14. Assesses Kadohata's skill in creating a convincing representation of a dystopian future and of the characters who populate the novel's fictional world.

*Nicholas Birns*

# INDIAN AFFAIRS

*Author:* Larry Woiwode (1941-    )
*Type of plot:* Psychological realism
*Time of plot:* 1971
*Locale:* Northern Michigan
*First published:* 1992

> *Principal characters:*
> CHRISTOFER VAN EENANAM, a part Native American Indian graduate
> student of English who is writing his dissertation on the poetry of
> Theodore Roethke
> ELLEN STROHE VAN EENANAM, Chris's wife of seven years
> BEAUCHAMP NAGOOSA, Chris's Indian friend, a poet and a petty thief
> GAYLIN, a young Indian from the local village, an arsonist

*The Novel*

*Indian Affairs* describes the internal and external events experienced by Chris and Ellen Van Eenanam as they live under primitive conditions in her grandparents' hunting lodge in the wilderness of northern Michigan during a freezing winter in 1971. The novel is subtitled *Book Two: The Native Son*, identifying the work as the second volume of a planned trilogy by Woiwode. The first part, *What I'm Going to Do, I Think, Book One: The Boy*, published in 1969, tells the story of Chris and Ellen's courtship, marriage, and honeymoon at the same hunting lodge in Michigan. Much of the background of the characters in *Indian Affairs* is provided, and although the second volume may be read independently of the first, familiarity with *What I'm Going to Do, I Think* greatly enhances the reading of *Indian Affairs*.

By the end of the first novel, Chris has decided that in order to provide financially for his wife and their expected child, he will not return to the graduate school where he has been studying mathematics. The child, however, arrives prematurely and dies shortly after birth. *Indian Affairs* opens with the couple returning to the hunting lodge in the dead of winter; six years have passed since the action of *What I'm Going to Do, I Think*. Chris has returned to graduate school, this time to study English literature, and plans to finish his dissertation on the poetry of Theodore Roethke. Ellen intends to write a personal journal that explores her feelings about the death of their child and their continuing childlessness.

Shortly after their arrival, Chris and Ellen learn of a fire that has burned down a shack in a small Indian village nearby. This is the first in a series of mysterious fires—apparently the work of an arsonist—that occur throughout the novel. Along with this mystery, Ellen and Chris have another: a prowler, possibly a peeping Tom, has been stalking about outside their cabin at night. A gang of young Indian toughs has repeatedly been threatening Chris because he has refused to buy them the liquor that are too young to buy for themselves. Ellen is lured to secret "women's lib" meetings, held at the local library, by an oddly interested stranger.

As the plot relies on these events for its forward movement, the internal lives of the two main characters, and especially of Chris, are explored. Chris speculates philosophically on the nature of life, death, and of nature itself, inspired by the poetry of Roethke. Chris's friend Beauchamp Nagoosa has provided him with peyote, a hallucinogenic substance, with which both Chris and Ellen experiment. Chris's encounters with the local Indians, his studies of the historical and persistent injustices suffered by Native Americans, and his exploration of their current ways of life lead him to come to embrace his own Native American heritage. His final thought in the novel, a line from Roethke, is *"I'll be an Indian."*

Ellen, brought up by her grandparents from a very young age after her own parents were killed in a mysterious "accident," comes to understand that her beloved Christian Scientist grandparents are extremely prejudiced anti-Semites and that her father was most likely Jewish. She believes that this conflict may have driven her parents to suicide and that, most likely, the automobile "accident" was actually a deliberate and calculated act. By the novel's end, Ellen has, like Chris, realized that she must come to terms with her family history and her ethnic heritage.

The climax of the novel is reached after the mysteries of the prowler and the arsonist are solved and after Chris has achieved a tentative truce with the local roughnecks. He has finished his dissertation, and Ellen has completed her journal. She is pregnant. On the day they are to leave for New York to begin a new life, they stop to attend the funeral of Jimmy Jones, a local Indian who was killed in the most recent house fire. Because Jimmy is a war veteran, an incongruous color guard from the American Legion attends the funeral and honors the deceased with a twenty-one-gun salute. The genuine terror of the Indians at the sound of the gunshots, the sight of men, women, and children falling to the ground as they must have done at Wounded Knee, evokes images of Judgment Day and so horrifies and moves Chris that he feels a sudden sense of conviction that settles his life: the absolute surety of the resurrection of the dead, of the life of the world to come. This, finally, is the only way that justice may be truly had for all.

*The Characters*

Christofer Van Eenanam is a hero alienated from the world—even, it seems, from his own wife. The final pages of *What I'm Going to Do, I Think* strongly suggest that the character is leaning toward suicide; there is a distinct emptiness in Chris Van Eenanam's soul at the end of the first novel. By the time *Indian Affairs* opens, six years later, Chris has given up working for the "Establishment" in a brokerage firm, a period of his life that now is a source of embarrassment to him. His choice of English literature over mathematics as a field of study further reflects this change in his temperament. He feels the need to understand himself, to explore his heritage, and to find some deeper meaning to his life. Woiwode's often disjointed plot line and the obscurity of Chris's reasoning help to render his sense of confusion and of aimlessness throughout the novel.

Woiwode renders the conflicts in his main character's life in a number of ways. Almost immediately, the uneasy relations between Chris and his wife are dramatized. Chris has apparently been drinking more than Ellen would like, and she disapproves of his buying liquor for underage locals. Chris's thoughts ramble widely, now focused on cutting down a tree, now following a train of thought that leads to a childhood memory. From the beginning, Chris is established as a complex, confused, self-centered young man.

It is not until the final pages of the novel that Chris begins to feel a sense of self, as the threads of all of his experiences and interests come together. Finally, he feels that he has found some meaning in his life. He is reconciled with his now-pregnant wife and with his Indian heritage, which he finally acknowledges publicly and has come to accept. He also finds spiritual satisfaction, not in the doctrines of any established religion but in the certainty of the resurrection of the dead. Belief in this fundamentally Christian doctrine, whether or not it is arrived at through association with the Christian church, Woiwode suggests, is the only way in which the great evils and injustices of the world may be reconciled with the belief in a loving God.

Ellen, Chris's wife, is seemingly as self-centered as her husband at the novel's opening. She is still obsessed with her childlessness, and she appears to resent Chris for this reason. She is unable to break the emotional stranglehold that her grandparents—particularly her grandmother—have over her. Ellen's disenchantment with Chris reaches a climax with the discovery that the mysterious prowler, Peggy, is one of Chris's former lovers who seems to have a kind of "fatal attraction" for him.

Beauchamp Nagoosa is a Native American who is a poet and a thief. He is by turns sympathetic and nonsympathetic. At times a poet in love with nature, indignant at the exploitation of the Native American by whites, he exploits that same history to justify his own stealing and "squatting" in a house that does not belong to him. He eagerly takes the teenaged daughter of a neighborhood prostitute into his bed. Beau demonstrates both the best and the worst traits of modern American Indians.

Gaylin, a young man from the village, takes on the role of temporary son to Chris. Chris acts as Gaylin's "guide" when the boy first experiences the effects of peyote. Chris teaches Gaylin to build a teepee in the traditional manner, an episode that turns out to be as much an initiation rite for Chris as it is for the boy. These experiences compel Chris to rediscover and accept his own Native American heritage.

*Themes and Meanings*

Woiwode is a Christian author, and despite the book's Native American themes, the ultimate consolation for the main characters in the novel is also a fundamental Christian belief, the very foundation of Christianity: the resurrection of the dead. This belief is the only hope for one who needs to keep faith with a benevolent God. It is with this act of faith that Chris accepts both his heritage and his destiny.

In the meandering plot of the novel, the senseless and violent acts of the teenage Indians, the arson of Gaylin, and the deaths and injuries sustained by this violence can in no way be morally justified. The irrational hatred of the implied anti-Semitism of

Ellen's grandparents, a hatred that seemingly is so strong that it drove her parents to suicide, is especially ironic as it comes from a supposedly devout Christian Scientist couple. The willingness of the book's Native Americans to exploit their own customs and religion for profit belies their indignant protestations of having been ravaged by whites. For Woiwode, it seems, this senseless perpetuation of injustice can never be understood in this life. The only hope for true understanding is in the afterlife.

Family dynamics are also explored in the novel. The pain experienced by the death of a child and the rift that such an event can create in a marriage becomes clear as the issue continually arises but is never discussed by Chris and Ellen. It is a seemingly unresolvable pain. Chris's inability to break away from his family history is clear with his final reconciliation to his heritage. The emotional stranglehold that parents are capable of inflicting upon their children is seen in the Strohes' relations with Ellen. Woiwode never overtly praises or condemns his characters, however; he merely renders them in action and dramatizes the consequences.

The theme of death predominates in the novel. The death of Chris and Ellen's firstborn son precedes the events of the novel. The death of Ellen's parents is still something with which she must come to terms even twenty years after the event. Thoughts of Chris's dead mother arise briefly throughout the novel. The death of Ellen's grandfather seems imminent. Ellen feels that the revelation of the mysterious Peggy has caused her to feel the death of the person she believed Chris to be. Jimmy Jones is killed in a fire set by one of his kinsmen. The climax of the novel occurs at his funeral, during which the images of the massacre at Wounded Knee are evoked. All of these deaths, including that of Beau's dog, are devastating to the survivors and are senseless.

Yet there is also hope. Ellen is once again pregnant. If the Chris she had known is dead for her, her husband now lives in a different way, a more positive way. Ultimately, moreover, the dead of all ages will live again on Judgment Day.

*Critical Context*

Woiwode's first novel, *What I'm Going to Do, I Think*, published in 1969, was an enormous critical success for which he received a William Faulkner Award and an American Library Association Award. He was also awarded Guggenheim Fellowships in 1971 and 1972. Woiwode went on to publish other successful works, including the novels *Beyond the Bedroom Wall* (1975) and *Born Brothers* (1988) and the collection *The Neumiller Stories* (1989). He has also published a volume of poetry, *Even Tide* (1977).

Although twenty-three years have elapsed between *What I'm Going to Do, I Think* and its sequel, *Indian Affairs*, the two novels are intimately related. Many of the characters, themes, and story lines of the second volume appeared in the first. *Indian Affairs*, although more complex, is also more obscure than its predecessor, a literary trait of Woiwode's that has been alternately praised and criticized. For this reason, the book has received mixed reviews, and a reading of *What I'm Going to Do, I Think* may be necessary for a complete understanding of *Indian Affairs*.

*Bibliography*

Block, Ed, Jr. "An Interview with Larry Woiwode." *Renascence* 44, no. 1 (Fall, 1991): 17-30. Woiwode discusses the circumstances of his conversion experience. He also declares the central importance of the family as an expression of values in his work and discusses his use of fragmentation to encourage a sense of struggle within the reader. Includes a brief reference to *Indian Affairs*: "It's a comedy."

Jones, Timothy. "The Reforming of a Novelist." *Christianity Today* 36, no. 12 (October 26, 1992): 86-88. Jones gives a brief background on Woiwode and *Indian Affairs* before the interview proper. Woiwode answers questions regarding his own Christianity and the role of faith in his fiction.

Woiwode, Larry. "Homeplace, Heaven, or Hell." *Renascence* 44 (Fall, 1991): 3-16. Woiwode explores the positive aspects of writing within a specific, detailed regional landscape and how such specifics are inherently universal. The author also gives a personal account of the circumstances surrounding his decision to move his family to North Dakota and provides some insight into his religious beliefs. Sheds some light on Woiwode's Christian ethics and thus on the philosophical meanderings of *Indian Affairs*.

_____ . *What I'm Going to Do, I Think*. New York: Farrar, Straus and Giroux, 1969. Woiwode's first novel and the first part of the intended trilogy of which *Indian Affairs* is the second installment. Recommended reading for a fuller understanding of *Indian Affairs*. It is interesting to compare stylistic and philosophical points of view from the two books.

_____ . "What I'm Going to Do, I Think." *Library Journal* 94 (February 1, 1969): 579. The author gives a brief summary of his background. He cites Leo Tolstoy as the single greatest influence on his writing and states that his intention in writing is not to be deliberately obscure but "to tell the truth as clearly as I can."

*Diane Almeida*

# THE INDIAN LAWYER

*Author:* James Welch (1940-    )
*Type of plot:* Suspense
*Time of plot:* 1989
*Locale:* Western Montana
*First published:* 1990

> *Principal characters:*
> SYLVESTER YELLOW CALF, the "Indian lawyer," once a star athlete on the reservation, now a city attorney
> JACK HARWOOD, an intelligent but desperate inmate whose parole Sylvester denies
> PATTI ANN HARWOOD, Jack's wife, an innocent and loving woman caught in her husband's schemes
> LENA OLD HORN, Sylvester's high-school guidance counselor, who inspires him to succeed

*The Novel*

Set in the cell blocks of a state prison and the back rooms of state politics, *The Indian Lawyer* depicts one man's effort to survive the penal system and another's search for the best way to represent the interests of Native Americans and others whom the political system neglects. The novel contains sixteen chapters that move freely between the main characters' points of view. The plot progresses chronologically, but it is interrupted by reminiscences that take characters back to such pivotal moments in their pasts as Sylvester's basketball championships and Jack's courtship of Patti Ann.

The book begins with Jack Harwood's parole hearing. Jack is serving a long sentence for armed robbery and is beginning to crack under the pressure of incarceration. Sylvester is a board member, and Jack is drawn to him because he is a Blackfeet. Jack has had problems with the Indian inmates who rule the violent prison. Insufficiently repentant and a onetime escapee, Jack is denied release. That afternoon, visiting with Patti Ann, Jack asks his wife to dig up information on Sylvester.

Back in Helena after the parole hearings, Sylvester, with his girlfriend Shelley, attends a party at Buster Harrington's mansion. Buster, the founder of a law firm that is ready to make Sylvester a partner if he will agree to run for Congress, has arranged for a meeting with Fabares, a Democratic Party official. Sylvester is encouraged by his discussion with Fabares and tells Shelley that he is seriously considering becoming a candidate.

Patti Ann contacts Sylvester at his office. She is lonely from the years without Jack and has been traumatized by a series of miscarriages and a hysterectomy, but her vitality is restored in Sylvester's presence. She manages to interest him in her phony story of a contested will, and Sylvester promises to investigate the situation. Jack phones Patti Ann and instructs her to see Sylvester socially, to intensify her relationship with the lawyer. Awakened by Sylvester, but fantasizing about adopting a child and rearing a family with a freed Jack, Patti Ann agrees.

When a meeting with Sylvester in a restaurant bar leads to her bedroom, Patti Ann knows she should feel guilty, but she does not. She is revived by their intimacy, but Sylvester is bothered. He does not know why he would risk shaking up his life at such an important juncture or why he is letting his relationship with Shelley deteriorate. He drives to Browning, to the Blackfeet reservation where he grew up. He visits Lena Old Horn, hoping that she will encourage his political ambitions. Somewhat reluctantly, Lena tells Sylvester, her former student, that she has faith in him.

Strengthened by his trip home, Sylvester returns to Helena and tells Buster that he will run. As the campaign begins to take shape, Jack Harwood's plans also unfold. Although Jack wanted Patti Ann to sleep with Sylvester, the fact that she did enrages him. His plot is no longer merely for the purpose of escape. When he thinks of his tormentors in the prison, Jack realizes that he seeks revenge against Sylvester in particular and against Indians in general. After receiving sinister phone calls, Patti Ann knows that Jack's contacts on the outside are working to blackmail Sylvester into granting Jack's freedom. The affair with Patti Ann is a breach of legal ethics, a political disaster. When Jack's contacts, Woody Peters and Robert Fitzgerald, decide to cut Jack out of the plan and make Sylvester pay for their silence, Sylvester's political ambitions, his entire career, and Patti Ann's safety are threatened.

Patti Ann and Sylvester are able to run Peters and Fitzgerald off, but Sylvester is afraid the former convicts will make trouble for him down the road. He decides not to run for Congress and risk a future humiliation. Buster and Shelley tell Sylvester that his chance will come again, and Buster quickly withdraws Sylvester's candidacy. Shelley walks out after hearing of Sylvester's affair. Sylvester helps Patti Ann by arranging a safe way for Jack to serve out his sentence and work toward parole. Buster tells Sylvester to take time off and travel to Europe. Instead, he goes to a Sioux reservation in North Dakota, where he helps the tribe with a water-rights dispute. Sylvester remains immersed in his work for the Sioux until he is called back to Browning for his grandfather's funeral. The novel ends as Lena Old Horn watches Sylvester play basketball in a spring snowstorm. Lena knows that, playing all by himself, Sylvester is challenging the only person who ever stood in his way.

*The Characters*

Sylvester is the central focus of *The Indian Lawyer*. The other characters in the novel exist primarily as foils; they illuminate aspects of Sylvester through their interaction with him.

Sylvester is a man of both physical and intellectual prowess who is accustomed to achieving his goals. From the basketball court to the courtroom, Sylvester's victories have been of heroic proportion. He is never sure whether he competes for his own glory or for the sake of the tribe and race he always represents but from which his success has made him feel detached. This distance between Sylvester and his people creates a sense of loneliness that is the hero's tragic flaw. Giving way to the temptations of Patti Ann is a mistake that costs Sylvester his biggest game, the congressional election. His defeat strengthens him, however, and the novel suggests that the Indian lawyer has regained his sense of cultural mission by joining the Sioux's legal battle.

Jack Harwood is not a typical convict. He is more intelligent and compassionate than his fellow inmates. His fascination with the concepts of crime and punishment, not a truly criminal nature, seems to have led him to prison. Subject to the harshness of incarceration, Jack gradually loses his strength and assuredness until he is reduced to the role of a cornered animal. Flashbacks to better times, to the days when he was able to protect himself from prison predators—or, better still, to his happiness with Patti Ann—contrast with the vulnerable, desperate state of mind in which Jack now finds himself. Through this comparison, the novel depicts how easy it is for an individual to fall from grace, a descent Sylvester narrowly escapes.

Patti Ann illustrates the process by which an individual reawakens to the world. A small-town girl before her first marriage, Patti Ann is quickly overwhelmed by the pressures of adulthood. After twice miscarrying and being abandoned by her husband, Patti Ann is rescued by Jack's love. When Jack is sent to prison, Patti Ann slips into limbo, waiting for the happiness she remembers to return. Her affair with Sylvester tests Patti Ann's innocence, but she endures, helping Sylvester to bluff his way out of the blackmail plot and committing herself to wait for her husband's expected release. The novel hints that Patti Ann will be able to reclaim her former happiness with Jack.

Significantly, it is through the wearied perspective of Lena Old Horn that Sylvester is last shown. Lena knows that she will always be a Crow in Blackfeet country, a member of a strange tribe. Like Lena, Sylvester will always be an outsider, an Indian in the courtroom and a lawyer in Indian country. Lena's inability to conquer the loneliness of the outsider suggests to the reader that Sylvester's battle with alienation is far from over.

*Themes and Meanings*

*The Indian Lawyer* focuses on the issue of assimilation, the merging of once-separate cultural groups. As a boy playing basketball with other members of his tribe, Sylvester displays exceptional athletic ability that allows him to envision a life beyond the boundaries of the Blackfeet reservation. When a sports journalist writes a column exhorting Sylvester to become an inspiration to his people by rising above the "degradation" so often associated with reservation life, his teammates react with resentment and distance themselves from the group's new star. This is the first suggestion in the novel that by moving toward his goals in mainstream society, Sylvester will have to sever, or at least weaken, his cultural roots.

A basketball scholarship to the University of Montana leads Sylvester to law school, but time spent learning courtroom procedure is time spent forgetting Blackfeet history and ritual. Welch makes sure the reader knows, even if Sylvester does not, that a grandson who learns his tribal history from textbooks instead of taking time to listen to the elders speak is a source of secret shame for Mary Bird. The most profound symbol of Sylvester's neglect is the war medicine, a hide pouch with secret contents, worn by his great-great-grandfather. Mary had presented the pouch to Sylvester before he left for college. Instead of cherishing the relic, which represents the strength and nobility of his ancestors, Sylvester leaves it behind, hidden in a bookcase. Later, as Sylvester prepares to announce his candidacy, his grandmother again places the war medicine where Sylvester can see it. This time, he accepts the link to his cultural heritage. While in possession of the pouch, Sylvester begins to understand that a congressional campaign backed by Buster's wealth and the Democratic Party machine may be a step too far removed from the people he wants to help. The war medicine takes Sylvester not to Congress but to the Sioux reservation. For once, the Indian lawyer balances his heritage with his future as he tries to make sense of his own cultural identity.

In poignant contrast to Sylvester's attempt to adjust to life outside his ancestral home stands Jack Harwood's struggle to adapt to the demands of an existence on the inside of prison. Welch reverses the reader's cultural assumptions concerning identities that represent power and influence and those that are assumed to stand for disenfranchisement. Furthermore, the white Jack Harwood becomes a racial minority in the predominantly Indian prison population. This irony demonstrates the considerable influence of circumstance, of capricious fate, over the lives of individuals. Harwood must learn a set of "con-codes" for behavior, without which survival is almost impossible. At first, Jack learns his lesson so well that he is able to teach new inmates the ropes. He is unable to alter his inmate façade even long enough to win his freedom at a parole hearing. Soon, like Sylvester, Jack begins to crack under the pressure of an alien environment. The way in which Sylvester and Jack escape the dangerous tangle in which they have become involved focuses attention on the presence of women in the novel.

In *The Indian Lawyer*, men receive invaluable aid and comfort from women. Without the contributions of his grandmother, Lena Old Horn, and Shelley, Sylvester would not be in a position to contemplate running for Congress. Even though she seems to trap Sylvester and betray Jack, Patti Ann's nearly angelic support eventually saves both men from the violence that threatens them. This aspect of the novel suggests a belief in the ultimate importance of the affection and trust to be gained from the union of man and woman, from primary human relationships.

*Critical Context*

James Welch grew up in Montana. He attended reservation schools and has taught English literature and Indian studies at the University of Washington. Many of Welch's life experiences are reflected in *The Indian Lawyer*; he sat for years on the Montana State Board of Pardons, and the portrait of Sylvester Yellow Calf, a Native American man who achieves what other members of his tribe have not been able to, is particularly poignant in relation to the author's life.

In his third novel, *Fools Crow* (1986), Welch continued to explore themes of success and responsibility. The hero of that moving historical novel asks, "what good is your own power when the people are suffering. . . . ?" In *The Indian Lawyer*, Welch gives Sylvester the insight to arrive at, and begin answering, the same difficult question. The importance of the character of the Indian lawyer, the new warrior, to the body of Welch's work is clear from Sylvester's name. "Yellow Calf" is the name of the protagonist's revered grandfather, a redemptive figure in Welch's first novel, *Winter in the Blood* (1974). A moving passage in *Fools Crow* describes a yellow calf that embodies all the beliefs cherished by a dying warrior who wants to take the animal's name for his grandson. By bestowing the name on the hero of *The Indian Lawyer*, Welch creates a symbol of the ancient beliefs in an empowering modern form.

*Bibliography*
Brosnahan, John. "The Indian Lawyer." *Booklist* 87 (October 15, 1990): 417. Brosna-
    han is one of a number of critics who do not find *The Indian Lawyer* to be as
    significant an achievement as Welch's other novels. Treated as a work of suspense,
    however, the book earns high marks.
Hoagland, Edward. "Getting off the Reservation." *The New York Times Book Review*,
    November 25, 1990, 7. Hoagland is one of the few critics who find the novel to be
    as accomplished as Welch's previous works. He praises the novel's construction
    and character development. Particular attention is paid to the uplifting aspects of
    the book's conclusion.
Lemon, Lee. Review of *The Indian Lawyer*, by James Welch. *Prairie Schooner* 65
    (Summer, 1991): 130-131. Lemon considers *The Indian Lawyer* alongside several
    other works of contemporary fiction that deal with the theme of ethnicity and
    bigotry, including another novel that focuses on Native American themes, Linda
    Hogan's *Mean Spirit* (1990).
Parins, J. W. "The Indian Lawyer." *Choice* 28 (March, 1991): 1139. Highlights the
    psychological portraits contained in the novel. The impact of prison life is a special
    concern.
Seals, David. "Blackfeet Barrister." *The Nation* 251 (November 26, 1990): 648. Seals,
    himself a Native American author, places Welch's novel within the context of other
    recent works of Native American fiction, sometimes finding fault with the book's
    sophisticated construction. Seals wonders if the novel's discussion of assimilation
    is provocative enough, suggesting that there are many Native Americans in law
    firms. He goes on to assess literature's capacity to reflect a culture's value system.

*Nick David Smart*

# THE INNOCENT

*Author:* Richard E. Kim (Kim Eun Kook, 1932-    )
*Type of plot:* War
*Time of plot:* 1953
*Locale:* South Korea
*First published:* 1968

> *Principal characters:*
> MAJOR LEE, a young officer in the South Korean army, a brilliant military
>     strategist philosophically opposed to any but the most unavoidable
>     violence
> COLONEL MIN, a revolutionary of great integrity and courage who grimly
>     accepts responsibility for bloodshed as the price demanded by justice
> COLONEL MCKAY, an American CIA officer who keeps largely in the
>     background but abets Colonel Min's coup efforts
> GENERAL MAH, head of Armed Forces Intelligence, the Presidential
>     Brigade, and the Metropolitan Police of Seoul

*The Novel*

*The Innocent* takes its title from the almost paradoxical reluctance to take human life of Major Lee, an army officer who is masterminding the overthrow of his own government. Major Lee's respect for law, order, and human life pits him in an allegorical struggle with Colonel Min, the military leader of the coup to which the novel builds up. The conflict between the two officers dominates the story, which is narrated by Lee himself. Lee's idealism is understandable for someone so obviously dedicated to his country, but his innocence often appears to be sheer naïveté in a military genius. Colonel Min is Lee's antagonist, but Min is not a bad man; he is, in fact, an exceptionally good one, although he is at times given to an unconvincing Byronic brooding over the metaphysical conundrums of guilt, fate, and necessity.

Given these narrative weaknesses, *The Innocent* reads best, perhaps, as a version of the medieval psychomachia, a battle of allegorical abstractions. Major Lee thus becomes Colonel Min's conscience, and the real conflict becomes the painful tug of opposed impulses in the psyche of a good man of whom history makes difficult demands for action. At crucial moments, Min acts to preserve Lee's innocence by doing the dirty work himself—even sending Lee to Japan under virtual house arrest while the coup is being fought—and he seems to admire Lee's pure-mindedness, even though he finds it ineffectual.

As for the long, drawn-out buildup to the coup itself (which finally comes to pass three-fourths of the way through this almost four-hundred-page work), it consists not so much of action scenes as of long conversations in which the major characters, who are not always sharply differentiated, explain to one another various events from the past or analyze the motives of their fellow officers. Despite the potential for boredom in this narrative procedure, the intricacy of the intrigues actually holds it all together. The coup itself is never described at first hand but is summarized in a lengthy news dispatch that effectively catches the tone and style of such reports.

*The Innocent* is told in retrospect by Major Lee, and it opens in 1953, shortly after the end of the Korean War, with a dialogue between Major Lee and Reverend Koh, an army chaplain and an old friend of Lee's from the recent war. Lee is about to leave for an officers' course at Fort Benning, Georgia, and Reverend Koh has come to bid him a good voyage and ask him why, with a good university teaching career ahead of him, Major Lee has chosen to stay in the army. The scene establishes Lee's patriotism and idealism—ironically revealing the chaplain to be the more cynical of the two—and sets the tone for Lee's behavior throughout the novel.

Lee's reminiscences then reveal that several years have passed, during which he has completed his tour at Fort Benning, studied at the Command and General Staff College at Fort Leavenworth in Kansas, and served as a military attaché in Southeast Asia and Europe. With this exposition out of the way, the novel proper opens in chapter 2 on August 18 of an unidentified year, "four days before the coup." Major Lee has just been ordered home from Turkey and assigned to the Joint Chiefs of Staff in Seoul, where he has apparently just planned the impending coup.

The coup has been hatched among a small group of general officers led by Lieutenant General Hyun. A command group of nine officers carries out the actual planning and execution under Colonel Min, special assistant to General Hyun. Before the coup can actually take place, various political problems with renegade general officers must be overcome. The jockeying for position with these corrupt dissidents leads to an extended and truly engrossing scene: a night-time showdown between a large force led by Colonel Min (abetted by Colonel McKay, the Central Intelligence Agency operative) and the treacherous Major General Mah, head of Armed Forces Intelligence, who wants to cut a deal to save himself from a post-coup court-martial and probable execution.

The dramatic—and well-told—confrontation with General Mah occurs halfway through the novel. With Mah out of the way, Min senses that the way is clear for the coup, and he orders Major Lee back to Japan, under supervision by the Central Intelligence Agency (CIA). Min's motive is apparently to remove Lee from the scene of bloodshed and preserve by force the major's idealism and innocence. The coup, although bloody, succeeds except for the machinations of the vicious General Ham, who takes a group of hostages.

Ham thinks he has the CIA's support, and, indeed, Colonel McKay does not want to see a civil war break out. He brings Lee back to Seoul to negotiate peacefully. Yet McKay also wants Colonel Min to give him, for intelligence purposes, two officers who have turned out to be Communist infiltrators from North Korea, and so McKay and Min agree on a swap: Min can have Ham if McKay can have the two officers. The hostages are murdered by rebels in Ham's group, however, leaving Ham with no trump card, and he dies when his plane is shelled as he tries to leave the scene of a parley with Min.

The coup is complete, then, but in a bloody finale, Min is assassinated in his automobile, and the peacemaker Lee kills the last assassin with a grenade. These events spell the end of Major Lee's idealism. The novel ends as it began: with Lee, now a civilian, engaged in an earnest farewell dialogue with Chaplain Koh before leaving his country for what may be forever.

*The Characters*

Only two characters in *The Innocent* demand any consideration: the narrator, Major Lee, and Colonel Min. Lee is by temperament and training more of an academic than a military officer, but love of his country impels him to take up a military career after the Korean War ends. Lee met Colonel Min during their teaching days together at a university in Seoul. After the war, a year before the coup, both Lee and Min were in Paris, where Min conceived of the plans for the coup in a sidewalk café. Their relationship thus has a long history.

The idealist Lee is haunted by a story about Min that he is told by a young officer from Min's village. Min is rumored to have shot and killed a North Korean officer in cold blood in the time immediately following World War II. The true story turns out to have been that Min had been in Manchuria with Korean units fighting with Communist Chinese forces, and that these Korean forces had become the vital cadre of the new North Korean Army. Min, however, simply left his unit and went home, only to have a North Korean major come and take him under arrest to a nearby Russian garrison. The North Korean major was an intensely patriotic Communist who wanted Min to come back and work with the Korean Communists.

What happened at the Russian garrison became the basis for the rumor of Min's brutality. In the presence of the Russian commander, a major, and a Russian lieutenant, the North Korean major had given Min a cruel lashing with a whip. The North Korean major, already in a frenzy, became infuriated by the Russian officers' laughter at the abuse of Min and had suddenly grabbed the Russian major by the neck and strangled him. Min, meanwhile, had whipped and shot the Russian lieutenant. Min and the North Korean had then driven away to Min's village, and Min left the major in the jeep while he roused friends. When Min returned to the jeep, however, he found the major apparently dead from his own pistol.

Later, after the coup, Colonel McKay explains to Lee that the North Korean major did not die from his wound after all but was taken to a Russian hospital to recover. The Russians naturally thought that the two dead Russians and the wounded North Korean were Min's doing, and Min thus gained his reputation as a ruthless killer. Major Lee learns all this about his friend with great relief.

*Themes and Meanings*

The tension of the relationship between Colonel Min and his conscience, Major Lee, holds the narrative together. Colonel Min carries his reputation and his responsibilities with much solemnity. He has, of course, killed other men when the situation demanded it, and he is weighed down by the cruelties inflicted by war. In his brooding,

Byronic moments, he sits in his quarters in the dark, listening to somber music. His long friendship with the idealistic Lee makes Lee his natural conscience. At one point after the coup, Min actually tells Lee: "There are many things we have to do together, do you understand? I suppose I can afford to have one prosecutor and one judge all put together in you?" Lee parries, "I am not your prosecutor and your judge!" Min, however, insists, "Ah, but you are, yes, you are!"

The strain of their complementarity sometimes becomes extremely difficult for both men. After the coup, when they are trying to put down General Ham's rebellion, Min loses patience with Lee and tells him, in effect, to shut up. Min then lectures Lee: "If I always listened to your voice, Major, I would never, never get anything done in this maddening world! This world, do you understand, this world full of idiots like me in flesh and blood—not pale lifeless saints like you!" After Min has finally had to kill Ham and his men, Lee arouses Min's extreme anger by calling him a murderer, and Min erupts by blistering Lee's "tear-jerking, mushy, holier-than-thou self-righteousness and melodrama" and sneering at his "pure heart," his "clean conscience," and his precious "innocence."

With the bloody denouement, in which Min dies and Lee blows a man to bits with a grenade, Lee's long and exhausting apprenticeship to an absurd world ends with him completely disillusioned. When he says goodbye to Chaplain Koh, he is a changed man, and he cannot put much faith in such traditional pieties as the chaplain's insistence that "Colonel Min did not die in vain." Min states his existential philosophy when he tells Lee, "There is nothing out there in the heavens, Major. Remember? We have only ourselves." This bleak credo is perhaps the main theme of the novel.

*Critical Context*

In *The Innocent*, Richard E. Kim writes of a world he knows well. He was born in Hamhung, Korea, in 1932, and during the Korean War he served as liaison officer to the U.S. Army and as an aide-de-camp in the Korean military. After the war, he took graduate degrees from Middlebury College, the State University of Iowa, and Harvard University.

Kim's first novel was *The Martyred* (1964), a philosophical speculation on goodness and truth set in Seoul shortly after the North Korean invasion. The martyrs of the title are twelve Christian missionaries shot to death in Pyongyang by Communists. Two other missionaries are spared, however, and their good fortune becomes the subject of speculation and the basis of a probing examination of moral and spiritual issues that foreshadows the theme of *The Innocent*.

In *Lost Names* (1970), Kim re-creates, in the words of his subtitle, "Scenes from a Korean Boyhood." These seven scenes are set during World War II in a Korea that is occupied by the Japanese, and the "lost names" are names that Koreans have to give up and replace with officially registered Japanese names. The Kims' new name becomes Iwamoto, or "rock foundation." These seven essays recover movingly a period and place little thought of by most Westerners and do much to illuminate the sensibility behind Kim's two philosophical novels.

*Bibliography*

Clark, Colin. Review of *The Innocent*, by Richard E. Kim. *Library Journal* 93 (October 1, 1968): 3578. Very critical of the novel's lack of action, background, and development. The conversations are "stilted" and the characters are "a faceless pack of colonels and generals."'

Gropman, Donald. Review of *The Innocent*, by Richard E. Kim. *The Christian Science Monitor*, October 31, 1968, 13. Judges Colonel Min to be more believable than Major Lee in a novel that fails to convince the reader that its characters could be real people.

Nichols, Christopher. "The Tough and the Tender." *National Review* 21 (February 25, 1969): 183-184. The longest and most flattering review of "Mr. Kim's vivid, timely and courageous rendering of his native land's ordeals." Nicholas responds pugnaciously to a negative review in *The New York Times*, lauding the "basic Christian theme" that animates *The Innocent* as well as its "secular insights."

O'Brien, R. E. Review of *The Innocent*, by Richard E. Kim. *Best Sellers* 28 (October 15, 1968): 288. Praises everything about the novel: its insights and suspense, its artistically handled theme, and its excellent dialogue.

Simpson, H. A. Review of *The Innocent*, by Richard E. Kim. *Saturday Review* 51 (November 23, 1968): 66. Complains about the long stretches of dialogue that do not advance the plot, but judges *The Innocent* a "worthy successor" to *The Martyred*, if not ultimately as good as the earlier novel.

*Frank Day*

# THE JAILING OF CECELIA CAPTURE

*Author:* Janet Campbell Hale (1947-      )
*Type of plot:* Psychological realism
*Time of plot:* 1980
*Locale:* Berkeley, California; Spokane and Tacoma, Washington; and reservations in Idaho and Washington
*First published:* 1985

> *Principal characters:*
> CECELIA CAPTURE WELLES, a thirty-year-old Indian woman in her second year of law school
> MARY THERESA CAPTURE, her mother
> WILL EAGLE CAPTURE, her father
> BRIAN (BUD) DONAHUE, her first lover and the father of her son
> NATHAN WELLES, her husband, a teacher in Spokane

*The Novel*

Drawn from the author's experiences of growing up as a Native American in a white-dominated society, *The Jailing of Cecelia Capture* consists of the reflections of the title character, who is spending a weekend in jail after her arrest for drunk driving. She scans her entire life, discovering that in many ways she has been repeatedly imprisoned by her society and culture.

The novel begins in jail. Cecelia's immediate fears center on the compulsory mugshots: They will make her look ugly, because she could not fix her face and hair. She recognizes that only a woman would care about this, and only in a culture that disproportionately glorified female attractiveness. In a cell with a white prostitute and a black thug, Cecelia realizes that, like them, she has spent her life trying to attract men. She bypasses the chance to call her husband for help, reassured that she will be released as soon as she sobers up.

Gradually, she pieces the past day, her birthday, together. As usual, she had forced herself through the deadening routine of law school, alleviating the pain with a rare thermos of wine to celebrate the day. The alcohol brings little relief; only the pressures of professional school keep at bay the emptiness of her life. She lives in a shabby apartment with few pleasantries; her husband—by now a husband in name only—and children are hundreds of miles and several months away; she has no transportation in the rainy winter of San Francisco Bay; her life consists of unrelieved study; she feels overweight and unattractive. Her most recent effort at romance lasted one night with a nameless man. At school, she has to confront a lover whom she reluctantly left after learning he already had a permanent relationship. Yet the wine at least gets her through the day.

After school, she makes the rounds to celebrate. She toys with a man who tries to pick her up. The experience reminds her of a game she plays with her husband in which they act like strangers who discover each other in bars. Remembering Nathan, she recalls what their marriage has become. That thought drives her in tears out of the bar. Her car is stopped before she gets home.

While waiting in her cell to be interviewed, Cecelia recollects her childhood on various reservations. She had been the last surviving child of an Indian father and a white mother. Her mother had belittled her because she was darker and coarser-haired than her older sisters; her mother's whole side of the family shunned their Indian relations. She insisted that the girl's dreams were ridiculous; like all women, Cecelia could rely only on her looks to make her way. Cecelia's father, however, was exceptional among his race because of his education, and he drove this last daughter to become an example of success. Because he had failed at that himself, having dropped out of college before fighting in World War II, he now spent every evening getting drunk. Cecelia grew up desperate to escape the squalor of a reservation life made worse by an alcoholic father and a physically and emotionally crippled mother.

Cecelia is stunned to learn that she is not being released because of an old charge of welfare fraud. After she had fled her home at the age of sixteen for the Summer of Love in 1967 San Francisco, she had met a gentle college-age man at one of the park "events" of the period. Under the influence of drugs, alcohol, and the spirit of the time, she had taken him as her first lover. After a single weekend, he had disclosed that he had been drafted; his ship was leaving for Vietnam immediately. She was bearing his child when he died there. In the early years of single motherhood, she was caught working while on welfare, and she skipped town before repaying the entire assessment. Later, she completed college and met her present husband.

Now she has to call him. On the day he bails her out, they agree to divorce. Before the hearing, Cecelia buys a gun; she will kill herself rather than return to jail. Her case, however, is dismissed because of time limitations. The novel ends when she drops the bullets at the grave of Bud, her first lover.

### The Characters

The novel has essentially only one character, Cecelia herself, Although the book is narrated in the third person, Cecelia is the only character presented internally as well as externally; hers is the only consciousness readers enter. All other characters— including those with direct bearing on the action—appear only as they affect her. This close-up technique highlights and heightens Cecelia's persona, enabling the reader to identify easily with her, to experience events through her. Because the novel is an exercise in ethnic consciousness-raising, this succeeds: Readers certainly learn the problems in development faced by Native American women. Yet the approach also reduces the status of all other characters and possible points of view.

Cecelia is complex enough and her situation difficult enough to deserve central staging in a work devoted to her. Simply describing that situation illustrates the complexity and difficulty. She is a thirty-year-old, reservation-reared, codependent Native American woman in her second year of law school. She thus exemplifies at least six levels of social and cultural dislocation, six barriers to her chosen goal.

Reared in segregation, she begins with the burdens of inferior education and inadequate role models, conditioned to accept secondary, or even tertiary, status. With an alcoholic father and disabled mother, she has grown up assuming that such deficiencies are normal. Membership in an ethnic minority reinforces many of these patterns, as does being female; both compound the prejudice she encounters trying to overcome them. She is an older student; even her Ph.D.-pursuing husband skips her university graduation, apparently because he finds something distasteful about her failure to graduate until the age of twenty-six.

Furthermore, she has dropped out of both high school and law school; she has a history of failure. Moreover, she has two school-age children, the older already in academic and social trouble, supposedly because of his absentee mother. Moreover, this is only a partial list of her problems. Looming over all is the fact that the program of study she is pursuing involves a partial betrayal of her heritage. She is becoming expert in the legal system that justified the brutal depredation of her ancestors, and she is running the risk that she may use her education to turn her back on her people. Her own personal history seems likely to trip her up, if not trap her completely. Her story begins with a drinking bout, merely the last of a long series, and she fails to find a single stable love relationship by the age of thirty. If life were a baseball game, she would have struck out before ever getting to the plate.

Yet all this serves only to spotlight her saving quality: Cecelia Capture simply will not quit. She is indomitable, a pillar of resolution. What makes this more remarkable is that she clearly does not enjoy what she is doing. Law school is drudgery for her; she suffers it only because it alone will get her what she wants. The discipline is so uncongenial that her only effective recitation occurs when she has drunk enough wine to anesthetize her normal tensions. Her classmates find her aloof and disconnected, and she has no close relations with any of them. She hates being separated from her children, especially because she knows her absence is hurting them. Exactly what motivates her is not clear. She does what she does partly to fulfill her father's ambitions, but more to overcome the limitations imposed on her by family, race, and culture. She simply will not be stopped.

*Themes and Meanings*

*The Jailing of Cecelia Capture* is an apologia, an explanation and justification of the central character. Its objective is to illustrate how and why Cecelia came to be the way she is, in herself and in relation to her culture. Since her major quality is perseverance, the novel seems at times almost like a promotional manual for that trait. Cecelia's life is a progressive and continuing overcoming; her motto might well be, "That won't stop me."

This focus, however, is not as transparent as it seems in summary, primarily because the novel establishes starkly just how formidable the obstacles facing her are. The example of her father is constantly before her. He had been, after all, a respected elder of the tribe, often a member of the tribal council before he was impeached for drinking in office; he had volunteered for service during World War II, at a time when Indians were not American citizens and had to give up their native names to enter the Armed

Forces; and he had a career as a prizefighter. Yet he did not live up to his own father's measure; Eagle Capture had served as tribal judge, designing the legal norms that gained status for the tribal government under the laws of the country. Will was educated at the white high school, entirely so than he could gain the college degree expected of his father's son. Even though his football skills earned him a college scholarship, however, he proved unable to keep up academically, and his decline into alcoholism seemed inevitable. Now, however, he was expecting his daughter to succeed where he, a male, had failed.

The book emphasizes that the problems multiply for each new generation, if only because the expectation of personal defeat becomes the norm. Cecelia's parents fell short of their parents' achievements. The loveless, abusive, codependent life they lead forms part of the context of Cecelia's consciousness; in fact, one major episode relates her attempt to break herself and her mother free of her father's abuse. This attempt fails. Her family is too snared in traps of their own fashioning to accept liberation. Yet the failure teaches Cecelia that the limitations of her parents and siblings are not necessary, and certainly not inescapable. It also teaches her the cost of liberation: Realizing herself will be possible only at the sacrifice of her family and others who demand her subordination. Having come so far, against such odds, can she now accept less?

## Critical Context

*The Jailing of Cecelia Capture* is possibly more important as a cultural document than as a novel. Published in 1985, long after the energies of the radical American Indian Movement of the 1960's and 1970's had largely burned out, the book demonstrates that self-realization and cultural integrity for Native Americans remain possible even under the jurisdiction of the United States. The novel shows that a person can work for her people while giving up only—or mainly—the limitations they confuse with their culture—and also shows how lonely such a passage can become.

The book is hard-eyed and uncompromising. Its depiction of common reservation life pulls few punches: The majority appear alienated from the ways of the past, which require too much effort to sustain, and mired in the unnourishing bread and pompous circuses of American commercial culture. The tribes seem caught in a world compounded of the dregs of two societies, able to function in neither. Cecelia gains only credit for turning her back on the shabby mobile-home and junked-car surroundings of her parents and siblings, but the urban American Dream, on close inspection, seems hardly congenial. Upward mobility into material culture is not Cecelia's ambition, but it is about all she is offered. None of the men she meets is capable of recognizing her for herself. Her most positive encounter is with another Indian, who offends her by referring to her as a squaw with an education. Eventually, she discovers that even her Ivy League-educated *Mayflower*-descended husband has chosen her not for what she is but for what she represents to him—the victim of the crimes of his ancestors. Yet it is precisely her self, her embattled self, that she finally discovers as worth preserving from assaults from two cultures leagued together to deprive her.

*Bibliography*
Bataille, Gretchen M. and Kathleen M. Sands. *American Indian Women: A Guide to Research*. New York Garland, 1991. This standard reference work lists all of Hale's publications in books to 1991 and directs students to relevant studies of her culture and background.

Bruchac, Joseph, ed. *Songs from This Earth on Turtle's Back: Contemporary American Indian Poetry*. Greenfield Center, N.Y.: Greenfield Review Press, 1983. Bruchac collects several poems by Hale, including some that connect with the world of Cecelia Capture.

Hale, Janet Campbell. *Bloodlines: Odyssey of a Native Daughter*. New York: Random House, 1993. This is not a strict autobiography but rather a collection of semiautobiographical essays that shed light on Hale's personal and tribal background. In many, she touches on connections between her actual experiences and the fictional ones of Cecelia Capture and reflects on the situation of the Native American caught between cultures. She also illuminates many tribal customs and traditions, particularly those concerning women.

_____ . *Custer Lives in Humboldt County and Other Poems*. Greenfield Center, N.Y.: Greenfield Review Press, 1978. Hale's first volume of poetry, this book includes many reflections on the status of women in Native American societies. In particular, it documents the intrusion of the white world and the difficulty of Indian women in coming to terms with it. The poems are quite accessible, drawing on long-established traditions of Indian song.

_____ . *The Owl's Song*. Garden City, N. Y.: Doubleday, 1974. Hale's first novel, aimed at juvenile readers, was an award-winning account of the problems faced by a fourteen-year-old Indian boy in entering puberty and undergoing rites of passage in two cultures simultaneously. It is most striking in its depiction of the continuing nourishment drawn by Native Americans from their ancient foundations. The protagonist learns that the old ways survive transplanting, even in the hostile ground of the white world.

Wiget, Andrew O. "Native American Literature: A Bibliographic Survey of American Indian Literary Traditions." *Choice* 23 (June, 1986): 1503-1512. Contains little direct information about either Hale or the novel, but does place both in the burgeoning context of Native American literature. A useful forging of lineages.

Wolitzer, Meg. "The Jailing of Cecelia Capture." *The New York Times Book Review* 90 (April 7, 1985): 14. Wolitzer summarizes the plot neatly, focusing on the series of repressions suffered by Cecelia from unhappy childhood to parental programming to loveless marriage.

*James Livingston*

# JAPANESE BY SPRING

*Author:* Ishmael Reed (1938-    )
*Type of plot:* Satire
*Time of plot:* The 1990's
*Locale:* The fictitious Jack London College in Oakland, California
*First published:* 1993

>  *Principal characters:*
>  BENJAMIN "CHAPPIE" PUTTBUTT, a black conservative, son of career Air
>  Force officers, professor of "Humanity" at Jack London College
>  ISHMAEL REED, the author himself, who appears as a character in the
>  novel
>  DR. YAMATO, Puttbutt's Japanese instructor, who later becomes president
>  of Jack London College
>  JACK ONLY, the billionaire patron of a conservative think tank opposed to
>  multiculturalism
>  DR. CRABTREE, a conservative English professor who opposes multicul-
>  turalism (and Puttbutt's tenure) but later has a change of heart
>  ROBERT BASS, JR., a student at Jack London College who edits the racist
>  newspaper that lampoons Puttbutt
>  ROBERT HURT, the dean of Jack London College, who defends multicul-
>  turalism
>  BRIGHT STOOL, the president of Jack London College, fired when a
>  Japanese group buys the college
>  MARSHA MARX, the chair of the women's studies department at Jack
>  London College

## The Novel

A satiric interpretation of Ishmael Reed's America in the early 1990's, *Japanese by Spring* is the story of a typical (though fictitious) California college in the final years of the George Bush Administration. *Japanese by Spring* is written in three parts of unequal length, and concludes with an epilogue. Part 2 could be considered merely a brief interlude (at ten pages, it is half the length of the epilogue), except that it advances the plot sharply and is a focal point of the action in the novel.

The story begins with a brief biography and character sketch of the protagonist, Benjamin "Chappie" Puttbutt. The son of two African American career Air Force officers, Puttbutt was sent to the Air Force Academy in the 1960's. There, Puttbutt went through a rebellious black consciousness stage, but he took a conservative turn after a tragic love affair with the wife of his Japanese professor. Unnerved by the experience, Puttbutt becomes a pacifist and ends up teaching English at Jack London College.

As the novel opens, a decision is pending on whether or not Puttbutt will be granted tenure. The tenure decision dominates the entire first section of the novel. Puttbutt does everything he can to appear to be a team player: When black students are lynched on campus, Puttbutt tells the press that the students deserved their beatings because of their excessive demands. Yet there are signs of trouble for Puttbutt.

The first sign is in the classroom. Some of the more bigoted white students, notably Robert Bass, Jr., the son of a local industrialist who contributes heavily to the college, openly ridicule him in class.

Puttbutt tries to be conciliatory on all fronts: Many liberal professors (especially the dean of "Humanity," Robert Hurt) are outraged at the blatant racism of the attack on Puttbutt, but the college president, Bright Stool, quiets demands for Bass's expulsion. The chair of the African studies department, Dr. Charles Obi, who should be most sensitive to attacks on a black professor, asks Puttbutt not to rock the boat. Puttbutt himself defends Bass's racist cartoons and remarks as protected forms of free speech.

Other threats to Puttbutt's security as a black conservative scholar arise from his past. His father, still an active-duty general, warns him that his grandfather, the only Puttbutt who did not serve in the military, and who in fact sympathized with the Japanese in World War II, may be trying to contact him. Grandfather Puttbutt in fact kidnaps his grandson with a gang of Japanese toughs and outlines a seemingly paranoid plan to side with the Japanese in an upcoming global economic conflict. Just as he is told that he may be on the losing side, Puttbutt returns to campus to receive the crushing blow that ends the first section: His tenure has been denied.

The pace of the plot quickens precipitously in part 2: still reeling from his denial of tenure, Puttbutt learns that Bass's father, angry over the threatened suspension of his son, has pulled his financial backing from the college, and his corporate friends follow suit. Japanese investors buy the college and institute radical changes, including hiring a new president and naming Puttbutt vice president. Part 2 ends melodramatically with the revelation that the new president is Puttbutt's former Japanese tutor, Dr. Yamato.

For the first few chapters of part 3, Puttbutt enjoys his reversal of fates: People who once held authority over him are now under his authority. Robert Bass, Jr., apologizes to Puttbutt and becomes his household servant. Angry mobs who threaten Puttbutt are beaten back by Ninja warriors. Yet revenge is not sweet for Puttbutt, who grows increasingly uneasy.

At this point, Ishmael Reed himself becomes a character in the novel, reversing the point of view from Puttbutt's Western cultural chauvinism to Reed's embrace of multiculturalism. After Reed's point of view is established, he meets Puttbutt in the faculty club at Jack London College. Returning to his office, Puttbutt finds the college's name changed: Instead of being named for Jack London, who is presented in the novel as anti-Asian, the school is now named for Hideki Tojo, the prime minister of Japan during World War II.

As the changes come more and more rapidly, Puttbutt becomes more and more opposed to the new administration. They institute new intelligence tests for students, with questions weighted toward Japanese culture. Japanese American students are expelled for having become too Westernized. When Reed protests, he is fired.

Organizing a faculty protest, the pacifist Puttbutt faces his first battle since leaving the Air Force Academy, but his father intrudes, bringing armed troops to subdue President Yamato. Yamato is arrested (the charge is not specified) but is soon free, showing up in Puttbutt's house and telling him about an impending struggle for control of the United States. The novel ends with an epilogue describing the country in 1992 from Reed's point of view.

*The Characters*

Benjamin "Chappie" Puttbutt represents a departure in characterization for Reed, whose protagonists are usually close to his own point of view. Puttbutt is very nearly Reed's opposite in many areas: a conservative from a military family, opposed to multiculturalism, defending Western cultural values. Reed builds up readers' sympathy for Puttbutt by making him the underdog but then undermines that sympathy when Puttbutt gains power. Puttbutt's pacifism, which arises partly from chafing at the role his parents have chosen for him and partly from shock at his lover's suicide while he is at the Air Force Academy, is shown to be mere capitulation to whoever is in power. The most subtly drawn of the characters in the novel, Puttbutt changes during the course of the book, learning how to rise above cultural parochialism. Nevertheless, the story leaves him just at the point of discovery of his limitations: His future is left open to question.

Ishmael Reed, the author appearing as a character in the novel, serves as a foil to Puttbutt—or vice-versa. Their opposition is not antagonistic: Both are African American men of letters, both have been attacked by feminist groups, both are studying difficult foreign languages. Yet the differences are telling, and crucial to the plot: Reed has staked his career on a multicultural philosophy that Puttbutt has opposed as a threat to Western cultural values.

Dr. Yamato, who is first seen simply as Puttbutt's Japanese instructor, is something of a mystery. His diatribes on the cultural supremacy of Japan are disturbing for Puttbutt, who sees them as cultural chauvinism and bigotry—though he does not see, as the reader does, that they closely mirror Puttbutt's own claims for Western cultural supremacy. When Yamato becomes president of Jack London College, his contempt for Western culture becomes more overt.

Jack Only, a mysterious billionaire, is now so old and decrepit that his black chauffeur has to carry him around. Reed describes Only as "a giant, craggy-faced cucumber with flippers where legs and arms should have been." He speaks through an electronic box. Only's misshapen form represents the moral shrivelling resulting from his bigotry. His name suggests the exclusivity of his cultural ideal. Only believes that civilization is threatened by multiculturalism, and he pays his think tank to prove it. When Reed demonstrates that multiculturalism can be big business, however, Only listens. His love of money overcomes his aversion to minorities.

Robert Hurt, the dean of "Humanity" at Jack London College, is a passionate defender of liberal causes. This puts him in an ambiguous position when Puttbutt is attacked by Robert Bass, Jr., in the racist student paper *Koons and Kikes*. On the one hand, Hurt cannot tolerate a racial slur against a black faculty member; on the other hand, the target of the slur, Puttbutt, believes that the attack is justified by white frustration.

Dr. Crabtree is a professor of English literature who secretly opposed Puttbutt's tenure. A champion of the "classics," Crabtree snubs Puttbutt until the tables turn and Puttbutt becomes his superior; then he curries favor, but to no avail. Puttbutt condemns him to teach "Freshman Yoruba." Yet Crabtree learns from the experience, and changes: By learning the African language, he begins to appreciate another culture, and the scales fall from his eyes. Reed's surprisingly sympathetic portrait of a white bigot suggests that Crabtree's bigotry was only ignorance, not blind hatred.

Robert Bass, Jr., becomes another redeemed bigot in the course of the novel. The leader of student ridicule of Puttbutt, his humiliation and punishment result not in greater hatred toward the black professor but in the discovery that, like Crabtree's, his bigotry was simply lack of understanding.

*Themes and Meanings*

*Japanese by Spring* is a satire on contemporary American attitudes toward cultural diversity, especially on college campuses. The title comes from the name of a language instruction book that promises the protagonist quick mastery of Japanese. The book, which soon becomes abbreviated to "J.B. Spring," and finally just "J.B.S.," is a symbol of the consumer attitude to other cultures that many characters in the novel exhibit. The main character, Benjamin Puttbutt, for example, seems to be studying Japanese simply to make himself more marketable.

Reed makes the satire much more amiable than some of his earlier novels by making the villain cultural elitism itself rather than any one character. The enemies of cultural diversity are not evil, merely crippled by various forms of chauvinism, from which many characters recover. It is not only the defenders of the white status quo who are carriers of this disease: The Japanese educators who take over the college end the elevation of Western culture in the curriculum, but they threaten to replace it with an equally narrow, Japan-centered vision of the world. The African studies department is run by an "Afrocentrist" who believes that Africa is the source of all good and that African culture is morally superior to any other.

Stylistically, Reed continues a trend in his novels toward realism, though there is a touch of his earlier fantasy style in making the character Jack Only "a giant cucumber with flippers." Characterization is muted in the novel, as is usual with satire and with Reed's fiction in general. Characters tend to be readily recognized types, probably drawn from Reed's own experience as a college professor in Berkeley, California. There are several touches that echo Reed's own experience: He, too, was involved in a bitter and public battle over tenure at the University of California at Berkeley. He, too, has come under fire by enemies of diversity in all camps, European, African, and Asian. Yet the major intent of the book is not autobiographical, despite the fact that the character "Ishmael Reed" plays an important role in it.

Another aspect of realism in the novel is the presence—sometimes oppressive—of names and events from the real world. At times, passages can read like a 1992 newsmagazine, dropping names in the news such as Anita Hill, Rodney King, and Dan Quayle. Often, the names seem mere attempts to lend legitimacy to whatever claim the narrator is making, in the manner of an authoritative footnote. There are about thirty fictional characters in *Japanese by Spring*, most of them minor; there are more than a hundred real people mentioned and quoted, most of them contemporary, and most mentioned only once. This obsessive referencing to the world outside the novel at times threatens to destroy the illusion of Jack London College, which may be Reed's intention.

It can be argued that multiculturalism itself is the novel's protagonist, for though Chappie Puttbutt is the point-of-view character, he is not the moral center. He is a ghost of what Ishmael Reed might have become under other circumstances. The fictive symbiosis of the characters of Reed and Puttbutt, in fact, is a major point of interest in the novel. Both are African American academic intellectuals, Reed a pro-multicultural poet and novelist, Puttbutt an anti-multicultural literary critic. Though Reed is held in the background for the first half of the novel, he is first seen in scenes that parallel Puttbutt's: struggling to learn a difficult tonal language (in Reed's case Yoruba, in Puttbutt's Japanese). Despite the fact that Puttbutt is Reed's opposite in many political and cultural issues, he is shown as victimized by some of the same forces that oppose Reed. Reed takes great pains to make his reader sympathize with a protagonist who is nearly the opposite of himself.

*Critical Context*

Chappie Puttbutt represents a new development in characterization for Reed. Protagonists such as the Loop Garoo Kid in *Yellow Back Radio Broke-Down* (1969), PaPa La Bas in *Mumbo Jumbo* (1972), and Raven Quickskill in *Flight to Canada* (1976), while not autobiographical characters, represent Reed's point of view: The values of these characters are the values of their respective novels. Beginning with the character of Ian Ball in *Reckless Eyeballing* (1986), however, Reed began to develop characters who did not completely embody the point of view of the novel or the novelist. Like Puttbutt, Ball had adjusted his beliefs to fit those of the people who could most help his career.

Perhaps one reason for an avoidance of what Reed elsewhere calls a "Neo-Hoodoo," or Africa-conscious, protagonist is that characters such as PaPa La Bas or Loop Garoo, steeped in African tradition, might upset Reed's carefully crafted cultural balance in the novel. Reed's earlier Neo-Hoodoo aesthetic championed African art forms as they appeared in African American works. The aesthetic of *Japanese by Spring* is subtly different: It champions *all* cultures, never one at the expense of another. While it is possible to celebrate African elements in American art and letters without becoming Afrocentric—in fact, elsewhere Reed has done so—it would be easy for an audience to misread such celebration as cultural chauvinism, which would be contrary to the spirit of *Japanese by Spring*.

In turning away from the biting satire and wild fantasy of his earlier period, Reed is also turning away from much that gave his fiction its power. A devil's advocate for this novel might say that its satire is more subtle, more sophisticated, and therefore represents a sharpening of Reed's powers. To critics such as Gerald Early in *The New York Times*, however, this mellowing is merely a blunting of Reed's rapier. Evidence for the former view, and perhaps a reason for it, may be found in the epilogue to the novel, which is written from Reed's own point of view.

The epilogue is as broad in focus as the whole novel. In essence, it is a picture of the multicultural America of the twenty-first century, imaged in the California Reed saw in 1992. The epilogue centers, however, around a single plot element, a specific ritual of an African church in Oakland, California, on June 7, 1992. The ritual involves the resurrection of a god of the Yoruba people with whom Reed says, African Americans have lost touch. Reed's fiction in the 1960's and 1970's demonstrated the influence of the African Vodun ("voodoo" or "hoodoo") religion on American popular culture; *Japanese by Spring* notes the importance of recovering another "lost" religion.

This time, however, there is a difference: Reed is presented as an impartial observer at the ritual, not as a partisan in the struggle between African gods and Jahweh. In fact, it is in the context of the ritual that Reed experiences a change of heart toward the African Methodist Episcopal Zion church of his stepfather. He realized that this African American church, founded forty years before American slaves were freed, preserved many of the Nigerian religious practices in a different form.

This change of heart affects the whole tone of Reed's satire in *Japanese by Spring*, but it does not in any way lessen the intensity of his denunciation of injustice in his culture. It only makes it less shrill. There are no villains in *Japanese by Spring*, at least, none who cannot be redeemed by learning to appreciate other cultures. Reed continues to challenge the way readers see themselves and others, and *Japanese by Spring* does so in a more subtle way than do his other novels, but no less effectively.

*Bibliography*
Beauford, Fred. "A Conversation with Ishmael Reed." *Black Creation* 4 (1973): 12-15. An early interview with Reed that still offers valuable insight into his ideas and methods.
Bryant, Jerry H. "Old Gods and New Demons: Ishmael Reed and His Fiction." *The Review of Contemporary Fiction* 4 (Summer, 1984); 195-202. Bryant looks at Reed's fiction as an expression of the African religions about which he writes. Bryant uses the terminology of contemporary fiction to talk about Reed, which is not always helpful. This study, though, is important as one of the few serious scholarly studies of Reed at a time when his critical reputation seemed to wane elsewhere.
Hume, Kathryn. "Ishmael Reed and the Problematics of Control." *PMLA* 108 (May, 1993): 506-518. Written for a scholarly journal, this essay's academic jargon may pose a problem for some readers, but it is valuable as a cogent summary of many

attacks, largely feminist, on Reed's fiction. Viewing the theme of power and control as one of Reed's major contributions to contemporary fiction, Hume demonstrates that Reed's use of the theme reveals as much about him as it does about America. Reed's frequent use of grotesque violence is explained as a function of the theme of control.

McConnell, Frank. "Ishmael Reed's Fiction: Da Hoodoo Is Put on America." In *Black Fiction*, edited by A. Robert Lee. New York: Barnes & Noble, 1980. Mostly on the style of Reed's earlier fiction, this article nevertheless provides an accurate guess of the directions Reed's fiction would take after 1980. McConnell was one of the first critics to recognize that Reed's writings had gone beyond the "Neo-Hoodoo" aesthetic of his earliest fiction. McConnell is also successful at demonstrating that traditional critical tools do not do justice to Reed's fiction.

Reed, Ishmael. "The Great Tenure Battle of 1977." In *Shrove Tide in Old New Orleans*. New York: Avon Books, 1978. This account of Reed's struggle for tenure at the University of California at Berkeley provides interesting background to the fictional tenure battle described in *Japanese by Spring*. Though Reed's real-life tenure battle occurred fifteen years before the fictional one, many of the concerns are the same.

*John R. Holmes*

# JASMINE

*Author:* Bharati Mukherjee (1940-　　)
*Type of plot:* Bildungsroman
*Time of plot:* 1965-1989
*Locale:* India, New York City, and Iowa
*First published:* 1989

> *Principal characters:*
> JASMINE, the protagonist and narrator, a young Hindu woman from India who illegally enters the United States
> PRAKASH VIJH, Jasmine's husband, killed by a Sikh fanatic's bomb in India
> LILLIAN GORDON, an elderly Quaker woman who teaches Jasmine how to act American
> DEVINDER VADHERA, Prakash's former Indian professor, now living in New York
> KATE GORDON-FELDSTEIN, Lillian's daughter, who introduces Jasmine to Taylor and Wylie Hayes
> TAYLOR HAYES, a Columbia University professor, Jasmine's first American employer and lover
> WYLIE HAYES, Taylor's professional wife
> DUFF, the adoptive daughter of Taylor and Wylie Hayes
> BUD RIPPLEMEYER, an Iowa banker with whom Jasmine lives as his common-law wife
> DU THIEN, a Vietnamese refugee boy adopted by Bud and Jasmine
> DARREL LUTZ, a young Iowa farmer in love with Jasmine

## The Novel

*Jasmine* is a novel of emigration and assimilation, both on physical and psychological levels. In this novel, Bharati Mukherjee fictionalizes the process of Americanization by tracing a young Indian woman's experiences of trauma and triumph in her attempt to forge a new identity for herself.

The story is told from the first-person point of view by the female protagonist, who undergoes multiple identity transformations in her quest for self-empowerment and happiness. Mukherjee uses the cinematic techniques of flashback and cross-cutting to fuse Jasmine's past and present. The novel is steeped in violence.

The book begins with the twenty-four-year-old narrator, Jane Ripplemeyer, living as the common-law wife of Bud Ripplemeyer, a fifty-four-year-old invalid banker in Baden, Elsa County, Iowa. Through flashbacks, she recalls her story from childhood in Hasnapur, a village in Jullundhar District, Punjab, India, where she was born as Jyoti, the unwanted fifth daughter in a poor, displaced Hindu family. When she was seven, an astrologer predicted that she was doomed to widowhood and exile. Determined to fight her destiny, Jyoti begins to empower herself through learning English, for "to want English was to want more than you had been given at birth, it was to want the world."

Her first notable transformation begins when, at fourteen, she marries Prakash Vijh, an engineering student and a modern city man who does not believe in the subservient role of the Indian wife. "To break off the past," Prakash renames her "Jasmine" and gradually moulds her to become a new woman, untrapped by the traditional beliefs of a feudal society. He implants the American Dream in her mind, and both plan to leave for America to begin a new life. When Prakash falls victim to a Sikh extremist's bomb, she decides to emigrate to the United States to fulfill her husband's dream.

Her American odyssey accelerates the process of her metamorphosis. Upon her arrival in Florida, when she is brutally raped by a monstrous skipper, she symbolically turns into the goddess Kali to slaughter her assailant. She also burns her husband's suit outside her motel, as if to burn her Jyoti-Jasmine self and her Indian past. With help from a kindly mentor, Lillian Gordon, she reinvents herself into her first American identity, "Jazzy in a T-shirt, tight cords, and running shoes."

After her initiation into the American way of life, Jasmine moves on to New York. She lives temporarily with the family of her late husband's professor, Devinder Vadhera, but she feels stifled by the pseudo-Indian cultural environment in the Vadhera household. To distance herself further from India and everything Indian, she seeks the help of Lillian's daughter, Kate, to secure the job of a live-in "day mommy" for Duff, the adoptive daughter of a Columbia University couple, Taylor and Wylie Hayes.

In her emancipating position as the couple's au pair, Jasmine starts living the American Dream. She falls in love with Taylor and his world of ease and comfort. Taylor accepts her without sanitizing her foreignness and gives her a new identity, "Jase," a woman who lives for today and becomes aware of the plasticity and fluidity of American culture. Her happiness, however, ends when, by a strange quirk of fate, she happens to spot her husband's killer in a New York park. To escape her past, she flees New York and ends up in rural Iowa, to be reincarnated as "Jane Ripplemeyer."

Even in Elsa County, however, fates seem to be intertwined. She and Bud adopt Du Thein, a Vietnamese refugee boy who constantly reminds her of her own past. She thinks of Du as the son that she and Prakash might have had, but she is carrying Bud's child. When Bud is shot and crippled by a distraught farmer, she refuses to marry him, because she hopes to save him from what she believes is her destiny. She also resists Darrel Lutz, her tormented lover, who wants to run away with her. When Du leaves for California to be with his sister's family, however, she realizes that she will not be far behind. Darrel's suicide reaffirms that Iowa is closing in on her. She feels totally isolated as Jane Ripplemeyer and hopes that Taylor will come to her rescue.

When Taylor and Duff finally track her down, she walks out on her life with Bud and is headed toward California, "greedy with wants and reckless from hope," to set up "an unorthodox family" with Taylor, Duff, and Du.

## The Characters

Jasmine is a complex, resourceful, and dynamic character who undergoes dramatic changes throughout the novel. A young, daring woman from India, she represents Bharati Mukherjee's concept of "the new breed" of Americans from non-European countries who are imperceptibly changing the face of America. Endowed by nature with good looks and a good mind, she uses them both to her fullest advantage to seek happiness and self-fulfillment. With her remarkable willpower, she fights an undesirable fate as she resists the hold of a feudal and patriarchal family. Her marriage to Prakash allows her to break the mold of the traditional female role in Indian society and strengthens her hopes for a bright future. When Prakash decides to go to school in America, she sees this as a possible way to subvert the fate predicted by the astrologer. Even her husband's death does not deter her from realizing her American Dream. Her arduous voyage to America shows her stubborn will to survive and her determination to re-create her destiny. She goes through several rebirths to become all-American. Her adaptability and readiness to reinvent herself aid her assimilation into American society.

Prakash Vijh, Jyoti's husband, impresses the reader with his modern outlook and revolutionary ideas. He liberates Jyoti from her feudal past and transforms her into a new kind of modern woman, capable of independent thought. He renames her Jasmine and stirs her mind with new possibilities. Jyoti rightly thinks of him as her Pygmalion.

Lillian Gordon, an old white Quaker woman who provides sanctuary to refugees and illegal aliens, represents the best in the American spirit of compassion, tolerance, and philanthropy. She facilitates Jasmine's assimilation into mainstream America.

Professor Devinder Vadhera, an Indian expatriate living in New York, embodies the conflict between assimilation and cultural preservation. As Prakash's former teacher, he serves as Jasmine's American connection. Yet Jasmine rejects the stifling aloofness of his Indian world to merge into the great American melting pot.

Kate Gordon-Feldstein, Lillian's daughter and the author of a book on migrant workers, is the first person to applaud Jasmine's expression of will. By helping her to find a job with the Hayeses, Kate opens up new possibilities for Jasmine to fulfill her dream.

Taylor Hayes, an academic who falls in love with Jasmine and calls her "Jase," teaches her how to take charge of her life and harmonize her Hindu concept of destiny with her American expression of will. Most important, he does not fear her foreignness and accepts her as she is. Under Taylor's loving tutelage, as Jasmine puts it, "I bloomed from a diffident alien with forged documents into adventurous Jase." It is Taylor who eventually leads her to "the promise of America."

Bud Ripplemeyer, the disabled banker, offers Jasmine a haven of economic security and the prospect of motherhood, but he cannot offer her "adventure, risk, transformation," for which she craves. Though he wins Jasmine's deep affection and admiration, he fails to satisfy her emotional needs.

Du Thien, the Vietnamese boy adopted by Bud and Jasmine, plays an important part in Jasmine's emotional life. He constantly reminds her that she is living in exile among strangers. She regards Du as the son she and Prakash might have had.

*Themes and Meanings*

Primarily an immigrant narrative, *Jasmine* explores the process of Americanization and brings out the conflict between assimilation and cultural preservation. It is a poignant story of survival, expediency, compromises, losses, and adjustments involved in the process of acculturation to American life. As Jasmine says in the novel, "There are no harmless, compassionate ways to remake oneself. We murder who we were so we can rebirth ourselves in the images of dreams."

The process of rebirth, even in a metaphoric sense, his been extremely painful for both Jasmine and Du. Both have confronted death closely, endured severe hardships, suffered horrible indignities, and survived. Jasmine calls her own transformation "genetic," whereas Du's was "hyphenated." In her desire for assimilation into mainstream America, Jasmine immolates her Jyoti-Jasmine self to burn her Hindu past. To accomplish her genetic transformation, she conceives a child by a white American from the heartland and feels potent in her pregnancy, as if she is "cocooning a cosmos."

Du, on the other hand, has retained his identity as a Vietnamese American. A survivor and an adapter, he learns to camouflage himself within the expectations of others, but he instinctively resists the idea of the American melting pot. Although it seems that he is fast becoming all-American, he keeps his language and ethnic heritage alive by secretly keeping in touch with the Vietnamese community. Like Jasmine, he too experiences three lives—one in Saigon, the other in a refugee camp, and the third as Yogi Ripplemeyer—but he never severs his connection completely from his roots. Du's character exemplifies that in a multicultural society one does not have to erase one's ethnic identity entirely to become an "American."

The novel also portrays the problems of immigrants who arrive in the United States with dreams of wealth and success but find it difficult to adjust to the new environment and ethos. Mukherjee probes such troubles through the character of Professor Devinder Vadhera, once a scientist in India, now working as an importer of human hair in Flushing, New York. He does not like his job, but he needs to work to support his wife and old parents. To adapt to his new environment, he undergoes a name change and becomes a diminutive "Dave." He lives in a ghetto, always feels stressed, and complains that America is killing him. He regards Flushing as a neighborhood in Jullundhar and encloses himself in "the fortress of Punjabiness," artificially created in his home environment. According to the narrator, Vadhera "had sealed his heart when he'd left home. His real life was in an unlivable land across oceans. He was a ghost, hanging on."

The novel obviously moves from Vadhera's cultural isolation to Jasmine's intense longing for assimilation. Since the novel focuses on the physical, emotional, and intellectual growth of the female protagonist and her quest for self-determination and identity, it can also be viewed as a *Bildungsroman*, or rite-of-passage novel.

*Critical Context*

Acclaimed as brilliantly written and superbly crafted, *Jasmine* grew out of a short story of the same title in *The Middleman and Other Stories* (1988), which won Mukherjee the prestigious National Book Critics Circle Award. In *Jasmine*, the author successfully employs a number of narrative strategies, such as the use of a first-person point of view (unlike the omniscient perspective of her previous novels), singular and plural narrative voices, flashbacks, introspective asides, and cross-cutting, which allow the reader to roam in time, within a chapter, even within a paragraph, from one continent to another. Mukherjee also experiments with the form of the novel by creating a female *Bildungsroman* in the picaresque mode.

Thematically, *Jasmine* is central to Mukherjee's mission as a writer. "My material," as she has stated, "is the rapid and dramatic transformation of the United States since the early 1970s. . . . My duty is to give voice to continents, but also to redefine the nature of *American* and what makes an American." *Jasmine* is basically a story of transformation. Like Mukherjee's first two novels, *The Tiger's Daughter* (1972) and *Wife* (1975), and her first collection of short stories, *Darkness* (1985), it deals primarily with the South Asian immigrant experience. Whereas these earlier works dramatize cultural disorientation and alienation, however, *Jasmine* celebrates the process of assimilation and Americanization prefigured in *The Middleman and Other Stories*. Her novel *The Holder of the World* (1993) traverses the continents.

In addition to her novels and two collections of short fiction, Mukherjee has written a travel memoir, *Days and Nights in Calcutta* (1977; coauthored with her husband Clark Blaise); a documentary, *The Sorrow and the Terror: The Haunting Legacy of the Air India Tragedy* (1987, in collaboration with Blaise); a political treatise, *Kautilya's Concept of Diplomacy* (1976); and a number of essays, articles, and reviews. Her work has appeared in several newspapers, magazines, and anthologies. Her immigrant narratives, chronicling the saga of "new Americans," are contributing to the literature of American multiculturalism and have won for her a distinctive place among first-generation North American writers of Indian origin.

*Bibliography*
Boire, Gary. "Eyre and Anglos." *Canadian Literature*, no. 132 (Spring, 1992): 160-161. In this highly suggestive review, Boire views *Jasmine* as "the paradigmatic 'postcolonial' narrative." He points out that young Jyoti's abandonment of two British novels, Charles Dickens' *Great Expectations* (1860-1861) and Charlotte Brönte's *Jane Eyre* (1847), because she found them too difficult to read, is significant because it symbolizes the author's "own need to 'rewrite' past literary and political wrongs" by rejecting well-known icons of the British Empire.
Chua, C. L. "Passages from India: Migrating to America in the Fiction of V. S. Naipaul and Bharati Mukherjee." In *Reworlding: The Literature of the Indian Diaspora*, edited by Emmanuel S. Nelson. Westport, Conn.: Greenwood Press, 1992. Chua offers a perceptive analysis of *Jasmine*, stressing "survival and reincarnation" as the book's integral themes. He also points out apparent similarities between *Jasmine* and *Jane Eyre*. The concluding section traces Mukherjee's evolution as an artist.

Kaye-Kantrowitz, Melanie. "In the New New World." *The Women's Review of Books* 7 (April, 1990): 8-9 Calls the novel "a witty, dazzling fairy tale disguised by naturalism." Kaye-Kantrowitz demonstrates, with textual evidence, the novel's three themes: identity, hovering mortality, and "the contrast between the escapee/immigrant vision of America and the vision of the protected American."

Koening, Rhoda. "Passage from India." *New York* 22 (September 25, 1989): 132. Tracing the protagonist's passage from her native village to the city and thence to America, Koening shows how "first with love, then with courage and cunning," Jasmine "creates her destiny."

Schaumburger, Nancy Engbretsen. "Chaos and Miracles." *Belles Lettres: A Review of Books by Women* 5 (Summer, 1989): 29. Gives a summary of the novel, highlighting the young heroine's different identities, which "the various circumstances and men in her life have bestowed upon her."

*Chaman L. Sahni*

# JAZZ

*Author:* Toni Morrison (1931-     )
*Type of plot:* Social realism
*Time of plot:* The 1920's, with flashbacks reaching back to 1873
*Locale:* Harlem, New York, and rural Virginia
*First published:* 1992

> *Principal characters:*
> JOE TRACE, an amiable fifty-three-year-old salesman of beauty products
> VIOLET TRACE, Joe's wife, an emotionally volatile fifty-year-old hairdresser
> DORCAS, Joe's mistress, an impressionable eighteen-year-old orphan
> ALICE MANFRED, Dorcas' aunt and Violet's confidante, a dignified fifty-nine-year-old widow
> ROSE DEAR, Violet's mother, a suicide
> TRUE BELLE, Violet's grandmother, maidservant to Vera Louise Gray
> VERA LOUISE GRAY, an eccentric white woman, mother of Golden Gray
> GOLDEN GRAY, Vera's blond, light-skinned mulatto son
> HUNTER'S HUNTER (HENRY LESTORY), the father of Golden Gray and hunting mentor of Joe Trace
> WILD, Joe's mother, a feral woman who lives in the woods
> FELICE, Dorcas' friend, a seventeen-year-old girl

*The Novel*

*Jazz*, Toni Morrison's sixth novel, is a lyrical, multifaceted narrative that explores the Harlem lives and back-country roots of a number of African American characters in the years from 1873 to 1926. In keeping with the loose, improvisational nature of the music that gives the book its title, *Jazz* is composed of ten untitled, unnumbered chapters. The principal first-person narrator is an unnamed omniscient observer with a distinctly subjective personality who knows Harlem and the main characters well. The novel also includes first-person passages narrated by Joe, Violet, Dorcas, and Felice, that give the reader a rich and sometimes conflicting range of perspectives on the characters and action.

The main events of the novel take place in the six months or so from fall 1925 to spring 1926. The locale is Harlem, site of the 1920's Harlem Renaissance, a legendary period of African American creativity in fiction and poetry. Morrison's emphasis, however, is on jazz, the distinctively urban African American music that reached an early peak in this period. Her novel begins *in medias res* in January, 1926, with an anecdote that seems the novelistic equivalent of such blues ballads as "Frankie and Johnny." Joe Trace, a married man in his fifties, has a "deepdown, spooky love" for eighteen-year-old Dorcas, but when their three-month-old affair goes awry, he shoots her at a party. (The reader later learns that Joe is never arrested for this murder because no one will admit to witnessing the crime.) Joe's wife, Alice, then takes a strange revenge by bursting in on Dorcas' funeral and trying to slash the dead girl's face.

Playing off this sensational opening anecdote, Morrison's mercurial narrative ranges in many directions, much as a jazz musician might improvise on the opening statement of a melody. In a vividly sensuous style, the author brings to life both the excitement of Jazz Age Harlem and the racism, violence, and unresolved mysteries of the places its citizens had left behind—the rural South and the cities of the Midwest.

The early chapters focus on the midlife crises of Violet and Joe that lead to their desperate actions. As Violet reaches the age of fifty, she begins to feel more keenly the lack of a child in their marriage. Her despair causes her to withdraw into silence and to bouts of insane behavior, including an impetuous attempt to steal another woman's baby. Joe, on the other hand, yearns to regain the excitement that he and Violet had when they "train-danced" into Harlem in 1906. Once he has gained Dorcas as his mistress, however, he finds that it is not the excitement of youth that he needs so much as someone to whom he can talk.

In later chapters, Morrison explores the troubled family pasts of Violet and Joe through an intricately interwoven series of flashbacks set in fictional Vesper County, Virginia. Violet is left to endure the memories of her father's abandonment of his family when she was a young girl, of her family's eviction from their home by whites when she was twelve, and of her mother True Belle's suicide when Violet was sixteen. Joe, also an orphan, is haunted by the memory of his search for his mother, Wild, a feral woman who lived in the woods. Though he learns how to stalk from tracking expert Hunter's Hunter, Joe is never able to catch a glimpse of his mother. In a related subplot that reaches back even earlier, Golden Gray, a young mulatto, travels from Baltimore, where he lives with his white mother Vera Louise Gray, to Vesper County in search of his black father, Hunter's Hunter. En route, Golden Gray rescues Wild when she knocks herself unconscious against a tree, and Golden and Hunter help the feral woman to deliver a baby (Joe Trace).

Like Violet and Joe, Dorcas is also suffering from the loss of her parents, both of whom were killed in the East St. Louis riots of 1917. Harlem transforms Dorcas from a sorrowful nine-year-old into a reckless flapper enraptured with Harlem's flashy styles and uninhibited attitudes. Yet Dorcas allows herself to be drawn into an affair with Joe partly because he serves as a father figure.

In contrast to Violet, Joe, and Dorcas, who let their emotions and their haunted pasts propel them into destructive or self-destructive behavior, is Alice Manfred, Dorcas' dignified aunt. Early in the novel, Alice tries unsuccessfully to prevent her niece from losing herself in Harlem's immoral sensuality. Later, Alice generously befriends Violet (the violator of her niece's funeral) and helps Violet to gain an old-fashioned but stabilizing sense of herself.

Toward the end of the novel, Joe and Violet move closer to each other by embracing a quiet domestic existence. Even Felice, the teenaged best friend of Dorcas who shared her appetite for Harlem's frenzied nightlife, seems to find the happiness that her name denotes by gradually accepting a cozy role as Joe and Violet's surrogate daughter.

*The Characters*

Joe Trace, a middle-aged salesman, gains the reader's sympathy despite his seemingly perfidious acts that begin the novel. A charming, avuncular man, trusted in his community, Joe nevertheless takes an eighteen-year-old girl as his mistress. He drifts into this unsavory behavior because of his wife's emotional withdrawal and his own midlife melancholy, but also because he sees Dorcas as a needy, vulnerable girl whom he wants, in his own odd way, to protect. The reader feels sorry for Joe in the flashback passages when he is tracking Wild, his inaccessible mother; despite his grimmer purpose, Joe's tracking of Dorcas, when he has lost control of their relationship and of himself, retains some of that pathos from earlier in his life.

Violet Trace is a fifty-year-old hairdresser who is hardworking but subject to spells of emotional derangement. The reader's attitude toward Violet shifts from shock over her desperate violence at Dorcas' funeral to sympathy when one learns of the traumas of Violet's past, particularly her mother's suicide. Ironically, after striking out in hate against Dorcas' corpse, Violet then becomes preoccupied with the life of the dead teenager. Fortunately, Violet finds Alice Manfred to be the kind of caring maternal figure that Violet has missed having in her life, and with Alice's help, Violet regains her emotional balance.

Dorcas, the catalyst for the most violent acts in the novel, is viewed differently by different characters. The narrator presents her as an emotionally damaged adolescent who chases the thrills of Harlem to escape her painful past, while on a deeper level she actually wants to die. Alice sees Dorcas as the defenseless victim of an older man's seduction; Violet sees her as the beautiful daughter she wishes she could have had. To her best friend Felice, Dorcas seems an unscrupulous, less-than-attractive girl who habitually uses people, while Joe is struck by her softness, beauty, and neediness.

Alice Manfred serves as the moral pivot of the novel. A maternal figure who embodies an old-fashioned sense of morality, she fails to keep Dorcas from succumbing to Harlem's temptations; after Dorcas' funeral, however, Alice helps Violet to regain control of herself as a "lady." This change in Violet revives her marriage with Joe, and they in turn serve as stabilizing parental figures in the life of Felice.

Though they are not characters in the conventional sense, two other important personalities in the novel should be noted: the City and the narrator. Curiously, in *Jazz* Morrison almost never uses the word "Harlem." Instead, throughout the novel she refers to this section of New York as "the City," a place of mythic power that exerts strong influences on its inhabitants. For example, Joe's decision to take a mistress seems as much an aspect of his love for the City as an attraction for a particular woman. Joe begins his affair with Dorcas in October, a time of special beauty in the City's weather; and the main action moves from this golden October, through the cold January of Dorcas' murder and Joe and Violet's despair, to the "sweetheart weather" of early spring, when life begins to blossom in the City and for Joe and Violet once again.

Morrison's first-person narrator undergoes curious changes in her views of the characters, the City, and even of the plot and of herself. At first, she speaks with a confident voice that ranges from a gossipy, sensationalistic view of the characters' perversities to a lyrical celebration of her love for the City. Early on, she also raises the suspense level of the plot by stating that there will be another shooting later when Felice arrives at the home of Joe and Violet. Yet a strange irony of the novel is that as Violet, Joe, and Felice become more stable in the final chapters, the narrator seems to become emotionally unhinged. The foreshadowed ending is changed so that no second shooting occurs, and the narrator proclaims herself unreliable and helpless.

## Themes and Meanings

Toni Morrison has stated that the overarching purpose of her novels is to show readers "how to survive in a world where we are all of us, in some measure, victims of something." She begins *Jazz* with an anecdote in which Dorcas seems to be the clear victim of the actions of Joe and then Violet. By the end of the novel, however, Morrison has shown how all the characters are victims, for all are scarred by their pasts—often by the racism, dispossession, and violence that are the heritage of slavery. Most of the characters are thus preoccupied with a search for self that involves working out the complex family patterns that haunt them. Some characters, such as Joe and Golden Gray, conduct an actual search to find a parent. On a less conscious level, most of the characters—including Joe, Violet, Dorcas, Alice, and Felice—are searching for people who will fill the gaps left by the relatives they have, in one way or another, lost. For example, as a result of her mother's suicide, Violet loses both her mother and her desire to become a mother; yet she comes to find in Alice and in Dorcas (and then Felice) both the mother and the daughter that she longs to have in her life.

Even the narrator is the victim of her own illusions and mistaken projections. She finds that she must partially give up the romantic view of the City, presented early in the novel, as a place of ideal liberation where people are inspired to become "their stronger, riskier selves." As the novel proceeds, the narrator must also consider the havoc that the City's passions wreak in the characters' lives, and she must admit that the old-fashioned values of Alice Manfred and the quiet domesticity embraced by Joe, Violet, and Felice at the end ultimately lead to a richer kind of happiness. Thus the narrator learns that the characters have outgrown the need for violence and that the shooting scene involving Joe, Violet, and Felice that she foreshadowed at the beginning of the novel no longer fits the way that the characters have evolved.

Ultimately, the great achievement of *Jazz* is that Morrison goes beyond the mere illustration of how her characters are victims who survive; she dramatizes how they move beyond their victimization and grow in moral stature. When Violet is in the depths of her despair, Alice advises her, "You got anything left to you to love, anything at all, do it." In their various ways, Joe, Violet, Felice, and the narrator all eventually absorb this all-important lesson: They learn to give and to receive a mature kind of love.

*Critical Context*

In 1987, Toni Morrison achieved a decisive plateau in her career with her fifth novel, *Beloved*, a Pulitzer Prize-winning best-seller that solidified her position as the leading African American novelist of her generation. With *Jazz*, on the other hand, Morrison dared to risk her established position by writing a novel that is less masterful and confident, more exploratory and tentative.

One measure of Morrison's adventurousness in *Jazz* is her choice of setting. She begins the novel not in the rural and small-town settings that have been her recognized forte, but rather in 1920's Harlem; she uses the novel to explore her ambivalence toward that legendary time and place. On the one hand, Morrison enjoys celebrating Harlem and its jazz as a metaphor for the exhilarating liberation felt by blacks who moved to Northern cities after World War I, when it seemed as if racism and war might be things of the past. On the other hand, she is also honest enough to recognize that the excitement and sensuality of the City lured people away from the kinds of love and maturity that could truly heal them.

*Jazz* is also audacious in the lengths that Morrison is willing to go to make her narrator fallible. Rather than excising the early passage that mistakenly foreshadows a second shooting, Morrison chooses to leave the passage in and to dramatize the feelings of anxious inadequacy that this dissonance in the plot brings up in the narrator. In this way, Morrison provides the narrator with the same opportunity that the characters have enjoyed: the chance to realize her mistakes and to renew and reinvent herself on a stronger footing.

Though *Jazz* seems at times less in control than Morrison's other novels, its adventurousness and inventiveness are exhilarating, and its many stories, characters, and perspectives are richly imagined and frequently moving. Ultimately, *Jazz* shows Toni Morrison to be a great American writer who is not content to let her past successes become formulas for her future works. In 1993, her achievements were recognized with the 1993 Nobel Prize in Literature.

*Bibliography*

Gates, David. "America Means Black, Too." *Newsweek* 119 (April 27, 1992): 66. Gates expresses reservations over the excesses of Morrison's arty style and self-conscious use of her narrator in *Jazz*. Overall, however, Gates celebrates the way Morrison's prose creates a vividly convincing world. He believes she may be "the last classic American writer."

Hulbert, Ann. "Romance and Race." *The New Republic* 206 (May 18, 1992): 43-48. Hulbert criticizes *Jazz* as a failed experiment in self-conscious improvisation. She argues that Morrison's characters are flat and her descriptions clichéd. According to Hulbert, although Morrison intends to avoid romanticizing blackness, she instead ends up sentimentalizing family domesticity.

Leonard, John. "Her Soul's High Song." *The Nation* 254 (May 25, 1992): 706-718. This discussion of *Jazz* in relation to Morrison's other novels finds her dominant theme to be "identity-making" in a black culture of broken families and failed dreams. Leonard admires *Jazz*'s wealth of characters, its exploration of their Southern roots, and its witty use of a self-conscious narrator. According to Leonard, Morrison is "the best writer working in America."

O'Brien, Edna. "The Clearest Eye." *The New York Times Book Review*, April 5, 1992, 1, 29-30. O'Brien admires the virtuosity of Morrison's style—her shifting perspectives and lyrical sentences. She praises Morrison's ability to express her anger at the injustices done to African Americans while also bringing her characters into complex, dramatic life. Nevertheless, O'Brien feels that *Jazz* fails to deliver the ultimate moments of profound feeling that are the hallmark of great literature.

Wood, Michael. "Playing in the Dark: Whiteness and the Literary Imagination." *The New York Review of Books* 39 (November 19, 1992): 7-10. Wood's analysis of *Jazz* in the context of Morrison's other novels finds it to be the first in which her African American characters achieve a genuine escape from white cultural oppression and their own tendency to react perversely to it. He also criticizes Morrison's self-conscious mannerisms and occasional talkiness. Overall, however, he admires the rich interplay of her language and overall design.

*Terry L. Andrews*

# THE JOY LUCK CLUB

*Author:* Amy Tan (1952-    )
*Type of plot:* Family
*Time of plot:* The twentieth century
*Locale:* China and Northern California
*First published:* 1989

> ### Principal characters:
> JING-MEI WOO, also named JUNE, the daughter of Suyuan and Canning Woo
> WAVERLY JONG, nicknamed MEIMEI, the daughter of Lindo and Tin Jong
> LINDO JONG, a mother and Suyuan Woo's rival
> LENA ST. CLAIR, the daughter of Ying-ying and Clifford St. Clair
> YING-YING ST. CLAIR, also named BETTY, a mother
> ROSE HSU JORDAN, the daughter of An-mei and George Hsu
> AN-MEI HSU, a mother and the most recent host of the Joy Luck Club

## The Novel

*The Joy Luck Club* is a collection of sixteen stories narrated by three mothers and four daughters. Divided into four groups or sections, the stories constitute a dialogue between the Chinese mothers and their American daughters as they attempt to connect. The same events are often narrated or mentioned by two or more of the characters. So connected are the stories, in fact, that they can be viewed as chapters in a polyphonic novel, a novel of many voices.

The first section is entitled "Feathers from a Thousand *Li* Away." The feathers symbolize the hopes that the mothers brought with them from China and the value of their Chinese heritage. In the first story, "The Joy Luck Club," Jing-mei Woo, a daughter, narrates her first night as a member of the Joy Luck Club, a mah-jongg group started by her mother in San Francisco in 1949. The next story, "Scar," is told by An-mei Hsu, a mother, who remembers her first two encounters with her own mother, who had been disowned by her family for dishonoring her widowhood. In "The Red Candle," Lindo Jong, a mother, reveals the circumstances of her arranged marriage to a spoiled boy and the clever way she freed herself without disgracing her family. The final story, "The Moon Lady," is told by Ying-ying St. Clair, a mother, who recalls the night she feel into a river and "lost" herself, later to be disillusioned by an encounter with the legendary Moon Lady. The "feather" stories probe the childhood experiences of the Joy Luck "aunties," defining their characters and culture.

The title of the second section, "The Twenty-Six Malignant Gates," refers to a Chinese book that enumerates the many harms that can befall children who stray from their mothers' protection. In the first story, "Rules of the Game," Waverly Jong, a daughter, reminisces about her years as a chess prodigy and the strain it placed on her relationship with her mother. Narrated by Lena St. Clair, a daughter, "The Voice from the Wall" recounts Ying-ying St. Clair's deteriorating mental health and the unhappiness of the St. Clair home during Lena's adolescence. In "Half and Half," Rose Hsu Jordan, a daughter, attributes her crippling indecision and the failing of her marriage to the tragic death of her brother, Bing, who years earlier had drowned while under her supervision on a family outing. The final story, "Two Kinds," is narrated by Jing-mei, who reflects on her mother's frustrated attempt to turn her into a prodigy: countless piano lessons, a disastrous talent show, and finally an angry confrontation between mother and daughter. All narrated by American daughters, the "gate" stories depict the childhood estrangements of the daughters from their mothers.

The third section is entitled "American Translation" because the daughters are, in effect, American versions of their mothers. In the first story, "Rice Husband," Lena St. Clair realizes the inadequacy of her marriage during a visit from her mother. The next story, "Four Directions," is narrated by Waverly Jong, who introduces her fiancé to her parents and finally begins to understand herself and her mother. In "Without Wood," Rose Hsu Jordan is emotionally paralyzed by her faltering marriage until she learns to stand up for herself—with her mother's help. The final story, "Best Quality," relates Jing-mei's humiliation at the hands of Waverly Jong during a holiday dinner. To restore her daughter's self-confidence, Suyuan gives Jing-mei a jade pendant signifying her "life's importance." The "translation" stories present the daughters as vulnerable adults in need of guidance and on the verge of connecting with their mothers.

In the last section, entitled "Queen Mother of the Western Skies," the mothers and daughters finally connect. The first story, "Magpies," begins where "Scar" leaves off. After the death of her grandmother, An-mei returns to Tientsin with her mother, who later commits suicide to ensure An-mei's security and prosperity as the honored daughter of Wu Tsing. In "Waiting Between the Trees," Ying-ying recalls her first marriage to a bad husband, her abortion, and her second marriage to Clifford St. Clair, who brought her as a "ghost" to America. The third story, "Double Face," is a continuation of "The Red Candle." Lindo Jong remembers her early years in America as a factory worker and her friendship with An-mei, who introduced her to Tin Jong, her second husband. Jing-mei narrates the final story, "A Pair of Tickets," in which she travels to China with her father and discovers her late mother in the gestures and visages of her mother's long-lost Chinese daughters.

## The Characters

Jing-mei Woo, the daughter of Suyuan and Canning, is the novel's protagonist. Unlike the other characters, she narrates four stories, two for herself and two for her deceased mother. Her mother claimed that Jing-mei was born with an excess of water and therefore flows in too many directions. In college, she majored in biology at first, then changed to art, and finally dropped out to become a secretary, then a copywriter for a small-time advertising agency. Her name, Jing-mei, means "sister of best quality."

Waverly Place Jong, the daughter of Lindo and Tin, functions as Jing-mei's antagonist, always asserting her superiority and humiliating her rival. She was named after her family's street in San Francisco so that she would never forget her home. As a child, she was a national chess champion. Her picture appeared in *Life* magazine along with a quote from Bobby Fischer. A tax attorney by profession, she is clever, analytical, strong-willed, and occasionally arrogant. She is the most balanced and stable of the four adult daughters.

Lindo Jong, the mother of Waverly and the wife of Tin, embodies strength and cunning. She was Suyuan Woo's best friend and archnemesis, encouraging competition between Waverly and Jing-mei. Born into a poor family, she was betrothed and later married to a cruel boy in a wealthy family. The ordeal enabled her to discover her inner strength and worth, which she later tried to pass on to her daughter. Like her daughter, she is proud, impatient, aggressive, and clever—an excellent mah-jongg player.

Lena St. Clair, the daughter of Ying-ying and Clifford, is characterized by her passivity, fear, and low self-esteem. As a child, she was ashamed of her Chinese heritage and especially of her eyes, which betrayed her ethnicity. An architect by profession, she married one of her colleagues, Harold, and they agreed to share expenses, such as rent and gasoline, even splitting the cost of ice cream. Lena earns considerably less money than Harold, however, and she considers their arrangement to be unfair, but she has been reluctant to complain. At her mother's prodding, she finally confronts her husband.

Ying-ying St. Clair, also named Betty, is the mother of Lena and the wife of Clifford. Described by Jing-mei as the "weird auntie," she is patient, kind, and funny but also "hard of listening." Because her family in China was upper class, she enjoyed the luxuries and leisure of wealth, but a bad marriage crushed her *chi* (spirit), and she became a ghost of her former self. Her identity was further confused by her second husband, Clifford, who on her immigration papers changed her name to Betty and her birth year from 1914 to 1916. Born a tiger, she became a dragon in the stroke of a pen.

Rose Hsu Jordan, the daughter of An-mei and George, was born without wood and consequently bends too easily to other people's suggestions. To compensate for her indecisiveness, she married a confident man, Ted, and allowed him to make decisions for her. Ted's confidence was shaken when he lost a malpractice suit, however, and their marriage began to disintegrate. The resulting separation paralyzed Rose emotionally. By the end of her second story, she is finally able to stand up to her husband and demand their house in the divorce settlement.

An-mei Hsu, the mother of Rose and the wife of George, has no spine, but she is not stupid. For nine years, she lived with her grandmother, Popo, in her uncle's house. After Popo's death, she went to live with her mother, Nuyer, who was the third concubine of a wealthy man. She enjoyed the opulence of her surroundings but also had to bear the stigma of her mother's concubinage. Her mother's suicide had a profound effect on her, teaching her to "shout." Years later, the death of her son, Bing, effectively silenced her, destroying her faith in the Christian God.

*Themes and Meanings*

In four sections of four stories each, the mothers and daughters engage in what might be called tag-team narration. Four is the number of corners at a mah-jongg table, and the structure of the novel seems to be patterned loosely on the game of mah-jongg. The three mothers and Jing-mei, substituting for her late mother, narrate the stories in the first and last sections of the novel. The daughters' stories, coming in the middle two sections, are framed by the mothers' stories, suggesting that the daughters are inside their mothers (a womb image) and their mothers inside them.

Jing-mei narrates the first and last stories of the novel and the last story of each of the two middle sections. She functions as an important link between the generations and as an "anchor" in the last three sections. Each of the other characters—mothers and daughters—narrates two stories, one about childhood and the other about adulthood. The first two sections focus on the characters as children, while the last two sections focus on the mothers and daughters as adults.

This contrapuntal structure is complemented by numerous contrasts: Chinese and American, mother and daughter, past and present, pride and shame, forgetting and remembering. Opposition organizes the plot, as the characters search for resolutions to their differences. Remembering their own mothers, the Joy Luck "aunties" are frustrated because their daughters are not connected to them in the same way that they were connected to their own mothers. They fear that their heritage will be lost after they die and that their daughters will forget them. As China is separated from America by a vast ocean, so the mothers are separated from their offspring by age, culture, and language.

Tan's novel is very much concerned with language and communication. Important motifs include translation, orality, misinterpretation, and silence. Whereas the mothers speak fluent Chinese and imperfect English, their daughters speak perfect English and only some Chinese. Jing-mei must travel to China to translate her mother's speech for her half-sisters. Clifford often misunderstands and mistranslates his wife's meaning. An-mei says "faith" and Rose hears "fate" because her mother cannot make the "th" sound in English. Ying-ying's silence causes Lena pain as a child and cripples her as an adult.

Of course, the obstacles to communication are not only lingual but also cultural and generational. Jing-mei sees but cannot understand her aunts' loyalty to her mother. Popo tells An-mei stories that she cannot understand because of her age. Ultimately, the novel is about the struggle of the mothers and daughters to understand each other, to overcome the cultural and generational barriers that separate them. Waverly and Jing-mei seem to achieve this goal by the end of the novel, while Rose and Lena are apparently very close to it.

*Critical Context*

Formerly a freelance business writer, Amy Tan decided in 1985 to take up fiction writing as a hobby. She was inspired by Native American author Louise Erdrich's *Love Medicine* (1985), a critically acclaimed collection of short stories. Tan's first story, "Endgame," was good enough to get her into a recognized writing program, where she became friends with Amy Hempel and Molly Giles, both fiction writers. Giles advised her to send "Endgame" to *FM* magazine, which eventually published the story. When *Seventeen* magazine paid to republish the story, Tan knew she had joined the ranks of professional fiction writers. "Endgame" later became "Rules of the Game" in *The Joy Luck Club*.

Published in 1989, *The Joy Luck Club*, is Tan's first novel. The book was originally entitled *Wind and Water*, but her agent suggested a title change. Several of the stories were published first in national magazines such as *The Atlantic* and *Ladies' Home Journal*. All of the stories are faintly autobiographical. For example, Tan's name in Chinese is An-mei. Her grandmother, Jing-mei, was raped and forced into concubinage and later committed suicide, like An-mei Hsu's mother in "Magpies." Like Jing-mei in "A Pair of Tickets," moreover, Tan traveled to China in 1987 to investigate her heritage.

After *The Joy Luck Club*, Tan published *The Kitchen God's Wife* (1991) and *The Moon Lady* (1992). The former is a novel about an aging matriarch's colorful life in China and her effort to connect with her daughter. The latter, a children's book, is a retelling of Ying-ying's first story in *The Joy Luck Club*. Critics reacted favorably to *The Kitchen God's Wife* and unfavorably to *The Moon Lady*, which fails to capture the magic and subtlety of the adult version.

*The Joy Luck Club* is often compared with Maxine Hong Kingston's *The Woman Warrior* (1976), a collection of related stories juxtaposing the author's memories of her childhood in San Francisco with fantastic tales about female warriors. Tan's novel can also be grouped with Gus Lee's *China Boy* (1991), Gish Jen's *Typical American* (1991), and David Wong Louie's *Pangs of Love* (1991), contemporaneous works of fiction by and about Chinese Americans.

*Bibliography*
Angier, Carole. "Chinese Customs." *New Statesman and Society* 2 (June 30, 1989): 35. Angier implies that *The Joy Luck Club*'s success in America is based on "ideological correctness" rather than "intrinsic qualities." Characterizing Chinese culture as cunning and crafty, Angier argues that Tan's novel, because it is "cunningly crafted," disproves its own theme that "American children lose Chinese values."
Bain, Carl E., et al. "Amy Tan's 'A Pair of Tickets.'" In *The Norton Introduction to Literature: Instructor's Handbook*. 5th ed. New York: W. W. Norton, 1991. Provides a detailed and insightful explication of the novel's final chapter. The editors emphasize setting as the key to understanding Jing-mei's story. Particularly interesting is the editors' discussion of personal and place names in China.
Miner, Valerie. "The Daughters' Journeys." *The Nation* 248 (April 24, 1989): 566-569. Miner observes that the narration progresses horizontally (from friend to friend) as well as vertically (from mother to daughter). She contrasts the epic journeys of the mothers with the domestic journeys of the daughters and accurately

characterizes the daughters as their mothers' "guardian angels" in an alien culture.

Pollard, D. E. "Much Ado About Identity." *Far Eastern Economic Review* 145 (July 27, 1989): 41-44. Pollard identifies the novel's movement as "a kind of anagnorsis without dénouement"—in other words, a process of gradual understanding or recognition without a final outcome. Failing to take into account the shifts in point of view, Pollard complains that the mothers speak "broken English" in the "daughters' narrations" but perfect English in their own stories. He also accuses Tan of misusing Chinese expressions.

Shear, Walter. "Generational Differences and the Diaspora in *The Joy Luck Club*." *Critique* 34 (Spring, 1993): 193-199. Shear identifies the novel's organizational scheme as "generational contrast" and praises "the multiplicity of first-person narratives" for giving voice to two generations instead of just one. Kingston's *The Woman Warrior* serves as Shear's touchstone for evaluating the success of Tan's novel; he compares and contrasts the two works throughout his analysis.

*Edward A. Malone*

# KATE VAIDEN

*Author:* Reynolds Price (1933-      )
*Type of plot:* Psychological realism
*Time of plot:* 1937 to 1984
*Locale:* North Carolina and Virginia
*First published:* 1986

> *Principal characters:*
> KATE VAIDEN, a fifty-seven-year-old woman suffering from cervical cancer
> FRANCES VAIDEN, Kate's mother
> DAN VAIDEN, Kate's father, who murders his wife, then commits suicide
> CAROLINE, Frances Vaiden's sister, who rears Kate
> HOLT PORTER, Caroline's husband
> SWIFT PORTER, Holt and Caroline's son
> WALTER PORTER, Holt and Caroline's son
> GASTON STEGALL, Kate's first love
> DOUGLAS LEE, a boy who impregnates Kate when they are both in their teens

## The Novel

*Kate Vaiden*'s protagonist is an aging woman trying to exorcise the demons of her past. She needs to recount the events of her troubled life to the son she abandoned more than forty years ago, when he was four months old, to win his forgiveness. In piecing together her story, Kate discovers much about herself and reveals an impressive inner strength.

In 1984, Kate Vaiden is recovering from cancer surgery. Her life-threatening cervical carcinoma causes her to reflect upon her life and makes her determined to find the son she, as a frightened, unmarried, ashamed seventeen-year-old in a small Southern town, left in the care of her aunt, Caroline Porter. Kate lives near Macon, North Carolina, where her son is reared, but she has suspended all contact with her family there.

From age eleven, Kate's life is melodramatic. Price, however, succeeds in raising the story above its surface sensationalism by focusing on universal truths that direct Kate's life. The only child of Dan and Frances Vaiden, Kate was reared by her Aunt Caroline, Frances' sister.

Early in the novel, Kate has come with her mother from Greensboro, where they live, to Macon, the small town near the Virginia border where Frances was reared, for the funeral of cousin Taswell Porter, recently killed in a motorcycle accident. Frances' husband, however, has refused to attend the funeral, and he is enraged when his wife insists on going. Kate learns late in her life that her father suspected Frances of having an affair with her cousin, Swift Porter, who would surely attend the funeral.

The day after Taswell's burial, Swift asks Frances to go with him to check the grave.

Dan Vaiden, smoldering with jealousy, has come to Macon and is stalking his wife. He follows her when she goes into the woods with Swift and, confronting her, fires his revolver, wounding her fatally before turning the gun on himself.

Kate, orphaned at age eleven, is overcome by sorrow, confusion, and guilt. She thinks that if she had accompanied her father when he went to look for her mother, as he asked her to, the deaths might have been avoided. She is too innocent to realize that if she had done so, she too might be dead. The events of this memorable day fester in Kate's troubled mind and color her existence. Price, who in several of his other works has been intensely concerned with how the sins of the fathers are visited upon their children, clearly demonstrates that after the events Dan precipitated, Kate must bear a crushing burden from which she will never be free.

As a result of Kate's early life, she has never been able to trust people. The shattering blow of her parents' deaths heightens her distrust and makes her distant. When she is thirteen, however, Kate has an affair with a sixteen-year-old neighbor, Gaston Stegall. She grows to love Gaston. Just when Kate has begun to find some stability in a relationship, Gaston, now eighteen, joins the Marines. When he is killed during a training exercise, Kate becomes more withdrawn and suspicious than ever. Kate's mother once made her a penny-show garden with a slogan, "People will leave you," that seems prophetic for Kate. If the people she loves do not run away, death will snatch them from her.

Shortly after Gaston's death, Kate is impregnated by Douglas Lee, a youth whom her cousin Walter has rescued from an orphanage and taken to Norfolk to live with him. Walter uses Douglas sexually; Douglas, defiant and retaliatory, impregnates Kate. Rejecting Walter's suggestion that all of them live together in Norfolk after she bears the child, Kate sets out for Raleigh with Douglas.

Fearing, however, that living with Douglas will not work out, she bolts when the train stops in Macon, returning to Aunt Caroline, who sees her through her pregnancy. Kate then tracks down Douglas Lee, now a chauffeur to Whitfield Eller, a blind piano tuner in Raleigh. Soon, Eller is brutally attacked by an unidentified intruder—most likely Douglas, who disappears. Kate takes Douglas' place chauffeuring Eller, who begins to have romantic inclinations toward Kate. Later, Douglas is found dead by his own hand in Eller's bathtub.

Kate goes to Greensboro. She finishes high school by correspondence and works for the next forty years, never communicating with her family. As the novel closes, Kate has established contact with her son, now past forty, who has inherited Walter Porter's house in Norfolk, where he lives and serves in the Navy. Kate is preparing to meet him and tell him her story. The novel ends before they meet. One thing, however, is clear: Kate Vaiden is facing realities that she could not face from the time her parents' violent deaths robbed her of her childlike innocence and confirmed her inherent distrust of people.

## The Characters

Kate Vaiden recounts her first-person narrative partly as a means of dealing with her tortured past and partly as a rehearsal of what she will tell her long-lost son, Lee. Price presents Kate as a woman who fears intimacy, who runs from commitment. The people young Kate admits into her life and emotions die: her parents, Gaston Stegall, and Douglas Lee. In her convoluted way, she feels guilt for these deaths. Life for her is easier if she strikes out on her own and shrinks from intimacy, because intimacy— even platonic closeness—threatens her. People are drawn to Kate, but as a part of her self-protective mechanism, she eventually must shun them.

Aunt Caroline Porter is extremely interesting. She is a saintly woman but nobody's fool. She always steps into the breach when she is needed. She rears the orphaned Kate, she sees Kate through her pregnancy, and she ultimately rears Kate's child. On the surface, she seems self-sacrificing, but underlying her actions is deep-seated guilt. Caroline has some inkling that Kate's parents are dead because of her son Swift's romantic involvement with Frances. This is why she insists that Swift break the news of the murder-suicide to Kate. She also realizes that the intentions of her son Walter are not entirely pure when he takes Douglas Lee from the orphanage to live with him. Her good deeds can be viewed as an expiation for her son's bad deeds. Readers learn more about Caroline Porter from what she does than from what she says.

Douglas Lee has a temper, but readers see little of it. He once cut Walter's hand with a knife and, almost certainly, he has beaten Whitfield Eller, the blind piano tuner, although he is never directly accused of the attack. Douglas seethes with internalized anger. He seduces Kate to retaliate for the sexual liberties Walter takes with him. Douglas' suicide is aimed directly at hurting three people: Kate, Walter Porter, and Whitfield Eller.

Gaston Stegall is a sympathetic character who joins the Marines to serve his country in time of war. He never sees active duty; during a training exercise, he unaccountably stands up in the line of fire and is killed. His death is officially labeled a training accident but can legitimately be called a suicide. Price offers no overt motivation for Gaston's brash act; the episode, however, certainly helps the author to build his characterization of Kate Vaiden, because her reaction to Gaston's suicide leads ultimately to her pregnancy and her forty-year absence from Macon.

Holt Porter, Caroline's husband, although a minor character, plays a definite part in building the milieu in which *Kate Vaiden* takes place. Caroline runs the household and makes the decisions. Holt goes along with them, although they certainly cost him both money and the freedom that many people crave in later life. Holt is not exactly the henpecked husband, but he is compliant and dutiful, never complaining, never running from responsibilities that really should never have fallen to him.

*Themes and Meanings*

In her critical biography of Reynolds Price, Constance Rooke suggests that Price's work is characterized by two conflicting problems, which very much influence his themes and his resolution of those themes. According to Rooke, Price wrestles with the paradox of how one can live a solitary existence without longing for the company of others. People who escape their solitary situations, ironically, quickly realize that they have sacrificed much of their individuality and personal autonomy.

Kate Vaiden is a striking example of Rooke's contention, reached three years before the publication of *Kate Vaiden*. Kate wants, even seeks, love. Every time she allows her heart to become involved with someone else, however, that person leaves her, not infrequently through the most permanent departure of all—death. By the time Kate is eighteen, she loses the four people who mean the most to her.

Rather than jeopardize her emotions again. Kate allows relationships to progress just to the point that they might stand a chance of permanence; then she withdraws. Whitfield Eller begins to think romantically of Kate, but after Douglas kills himself, she takes Eller to the Great Smoky Mountains and leaves him with his aunt.

Kate has a romance with a veteran returned from World War II. Shortly before they are to marry, she tells him her whole life story, which causes him to flee. After she returns to Raleigh as a legal secretary, Kate ceases to pursue romance or to allow it to enter her life.

In much of his writing, particularly in such novels as *The Surface of the Earth* (1975), *The Source of Light* (1981), *Good Hearts* (1988), and *The Tongues of Angels* (1990), Price is obsessed with death and with how it affects the living. He is fascinated as well with the biblical notion that the sins of the fathers are visited upon their children, a theme that cries out from almost every page of *Kate Vaiden*.

Using the cohesive family as a base, Price makes Kate's separation from it more pitiful than would be a relative's separation from a family less steeped in Southern familial tradition. Caroline is the glue that holds the family together, but death, disappointment, and guilt are the forces Price uses to unglue Kate from her family for forty years.

Kate, however, cannot overcome the family ties in which Price so strongly believes. As the novel ends, she is on the brink of forging a new beginning with her son. She has already made her peace with Swift, whose sexual aggressiveness led to her parents' death and to her leaving Macon (because of Swift's advances to her) for Norfolk, where she stayed with her cousin Walter and his ward, Douglas Lee.

*Critical Context*

Reynolds Price published thirteen books before *Kate Vaiden* appeared. Five of these were novels, including his much-heralded *A Long and Happy Life* (1962). He had produced as well two collections of short fiction, two of poetry, a translation of thirty stories from the Bible, two plays, and a collection of essays.

He finished the first third of *Kate Vaiden* the day before he had surgery for a spinal cancer that nearly killed him, the aftermath of which left him without the use of his legs. In an effort to control the incredible pain he was enduring, Price underwent a course of hypnotism that was aimed at helping him control his pain through posthypnotic suggestion.

The result of this treatment was that Price was put in touch with vivid memories of his early life, going back as far as the first few months of his existence. The result was an outpouring of writing, including his autobiography, *Clear Pictures: First Loves,*

*First Guides* (1989). *Kate Vaiden* assumed a new shape following Price's hypnotism and, upon publication, became both his greatest commercial success and a notable artistic triumph, winning the National Book Critics Circle Award in fiction.

In *Kate Vaiden*, Price connects with many of the feminist concerns of the 1980's, although he does so without overt intention: that is, he did not set out to write a feminist tract. Rather, his picaresque narrative, his occasional use of epistolary technique in the revelation of plot, and his graceful use of flashbacks all result in a book that was precisely right for its time.

*Bibliography*
Drake, Robert, ed. *The Writer and His Tradition*. Knoxville: University of Tennessee Press, 1969. Drake considers Price and his work in relation to Southern tradition. Although the book was published before some of Price's most important work had been published, Drake offers valuable insights into such novels as *A Long and Happy Life* and *A Generous Man*. Places Price in a useful and appropriate literary context.

Humphries, Jefferson. "'A Vast Common Room': Twenty-five Years of Essays and Fiction by Reynolds Price." *The Southern Review* 24 (Summer, 1988): 686-695. Despite its brevity, this overview of a quarter-century of Price's writing is an indispensable resource. Calls *Kate Vaiden* a "fictional autobiography," revealing that in 1983, Price decided to make the protagonist female rather than the male he had been developing in that role.

Kimball, Sue Laslie, and Lynn Veach Sadler, eds. *Reynolds Price: From a Long and Happy Life to 'Good Hearts.'* Fayetteville, N.C.: Methodist College Press, 1989. This 154-page collection of essays on Reynolds Price and his work is diverse and well balanced. The contributions on *Kate Vaiden* are germane. Many of the contributors are Southerners who know Price's locale intimately.

Rooke, Constance. *Reynolds Price*. Boston: Twayne, 1983. This first full-length consideration of Price provides a biographical overview, an analytical reading of Price's major works, and a useful, though dated, selected bibliography. Rooke identifies the major problems Price confronts in most of his books.

Rushman, Michael. "A Writer at His Best." *The New York Times Magazine* 137 (September 20, 1987): 60. Draws heavily upon an exhaustive 1987 interview with Price. Shows how paraplegia following spinal surgery in 1984 marked a period of productivity in Price's life unlike any he had previously experienced.

Tolson, Jay. "The Price of Grace." *The New Republic* 198 (July 4, 1988): 34-39. In his overview of Price's writing, Tolson calls *Kate Vaiden* the best of his novels to date. This capsulized summary of Price's career to 1988 is useful.

Wright, Stuart, and James L. W. West, III. *Reynolds Price: A Bibliography, 1949-1984*. Charlottesville: University Press of Virginia, 1986. This extensive bibliography, which includes *Kate Vaiden*, is splendid but needs updating. Exhaustive for the three and a half decades it covers.

                                                                    *R. Baird Shuman*

# THE KING

*Author:* Donald Barthelme (1931-1989)
*Type of plot:* Alternative history
*Time of plot:* The early 1940's
*Locale:* Great Britain
*First published:* 1990

> *Principal characters:*
> KING ARTHUR, the legendary British leader, who is pictured as still living
>     in 1940
> GUINEVERE, the queen, his wife
> LAUNCELOT DU LAC, the queen's lover and chief general of King Arthur
> LORD HAW HAW, a German radio propagandist
> SIR KAY, Arthur's aide
> SIR ROGER DE IBADAN, the Black Knight, a visiting knight from Africa
> VARLEY, Guinevere's maid
> LYONESSE, the queen of Gore
> LIEUTENANT EDWARD, a former plasterer, Lyonesse's lover
> MORDRED, Arthur's bastard son, a traitor
> THE BROWN KNIGHT, a knight from Scotland
> THE YELLOW KNIGHT, Sir Colgrevaunce of Gore
> THE RED KNIGHT, Sir Ironside of the Red Lands, a Communist
> THE BLUE KNIGHT, a man searching for the Grail, the ultimate weapon

*The Novel*

*The King* is an attempt to fit the Arthurian tales of Sir Thomas Malory to the situation during the Battle of Britain. In a series of small, unnumbered chapters, Donald Barthelme delineates, in an almost offhand, oral style, the concerns of Arthur, Guinevere, Lancelot, and many minor characters.

The first chapter, written in a parody of the medieval Malory's convoluted style, describes Launcelot riding about furiously in a state of wild and random action. It becomes clear that this story will be something different, however, when Guinevere is shown in the next chapter sitting with her maid listening to Lord Haw Haw, a historical English traitor who broadcasts propaganda for the Germans in World War II.

The story, what there is of one, is told as a series of conversations by an ever-widening number of characters who discuss the Battle of Britain, worry that the war is not going well, and intersperse their comments with talk of love affairs and politics. The main plot is the attempt of Arthur and the few knights to deal with World War II, especially the Battle of Britain. They endure two radio harassments: Lord Haw Haw, the legendary English traitor trying to convince the English to surrender, seems to concentrate his satire on Queen Guinevere, continually harping on her infidelities to Arthur and her frivolous lifestyle. Readers wonder how he seems to know every one of her deviant actions. The other radio annoyance is known only as Ezra, an obvious reference to Ezra Pound, the famous American poet who made pro-Axis broadcasts. He harps on anti-Semitic propaganda, blaming World War II on the Jews. The characters all seem to listen carefully to these men and then ignore them.

Side plots erupt. The lady Lyonesse, Queen of Gore (wherever that is), falls in love with a medical officer, a Lieutenant Edward, who in civilian life is a plasterer. Sir Roger de Ibadan, the Black Knight from Dahomey, tells tales of his native land, with its evil king and its love of sculpture. He in his turn falls hopelessly in love with a ruthless highwaywoman named Clarice. A quasicommunist crusade is preached by a homeless beggar named Walter the Penniless; another communist, the Red Knight, advocates the overthrow of Arthur, whom he derides as an anachronism. The Blue Knight, on the other hand, has a solution for the war: The Holy Grail. It is a bomb, he says, a blue bomb made of cobalt that is bigger than all the other bombs of the world and will successfully end the war.

In the spring, Guinevere decides to leave the government in the hands of Mordred, whom everyone knows is no good. The young Mordred immediately has dreams of power and plots to overthrow Arthur. Arthur is in military headquarters with Sir Kay, lamenting the loss of Tobruk to General Rommel and having trouble reconciling his plans with the interference of Sir Winston.

Sir Kay, worried about the outcome of the war, wants to look at the prophecies of Merlin, which only Arthur is supposed to see. Arthur, after much cajoling, allows Sir Kay a brief look at the next few years of the prophecy. All readers of Malory's original story know that Arthur's reign is supposed to end in an immense battle with Mordred in which almost everyone, including Arthur and Mordred, is killed. The battle is indeed held, and Mordred is indeed killed, along with almost all the others involved, but Arthur is not. Kay, surprised, asks Arthur about his; Arthur explains that he didn't like the prophecy the way it was, so he rewrote it.

The war seems to recede into the distance, even though there is mention that it ends much as the real war did, through the intervention of rather unsympathetic Americans. The King and Queen go back to playing their mythic roles, and the book ends as it began, with an adventure of Sir Launcelot told in the language of Malory.

## The Characters

King Arthur, the legendary leader of Great Britain is a somewhat shadowy character. He leaves politics to "Winston" and the propaganda machines and interests himself in the military. He vaguely feels that his kingly role has outlived its usefulness and feels keenly the loss of the old, romantic Round Table.

Guinevere plays the part of the bored and spoiled queen, a characterization Barthelme appropriated from Malory. Like all the characters, she is not rounded out, because the purpose of the novel is not the characterization but the reaction of the characters to the situation. Guinevere seems to accept the accusations of Lord Haw Haw, the radio traitor, that she is "dallying" with Sir Launcelot, even though during the period of the book she is sleeping with the Brown Knight and not with Launcelot.

She feels weary and bored and perhaps understands that the romantic role of queens is dead. She does insist, however, that "all myths come from queens."

Sir Launcelot du Lac is a sort of noncharacter. The book opens with his fighting, and his character seems to be defined by his first jousting with and then befriending a strange knight. The book ends with his dream of "the softness of Guinevere." He is concerned only with Malory's two principal themes, fighting and love.

Sir Kay is King Arthur's aide-de-camp and is primarily a sounding board for Arthur's discussions of war and kingship. He worries about Merlin's prophecies because, although he has never read them, he knows that there is an upcoming battle with Mordred.

Sir Roger de Ibadan, the Black Knight, is a visitor from the African country of Dahomey, where "white people are regarded as freaks of nature." There seems to be little prejudice here, however; Launcelot invites him to join "our side." Sir Roger is a vaguely passionate fellow who falls "tragically" in love with the female thief, Clarice, to whom he is second only to her thieving in importance.

Lyonesse is the Queen of Gore and is the wife of King Unthank. She claims that her husband does not love her and treats her badly, so she seeks comfort in the arms of Lieutenant Edward. She seems to stand for the dislocation of people and the dissolution of families that inevitably occur in wartime.

Lieutenant Edward is the soldier freed from the bonds of duty and family, footloose and confused. In civilian life, he was a plasterer, and he feels quite ashamed of his common upbringing, especially after he falls in love with the queen of Gore.

Less developed characters include the Red Knight, a communist who spouts the party line about parasitic nobles stealing money from the people; the Blue Knight, who urges Arthur to seek the Grail, an atomic bomb; the Brown Knight, a Scotsman with bad taste who sleeps with Queen Guinevere; and a crusading fanatic named Walter the Penniless who lashes out in a sermon at the "Pomp and Orgulity" of Arthur and his knights.

*Themes and Meanings*

*The King* is a delicate attempt to communicate the fragile relationship between romance and reality. By combining the romantic tale of Arthur and his knights with a horrible twentieth century reality, the Battle of Britain, Barthelme slowly draws out the consequences of the relationship.

Arthur is a no-nonsense romantic, if there is such a thing. He understands that against the propaganda machines and manipulativeness of modern politics, not much can be done, but he seems to continue on anyway, with a romantic sense of duty. Guinevere and Launcelot try to keep up the good old days of athletic combat and "Maying"; they sigh a lot because these activities are no longer appreciated.

In short, all the knightly characters pursue a life of love and beauty in the face of a world that holds their pursuits of no account. The Brown Knight even apologizes for wearing brown armor on a black horse, for in the world of knighthood, bad taste is a no-no. Barthelme is neither satirizing nor endorsing the "lifestyle" (if anything so tenuous could be so called) of the Arthurian characters. Yet the world they are fighting—represented by Lord Haw Haw, the Germans (who are "insane"), and even Sir Winston—are dull by comparison.

Other forces impinge on their world: The Blue Knight wants to achieve the Grail, which his cobalt blue armor helps to identify as the big bomb. This, he says, will win the conflict and utterly destroy the enemy, making England safe for knighthood. Then there is the communist, the Red Knight, who has the party line down pat. He wants to overthrow the government (such a wisp of a government as it is) and give the power to the working man. Since the only working man in the book is the former plasterer Lieutenant Edward, who is wooing the aristocratic Queen of Gore, his message seems vaguely vacant.

Is there then a specific positive theme of the novel? The peculiar ending perhaps gives a clue. Arthur, having shown Sir Merlin's prophecy to Sir Kay, rewrites the prophecy so that he wins, creating a happy ending. Launcelot, disgusted by the slaughter of the last battle in which Mordred is defeated, rides off by himself despite Guinevere's pleas. Arthur and Guinevere then have a conversation about their roles, which they affirm as romantic foci of the human dream: peace, family, and justice. The book ends with Launcelot dreaming, under a tree, of the beauty of Guinevere; she "enters the dream in her own person," bringing a bottle of wine to drink with Launcelot "under an apple tree." This is the story of Eden, the great tragic, romantic love story of humanity, the continuing attempt of fragile, rather comic people to achieve peace and justice, joy and beauty, and their continual and tragic failure.

*Critical Context*

Barthelme identified his primary influence as Samuel Beckett. From the beginning of his career, however, he has been identified as a postmodernist, one who has absorbed the techniques of Ernest Hemingway, William Faulkner, D. H. Lawrence, and James Joyce and gone "beyond" them. His writing technique seems to be that of the collage, a form borrowed perhaps from modernist painters. In his use of this form, Barthelme joins literary allusions, attitudes, and clichés, often of a romantic nature, in a sort of upside-down way to modern moral and social problems. His method demonstrates, in an inappropriateness of the fit, how badly such romantic formulae illuminate the modern world.

*The King* seems to be a mellower version of this constant practice. The merging of a romantic Camelot with the Battle of Britain creates a strange, inappropriate world. The romantic clichés seem inadequate, and the more modern situation seems banal and not to the point.

The tone of the novel is less harsh than in many of Barthelme's earlier stories; the author seems to be saying that this is certainly not the way to run the world, but that he cannot think of another way. Such a tone is perhaps more in tune with more optimistic postmoderns such as Frederick Turner. There is, for example, a sense of affirmation in Guinevere's assertion that queens are myth-makers, and Arthur almost accepts the fact that a mythic structure shapes his life.

The novel's impact has been small. Barthelme's popularity has never been overwhelming; in fact, he has often been accused of elitism, of appealing only to the well-read and culturally chic. In the wake of his death, his works have been removed from some anthologies in favor of works by such writers as Raymond Carver, James Allen McPherson, and Bobbie Ann Mason. Such a practice indicates that the editors of anthologies, at least, believe Barthelme to have been no more than a minor writer.

*Bibliography*
Carver, Robert. "Knights Shift." *New Statesman and Society*, 4 (March 1, 1991): 38. This review claims that the book's idea resembles that of Raymond Queneau's *Les Fleurs bleues* (1965; *The Blue Flowers*, 1967). Carver remarks that Barthelme's constant jokiness becomes wearing, even though some of the jokes are good. Carver also decries the book's lack of continuity and of plot and character development.

Davenport, Guy. "Style as Protagonist in Donald Barthelme." *The Review of Contemporary Fiction* 11 (Summer, 1991): 69-74. Stresses the dominance of Barthelme's style over structure and content. Davenport points out that allusions, many of them esoteric, make up much of Barthelme's writing, but that the allusions are in tension with the structure and content. Davenport finds one value in Barthelme's work: the father as self, teacher, artist, God, and civilization

Davis, Alan R. Review of *The King*, by Donald Barthelme. *America* 163 (December 29, 1990): 517-518. Claims that Barthelme's forte is portraying the "loss of soul in a supermarket world." Davis, however, demurs that the subject is missing in *The King*. He evaluates the novel as a rather tenuous work that merely celebrates that romance can still be enjoyed in fiction.

Koger, Grove. Review of *The King*, by Donald Barthelme. *Library Journal* 115 (April 1, 1990): 134. Laments the "tired irony" and the facile whimsy of Barthelme's style. Koger argues that only faithful fans of Barthelme will be pleased with the book.

Molesworth, Charles. "The Nasciemento Effect and Barthelme's *The King*." *The Review of Contemporary Fiction* 11 (Summer, 1991): 102-107. Emphasizes the effect of the use of fragmented forms in Barthelme's work, especially *The King*. The "Nasciemento effect," named after a Brazilian singer, is a coinage of Molesworth's referring to the insertion of one's own words into the interruptions of a broadcast caused by static. Molesworth argues that the news of World War II is the "static" interfering with the retelling of the Arthurian story.

*Robert W. Peckham*

# THE KITCHEN GOD'S WIFE

*Author:* Amy Tan (1952-    )
*Type of plot:* Family
*Time of plot:* The 1980's (in the United States) and the 1920's to the 1940's (in China)
*Locale:* Northern California and China, particularly Shanghai
*First published:* 1991

> *Principal characters:*
> JIANG WEILI (WINNIE), a woman who seeks a deeper understanding with her daughter by telling her about the past
> WEN FU, Weili's first husband, who turns out to be a liar, gambler, coward, and womanizer
> JIMMIE LOUIS, Weili's second husband, who brings her to the United States, out of Wen Fu's clutches
> PEARL, Weili's American-born daughter, who conceals her life-threatening illness from her mother
> HULAN (HELEN), Weili's best friend in China, who runs a flower shop with her in California
> PEANUT, a relative with whom Weili is reared who eventually shows her how to escape her despotic husband

*The Novel*

   *The Kitchen God's Wife* is about a mother and daughter who have mutually reinforcing secrets. Their inability to communicate is based partially on their different backgrounds. The mother was reared in China and emigrated to California later in life, while her daughter was born and reared in the United States. In the beginning, the story is told by the daughter, Pearl, who has informed everyone but her mother that she has multiple sclerosis. Pearl is afraid that her mother, Winnie, will get overexcited by the news. Pearl feels especially guilty about covering up the information because she believes that her mother would never hide anything from her.

   Most of the story, however, is given in the voice of the mother, whose Chinese name is Jiang Weili (in Chinese, the family name is given first). Out of an unrealistic fear of her former husband Wen Fu's reappearance—especially unrealistic since he is in China and she in California—Weili has never told her daughter anything but generalities about her first marriage. Now that Wen Fu has died, she tells her story, in the process revealing certain long-veiled circumstances of Pearl's nativity.

   When Weili is six years old, her mother deserts the family, bringing shame on the house. Weili is sent to live in her uncle's residence so that she will not be a constant reminder of her mother's betrayal. In her new home, she plays second fiddle to her uncle's children, which is particularly galling in relation to Peanut, the daughter, who is Weili's junior by a year. Thus, Weili jumps at the chance to marry Wen Fu, a local boy who begins by romancing Peanut but who switches matrimonial targets when he learns that Weili is from the richer branch of the family.

At the time of the couple's marriage, China is in a skirmishing war with Japan, and the newlyweds pack off to live at the Chinese Air Force Academy, where Wen Fu is a pilot. As she lives with him, Weili comes to understand her husband's perversity. With his friends, he is quick witted, generous, brash, and gutsy. To his wife, he is cruel, spiteful, and overdemanding sexually. Moreover, he is a coward who turns tail whenever the other fighter pilots fly into combat. Perhaps as a compensation for his increasingly ill-concealed derelictions of duty, he plays the bully with his wife. He takes possession of some of her personal savings and wastes them, and he begins to flaunt his extramarital affairs, to the point of moving his mistresses into the house. These actions do not merely personally affront Weili; since the couple must share their housing with another married couple, they also cause her to lose face.

The rapid deterioration of their marriage takes place against the backdrop of China's collapsing defense against a Japanese invasion. Wen Fu's air force unit repeatedly relocates, moving deeper into China's interior as the Japanese blitzkrieg continues. Meanwhile, new personal disasters harden the marriage partners' hearts against each other. Wen Fu loses an eye in a jeep mishap and so loses both his looks and the status of being a pilot. Weili loses the last vestiges of feeling for her spouse when he prevents a doctor from seeing their daughter, who is struck by a sudden sickness and dies. For Weili, aside from her children, the only bright spots during the war years are her deepening friendship with a fellow pilot's wife, Hulan, and an enchanting meeting with a Chinese American translator, Jimmie Louis.

Back in Shanghai after the war, two encounters persuade Weili to leave her marriage. She finds Peanut, who has left her husband and set up a house for runaway wives, and meets Jimmie Louis again and falls in love with him. She does escape her husband and, after a series of misadventures that include being thrown in jail on trumped-up charges preferred by Wen Fu, joins Jimmie in California as his wife. On the day before she leaves for America, however, Weili is surprised and raped by Wen Fu. Pearl is born about nine months later, and the question of her father's identity is left open.

Now, however, after years of doubt, Weili is convinced that Jimmie Louis, who has died, is Pearl's true father, a fact that Weili tells her daughter as she brings her narrative to a close. Overwhelmed by her mother's history and by her courage in revealing it, Pearl reciprocates by informing her mother of her own sickness. The novel ends with a flow of trust between mother and daughter. Each has been brought abreast of the other's heartaches, the mother's found in an unhappy past and the daughter's in a straggling, uncertain future.

## The Characters

Jiang Weili (Winnie), who tells most of the story, is a woman who, it is said, combines weakness and strength. Plucked out of her home and placed in her uncle's house when her mother deserts the family, she grows up taught to defer to her uncle's children. Yet her first years with her mother, who spoiled her, have given her an ineradicable sense of self worth. When Weili makes a poor marriage to Wen Fu, she at first acts docilely, putting up with his abuse. Her repression of her better instincts in this relationship acts as one of the book's sharper critiques of the man-as-master ideology of old China. Later, Weili revolts and escapes her first marriage. At the time of the story's telling, it is her past that separates her from her daughter; Weili does not want to reveal her history, which would show her weaknesses. Eventually, however, Weili unburdens herself and draws her daughter to her in the process.

Wen Fu, Weili's first husband, is the villain of the piece. He seems to have little but the most superficial qualities, such as surface good humor and bravado, to recommend him. At bottom, he is a domestic tyrant, gambler, and womanizer. Although Tan makes him unsympathetic, she does allow the reader to glimpse some of the bases for his cruelty. He is obsessed with his status as a "war hero," yet he is not a hero but a drunken coward; his self-esteem is therefore rooted in self-deception. His character can be taken as symbolic of the Chinese military as a whole, since his shallow bluster reproduces the widely proclaimed but largely illusory effectiveness of their war effort. In the end, Wen Fu loses out to both Weili, who escapes his power, and to his own greed, since he wrecks his house looking for an imaginary hidden fortune.

Pearl, Weili's daughter, is a foil to her mother. Although she is a well-developed character who constantly mediates between the demands of her mother (who Pearl thinks is too meticulous in observing family conventions) and her American husband (who she thinks is too nonchalant in regard to Chinese culture, Pearl is not as well-rounded as her mother. What Pearl is afraid to tell her mother acts as a minor counterpoint to her mother's more resonant secret, Weili's whole unrevealed youth. After her mother tells all, Pearl is enabled to divulge what is in her own heart, leading to a richer understanding of both her mother and the family history.

Hulan (Helen) is, with Weili, the co-owner of a flower shop in California. She meets Weili while their husbands work together in the Chinese air force. The outspoken, bossy Hulan is a conservative counselor to Weili, telling her to try to endure her husband. Finally, she comes to adopt Weili's more progressive views on marriage, although she continues to lecture her on right living.

Jimmie Louis, Weili's second husband, is a Chinese American who meets and falls in love with her when he is working in China. He is romantic and loyal, but he is ineffectual in dealing with the Byzantine complexities of the Shanghai bureaucracy. He helps Weili to get away from Wen Fu, but he has to leave her when he is called back to America. Once they are reunited, they have a few years of marital bliss before his untimely death from cancer.

*Themes and Meanings*

*The Kitchen God's Wife* is structured around two interrelated dichotomies: between China and the United States and between mother and daughter. At first, it would seem that China has little to offer Weili and other immigrant women except nostalgic memories of its food and landscapes. As wives in prerevolutionary China, women have little voice in running their families; if they have made bad marriages, they must put up with husbands who may be sadistic or uninterested. Divorce initiated by a woman is unthinkable. Women are often forced into bad marriages, because as daughters they have limited say in whom they will marry and little chance to get to know their prospective partners. Moreover, people in wartime China have to put up with extreme political instability. As the story unfolds, for example, Weili and her husband must keep relocating as Japanese troops keep occupying new parts of the country.

Life in the United States, where women have more equality with men and political conditions are generally calm, seems like paradise compared to existence in China. Yet there is a definite critical undertone to Tan's discussion of the American environment.

Pearl is something of an epitome of American life, with her petty trials and triumphs, her bickering with her husband and children, and her mostly picayune concerns. Yet she seems to be living on a small scale. Her mother's life journey of catastrophe, heartache, violence, and passion in China has tested her to the utmost and bonded her friends to her with ties forged in adversity. In the United States, in contrast, most potentials remain unrealized. Women have security and formal equality but little chance to develop their independence, as Weili has, through resistance to authority and oppressive customs.

The difference in each woman's upbringing leads to an unspoken rupture in their familial connection. Each conceals a secret because each believes the other does not really recognize the true mortar of culture. For Weili, this mortar is the complex configuration of established deference patterns that should guide interfamilial relations. Her daughter's lack of openly displayed grief at her father's funeral—a display that should have been made whether the girl felt grief or not—symbolizes Pearl's lack of appreciation for custom. How, Weili thinks, can her daughter understand the choices her mother made in her life if she does not honor these traditions?

Meanwhile, Pearl thinks her mother cannot comprehend the emotional shadings that govern American life. Although Pearl was devastated by her father's death, she could not express her feelings at the funeral, and her mother's demand for tears seemed to violate her emotional integrity. Pearl thus anticipates that if she tells her mother about her illness, her mother will make a scene—that is, respond in an emotionally inauthentic manner.

Each sees the other as lacking in sensitivity to either cultural or emotional nuance. It is the mother, the more daring, who saves the situation by telling her story. In a way, she trumps her daughter by revealing that, while steering meticulously through the protocols of Chinese tradition, she has had as rich and adventurous of an emotional life as Pearl has. What Weili basically establishes by her tale, however, is that custom and emotion can fruitfully work together. To approach each other, the two women have suspended disbelief about the values of Chinese and American principles and have become willing to see that each has something to offer a harmoniously integrated life.

*Critical Context*

*The Kitchen God's Wife* was Tan's second novel. Her first, *The Joy Luck Club* (1989), brought her success and critical acclaim; Tan, however, did not attempt to re-create her earlier triumph by rewriting her first book. Her second novel departs substantially from the first in structure, in the weight given to the different claims of China and the United States, and in approach.

*The Joy Luck Club* is told by eight narrators—four mothers and four daughters, all friends—whose stories jump around in time and space, leaving the reader to sort out their chronologies and relationships. In contrast, *The Kitchen God's Wife* has the relatively simpler structure of a tale within a tale. Further, the first novel gives equal attention to the lives of the American daughters and Chinese mothers, while the second work concentrates on Weili in China.

The most important departure in the second book is that Tan has exchanged her earlier Magical Realism for a realistic tone. Magical Realism, first associated with Latin American writers, is a style that remains realistic but constantly skims near the edge of fantasy. It dwells on plausible but unusual events involving pageantry, humor, and hints of folklore. In the United States, Magical Realism has been associated with African American women writers such as Toni Morrison. More to the point, however, it was the chosen style of Tan's most prominent Chinese American literary predecessor, Maxine Hong Kingston, who in books such as *The Woman Warrior* (1977) captured the history of Chinese immigrants in a fabulist style.

*The Joy Luck Club* blends Magical Realist passages about old China with less extravagant narrative strands describing San Francisco's Chinatown. *The Kitchen God's Wife*, on the other hand, though set largely in China, opts for a thoroughgoing realism. The times themselves are often extraordinary, but Tan avoids her earlier dreamlike tone and settles on a sober, steady, fearless examination of circumstances. In truth, the most notable remaining touch of Magical Realism in the second book occurs in the recounted legend of the Kitchen God that gives the book its title.

Feminism finds strong spokeswomen in all of Tan's major characters, especially those who come from China. These women are (or grow to be) spirited, assertive, and decisive. The American-born heroines of Tan's novels aspire to these same qualities, although their dual heritage often undermines their self-assertion by plaguing them with ambivalence.

Tan's books also touch on issues of ethnic pride and multiculturalism. Advocates of multiculturalism seek to highlight the intrinsic value of each immigrant ethnic culture rather than to see each as merely a contributor to the larger U.S. culture. Within this general framework, Tan takes a moderate position, pointing immigrants and their children neither toward Americanization nor toward a complete return to ethnic roots. Rather, she describes characters who struggle to integrate the psychic demands of two worlds.

*Bibliography*
Kim, Elaine H. *Asian-American Literature: An Introduction to the Writings and Their*

*Context*. Philadelphia: Temple University Press, 1982. Though the book does not discuss Tan's work, it is a useful guide for those who want more background on the tradition from which she springs. It focuses on the interwoven immigrant experiences of the Japanese and the Chinese in the United States. It details both the stereotypes of Orientals in American literature and early attempts by Asian Americans to combat them.

Tan, Amy. "Angst and the Second Novel." *Publishers Weekly* 238 (April 5, 1991): 4-7. In this essay, Tan dissects the problems facing an author who has to live up to a huge first-novel success. She mentions other writers' cautions about publishing a second book, such as the warning that critics are harder on a second effort. She also discusses the generally useless advice she received on writing a second novel, and she details her false starts on the trial to writing *The Kitchen God's Wife*.

——————— . "Double Face." In *Home to Stay: Asian-American Woman's Fiction*, edited by Sylvia Watanabe and Carol Bruchac. Greenfield Center, N.Y.: Greenfield Review Press, 1990. This anthology includes a selection by Tan taken from *The Joy Luck Club*. The excerpt is prefaced by a statement by Tan that tells about her own extraordinary life, which was much more unconventional than that of her Chinese American characters. The anthology also has generous selections from Chinese American female writers, whose work can be read to locate Tan's work within a developing tradition.

——————— . "Lost Lives of Women." *Life* 14 (April, 1991): 90-91. Tan describes a photograph which is blown up and reproduced along with her comments, that depicts a group of women and girls at a Buddhist retreat in Hangzhou, China, in 1992. The picture shows Tan's mother and other relatives. She describes many horrifying incidents from their lives, some of which were reworked for scenes in the *The Kitchen God's Wife*.

Young, Pamela. "Mother with a Past." *Maclean's* 104 (July 15, 1991): 47. This discussion of *The Kitchen God's Wife* focuses on Tan's problems writing a follow-up book to her first spectacular success. Tan made false starts, such as beginning and abandoning books on the San Francisco earthquake and on immortality. Young compliments Tan on her second book, which, the critic argues, shows incredible deftness at switching styles to capture different types of scenes.

*James Feast*

# LaBRAVA

*Author:* Elmore Leonard (1925-      )
*Type of plot:* Detective and mystery
*Time of plot:* The 1980's
*Locale:* South Miami Beach, Florida
*First published:* 1983

> *Principal characters:*
> JOE LABRAVA, a freelance photographer of the Miami Beach street scene,
>     formerly a Secret Service Agent and Internal Revenue Service investi-
>     gator
> MAURICE ZOLA, an elderly hotel owner-manager who was a photographer
>     years ago
> JEAN SHAW, a former motion-picture star, Zola's friend and business
>     associate
> RICHARD NOBLES, a sociopathic he-man, thief, and private security guard
> CUNDO REY, a Cuban expatriate, nightclub go-go dancer, and car thief

## The Novel

*LaBrava*, Elmore Leonard's tenth crime novel, takes place in the 1980's in South Miami Beach, Florida, a resort that is a decadent remnant of its Art Deco heyday. Into this seedy milieu the author places a varied group of characters, including such grotesques as a hustler who preys upon women and a psychopathic Cuban refugee who is a go-go dancer and car thief. Joe LaBrava, the title character, an erstwhile Secret Service man who guarded former First Lady Bess Truman, is a freelance photographer in his late thirties who prowls the streets with camera in hand.

Through his friendship with hotelman Maurice Zola, LaBrava finally meets Jean Shaw, a fiftyish former film star with whom he recalls having fallen in love when he was twelve years old. When she is brought drunk to a county crisis center one night, LaBrava takes Zola there to get her released. Richard Nobles, a private security guard and all-around thug who comes there for the same purpose, challenges LaBrava, but the physically imposing hulk is no match for the photographer, who flattens him. After a quarter of a century, LaBrava is still smitten with Shaw, and they become sexually involved. Unclear, however, is whether he is attracted to the woman or to her film images, which he vividly recalls from childhood. Adding intriguing complexity to Leonard's carefully woven plot and characterizations is the fact that Shaw herself often confuses film fiction with real life, seemingly reenacting old screenplays in actual situations.

By winning the battle over Shaw, LaBrava earns Nobles' enmity. The sociopath starts tailing the photographer and eventually decides to kill him with his crony Rey's assistance. (Rey already has killed Nobles' vengeance-seeking uncle, who believed his nephew's false testimony led to a son's lengthy prison term.) LaBrava, meanwhile, also stalks Nobles, unnerving his prey by surreptitiously taking pictures of him, which he uses to forestall an attempt by Nobles and Rey to shake down local merchants. Paralleling this petty extortion scheme, which amounts to a few hundred dollars per store, is a much more ambitious plan. Nobles also has been preying upon Jean Shaw after she had encouraged his attention. Her attitude toward him is ambivalent, but they soon become partners in crime, although she may be setting him up for a big fall. This lack of certainty about Shaw's motives and the ambiguous morality that is central to her character is an aspect of the illusion-versus-reality motif that Leonard develops throughout the novel. All of this adds depth and resonance to the novel, qualities not often present in crime fiction.

In the main story line, Shaw receives a crudely typed extortion note threatening her with death unless she follows subsequent instructions demanding the payment of $600,000. Since she barely has enough income on which to live, such a sum is far beyond her means to raise, so she looks to Zola. The police are certain that Nobles is a key player in the scheme and believe that, since he is an inveterate bumbler, their task of catching him in a self-incriminating act should be simple. Leonard, though, has laid the groundwork for necessary complications: the odd relationship between Nobles and Shaw, the focus upon her motion-picture career, and her tendency to infuse much of her conversation with lines from old films. In the event, LaBrava and the others realize, Nobles is neither orchestrator nor dupe, but rather accomplice and front man in a scam too complex for him to have concocted. Jean Shaw is the brains behind the alleged extortion, but rather than a product of her imagination, it is primarily a reworking of a plot from *Obituary*, a film in which she starred with Tyrone Power.

Leonard is full of surprises in *LaBrava*, not the least of which is his conclusion. Though Jean, it finally is clear, has double-crossed and tried to swindle Maurice, the two are going to get married. Maurice promises, "I'm gonna take good care of her," which is precisely what he has been doing for years. Evidently putting her celluloid past wholly behind her and ready at last to embrace real life, Jean tells LaBrava, "It's not the movies, Joe." This statement can also explain the relevance of numerous minor characters and subplots that flesh out the novel. Inherently interesting, they do more than merely increase the number of perilous scenes, for just as Joe LaBrava's photography eschews illusion in favor of raw realism, the minor players and incidents focus attention upon and enhance the reality that ultimately becomes the controlling force in the main characters' lives.

### The Characters

Maurice Zola describes Joe LaBrava as "one of those quiet guys, you never know what he's gonna do next." As a photographer, according to Zola, LaBrava "shoots barefaced fact. He's got the feel and he makes *you* feel it." The skills emerge from his keen understanding of people, because his eye, like the lens of his camera, penetrates to the essence of those he meets. These qualities, as well as his ubiquitous picture-taking, help him to solve the crimes that occur. LaBrava also inspires confidence and trust in people, such as canny Maurice Zola (who confides, "I'm going to tell you a secret I never told anybody around here") and worldly-wise women like cosmetic salesperson Franny Kaufman and actress Jean Shaw. Although he lives in Zola's Della Robbia Hotel and becomes deeply involved (sexually and otherwise) with its residents, LaBrava remains an outsider, fundamentally detached, and thus can credibly function as the moral center and conscience of the novel. He is a touchstone by which others are measured.

Maurice Zola, about eighty years old, has had several careers before settling upon hotel ownership and management. A onetime bookmaker and railroadman, in the 1930's he was a photographer for the Farm Security Administration, "documenting the face of America during the Depression." Part of the south Florida scene for half a century, he has experienced it all: women, scams, good times and bad. He has made a lot of money and lost some of it, but he still has plenty left. Given all he has been through, he retains a surprising amount of trust for people and looks out for the well-being of those he admires, especially LaBrava and Jean Shaw. Maurice's knowledge of the milieu, his patience, and his sound common sense are vital to the former's efforts and help to rein in the latter.

Jean Shaw, the onetime actress, who portrayed beautiful but dangerous seductresses (in the manner of Bette Davis, Mary Astor, and Veronica Lake), continues to live in a make-believe world, watching her old films and luring young men. Her motives for bringing to life an old film extortion plot are not fully clear but probably have as much to do with her obsession with reliving past cinematic glories as with her need for money. She may also be attracted to the scheme by the realization that Maurice, her devoted protector, could and would provide the payoff. Seen as vulnerable through much of the novel, she does kill Nobles in a coldly deliberate manner, but mitigating the shock is the fact that it is a precise replay of a scene from her film *Obituary*.

The real villains of the piece, Richard Nobles and Cundo Rey, are stereotypical hustlers, partners in crime but untrusting of and disloyal to each other. Though they possess the requisite fearlessness and determination of thugs, ineptness and lack of vision inhibit their dreams of grandeur. Big and muscular Nobles, in his mid-thirties, is a fellow LaBrava "knew by sight, smell and instinct" who "pumped his muscles and tested his strength when he wasn't picking his teeth." A brute who preys on women and boasts of having eaten a snake and an eagle, he has had a varied career and once acted as an informer against his cousin for the federal Drug Enforcement Agency. Cundo Rey, his sidekick, is a bisexual murderer whose criminality makes him a willing accomplice in just about anything, as long as money is to be made. One of his guiding principles is that anger is good if one can "use it right away" and "let it pick you up and carry you." Ironically, he rarely exhibits the emotion, and the maxim more appropriately describes Nobles. Significantly, both men are undone by the same nemesis, LaBrava, who personifies calmness. In his climactic battle of wits and pistols with LaBrava, Cundo is dead moments after boasting, "I say to St. Barbara I believe this is my day."

## Themes and Meanings

The novel develops according to a standard Leonard pattern: An ordinary, fundamentally good man gets caught up in a crime but eventually prevails over those who are greedy, evil, and amorally ambitious. What distinguishes Joe LaBrava is that when challenged, he cannot remain the dropout he had become and is impelled to involvement by a strong social conscience, romantic nature, loyalty to a friend, and innate curiosity. At the end, though, he is still merely a solitary freelance photographer, someone who has been in a peck of trouble but has emerged basically unchanged, although disillusioned, by his experiences.

*LaBrava* is a fast-paced narrative with noteworthy verisimilitude, a result of Leonard's keen ear for spoken language and his grimly realistic settings, whether a hotel inhabited by old widows or a county crisis center filled with alcoholics and assorted psychotics. Counterpointing and in contrast with this realism is the pervasive illusion theme, centered around the nostalgia enveloping Jean Shaw, whose words and actions are so intertwined with the film lines she spoke and roles she played years ago that there is no discernible boundary between make-believe and reality. Leonard suggests, though, that everyone needs illusions to survive, whether one is an aging film star or simply an ordinary old lady using Franny Kaufman's Bio-Energetic Breast Cream. Even levelheaded Joe LaBrava has been sustained for twenty-five years by cinematic illusion, his childhood love for a film actress whose name he could not even remember.

In addition to the security that their illusions provide, perhaps as escape from the dismal reality surrounding them, these people need one another. Even the villains, Nobles and Rey, almost always operate as a team. Zola and Shaw long ago forged an odd yet useful symbiotic relationship. Although LaBrava at the end is as much a loner as at the start, his vocation keeps him amid people, even if he is separated from them by a camera lens, and he is quick to form close, if usually temporary, relationships. When he agrees to be best man at the Zola-Shaw wedding, he gives the couple a smile and thinks to himself, "Why not?" This slight suggestion of wistfulness coupled with ambivalence is appropriate, given all that has transpired and the questions that remain about Shaw. Zola must be speaking for the author on the last page of the novel when he stops speculation about the mystery by saying that "you always got a few loose ends. Who needs to know everything?" Using film language to reinforce Zola's statement, Shaw ends the discussion by agreeing, "It's a wrap."

## Critical Context

Elmore Leonard was a successful writer of Western fiction in the 1950's and early 1960's, producing five novels and many stories, including *Hombre* (1961), which the Western Writers of America named one of the twenty-five best Westerns of all time and which was made into a film starring Paul Newman. Thinking the market for Westerns was diminishing, Leonard turned to crime fiction, but numerous publishers rejected his first such novel, *The Big Bounce*, before it finally came out as a paperback original in 1969. Though he averaged a crime novel a year during the 1970's,

Leonard did not become a popular and critical success until *Stick* (1983) and *LaBrava*, the latter of which won the Mystery Writers of America Edgar Allan Poe Award in 1984. Widely praised, it secured his reputation as one of the major American crime writers, though he has said, "I think that I'm really writing novels, not mysteries, but I don't want to sound pretentious."

Leonard's crime fiction stands apart from much else in the genre: His characters are less stereotypical and more substantive; he does not have a recurring detective who confronts cases in a predictable manner; and his locales and casts change considerably from book to book (though the Detroit area is the setting of a number of his novels, and *LaBrava* is the fourth set in the Miami Beach area). Partly by avoiding adherence to formula writing, he has advanced beyond the genre author label into the mainstream of American fiction.

One of his major influences is Ernest Hemingway, and Leonard has acknowledged that a close reading of Hemingway's *For Whom the Bell Tolls* (1940) focused his attention on the importance of dialogue and narrative point of view. Leonard has recalled being especially struck by how Hemingway "told so much just in the way a character talked." Yet Leonard says that he differs from Hemingway in important respects, claiming to see more absurdity, to like people more, and to be more tolerant. In terms of attitude (sardonic humor, for example), Leonard can be compared to contemporaries such as Mark Harris and Kurt Vonnegut, Jr., both of whom he has praised; he also has spoken of the influence on his work of George V. Higgins' *The Friends of Eddie Coyle* (1972), primarily for its use of dialogue and monologues as means of increasing realism, and of John O'Hara and John Steinbeck. He has disclaimed being influenced by the leaders of the "hard-boiled" school of American crime fiction—Raymond Chandler, Dashiell Hammett, and Ross Macdonald—but his depictions of urban realism and physical violence and his pervasive morality link him unmistakably to the hard-boiled genre.

*Bibliography*
Geherin, David. *Elmore Leonard*. New York: Continuum, 1989. The first full-length study of Leonard. Starts with a short biography and then summarizes and analyzes the novels and some stories. The last chapter, "Why Is Elmore Leonard So Good?", makes a good case for Leonard as a major American writer, and the bibliography is a useful research tool.
Prescott, P. S. "Making a Killing." *Newsweek* 105 (April 22, 1985): 62-64. Focusing upon Leonard's belated emergence as a widely recognized popular writer, this article also provides a useful review of his themes.
Reed, J. D. "A Dickens from Detroit." *Time* 123 (May 28, 1984): 84-85. One of a number of 1984 articles on Leonard in nationally circulated publications, this piece discusses *LaBrava* and then considers themes and techniques.
Shah, Diane K. "For Elmore Leonard, Crime Pays." *Rolling Stone* (February 28, 1985): 33-34. A useful biographical as well as critical piece. Includes an interview with the author in which he is characteristically frank.

Sutter, Greg. "Advance Man: Researching Elmore Leonard's Novels, Part 2." *The Armchair Detective* 19 (Spring, 1986): 160-172. The second of Sutter's explanatory pieces. The two articles reveal much about Leonard's methods.

—————— . "Getting It Right: Researching Elmore Leonard's Novels, Part 1." *The Armchair Detective* 19 (Winter, 1986): 4-19. Sutter, a researcher for Leonard, tells about his work in this two-part article. The verisimilitude present in Leonard's novels, Sutter makes clear, is the result of visits to locales and much legwork.

Yagoda, Ben. "Elmore Leonard's Rogues' Gallery." *The New York Times Magazine*, December 30, 1984, p. 20. A well-informed and in-depth review of Leonard's career and literary production. Yagoda's emphasis is on Leonard's crime fiction.

*Gerald H. Strauss*

# LEAVING HOME

*Author:* Lionel G. Garcia (1935-      )
*Type of plot:* Psychological realism
*Time of plot:* The early 1940's
*Locale:* Southern California
*First published:* 1985

> *Principal characters:*
> ADOLFO, a former major-league baseball pitcher who realizes too late that
>    he has wasted his life
> MARIA, Adolfo's cousin, who wants to keep all of her family at home
> CARMEN, the daughter and favorite child of Maria, an intelligent young
>    woman who wants and achieves a better life than anyone in her family
> THE PROFESSOR (MANUEL GARCIA), a sidekick of Adolfo, a former
>    elementary-school teacher
> ISABEL, Adolfo's former lover, who takes in Carmen and helps her find a
>    job

*The Novel*

Lionel G. Garcia's *Leaving Home* offers an intimate view of one Latino family in the early 1940's. The novel examines the pain of breaking family ties, identity crisis, and racism.

In *Leaving Home*, Garcia is the narrator, telling the story almost entirely in a third-person omniscient voice. At one point in the novel, the author intrudes into the action using the first-person voice, and at another point, he addresses the audience directly in the second person.

As the novel opens, the aging Adolfo, a former major-league baseball pitcher who ruined his career with alcohol, is preparing to move to San Diego, away from the home of his cousin, Maria, in the Imperial Valley. He is a poor man who has little to live for but his memories. He hopes to move in with his former lover, Isabel, the mother of his son. Carmen, Maria's daughter, goes with Adolfo, hoping to move in with an aunt in order to find a better job. Maria, determined to show her family that no one loves them as much as she does, has burned the letters that Adolfo and Carmen asked her to mail to announce their respective arrivals. Maria hopes that the two will have to move back in with her.

Turned away by her aunt, Carmen is allowed to stay with Isabel. Adolfo, however, is forced to return to Maria's house. Upon his return, Adolfo discovers that he has been swindled out of his beer joint and that he has no prospects for work. Maria promises to help Adolfo find a job, but he is a proud man who considers himself to be a celebrity, and he refuses to work in the fields. Adolfo finally agrees to work as a gardener for a priest, but he soon finds the work demeaning and quits.

Adolfo then travels to Los Angeles, planning to stay with some old friends. On the trip, he meets Antonia, a con artist who easily persuades Adolfo to move in with her so she can get his pension checks. He lives unhappily with Antonia until he gives in to his craving for alcohol, after which she throws him out.

Adolfo then moves in with the Professor, another victim of Antonia's scam. When the health department condemns the men's house, Adolfo and the Professor move into a boarding house, at which they pay their rent in the form of sexual favors to the owner, Anna, a widow.

After the United States enters World War II, the Professor decides that he wants to return to Tijuana to avoid the draft. Even though he is much too old to be drafted, he remembers that during World War I, Hispanics were drafted before whites. The Professor plans to live with his sister, Yolanda. Adolfo accompanies him. In Tijuana, after another failed attempt at love, Adolfo marries a prostitute. He soon leaves her, however, and returns to Maria's house.

While Adolfo travels, Carmen succeeds in improving her life. She contracts tuberculosis while working at a film theater and must go to a state sanitarium to heal, but she discovers through this misfortune that she wants to be a nurse.

Upon her release, Carmen applies for a job at the Navy hospital in San Diego. After some struggle because of her race and her former illness, she is hired to wash pots. She is soon promoted to orderly and shortly thereafter is recommended for nurses' training in the U.S. Navy. She is graduated at the top of her class and becomes an officer. Although Carmen is capable, her promotion is based on the fact that she is Hispanic. The Department of Defense uses her as a symbol.

While visiting her mother, Carmen realizes the differences between the clean, organized military base and her mother's dusty house. Although she loves her mother dearly, Carmen suggests that Maria has not been keeping the house clean. Maria knows that the family tie to Carmen has been broken. When Carmen becomes engaged to a white naval officer in the Philippines, Maria believes that she has lost Carmen.

Maria experiences significant changes. She begins to question God's judgment when Carmen gets sick. When Arnoldo, one of Maria's sons, is killed in battle, she loses her faith in God. As her family falls apart, so do her beliefs. She is left alone and lonely. When Adolfo returns, Maria feels happy again. The two agree that Adolfo has wasted his life, but they are happy to have each other. The novel ends on this positive note.

## The Characters

Adolfo, the former baseball pitcher, is full of contradictions. At once comic and pathetic, he cannot see himself as others see him, as an old man who lives in the past and talks too much. He is absurdly fastidious, as can be seen when he is offended by the sound of his lover urinating, yet he wants to project a macho image. He sees himself as a ladies' man, but at one point he is described as wearing a shrunken wool suit and canvas shoes with holes purposely cut in them to allow room for his corns. He frequently fails to wear his dentures. He is disgusted by ignorance but can barely read. Adolfo is a dreamer, and as such, he leaves the stability of Maria's house in search of a better, more prosperous life of love and leisure. Having been born talented, he believes he deserves such a life. He also believes that Carmen deserves a better life and encourages her to stay with Isabel to gain opportunities. By the end of the novel, Adolfo recognizes himself as a failure and returns to Maria's house. Garcia uses interior monologues to show Adolfo's development.

Maria is the hub of the family, trying to keep the family connected. She does not have strong matriarchal qualities, but she is a strong woman who survives many hardships, including the judgment of the Hispanic community against women such as herself who become pregnant out of wedlock. She wants desperately to keep her family together to keep from being alone. Through her conversations, she reveals a belief in witchcraft that coexists with her belief in God. She sees herself as able to punish God by ignoring Him or breaking a promise to Him, but she fears divine power. She relies on God to keep her family safe, and when she thinks that God has begun taking family members from her, she becomes angry with Him. She begins not to care what her children do because she believes that they have forsaken her. By the end of the novel, Maria has grown bitter.

Carmen changes from a shy, indecisive child to a mature woman who knows what she wants. Carmen is Maria's favorite child. Although she loves her mother, Carmen feels no sadness when she leaves Maria. Carmen understands that in order to break out of the poverty in which she has grown up, she must move to the city and find more profitable work. In the sanitarium, she meets Luz, who tells her to do more than is expected of women, to make something of her life rather than accept the common fate.

The Professor, Adolfo's friend, is a flat character, but he is important in advancing the plot. The former elementary-school teacher shares his money with Adolfo, listens to Adolfo's stories, and takes him to Tijuana, where Adolfo meets a woman whom he believes he loves more than he loves Isabel. After being spurned by the Professor's sister and marrying a prostitute, Adolfo decides to return to Maria's house.

*Themes and Meanings*

*Leaving Home* is an examination of poverty, racism, and the family. Garcia presents a group of related individuals in the midst of a changing society. Hispanics had begun to achieve equal rights in the 1940's but were not yet considered to be equal to whites, and hostility against them remained. Not all the characters in the novel want to break away from traditional lives of working all day and drinking all night.

In his novel, Garcia shows a family of diverse personalities. Adolfo was born with talent, a cruel fate according to Maria. Because of his ability to pitch well, Adolfo is able, temporarily, to rise above the expected poverty of his race. His experiences as a famous pitcher cause him to continue to seek better things for himself and his family. After his baseball days, however, Adolfo is never again able to rise above poverty. Maria, on the other hand, is willing to accept her fate. She believes that she should not ask for anything more than she has. She cannot understand Adolfo's pride. When she helps him find a job, it is clear that she does not see a job as a measure of a person's worth.

Garcia presents the plight of farmworkers and those forced to live on pensions. Farmworkers work long hours, yet make barely enough money to live on. Maria lives next to a dump where the children use old tires for toys. Adolfo is not surprised by the shabby furniture at Antonia's house because that is what he is accustomed to. People do not paint their houses, and junked cars litter yards.

The author also shows that Hispanics were treated as second-class citizens, citing the U.S. military's supposed policy of drafting minorities before whites. In the job market, Garcia depicts blatant racism, as Carmen is told that not many people of her race become nurses.

*Leaving Home* is also about breaking family ties and about abandoning the predictable for the unpredictable. Garcia presents various leave-takings throughout the novel. Adolfo and Carmen leave Maria's house to improve their lives. Carmen, unlike Adolfo, almost completely severs the tie to Maria. Another of Maria's daughters, an illegitimate child also named Maria, leaves home several times because she gets angry with her mother, but she always comes back. The death of Maria's son Arnoldo causes a further breakup of the family, almost pushing Maria to insanity. Adam, Maria's other son, also takes permanent leave. Arnoldo dies a hero, but Adam, a victim of syphilis, dies a scoundrel. Arnoldo's death gives Maria much pain, while Adam's gives her relief.

Garcia's novel reveals that in a society of growing equality, people must be willing to take chances, to ignore the fate of their race, to leave home. Doing so may result in success and greater happiness. Such action, however, may also result in anxiety and unhappiness.

*Critical Context*

*Leaving Home* is Garcia's first published novel. While the novel was in progress, Garcia won the 1983 PEN Southwest Discovery Prize. *Leaving Home* was well received by critics, who forecast a promising future for Garcia. His ability to create believable, sympathetic characters can be seen in his short stories.

In this novel, Garcia uses several literary techniques. A shifting point of view is evident in the author's use of third-person omniscient, first-person, and second-person points of view. The author also uses indirect interior monologue. Fragmented time sequences add complexity to the novel.

Garcia's theme of moving out of poverty is prevalent in his other novels *A Shroud in the Family* (1987) and *Hardscrub* (1990). The author bases his works on human experiences and is inspired by his own familial experiences. *Leaving Home* is part of the body of literary social criticism that examines racism, poverty, and the family.

A practicing veterinarian in Seabrook, Texas, Garcia writes and publishes regularly. Several of his short stories have been published in various magazines. By the early 1990's, he had begun writing and publishing reminiscences revealing the strong ties in his own family.

*Bibliography*
Garcia, Lionel. "Table Manners." *Texas Monthly* 18 (October, 1990): 44-45, 49-50.
Although this article does not directly relate to *Leaving Home*, its reminiscences
describe real people who bear a strong resemblance to the characters in the novel.
For example, the depiction of Tío Nano carrying two heavy suitcases is similar to
a scene in which Adolfo carries suitcases for Antonia. The grandmother in the
reminiscence, always willing to help the less fortunate, is very much like Maria.
_____ . "The Wedding." In *Cuentos Chicanos: A Short Story Anthology*,
edited by Rudolfo A. Anaya and Antonio Marquez. Albuquerque: University of New
Mexico Press, 1984. A short story by Garcia. The section of this anthology
describing the contributors provides valuable information on Garcia's life but
contains no information on *Leaving Home*. The information is useful for some types
of criticism.
"Leaving Home." *Booklist* 81 (August, 1985): 1630. This favorable review gives a
brief summary for a general audience. The review is helpful for understanding the
plot and suggests that the work is important because it is about a group of people
who need more attention from society.
Taylor, Pat Ellis. "Sons and Lovers." *Texas Observer*, April 20, 1990, 16. Ellis' review
focuses on Garcia's novel *Hardscrub*, but there is some discussion of *Leaving
Home*. The review suggests a common theme of the two novels of upward socioeconomic mobility.
Wilson, Patricia J. "An Interview with Lionel G. Garcia." *Texas Library Journal* 68
(Spring, 1992): 22-24. Provides insight into Garcia's writing techniques. The article
contains little information on *Leaving Home*, but Garcia discusses where he gets
ideas for his characters.

*Wilma Shires*

# A LESSON BEFORE DYING

*Author:* Ernest J. Gaines (1933-    )
*Type of plot:* Social realism
*Time of plot:* 1948-1949
*Locale:* The former slave quarter on a plantation in rural Louisiana
*First published:* 1993

> *Principal characters:*
> GRANT WIGGINS, a young black teacher in the quarter school
> JEFFERSON, a young man convicted of murder and awaiting electrocution
> TANTE LOU, Grant's aunt and benefactor
> EMMA GLENN, Jefferson's godmother and friend to Tante Lou
> REVEREND MOSE AMBROSE, the pastor of the quarter church
> MATTHEW ANTOINE, a Creole, Grant's former teacher
> VIVIAN, Grant's love, a Creole teacher in Bayonne
> HENRI PINCHOT, the plantation owner and brother-in-law to Sam Guidry
> SAM GUIDRY, the St. Raphael Parish sheriff
> PAUL, a humane deputy

*The Novel*

In *A Lesson Before Dying*, Ernest Gaines once again takes his reader to a familiar fictional setting based on his boyhood home in Point Coupée Parish near New Roads, Louisiana, which becomes the fictional St. Raphael Parish, with Bayonne as its parish seat. A small town of about six thousand inhabitants, Bayonne is one of the two main settings in the novel. The other is the old slave quarter on an antebellum plantation owned by Henri Pinchot located a few miles away, near the St. Charles River. The year is 1948, a time when segregation and racial injustice were oppressive realities for Southern blacks, a time, too, when most of them did not know that the winds of change, if ever so slightly, were beginning to stir.

The basic plot is simple. A young, semiliterate black man, Jefferson, is tried for the murder of a white store owner, old Mr. Gropé; although Jefferson is innocent, the all-white, all-male jury sentences him to death in the electric chair. In pleading for his client's life, Jefferson's white lawyer argues that it would make no more sense to electrocute Jefferson than it would to execute a hog or some other dumb animal.

That assessment of Jefferson's human worth deeply troubles his godmother, Emma Glenn, who enlists the aid of her friend, Tante Lou, to pressure Tante Lou's nephew, Grant Wiggins, into trying to help Jefferson face death like a man, with dignity and courage. Grant, the sole teacher at the church school in the quarter, is reluctant to help, but he yields in the face of his aunt's strong moral cajoling and the insistence of his friend Vivian, with whom he is in love.

Before he can even visit Jefferson at the jail in Bayonne, Grant must approach the plantation owner, Henri Pinchot, who, because he is Sheriff Sam Guidry's brother-in-law, can intercede to obtain Guidry's permission. The prospect of asking Pinchot for help rankles Grant, because he knows he will have to pay a steep price—some of his fragile pride.

But even more troubling are his own persistent doubts about the efficacy of any effort to transform Jefferson into a man. Grant's sense of purpose as teacher, like his pride, is very brittle. His former teacher, Matthew Antoine, preaching nihilistic futility, had already severely damaged it, and it is soon apparent that Grant would likely bolt and run were it not for Vivian, who cannot leave with him until she has obtained a divorce from her estranged husband.

Grant's biggest problem, however, is Jefferson himself. During the initial visits to the parish courthouse in Bayonne, when Miss Emma accompanies Grant, Jefferson is almost catatonic, unwilling to communicate with either of them. When, in a subsequent visit by Grant, he does break out of his shell, his behavior shows that he has accepted his lawyer's conception of him as subhuman. He snorts and grunts, rooting on the floor of his cell and gobbling his food like a hog—behavior that greatly distresses Grant, for it seems to confirm everything that Antoine had said.

Still, Grant does not give up. Although he has no idea of how to go about restoring some pride in Jefferson, his resolve to do so gradually grows. He opts for simple kindness, believing that Jefferson's sense of self-worth must come from a belief that others care. Grant's nemesis, the Reverend Ambrose, chagrined by Grant's apparent agnosticism, pulls against him, convinced that Jefferson can find comfort only in the revealed word of God.

With patience, Grant finally begins to break through to Jefferson. He gives the condemned man a small portable radio, which Jefferson takes as a kind, caring gift, more, in fact, than he had ever before received. Then Grant encourages him to write down his thoughts and feelings, which Jefferson, in halting words, does, finally confirming his humanity. Clearly, before his date with Gruesome Gertie, the portable electric chair, he redeems his manhood; in the process, Jefferson helps Grant to find himself and earn the respect and proffered friendship of Paul, a white but sympathetic deputy. Thus, despite the awful miscarriage of justice that is the central fact of the novel, *A Lesson Before Dying* ends on a hopeful note.

*The Characters*

Grant Wiggins, the protagonist, is also the novel's primary narrator, so it is chiefly his thoughts that the reader audits. He is a seeker cut adrift from his communal moorings by his education, which, ironically, seems to limit rather than expand his options. Given his time and place, he can be little other than a teacher, but his doubts about the value of trying to help the quarter children make him harsh and perfunctory, almost a martinet. Initially, he seems destined to fulfill the fate that Matthew Antoine has told him is in store for him, to become "the nigger" he was "born to be."

For Grant, Jefferson's plight is all too typical of what a young, ignorant black male might expect in a white man's world, and Grant sees little point in trying to help him. He gradually warms up to his charge, however, not so much from the moral cross

Tante Lou has tried to make him shoulder as his desire to prove Sheriff Guidry and others wrong. Blinded by pride, palpable resentment, and doubt, Grant does not fully understand that, in helping Jefferson, he has set out on his own spiritual odyssey, one that finally proves Matthew Antoine wrong. The reader understands, however, and knows that Paul's visit to the quarter, made from respect and admiration for Grant, signals an enduring, hopeful change.

Although Grant is hostile to Tante Lou's moral arm-twisting, she is the first important catalyst in his transformation. She will not let Grant wheedle out of what she perceives as both his Christian and communal responsibility. His education has led him to question her beliefs, but Grant's residual sense of guilt is tapped by his aunt, for whom he has both affection and grudging reverence. She, of course, is bound to the community by traditional ties based in an abiding faith that Grant, in his modern enlightenment, has almost entirely rejected. He cannot, however, refuse her on a personal level.

Vivian is the other important catalyst. Her love offers Grant solace and hope in his darker moments, when the pointlessness of trying to help seems confirmed by Jefferson's actions. She also keeps Grant anchored to his job, because she is not free to leave with him until she obtains her divorce. Her own strong sense of responsibility, rooted in more private feelings of pride and dignity, nicely balances Tante Lou's.

While Grant's main conflict lies within, it is to an important degree objectified in the person of Jefferson, the novel's victim. To raise him up, Grant must overcome Jefferson's self-loathing, inculcated by whites who have repeatedly told him that he is no better than an animal. It is that same self-effacement and contempt from which Grant has tried to run, evading rather than coping with it. In helping Jefferson, he is at last forced to face up to and triumph over it. Jefferson, going to his death with manly dignity, provides an outer measure of Grant's own spiritual growth.

## Themes and Meanings

In *A Lesson Before Dying*, the personal problems of the black and Creole characters are the bitter fruit grown from seeds sown in the soil of racial bigotry. For them, the injustice of the caste system is the central, inescapable burden that weighs them down with poverty and ignorance, often with little hope of amelioration. That fundamental fact of their life is gleaned at the novel's outset, when, with prophetic resignation, Grant explains that he did not go to Jefferson's trial because he knew what the verdict would be, what it inevitably had to be.

What Gaines shows is that even in the face of such abysmal conditions, a man or woman can reveal courage and dignity—or even, like Jefferson, regain them when they are lost. Some of the novel's characters, especially Tante Lou, define their humanity by their faith both in God and tradition. Others, such as Grant, must define it on their own terms through personal exorcism, not of the devil, but of doubt and despair, and through contact with their own innate decency.

*A Lesson Before Dying* reads a bit like a sophisticated morality drama. It is not, of course, a religious allegory in the mode of the medieval morality plays, but like them, it involves an outward test that reflects the psychomachia, or mind struggle, within the protagonist. Grant's inner conflict is between despair, articulated by Matthew Antoine, and hope, held out by Vivian. At stake is his secular redemption, and the challenge he must meet and overcome in achieving it is objectively manifest in Jefferson, who has been reduced to the very thing that Antoine had claimed Grant was fated to become. Grant must redeem Jefferson to redeem himself, and he must accomplish this from an initial condition of existential uncertainty that approaches despair.

Through education, Grant has distanced himself from the faith that steadies Tante Lou and fires the righteous anger of Mose Ambrose. He is the new Southern black, struggling to redefine himself in the face of changes that are eroding a way of life that for prior generations had at least allowed a modicum of pride and self-respect. The time is not yet right for collective action, the boycotts and sit-ins of the next generation; for Grant, therefore, the only hope seems to lie in his love for Vivian and their anticipated flight.

Ironically, it is Vivian's situation that keeps him at his school, not any sense of self-sacrifice or humanistic concern for his charges. In fact, at first he seems to have accepted Antoine's assessment of his worth, much as Jefferson, in jail, accepts the view of himself as hog. Like Jefferson, Grant must learn in his own prison, his racially inherited place under a brutal Southern sun, that it is possible to find both dignity and hope.

*Critical Context*

In some important ways, the artistic antecedents of *A Lesson Before Dying* lie in Gaines's first novel, *Catherine Carmier* (1964). There are, for example, close parallels between character pairs, notably Tante Lou and Grant Wiggins and the earlier book's Aunt Charlotte and Jackson Bradley. The two spinster aunts, spiritually identical, are moral preceptors for their searching, disillusioned nephews, both of whom attempt to find themselves in romantic entanglements with Creole women.

The principal locales of the two novels are much the same, except that *Catherine Carmier* is set in the early 1960's, when a young, educated black man such as Jackson had some alternatives to teaching. Despite the pain it causes for his aunt, Jackson rejects the option in his quest for a new, personally rewarding identity. Grant, facing the less hopeful world of 1948, at least goes through the motions of teaching, though he longs, however vaguely, for something better.

Racial injustice permeates both novels. Both books relate that injustice to a generational change and conflict between the older, tradition-bound members of the community and the increasingly alienated youth, who can find nothing to bind them to their heritage. Further, both works treat that passing of a way of life with a mixture of relief, sadness, and some compensatory humor.

In *A Lesson Before Dying*, Gaines also returned to a simpler method of presenting his story. In the novel's immediate predecessor, *A Gathering of Old Men* (1983), he used the collective point of view of more than a dozen voices, but in *A Lesson Before*

*Dying*, he confines point of view primarily to the single voice of Grant Wiggins. The novel thus shares the narrative directness of *Catherine Carmier*. It is similar, too, in its plain but lyric style—rich in colloquial speech, understatement, and bare diction—and in its characteristically even-tempered handling of the passionate issue of racial intolerance.

*Bibliography*

Babb, Valerie Melissa. *Ernest Gaines*. Boston: Twayne, 1991. A major critical introduction to Gaines, with a chronology and bibliography. The best general introduction to Gaines published before *A Lesson Before Dying*. Strongly recommended as starting point for further study.

Rubin, Merle. "Convincing Moral Tale of Southern Injustice." *The Christian Science Monitor*, April 13, 1993, 13. A review for the general reader. Gives a synopsis of the novel and an upbeat appraisal typifying the book's reception in most reviews. For Rubin, *A Lesson Before Dying* is an important "moral drama."

Senna, Carl. "Dying Like a Man." *The New York Times*, August 8, 1993, p. G21. An enthusiastic review that helps illuminate the racial lines and tensions among the book's black, white, and Creole characters. Senna does claim that the novel has an occasional "stylistic lapse" but gives no specific examples.

Sheppard, R. Z. "An A-Plus in Humanity." *Time* 141 (March 29, 1993): 65-66. Reviews *A Lesson Before Dying*, giving a short plot synopsis. Praises the author's level-headed ability to convey the "malevolence of racism and injustice without the usual accompanying self-righteousness."

Summer, Bob. "Ernest J. Gaines." *Publishers Weekly* 240 (May 24, 1993): 62-64. Based on an interview with Gaines. Offers insights to the author's preparations as a writer. Valuable for relating the novel to its author's methods and artistic vision.

Yardley, Jonathan. "Nothing But a Man." *The Washington Post Book World* 23 (March 28, 1993): 3. A brief but excellent explication of the novel. Focuses on Grant as protagonist and notes that the lesson referred to in the work's title is one learned by him as well as by Jefferson. Also remarks on Gaines's admirable restraint in treating racial themes.

*John W. Fiero*

# LET THE CIRCLE BE UNBROKEN

*Author:* Mildred D. Taylor (1943-    )
*Type of plot:* Historical realism
*Time of plot:* The 1930's
*Locale:* Rural Mississippi
*First published:* 1981

> *Principal characters:*
> DAVID LOGAN (PAPA), the head of a landowning African American family in rural Mississippi
> MARY LOGAN (MAMA), David's wife, the mother of Stacey, Cassie, Christopher-John, and Little Man
> CASSIE LOGAN, the nine-year-old narrator
> HORACE GRANGER, the white owner of a large plantation
> LEE ANNIE LEES, an elderly African American woman
> WADE JAMISON, a white lawyer and friend of the Logans
> STACEY LOGAN, Cassie's older brother
> T. J. AVERY, Stacey's best friend

*The Novel*

Based on experiences typical of those endured by the author's parents, *Let the Circle Be Unbroken* is a fictionalized portrayal of how a rural Mississippi community, and the Logan family in particular, faced adversity and survived during the Depression of the 1930's.

The novel contains fourteen chapters that separate major episodes or denote passage of time. Cassie Logan, the nine-year-old daughter of David and Mary Logan ("Mama" and "Papa"), narrates the story.

The opening chapter establishes a theme of discrimination and abuse of the community's black families. T. J. Avery, Stacey's classmate, is unjustly accused of killing a white store owner. The black families wonder whether T. J. can get a trial at all, and, if so, whether it can possibly be a fair one. Wade Jamison, a white lawyer whom the Logans respect, attempts to get T. J. acquitted, but he is unsuccessful; T. J. is sentenced to death.

As winter comes, the plight of both black and white sharecroppers and day laborers is revealed. Most of the area's families live in one-room shacks with dirt floors. Even Papa, a landowner who has a nice five-room house and admits to being better off than many others, is worried about paying the taxes on his land. Papa has been cheated out of payment for his cotton crop by Horace Granger, the wealthy white owner of a six-hundred-acre plantation.

Meanwhile, Lee Annie Lees, the sixty-five-year-old aunt of a local black family, announces as she turns sixty-five that she will study for the voter-registration test. Cassie helps her to memorize all laws in the Constitution in preparation for the test, aware, however, that Horace Granger, for whom Lee Annie's relatives are sharecroppers, can control her fate.

When representatives of a Farm Workers' Union solicit Papa's support for an effort for "both black and white" he promises to "think it through," but his enthusiasm for the union is diminished by his suspicion that black farmers would not really be protected by the organization.

As tax-payment time approaches, Papa considers working temporarily on the railroad and later does so. Stacey realizes that times are hard and begs to quit school to get a job, but the Logans forbid it, insisting that they will make ends meet somehow.

Several times Papa's brother Hammer comes from the North to visit, as does Bud Rankin, Mary Logan's nephew. When it becomes known that Bud has a white wife, there is tension between Bud and Hammer in particular, but Bud asks the Logans if his daughter Suzella can visit. Encouraged by her mother, Suzella has often passed for white so things "won't be so hard" for her. Cassie has trouble accepting her: she resents giving up her bed and seeing Stacey give Suzella all his attention, but she grudgingly tolerates her.

Things worsen when the county agent requires some families to plow up the parts of their cotton crop that are over the quota. Stacey finally feels compelled to do something to help, so he and a friend, Moe, run away to take jobs cutting cane. The family is distraught; Mama sends for Papa, but it is difficult to know how to look for the boys. Cassie questions how the adults can pretend that everything is all right, but Mama reminds her that "life goes on no matter what."

As feared, Granger sees to it that Lee Annie is told that she has failed the voter registration test she had vowed to take. On New Year's Day, news finally comes that Stacey and Moe have been located. Again, Mr. Jamison helps the Logans; he finds Stacey, who is reunited with his family. Cassie remembers her mother's saying that one day Stacey would be her friend again, and she sees that her mother's prediction is true.

*The Characters*

David Logan (Papa) is a fully human man with a strong sense of values and strength of character that have earned him the love and respect of his family and his community. While fortunate to have acquired four hundred acres of land, he is never arrogant or indifferent to the needs of his less fortunate neighbors. He possesses the wisdom to know when and how to speak up and when to remain silent. Although he is a thoroughly admirable character, his goodness never seems contrived or artificial.

Mary Logan (Mama) is the author's mouthpiece for voicing her feelings about the unjust treatment of blacks in the 1930's. Moreover, Mama is a warm, loving mother who wants her children to understand what it means to be black in a white-dominated world and to learn to deal with it. She believes in education and in self-improvement, and she hopes that one day the children will be spared the racial discrimination she has known.

Cassie, a fifth-grader at the beginning of the story, experiences the gamut of feelings that a young girl coming into adolescence has. Capable of hurt feelings and jealousy, she is also sensitive: to harmonica music, to T. J., even to Suzella at times. She is clever; in a game of marbles, she plots to win the prize blue one, risking punishment afterward since Papa has said that "marbles might lead to gambling." She feels the sting of being treated like a child by her eldest brother when he becomes a teenager.

Stacey is a lovable, serious-minded preteen. He feels a responsibility to family, even to the point of sacrificing his own comfort and disobeying and worrying his parents in order to try to help them. He shows courage in taking the necessary risks to do what he feels is right.

Wade Jamison is a truly sympathetic character. Though shunned by other white people in the community for trying to get justice at T. J.'s trial, he has a genuine sense of justice. He faces reality squarely, however; he knows that his just behavior toward the black families cannot cancel the years of abuse they have received from other whites.

Horace Granger, the white owner of a six-thousand-acre plantation, is predictable. He is a prejudiced, powerful white man who seems truly to believe that racial equality is unthinkable. Perhaps a product of his own upbringing, he measures success in terms of power over, and manipulation of, both black and white sharecroppers.

Suzella Rankin experiences the dilemma of one who must live in two worlds. She admits the advantages of being able to pass as white, but she loves her black father even when she feels ashamed of him. The fact that she is too advanced to remain at her grade level in the rural Mississippi school demonstrates the contrast in education and opportunity between the North and the South.

Lee Annie, though aunt to the Ellis family by blood relationship, is "aunt" to the community. Loved by all, she shows courage and strength of character when she decides that, at age sixty-five, she will do what she has always longed to do: register to vote.

*Themes and Meanings*

Based on experiences of the author's own parents' generation, *Let the Circle Be Unbroken* depicts perceptively the plight of black families in rural Mississippi during the Great Depression. The book shows the clash between well-intentioned New Deal politics, the politics of white Mississippi, and the threat of unionism in this context.

The novel is a powerful and moving story of strength, love, dignity, and integrity against almost unbeatable odds. David and Mary Logan, well acquainted with the injustice of racial prejudice, provide the love and support that will help their children to know the truth about growing up black and not being defeated by it.

The sting of injustice runs throughout the novel. The black families who dare to attend T. J.'s trial see him sentenced to die for a murder he did not commit. Sharecroppers weep as they plow under cotton because a county agent has miscalculated the quota, and they see their meager profit being destroyed. Lee Annie dares to take a stand by memorizing the laws of the Constitution for a voter-registration test, only to be rejected and see her family dismissed from the Granger plantation. Stacey, determined to help his family, is not paid for his ceaseless labor.

David Logan demonstrates dignity and wisdom in managing his affairs. Knowing Horace Granger's power in the community, Papa thinks things through before making decisions. He does not accept offers that do not ring true; under difficult circumstances, he works to pay the taxes and keep his land. In spite of injustice, Papa is fair. He is able to separate strength of character from color of skin, recognizing that Wade Jamison is "a rare man" who, though white, is a friend and is fair. He knows that T. J. has acted foolishly in going with two white boys to break into a store, although he dares to hope that the boy can have a fair trial and keep his life.

Suzella portrays the dilemma of being caught in two worlds; having mixed blood isolates her in both groups. She recognizes the social advantages of passing as white, and she feels the strength and love of her black relatives. Ultimately, however, she returns North to her white mother because she cannot cope with being black in a white world.

The novel is also a story of growing up. Stacey longs to be grown and to help support the family, while Cassie resists the inevitable and longs for things to remain the same. Each learns in time that the wisdom of their parents is to be trusted.

Through all the misery and mistreatment, the families learn that, by looking to the traditions and the heritage of their past, the community members can sustain one another even in times of trial. One endures for the sake of the next generation. The Logan family learns that love is stronger than adversity even in the difficult environment of rural Mississippi.

*Critical Context*

*Let the Circle Be Unbroken* is the third of Mildred D. Taylor's books; her first, *Song of the Trees*, was published in 1975. The next year, she published *Roll of Thunder, Hear My Cry*, and *Let the Circle Be Unbroken*, which followed in 1981, is a sequel to that book. Additional novels including *The Friendship* (1987) and *The Road to Memphis* (1990) continue the story of the Logan family.

Rather than experimenting with innovative techniques, Taylor opts to use her natural language skills to let the young Cassie Logan tell her story. The novel flows with a smoothness and clarity that helped to establish Taylor's reputation. It is both humorous and capable of evoking deep emotional reactions. The fact that the author bases her novels on the kinds of experiences that her own parents lived through may well contribute to the power and compassion that she brings to her work. Also, Taylor's own Peace Corps experience in Ethiopia as a teacher further broadened her base of knowledge and sensitivity.

Some critics have suggested that *Let the Circle Be Unbroken* and the Logan family series belong alongside other classics such as Mark Twain's *The Adventures of Huckleberry Finn* (1884) and Laura Ingalls Wilder's *Little House on the Prairie* (1869). Taylor has received formal recognition for the Logan family series, including *The New York Times* Outstanding Book of the Year Award for her first work, *Song of the Trees. Roll of Thunder, Hear My Cry* won the American Library Association's Notable Book award and the Newbery Medal in 1977 and was a finalist for the National Book Award.

*Bibliography*
Eiger, Melanie. Review of *Let the Circle Be Unbroken*, by Mildred D. Taylor. *Best Sellers* 41 (February, 1982): 444. Eiger suggests that *Let the Circle Be Unbroken* could have a positive influence on the younger reader, white or black, in dealing with problems of racial discrimination and injustice. She notes that the example of the Logan family provides instruction in courage, dignity, and the value of passive resistance.
Heins, Ethel L. Review of *Let the Circle Be Unbroken*, by Mildred D. Taylor. *The Horn Book Magazine* 58 (April, 1982): 173. Comments that Taylor demonstrates sensitivity in her treatment of the injustice and suffering that African Americans endured during the Depression. The reviewer observes that Cassie's narration captures something of the transition from childhood innocence to an awareness of the black condition.
Harper, Mary Turner. "Merger and Metamorphosis in the Fiction of Mildred D. Taylor." *Children's Literature Association Quarterly* 13 (Summer, 1988): 75-80. Harper identifies the rich oral tradition of African American folktales as a source for Taylor's works. The characters draw courage and strength from such folk songs as the one that inspires the novel's title.
Jordan, June. "Mississippi in the Thirties." *The New York Times Book Review* 86 (November 15, 1981): 55, 58. Jordan praises Taylor's ability to deal with the effects of New Deal politics and 1930's racial discrimination in language and style that is appropriate for the younger reader. The sharing of true community, the risk-taking, and the courage of the Logans even in the face of humiliation, Jordan says, make the novel worthy of being called a classic.
McDonnell, Christine. "Powerful Lesson of Family Love." *The Christian Science Monitor* 73 (October 13, 1981): B1, B11. Notes that *Let the Circle Be Unbroken* appeals to readers of all ages, although its main thrust is toward the young. Observes that Taylor uses contrast as a major means of organizing her commentary on the cruel conditions of the rural black family in Depression Mississippi.

*Victoria Price*

# LIBRA

*Author:* Don DeLillo (1936-      )
*Type of plot:* Psychological realism
*Time of plot:* The 1950's and the 1960's
*Locale:* The United States, Japan, and the Soviet Union
*First published:* 1988

*Principal characters:*

NICHOLAS BRANCH, a retired member of the CIA
WALTER "WIN" EVERETT, JR., a member of the CIA relegated to teaching college
DAVID FERRIE, a flamboyant pilot with connections to the CIA
T. J. MACKEY, a renegade CIA agent
LEE HARVEY OSWALD, a maladjusted young man
MARGUERITE OSWALD, Lee's manipulative mother
LAURENCE "LARRY" PARMENTER, a CIA agent
JACK RUBY, a Dallas nightclub owner with connections to the underworld

*The Novel*

*Libra* is Don DeLillo's fictional re-creation of the life of Lee Harvey Oswald, alleged assassin of President John F. Kennedy, and of the conspiracy that many believe lay behind the assassination.

DeLillo has woven his novel from three major strands. The first is the story of Oswald himself, from his childhood in New York City until his death at the hands of Jack Ruby. The second strand follows the growth of a conspiracy to commit some act that will focus the anger of the U.S. government on Cuban dictator Fidel Castro. The plot is originally intended to fail; as DeLillo notes, however, "There is a tendency of plots to move toward death." In the third and simplest strand of the novel, retired CIA analyst Nicholas Branch is trying years later to write a classified history of what took place.

As *Libra* opens, young Lee Harvey Oswald is living in the Bronx with his widowed mother, Marguerite Oswald. Her efforts at finding another husband have failed, as have her attempts to make a home with relatives. In what will become a familiar pattern, Lee and his mother always seem to be on the move to increasingly cheaper apartments. Eventually, mother and son return to New Orleans. Lee was born there, and Marguerite's sister still lives there, but once again there seems to be no home for them.

Along the way, Lee discovers Marxism, which offers him an explanation for his marginalized situation in society, but he also enlists in the Marines. He is assigned to Atsugi Naval Air Station in Japan, from which U2 spy flights are launched over the Soviet Union. In Japan, he also begins an affair and makes contact with Soviet agents, expressing his belief in Marxism and offering to defect.

When he learns that his unit is scheduled to leave Japan, Lee shoots himself in the arm in a vain attempt to remain behind. A second incident—a fight with a sergeant— earns him a court martial and a brief sentence in the brig.

When Marguerite suffers a minor accident, Lee secures an early separation from the Marines. Rather than take care of his mother, however, he travels to the Soviet Union to defect. There, he marries but fails to find a meaningful role. Repeating the pattern established in his youth, he returns to the United States only to pass through a series of dead-end jobs. He becomes obsessed with making a place for himself and becoming a part of history. His attempt to assassinate right-wing General Edwin A. Walker fails, but he attracts the attention of conspirators plotting a far more important crime. The group needs a patsy with ties to the Communist world, and Oswald seems made for their purposes.

The conspirators are Win Everett, Larry Parmenter, T. J. Mackey, and David Ferrie. Bitter at American failure to support a rebel invasion of Cuba at the Bay of Pigs, Everett concocts a phony assassination attempt, complete with carefully planted clues that will lead to Fidel Castro's doorstep. Parmenter uses his contacts in the Central Intelligence Agency (CIA) to identify a likely patsy, a young man with increasingly violent tendencies who has recently returned from the Soviet Union. Mackey assembles a backup team of assassins. Unknown to Everett and Parmenter, however, Mackey neglects to explain to his team that they are supposed to miss.

Years later, CIA historian Nicholas Branch concludes that the assassination of JFK was largely a matter of chance. The conspirators focus their plans on Miami, but chance dictates that the Secret Service increase its security in Miami. Chance then takes the President to Dallas, placing him in a motorcade scheduled to pass by the very building, the Texas School Book Depository, where Oswald now works. Conspirator David Ferrie, who knew Lee as a child, persuades the increasingly unbalanced young man that fate is handing him his next target.

By November 22, 1963, Lee has fallen in with Ferrie's plan. From his window in the depository, he fires three shots at the presidential motorcade. The first hits Kennedy near the neck, the second strikes Texas governor John Connally (riding in the limousine with Kennedy), and the third misses completely. A member of Mackey's team actually fires the fatal shot to Kennedy's head. Lee flees the building for his rendezvous point, the Texas Theater. On the way, he is stopped by Patrolman Tippit, whom he shoots. Mackey plans to have Lee murdered in the theater, but police apprehend him before the murder can take place.

Suddenly in need of help, the conspirators approach Dallas nightclub owner Jack Ruby. Knowing that Ruby owes thousands of dollars in back taxes, they promise to loan him money and forgive the debt. Genuinely distraught over Kennedy's death, Ruby is easily persuaded that the public will idolize him for murdering the president's assassin. Ruby slips into the Dallas jail, where he is a well-known local figure, and shoots Lee. *Libra* concludes with a rambling, embittered soliloquy by Marguerite Oswald over the grave of her dead son.

## The Characters

Lee is the "Libra" of the novel's title, the primary character around whom DeLillo builds his plot and its meaning. The astrological sign for the Libran is a pair of scales, a highly appropriate symbol for Lee, who by novel's end is ready to be tipped either way. Ambivalence has marked much of Lee's life. An avowed Marxist, he nevertheless joins the U.S. Marines. He longs for life in the Soviet Union, but once there is disappointed and returns to the United States. He admires and identifies with Kennedy, and in his growing delusional state, he believes that assassinating the president will irrevocably complete the identification.

Marguerite Oswald is, next to Lee, the novel's most compelling character. Even more than Lee, she sets the novel's tone. She is presented not so much through her actions as through her distinctive manner of speech. She often addresses some ultimate judge ("your honor") to explain her poverty and her son's problems. She is both fascinating and repellent; early on, readers sense Lee's need to escape the manipulative web of words his mother seeks to spin around him.

Conspirators Win Everett, Larry Parmenter, and T. J. Mackey exemplify varying degrees of divergence from the controls of the CIA. Attempting to carry on the work of invasion after the disastrous Bay of Pigs episode, Everett has been found out and banished to Texas Woman's University, ostensibly to identify potentially friendly students. Equally guilty but less conscience-stricken, Parmenter has managed to carry on smoothly within the agency. Mackey (who reminds Everett of a cowboy) also retains the agency's full confidence, but Mackey has given himself over completely to the Cuban rebels' cause. Conspirator David Ferrie operates as a free agent. A commercial pilot until his sexual involvement with boys costs him his job, he is obsessed with patterns, signs, and methods of control. At one point he assures Lee that he believes in everything.

Nightclub owner Jack Ruby is, like Lee, an essentially weak individual ripe for manipulation. Like Lee, he comes to identify with his target; after his imprisonment for shooting Lee, Ruby becomes convinced that he himself is responsible for assassinating the president. Like Marguerite Oswald, Ruby comes alive for the reader through his peculiar and idiosyncratic speech patterns.

Nicholas Branch is a puzzled, wary researcher who finds himself—perhaps like many readers—drawn into the mystery of the assassination. Overwhelmed by a library of data, he nevertheless comes to the tentative conclusion that Kennedy died as a result of a combination of conspiracy and chance. Within the fictional world DeLillo has created, the reader comes to the same conclusion.

## Themes and Meanings

At its most obvious level, *Libra* recounts the life of Lee Harvey Oswald. DeLillo clearly has studied the vast assassination literature carefully. Those familiar with the case will recognize many of Lee and Marguerite's actual words, but even informed readers will have a hard time determining where the public record ends and DeLillo's fiction begins. On another level, *Libra* provides a plausible psychological and social context in which Lee's character could have developed and the assassination could have taken place. The novel succeeds brilliantly on both levels, offering as it does so a penetrating critique of a society controlled by new and little-understood forces.

In broad terms, Lee's life is a search for some system, political or otherwise, that will give his life meaning. American capitalism seems to offer him only a marginal existence, so his discovery of Marxism provides him with a measure of hope. Once in the Soviet Union, however, he finds only a grayer version of life in the West. By the end of the novel, he is fantasizing that there may be a place for him and his family in Fidel Castro's Cuba.

Yet nonpolitical systems are what snare Lee and in the end define his life. Marguerite Oswald's web of words, her litany of excuses and grievances, constitute one such system—one that Lee strives constantly to escape.

Without quite realizing it, however, Lee has already defined himself through another pattern, that of the images constantly projected by the media. Lee frequently conceives of himself in B-film terms. At one point, he attempts to commit suicide rather than be expelled from the Soviet Union. He sees himself draw the razor across his wrist while (as he describes it later in his diary) a violin plays somewhere offstage. After being shot by Jack Ruby, Lee sees himself on television, imagining how the shot must have looked to the cameras. As his consciousness fades, he watches himself from "a darkish room, someone's television den."

Three other forces define Lee. The first is the conspiracy itself, in which Lee is only dimly aware that he is playing an important role. This particular, rather limited action scarcely qualifies as a system, of course, but DeLillo clearly intends it to be emblematic of wider, perhaps even more mysterious forces. The assertion that "there is a world within the world" runs like a refrain through the novel.

The mirror image of the conspiracy concocted by Everett and Parmenter and Mackey is coincidence. In *Libra*, coincidence is elevated to a principle. It is by coincidence that Lee fits the profile required by the conspirators, by coincidence that the presidential motorcade passes by his new place of employment. At one point early in the novel, a character remarks that the science of coincidence is still waiting to be discovered.

Lee exists in one final pattern: He is a character in history. Known all of his life as Lee or Lee Oswald, he is transformed at the moment of his arrest into Lee Harvey Oswald, the character familiar from television and newspaper reports and the seemingly endless stream of books that have been written about the assassination. Lee senses something of this as he sits in his cell in Dallas, planning his encounters with lawyers, historians, and psychologists. While he may be wrong about the details, Lee is correct about finally having entered history.

*Critical Context*

Upon its appearance in 1988, *Libra* became Don DeLillo's most successful novel. DeLillo's earlier novels had explored the various forces responsible for shaping and misshaping contemporary American society, including advertising, the media, technology, and drugs. This first phase of his career culminated with the publication of *White Noise* in 1985. *White Noise*, which described the effects of an "airborne toxic event," won the American Book Award and a nomination for the National Book Critics Circle Award.

*Libra* was nominated for both these awards and became a best-seller as well, perhaps in large part because of its subject. Polls confirm that most Americans discount the verdict of the Warren Commission—which concluded that Kennedy was killed by a lone gunman—and believe instead that a conspiracy was involved. In an author's note, DeLillo stresses that his novel is "a work of imagination," but he goes on to explain that it provides "a way of thinking about the assassination." Clearly, many readers have welcomed this opportunity.

*Bibliography*
Cain, William E. "Making Meaningful Worlds: Self and History in *Libra*." *Michigan Quarterly Review* 29 (Spring, 1990): 275-287. A long, thoughtful, detailed review aimed at readers somewhat familiar with DeLillo's other novels. Praises DeLillo's "astute, off-beat, defamiliarizing curiosity about everyday life."

Curtis, Anthony. "'An Outsider in This Society': An Interview with Don DeLillo." In *Introducing Don DeLillo*, edited by Frank Lentricchia. Durham: Duke University Press, 1991. DeLillo discusses *Libra* in relationship to his other work. An expanded version of an interview that appeared in *Rolling Stone* magazine in 1988. DeLillo grants few interviews, making this example especially important.

DeLillo, Don. "American Blood: A Journey Through the Labyrinth of Dallas and JFK." *Rolling Stone*, December 8, 1983, 21-22. An early article by DeLillo stressing "our uncertain grip on the world." Provides an opportunity to examine the materials the author would assemble into a novel five years later.

Lentricchia, Frank. "*Libra* as Postmodern Critique." *South Atlantic Quarterly* 89 (Spring, 1990): 431-453. Examines *Libra* as a novel of "social destiny," but one in which images have come to play a more important role than such factors as class and race. Also appears in Lentricchia's *Introducing Don DeLillo*.

Tyler, Anne. "Dallas, Echoing Down the Decades." *The New York Times Book Review*, July 24, 1988, 1. A long, accessible review by a fellow novelist. Stresses DeLillo's mastery of the commonplace events of his characters' lives and calls the book "a triumph."

*Grove Koger*

# LIKE WATER FOR CHOCOLATE
## A Novel in Monthly Installments with Recipes, Romances, and Home Remedies

*Author:* Laura Esquivel (1950-    )
*Type of plot:* Romance
*Time of plot:* The 1910's to the early 1930's
*Locale:* Near Piedras Negras, Mexico
*First published: Como agua para chocolate*, 1989 (English translation, 1992)

> *Principal characters:*
> TITA DE LA GARZA, the novel's heroine, a fabulous cook
> PEDRO MUZQUIZ, Tita's true love, who marries her sister Rosaura
> MAMÁ ELENA, Tita's tyrannical widowed mother with a dark past
> ROSAURA, Tita's unattractive sister, Pedro's wife and the dutiful daughter of Mamá Elena
> GERTRUDIS, the rebellious illegitimate daughter of Mamá Elena
> JOHN BROWN, the family's kind doctor, Pedro's rival for Tita's love
> NACHA, an Indian cook at the ranch, a maternal figure for Tita

*The Novel*

   *Like Water for Chocolate* combines the story of a forbidden romance between Tita de la Garza and Pedro Muzquiz with a collection of traditional, mouth-watering Mexican recipes. The title, from a Spanish expression meaning "boiling mad," refers to Tita's anger that an absurd family tradition prevents her from marrying and dictates that, as the youngest daughter, she remain at home to care for her mother, Mamá Elena. Like the title, all the incidents in the novel are related to cooking.

   Organized like a recipe calendar, each chapter corresponds to a month of the year and begins with the name and list of ingredients for one of Tita's recipes along with the method of preparation. In its form, the book also imitates the romantic novels presented in monthly installments in women's magazines; each chapter ends with the note "to be continued. . . ." The narrator is Tita's grandniece, who reconstructs Tita's recipes and her love story from the diary in which the protagonist recorded her recipes along with the events that occurred when she prepared each of them.

   The novel's plot revolves around the tension between Tita's love for the kitchen, where she creates magic with food, and her rebellion against the tradition that confines her there. The novel opens with the proper method of chopping onions for the January recipe and connects the tears caused by the onions to the flood of tears that accompanied Tita's birth on the kitchen table. The narrator explains that Tita cried her way into the world because she somehow knew her fate, and her tears at birth produced ten pounds of salt for cooking. This beginning typifies the relationship between cooking and the events in Tita's life and introduces into the narrative the recurrent Magical Realism common in modern Latin American fiction.

In the first chapter, Tita's true love, Pedro Muzquiz, requests her hand in marriage. When Mamá Elena explains that Tita cannot marry and suggests Tita's sister Rosaura instead, Pedro accepts in order to remain as near to Tita as possible. The rest of the novel recounts Tita and Pedro's attempts to be together in defiance of authoritarian Mamá Elena and how Tita rebels through her culinary artistry and the unexpected and dramatic reactions her recipes provoke. For example, Tita sheds tears in the batter when forced to prepare Rosaura and Pedro's wedding cake. Her sadness, baked into the cake, afflicts the wedding guests with desperate nostalgia for lost love that causes a mass eruption of vomiting that spoils the wedding reception. One casualty of this nostalgia is the ranch's Indian cook, Nacha, who had nourished and entertained Tita in the kitchen and taught her the secrets of cooking. Later, when Pedro presents Tita with roses to celebrate her first anniversary as the ranch's new cook, the dish Tita prepares with the flowers unleashes such erotic euphoria in Tita's sister Gertrudis that she abandons her family and rides off on horseback, naked, with a revolutionary soldier. Gertrudis ultimately satisfies her lust as a prostitute, then marries the soldier and serves with him in the army.

Tita's sister Rosaura, inept and fearful in the kitchen, cannot even produce milk to nurse her first child, Roberto. Tita rescues him from starvation, but Mamá Elena, suspicious of Pedro and Tita's love, sends Rosaura's family to Texas. Roberto, deprived of Tita's milk, soon dies. Tita suffers a nervous breakdown but recovers in the care of the family's physician, John Brown, who falls in love with and proposes marriage to Tita. Mamá Elena represses Tita until her death from the emetic she uses to counteract poison that she suspects Tita is putting into her food. With Mamá Elena gone, Tita is free to marry John but refuses his offer because of her love for Pedro. Meanwhile, Rosaura attempts to perpetuate the family tradition with her own daughter Esperanza. Tita feeds her from infancy and instills in her an independent spirit. Rosaura eventually suffers a horrid death from intestinal disorders. Esperanza then marries John's son, and at the sumptuous wedding feast prepared by Tita, Tita and Pedro are at last united. Their flames of passion, fanned by the food Tita serves, engulf the lovers in a fire that destroys the entire ranch. Only Tita's diary survives intact. The narrator, Esperanza's daughter, closes the novel with the promise that Tita will live on as long as people continue to prepare her recipes.

*The Characters*

Tita de la Garza, the youngest daughter in her family, wins the reader's sympathy immediately as the victim of the repressive family tradition that prevents her from marrying. Like most of the characters in the novel, in certain respects she resembles someone from a fairy tale. Beautiful, desirous of pleasing her mother, enormously talented, but cursed by an unfortunate destiny and a wicked mother and sister, Tita can be likened to Cinderella. She propels the novel's action forward through the effects produced by the dishes she prepares. Tita represents a model of female liberation because, rather than rejecting the domestic space that confines her, she employs the resources of the kitchen to obtain self-fulfillment.

Mamá Elena, Tita's cruel mother, like most female characters in the novel, is characterized largely by her relationship to the activities of the kitchen. In contrast to Tita, who uses ingredients creatively and generously, Mamá Elena displays and demands rigid obedience to rules in cooking. She is the principal villain, notorious for loving any destructive culinary activity, such as dividing, dismembering, detaching, or carving. She inspires a modicum of sympathy after her death, when Tita discovers Mamá Elena's secret: Before and during marriage, she had enjoyed an affair with a mulatto until her scandalized family had the lover murdered. Readers interpret her authoritarian ways as the tragic result of being so severely punished herself for defying repressive societal rules.

Rosaura, the unattractive and inept sister obsessed with keeping up appearances, resembles a fairy-tale wicked stepsister and thus gains virtually no sympathy from the reader. Diametrically opposed to Tita, she shows her lack of creativity in her fear of the kitchen. Her death is an act of poetic justice, punishment for unquestioning allegiance to societal norms.

Gertrudis, the rebellious, unfettered daughter of Mamá Elena and her mulatto lover, is depicted in stark contrast to Rosaura. She fully appreciates Tita's talents and observes that an entire family history is contained in Tita's recipes. She is the receptacle for the erotic response that one of Tita's recipes provokes and is the embodiment of unbridled female freedom.

Nacha, the ranch's Indian cook, serves as a kind of surrogate mother to Tita. She is the representative of a centuries-long tradition of culinary art that is transmitted only orally until Tita begins writing down her recipes. Through this character, Esquivel pays tribute to the contributions of Mexico's indigenous female population.

Pedro Muzquiz, Tita's lover and Rosaura's husband, like all the male characters in the novel, remains relatively undeveloped. He exists principally as the object of Tita's quest for romantic happiness and as the lens through which to admire Tita's beauty and talent.

John Brown, the family doctor and Pedro's rival for Tita's affections, is a relatively bland stock character, as his name might suggest. His kindly presence serves to highlight Tita's virtues and to introduce tension into Pedro and Tita's love story.

*Themes and Meanings*

*Like Water for Chocolate* playfully imitates the steamy romances included in Hispanic women's magazines and simultaneously pays tribute to the arts of the kitchen. The novel begins and ends in the kitchen, where Tita's grandniece prepares one of Tita's recipes, illustrating that the plot is above all a vehicle for the author to celebrate food and cooking as the center of daily lives and destinies. This message is also evident in the fact that cooking is the root cause for the events of Magical Realism or fantasy that pervade the novel. The importance of freedom for women is the novel's central feminist theme.

Tita learns the most important lessons about life in the kitchen from the Indian cook Nacha. As in the book's title, descriptions of how characters feel in various situations are presented in imagery from food and cooking. In addition, the unique ways in which food is prepared and the ingredients employed are shown as determining or redefining people's fates, as with the wedding cake prepared by Tita that spoils Rosaura's reception and destroys Nacha's life. The novel equates understanding these secrets of the power of food with understanding life. In its language, food-related events, characterization in terms of attitudes toward food and cooking, and cookbook-like form, this novel makes culinary activity itself the captivating stuff of literature.

Central to conveying a message of liberation for Mexican women is the choice of a traditionally female space in Mexican society, the kitchen, as defining characters' lives. To this end, the novel's action is set temporally around the time of the Mexican Revolution, when women's rights in Mexico were also being redefined and reevaluated. Clearly, however, it is not the kitchen but societal codes that have restricted women's independence. Mamá Elena's miserable death from poisoning and Rosaura's grotesque demise testify to the evils of unquestioning allegiance to tradition in the name of keeping up appearances. The novel suggests that Gertrudis' uninhibited happiness, by contrast, is the direct consequence of her rebellious freedom. The plainest evidence of this novelistic message of liberation, even if it applies principally to amorous freedom, appears in the marriage of Rosaura's daughter Esperanza, who, through Tita's guidance, refuses to succumb to the family tradition that has enslaved her aunt.

In the end, the blending of culinary and literary arts, which triumphs most obviously in the survival of Tita's cookbook and diary at the novel's conclusion, offers would-be cooks and writers new recipes for creative expression.

*Critical Context*

*Like Water for Chocolate*, Laura Esquivel's first novel, was a runaway best-seller in both the Spanish original and in English translation. In addition to its wide acclaim among nonacademic audiences, the novel was embraced by feminist scholars as a unique and significant contribution to the burgeoning field of Latin American women's writing. In its focus on the kitchen, Esquivel's work finds antecedents in her compatriot Rosario Castellanos' 1971 short story "Cooking Lesson," which denounces how the kitchen imprisons and stereotypes women, and in Puerto Rican writer Rosario Ferré's 1984 essay "The Writer's Kitchen," in which she acknowledges the parallels between recipes for cooking and for creative writing. Esquivel's book introduces novelty both in her narrative technique, which artfully blends recipes into an archetypal love-story plot, and in her lighthearted appropriation of literary genres typically associated with women, the recipe collection and the romance. Other writers who explore the similarities in the creative processes of writing and cooking have not achieved the widespread appeal among diverse audiences that Esquivel enjoys; however, this topic has attracted the attention of female writers both in Latin America and in the United States. Esquivel joins these women in marking a new phase in feminist thought. Instead of rejecting the kitchen as a space that impedes women's freedom, they adapt the kitchen's secrets to literary production.

Esquivel established her reputation as a screenwriter before embarking on her successful foray into fiction writing. In 1985, her screenplay for Chido One received a nomination for the Ariel Award from the Mexican Academy of Motion Picture Arts and Sciences. Esquivel also collaborated with her husband on the screenplay for the film based on *Like Water for Chocolate*, which has also enjoyed great praise, capturing eleven awards in Mexico in 1992.

*Bibliography*
Castellanos, Rosario. "Cooking Lesson." In *A Rosario Castellanos Reader*, edited by Maureen Ahern. Austin: University of Texas Press, 1988. Castellanos' story of a newlywed woman's revelation about life as she burns a piece of beef set a precedent for Esquivel's work. This story from 1971 presents a well-educated heroine entirely unschooled in culinary techniques who condemns societal conventions that entrap women in the domestic sphere.
Ferré, Rosario. "The Writer's Kitchen." In *Lives on the Line*, edited by Doris Meyer. Berkeley: University of California Press, 1988. The Puerto Rican writer's autobiographical testimony of her transformation from a housewife into a writer uses culinary imagery to describe the creative process. She discusses striking parallels between cooking and writing in the context of women's search for creative freedom. As evidenced in her analogy between these two activities, she concludes that differences in women's and men's literature are especially prominent in the themes they explore.
Franco, Jean. *Plotting Women*. New York: Columbia University Press, 1989. This book traces the history of Mexican women's writing and how the narrative forms employed by them differ from those used by men. Plotting refers both to narrative technique and to the skillful transgressions necessary for these women to make themselves heard. Franco includes discussion of female writers' confrontations with the confines of domesticity.
Jaffe, Janice A. "Hispanic American Women Writers' Novel Recipes and Laura Esquivel's *Como agua para chocolate (Like Water for Chocolate)*." *Women's Studies* 22 (March, 1993): 217-230. Esquivel's use of the kitchen is depicted as liberating and creative for women. The novel is placed in the context of literature by female writers that envisions the kitchen as a space of female repression or, alternatively, of community and creativity. Concludes that Esquivel's positive appropriation of the kitchen was possible only after earlier feminist writers' denunciation of how domestic chores enslaved generations of women.
McMurray, George. "Two Mexican Feminist Writers." *Hispania* 73 (December, 1990): 1035-1036. McMurray briefly outlines the novel's plot, emphasizing the Magical Realism. He attributes the book's popularity to Magical Realism and traces this aspect of the novel to the work of Gabriel García Márquez. Also discusses a novel by Mexican writer Angeles Mastretta that McMurray views as representative of contemporary feminist trends in Latino literature.

*Janice A. Jaffe*